D1555313

Prison Pictures from Hollywood

For Evelyn and Arthur Wilton
who have always cared

PRISON PICTURES FROM HOLLYWOOD

Plots, Critiques, Casts and Credits for 293 Theatrical and Made-for-Television Releases

by

James Robert Parish

McFarland & Company, Inc., Publishers
Jefferson, North Carolina, and London

Acknowledgments

Academy of Motion Picture
Arts & Sciences Library
Kathy Bartels
Beverly Hills Public Library
John Cocchi
Film Favorites (Karin Martin)
David Hayes
Hollywood Film Archives
(Richard Baer)
Kim Holston
Doug McClelland
Alvin H. Marill
Lee Mattson

Jim Meyer
Michael R. Pitts
Howard H. Prouty
Linda J. Sandahl
Arleen Schwartz
Les Schwartz
Margie Schultz
Super Sleuth Videos
(Robert W. Johnson)
Dr. Bryan Taylor
Vincent Terrace
Donald A. Weinblatt

Editorial Consultant: T. Allan Taylor

British Library Cataloguing-in-Publication data are available

Library of Congress Cataloguing-in-Publication Data

Parish, James Robert.
Prison pictures from Hollywood : plots, critiques, casts and
credits for 293 theatrical and made-for-television releases / by
James Robert Parish.
p.   cm.
Includes index.
ISBN 0-89950-563-5 (lib. bdg. : 50# alk. paper) ∞
1. Prison films—Catalogs.   I. Title.
PN1995.9.P68P37   1991
016.79143'655—dc20
90-53519
CIP

©1991 James Robert Parish. All rights reserved

Manufactured in the United States of America

McFarland & Company, Inc., Publishers
Box 611, Jefferson, North Carolina 28640

Contents

v

Introduction

Every film genre has its special conventions. However, few are as well defined as prison movies. Like combat and police movies, prison pictures reflect a stringent way of life in which strict rules and protocol control daily activity. As filmmakers have replicated (or "glamorized") the extremely structured existence of life within penitentiaries and reformatories, many elements of these motion pictures have grown into clichés. For example, there is the induction of new inmates into the prison system; the unique convict jargon; the milling, restless prisoners in the exercise yard; the abnormal regimen of eating, sleeping and working under constant surveillance and always with restricted freedom; the death row melancholy of condemned inmates; the tough and or sympathetic warden and his guard staff; and of course, the constant friction and outbreaks of violence between the keepers and their charges.

One of the strange results of scriptwriters' focusing on prisoners as prime subjects for motion pictures has been that they have often converted their convict characters into screen "heroes." By striving to create sympathy for the plight of inmates on camera, scenarists and audience alike frequently lose sight of the fact that, in most instances, these people have chosen (for whatever reason) to break laws for their own purposes. This realization provides prison movies with a strange flavor all their own.

Prison films do not focus only on prisoners. They also deal with the complex personalities and temperaments of administrators and guards who have chosen to work in tough penal environments. And not to be overlooked are those civilians who must cope with having their relatives or loved ones locked up in prison, and the traumatic effect this has on their own lives.

Over the decades, there have been distinctive changes in the tenor of prison movies. These changes usually reflect the average citizen's attitude toward penal rehabilitation and retribution in general and with capital punishment. Many of the most powerful prison motion pictures and telefeatures have dealt with abuses in the penal system and the need for reform, ironically often using the occasion to exploit these inhumanities against mankind for the titillation of moviegoers.

There are many reasons why prison movies have been such a favorite with filmgoers for decades. They provide an opportunity to view (even in distillation) and to vicariously experience a subculture that the average viewer will never know firsthand. As such, prison movies pander to human fascination with the grueling existence of incarcerated convicts in which freedom may be days, years or an eternity away. This mystique of bravery, deprivation and endurance has its appeal to some audiences. Then too, action enthusiasts are drawn to prison movies because they provide frequent opportunities for rough encounters as caged and frustrated inmates clash with each other and with their guards. Additionally, the strained, abnormal existence of locked-up human beings allows viewers the chance to enjoy watching favorite stars exercising machismo (Burt Lancaster in *Brute Force,* Sylvester Stallone in *Lock Up*) and high dramatics (Eleanor Parker in *Caged,* Susan Hayward in *I Want to Live!*). More recently, a strong subculture of softcore pornography movies has developed, dealing expressly with women behind bars, and pushing voyeurism to new heights.

Because the prison film has so insistently intrigued American filmmakers for so long, I have focused primarily on genre pieces produced by Hollywood. Because there is such richness and variation of thematic material dealing with prisoners behind bars, I have limited this book to a discussion of those full-length feature films and made-for-television movies whose chief focus is on prison inmates. As such, this book does *not* deal with the world of the paroled ex-convict. The study of individuals confined to prisoner-of-war camps or to mental institutions are subjects requiring separate investigation unto themselves.

As always, I would appreciate learning readers' response to this book, whether it be suggestions, additions or corrections.

James Robert Parish
April, 1991

Prison Shows on Television

Compiled by Vincent Terrace

Camp California (Pilot). September 9, 1989, ABC, with Ted Wass, Garrit Graham, Barry Corbin, Valerie Mahaffey, Luis Avalos (originally titled *Club Fed*).

Mariah. April 1, 1987, to May 13, 1987, ABC (a.k.a. *Mariah State*), with John Getz, Tovah Feldshuh, William Allen Young, Susan Brown, Renee Lippin, Chris Wiggins.

Maximum Security. March 9, 1985, to April 23, 1985, HBO, with Geoffrey Lewis, Jean Smart, Trinidad Silva, Teddy Wilson, Stephen Elliott.

Prisoner: Cell Block H. 1979–1980, Syndicated, with Peita Toppano, Kerry Armstrong, Carol Burns, Val Lehman, Elspeth Ballantyne, Patsy King, Fiona Spence, Sheila Florance.

The Warden (Unaired Pilot). Produced in 1963, with Robert Webber, Gene Evans, Tige Andrews, Nancy Rennick, Lane Bradford, Greg Morris.

Willow B: Women in Prison (Pilot). June 29, 1980, ABC, with Carol Lynley, Debra Clinger, Trisha Noble, Sally Kirkland, Liz Torres, Lynne Moody, Ruth Roman.

Women in Prison. October 11, 1987, to April 2, 1988, FOX, with Julia Campbell, Peggy Cass, Antoinette Byron, Wendie Jo Sperber, C. C. H. Pounder, Blake Clark.

Prison movies are unfair. Whether they are good or bad, they can grab and hold our interest. Conflict is built into them. It's as much a part of the prison landscape as cellblocks, walls, the presence of the guards, the tensions of the prisoners.... I've sat through lots of them, some quite terrible, and never once thought of walking out. Something is always bound to happen in a prison movie — and you can't say that about every movie set in the wide-open spaces.

— Vincent Canby (*New York Times*) reviewing *On the Yard* (January 19, 1979)

The Films

1. *The Accusing Finger* (Paramount, 1936), 61 min.

Producer, A. M. Botsford; director, James Hogan; screenplay, Madeleine Ruthven, Brian Marlow, John Bright, Robert Trasker; music director, Boris Morros; camera, Henry Sharp; editor, Chandler House.

Marsha Hunt (Claire Patterson); Robert Cummings (Jimmy Ellis); Paul Kelly (Douglas Goodwin); Kent Taylor (Jerry Welch); Harry Carey (Senator Nash); Bernadene Hayes (Muriel Goodwin); Sam Flint (District Attorney); DeWitt Jennings (Warden); Ralph Harolde (Spud); Fred Kohler (Johnson); Hilda Vaughn (Maid).

For decades concerned citizens and politicians have debated the pros and cons of the death sentence as a deterrent of capital offenses. Not to be left out, Hollywood has entered the controversy on several occasions. This mild programmer from Paramount Pictures sought to be a vigorous statement supporting the abolition of prison executions. Unfortunately, it was too ineffectual a drama to have the desired effects. "Only on two occasions does it stir the spectator — once where a young convict in the death house speaks about his approaching death, and at another time when he is shown being taken to the death cell" (*Harrison's Reports*).

Overzealous state prosecutor Douglas Goodwin (Paul Kelly) has an admirable record of convictions, especially those sending capital offense defendants to the electric chair. Goodwin happens to be at the apartment of his estranged wife, Muriel (Bernadene Hayes), when she is killed by a jewel thief. Because of circumstantial evidence, he is convicted and sentenced to be executed. While awaiting his death sentence, he reflects on his career and the possibility that some of the people he prosecuted may have also been innocent victims of fate. After talking with Jimmy Ellis (Robert Cummings), one of the men he had tried, he is converted to believing that capital punishment is bad. Meanwhile, Senator Nash (Harry Carey) is making a drive to abolish the death sentence and he brings Goodwin before the group where he makes an impassioned plea. Thanks to the efforts of assistant prosecutor Jerry Welch (Kent Taylor) and Goodwin's secretary, Claire Patterson (Marsha Hunt), the real killer is found and Goodwin is released.

Variety disliked the picture, explaining, "*The Accusing Finger* is a glaring example of too many chefs having a finger in the broth.... Main fault is that the film fails to pertinently develop several plot angles introduced.... Whoever conceived the finale and the prison material should have been permitted to re-write and subordinate the other themes because they detract and weaken the entire structure."

2. *Alcatraz: The Whole Shocking Story* (NBC–TV, Nov. 5–6, 1980), color, 200 min.

Executive producer, Pierre Cossette; producers, James H. Brown, Ernest Tidyman; director, Paul Krasny; story, Clarence Carnes, Don DeVevi; teleplay, Tidyman; production designer, William L. Campbell; set decorator, Charles Graffed; costumes, Michael Lynn; makeup, John Norin, Greg La Cava; music, Jerrold Immel; music editor, Echo Film Service; assistant director, Robert Jefford; sound, Maury Harris; sound editor, Don Ernst; special effects, John Frazier; camera, Robert B. Hauser; editors: Donald R. Rode (part one), Les Green (part two).

Michael Beck (Clarence Carnes); Art Carney (Robert Stroud); Alex Karras (Jughead Miller); Telly Savalas (Cretzer); Will Sampson (Clarence's Father); Ronny Cox (Bernard Coy); Richard Lynch (Sam Shockley); Robert Davi (Hubbard); John Amos (Bumpy Johnson); James MacArthur (Walt Stomer); Ed Lauter (Frank Morris); Joe Pantoliano (Ray Neal); Louis Giambalve (Clarence Anglin); Jeffrey Tambor (Dankworth); Paul Mantee (Ordway); Charles Aidman (Warden Johnson); Jack Rader (Weinhold); Walter Mathews (Corwin); Spencer Milligan (Fred Haskell); Sidney Clute (Miller); Redmond Gleeson (Jackson); Brad English (Thompkins); Antony Ponzini (John Anglin); Paul Picerni (Lieutenant Lagason); Burt Marshall (Guard); Lois Red-Elk (Clarence's Mother); Arthur Taxier (Connelly); David Boyle (Guard); G. W. Bailey (Holfeld); Sandy Ward (McIntire); Stack Pierce (Presser); Tom Lupo (Dunslay); Roger Hackett (Male Nurse); Ken Letner (Armory Lieutenant); Tom O'Neill (Guard); Al Gingolani (Carroll); Bob Hoy (Myron Thompson); Peter Coyote (Courtney Taylor); John Wagoner (Alvin Tucker); Wiley Marker (Judge Goodman); John Chappell (Sheriff's Deputy); Peter Jason (Lieutenant Micklin); Hoke Howell (Store Owner); Jocko Marcellino (Prisoner); Roger Hampton (Hampton); James Harrison (Dumpy); Jim Steck (Guard Crayden); Pat Valentino (Colman); W. T. Zacha (Baggett); David DeLange (Lieutenant Stanfield); Frank McCarthy (Lieutenant Holmby); James Jeter (Guard Fairgate); Angelo Grisante (Convict); Jim Haynie (Salkin); Nick Eldredge (Larwin); Johnny Weissmuller, Jr. (Felish).

Like the U.S. Marine Corps, which prides itself on being the toughest military regimen for men, Alcatraz Prison, since its inception in the mid–1930s, rightfully had the reputation of being the most rugged disciplinary environment that American penal authorities could devise to impose on male prisoners. Among (ex) convicts, having served a "stretch" at Alcatraz was its own (inverted) badge of courage and respect. The fact that the prison was touted as escape-proof provided a ready challenge to decades of enterprising prisoners who intended to prove the authorities wrong.

The general public has long been intrigued with the stark conditions that existed at the hellhole known as Alcatraz. To exploit this (perverse) fascination and to gain high ratings, this overdrawn telefeature aimed at being both exploitive and action-filled. What emerged, however, was a lengthy, humdrum chronicle in the lackluster tradition of a "B" movie. It generally failed to live up to the "shocking" premise of its title. "Any film that encourages us to root for convicted criminals is somewhat suspect—[Ernest] Tidyman's script circumvents this complexity by simply not delving into the crimes committed by potential escapees" (Gail Williams, *Hollywood Reporter*).

The focus of this lengthy drama (originally shown over two nights of prime time TV) is Clarence Carnes (Michael Beck) a youthful Oklahoma Indian (of the Choctaw tribe) who is drawn by a friend into helping rob a gas station. When a murder occurs during the holdup, Carnes is convicted and sentenced to life imprisonment. He keeps trying to escape from custody (jail, the chain gang, etc.) and finally his keepers decide to ship him off to Alcatraz.

Just before being relocated to the San Francisco Bay prison, authorities inform the convict, "If nothing else can hold you Carnes, Alcatraz will. Nobody else has escaped and neither will you." The stage is set for the youngest prisoner in Alcatraz's history to meet his match. Upon arriving at the bleak island fortress in the late 1930s, Clarence and the other new inmates are warned by a stern guard (Alex Karras) of the ironhanded rules that govern life in this strictest of all American prisons:

> You're gonna be searched inside and out and if anybody is taking anything into Alcatraz, he'll go straight to the hole and he'll wish he were in hell. Now this is the rock... You are here because you're useless and worthless both in society and the prison system and here you'll stay until the day you die or you get paroled. There is no escape! Swim and the current will drown you or the sharks will eat you. Smart cons don't even try.
>
> You lay one finger on any of these guards and it's the gas chamber. Now, you're allowed one visitor a month, if you follow the rules, two showers a week, one haircut a month. That's all the privileges you'll ever get on the rock.

If the authoritarian warnings and the rugged convict regimen have not already convinced the impressionable Carnes of his fate, another prisoner, Bernard Coy (Ronny Cox), underlines the young man's plight. "This is the last stop on the hardest line in the prison system and it's the worst and that's how they treat you. You try to fight that and you'll end up dead or crazy." Coy also gives Clarence some practical advice, "Tell the man [i.e. authority figures] what you want, but don't look eager. They'll figure saying no is good for you."

Carnes's father (Will Sampson) relocates to San Francisco where he takes a job in the local shipyards so he can be close enough to visit his son. While the two meet monthly, more than the glass window barrier in the visitors' room separates the proud, baffled Indian elder from his feckless son, the latter feeling himself a worthless pawn in the social strata of a prejudiced America.

Eventually the rebellious, dispirited Carnes settles into the tedium of Alcatraz existence where "working is a privilege." He earns a job in the laundry room. Meanwhile, in 1946, Sam Shockley (Richard Lynch), a mentally disturbed inmate, foments one more escape plan. Coy, who works in the library and delivers magazines to the convicts' cells, is the communications link for the scheme, while rugged Cretzer (Telly Savalas) is the "brains" behind the plot. Cretzer wants Carnes, who has a knowledge of the outdoors, to help with the breakout, especially to guide the thirty escapees through the woods which surround the fortress. Carnes is eager to escape this hell on earth, "I'd try to get out of here with the devil if he asked me." On the other hand, veteran convict Robert Stroud (Art Carney), known as "The Birdman of Alcatraz" for his prison-obtained education in ornithology, refuses to join in the break-to-freedom. He points out to the stir-crazed Carnes, "There's one thing worse than not being free and that's no life at all. Think of that."

When the convicts make their bid for freedom, several guards are taken hostage. The warden (Charles Aidman) calls in the Bureau of Prisons and the FBI, as well as a detachment of San Francisco–based Marines. The bloodthirsty Cretzer shoots several of the guards and orders Carnes to take a knife and slit the throats of any hostage survivors. Bearing Stroud's words in his mind, Clarence spares the surviving guards and returns to his cell. Meanwhile, prisoners Cretzer, Coy, Shockley and Hubbard (Robert Davi), in particular, hold out against the assault team which now is drilling into the walls to blast the prisoners out with tear gas.

In the midst of the chaos, level-headed Stroud acts as an intermediary to save the noncombatant convicts in D Block from further harm. Eventually, the riot is quelled with two of the survivors, Shockley and Thompkins (Brad English), tried for their bloody escape attempt and sent to the gas chamber at San Quentin Prison in 1948, while Carnes remains at Alcatraz for ninety-nine years *plus* life. He is reassigned to cell #39, next to Robert Stroud's and the two become friends.

The narrative jumps to January 1954 at a point where the veteran Stroud observes to Carnes, "They're letting a second-rate bunch of cons in these days." While Stroud remains in lock-up (isolated to his cell) because he cannot stand the tension of being back amongst the general population (allowed to mingle in the exercise yard, eat in the general dining hall, etc.), Carnes has quelled his rebellious nature. Having been in the isolation "hole" forty-two times, he now has calmed down and is moved from his job in industry to the library. In the late 1950s, convicts Walt Stomer (James MacArthur), Frank Morris (Ed Lauter) and the Anglin brothers, Clarence (Louis Giambalve) and John (Antony Ponzini), hatch a new escape plan. Bumpy Johnson (John Amos), a former Harlem big shot hood, does not want to take the chance of escaping himself, but agrees to help the men with outside contacts should they reach freedom. Carnes's rationale for assisting Stomer *et al.* is his belief that, if at least one convict escapes "the rock," then the dreadful Alcatraz will have to be closed down. However, because Carnes was involved in the 1946 riot, he is watched too closely to attempt escape himself. Finally, on the night of June 11, 1962, the breakout is attempted. At the last minute, Stomer is unable to break out of his cell in time to join up with the others and must remain behind. However, Morris and the Anglins do escape and are never found. A postscript advises that on May 15, 1963, Alcatraz Prison was closed by order of Attorney General Robert F. Kennedy. Clarence Carnes was transferred from Alcatraz to Leavenworth Prison and was paroled finally in 1973.

A preface to this telefilm had stated, "This motion picture is based on a true story, but some names, places and incidents have been changed for dramatic effect." Herein lay the entertainment problems with *Alcatraz: The Whole Shocking Story*. What was factual had been told better before (e.g. *Birdman of Alcatraz*, 1962, and *Escape from Alcatraz*, 1979, qq.v), and what was fictional was bland and hackneyed. Finally, what was missing most of all was the gritty sense of reality, something that even a programmer like *Alcatraz Island* (1937), q.v., had captured far better. The details of the 1946 escape attempt would be documented yet again in the middling telefeature *Six Against the Rock* (1987), q.v.

3. *Alcatraz Island* (Warner Bros., 1937), 64 min.

Supervisor, Bryan Foy; director, William McGann; based on the story "Alcatraz" by Crane Wilbur; screenplay, Wilbur; art director, Esdras Hartley; gowns, Howard Shoup; camera, L. W. O'Connell; editor, Frank Dewar.

John Litel (Gat Brady); Mary Maguire (Ann Brady); Ann Sheridan (Flo Allen); Gordon Oliver (George Drake); Dick Purcell (Harp Santell); Ben Welden ("Red" Carroll); Addison Richards (Fred MacLane); George E. Stone (Tough Tony Burke); Vladimir Sokoloff (Flying Dutchman); Peggy Bates (Miss Toliver); Charles Trowbridge (Warden Jackson); Janet Shaw (Sally Carruthers); Doris Lloyd (Miss Marquand); Veda Ann Borg (The Red Head); Matty Fain (Butch); Anderson Lawler (Whitey Edwards); Walter Young (Federal Judge); Edward Keane (Crandall); Ed Stanley (U.S. Attorney); Granville Owen (Gat's Secretary); Sol Gorss (Gat's Bodyguard); Sam Cohen (Maury Schwartz); Milton Kibbee, Perc Teeple (Court Clerks); Myrtle

Stedman (Woman); Mike Lally, Al Herman, Jack Gardner, Alan Davis (Convicts); Guy Usher (Principal Keeper); Cliff Saum, Henry Otho, Pat O'Malley, Ralph Dunn, Galan Galt, Ted Oliver (Guards); Francis Sayles (Bailiff); Earl Dwire (Judge); and Ethan Laidlaw.

Alcatraz Prison, on Angel's Island in San Francisco Bay, had been taken over by the Federal Bureau of Prisons in 1934 and converted from a military prison facility into a maximum security complex for the most incorrigible prisoners in the U.S. penal system. The still fresh novelty of the locale was exploited by Warner Bros. in this continuation of its latest cycle of jail dramas ("ripped from the headlines") which had led off with *San Quentin* (1937). This film also featured studio contract player Ann Sheridan.

Regarding this entry from Bryan Foy's "B" unit at Warner Bros., *Variety* assessed, "Every effort is made to give the picture an authentic Alcatraz background, as has characterized other Warner prison releases, but, due to weakness of story, an average directorial job and failure to inject desired menace, it has its drawbacks as entertainment."

Smooth racketeer Gat Brady (John Litel) has been enjoying the good life, including having a caring fiancée, Flo Allen (Ann Sheridan). One of his henchmen, Red Carroll (Ben Welden), asks Gat to help out his brother who was wanted for murder, but Brady refuses. As a result Red swears to get even with Brady. Meanwhile, the federal government is investigating Brady and the adverse publicity causes the swank boarding school which his daughter Ann (Mary Maguire) is attending to ask her to leave. Just as Brady and Ann really get to know each other and are planning to leave for a European trip, he is arrested by federal agents for income tax evasion. He is convicted for a five year term and sent to Leavenworth Prison.

Soon Red is incarcerated at Leavenworth on a charge of having attempted to kidnap Ann. When Carroll taunts Brady into fighting with him, the latter is labeled an incorrigible prisoner and is transferred to Alcatraz Island. Before long, Red manages to get himself sent to Alcatraz and again stirs up trouble with Gat. Later Carroll is found stabbed to death and Gat is the logical suspect. However, Ann, assisted by district attorney George Drake (Gordon Oliver), as well as Flo Allen, work to prove Gat's innocence. A federal agent (Dick Purcell) is sent undercover to pose as a prisoner and forces a confession from a convict (Vladimir Sokoloff) who had held a grudge against Red. Gat is freed from the murder charge.

The most solid aspects of this minidrama were the unmannered performances of the cast, especially George E. Stone in a subordinate comic convict role, and the subtle way the storyline exploited the grimness of prison life in general, and the spartan existence at Alcatraz in particular.

The trade paper *Harrison's Reports* noted of the contrived, coincidence-filled premise, "In spite of the fact that the hero is a racketeer, one is in sympathy with him because he is not shown stooping to low tricks or injuring any one. Human appeal is aroused by the devotion between the hero and his daughter."

4. *Angels with Dirty Faces* (Warner Bros., 1938), 97 min.

Producer, Sam Bischoff; director, Michael Curtiz; story, Rowland Brown; screenplay, John Wexley, Warren Duff; art director, Robert Haas; gowns, Orry-Kelly; music, Max Steiner; orchestrator, Hugo Friedhofer; song, Fred Fisher and Maurice

Spitalny; music director, Leo F. Forbstein; assistant director, Sherry Shourds; dialogue director, Jo Graham; technical adviser, J. J. Devlin; sound, Everett A. Brown; camera, Sol Polito; editor, Owen Marks.

James Cagney (William "Rocky" Sullivan); Pat O'Brien (Jerry Connelly); Humphrey Bogart (James Frazier); Ann Sheridan (Laury Ferguson); George Bancroft (Mac Keefer); Billy Halop (Soapy); Bobby Jordan (Swing); Leo Gorcey (Bim); Bernard Punsly (Hunky); Gabriel Dell (Patsy); Huntz Hall (Crab); Frankie Burke (William "Rocky" Sullivan as a Boy); William Tracy (Jerry Connelly as a Boy); Marilyn Knowlden (Laury Ferguson as a Girl); Joe Downing (Steve); Adrian Morris (Blackie); Oscar O'Shea (Guard Kennedy); Edward Pawley (Guard Edwards); William Pawley (Bugs the Gunman); Charles Sullivan, Theodore Rand (Gunmen); John Hamilton (Police Captain); Earl Dwire (Priest); The St. Brendan's Church Choir (Themselves); William Worthington (Warden); James Farley (Railroad Yard Watchman); Pat O'Malley, Jack C. Smith (Railroad Guards); Roger McGee, Vince Lombardi, Sonny Bupp, A. W. Sweatt (Boys); Chuck Stubb (Red); Eddie Syracuse (Maggione Boy); George Sorel (Headwaiter); Robert Homans (Policeman); Harris Berger (Basketball Captain); Lottie Williams (Woman); Harry Hayden (Pharmacist); Dick Rich, Steven Darrell, Joe A. Devlin (Gangsters); Donald Kerr, Jack Goodrich, Al Lloyd, Jeffrey Sayre, Charles Marsh, Alexander Lockwood, Earl Gunn, Carlyle Moore (Reporters); Lee Phelps, Jack Mower (Detectives); Belle Mitchell (Mrs. Maggione); William Edmunds (Italian Storekeeper); Charles Wilson (Buckley the Police Chief); Vera Lewis (Soapy's Mother); Eddie Brian (Newsboy); Billy McClain (Janitor); Claude Wisberg (Hanger-On); Frank Hagney, Dick Wessel, John Harron (Sharpies); Wilbur Mack (Croupier); Frank Coghlan, Jr., David Durand (Boys in Poolroom); Mary Gordon (Mrs. Patrick McGee); George Offerman, Jr. (Older Boy in Poolroom); Joe Cunningham (Managing Editor); James Spottswood (*Record* Editor); John Dilson (*Chronicle* Editor); Charles Trowbridge (Norton J. White); Tommy Jackson (*Press City* Editor); Ralph Sanford, Galan Galt (Policemen at Call-Box); Emory Parnell, Wilfred Lucas, Elliott Sullivan (Police Officers); William Crowell (Whimpering Convict); Lane Chandler, Ben Hendricks (Guards); Sidney Bracey, George Taylor, Oscar G. Hendrian, Dan Wolheim, Brian Burke (Convicts); John Marston (Well-Dressed Man); Poppy Wilde (Girl at Gaming Table).

In a year filled with superior Hollywood film fare, *Angels with Dirty Faces* stands out as a marvelous example of the Warner Bros. production line at its finest. It definitely lived up to its advertising slogan, "A big time cast in a big city drama destined to be the biggest hit in years!"

Expertly supervised by veteran director Michael Curtiz, the ninety-seven minutes of drama and action in *Angels with Dirty Faces* rushes by pell-mell, scarcely leaving the viewer time to absorb it, let alone realize that this story of two boyhood pals who grow up on the opposite sides of morality is a thinly veiled variation of the format pioneered by Metro-Goldwyn-Mayer in *Manhattan Melodrama* (1934). Despite its plotline derivativeness, *Angels with Dirty Faces* easily stands on its own merits. It is a masterful blend of a gun-happy gangster yarn with a sociological study of the effects of environment (the slums of East Side New York) on neighborhood youths. Tossed into the mix are assorted love interests. There is the gangster hero's yearning for his childhood sweetheart, a priest's devotion to his congregation in general and a group of teenaged toughies in particular, and the clergyman's loyalty to his boyhood chum who took a wrong turn morally years before.

This film boasts several cinema history notable statistics: it was the sixth of eight crackerjack buddy pictures made by Pat O'Brien and James Cagney at Warner Bros., the first of three studio movies to co-star the wisecracking love team of

Opposite: Quelling a riot in *Alcatraz Island* (1937).

Cagney and Ann Sheridan, one of several celluloid underworld actioners to pit Humphrey Bogart in a losing battle against Cagney and O'Brien, and the third Hollywood motion picture to feature the "Bowery Boys," who had come to the studio earlier in the year for *Crime School* (1938), q.v. Additionally, *Angels with Dirty Faces* contains one of the American cinema's most memorable prison death house execution scenes.

As youths on Manhattan's Lower East Side in the early 1920s, young Rocky Sullivan (Frankie Burke) and Jerry Connelly (William Tracy) are two punks who neither respect the law nor the girls on the block. One day, the daring duo is intercepted by a railroad yard watchman while breaking into a boxcar filled with fountain pens. The youths break for freedom, with Jerry getting away. Rocky, however, is captured and sent to a reformatory. In subsequent years, Rocky falls into a life of crime, eventually becoming a big time hood (James Cagney), while Jerry, who remains loyal to his pal, becomes a priest (Pat O'Brien) and is assigned to their childhood parish in the tenderloin district in Manhattan. After being released from his latest jail stay, Rocky returns to his old neighborhood and rents a room in a boardinghouse in which his former childhood playmate, Laury Ferguson (Ann Sheridan), resides. Rocky quickly becomes the idol of the latest gang of slum kids (the Dead End Kids), who all too quickly emulate his reckless style. At Father Jerry's pleadings, Rocky does persuade the youths into attending the parish recreation center. Meanwhile, Rocky contacts his lawyer-partner James Frazier (Humphrey Bogart) who had been supposedly holding in trust $100,000 of the two's money. Rocky discovers that Frazier is in cahoots with underworld figure Mac Keefer (George Bancroft) in operating a prosperous club and in other rackets and intends to renege on his deal with Rocky. When an attempt to have Rocky killed fails, Sullivan kidnaps Frazier, takes the money, and, for added insurance, grabs a parcel of incriminating documents. This action leads to the three hoodlums working together, but definitely not trusting one another. Later, Father Jerry inaugurates a media campaign to rid the community of the crime craze. When Rocky overhears his confederates planning to eradicate Father Jerry, he kills them instead. Eventually, Rocky is captured and sentenced to death in the electric chair.

Father Jerry, with his soulful eyes brimming over and a catch in his Irish brogue, visits Rocky for the last time in his death row cell. What follows is a masterful screen interlude guaranteed to captivate viewers. It allows moviegoers the titillating vicarious experience of observing a cocky hoodlum prepare to go to the electric chair, while, at the same time, it plays out the final chapter in a complex buddy relationship that has endured throughout this sentimental chronicle. Because the film has been structured to make *both* the pugnacious gangster *and* the street-wise clergyman equal heros to the audience, the interplay is even more gripping. It does more in explaining the mentality of an unremorseful condemned man than any other genre film to date.

FATHER JERRY: I want to ask you one last favor.

ROCKY: There's not much I could do, kid.

FATHER JERRY: Yes there is, Rocky. Perhaps more than you could do under other circumstances. If you have the courage for it and I know you have. . . .

ROCKY: You mean walking in there? That's not going to take much.

FATHER JERRY: I know that Rocky.

ROCKY: It's like sitting in a barber chair. They're going to ask me, "Got anything to say?" and I say, "Sure. Give me a haircut, shave and a massage. One of those nice new electric massages. (He laughs). Heh. Heh."

FATHER JERRY: But you're not afraid, Rocky.

ROCKY: They'd like me to be, wouldn't they? I'm afraid I can't oblige them, kid. You know, Jerry, I think to be afraid you've gotta have a heart. I don't think I've got one. That got cut out of me a long time ago.

FATHER JERRY: Suppose I asked you to have the heart to be scared. Suppose at the last minute the guards dragged you out of here screaming for mercy. Suppose you went to the chair yellow?

ROCKY: Yella? Say, what the matter with ya? You've been worrying about my courage.

FATHER JERRY: This is a different kind of courage, Rocky. The kind, well, that's born in heaven. Oh not the courage of heroics or bravado, the kind that you, God and I know about.

At this juncture, the priest explains further:

FATHER JERRY: I want you to let them [the neighborhood youths] down. You see, you've been a hero to these kids and hundreds of others all through your life and now you're going to be a glorified hero in death and I want to prevent that. They've got to despise your memory. They've got to be ashamed of you.

ROCKY: You're asking me to throw away the only thing I've got left, the only thing they haven't been able to take away from me. You want me to give the newspaper sob sisters a chance to say, "Another rat turned yella." . . . You're askin' a nice little favor, Jerry. Asking me to crawl on my belly. The last thing I do in life. . . . Nothing doing. You've got to figure out some other way . . .

Seemingly having failed to persuade his belligerent pal, a resigned Father Jerry follows Rocky as he is taken from his cell and is led to the execution room. As Rocky reaches the death room, the priest says, "Goodbye, Rocky. May God have mercy on you."

Suddenly in a sharp change of posture, Rocky turns into a whimpering, squirming coward as he is dragged to the hot seat. With James Cagney's bravura performance, this remarkable sequence is unforgettable, as he screams hysterically: "Oh no. I don't want to die, please. Don't make me burn. Oh, please! Oh please. Don't do this! Please! Oh please, don't kill me!"

In a quick montage thereafter, newspaper headlines boast, "ROCKY DIES YELLOW! KILLER, COWARD AT END!"

The finale has Father Jerry returning to the basement clubhouse of the young neighborhood toughies. He insists to the unbelieving teenagers, "It's true boys. Every word of it. He died like they said." (The shock of realization in the kids' eyes concludes the film's twisted do-good message: don't make heroes of villains.) The next words by the priest are among the most famous closing lines in movie history: "All right fellas. Let's go and say a prayer for a boy who couldn't run as fast as I could."

The critics were equally as enthusiastic as the public about *Angels with Dirty Faces*. "The film proceeds racily, overcoming the familiarity of the ground it is covering by its surprising twists of plot and character, and it emerges as one of the most picturesque and dramatic of this year's crime studies" (Frank S. Nugent, *New York Times*). *Variety* endorsed, "With few exceptions the picture is skilfully and handsomely produced. . . [I]t is forcefully told. Also the screenplay contains many effective cinematic touches." In her 3 ½ star *New York Daily News* review, Kate Cameron noted that Cagney "achieved the sensitive, rounded and menacing characterization which is the mainspring of this fiction." Cagney was Oscar-nominated for his performance, but lost the Best Actor Academy Award to Spencer Tracy of MGM's *Boys Town*, q.v.

James Cagney would return to the prison genre in *Each Dawn I Die* (1939) and *White Heat* (1949), qq.v., while Pat O'Brien would make *Castle on the Hudson* (1940), q.v., and the Dead End Kids would appear in the later boys' reformatory exposé, *Hell's Kitchen* (1939), q.v. For the record, Warner Bros.' *Angels Wash Their Faces* (1939), which starred the Dead End Kids, Ronald Reagan and Ann Sheridan, is *not* a sequel to *Angels with Dirty Faces*.

5. *Ann Vickers* (RKO, 1933), 72 min.

Executive producer, Merian C. Cooper; producer, Pandro S. Berman; director, John Cromwell; based on the novel by Sinclair Lewis; screenplay, Jane Murfin; art directors, Van Nest Polglase, Charles Kirk; music director, Max Steiner; sound, Paul F. Wiser; camera, David Abel, Edward Cronjager; editor, George Nicholls, Jr.

Irene Dunne (Ann Vickers); Walter Huston (Judge Barney Dolphin); Conrad Nagel (Lindsey Atwell); Bruce Cabot (Captain Lafayette (Resnick); Edna May Oliver (Dr. Malvina Wormser); Sam Hardy (Russell Spalding); Mitchell Lewis (Captain Waldo Drindle); Murray Kinnell (Dr. Slenk); Helen Eby-Rock (Kitty Cognac); Gertrude Michael (Mona Dolphin); J. Carrol Naish (Dr. Sorell); Sarah Padden (Lil); Reginald Barlow (Chaplain); Rafaela Ottiano (Frieda Feldermus); Irving Bacon (Waiter); Geneva Mitchell (Leah Burbaum); Mary Foy (Matron); Frederic Santley (Sam, Reform Assistant); Wally Albright (Mischau); Edwin Maxwell (Defense Attorney); Larry Steers (Prosecutor); Arthur Hoyt (Mr. Penny); Jane Darwell (Mrs. Gates).

Best-selling novelist Sinclair Lewis had already written *Main Street* (1920), *Babbitt* (1922), *Arrowsmith* (1925), *Elmer Gantry* (1927) and *Dodsworth* (1929), when his *Ann Vickers* was published in 1933. In his newest book, Lewis, in his typical satirical style, continued his mocking the hypocrisies of contemporary American society, as well as interweaving social protest (women's rights, prison reform) into his romance yarn. RKO purchased the property as a vehicle for its contract star Irene Dunne and announced boastfully, "These are the times of overturning. RKO Radio does not believe that the truth should be suppressed. The screen dares to produce what Lewis dared to write. The picture now pleads guilty to destroying human faith in certain pleasant lies. It will inflame the nation like purifying fire. But *Ann Vickers* is not a sermon!!"

The chronicle opens during World War I with zealous Ann Vickers (Irene Dunne) becoming the assistant Head Resident at the Corlears Hook Settlement House in New York City. Unlike the typical woman of the day, Ann is career-oriented, a professional do-gooder. (She is a college graduate who underwent nurse's training, joined the suffragette movement and later became a social

Edna May Oliver and Irene Dunne in *Ann Vickers* (1933).

worker.) As her friend, Dr. Wormser (Edna May Oliver), observes, "Ann has a passion for helping people. She is going to make the world over if it takes all winter." But then at a Settlement House party Ann meets dashing young Captain Lafayette Resnick (Bruce Cabot). She abandons her plan of going out west to "do more important work" in order to be near Resnick. Later, she succumbs to his advances, becomes pregnant and then has a miscarriage. While Malvina remains her constant support throughout, Resnick quickly drops Ann to find new conquests. Shaken by the traumatic turn of events in her life, Ann has a revelation of sorts: "I've discovered you can read into someone else all the things you want them to be and you can love those things and think you're loving the person...."

Ann accepts a post out west at the Copperhead Gap Prison, determined to conquer new terrain — this time to learn about penology. Her highfalutin suitor, stuffy attorney Lindsey Atwell (Conrad Nagel) thinks Ann's new crusade is merely a lark. "When do you start your stretch?" he inquires. Although she is a zealous reformer, there is more than a hint that this modern woman retains some primitive, old-fashioned instincts. When refusing Atwell's too polite offer of marriage, she explains, "Grabbing me is the only way I'll be gotten." She also tells him, "Copperhead Gap may be terrible, but I won't have to use women's wiles on it." Clearly Ann is a very strange breed of reformer.

Arriving at the austere prison, the officious warden (Murray Kinnell) admits to the bewildered Ann that the crude, sadistic Captain Waldo Drindle (Mitchell Lewis) "is the real boss of the prison. I'm just the gadabout. I contact the citizens and officials and find out what they want us to do. But it's Captain Waldo that really carries it out." Thinking the newcomer a misguided fool, the warden tells

Drindle, "Miss Vickers is in for the comparatively minor crime of being a sociologist, Captain, so let her off easy. So don't give her the dark cells, at least not yet."

Drindle is not impressed by this refined female interloper and quickly confides to Ann his own theories of "modern" penology. "I've been in prison work for thirty-two mortal years and I tell you the only way to handle prisoners is to put the fear of God in them. Of course, the warden ain't supposed to know everything I do around here. He passes the buck to me.... I'd like to get back some of the good old punishment. If I could brand incorrigibles, slash them ... a little trophy so that it would be a warning to everybody.... Use a real cat-o-nine-tails.... Say, if I could do that I'd sure cure crime in a jiffy."

Ann is installed in the women's section of the prison and, through a montage, the viewer shares with her a succession of jail hourse horrors being carried out on the prisoners by the stern matrons who carry canes to beat the convicts into submission. Midst the grim daily prison life, Ann also witnesses the hanging execution of a black woman. Angered by all she has seen, Ann protests to the warden and Drindle. Their response is to blackmail her with staged compromising photographs. She soon leaves the prison, having gained very few concessions for the inmates. Later she writes *99 Days & Nights in Prison,* a best-seller exposé of the human cruelty she observed at Copperhead Gap.

The remaining segment of the melodrama finds Ann returning to New York and becoming the head of Stuyvesant Industrial Home, a sort of women's reformatory. As was typical of many reformers of this period, Ann has a very cavalier attitude towards her subject, guided more by noblesse oblige than by any real empathy. This flaw is illustrated perfectly when Kitty Cognac (Helen Eby-Rock), a former inmate of Copperhead Gap, arrives at Ann's institution as a new charge. Ann discovers that her ward is a dope addict. Ann casually tells the dependent Kitty, "We'll have to get you off the snow, cold turkey. I hate to have to do it this way." With that, Ann sweeps out of the room, bound for more important matters. Later Ann falls in love with a married man, the salty Judge Barney Dolphin (Walter Huston) of the New York State Supreme Court. He is amused yet amazed by the dedicated and seemingly ageless Ann, who is certainly not his vision of a warden.

> BARNEY: You, reformatory superintendent? Nonsense my dear girl. Where are the glasses? The bad smell? Where's the patient martyred expression?
>
> ANN: I'm worse yet. I mother the poor souls and they have to stand for it.

Ironically, the judge is soon convicted of receiving bribes and is sentenced to six years at hard labor at Fielding Penitentiary, putting a seemingly insurmountable block in the way of the growing love between him and Vickers. The faithful Ann visits him there and learns from the warden that Barney has become a model prisoner; in fact, he enjoys making gunny sacks and has turned down an easier clerical job. Meanwhile, the pious Board of Reformatory decides that Ann's personal life is not above approach and demands her resignation from the Home. While waiting for the judge to be released, she cares for his young son and earns her living writing syndicated newspaper articles on prison reform. At the finale Barney and Ann are reunited.

While *Variety* lauded Irene Dunne's performance, the trade paper pinpointed some of the film's problems, "It is too sketchy.... Ann's experiences in the prison reform movement are told in a few short sequences tied together with symbolic lap-dissolves. Too much that happens to her seems casual and off-hand, although the implications of soul upheaval are contrariwise." Mordaunt Hall (*New York Times*) concurred, "More often than not the natures of the persons involved are hinted at rather than adroitly delineated, and the narrative, which touches on many phases of Ann's eventful career, is somewhat too episodical."

6. *Attica* (ABC–TV, March 2, 1980), color, 100 min.

Producer, Louis Rudolph; director, Marvin J. Chomsky; based on the book *A Time to Die* by Tom Wicker; teleplay, James S. Henerson; art director, Tracy Bousman; music, Gil Melle; sound, Don Johnson; camera, Don H. Birnkrant; editor, Paul LaMastra.

Henry Darrow (Herman Badillo); Charles Durning (Russell Oswald); Joel Fabiani (Senator Gordon Conners); Morgan Freeman (Hap Richards); George Grizzard (Tom Wicker); David Harris (T. J.); Roger E. Mosley (Frank Green); Arlen Dean Snyder (Superintendent Vince Mancusi); Glynn Turman (Raymond Franklin); Anthony Zerbe (William Kunstler); Andrew Duncan (Lieutenant Driscoll); Ron Foster (Leon Clay); William Flatley (Dudley); Noble Lee Lester (Bobby Seale); Paul Lieber (Art Silver); M. B. Miller (McLaughlin); Earl Rowe (Captain Cowan); Maurice Woods (Lumumba).

In February, 1980, a month before this timely telefeature debuted, a prisoner riot at the New Mexico State Penitentiary at Santa Fe resulted in twelve correctional officers being held hostage. Before the bloody fracas ended there, thirty-six people were dead (of which thirty-three were inmates), and there had been millions of dollars of damage done to state property. It was the worst such incident since the convict rampage at New York's Attica State Prison in September 1971 which resulted in forty-three deaths. This stark made-for-television recreation of that Attica siege was based on a series of articles by Tom Wicker, the *New York Times* associate editor who was an eye witness to the violent conflict. (The articles were translated into the book *A Time to Die* [1975].)

Russell Oswald (Charles Durning) is the Prison Commissioner appointed by Governor Rockefeller to investigate the deteriorating conditions at Attica State Prison. The stage is soon set for an explosive revolt at the maximum security penitentiary, where the inmates orchestrate a grisly protest, ironically to achieve more humane treatment at the hands of the correctional officers and Superintendent Vince Mancusi (Arlen Dean Snyder). One of the black convict leaders is burly Frank Green (Roger E. Mosley), who after the guards are taken hostage and blindfolded, demands complete amnesty in exchange for the guards' release. Hap Richards (Morgan Freeman) is a jailhouse lawyer who tries unsuccessfully to reason with the men, while radical civil liberties attorney William Kunstler (Anthony Zerbe) is an outside negotiator caught up in the havoc. The latter must counter the cautionary viewpoint of another arbiter, Bobby Seale (Noble Lee Lester). One of the reporters at the scene of the mayhem is *New York Times's* journalist Tom Wicker (George Grizzard) who finds himself powerless to stop the rampaging events, and can merely record the facts.

In reviewing this unadorned and often gripping drama, *Variety* noted the production "catches the feeling of inevitable doom" and added, "the telefilm is a brilliant study in manipulation of groups of people ... but the two-hour exchanges of views are ultimately depressing."

Marvin J. Chomsky won an Emmy Award for his direction of this made-for-television movie, while nominations went to Charles Durning (Outstanding Supporting Actor), James S. Henerson (teleplay adaptation), Paul LaMastra (editor) and to the project's team of sound editors.

7. *The Avenging Shadow* (Pathé, 1928), 45 min.

Director, Ray Taylor; story/continuity, Bennett Cohen; titles, Ray Doyle; camera Harry Cooper, David Smith; editor, Thomas Malloy.

Ray Hallor (James Hamilton, a Young Bank Clerk); Wilbur Mack (Worthington, his Assistant Cashier); Clark Comstack (Sheriff Apling); Howard Davies (Tom Soomers, the Prison Warden); Margaret Morris (Marie, his daughter); LeRoy Mason (George Brooks, a Deputy Warden); Grey Boy (Klondike, the Dog).

"Strictly for the nuts who believe in the dog films" (*Variety*).

In the "flapper" era of the twenties and early thirties when penal reform was not a prime topic of concern for the average citizen, Hollywood used prisons as a catch-all plot device to sidetrack the hero or to have him encounter an assortment of types who may prove useful in his later life.

Falsely convicted of stealing a factory payroll, bank clerk James Hamilton (Ray Hallor) is sentenced to prison. Actually the culprits are Worthington (Wilbur Mack), an assistant at the bank and George Brooks (LeRoy Mason), a deputy warden at the prison. The true hero of the piece proves to be Klondike, a police dog (Grey Boy), who helps Hamilton prove his innocence. Meanwhile, Hamilton falls in love with the warden's daughter, Marie (Margaret Morris).

8. *Back Door to Heaven* (Paramount, 1939), 81 minutes.

Producer, William K. Howard; associate producer, Johnnie Walker; director, Howard; screenplay, Howard, John Bright, Robert Tasker; assistant director, Harold Godsoe; camera, Hal Mohr; editor, Jack Murray.

Aline McMahon (Miss Williams); Jimmy Lydon (Frankie as a Boy); Anita Magee (Carol as a Girl); William Harrigan (Mr. Rogers); Jane Seymour (Mrs. Rogers); Robert Wildhack (Rudolph Herzing); Billy Redfield (Charley Smith as a Boy); Kenneth LeRoy (Bob Hale as a Boy); Raymond Roe (John Shelley as a Boy); Al Webster (Sheriff Kramer); Joe Garry (Reform School Superintendent); Wallace Ford (Frankie as an Adult); Stuart Erwin (Jud); Bert Frohman (The Mouse); Kent Smith (John Shelley); Bruce Evans (Charley Smith); George Lewis (Bob Hale); Doug McMullen (Wallace Kishler); Helen Christian (Mrs. Smith); Robert Vivian (George Spelvin); Hugh Cameron (Penitentiary Warden); Iris Adrian (Sugar); Georgette Harvey (Mrs. Hamilton).

By the late 1930s it had become an established Hollywood assertion that, frequently, it was environment, *not* bad traits, which caused a youth to go wrong in life and to end up incarcerated in prison. Such was the case with the maudlin *Back Door to Heaven*. So contrived was this melodrama that Frank Nugent *(New York Times)* described this production co-written, produced and directed by William K. Howard as, "Certain descriptives come readily to the finger tips: banal, outrageous and maladroit would be the least impolite."

In the eighteen-minute prologue, Frankie (Jimmy Lydon) is a hapless Ohio youth born on the wrong side of the tracks. Before long this grammar school youth has stolen a harmonica. He is sent to reform school and begins on a path of crime that leads to his becoming an automobile thief and serving a five year term in the state penitentiary. Later, he intends to make a fresh start in life, but becomes innocently tangled in a holdup and homicide committed by two friends. Railroaded back into prison, he escapes from the death house, bent on attending a reunion of his grammar school classmates. Once there and having bid farewell to his school chums, he is determined to return to prison to meet his fate. However, pursuing prison guards surround the schoolhouse and Frankie is gunned down by law enforcers.

For his John Garfield–like, victim-of-the-Depression role, *Variety* applauded Wallace Ford who "presents a fine and vigorous characterization of the boy who tried hard to go straight, but continually encountered bad breaks." Others in the cast included Aline McMahon as the sympathetic school teacher, Patricia Ellis (who sings two songs) as Ford's love interest, and Stuart Erwin and Bert Frohman as two of Ford's prison pals.

9. *Bad Boy* (Allied Artists, 1949), 85 min.

Producer, Paul Short; associate producer, George Berthelon; director, Kurt Neumann; story, Robert Hardy Andrews, Short; screenplay, Andrews; additional dialogue, Karl Kamb; production designer, Gordon Wiles; art director, Theobold Holsopple; set decorator, Raymond Boltz, Jr.; costumes, Lorraine MacLean; makeup, Charles Huber; music/music director, Paul Sawtell; assistant director, Frank Heath; dialogue director, Clarence Marks; technical adviser, William O'Donnell; sound, Earl Scamera, Karl Struss; supervising editor, Otho Lovering; editor, William Austin.

Lloyd Nolan (Marshall Brown); Jane Wyatt (Mrs. Marshall Brown); Audie Murphy (Danny Lester); James Gleason (The Chief); Stanley Clements (Bitsy Johnson); Martha Vickers (Lila Strawn); Rhys Williams (Arnold Strawn); James Lydon (Ted Hendry); Dickie Moore (Charlie); Selena Royle (Judge Florence Prentiss); Tommy Cook (Floyd); William Lester (Joe Shields); Walter Sande (Texas Oil Man); Stephen Chase (Sheriff Wells); Charles Trowbridge (Dr. Fletcher); Francis Pierlot (Mr. Pardee); Florence Auer (Mrs. Meechan); George Beban (Bell Captain); Bill Walker (Ollie); Barbara Woodell (Mrs. Strawn).

"Neither the thinking of the public nor the state of society will be improved by this weakly contrived little pretense at discussing juvenile crime" (Bosley Crowther, *New York Times*).

Texas-born Audie Murphy, America's most decorated soldier in World War II, was twenty-five years old and making his third feature film when he starred as a juvenile delinquent in *Bad Boy*. The movie was based on factual cases from the files of Variety Clubs International's Boys' Ranch at Copperas Cove, Texas. As *Variety* pointed out about this motion picture, "There are good exploitation possibilities in the title and story. . . . [Murphy] has an ingratiating personality and some latent thespic ability that should register with the younger set of filmgoers." But the trade journal also warned, "Deficiencies are largely plot holes that leave some of the motivation foggy."

Seventeen-year old Danny Lester (Audie Murphy) is a tough punk who has a police record of sixty-two separate charges when he is caught robbing a crap game at a downtown hotel. At the Dallas County courthouse, Judge Florence Prentiss (Selena Royle), angered that Lester will not reveal the whereabouts of his criminal associate, wants to remand the juvenile to the state reformatory until he is eighteeen, when he will be sent to the state prison to complete his twenty-year sentence. Appearing on the scene is Marshall Brown (Lloyd Nolan) who with his wife (Jane Wyatt) runs the Boys' Ranch at Copperas Cove. The idealistic Brown insists to the cynical judge, "I don't believe there are any hopeless boys, only people who grow hopeless."

Brown is persuasive enough to have Danny released into his custody and the wayward boy is driven to the ranch, 4,200 acres of wide open space with no walls and no guards. Marshall seeks to impart his enthusiasm for the ranch's rehabilitaton philosophy to Danny, "So much work, so much play, so much study, so much fun and any boy who really wanted to get himself straightened out and squared out with the world could do fine, that is if he wanted to." However, young Lester, who mysteriously ran away from home when he was thirteen, is anti-social and refuses to fit in with the eighty other youths at the working ranch. Soon Danny is at loggerheads not only with his peers, which include Ted Hendry (James Lydon), Charlie (Dickie Moore) and Bitsy Johnson (Stanley Clements), but with Brown's chief assistant, the wisecracking, but soft-hearted The Chief (James Gleason). The only one with whom Danny relates is Mrs. Brown, who agrees to allow him to work at the main house. Meanwhile, on several nights, Danny sneaks out from the facility and goes into town where he commits assorted burglaries and later steals a gun from a gun shop. Throughout the tense situation between Danny and the ranch folk, Marshall retains his faith in Danny. He has a hunch that a trauma in the boy's childhood caused him to take a wrong turn. After much investigation Marshall uncovers that Danny's stepfather (Rhys Williams) and stepsister (Martha Vickers) had allowed the youth to mistakenly believe that he was responsible for his mother's (Barbara Woodell) death, by having given her medication he stole from the pharmacy where he had an after school job. After Danny's confederate (William Lester) is captured, the troublesome Lester is given a second chance by Judge Prentiss to make good at the ranch. A postscript advises that Danny later attended Texas A & M University, studying engineering.

Because *Bad Boy* was produced at a time when there was a general belief that humane prison reformatories could rehabilitate youths, the film had a far more upbeat approach than similar pictures of a decade earlier, such as *Crime School* (1938) and *Boy Slaves* (1939), or the more genteel *Boys Town* (1938), qq.v.

10. *Bad Boys* (Universal, 1983), color, 123 min.

Producer, Robert Solo; associate producer, Martin Hornstein; director, Richard Rosenthal; screeenplay, Richard Diello; production designer, J. Michael Riva; set designer, Maher Ahmad; set decorator, Richard Reams; costumers, Mickey Antonetti, Jay Hurley; makeup, Jay Cannistraci; music, Bill Conti; music editor, Doug Lackey; assistant directors, Tom Mack, Pat Kehoe, Bill Elvin, Katterli Frauenfelder, Robert Roe; stunt coordinator, Chuck Waters; special effects, Bob Shelley; sound, Jack Wiener; sound rerecording, Don MacDougall, Dave Dockendorf, Richard Tyler; sound editor, John Elizalde; camera, Bruce Surtees, Donald Thorin; editor, Antony Gibbs.

Sean Penn (Mick O'Brien); Reni Santoni (Ramon Herrera); Jim Moody (Gene Daniels); Eric Gurry (Horowitz); Esai Morales (Paco Moreno); Ally Sheedy (J. C. Walenski); Clancy Brown (Viking Lofgren); Robert Lee Rush (Tweety); John Zenda (Wagner); Alan Ruck (Carl Brennan); Tony Mockus (Warden Bendix); Erik Barefield (Terrell); Dean Fortunato (Perretti); Lawrence Mah (Ricky Lee); Jorge Moa (Carlos); Ray Caballero (Pablo); Martha De La Cruz (Mrs. Moreno); Ray Ramirez (Mr. Moreno); Eugene J. Anthony (Robert Walenski); Andrew Gorman (Detective Moran); Marco A. David (Pacito); Donald James (Black Gang Leader); Jane Alderman (Woman Victim); Richard L. Rosenthal (Judge); Fran Stone (Vicki O'Brien); Omar S. Saunders (Johnson); Kevin Springs

(Roberts); Eric David (1st Line-Up Boy); John San Juro (2nd Line-Up Boy); Adam Pelty (Teen Gun Dealer); Marvin Townes (1st Bad Dude); Aaron Holden (2nd Bad Dude); Bill Martin, Jr. (Truck Driver); Myles O'Donnell (Worker); Robin Coleman (Squad Car Cop); Edward Kearns (Line-Up Sergeant); Brenda Joyce Minor (Policewoman); Richard Lee Padget (Guard); Peter Kirkpatrick (1st Mess Hall Supervisor); David Barrett (2nd Mess Hall Supervisor); Peter Kobernik (Food Supervisor); Dick Sollenberger (Van Driver).

In the thirties the gospel according to MGM and Warner Brothers preached that there was no such thing as a bad boy: there were ony bad influences. Give a troubled adolescent some hard-nosed but loving moral authority from the likes of Spencer Tracy or Pat O'Brien and he'd rehabilitate himself.... Judging from *Bad Boys,* young punks of the eighties are perceived less as angels with dirty faces than as sociopaths with superior firepower. Indiscriminately violent, sexually sophisticated, and ruthlessly acquisitive, the new breed of teen menace seems to bring out the nascent Dirty Harry in nervous liberals.

(Tom Doherty, *Film Quarterly* magazine)

In the Chicago slums, sixteen-year-old Mick O'Brien (Sean Penn) joins with Carl Brennan (Alan Ruck) in robbing drugs that a Puerto Rican youth gang is selling to a rival black group. In the process, Brennan is shot dead and Mick, while attempting to escape in a car chase, accidentally kills the younger brother of Paco Moreno (Esai Morales), the leader of the Puerto Ricans. O'Brien is captured and sent to Rainford Juvenile Correctional Facility where he is to remain until he is rehabilitated.

While Rainford may look depressingly glum from the outside, the inside is a hellhole, even for the most hardened teenage criminal. Disillusioned administrator Gene Daniels (Jim Moody), operating in a rote mode, indoctrinates a blasé Mick to the new environment where containment, not rehabilitation is the modus operandi.

You have been assigned to Dorm C. That's our special circumstances dormitory for critical offenders. Your fellow inmates are murderers, armed robbers, rapists and mental defectives just like yourself. They've graduated at the top of the class. You will be treated with respect if you treat others with respect. I suggest you stay cool and follow all the rules. Your crime is not that you got caught, but the crime itself. Hopefully, you will realize what you did was wrong. Hopefully, you will never do anything like that again. This is the juvenile facility. That means you are not in charge of the zoo, we are. If you think you're hip, you're not. If you were, you wouldn't be here. Have I made myself understood?

Dorm C, a caged two-tier cell block dormitory housed in a bleak warehouse-like structure has its own set of regulations, geared to demerit points: Running for the fence = 2,000 points; Drugs or alcohol = 1,500 points; Dangerous activities = 1,000 points; Fighting = 700 points; Sexual harassments = 400 points; Smoking = 400 points.

It is soon evident to the street-wise Mick O'Brien that being corralled in Dorm C is more life-threatening than surviving in the gang-infested slums. In fact, it is more hazardous than being incarcerated in an adult prison. For these impulsive, hardened youths, ever anxious to prove their masculinity, to establish their domination, and unable to comprehend their mortality, scarcely fear anything or anyone. These are rebellious teenagers of the roughest sort.

Rene Santoni and Sean Penn in *Bad Boys* (1983).

Mick's cellmate is the precocious arsonist Horowitz (Eric Gurry), whom he befriends. On the other hand, Mick quickly comes into a power struggle with Viking Lofgren (Clancy Brown) and Tweety (Robert Lee Rush) who are the inmate chiefs of Dorm C. Danny receives letters form his neighborhood girlfriend J. C. Walenski (Ally Sheedy), while Paco, who has sworn to get even with Mick, kills one of the black gang. In the reformatory, O'Brien witnesses Tweety kill a black youth (Erik Barefield) whom he has just raped. Later, Mick not only survives an attack by Viking and Tweety, but he outmaneuvers them and is soon elected "barn boss" by his peers, with Horowitz as his enterprising partner. As "smacks" (trustees) they have the run of the dorm and control the flow of illegal goods distributed to their fellow inmates. After Mick learns that Paco has raped J. C., he escapes but is caught soon after he visits her. His captor, Rainford Correctional Officer Ramon Herrera (Reni Santoni), later tells him that due to a bureaucratic error, the now-jailed Paco is to be sent to Rainford. Ramon warns Mick not to jeopardize his future parole (in six months) by causing trouble with Paco. Thereafter, both Paco and Viking (Tweety has been paroled but is killed in a store robbery) set out to murder Mick, with the intrigued inmates placing bets on who will be the survivor. Viking is eliminated when he is almost killed by a booby-trapped radio engineered by Horowitz. On the night before Paco is to be transferred to another facility, he knocks out Ramon, who is dorm chief that evening, and starts a bloody fight with Mick. The latter is the victor of the vicious match. However, instead of killing Paco as the chanting mob of inmates urge, he returns to his cell, while the recovering Ramon looks on.

The critical reaction to this grim, vicious study was downbeat. David Denby (*New York* magazine) assessed, "The movie bears some resemblance to the old Warner Bros. prison pictures ... which also mixed violence, romance, and cornball social consciousness in about equal measure, but it's coarser and grislier—more frightening than entertaining." Rex Reed (*New York Post*) judged, "*Bad Boys* is one of those violent teenage reform school movies that shows how far we've sunk since Mickey Rooney in *Boy's Town*"). Steve Jenkins (British *Monthly Film Bulletin*) weighed, "Director Rick Rosenthal (*Halloween II*) is unable to overcome some basic structural weaknesses (the continuing narrative outside the Rainford Facility, which dissipates any claustrophobic tension on the inside; the plot's protracted final stage). . . ." Sheila Benson (*Los Angeles Times*) argued, "The picture's greatest gift is the performance of Sean Penn, who manages to surmount his lack of revealing lines and turn a glower into something approaching a characterization." In *Newsweek* magazine, David Ansen evaluated, "you can sense that the filmmakers would like to make something more than an exploitation movie—and can't." Ansen admitted, "it's unsentimental about its teen-age hoods and unsparing about the nastiness of juvenile jails." He also perceived that the prison movie has a long lineage. "The slammer imposes its own microcosmic set of rules, and they've helped make the prison movie one of the most formalized and durable genres in the business. What changes over the years is the style and level of brutality. It's impossible to deny the Roman-circus aspects of these spectacles, and one can read them as a fairly accurate reflection of the public's current level of bloodlust. Inside the obligatory framework of Social concern . . . is the carnival barker's pitch: 'Hey, you want to watch some dudes get royally wasted?'"

Filmed at St. Charles Youth Correctional Facility and Statesville Adult Correctional Facility in Illinois, *Bad Boys* earned $5,544,476 in domestic rentals paid to the distributor.

11. *Bad Girls Dormitory* (Films Around the World, 1985), color, 95 min.

Executive producer, Cynthia DePaula; associate producer, Sam Silverstein; director/screenplay, Tim Kincaid; wardrobe, Derex Ritchie; makeup, Steve Reitey; music, Man Parrish; songs, Parrish and Beth Rudestsky; special effects, Matt Vogel; camera, Arthur D. Marks.

Carey Zuris (Lori Christianson); Teresa Farley (Marina); Natalie O'Connell (Paige); Rick Gianasi (Don Beach); Marita (Miss Madison); Jennifer DeLora (Lisa); Donna Eskra (Rebel); Dan Barclay (Dr. DeMarco); Rebecca Rothbaum (Nurse Stevens); Rachel Hancock (Harper); Charmagne Eckert (Valeska); Frances Raines (Barb); Jane Donadio (Jen); William Peterson (McCoy); Renata Cobbs (Eula); Sherry Hard (Gloria); David Sotolongi (Zulu); Marc Umile (Tom); Dave Mlotok (Mr. Garfield); Sandor Black (Billy); Ryan Sexcto (Ray); Shawn Carroll (Paul); Lynnea Benson (Kitty); Tom Billett (Big Guard); Debra Laster (Sperrazzae); Camille Validum, Mark Legan (Guards); Dick Biel, Jonathan Putnam (Vice Cops); Alvin Hippolyte, Ben Lizza (Narcotics Officers); Steven Kanterman (Lee); Harve Soto (Roland); Lance Brett (Jalk); Maggie Wagner (New Girl); Chuck Murdoun (Man in Restaurant); John Abbato (Waiter); Marie Loffredo (Counter Lady); Lovell Dixon (Gloria's Baby); Kate Mcamy (Dottie); Parri Shashmanesh (Deke); Cathryn Bibbell (Lenka); Meredith Rush, Christine Solazzi, Camille Welles, Cheryl Costa, Elisa London, Carole Lynn Arnold, Leeane Baker (Dorm Girls).

Regarding this low-budget effort, *Variety* noted, "There is an almost antiseptic air about the proceedings, and very little heart." Concerning its efforts to be more than the usual women-behind-bars entry, the paper added that whenever director Tim Kincaid "gets maudlin and socially indignant over the cruel fates of his young inmate-protagonists, he loses his otherwise calm grip on dramatic narrative...."

As far as the deliberately soft-core pornography aspects went, *Variety* wondered about "...the way it pulls its punches so it is never allowed to veer into outright porn or gut-ripping gore."

Following the precepts set for the genre years before in *Caged* (1950), q.v., *Bad Girls Dormitory* focuses on young Lori Christianson (Carey Zuris), another victim of being in the wrong place at the right time. She is sentenced to a term at the New York Female Juvenile Reformatory. Before long she is pulled into the degrading battle for survival among the other toughened inmates and the corrupt staff. Warden Marina (Teresa Farley) offers platitudes and very little assistance to her downtrodden wards, while the staff physician, Dr. DeMarco (Dan Barclay), is a drug addict with an overzealous interest in providing his female patients with physical examinations. There is also the sadistic and overly butch guard Harper (Rachel Hancock). Every few hours, the various factions among the inmates battle it out for supremacy. The only bright light in Lori's dim existence is social worker Don Beach (Rick Gianasi) who attempts to help her. However, he is defeated by the deadening system which has a hold on Lori. Quickly exposed to the brutal side of life, including having one of her fellow inmates hang herself, Lori realizes she must adapt to her vicious surroundings or die. Later, she understands that she is becoming too successful with her bid for survival. She wonders, "Oh God, what's happening to me? I don't feel anything." As the film concludes, a new girl arrives at the facility and the now-toughened Lori, as hardened as the other veteran inmates, makes advances to the newcomer, just as had happened to her months before.

Not only are the production values slipshod in this cheaply assembled feature, but many of the performers are rank amateurs whose dialogue appears to have been (re)dubbed after the filming. Among the songs in the undistinguished score is one number entitled "Hose Me Down," which given the earnestness of the overall effort is not intended (intentionally) to be funny.

12. *The Bad One* (United Artists, 1930), 70 min.

Presenter, Joseph M. Schenck; supervisor, John W. Considine, Jr.; director, George Fitzmaurice; story, John Farrow; screenplay, Carey Wilson, Howard Emmett Rogers; art directors, William Cameron Menzies, Paul French; costumes, Alice O'Neill; music arranger, Hugo Riesenfeld; assistant director, Walter Mayo; sound, Frank Grenzbach; camera, Karl Struss; editor, Donn Hayes.

Dolores Del Rio (Lita); Edmund Lowe (Jerry Flanagan); Don Alvarado (The Spaniard); Blanche Frederici (Madame Durand); Adrienne D'Ambricourt (Madame Pompier); Ullrich Haupt (Pierre Ferrande); Mitchell Lewis (Borloff); Ralph Lewis (Blochet); Charles McNaughton (Petey); Yola D'Avril (Gida); John Sainpolis (Judge); Henry Kolker (Prosecutor); George Fawcett (Warden); Victor Potel, Harry Stubbs, Tom Dugan (Sailors); Boris Karloff (Guard).

The Bad One relied on the still novelty of sound to excuse its many shortcomings, including a wildly improbable plot and very self-conscious performances from the leads. *The Bad One* was Dolores Del Rio's talking film debut and rematched her with Edmund Lowe, her co-star in the well-regarded *What Price Glory?* (1926). With much of its action set on a French penal island, *The Bad One* was too reminiscent of *Condemned* (1929), q.v., to be original even in its cavalier depiction of the harsh life at a prison colony.

Sultry Spanish dancer Lita (Dolores Del Rio) sings and dances in a Marseilles café, where she draws the attention of rambuctious Jerry Flanagan (Edmund

Lowe), a Brooklyn-born Don Juan who has a girl in every port and refuses to settle down with one woman. However, he is soon captivated by the fiery Lita and agrees to marry her. One of Lita's old beaus arrives on her wedding day and Jerry gets in a scuffle with him, leading to the other's death when he falls and hits his head. Jerry is sentenced to hard labor at a French penal island. Being tough-natured he accepts his fate, angered only that Lita has seemingly betrayed him by her honest testimony at his trial. On her part, Lita is heart-broken at the turn of events and demanding a strange sort of penitence for herself, she arrives at the prison isle where she becomes friendly with the warden's wife (Blanche Frederici) and begins a romance with Pierre Ferrande (Ullrich Haupt), reputed as the toughest, most sadistic guard at the stronghold. (Pierre is known as "the bone-breaker" for his vicious treatment of the prisoners.) Later, during a convict riot instigated by Blochet (Ralph Lewis), Jerry comes to the defense of the Warden (George Fawcett) and his men. For his bravery during the uprising, Jerry is pardoned. He and Lita, now reconciled, sail for the United States, planning to settle in Brooklyn.

Mordaunt Hall *(New York Times)* labeled the feature "a weird combination of reckless levity and ruddy melodrama." *Variety* was less diplomatic. "The story is one of those that could be terminated after every pair of reels. As the result it projects in a series of waves."

13. *Bars of Hate* (Victory, 1935), 63 min.

Supervisor/presenter, Sam Katzman; director, Al Herman; based on the story "Vengeance of the Lord" by Peter B. Kyne; screenplay, Al Martin; settings, Fred Preble; sound, Herb Eicke; camera, Billy Hyer; editor, Dan Milner.

Regis Toomey (Ted Clark, the Assistant District Attorney); Sheila Terry (Ann Dawson); Snub Pollard (Danny Wells); Molly O'Day (Gertie); Gordon Griffith (Jim Grant); Robert Warwick (Governor); John Elliott (Sheriff); Fuzzy Knight (Montague); Arthur Loft (Slim); Jack Cowell (Joe).

A bottom-of-the-barrel entry based on the Eccles Foster murder in Chicago in the late 1880s. This mini-action programmer, like so many silent features and quickie 1930s productions, used a prison angle in its plotline as an excuse for its exploitive title and to provide the motivation for the premise. *Variety* chided, "This is one indie that's an all-around weakie.... Production itself is 100% old-fashioned, 80% of the film being nothing more than auto, train and plane chases."

When her brother is convicted of murder, Ann Dawson (Sheila Terry) determines to prove his innocence. She (coincidentally) meets handsome Ted Clark (Regis Toomey), the assistant district attorney, and so convinces him of her mission, that he works to help free her brother. Ted even uses pickpocket Danny Wells (Snub Pollard) to obtain the needed evidence on the real culprits, a local racketeering gang.

14. *Behind Prison Gates* (Columbia, 1939), 63 min.

Executive producer, Irving Briskin; associate producer Wallace MacDonald; director, Charles Barton; screenplay, Arthur T. Horman, Leslie T. White; music diretor, Morris W. Stoloff; assistant director, William Mull; sound, Lambert Day; camera, Allen G. Siegler; editor, Richard

Fantl.

Brian Donlevy (Red Murray); Jacqueline Wells [Julie Bishop] (Sheila Murray); Joseph Crehan (Warden O'Neill); Paul Fix (Petey Ryan); George Lloyd (Marty Conroy); Dick Curtis (Captain Simmons); Richard Fiske (Lyman); George Pearce

(Dad Prentiss); Ralph Dunn (Guard Evans); James Craig (Jenkins); John Tyrrell (Martin); Ed LeSaint (Dr. Mason); George Anderson (Mathews); Al Hill (Betts); George McKay (Walsh); Ky Robinson (Guard Slade); Ernie Adams (Voight); Dick Boteller, Charles McMurphy, Al Herman, Douglas Williams, Ed Brady (Guards); Kit Guard, C. L. Sherwood, Jack Evans, Eddy Foster, Cy Schindell (Convicts); Earl Bunn (Machine Gun Guard); Shemp Howard (Waiter).

Appearances can be deceiving, as in the case of rugged Red Murray (Brian Donlevy) who is actually an undercover federal agent. He has had himself imprisoned, without even the warden (Joseph Crehan) knowing his real identity. Red's plan is to trick two bank-robbing, cop killers—Petey Ryan (Paul Fix) and Marty Conroy (George Lloyd)—into revealing where they have hidden the loot. Red soon pits Ryan against Conroy and, before long, escapes with one of them to retrieve the hidden money. The other breaks out and, in a shootout, both real convicts are killed, with the imposter Red saved by a fellow federal operative (Richard Fiske). By this time, Sheila Murray (Jacqueline Wells [Julie Bishop]), who is the sister of the real Red Murray (killed in a holdup attempt), has met and fallen in love with the bogus Red, whom she helps in his undercover detection work.

In the late 1930s, the prison film had become a too familiar staple at the box-office. B. R. Cristler *(New York Times)* insisted, "The gates of the prison picture continue to yawn for the unwary; in fact, even the unwary are beginning to yawn." *Variety* was less severe, "Usual threadbare convict stuff this time has enough twist to groove it for fair support rating.... Opus is grim and humorless. It's a manhunt, and wastes little time getting down to tacks in a prison yard...." *Harrison's Reports* acknowledged. "One is held in suspense during the closing scenes, —where the gangsters are shown learning of [the hero, Brian] Donlevy's connection with the federal bureau, for his life is endangered. The romance is incidental."

15. *Behind Prison Walls* (Producers Releasing Corp., 1943), 64 min.

Producer, Arthur Ripley; associate producer, Andre Dumonceau; director, Steve Sekely; story, W. A. Ulman, Jr.; screenplay, Van Norcross; music director, David Chudnow; dialogue director, Kurt Steenbart; assistant director, Chris Beute; sound, Ben Winkler; camera, Marcel Le Picard; editor, Holbrook N. Todd.
Alan Baxter (Jonathan MacGlennon); Gertrude Michael (Elinor Cantwell); Tully Marshall (James J. MacGlennon); Edwin Maxwell (Percy Webb); Jacqueline Dalya (Mimi); Matt Willis (Frank Lucacelli); Richard Kipling (Frederick Driscoll); Olga Sabin (Yette Kropatchek); Isabelle Withers (Whitey O'Neill); Lane Chandler (Reagan); Paul Everton (Warden); George Guhl (Doc); Regina Wallace (Mrs. Cantwell).

"One of the most intelligent and adult little satires ever to hit the independent market" *(Hollywood Reporter)*. *Harrison's Reports* noted, "the title of the picture is misleading, and tends to hurt its box-office chances; one believes it to be a sinister sort of picture." Don Miller in *B Movies* (1973), enthused, "It was a gentle, witty, somewhat intellectualized [entry].... An oddity from any company and a downright treasure coming from PRC, its soft-sell approach probably was the cause of its bypassing by most audiences.... For those who saw it, it was a pleasant surprise." Like the much later telefeature, *The Revenge of Al Capone* (1989), q.v., *Behind Prison Walls* demonstrated that incarcerated individuals still could retain great power on the outside.

Both James J. MacGlennon (Tully Marshall), steel magnate, and his over-intellectualized college-bred son Jonathan MacGlennon (Alan Baxter) are sentenced

Alan Baxter and Gertrude Michael in *Behind Prison Walls* (1943).

to prison for having withheld vital war materials. Jonathan, who had testified aginst his father at the trial, is full of social welfare schemes which he eagerly puts to work in prison, starting first with his pug-faced cellmate Frank Lucacelli (Matt Willis) who soon becomes a docile prison yard gardener. Meanwhile, even while behind bars, James MacGlennon schemes to expand his fortune and to find ways to combat Percy Webb (Edwin Maxwell), his unscrupulous vice-president who is trying to gain control of the corporation. With the help of Webb's secretary, Elinor Cantwell (Gertrude Michael), James maneuvers to retain power of his company. When the imprisoned magnate learns that Jonathan is about to be paroled for good behavior, he pretends to have undergone a reformation and asks his idealistic son to take control of the family business. As James anticipated, Jonathan's innovative social reforms do not appeal to the mercenary stockholders and Webb, among others, rush to sell their company stock. By now, Elinor, who has fallen in love with Jonathan, admits her complicity with his father. Thanks to newspaper accounts, Jonathan is erroneously regarded as a national hero for helping the "underdogs" of the work world. When Webb learns the truth of the situation, he uses a hired thug to attempt to keep Jonathan away from a crucial stockholders' meeting. However, James, now paroled, arrives in time to sabotage Webb's plot and to reaffirm his faith in his son.

The *Hollywood Reporter* also observed, "[Steve] Sekely's direction is completely of the tongue-in-cheek school. That trick of changing the scene during a close-up is adroitly employed, and for one of the first times on record the newspaper headlines regarding a court trial are shown in relative import to banner-lined war news."

This was the final film for versatile, veteran actor Tully Marshall (1864–1943) who had appeared in such landmark movies as *Intolerance* (1916), *The Covered Wagon* (1923), *Grand Hotel* (1932) and *This Gun for Hire* (1942).

British release title; *Youth Takes a Hand.*

16. *Behind Stone Walls* (Mayfair, 1932), 60 min.

Director, Frank Strayer; screenplay, George B. Seitz; camera, Jules Cronjager; editor, Byron Robinson. Robert Elliott (District Attorney John Clay); Eddie Nugent (Robert Clay); Priscilla Dean (Esther Clay); Ann Christy (Peg Harper); Robert Ellis (Jack Keene); George Chesebro (Leo Drugget).

Esther Clay (Priscilla Dean), the wife of district attorney John Clay (Robert Elliott), kills her racketeer boyfriend during a jealous rage. Her stepson, Robert (Eddie Nugent) thinking she is his real mother, accepts the blame for the homicide and is prosecuted by his father. Robert is sentenced to a life term in prison. Later, Esther attempts to kill a blackmailing pal of the late gangster, only to have John turn up at the scene and in the mêlée, he accidentally shoots his philandering wife. Robert is released from prison and returns home in time to defend his dad at the murder trial. He wins an acquittal for his father.

Variety judged of this weak potboiler which suffered from overall shoddy production values, "Several competent players struggle to give interest to this story, but the author has failed to throw proper interest to the theme...." Priscilla Dean, a popular silent screen star—best recalled for playing Cigarette in *Under Two Flags* (1922)—attempted a screen comeback in *Behind Stone Walls*. Unfortunately she overplayed her melodramatic assignment.

17. *Behind the High Wall* (Universal, 1956), 85 min.

Producer, Stanley Rubin; director, Abner Biberman; story, Wallace Sullivan, Richard K. Polimer; screenplay, Harold Jack Bloom; costumes, Bill Thomas; music, Joseph Gershenson; assistant directors, Ronnie Rondell, Jimmy Welch; camera, Maury Gertsman; editor, Ted J. Kent.

Tom Tully (Frank Carmichael); Sylvia Sidney (Hilda Carmichael); Betty Lynn (Annie MacGregor); John Gavin (Johnny Hutchins); Don Beddoe (Todd MacGregor); John Larch (William Kiley); Barney Phillips (Tom Reynolds); Ed Kemmer (Charlie Rains); John Beradino (Carl Buckhardt); Rayford Barnes (George Miller); Herbert C. Lytton (Professor Reese); Nicky Blair (Roy Burkhardt); David Garcia (Morgan); William Forrest (Corby); Frances Osborne (Mrs. Loomis); Peter Leeds, Jim Hyland (Detectives); Bing Russell, Dale Van Sickel, George Barrows, Ray Darmour (Guards).

As has been displayed by many Hollywood feature films over the decades, there are many reasons why a prison warden goes sour and thinks he is above the law. This entry was a remake of *The Big Guy* (1939), q.v.

Frank Carmichael (Tom Tully) rises from being prison guard to acting warden. He is hopeful of being appointed full warden, with the new salary needed to pay for medical care of his paraplegic wife Hilda (Sylvia Sidney). Just as he is expecting this career appointment, there is a prison break and Carmichael is dragged along as a hostage. Along the way, the escapees force garage mechanic Johnny Hutchins (John Gavin) to give them a ride in his truck. A motorcycle police officer gives chase and is killed by the lawbreakers. Later, the getaway truck crashes. Both convicts are killed and Carmichael shoots the prisoners' confederate, who is clutching a suitcase. Carmichael discovers the valise contains $100,000 in stolen cash. When the police arrives, he allows them to think the unconscious Hutchins is to blame for killing the cop and soon Hutchins is sentenced to die. Carmichael is declared a hero and named warden. His wife learns of these events and begs him to testify and save Hutchins's life. Later, when Hutchins makes a break from death row, Carmichael comes forward with a last-minute confession.

Variety disapproved of the lackluster proceedings, "This is a routine prison melodrama with only so-so entertainment values." Regarding Tom Tully's performance as the erratic, pressured prison warden, the trade paper allowed, "Tully's characterization of a prison warden fails to register, the poor performance contrasting quite sharply with the good work he has done in previous pix." Thankfully, veteran actress Sylvia Sidney gave meaning and intensity to her role as the wheelchair-bound wife.

18. *Betrayed Women* (Allied Artists, 1956), 70 min.

Producer, William F. Broidy; associate producer, A. R. Nunes; director, Edward L. Cahn; story, Paul L. Peil; screenplay, Steve Fisher; art director, George Troast; set decorator, Mowbray Berkeley; costumes, Tommy Thompson; makeup, Carlie Taylor; music, Edward J. Kay; assistant director, Bert Glazer; sound, Al Overton; camera, John Martin; editors, Ace Herman, Chandler House.

Carole Mathews (Kate); Beverly Michaels (Honey); Peggy Knudsen (Nora); Tom Drake (Jeff); Sara Haden (Darcy); John Dierkes (Cletus); Esther Dale (Mrs. Ballard); Paul Savage (Baby Face); Darlene Fields (Mrs. Mabry); John Damler (Mabry); G. Pat Collins (Hostage Guard); Burt Wenland (1st Guard); Pete Kellett (2nd Guard).

In the mid–1950s Hollywood was undergoing a fresh cycle of prison films, especially those dealing with the enticing (to some) subject of women-behind bars. Originally called *Women's Reformatory,* the picture was released in early 1956 with the more sensational title, *Betrayed Women. Variety* decided, "Performances of principals generally are persuasive enough to lend credence to story unfoldment, and subject shapes up handily for exploitation."

Because of the many reports of cruelties inflicted on inmates of the ancient Bayou Reformatory for Women in a southern state, the governor orders an investigation. He appoints an attorney, Jeff (Tom Drake), to study the situation. Jeff arrives at the prison farm at the same time as new inmate Honey (Beverly Michaels), a tough gun moll. The latter soon gets into conflict with forceful inmate leader Kate (Carole Mathews). Also at the prison farm is Nora (Peggy Knudsen), once engaged to Jeff, who is serving a term for having stolen funds to protect her brother. Among the farm's guards is the sadistic Darcy (Sara Haden). Meanwhile, Jeff comes into conflict with the stern Mrs. Ballard (Esther Dale), the veteran head of the prison who refuses to be sympathetic to her charges. Mrs. Ballard's brother, the moronic Cletus (John Dierkes) is in charge of the prison bloodhounds, and he is persuaded by Kate and Honey—who have temporarily joined forces—to help them escape. That breakout fails, but they try again, this time taking Jeff, Nora and Mrs. Ballard as hostages. When Kate breaks out her gangland lover Mabry (John Damler) hopes she will head to a hidden $50,000 from a prior robbery. As the police dragnet closes in, Mrs. Ballard dies of a heart attack. Kate is killed in the gunfire, and Honey forces Mabry to surrender. Honey gives up to the law enforcers, admitting that she forced Nora and Jeff to accompany her.

Appearing as the unyielding prison matron was Esther Dale (1885–1961), an expert at such roles, having played similar unsympathetic parts in such genre entries as *Condemned Women* (1938) and *Prison Farm* (1938), qq.v.

19. *The Big Bird Cage* (New World, 1972), color, 93 min.

Producer, Jane Schaffer; director/screenplay, Jack Hill; art director, Ben Otico; set decorator, Marshall Henry; makeup, Ray Solomon; music, William A. Castleman, William Loose; production supervisor, Carl B. Raymond; assistant director, Paul Mac-Lang; camera, Philip Sacadalan; editors, James Mitchell, Jere Huggins.

Pam Grier (Blossom); Anita Ford (Terry Rich); Candice Roman (Carla); Teda Bracci (Bull Jones); Carol Speed (Mickie); Karen McKevic (Karen); Sid Haig (Django); Marissa Delgado (Rina); Vic Diaz (Roccio); Andy Centenera (Warden Zappa); Rizza Fabria (Lin Tsiang); Wendy Gree (Gerdie); Subas Herrero (Moreno).

The 1960s and 1970s were particularly fertile decades for cross-breeding of film genres, including the black action species with the prison format. Black football-star-turned-movie actor Jim Brown had succeeded in *Riot* (1969) and *The Slams* (1973), qq.v., and on the distaff side, Pam Grier was featured in several behind-bars action adventures. Having made the popular *The Big Doll House* (1971), q.v., producer Jane Schaffer and director Jack Hill also shot *The Big Bird Cage* on the cheap in the Philippines. This time Hill was also responsible for the scenario as such.

Statuesque songstress Blossom (Pam Grier) performs at a tropical nightclub in the Philippines, one of those tough joints that sports a sign at the front door, "Check firearms here." One evening after the show, she and her comrades rob the club to finance their revolutionary cause. The multi-talented Blossom proves that she can not only handle a machine gun in an emergency, but she is equally adept at romancing her boyfriend Django (Sid Haig). Later, several of Blossom's female co-conspirators are captured by the police and sent to a government jungle work camp, somewhere outside of Manila. The institution is controlled by the sadistic Warden Zappa (Andy Centenera) who joyfully reminds the prisoners not to attempt escape because his assortment of snarling guard dogs "know who you are and they will always be able to find you no matter what or how far your run. The inmates include Terry Rich (Anita Ford) a curvacious actress jailed because of her indiscretions with politicians, the quiet black girl Mickie (Carol Speed) who committed crimes against the state; and lesbian Bull Jones (Teda Bracci). At the compound, those girls who fail to meet the work quotas in the field or who are caught stealing or lying are sentenced to work in the Big Bird Cage. This is an ominously imposing bamboo structure used as a sugar mill. "You don't ever come out for anything," warns one knowing inmate. It is custom at this facility for prisoners to hurl snitches from the heights of the Big Bird Cage. Blossom and Django penetrate the compound and stir up a bloody riot that turns into a massacre. They burn down the prison camp and escape down the rapids, with the prison guards (and dogs) in hot pursuit. A few of the girls survive the ordeal and eventually sail off to safety.

Addison Verrill *(Variety)* observed of this softcore pornography outing, "The women's prison epic is about as hardy a cinema chestnut as one can find these days, but it's a perfect showcase for the nudity, sex, violence, raw language and comic relief necessary in this type of exploitation programmer. All the ingredients are here.... Happily audiences for this type of feature couldn't care less about histrionics as long as blouses are kept unbuttoned." Beside the staunch Pam Grier, the personality honors in this action outing go to Bette Midler lookalike Teda Bracci, a tough bird who can find humor in the most perverse situation.

20. *The Big Doll House* (New World, 1971), color, 93 min.

Executive producers, Eddie Romero, John Ashley; producer Jane Schaffer; director, Jack Hill; screenplay, Don Spencer; production designer, Ben Otico; set decorator, Bobby Bautista; makeup, Antonio Artiesda; wardrobe, Felisa Salcedo; music, Hall Daniels; assistant director, Maria S. Abelardo; special effects, Teofilo C. Hilario; camera, Freddie Conde; supervising editor, Millie Paul; editor, Cliff Fenneman.

Judy Brown (Collier); Roberta Collins (Alcott); Pam Grier (Grear); Brooke Mills (Harrad); Pat Woodell (Bodine); Sid Haig (Harry); Christiane Schmidtmer (Miss Dietrich); Kathryn Loder (Lucian); Jerry Franks (Fred); Jack Davis (Dr. Phillips); Gina Stuart (Ferina); Letty Mirasol (Leyte); Shirley De Las Alas (Guard); and: Siony Cordona, Myrna De Vera, Kathy McDaniels.

Taking his cue from a rash of European-lensed women-behind-bars exploitation dramas (*99 Women, Barbed Wire Dolls, Wanda the Wicked Warden*), Jack Hill made several similar features for Roger Corman's New World Pictures, all lensed on the cheap in the Philippines. As Jim Morton, in his essay "Women in Prison Films" for *Re/Search: Incredibly Strange Films* (1986), perceived:

> By the end of the sixties the archetypal roles of the WIP [women in prison] films had been established, i.e.: The Queen Bee: dominant female prisoner who lords it over the others. The New Fish: usually the lead actress, in jail for the first time. The Sadistic Warden: more often than not the one who proves to be the root of all evil and unrest in the prison. The Hooker with the Heart of Gold: a street-smart dame who knows the ropes and befriends the New Fish, for better or worse. The Dyke Guard: sometimes named 'Ruby'; no WIP film would be complete with one.

Considering that it was shot for a paltry $125,000, *The Big Doll House* was a big moneymaker, earning $5,000,000 in domestic film rentals paid to distributors. It is a fully realized example of the sexploitation prison story that was and still is such a popular item in the softcore pornography film marketplace.

Well-mannered Miss Dietrich (Christiane Schmidtmer) is the warden of a seedy prison in the Philippines. Her chief cohort is the vicious Colonel Mendoza of the secret police. Among her subordinates is newcomer Dr. Phillips (Jack Davis), a humane individual who shocks Dietrich when he suggests the prisoners be treated better, including the discontinuation of guards torturing their wards. Among the inmates are political prisoner Bodine (Pat Woodell), the junkie Harrad (Brooke Mills) who murdered her baby, and Grear (Pam Grier), a prostitute whose benefactor worked for the government. Because Grear learned political news she should not have, she received a thirty-year sentence. Within this prison world, resilient Grear has a yen for red-headed prisoner Collier (Judy Brown) and makes no pretenses about her relationship with the other woman. As she informs Harry (Sid Haig), a driver who makes frequent deliveries to the compound, "All men are filthy. All they ever want to do is to get at you.... I'm not goin' to let a man's filthy hands touch me again!" The only person whom Grear fears is Lucian (Kathryn Loder), the extremely cruel prison guard who boasts a very tough demeanor. Later it develops that Grear is an informant for the warden, but this knowing convict is not above pilfering through Dietrich's private office, looking for information she can use in her power play or items she can sell. Eventually, Harry and Fred (Jerry Franks) help some of the inmates escape. En route, Harrad murders the informant Grear and is herself later killed by the pursuing guards.

The Big Doll House craftily misses no opportunity to exploit its cast for the sake of titillating its voyeuristic audience. Frequently within the scenario, the women convicts are stripped naked, take lengthy and recurrent showers, struggle for supremacy among themselves in bouts of mud wrestling and they are often tortured. One particularly memorable bondage sequence shows a prisoner bound to a rack and a cobra snake being lowered on to her. (The multi-leveled sexual implications of this segment are enormous!) Not overlooked are episodes of half-clad inmates being flogged. And, of course, much is made of the fact that these prisoners have sex-on-their-minds constantly. As Sid confides to Fred, "They are so horny.... Sometimes at night you can hear them honking." This is substantiated in the assorted lesbian and heterosexual couplings throughout the film. At a later point, during the prison escape, some of the fleeing women rape a male guard. Leaving no genre stone unturned, *The Big Doll House* focuses equal attention on the array of harsh female prison guards and the sleekly sinister prisoner supervisor, Miss Dietrich.

Much of the credit for the success of *The Big Doll House* is due to 5'8" Pam Grier who shortly thereafter became the queen of the short-lived black exploitation film craze. Unlike most participants in *The Big Doll House,* Grear displayed an innate acting talent and the ability to show both authority and vulnerability in her on camera characterization, such as in *Women in Cages* (1972), directed by Cirio Santiago and co-starring Judy Brown.

21. *The Big Guy* (Universal, 1939), 78 min.

Producer, Burt Kelly; director, Arthur Lubin; based on the story "No Power on Earth" by Wallace Sullivan, Richard K. Polimer; screenplay, Lester Cole; camera, Elwood Bredell; editor, Philip Cahn.

Victor McLaglen (Warden Whitlock);

Jackie Cooper (Timmy Hutchins); Edward Brophy (Dippy); Peggy Moran (Joan Lawson); Ona Munson (Mary Whitlock); Russell Hicks (Lawson); Jonathan Hale (Jack Lang); Edward Pawley (Chuck Burkhart); George McKay (Buzz Miller).

"Although story has a partial prison background, it neatly sidesteps utilization of too much penitentiary footage and concentrates on the human drama..." *(Variety).* The trade paper approved of the two leads: "[Victor] McLaglen is vigorous as the guard captain.... Cooper is excellent as the youth.... Cooper's dramatic scenes are highlighted with conviction...."

Young inventor Timmy Hutchins (Jackie Cooper) is tricked by Jack Lang (Jonathan Hale) into helping two escaped gangsters make their getaway. Timmy is forced at gunpoint to drive the culprits. When the car, pursued by the police, tumbles down a cliffside, one of the criminals is killed, while Warden Whitlock (Victor McLaglen), who had been taken hostage and knocked unconscious by the prisoners, awakens in time to kill the other fleeing convict. Whitlock finds that the gangster's suitcase contains a great deal of money, which he hides. He then arrests Timmy as the killer of a cop who had been murdered in the pursuit. Because Lawson lies on the witness stand at Timmy's trial, the latter is found guilty of homicide and sentenced to die. Eventually Whitlock's conscience gets the better of him and he has a change of heart. He goes to unearth the money and finds that the cache contains additional evidence that would prove Hutchins's protestations of innocence were true. Whitlock acknowledges Hutchins's innocence to Lawson (Russell Hicks), the attorney father of Timmy's girlfriend (Peggy Moran) and agrees to sign an affidavit, *if* he can be given a few days' grace period to escape with his wife before the police are alerted. At that crucial moment, Whitlock learns that the desperate Hutchins, on death row, has escaped from jail, accompanied by a trusty, Dippy (Edward Brophy). Whitlock pursues them and, in a shootout, Dippy kills Whitlock and then gives himself up. With the evidence on hand to substantiate his innocence, Hutchins is finally freed.

"This is a pretty gripping melodrama.... There are many exciting situations" *(Harrison's Reports)*. The story would be revamped (slightly) and remade by Universal as *Behind the High Wall* (1956), q.v.

A.k.a.: *Warden of the Big House.*

22. *The Big House* (Metro-Goldwyn-Mayer, 1930), 84 min. (Also silent version.)

Director, George Hill; story/screenplay/dialogue, Frances Marion; additional dialogue, Joe Farnham, Martin Flavin; art director, Cedric Gibbons; sound, Robert Shirley, Douglas Shearer; camera, Harold Wenstrom; editor, Blanche Sewell.

Chester Morris (John Morgan); Wallace Beery ("Machine Gun" Butch Schmidt); Lewis Stone (Warden James Adams); Robert Montgomery (Kent Marlowe); Leila Hyams (Ann Marlowe); George F. Marion (Pop Riker); J. C. Nugent (Mr. Marlowe); Karl Dane (Olsen); De Witt Jennings (Captain Wallace); Matthew Betz (Gopher); Claire McDowell (Mrs. Marlowe); Robert Emmett O'Connor (Donlin); Tom Kennedy (Uncle Jed); Tom Wilson (Sandy the Guard); Eddie Foyer (Dopey); Roscoe Ates (Putnam); Fletcher Norton (Oliver); Adolph Seidel (Prison Barber); and: Eddie Lambert, Michael Vavitch.

It is the ironic fate of most trendsetting motion pictures to seem derivative and cliched when viewed years later in retrospect. Such is the case with *The Big House*. However, when this rousing motion picture debuted in late June 1930, it was hailed a remarkable achievement in sound cinema. Not only was it timely (there had recently been a rash of riots at Auburn Prison and elsewhere), but it was a solid drama. Mordaunt Hall *(New York Times)* acknowledged, "It is an insight into life in a jail that has never before been essayed on the screen." Hall enthused further, "It is a film in which the direction, the photography, the microphone work and the magnificent acting take precedence over the negligible story ... it is a film that sweeps swiftly along...." *Variety* weighed the entry, "A he-man picture ... gripping with its stark drama.... Prison life on the half-shell is plainly exposed and with it a few of the problems which undoubtedly face every warden of every crowded prison institution...." The ads for *The Big House* proclaimed "See 3,000 desperate convicts in their break for freedom! Thrills!"

Twenty-four year old playboy Kent Marlow (Robert Montgomery) is brought to prison to begin serving his ten-year sentence for manslaughter. (He had been drunk on New Year's Eve and ran a man down.) The numb young man, now convict #48642, is ushered in before the egalitarian Warden James Adams (Lewis Stone). The paternalistic Adams gives Kent advice about dealing with his new environment. (Such indoctrination would become standard fare in prison dramas.)

> While you're not in the common sense of the word a criminal, I want to warn you against the influences you'll encounter here ... so you be careful of your conduct, your associations ... and remember this prison does not give a man a yellow streak. But if he has one, it brings it out.

Marlowe finds himself bunking in cell #265 with John Morgan (Chester Morris), a sleek forger, and with convicted killer Butch Schmidt (Wallace Beery), a gruff bruiser affectionately known as "Machine Gun." Butch, the veteran convict, takes it on himself to tutor the newcomer in the strange ways of life behind bars. As he insists, "I'll learn you a lot of things before we're through with you in here." Later, when the naïve and cowardly Kent squeals on a fellow convict, Butch warns him, "Well, Mr. Yellow Belly. You're goin' to get your first lesson right now. You can't squeal in stir." With that, Butch beats up the helpless Marlowe. Still later, Butch, a braggart who hides the fact that he cannot read and pretends to be receiving a rash of passionate letters from lovelorn girlfriends on the outside, admits to Morgan, "I'd go nuts if I didn't start trouble once in a while. I'd rather stand up and fight, even if I got the rope. It's better than sitting here rotting in this stinking hole."

Actually, among the cellmates, it is manipulative John Morgan who controls troublemaker Butch and who quickly views Marlowe as an annoyance. He too gives Marlowe a lesson in survival. "Now, you're in a tough spot. But you've got to learn that whining and double-crossing will get you nowhere.... If you're wise, you'll stand up and take your joe [punishment] like a regular guy."

After the restless Butch creates a disturbance in the dining hall regarding the crummy food, Warden Adams storms into the middle of chaos. He warns his charges, "You listen to me, you men. If you got any grievance within my power to correct, come to me. You can't gain anything by creating a row like this. I'm running this show and I'm ready for ya." Once having restored order, he has the instigator Butch put in the "dungeon" (solitary confinement) for thirty days on a diet of bread and water.

Further along, just as John Morgan is about to be paroled—he looks forward to "Bright lights, good food, women!"—Kent takes it on himself to hide Butch's knife in John's jacket. When the guards find the weapon and no explanation is forthcoming, Morgan is sent to the dungeon. He vows revenge on Marlowe. Later, he escapes in the prison morgue wagon, and once free, goes to see Marlowe's sister Ann (Leila Hyams) whom he had become attracted to just from seeing her picture. Before long he and Ann, who operates a bookshop, are in love. However, Morgan is soon recaptured and sent back to prison. But he now intends to change his ways, seeing a future for himself with Ann. The rambunctious Butch warns John, "Don't let that gang know you're going straight. They used to have a lot of respect for you."

The cumulative effects of overcrowding and unmanageable living conditions causes the convicts to plot a prison break set for Thanksgiving day. When Morgan learns of the plan, he tries unsuccessfully to dissuade Butch. The devious Marlowe, almost unhinged by this life in hell, alerts the warden of the scheduled riot, hoping it will reduce his sentence. The rampage gets underway when several guards are taken hostage and the warden refuses to give in to the convicts' demands. ("I'll see you in hell first," he tells the convicts. He then orders his own men to "Let 'em have it!") The bloody battle between the guards and convicts causes losses on both sides, with Army tanks soon arriving on the scene to quell the uprising. When Kent attempts to break away from the rioters, Butch shoots him. Morgan does his best to intervene between the two factions. After he is wounded by Butch, he returns the gunfire and kills Schmidt. Order is finally restored.

John Morgan is paroled for his valiant efforts. The warden advises him, "New

Chester Morris, Robert Montgomery and Wallace Beery in *The Big House* (1930).

friends, new surroundings, hard work. That's a man's salvation." As Morgan passes through the outer gates, a guard warns him, "See that you don't get homesick again."

There were many elements in the innovative *The Big House* that were to become standard elements within the genre. The soul-deadening sound of convicts garbed in drab prison uniforms shuffling out of their cells and plodding along to the dining hall, the cliques of men gossiping, plotting and observing in the exercise yard, the clanking of utensils as the prisoners sullenly shovel down their "food," the finite sound of cells slamming shut at the close of day. There is the endless succession of con games the convicts play on one another, the guards, and visitors. Within *The Big House* there is a steady dose of the unique prison jargon in which informants are called "snitches," the guards are labeled "screws" and cops are known as "bulls." Typically in such films, as in *The Big House,* the warden is both avuncular and stern. While he has the power of a mini-despot—a master over thousands of slaves—he generally realizes that he is always dealing with a potentially explosive situation. For even a conscientious prison warden, avoiding riots has a higher priority than rehabilitation. Such administrators know that coping with prisoners is a near-losing proposition. ("It's 3,000 idle men with nothing to do but brood and plot. You can't put them all in solitary," says Warden Adams). He realizes his job demands compromises, such as using convict informants to keep one step ahead of disaster. (Warden Adams admits, "Stoolies. I wish we could run the place without them.")

The Big House, certainly an uncharacteristic picture to be produced by glossy Metro-Goldwyn-Mayer, won two Academy Awards: for its screenplay and its sound recording. It received Oscar nominations for Best Picture (which went to *All Quiet on the Western Front*) and for Best Actor (Wallace Beery—who lost to George Arliss of *Disraeli*). *The Big House* was issued in both a sound and silent version. Additionally, in this time when Hollywood was making foreign language versions of many of its pictures, *The Big House* was reshot for a French version (*Révolte dans la Prison*) with Charles Boyer in the Chester Morris role and directed by Paul Fejos; as well as a German edition directed by Fejos and a Spanish version directed by Ward Wing. Originally, MGM star Lon Chaney was scheduled to star in *The Big House* as the bullying Butch, but he was then dying of cancer and was replaced by Wallace Beery. Shot on a forty-day production schedule at a cost of $414,000, *The Big House* earned a $462,000 profit.

Interestingly, MGM was led into producing *The Big House* because of the topicality of prison riots and because of the great success prison melodramas were then enjoying on the Broadway stage (i.e. *The Last Mile, The Criminal Code*). Having succeeded so admirably with this film form, MGM lost interest in the genre except for occasional outings (e.g., the Laurel and Hardy satire *Pardon Us,* 1931, and Edward G. Robinson's *Blackmail,* 1939, qq.v.). It would be proleterian Warner Bros. who would become the prime producer of genre pieces in the 1930s and thereafter.

23. *Big House, U.S.A.* (United Artists, 1955), 82 min.

Producer, Aubrey Schenk; director, Howard W. Koch; screenplay, John C. Higgins; costumes, George A. Thompson; music, Paul Dunlap; assistant director, Harold M. Klein; camera, Gordon Avil; editor, John F. Schreyer.

Broderick Crawford (Rollo Lamar); Ralph Meeker (Jerry Barker); Reed Hadley (James Madden); Randy Fan (Nurse Emily Evans); William Talman (Machinegun Mason); Lon Chaney, Jr. (Alamo Smith); Charles Bronson (Benny Kelly); Peter Votrian (Danny Lambert); Roy Roberts (Chief Ranger Erickson); Willis B. Bouchey (Robertson Lambert).

Using a pseudo-documentary style to trace the full case history of a crime from its inception to the punishment of the participants, *Big House, U.S.A.* was more ambitious in concept than execution. As Howard Thompson *(New York Times)* evaluated, "*Big House, U.S.A.* is an idea for a good crime melodrama gone wrong." Acknowledging the fine location work (Colorado's Royal Gorge Park) and the slow stretches of narration, *Variety* reported, "Plenty of violence is featured throughout in some rather chilling scenes, but fits the tough characters with which the story deals."

When a youngster (Peter Votrian) runs away from a summer camp, he is found by opportunist Jerry Barker (Ralph Meeker) who realizes the boy is the subject of a wide search by his wealthy father. Jerry demands $200,000 ransom from the twelve-year old's father (Willis B. Bouchey). The latter pays the money to Barker not knowing that his son is already dead (having accidentally fallen from the fire tower where Barker hid him). Taciturn Barker is caught, and although there is insufficient evidence to prove kidnapping, he is sentenced to prison for extortion. There, in "the big house," convicted bank robber Rollo Lamar (Broderick Crawford) and his cutthroat henchmen—including Alamo Smith (Lon Chaney, Jr.), Machinegun Mason (William Talman) and Benny Kelly (Charles Bronson)— make life difficult for the new convict. Snarling "pen boss" Lamar decides to break

Broderick Crawford in *Big House, U.S.A.* (1955).

out with his men and Barker, intent on getting the hidden ransom money that federal authorities never found. The breakout is a success, but soon the convicts fight among themselves and Rollo kills Benny. Later, the federal agents and Park rangers track down the escapees and in a pitched gun battle the convicts are killed.

In an era when Hollywood was competing desperately against the inroads of television and was attempting to be as sensational as possible to lure filmgoers, *Big House, U.S.A.* set a few standards of heightened violence. In the course of its eighty-four minutes, one convict is scalded to death in a prison boiler vat; another (Bronson) after being killed has his face and fingers disfigured by a blowtorch so his identity cannot be traced. Such excesses led the British *Monthly Film Bulletin* to complain, "The characters here depicted are so brutal as to anesthetize all sympathy, and their savagery is minutely explored by the director, Howard W. Koch, in a manner that leaves one shocked yet disinterested."

The prison scenes were shot at the Cascabel Island facility.

24. *The Big Shot* (Warner Bros., 1942), 82 min.

Producer, Walter MacEwen; director, Lewis Seiler; screenplay, Bertram Millhauser, Abem Finkel, Daniel Fuchs; art director, John Hughes; costumes, Milo Anderson; makeup, Perc Westmore; music, Adolph Deutsch; orchestrator, Jerome Moross; assistant director, Art Lueker; dialogue director, Harold Winston; sound, Stanley Jones; camera, Sid Hickox; editor, Jack Killifer.

Humphrey Bogart (Duke Berne); Irene Manning (Lorna Fleming); Richard Travis (George Anderson); Susan Peters (Ruth Carter); Stanley Ridges (Martin Feling); Minor Watson (Warden Booth); Chick Chandler (Dancer); Joseph Downing

(Frenchy); Howard Da Silva (Sandor); Murray Alper (Quinto); Roland Drew (Faye); John Ridgely (Tim); Joseph King (Toohey); John Hamilton (Judge); Virginia Brissac (Mrs. Booth); William Edmunds (Sarto); Virginia Sale (Mrs. Miggs); Ken Christy (Kat); Wallace Scott (Rusty).

Often the lines between a motion picture gangster tale and a prison melodrama are blurred. Such was the case with *The Big Shot,* a hastily assembled entry from Warner Bros. geared to cash in on the growing reputation of contract star Humphrey Bogart. *Variety* was unimpressed by the proceedings, "Conventional type gangster meller, pre-war formula, destined for dual-bill support spotting."

On his deathbed in a prison hospital, three-time loser Duke Berne (Humphrey Bogart) recalls the turn of events which caused his downfall. In flashback, he remembers that he wanted to avoid returning to criminal activities because a fourth conviction automatically means a life sentence. But his pals pressure him into joining them for an armored car robbery. Belatedly, he learns that the financier of the scheme is crooked criminal attorney Martin Fleming (Stanley Ridges), whose wife Lorna (Irene Manning) used to be Duke's girlfriend. Although Lorna, who still loves Berne, prevents him from participating in the holdup, a confused witness, nevertheless, insists Duke was one of the lawbreakers. After Fleming learns that Duke and Lorna are still in love, Fleming breaks Berne's alibi — George Anderson (Richard Travis) — and, as a result, both Duke and Anderson (whose only crime is perjury) are sentenced to prison. When Duke breaks out of prison, a guard is killed, and Berne heads to a mountain retreat with Lorna. However, when he learns that George has been charged with the guard's death and is now under death sentence at the prison, Berne determined to save his new-found friend. On the way, Lorna is killed by pursuing police and Duke, who shoots Fleming at his apartment, is fatally shot by the dying lawyer. Back in the present, Duke dies, as George and his fiancée (Susan Peters) look on.

25. *Big Town Ideas* (Fox, 1921), 50 min.

Presenter, William Fox; director, Carl Harbaugh; story-screenplay, John Montague; camera, Otto Brautigan.

Eileen Percy (Fan Tilden); Kenneth Gibson (Alan Dix); Jimmie Parrott (Spick Sprague); Lon Poff (Deputy); Laura La Plante (Molly Dorn); Leo Sulky (George Small); Harry De Roy (Bald-Headed Man); Lefty James (Warden); Larry Bowes (Governor); Paul Kamp (Grocer's Boy); Paul Cazeneuve (Show Manager); Wilson Hummell (Chef); Jess Aldridge (Governor's Bodyguard).

In a more innocent era when prisons were considered by most to be necessary and worthwhile institutions where inmates paid their debt to society and that was that, many silent filmplays used prisons as a change-of-pace setting to give flavor to a story. Such was the case with *Big Town Ideas,* which *Variety* judged was "a rare combination of heart interest, violent melodrama and comedy, with most of the subtitles written for humor."

Pert, young Fan Tilden (Eileen Percy) a waitress in a rural railway station restaurant hungers for the excitement of life in the big city. Her goals change when she encounters Alan Dix (Kenneth Gibson), a young man on his way to the local prison for having stolen bonds. She quickly comes to believe in his innocence and determines to put matters right. She maneuvers a chorine post in the variety show at the nearby prison and during the presentation she helps him to escape. The enterprising miss then goes after the real scoundrels, recoups the missing bonds, distracts the prison authorities from their search for Alan and finally convinces the governor to give her beau a pardon. As *Variety* championed of this breezy entry, "the story is worked out quite absorbingly and is replete with rapid-fire action."

26. *Birdman of Alcatraz* (United Artists, 1962), 147 min.

Presenter/executive producer, Harold Hecht; producers, Stuart Miller, Guy Trosper; director, John Frankenheimer; based on the book *Birdman of Alcatraz: The Story of Robert Stroud* by Thomas E. Gaddis; screenplay, Trosper; art director, Fernando Carrere; makeup, Robert Schiffer; music, Elmer Bernstein; assistant director, Dave Silver; bird handler, A. W. Kennard; sound, George Cooper; sound effects, Robert Reich, James Nelson; camera, Burnett Guffey, Robert Krasker; editor, Edward Mann.

Burt Lancaster (Robert F. Stroud); Karl Malden (Warden Harvey Shoemaker); Thelma Ritter (Elizabeth McCartney Stroud); Betty Field (Stella Johnson);

Neville Brand (Bull Ransom); Edmond O'Brien (Thomas E. Gaddis); Hugh Marlowe (Warden Albert Comstock); Telly Savalas (Feto Gomez); Whit Bissell (Dr. Ellis); Crahan Denton (Kramer); Leo Penn (Eddie Kassellis); James Westerfield (Warden Jess Younger); Lewis Charles (Chaplain Wentzel); Arthur Stewart (Guard Captain); Raymond Greenleaf (Judge); Nick Dennis (Crazed Prisoner); William Hansen (Fred Daw); Harry Holcombe (City Editor); Robert Burton (Senator Ham Lewis); Len Lesser (Burns); Chris Robinson (Logue); George Mitchell (Father Matthieu); Edward Mallory (John Clary); Adrienne Marden (Mrs. Woodrow Wilson); Harry Jackson (Reporter).

Undoubtedly, one of the most unique of all prisoners in the annals of American penology was Robert F. Stroud (1890–1963) who spent a total of fifty-four years in prison; forty-two of which were in solitary confinement. More amazingly, this school dropout, who killed one man in 1909 and in 1916 murdered a prison guard, became a noted ornithologist and author. *Birdman of Alcatraz*, based on the 1955 book by Thomas E. Gaddis, is a sturdy document of this remarkable individual. Starring Burt Lancaster in one of his most restrained performances, this movie is a landmark study in the prison genre. A. H. Weiler *(New York Times)* acknowledged this production is "a tribute to the iconoclastic courage needed to break the mold of the normal prison film drama." He lauded this movie "which stirs the emotions and remains in memory."

The narrative opens in 1959 as author Thomas E. Gaddis (Edmond O'Brien), who has written a best-selling book about a unique prisoner he has never yet met, is standing at a San Francisco wharf. He awaits the arrival of Robert F. Stroud (Burt Lancaster), the seventy-two year old convict, who is being transferred from Alcatraz Prison to a penal hospital facility at Springfield, Missouri. In a voice-over narration, Gaddis cites facts about this singular criminal who has spent the last seventeen years at Alcatraz. Stroud has existed for decades in solitary confinement in his various prison cells. The last time he broke bread with another person was in 1916. He has never used the telephone or ridden in an automobile. (In Gaddis's actual book, the author adds that Robert Stroud, the grandson of a judge, never got beyond third grade. "[H]e is probably the only convict in the history of Federal prisons who defied a government bureau and reversed a policy concerning himself, the conflict was over canary birds." Gaddis also notes ironically that the original name for the prison isle where Stroud was to spend so many years was Bird Island.)

The chronicle flashes back to 1912. Convict Robert F. Stroud, who killed a man in Juneau, Alaska in 1909 for making unwanted advances to a prostitute, is being transferred from the federal penitentiary at MacNeil Island, Washington to the "big time." Stroud is heading for the dank, imposing prison at Leavenworth,

Advertisement for *Birdman of Alcatraz* (1962).

Kansas which is geared to handle incorrigible prisoners. En route, the taciturn, handcuffed Stroud breaks a train car window. When asked what caused this act of rebellion, he responds, "I was thinking of my lungs. Even a prisoner has a right to breathe."

Once at the bleak Leavenworth stronghold, he is brought in to meet Warden Harvey Shoemaker (Karl Malden), the "god" on earth who now controls his every movement. The no-nonsense Shoemaker and the burly, glum Stroud quickly size each other up:

> SHOEMAKER: Such rights as you will enjoy are listed right here in my Rules and Regulations. There are eighty-six of them. I suggest you memorize them.
>
> STROUD: I know them. They're the same in all pens. They tell you when to eat, when to sleep, when to go to the privy.
>
> SHOEMAKER: Precisely. And what you'll do for twenty-four hours a day.... So with or without your cooperation, I intend to make a man of you.

At first, Stroud is assigned a cellmate, but quickly the two conflict, especially when the other picks up Stroud's framed photograph of his mother (Thelma Ritter). Later, while working in the laundry, Stroud and another inmate brawl over a comment the man made about Stroud's "mama." For this activity, Stroud is ordered to the hole, where he remains in solitary confinement for thirty days.

The iron-willed Shoemaker is determined to assert his influence over Stroud. Once he meets the prisoner's mother, Elizabeth Stroud, who has relocated 2,000 miles to live near the prison, he is convinced there is hope for Stroud. As he tells a subordinate, "I don't give up on a man that easily. He comes from good stock." But meanwhile, when Stroud is denied a visit with his devoted mama, with whom he shares an inordinately strong relationship, he rebels against a taunting, cruel guard (Crahan Denton). In a flash, Stroud stabs and kills the guard, cursing, "You ain't human, you're dog puke." (An interesting comment, since this is how most of the guards regard the inmates.) For this crime, Stroud goes on trial and is sentenced to death. However, his strong-minded mother campaigns to save her beloved "Robbie," even traveling to Washington, DC where she is granted a conference with the wife of ailing President Woodrow Wilson. Mrs. Stroud insists "My son is a person of worth," and her appeal is so persuasive, that Stroud's sentence is commuted to life. Shoemaker informs Stroud of the presidential commutation, adding, "I think you'll regret that this wire ever came. You are to spend the rest of your life in deep lock [a solitary confinement cell]."

As time passes, captor and captive fight for control of Stroud's soul, even after orders have come through for Shoemaker to be reassigned to a new federal prison commission in the nation's capitol.

> STROUD: I won't lick your hand and that's what eats you, ain't it keeper. A man ain't whipped till he quits and I'll never give you that pleasure.

> SHOEMAKER: I'll never forget you as long as I live. No matter what happens to me, no matter where I am, if I ever get a chance to punish you further I will do it.

More time passes and as the voice-over explains, "You sit and listen to your heartbeat and you hear your life ticking away. The thing that swells in your head until you lose your mind is you know absolutely for sure what's coming next." (Emphasizing this bleak observation is the barren sight of Stroud standing at the cell bars, staring into space and rocking back and forth.)

One day during his solitary exercise in the yard, Stroud finds a bewildered young sparrow struggling on the ground. He takes the bird back to his cell, where he begins tending to "Runty" who soon becomes a cherished pet and friend. Before long, Feto Gomez (Telly Savalas), another prisoner on solitary row, wants to have a bird, and thereafter several of the men in this block have canaries chirping in their cells. Quickly, Stroud becomes the authority on the care and feeding of these birds, and he even painstakingly constructs a bird cage for his own pet. Initially, the guards, especially Bull Ransom (Neville Brand), think the prisoners crazy for wanting birds in their cells, but soon see it as a way of pacifying these tough convicts. Over time, Stroud, who has a scanty education but a quick mind, asks for any and all literature from the prison library about the care of birds, and he discovers there is very little devoted to the subject. He begins to write practical but scholarly articles for bird journals.

One of the readers of his articles is Stella Johnson (Betty Field), of Shelbyville, Indiana who comes to deliver a bird he won in a contest she sponsored. The middle-aged widow is drawn to the dynamic Stroud and suggests she wants to move to Leavenworth, Kansas where she will manufacture and sell his bird remedies. He is agreeable to her marketing "Stroud's Specifics." Later, the two are married as a convenience so she will have more rights to visit him (although they are never allowed connubial rights).

Meanwhile, the new warden (Hugh Marlowe) at Leavenworth issues a directive that the men are to have no pets in their cells, nor engage in any profit-making enterprises. Undaunted, Stroud begins a publicity campaign to gain public support for his bird study. He enlists the aid of Stella, which angers Stroud's possessive mother. As a result of the nationwide support for Stroud's work, Harvey Shoemaker is dispatched from Washington to deal with this recalcitrant convict. The ever-resourceful Stroud is amused by the controversy he has created, especially this challenge to Shoemaker. Stroud refuses to back down on his demands, insisting he is "just an inmate protecting his rights." Stroud is victorious finally, but in the process angers his mother who cannot forgive that he let another woman, Stella, share in his life. As such, she turns bitter and voices damning statements to the press which militate against Stroud's bid for parole. Stroud tears up his mother's photograph and gets drunk on cell-brewed alcohol. In a dazed moment, he sets his many canaries loose, telling them, "Fly my aviation friends. I give you the illusion of freedom. Enjoy it!" Meanwhile, the warden is resentful of Stroud's growing, respectful reputation in the outside world, especially after the publication of his book *Stroud's Digest on the Diseases of Birds* (1942). The warden is angered because his celebrity convict "thinks he is a world unto himself" and insists that, Stroud's intellectual pursuits to one side, "We're keeping a killer locked up here."

Orders come through to transfer Stroud to Alcatraz Prison near San Francisco. Resigned to each new twist of fate which controls his every move in life, Stroud tells Stella he does not want her to follow him westward. "Don't waste your time grieving over me. When it's cut, it's cut. . . . So long friend." (She does come to visit him at Alcatraz for one final meeting, where he tells her "You fought your heart for me, but the sun has gone down and won't rise again.")

At Alcatraz, Stroud, prisoner #594, is housed in C Block, where he is placed in "segregation" (the new word for solitary confinement). He finds that Harvey Shoemaker is the new warden. The latter admits to him, "I don't suppose any of us truly enjoy living on this island. It wasn't designed for pleasure." Another reunion is with Feto Gomez, who has been at Alcatraz already for several years and is a trusty there. When Stroud was transferred he had not fought the fact that at Alcatraz he would not be allowed to have birds in his cell. He turns to other pursuits, studying languages (including Greek), current events, and to writing a book about the history of American penology and the many abuses of authority over the decades. Stroud feels he is an authority on the subject, "When you've lived in these manure piles for over thirty years as I have, you come to know everything's a mess." However, Shoemaker confiscates his manuscript, another challenge in their ongoing chess game of life. He threatens Stroud with more severe discipline if he continues to break rules (i.e. writing articles/books). The undaunted Stroud counters, "You know better than to try and frighten me at this late date." Wanting the last words, Stroud puts forth his theory on rehabilitation within the penal system:

> I wonder if you know what the word means. The definition . . . [is] to invest again with dignity. You consider that part of your job, Harvey, is to give a man back the dignity he once had. Your only interest is how he once behaved. You told me once a long time ago, and I'll never forget it, 'You'll conform to our ideas of how you

should behave' and you haven't retreated from that stand one inch in thirty-five years. You want your prisoners to dance out the gates like puppets on a string, with rubber-stamped values impressed by you — with your sense of conformity, your sense of behavior, even your sense of morality. That's why you're a failure, you and the whole science of penology, because you rob prisoners of the most important thing in their lives, their individuality. On the outside, they're lost, automatons just going through the motions of living, but underneath is a deep hatred for what you did to them. The first chance they get to attack society, they do it. And the result. More than half come back to prison.

In May 1946 during a prison break, which involves convicts Burns (Len Lesser) and Logue (Chris Robinson), Stroud refuses to participate in the break, preferring to remain in his unlocked cell. He later tends to a wounded prisoner, telling the injured man, "The first duty of life is to live." When the blood rampage between convicts and guards continues, Stroud mediates to end the battle.

More time passes. Harvey Shoemaker dies in 1953, replaced by a new warden. In 1959, Stroud, now an old man, leaves "the rock" to be transferred to another rock. As the motor launch reaches the San Francisco dock, the famous convict tells reporters, "Well, if you San Franciscans had any true civic pride, you'd blow that place out of the water instead of advertising it. What an eyesore!" When another newsman expresses surprise at Stroud's eruditeness, the prisoner retorts, "Just because a man is in prison, doesn't mean he's a boob." When asked if he can explains why he was not allowed to continue his bird study at Alcatraz, he responds, "In the eyes of the prison bureau, avian research is . . . for the birds." When Stroud and his biographer finally meet face-to-face for the first time, the former expresses enthusiasm for his new prison home-to-be. "I'm going to sleep in a room without a lock on the door. Think of it, to be able to walk in and out of a room anytime you want to. . . . It's going to be a swell place to live until I get my release."

A postscript details that Robert Stroud's petitions for parole have been denied yearly for twenty-four years. "He's now seventy, in his fifty-third year of jail."

There are many worthy aspects to this atypical prison film. Above and beyond the integrity of the scripting, direction and acting in retelling this unique prison story, *Birdman* effectively illuminates the many strange relationships and bonds that occur within prison. There is the link between warden and prisoner, the former the chief architect of the latter's very survival. Then there is the give-and-take between prisoners and guards, well illustrated here in the growing respect between Robert Stroud and his longtime guard, Bull Ransom (Neville Brand). In a very telling scene, Ransom expresses his frustration at Stroud who remains proud and unyielding, refusing to acknowledge Ransom's efforts at kindness or to treat him with any human warmth. It demonstrates how in some very deep psychological ways, the keepers (guards) are at the mercy of their charges (the prisoners), the latter who provide their very jobs. Another aspect of this intense study of a man's decades behind bars is to point out how each convict copes differently with his incarceration, the loss of his free will and his privacy. In Stroud's case, he survives years of deprivation in primitive settings, to emerge a learned man with advanced knowledge in many arenas.

There is much to commend about the somber, ungratuitous *Birdman of Alcatraz*. Granted it is self-consciously art, but it is generally an uncompromising study — filmed in black-and-white — which remains one of the most dignified and telling studies of incarceration on film. There are several small areas where this meticulous motion picture deviates from the real-life biography of Stroud, but, in the overall, they are inconsequential, (e.g., in real life, Stroud had two half-sisters and one brother Marcus, the latter who visited him at Leavenworth Prison.)

Variety lauded this remarkable motion picture, "Heretofore . . . the core of the 'prison picture' has been prison life itself, around which has been constructed dramatizations of those who were a part of that secretly sealed life on the negative side of society. . . . *Birdman* reverses the formula and brings a new breadth and depth to the form. . . . [It] achieves a human dimension way beyond its predecessors." On the other hand, Pauline Kael (*New Yorker* magazine) pointed out the movie's flaws. "Intelligent, affecting, clearly well-meaning — too well-meaning as it drones on and on, uplifghtingly. The [filmmakers] . . . are so sympathetic and discreet in their near-documentary approach . . . that they never solve the problem of how to dramatize the life of a convicted killer who spent more than forty years in solitary confinement. . . . We don't get enough understanding of Stroud . . . to become involved in how he is transformed over the years." As for Burt Lancaster's focal (and to many, mesmerizing) performance, Kael analyzed, "when he's cooped up like this and can't use his intense physicality he seems numb — half dead."

Because it was such an unglamorized, lengthy (147 minutes) character study, *Birdman of Alcatraz* was not typical fare for moviegoers seeking the rough-and-tumble thrills usually associated with the genre. The advertising campaign did its best to hype the "action" aspects of the film, proclaiming, "Inside the Rock called Alcatraz they tried to chain a volcano called 'The Bird Man.'" Much was made of the fact that Burt Lancaster had previously starred in another acclaimed prison drama, the very actionful, ferocious *Brute Force* (1947), q.v. Earning less than $4,000,000 in domestic film rentals paid to the distributor, *Birdman of Alcatraz* received four Academy Award nominations: Best Actor (Burt Lancaster), Best Supporting Actor (Telly Savalas), Best Supporting Actress (Thelma Ritter); Best Cinematography — Black-and-White.

The character of Robert Stroud would make a guest appearance in *Alcatraz: The Whole Shocking Story* (1980), q.v., this time played by Art Carney. In *Six Against the Rock* (1987), q.v., the Birdman would be portrayed by Dennis Farina.

27. *Blackmail* (Metro-Goldwyn-Mayer, 1939), 81 min.

Producer, John Considine, Jr.; associate producer, Albert E. Levoy; director, H. C. Potter; based on the story by Andre Bohem, Dorothy Yost; screenplay, David Hertz, William Ludwig; art directors, Cedric Gibbons, Howard Campbell; set decorator, Edwin B. Willis; wardrobe, Dolly Tree; music, Edward Ward, David Snell; second unit director, Charles Dorian; sound director, Douglas Shearer; camera, Clyde DeVinna; editor, Howard O'Neill.

Edward G. Robinson (John R. Ingram [John Harrington]); Ruth Hussey (Helen Ingram); Gene Lockhart (William Ramey); Bobs Watson (Hank Ingram); Guinn "Big Boy" Williams (Moose McCarthy); John Wray (Diggs); Arthur Hohl (Rawlins); Esther Dale (Sarah); Joe Whitehead (Anderson); Joseph Crehan (Blaine); Victor Kilian (Warden Miller); Gil Perkins (Kearney); Mitchell Lewis, Lew Harvey (Workmen); Willie Best (Sunny); Art Miles (Driver); Robert Middlemass (Desk Sergeant); Ivan Miller (Weber); Hal K. Dawson (Desk Clerk); Phillip Morris (Local Trooper); Charles Middleton, Trevor Bardette (Deputies); Joe Dominguez (Pedro); Everett Brown (Black Prisoner); Ed Montoya (Juan); Cy Kendall (Sheriff); Harry Fleischmann (Oil Worker); Eddy Chandler (Boss Brown); Lee Phelps (Guard); Wade Boteler (Police Sergeant).

With its hero a rough-and-tumble oil fire fighter who endures the rigors of chain gang life (for a crime he did not commit) and enjoys the love of a good woman (Ruth Hussey), one might have thought that Metro-Goldwyn-Mayer would have cast one of its contract stars—e.g., Clark Gable or Spencer Tracy—in the lead of *Blackmail*. However, the role went to Warner Bros.' Edward G. Robinson more noted for his characterizations as a lawbreaker (e.g., *Little Caesar*, 1930) than as a lawmaker (e.g., *I Am the Law*, 1938). This led Bosley Crowther (*New York Times*) to bemoan, "What a sad thing it is then, to see this distinguished inhabitant of the Rogues' Gallery, this Napoleon of crime, this indomitably amoral spirit who belongs with the Borgias, feebly trying to go straight in *Blackmail*." Robert W. Dana (*New York Herald-Tribune*), while no champion of this production, at least acknowledged the sociological aspects/virtues within this man's action picture: "The greater part of the film paints the villainy and inhuman treatment that exists in chain-gangs. It is not a pretty picture: it becomes a fairly real one, though, as Mr. Robinson and his unfortunate comrades conduct it. . . ."

Wrongly imprisoned for a crime he did not commit, John Harrington (Edward G. Robinson), escapes. He assumes the identity of John Ingram and quickly builds a profitable, albeit dangerous business in Oklahoma, of putting out oil fires. His wife Helen (Ruth Hussey) is aware of his clouded past, but supports his career ambitions and is the mother of their son Hank (Bobs Watson). Meanwhile, William Ramey (Gene Lockhart), who actually committed the crime for which John was sentenced, happens to see a newsreel photograph of Ingram and, being down on his luck, he comes to Ingram with a proposal. For $25,000, with which he intends to purchase a farm in Maine, Ramey agrees to provide evidence to clear John's name. No sooner does John give Ramey part of the sum and a promissory note for the balance, than Ramey destroys the confession and turns Ingram over to the law. Ingram is returned to prison, while Ramey now has a mortgage on Ingram's oil property. Surviving on the chain gang is difficult enough, but John is distraught when he learns that Helen and his son have been forced to give up their home and that his oil business is being destroyed by the incompetent Ramey. With the help of his one-time co-worker Moose McCarthy (Guinn "Big Boy" Williams), Ingram escapes again from the chain gang. This act causes Ramey to go into hiding from which he attempts to sell the now rich oil well which is on Ingram's once property. John tricks Ramey into returning to town. At the oil well—which has been set ablaze—Ingram forces a confession from Ramey which is overhead by others. By blasting the well, the property is saved. John and Helen are reconciled.

Actually *Blackmail* could have succeeded as a rugged action tale without its explicit section devoted to the struggle for survival on the chain gang. As *Variety* noted, "Chain gang camp sequences point up brutality and mental collapse of prisoners too graphically to fit into the composite whole." Nevertheless, Edward G. Robinson and the cast do admirably well in portraying the grim harshness dealt to the convict slaves on the chain gang. *Blackmail* does not make one forget the horrors depicted in southern prison camps in *I Am a Fugitive from a Chain Gang* (1932) and *Hell's Highway* (1932), qq.v., but Robinson's forceful portrayal of an innocent man coping with hellish treatment from sadistic guards is memorable unto itself. *Variety*, ever vigilant to box office grosses, noted, "The chain gang disclosures, however, may not be accepted by southern audiences."

28. *Blackwell's Island* (Warner Bros., 1939), 71 min.

Producer, Bryan Foy; director, William McGann; story, Crane Wilbur, Lee Katz; screenplay, Wilbur; art director, Stanley Fleischer; gowns, Howard Shoup; music director, Leo F. Forbstein; dialogue director, Harry Seymour; sound, Leslie G. Hewitt; camera, Sid Hickox; editor, Doug Gould.

John Garfield (Tim Haydon); Rosemary Lane (Sunny Walsh); Dick Purcell (Terry Walsh); Victor Jory (Deputy Commissioner of Corrections Thomas McNair); Stanley Fields (Bull Bransom); Morgan Conway (Steve Cardigan); Granville Bates (Warden Stuart Granger); Anthony Averill (Brower); Peggy Shannon (Pearl Murray); Charley Foy (Benny Farmer); Norman Willis (Mike Garth); Joe Cunningham (Rawden); Leon Ames (Special Prosecutor Ballinger).

Although an opening statement makes a disclaimer against this film being based on reality, the scenario of *Blackwell's Island* was based on actual events in the mid–1930s, when mobster/inmate Joey Rao had taken over the prison hospital on New York's Welfare Island and turned it into a comfortable retreat known as "politician's flat." Rao so controlled the institution that only those of the 1,700 inmates who could pay tribute to him were given "decent" food or shelter. The facts involving this outrageous situation, where a criminal was operating his gangland enterprises from inside a prison, were made known by the New York Commissioner of Corrections when he raided the compound in 1934. *Variety* ranked this social statement entry "One of the better prison mellers in the Warners' penal cycle, spiced and garnished this time with factual recording of almost unbelievable conditions in a penal institution."

Among many profitable gangland activities, mobster Bull Bransom runs the Waterfront Protective Association. He is supported by Steve Cardigan (Morgan Conway) a corrupt political figure tied into the current city administration. Because of the publicity surrounding his involvement in blowing up the vessel of a skipper who refused to pay off the Association, Bull and a few of his hoods are forced to accept a six month-to-three year sentence at the city penitentiary at Blackwell's Island.

No sooner does this hard core criminal reach the facility than he advises the warden (Granville Bates), "I didn't come here to sleep behind locked doors. Me and the boys will look over the joint and choose our own facilities." Because the unprincipled warden is only concerned with salvaging his pension, he is agreeable to anything, including allowing would-be bon vivant Bransom to turn the hospital dormitory into his private quarters, filled with personal effects, private phone lines, personal barber, etc. The crude Bull is afraid of no one, not even the tough guards. As he tells one keeper, "With all I got on you, you're lucky not to be in here yourself." When pressing matters make it necessary for Bull and the boys to return to the mainland, he casually steals out at night in a waiting speedboat.

Meanwhile, *New York Times-Dispatch* reporter Tim Haydon (John Garfield) is determined to expose the truth behind Bull's stay at Blackwell's Island. Tim creates a disturbance of the peace and is sentenced to six months at the facility. Even Haydon is amazed to find the true degree of corruption running rampant at the prison. Bull has put slot machines and pin games on all cell blocks and has turned part of the hospital ward into a gambling den. As head of the Prisoners Mutual Protective Association Bull has no opponents. Tim quickly makes his own reputation as a tough inmate and win's the admiration of Bransom. However, Bull learns of Tim's real purpose at the prison and tries to arrange his escape so he can have him liquidated. Tim does escape and tells the new Deputy Commissioner of

Corrections (Victor Jory) of the bizarre goings-on at Blackwell's Island. They make a surprise visit to the prison, verifying all of Tim's contentions. When Bull escapes in a speed boat, Haydon pursues him in another craft. In the chase, Bull's boat catches fire and he jumps overboard, only to be saved by Haydon. This time when Bransom is brought to trial, he is given the sentence he deserves — ninety-nine years in prison. Haydon is reunited with Sunny Walsh (Rosemary Lane) whose policeman brother (Terry) was killed by Bransom.

There is such a mixed tone to *Blackwell's Island* that it is often hard to fathom when the studio had tongue-in-cheek or was being serious with its social reform message. A good deal of the film plays like comedy, with the finale speedboat chase much like a serial chapterplay. Being produced in the socially-conscious late 1930s, the picture pays lips service to the need for reform in prisons and greater humanity to convicts. But for every sober moment of screen time, there is a contra-balancing comedy scene or quip, such as when Bull admits to the milquetoast warden, "I like it here or I wouldn't stay." The warden is not above such perversely humorous remarks as, "Convicts are always griping about something . . . making trouble is fun for them." It is hard to give this story full credence when, at the end, the denounced warden admits meekly, "I had to obey orders [from the political machine] or be kicked out. I should have resigned but I didn't. Now I have to take my medicine."

By this juncture, Warner Bros. was such an expert as churning out prison movies that it could whip together a concoction like *Blackwell's Island* easily. John Garfield, who would star in other prison entries (*Dust Be My Destiny,* 1939 and *Castle on the Hudson* 1940, qq.v.) brought more dimension to his facile hero's role than the part deserved, while Stanley Fields, a veteran at playing screen ruffians, obviously relished his no-holds-barred assignment. Rosemary Lane, as Garfield's love interest, was wasted.

29. *Blind Justice* (CBS–TV, March 9, 1986), color, 100 min.

Producer, Andrew Gottlieb; associate producers, Richard Yalem, Josephine Cummings; director, Rod Holcomb; teleplay, Cummings, Yalem; art directors, Albert Heschong, Joseph Nemec; set decorator, Chuck Korian; costumes, Linda Mathews; makeup, James R. Kail; music, Miles Goodman; music supervisor, Robert Drasnin; music editor, Robert Takage; assistant directors, Jeram Swartz, Charlotte Dreiman, Glen Sanford; stunt coordinator, Victor Paul; sound, Richard Goodman; sound editor, Sam Horta; camera, Thomas Del Ruth; editor, George B. Hively.

Tim Matheson (James William Anderson); Mimi Kuzyk (Cathy Anderson); Philip Charles MacKenzie (John Pierson); Tom Atkins (Officer Charles Kramer); Lisa Eichhorn (Carolyn Shefland); John Kellogg (Harold Anderson); Marilyn Lightstone (Dr. Carol Lathrop); Anne Haney (Joyce Anderson); David Froman (Officer Pike);

John M. Jackson (Detective Porter); Linda Thorson (Pamela Blake); Jack Blessing (Larry Richards); Ann Ryerson (Leslie Avery); Sam Dalton (Peter Hatman); Daniel Davis (Seth Thompson); Leonard Donato (Attorney Gregory Simpson); John H. Fields (Judge Robert Stanford); Tristan Hickey (Ray Carter); Richard Kuss (Judge Reuben Miller); Carlos Lacamara (Allen Sanders); Holly Lauren (Stacey Munge); Will MacMillan (Guard); Darcy Marta ("Fine Foto" Girl); Gary Pagett (Judge Richard Williamson); Michael Pniewski (Scott Carlson); Wendy Robbins (Janice Hanoway); Jon Shearin (Detective Stan Davis); Kurt Smildsin (Craig Willis); Diane Sommerfield (Newswoman); Joe Stone (Stuntman); Hugh Warden (Jury Foreman); Joseph Whipp (Detective Collier); Al White (Officer Paul Peterson); Dan Ziskie (Adam Carter).

As the opening credits to this telefeature impart, "The following is a dramatization based on true events. Though it is one man's story, it could happen to any one of us." Two of man's recurrent nightmares are being accused of a crime falsely *and* thereafter being jailed. This well-crafted, made-for-television feature ably depicts these fears becoming a frightening reality. "Director Rod Holcomb builds his case with attention to detail and is a portrait of middle-class life" (*Daily Variety*).

Told through a flashback, freelance photographer James William Anderson (Tim Matheson) recalls the event that triggered his Kafkaesque plight. He had been out jogging in the park when he needed to use the bathroom. Because the facility was locked, he took advantage of the cover of bushes to urinate, whereupon he was arrested for indecent exposure. He is irate at the situation and rather than pay the fine, is determined to reverse the charge. However, once at the police station a cop thinks he bears resemblance to a man wanted for the robbery of a photo booth store and the molestation of its female clerk. This puts into motion the "this can't be happening to me" syndrome. He has been married scarcely a year and neither he nor his wife Cathy (Mimi Kuzyk) can really afford either the bail money or retaining a lawyer, but they soon realize the necessity and hire Carolyn Shefland (Lisa Eichhorn). Matters deteriorate as it proves that the wanted man committed a rash of other robberies/rapes and one law enforcer in particular, Officer Charles Kramer (Tom Atkins) of Whitfield, makes a near vendetta of seeing that Anderson is booked and arrested each time a new warrant is issued. It becomes a near way of life for the harassed Anderson, who finds his domestic and business life falling apart, with no end to the nightmare in sight. Having spent a few nights in jails, he lives in constant dread that he could be convicted of each new charge and spend years in the much worse atmosphere of prison. Later a new lawyer (Philip Charles MacKenzie) takes charge of the case and eventually succeeds in clearing Anderson's record from each of the charges, although, off the record, this innocent defendant is damned by many judges, law enforcers, confused victims, and spectators. Finally, when all seems to have settled down, a new incident occurs and again Anderson is wanted by the police. However, it is discovered that Ray Carter (Tristan Hickey), who had been in jail on another charge for several months, is the guilty party.

A postscript details that Jim Anderson and his wife divorced and that he relocated to a southern city where he remarried and his photography career is flourishing. A final title card notes, "Although Jim was never convicted of any of the crimes for which he was accused, the memory of his ordeal will haunt him forever. . . ."

While very little screen time is devoted to Jim Anderson's ordeal in the local jail, its (after) effects are movingly real. A good deal of the credit for the success of this drama belongs to Tim Matheson, an actor best known for his light comedy assignments.

30. *Born Innocent* (NBC–TV, Sept. 10, 1974), color, 100 min.

Executive producers, Robert W. Christiansen, Rick Rosenberg; producer, Bruce Cohn Curtis; director, Donald Wrye; teleplay, Gerald DiPego; set decorator, Philip Abramson; costumes, Bruce Walkup; makeup, Bruce Hutchinson; music, Fred Karlin; music editor, Erma Levin; assistant director, Ken Swor; sound, David Ronne; camera, David M. Walsh; editor, Maury Winetrobe.

Linda Blair (Chris Parker); Joanna Miles (Barbara Clark); Kim Hunter (Mrs. Parker); Richard Jaeckel (Mr. Parker); Allyn Ann McLerie (Emma Lasko); Mary Murphy (Miss

Murphy); Janit Baldwin (Denny); Nora Heflin (Moco); Tina Andrews (Josie); Mitch Vogel (Tom Parker); Sandra Ego (Janet).

In the mid–1970s network censors were permitting more adult fare to be shown on prime time television. The TV networks soon turned to the shocking conditions of prison life as fertile material to expose for audiences' edification and voyeuristic gratification. An important, albeit lurid subgenre proved to be teenage-girls-in-reformatories, with a format that followed the guidelines established by *Caged* (1950), q.v. When initially telecast, *Born Innocent* was a controversial pathfinder in this delinquent youth screen category. It led to such explosive / exploitive followups as *Cage Without a Key* (1975) and *Love Child* (1982), qq.v.

In a western city, fourteen-year-old Chris Parker (Linda Blair) is brought to jail on a charge of being a runaway. (She has left home six times over the last two years; that is her only crime.) She spends the night in a dorm cell with an unsavory assortment of female lawbreakers of all ages and degrees of immorality. While innocent of face, Chris is street-wise enough to know to keep to herself. The next day she is made a ward of the court and remanded to a juvenile detention home where the well-bred Barbara Clark (Joanna Miles) indoctrinates the newcomer with a rote speech of "welcome" and explains the house rules:

> This isn't a jail. We have a fence here, but that's mainly to keep the intruders outside and we have locks on the doors. But the more progress you show here, the quicker you'll get rid of those locks. We try to provide a structure here. Easy steps for you to follow.... I'll tell you what we graduate here. Social people. People who can get along out there. Stay out of trouble.... Chris, the main thing here is to get along with the girls and the staff and not to get involved with any kind of fighting or anything like that. If you are aware of any kind of homosexual activity I'd like you to report it to the housemother. That is for your own protection. And if you can prove you can get along here, then it will be a short time before you reach Step Four and then you can go home, to a foster home or a group home.

Among the administrative staff at this very expansive but sterile rural facility is Emma Lasko (Allyn Ann McLerie), a middle-aged spinster who derives a disturbing gratification from controlling others' lives and from pretending that she has a real rapport with her young charges. She does not take kindly to Chris's bewilderment and quickly tries to force the impressionable girl into the institution's insensitive regimen.

Chris's roommate is Janet (Sandra Ego), a pregnant young Indian girl who had recently tried to cut her wrist. Chris is befriended by Josie (Tina Andrews), a black inmate who had been made a prostitute at the age of ten by her own mother. However, Chris soon comes into conflict with teenage lesbian Moco (Nora Heflin) and her entourage who sexually molest her in the showers. Frightened and overwhelmed by her surroundings, Chris attempts to escape, but is brought back where she is put in isolation and must again begin to build up good conduct points. Throughout her ordeals, Chris wavers between being a normal teenage girl with dreams of becoming a stewardess, to being a spiritless soul, old way beyond her years. Yet, there are moments when she regresses to being a confused child, sitting aimlessly on a swing wondering how her life has come to this.

Eventually Chris is given a four-day pass to visit her blue collar parents (Kim Hunter, Richard Jaeckel) who insist that the detention center is the best cure for their "wayward" daughter who cannot obey their household rules. Her weekend at home is a disaster, as the Parkers are suspicious of her every move. The weak-willed mother is more fearful of upsetting her husband than trying to reach out to her needful daughter. Chris runs away, taking a bus to Tucson where she hopes her older brother (Mitch Vogel) might take her in and end her stay at the center. However, he has his own problems and turns her over to the authorities. Heart-broken, she ends up back at the center in isolation again. Having abandoned any hope for her future, she takes an emotional turn for the worse. At one point she attempts suicide, but fails. Later, she and the other inmates rally when Janet is about to have her baby, but Janet suffers a miscarriage. This leads to a confronta-tion between the now-hardened Chris and Emma, and to a mini-riot among the girls. By now, Chris has learned to play the institution's games and is lost to any redemption.

Sue Cameron *(Hollywood Reporter)* acknowledged that this odyssey into hopelessness was a "massive, brutal, indictment of the juvenile justice system in the United States and also a statement against uncaring parents ... at times too sensationalistic, but basically [it is] a sensitive and successful attempt." As ex-pected, the most publicized moment in the production was Linda Blair's shower scene in which she is attacked by fellow inmates. The most touching sequence oc-curs while Blair is in solitary confinement and her supervisor/teacher (Joanna Miles) sits on the floor outside the room trying to reach out to this emotionally scared, confused young woman.

Linda Blair, who became a frequent star of exploitation features, would ap-pear in two later prison genre pieces *Chained Heat* (1982) and *Red Heat* (1985), qq.v., both presenting her in a by now-stereotyped role as an innocent young woman subjected to the dehumanizing horrors of the penal system.

31. *Boston Blackie* (Fox, 1923), 4,552'.

Presenter, William Fox; director, Scott Dunlap; based on the story "The Water Cross" by Jack Boyle; screenplay, Paul Schofield; camera, George Schneiderman. William Russell (Boston Blackie); Eva Novak (Mary Carter); Frank Brownlee (Warden Benton); Otto Matieson (Danny Carter); Spike Robinson (Shorty McNutt); Frederick Esmelton (John Gilmore).

Jack Boyle's enduring detective character, Boston Blackie, was a literary crea-tion of the 1910s and began its long stay in films in 1918 with Metro's *Boston Blackie's Little Pal* starring Bert Lytell and Metro followed it the next year with *Boston Blackie's Redemption* which featured the occasionally well-meaning lawbreaker being wrongly convicted and sent to prison where he endures tortures at the hands of a sadistic warden. The most famous screen exponent of the fictional sleuth was Chester Morris who portrayed the wise-cracking, girl-chasing crime buster in thirteen budget features for Columbia Pictures in the 1940s, as well as starring in a radio program dealing with Boston Blackie's ongoing adventures.

In Fox Film's *Boston Blackie's Redemption* (1919), adapted from Jack Boyle's 1919 story "The Water Cross," the resilient Boston Blackie (William Russell) has recently been let out of prison, having vowed to the brutalizing Warden Benton (Frank Brownlee) that he will crusade to have the man removed form his post for having tortured prisoners, including inflicting the "water-cross" torment on con-victs. Before he can make his threat reality, Blackie finds himself back in Benton's custody and about to suffer the hells of the "water-cross." Fortunately, his girlfriend Mary Carter (Eva Novak) reaches the governor and together they rush to the prison in time to save Blackie from further pain.

This adventure entry was another example of titillating the moviegoer with exploits situated in that forbidding setting—prison—where unspeakable physical and mental tortures were allegedly the rule, not the exception.

32. *Boy Slaves* (RKO, 1939), 70 min.

Producer, Pandro S. Berman; associate producer/director, P. J. Wolfson; story, Albert Bein; screenplay, Bein, Ben Orkow; art directors, Van Nest Polglase, Albert D'Agostino; music director, Frank Torvas; assistant director, Doran Cox; sound, Richard Van Hessen; camera, J. Roy Hunt; editor, Desmond Marquette.

Anne Shirley (Annie); Roger Daniel (Stoolie [Jesse Thompson]); James McCallion (Tim); Alan Baxter (Pete Graff); Johnny Fitzgerald (Knuckles); Walter Ward (Miser); Charles Powers (Lollie); Walter Tetley (Pee Wee); Frank Malo (Tommy); Paul White (Atlas); Arthur Hohl (Sheriff); Charles Lane (Albee); Norman Willis (Drift Boss); Roy Gordon (Judge); Helen Mackellar (Mother).

RKO was not about to be outdone in pursuing Hollywood's renewed interest in juvenile delinquents. If Warner Bros. could turn out *Crime School* (1938), q.v., and MGM could produce *Boys Town* (1938), q.v., then RKO had its *Boy Slaves*. Like *Crime School*, *Boy Slaves* dealt with the treatment (or herein brutal exploitation) of juvenile criminals. (In contrast, *Boys Town* focused on young hooligans who would end up in a reformatory if there was not a Father Edward J. Flanagan who created a refuge for tough neighborhood youths in his facility outside of Omaha, Nebraska.) Gratuitously conceived and paying lip service to the need for reform, *Boy Slaves* won no plaudits from *Variety*, "A preachment . . . devoid of essential entertainment factors. . . . It is more adaptable for presentation before welfare and social workers interested in abolishing various forms of child labor." The trade paper rated the production "ponderous, heavily dramatic and boring." *Boy Slaves* was part of RKO's then new budget economy features.

The film's preface states:

> Since the beginning of civilization, man's love and defense of his children has been a primary instinct. In America, fathers have fought and died on the battlefield so that they might hand down to their children a heritage of freedom. Yet today, in some isolated communities, hidden away from the law, there exist men who hold their love of money before humanity. Other men's young children labor for them from sunup and sundown. It is with these men this picture deals, with a hope that the mothers and fathers of America will search them out and expose them to the law.

Young Jesse Thompson (Roger Daniel) leaves his tenement home, determined to go out into the world and find a job so he can send money home to his needy mother. On the road, somewhere in the south, he encounters a group of young hobos and is with them when they are arrested by a rural sheriff for petty larceny. A local manufacturer of turpentine, Albee (Charles Lane), customarily is allowed to purchase the services of these delinquents for his own mercenary gain. As he fatuously tells the sheriff (Arthur Hohl) of his "charitable" action, "We'd both rather see these boys started on the road to self-respect rather than become jail birds." One of the gang, their leader Tim (James McCallion), prefers to remain in jail on a $100 vagrancy fine, rather than work at Albee's camp.

As it turns out, Albee's "camp" is surrounded by barbed wire fences and locked gates ("it's for your own protection boys," he tells them). The armed overseers govern the forced labor from dawn to dusk where they slave in gathering the ingredients for processing turpentine. They exist in primitive barracks/dormitories and any necessities they purchase (at exorbitant prices) at the company store are charged to their account. As a result, the youths are always in debt to their "benefactor." Later, Tim agrees to be bailed out by Albee, who charges the fee to the others' accounts. Tim joins his friends at the work camp. Also at the facility is Annie (Anne Shirley) a young servant who is Albee's badly treated cook/housekeeper and who is coveted by Pete Graff (Alan Baxter), Albee's foreman. Eventually, the youths go on strike, and one of them even attempts to write a letter of their plight to Mrs. Franklin D. Roosevelt. Later a fire breaks out in the boys' quarters and the boys escape with Annie. Jesse, who has been shot in a scuffle with Graff, dies. Some of the youths and Annie hole up at a farmhouse, with Albee and his henchmen closing in on them. In the nick of time, two police officers arrive and prevent a massacre of the remaining children. At a hearing, the judge (Roy Gordon) remands the boys to a state farm, where hopefully they will learn a trade. As for Albee and his cronies, he orders them to face charges of peonage.

This contrived minor offering tries its best to emulate the then fashionable statements of social protest by America's underprivileged. At one point, Tim says to Annie of their hopeless plight in the face of the seemingly uncaring establishment. "There are only them and us.... I'm sick of handouts." When Tim wants to battle Albee and his crew to the death, a frustrated Annie shouts out, "Go ahead and shoot. The way we are, we're worth nothing. Not even to each other." At the climactic courtroom hearing, the judge ruminates, "Has society come into this court with clean hands? Has society been just that it now demands justice from them?" As for the despicable Albee and his crowd, the judge enunciates, "I accuse these men of relentless and merciless cruelty."

Its allegedly noble purposes to one side, *Boy Slaves* is very weak tea. As Frank S. Nugent *(New York Times)* reported, "The supplementary story of a runaway small boy who is guardedly accepted by the gang, is marked down as a squealer and has to die to win their respect, is quite bathetic and not at all convincing." *Harrison's Reports* noted, "it seems as if the part played by Anne Shirley [then an RKO contract star] was written in as an afterthought—so as to have one well-known name to bolster up the weak cast...."

33. *Boys' Reformatory* (Monogram, 1939), 62 min.

Producer, Scott Dunlap; associate producer, Lindsley Parsons; director, Howard Bretherton; story, Ray Trampe, Norman S. Hall; screenplay, Trampe, Wellyn Totman; camera, Harry Newman.

Frankie Darro (Tommy); Grant Withers (Dr. Owens); David Durand (Knickles); Warren McCollum (Spike); Albert Hill, Jr. (Pete); Bob McClung (Blubber); George Offerman, Jr. (Joie); Frank Coghlan, Jr. (Eddie O'Mara); Ben Welden (Mike Hearn); Lillian Elliot (Mrs. O'Mara).

According to the more charitable *Harrison's Reports*, *Boys' Reformatory* was "A moving little melodrama, with fast action. What gives it its emotional quality is the young motherless hero's self-sacrifice; he prefers to go to jail rather than make unhappy the only mother he had ever known."

Teenager Tommy (Frankie Darro), an earnest and hardworking young orphan, is reared by Mrs. O'Mara (Lillian Elliot), to whom he is grateful. In contrast, his foster mother's son, Eddie (Frank Coghlan, Jr.) is a spineless ne'er-do-well who

Frankie Darro, David Durand and George Offerman, Jr. in *Boys' Reformatory* (1939).

spends all his time at the pool hall and who joins with his criminal pals in a robbery. When Eddie arrives home with the loot, Tommy takes the money and drives away, hoping to spare Mrs. O'Mara the shame of learning her real son has been involved in a crime. However, Tommy is caught by the police, and when he will not confess the actual facts, he is sentenced to the state reformatory. There, administrator Dr. Owens (Grant Withers) takes a liking to Tommy and soon makes him his assistant. Thereafter, Eddie arrives as a new ward of the institution; he later convinces Tommy that he has been going straight since that robbery episode, but that he was framed by Mike Hearn (Ben Welden), a gangster who had been using youths to carry out various tasks. Later Tommy escapes from the reformatory with one of Hearn's young stooges, convinced that he will be able to get incriminating evidence against Hearn. When the gangster learns Tommy's real purpose the boy's life is in danger. However, he manages to phone Dr. Owens who arrives in time with the police. The criminals are arrested. Tommy is cleared of any criminal charges and Eddie, who has been doing exemplary work at the reformatory, is put on probation. Both boys return home to be welcomed by Mrs. O'Mara.

Try as it would to carbon copy the successful Dead End Kids efforts at Warner Bros., this low-budget entry remained an unconvincing programmer. As *Variety* summed up *Boys' Reformatory,* "Has a mimeograph story without climactic punch or love interest, doesn't develop character or atmosphere, and it's shy on name value."

34. Boys Town (Metro-Goldwyn-Mayer, 1938), 96 min.

Producer, John W. Considine, Jr.; director, Norman Taurog; story, Dore Schary, Eleanore Griffin; screenplay, John Meehan, Schary; art directors, Cedric Gibbons, Urie McCleary; set decorator, Edwin B. Willis; music, Edward Ward; music arranger, Leo Arnaud; montage effects Slavko Vorkapich; camera, Sidney Wagner; editor, Elmo Vernon.

Spencer Tracy (Father Edward Joseph Flanagan); Mickey Rooney (Whitey Marsh); Henry Hull (Dave Morris); Leslie Fenton (Dan Farrow); Addison Richards (The Judge); Edward Norris (Joe Marsh);

Gene Reynolds (Tony Fonessa); Minor Watson (The Bishop); Victor Kilian (The Sheriff); Jonathan Hale (John Hargraves); Bobs Watson (Pee Wee); Martin Spellman (Skinny); Mickey Rentschler (Tommy Anderson); Frankie Thomas (Freddie Fuller); Jimmy Butler (Paul Ferguson); Sidney Miller (Mo Kahn); Robert Emmett Keane (Burton); Phillip Terry (Reporter); Gladden James (Doctor); Kane Richmond (Jackson, the Reporter); George Humbert (Calateri); Jay Novello (Gangster with Marsh); Johnny Walsh (Charley Haines).

If the other Hollywood studios could find pay dirt in "exploiting" the problems of wayward youths, then Metro-Goldwyn-Mayer was not to be left out of the sweepstakes. Taking a cue from Samuel Goldwyn's *Dead End* (1937) and Warner Bros.' *Crime School* (1938), q.v., the glittery MGM released its *Boys Town*. It was a high-toned morality play about Father Edward Joseph Flanagan (1886–1948), founder of the Omaha, Nebraska sanctuary for underprivileged and homeless youths who would otherwise end in a reformatory. Although Flanagan's oasis for victimized youths was *not* a state-sponsored correctional institution, the film cunningly falls within the genre, using all the conventions expected of this movie category. (A far lesser effort, Columbia's *Juvenile Court*, 1938, attempted to do the same thing in its tattered account of an idealistic young attorney [Paul Kelly] who takes it upon himself to organize a Police Athletic League to reform a bunch of hooligans—Frankie Darro in particular—aided by his understanding girlfriend [Rita Hayworth].)

Boys Town opens with the dedication:

> In tribute to a supreme achievement based upon a noble ideal, this picture is dedicated to the Rev. Father Edward J. Flanagan, the inspired founder of Boys Town, near Omaha, Nebraska ... and to the splendid work he is performing for homeless abandoned boys, regardless of race, creed or color.

To help misdirected youths, Irish-born Roman Catholic priest, Father Edward Joseph Flanagan (Spency Tracy) organizes a home as a harbor for tough neighborhood youths. His charges are hooligans who might otherwise be sentenced to a reformatory. It is Flanagan's creed that "...there isn't any such thing in the world as a bad boy. But a boy left alone, frightened, bewildered ... the wrong hand reaches for him. He needs a friend, that's all he needs."

Flanagan received spiritual support from his bishop (Minor Watson) and financial assistance from his pawnbroker pal, Dave Morris (Henry Hull). Before long, the rundown building which houses Father Flanagan's noble experiment is overflowing with his young wards. One Christmas Eve, when Flanagan is so overwhelmed by financial burdens that he cannot afford to purchase a tree, Morris comes to his assistance yet again.

Later, thanks to contributions from many sponsors, Father Flanagan establishes a haven for his boys on a 200-acre spread outside of Omaha, Nebraska. Meanwhile, just before he is to go to the state prison, Joe Marsh (Edward Norris) contacts the priest and gives him money to take care of his younger brother Whitey (Mickey Rooney), a neighborhood toughie who spends all his time hustling games in a pool hall. Once at Boys Town, the rebellious, smart-mouthed Whitey constantly fights every attempt at reformation and does his best to disrupt the running of the youth retreat where the boys have a self-government. At one juncture, he even runs away from Flanagan's town. However, the once-arrogant teenager finds humility (being defeated in a boxing match, losing his first bid to be the town's mayor, etc.) and redemption. Thereafter, he helps the priest and his peers capture a gang of bank robbers (pals of Whitey's brother who has escaped from prison), as well as coming to the rescue of his injured pal Pee Wee (Bobs Watson), who idolizes Whitey. Soon thereafter, Whitey is elected mayor of Boys Town. Thanks to the guidance and patience of Father Flanagan, Whitey emerges as an impressive example of the rehabilitative approach of Boys Town.

Made on a $1,000,000 budget, MGM promoted its new picture with: "Once in a year, perhaps once in a decade, comes a picture of such heartwarming sincerity and power ... such laughter and tears. ..." Other ad copy boasted, "More laughs than *Love Finds Andy Hardy*. ... More thrills than *Test Pilot*. ... More tears than *Captains Courageous*. ... With the stars that made them great. ... Spencer Tracy and Mickey Rooney!"

The critics responded enthusiastically to the picture. "It manages, in spite of the embarrassing sentimentality of its closing scenes, to be a consistently interesting and frequently touching motion picture. ... Spencer Tracy's performances of almost any one—is perfection itself and the most eloquent tribute to the Nebraska priest" (Frank S. Nugent, *New York Times*). As for Rooney's limelight-stealing performance, Nugent noted, "Mickey is the Dead End gang rolled into one. He's Jimmy Cagney, Humphrey Bogart and King Kong before they grew up or knew a restraining hand." The *New York Herald-Tribune* reported that *Boys Town* was "a film which is provocative as well as entertaining. It makes no bones about the fact that organized society invariably turns young tramps into hardened criminals and shows that even private charity is faced with innumerable obstacles in caring for them." *Variety* endorsed, "Though an intangible preachment for the Catholic priest, it has considerable mass appeal and is gripping entertainment most of time. ... Group of youngsters who figure importantly in Boys Town episodes are uniformly fine. ... John Meehan and Dore Schary have done an expert job in scripting the screen story, best portion being the indelible dialog fitting the varied characters."

Boys Town won Academy Awards for Best Actor (Spencer Tracy) and for Best Original Film Story. Mickey Rooney, primarily on the basis of his *Boys Town* performance, received a special miniature Oscar that year, along with Universal Pictures's Deanna Durbin for their "spirit and personification of youth." *Boys Town* was nominated for Best Picture but lost to *You Can't Take It with You*. It received other Oscar nominations for Best Director and Best Screenplay.

MGM did some location filming at the actual Boys Town in Nebraska and donated $5,000 to the charitable institution. Originally, the plot for *Boys Town* was to have incorporated a role for British contract star Freddie Bartholomew, but that concept was dropped from the final script. Spencer Tracy would later donate his Oscar to Father Flanagan, adding an inscription, "To Father Edward J. Flanagan, whose great human qualities, kindly simplicity, and inspiring courage were strong enough to shine through my humble efforts.

An intriguing sidelight to *Boys Town* is offered by Garson Kanin in his book *Tracy and Hepburn* (1972) in which he quotes Spencer Tracy reflecting late in life:

> I was sitting and watching *Boys Town* and there I am with this whole group and I realize that one of them a few days before — I'd seen in the paper — had been picked up for drunk driving, and one of them is off his rocker in an institution somewhere. Then there's two of them, they were friends back then, and somebody told me they've been picked up for pushing dope, and then there was poor little Mickey, and I've got my arms around all these characters and the camera's rolling in and I say, 'There *are* no bad boys!' I want to tell you I nearly fell out of this chair. Nearly, *hell,* I did.

To cash in on the success of *Boys Town*, MGM produced a sequel in 1941: *Men of Boys Town*, q.v., also starring Spencer Tracy and Mickey Rooney.

35. *Brass Knuckles* (Warner Bros., 1927), 68 min.

Director, Lloyd Bacon; screenplay, Harvey Gates; assistant director, Henry Blanke; camera, Norbert Brodine.

Monte Blue (Zac Harrison); Betty Bronson (June Curry); William Russell ("Brass Knuckles" Lamont); Georgie [George E.] Stone (Velvet Smith); Paul Panzer (Sergeant Peters); Jack Curtis (Murphy).

Better known for directing such musicals as *42nd Street* (1932), *Gold Diggers of 1937* (1936) and *I Wonder Who's Kissing Her Now?* (1947), Lloyd Bacon (1890–1955) also helmed a few prison melodramas, including *San Quentin* (1937), q.v., and *Brass Knuckles*. The latter was a production-line actioner, one of four silent features (and three short subjects) handled by director Bacon in 1927. Judged *Variety*, "This picture is lacking in qualities desirable for de luxe stands...."

In the course of an attempted prison breakout, "Fade-Away" Joe Curry murders the warden and is sentenced to die. Another participant, Brass Knuckles Lamont (William Russell) has his prison term extended. Lamont is particularly angry with another prisoner, Zac Harrison (Monte Blue) who is trying to go straight. Later when Zac and pal Velvet Smith (Georgie [George E.] Stone) are released, they visit Fade-Away Joe's daughter June (Betty Bronson) at an orphanage. She is so entranced with her visitors that she runs away to join them. Velvet strays into a criminal life again, but Zac encourages him to go straight. On June's birthday, the well-meaning Velvet takes June to an underworld café where Zac realizes that she is now almost an adult and that he loves her. Meanwhile, Lamont is paroled and learning of Zac's interest in June, informs the law that the two have an immoral relationship. While Zac is jailed, Lamont takes June into his custody. Later when Zac is released he must tell June the truth about her father, and accepting the facts, the couple is reunited.

Brass Knuckles was produced in a period when prison dramas and gangster melodramas overlapped greatly. It was also a time when the use of a penitentiary setting was not cause for statements of social concern and reform.

36. *Breakout* (NBC–TV, Dec. 8, 1970), color, 100 min.

Producer/director, Richard Irving; teleplay, Sy Gomberg; art director, Henry Larrecq; music, Shorty Rogers; camera, Ray Flin; editor, Milton Shifman.

James Drury (Joe Baker); Red Buttons (Pipes); Kathryn Hays (Ann Baker); Woody Strode (Skip Manion); Sean Garrison (Frank McCready); Victoria Meyerink (Marian); Bert Freed (Fletcher); Mort Mills (Middleton); William Mims (Banks);.

Harold J. Stone (Phil Caprio); Don Wilbanks (Mackey); Kenneth Tobey (Ranger); Ric Roman (Bianchi); Kent McCord (Hunter); Charles Lampkin (Cook); Teddy Quinn (Donnie); Buck Kartalian (Hogan).

The focus of this action entry was not especially on life behind bars in prison, but on the desire to break out of a maximum security fortress. (Ironically the most credible segments of this production were the interludes within prison.) Bank robber Joe Baker (James Drury) executes a crafty plan to escape, motivated by a desire to see his wife (Kathryn Hays)—who works at a nearby mountain inn—and to recoup the $50,000 in loot which was the cause of his imprisonment in the first place. He and fellow convict Skip Manion (Woody Strode) plan to make their break–aided by squeaky-voiced Pipes (Red Button)—while on a work gang detail. The scheme calls for running off through the woods and over adjacent mountains. When Manion is injured one day while working, Baker must substitute another convict for his two-man plan. His choice is Frank McCready (Sean Garrison), a snobbish but athletic fellow prisoner. Just when freedom seems to be his, Baker abandons his escape plan to save a lost youngster on a snowy mountaintop.

Evidently the producing studio, Universal Television, was not very pleased with this project, for it sat on the shelf for nearly two seasons before being televised. *Daily Variety* complained that it was "a standard prison break opus that came up with a new device to thwart the scheme—it talked itself to death."

37. *Breakout* (Columbia, 1975), color, 96 min.

Executive producer, Ron Buck; producers, Robert Chartoff, Irwin Winkler; director, Tom Gries; based on the novel *The Ten Second Jailbreak* by Warren Hinckle, William Turner, Elliott Asinof; screenplay, Howard B. Kreitsek, Marc Norman, Elliot Baker; art director, Alfred Sweeney, Jr.; set decorator, Ira Bates; costumes, Bill Thomas; music, Jerry Goldsmith; stunt coordinator, Dick Dial; sound, Al Overton, Jr.; special effects, Augie Lohman; camera, Lucien Ballard;

editor, Bud Isaacs.

Charles Bronson (Nick Colton); Robert Duvall (Jay Wagner); Jill Ireland (Ann Wagner); John Huston (Harris Wagner); Randy Quaid (Hawk Hawkins); Sheree North (Myrna); Alejandro Rey (Sanchez); Paul Mantee (Cable); Roy Jenson (Spencer); Alan Vint (Helicopter Pilot); Jorge Moreno (Soza); Sidney Clute (Henderson); Emilio Fernandez (The Warden).

Aspects of the mystique of life south-of-the-United States-border is examined in this near-mindless action yarn. It is simplistically geared to capitalize on Charles Bronson's macho superstar image, a status confirmed by his huge box-office hit, *Death Wish* (1974). Crass and obvious, *Breakout* panders to the stereotype concepts most Americans have about Mexican jails being filthy and very pregnable and their keepers being corrupt, unsophisticated and brutal. Its ironic subplots of greed and deception give the scenario whatever bite it possesses. As for the performances, Derek Elley (British *Films and Filming* magazine) commended Bronson for saving the cinematic day. "Bronson gently satirizes both himself and the set-up, while still maintaining the muscular pose for which he is famed." Not to be overlooked is the zesty, fleeting, appearance by Sheree North, the ex-sex bomb star of the 1950s, who had become a talented character star. With her world-weary demeanor and sardonic tone, she added a solid edge with her every onscreen moment.

Selfish tycoon Harris Wagner (John Huston) is fearful that his grandson Jay (Robert Duvall) is growing too powerful. He arranges for him to be jailed in Mexico

Robert Duvall and Charles Bronson in *Breakout* (1975).

on a contrived murder charge. Jay's wife Ann (Jill Ireland) brings him the money needed to bribe the warden (Emilio Fernandez) to get him out of incarceration, not realizing that the prison keeper runs a phony but lucrative escape gambit in which after the prisoners pay their bribes they are killed while escaping. Jay's attempt to break out is stymied, but because of the warden's deal with Harris, the Mexican jailers do not kill the American. Later, Ann meets with Harris in New York and he promises to finance future escape plans, which gives him access to information about Jay's activities. Going to Texas, Ann hires Nick Colton (Charles Bronson), a man with a price, to rescue her husband. Nick uses his business plane to fly to Mexico, but when he lands and attempts to rescue Jay who is working on a road gang, his efforts are aborted by gunfire from the guards. On his second attempt to free Jay—which calls for Nick's partner Hawk Hawkins (Randy Quaid) to infiltrate the prison disguised as a Mexican whore—the plan fails when Hawk is beaten up inside the stronghold.

Now demanding a much higher fee ($50,000), Nick devises a fresh plan which he keeps secret. He recruits a former playmate, Myrna (Sheree North), and a helicopter pilot, Harvey (Alan Vint), to assist him. Meanwhile, Jay is succumbing to the stress of his environment and his belief that Nick and Ann are having an affair (they are not) and is put in the prison hospital. However, he manages to be in the prison yard at the appointed time. When Harvey gets last minute jitters, Nick takes over piloting the helicopter, and while Myrna and Hawk create a diversion, Nick lands the copter, snatches up Jay and they make their escape (later avoiding an ambush by one of Wagner's men [Paul Mantee] at the border airport).

Jay is reunited with Ann, who pays his fee and hints by her action that she might later respond to his obvious attraction to her.

Tom Milne (British *Monthly Film Bulletin*) championed this surface entry, reasoning "Once over an atrocious opening sequence . . . *Breakout* develops quite pleasantly into an old-fashioned entertainment." Milne found that the movie remains, "consistently enjoyable, thanks partly to the fact that plot explanations take second place to excellent action sequences which are never allowed to go on too long . . . ." Far less enthusiastic was *Cue* magazine which jibed, "this is not a movie about adolescent acne. . . . There is enough noise and activity to keep a viewer awake, and enough noise and activity to give an alert viewer a headache. . . . [The] raison d'être of the entire exercise is to provide work for Mr. and Mrs. (Jill Ireland) Bronson, who apparently have the drawing power and muscle to lure escapists into the theatre. Caveat emptor."

The ad campaign for *Breakout* insisted *"The Greatest Escape Film Ever!* . . . . Sentenced to 28 years in prison for a crime he never committed. Only two things can get him out—A lot of money and Charles Bronson!" *Breakout* earned $7,528,000 in domestic film rentals paid to the distributor.

38. *Broadway Big Shot* (Producers Releasing Corp., 1942), 63 min.

Producer, Jed Buell; director, William Beaudine; associate producers, Dick L'Estrange, Charles Wayne; screenplay, Martin Mooney; camera, Jack Greenhalgh; editors, Robert Crandall, Guy Thayer.

Ralph Byrd (Jimmy O'Brien); Virginia Vale (Betty Collins); William Halligan (Warden Collins); Dick Rush (Tom Barnes); Herbert Rawlinson (District Attorney); Cecil Weston (Mrs. Briggs); Tom Herbert (Carnation Charlie); Stubby Kruger (Dynamite); Frank Hagney (Butch); Jack Buckley (Windy); Harry Depp (Ben Marlo); Jack Roper (Nipper); Al Goldsmith (Coffee Cake George); Joe Oakie (Sneaky); Alfred Hall (Dr. Williams); Jimmy Aubrey (Orderly); Dick Cramer (Reilly); Jack Cheatham (Tim); Jack Perrin (Ed).

It was a conceit of the entertainment arts, that newspaper reporters would and will do most anything to get a big scoop; even going to prison to find out the facts in an important case.

Fledgling reporter and former professional football player Jimmy O'Brien (Ralph Byrd) is determined to be a success in the newspaper game. His editor, Tom Barnes (Dick Rush), suggests that Jimmy allow himself to be framed to infiltrate a prison. It is the editor's scheme that once inside, Jimmy should make friends with a particular convict (who took the rap for highers-ups on the outside) and learn the truth about a corruption scheme involving major political figures. Jimmy agrees and, with the help of an obliging district attorney (Herbert Rawlinson), he soon finds himself inside the prison's walls. Once there, he learns the convict he must connect with has died. Barnes and the lawyer convince Jimmy to remain in prison to research the state of the penal system. Meanwhile, Warden Collins (William Halligan) decides that O'Brien is a model prisoner (he has been elected head of the convicts' Welfare League) and allows him to visit his home where he meets the man's daughter Betty (Virginia Vale). Still stuck in prison, Jimmy ferrets out the information for which he first went behind bars. Before Jimmy will give his newspaper the big story, Betty meets with Barnes and extracts a promise that he will now reveal his part in framing his employee. Now a free man, O'Brien agrees to play on the prison football team, helping the convicts win their first victory.

Made on the cheap by poverty row studio Producers Releasing Corp., *Broadway Big Shot* had pretensions of being a comedy. However, as Don Miller pointed out in *B Movies* (1973), the cast had "apparently no conception of what comedy is, or how to play it." *Variety* weighed, "Dramatic sequences fail to hit peaks, and general tenor of script allows yarn to roll along without too much effort."

39. *Brotherly Love* (Metro-Goldwyn-Mayer, 1928) 6,053'. (Also silent version.)

Director, Charles F. Reisner; based on the story "Big-Hearted Jim" by Patterson Margoni; screenplay, Earl Baldwin, Lew Lipton; titles, Robert Hopkins; sets, Cedric Gibbons; wardrobe, Henrietta Frazer; camera, Henry Sharp; editor, George Hively.

Karl Dane (Oscar); George K. Arthur (Jerry); Jean Arthur (Mary Brown); Richard Carlyle (Warden Brown); Edward Connelly (Coggswell); Marcia Harris (Mrs. Coggswell).

In the later 1920s tall, angular Danish actor Karl Dane made several feature films—very broad comedies—with diminutive Britisher George K. Arthur. One of these, *Brotherly Love,* paired the comedy team with Jean Arthur, then still in her apprenticeship period and yet to become the major film personality she did in the 1930s. *Brotherly Love* was issued in both a sound (talking sequences and sound effects) and silent version.

Based on a 1926 *Liberty* magazine story, *Brotherly Love* is a typically unrealistic comedy drama from the Roaring Twenties, when the unreality of film plots were only matched by the highs in the stock market. As presented here, prison was not a fearful place for segregation, repentance and rehabilitation, but a campus where romance and frivolity abounded. Decades later, on a scarcely more realistic level, Hollywood would conjure up a similar fantasy in Burt Reynolds's *The Longest Yard.*

Oscar (Karl Dane), a Newberry Prison guard, quarrels with a local barber, Jerry (George K. Arthur). All this leads to difficulty for Jerry who ends up being brought to the prison as a convict. Once there, both he and Oscar vie for the affections of comely Mary (Jean Arthur), the daughter of Warden Brown (Richard Carlyle). Anxious to show up Jerry, Oscar has the tiny convict assigned to the football squad. But the ploy backfires, as Jerry proves himself to be a gridiron hero. Later Oscar himself commits a misdeed and is sentenced to a competing prison. Meanwhile, Jerry is released but when he learns that Oscar's team will be playing the Newberry eleven, he schemes to return to his alma mater. He plays in the big game, helping the men to emerge victorious. He and Mary wed.

40. *Brothers* (Warner Bros., 1977), color, 104 min.

Executive producer, Lee Savin; in association with Robert H. Greenberg, Herb Forgash; producers, Edward Lewis, Mildred Lewis; in charge of production, Sidney Galanty; director, Arthur Barron; screenplay, Edward Lewis, Mildred Lewis; art director, Vince Creseman; wardrobe, Gerry Pumaia; music, Taj Mahal; assistant director, Michael Blum; sound editor, John Post; camera, John Morrill; editor, William Dornisch.

Bernie Casey (David Thomas); Vonetta McGee (Paula Jones); Ron O'Neal (Walter Nance); Rennie Roker (Lewis); Stu Gilliam (Robinson); John Lehne (Chief Guard McGee); Owen Pace (Joshua Thomas); Joseph Havener (Warden Leon); Martin St. Judge (Williams); Ricardo Brown (Morton);

Susan Barrister (Tina); John Zaremba (Judge #2); Alonzo Bridges (Guard); Al Turner (Henry Taylor); Samantha Harper (Joan Kline); Richard Collen (Davis Brother); Richard Peck (Davis Brother); Mercedes Alberti (Woman Guard); Thomas Bellen (Guard); John Shay (Judge #1); Robert Cortes (Stuart); Janet Dey (FBI Agent); Oliver Fletcher (Lacy); Sidney Galanty (Balaban); Trace Hunt (Mrs. Williams); Connie Morgan (Mrs. Thomas); Len Jewell (Mr. Thomas); Joan Lewis (Student); Bruce Simon (FBI Man); Alphonso Williams (Bill); Dick Yarmy (District Attorney Wayne); David Shaw (Newscaster).

Hollywood had nearly run its course with black exploitation features when *Brothers* was released by Warner Bros. in 1977. Opportunist filmmakers had so saturated the public with genre pieces that were violent, crude, anti-white tracts, that the few such quality entries as *Brothers* were bypassed by jaded and or outraged viewers. Even the critics tended to dismiss the above par *Brothers* as falling short of its mark. "With all of its good ingredients, it's a shame that a quality effort like this—stripped of all the usual exploitation elements that even many blacks have complained of—still falls back on 'Get Whitey' as its only lasting message." A. H. Weiler (*New York Times*) concurred that the film was slanted in its recitation of the historical facts, adding "Anger is the strident keynote." Even Connie Johnson (*Soul* magazine), who felt "*Brothers* is definitely a must-see for people who hunger for thought-provoking, sensitive and uncompromising portrayals of Black experience," agreed that the movie is "heavy-handed and depressing at times."

Brothers was promoted with the advertising campaign, "He was a nobody; a black man in a white man's prison. She was a somebody; a notorious, beautiful, radical black professor. Their love story shocked the nation. This film is that story. And it happened." The "somebody" was black political activist Angela Davis. In 1969 she was hired by the University of California, Los Angeles, to teach philosophy, but was dismissed the next year for her controversial/radical views and for her support of imprisoned black militants. She received tremendous publicity for her courtship/romance with black militant convict George Jackson (the "nobody" of *Brothers*), who was in San Quentin prison, convicted of bank robbery. When he attempted to escape during a hearing at the Marin County Courthouse (during which his younger brother Jonathan and a judge died), she was linked to the breakout effort. She went underground, later to be acquitted of conspiracy and homicide charges. Jackson himself would be killed in prison. In 1980 and 1984 Davis ran for vice-president of the United States on the Communist party platform.

A major thesis of *Brothers* is the inhumane existence suffered by convicts in overcrowded prisons. Another strong thread is demonstrating the discriminatory treatment of black convicts by white guards and fellow inmates. These themes, pushed to the front in *Riot* (1969), q.v., would be a recurring subject in prison films of the 1970s (e.g. *The Jericho Mile*, 1979, *Penitentiary*, 1979, qq.v.) and thereafter (*Brubaker*, 1980, *Fast-Walking*, 1982, qq.v.).

David Thomas (Bernie Casey) is arrested in Los Angeles for being an accessory to armed robbery of a gas station. He is sentenced to a term of one year to life, the length dependent on his prison behavior. Once jailed at Lincoln City Prison, he experiences the humiliation heaped on prisoners in general by guards and fellow inmates, and the additional intensified discrimination by white guards and convicts. His intellectual cellmate Walter Nance (Ron O'Neal) finally convinces the embittered Thomas that to brood over this dehumanization is futile. "You've been

doin' time instead of usin' time," he explains, urging his pupil to study Malcolm X and other such activists to learn a historical perspective about "who's been kickin' your ass." Awakened to a new level of thought, Thomas rises above the soul-damaging regimen of confinement and routine. He joins in publishing an underground prison newspaper for the black brothers. Meanwhile, Nance is beaten to death by a sadistic white guard. Later, Thomas's brother (Owen Pace) dies attempting to free him during David's trial for the murder of a guard (which he did not commit). Thomas later becomes involved in his own breakout bid and is killed in the process. Throughout much of his prison ordeal, Thomas is involved in a stymied romance with attractive activist Paula Jones (Vonetta McGee) who is drawn to Jackson the man and Jackson the victim of white prejudice. Their unrequited romance—full of words and significant looks—is played out in the visitors' room of the prison, always with a barrier between them and always within the surveillance of (suspicious) guards.

Putting aside the questionable reliability of the "facts" as presented by this feature film, both Bernie Casey and Vonetta McGee offer resilient performances, full of subtlety and intelligence. Not to be overlooked here is the screen work of Ron O'Neal (who had played *Super Fly*, 1972, during the peak of blaxploitation pictures) as Casey's long-oppressed cellmate. He gives dimension to the thesis that even in the worst of situations, a determined man can rise above a hell on earth by using his mind to grow.

41. *Brubaker* (20th Century–Fox, 1980), color, 132 min.

Executive producer, Ted Mann; producer, Ron Silverman; associate producer, Gordon Webb; director, Stuart Rosenberg; suggested by the book by Thomas O. Murton, Joe Hyams; story, W. D. Richter, Arthur Ross; screenplay, Richter; art director, J. Michael Riva; set decorator, John Franco, Jr.; costumes, Tom Bronson, Bernie Pollack, Aida Swinson; makeup, Gary Liddiard, Mike Moschella, Zoltan Elek; music, Lalo Schifrin; orchestrator, Jack Hayes; music editor, Robert H. Raff; assistant directors, Jon C. Anderson, Scott Easton; stunt coordinator, Mickey Gilbert; technical adviser, Murton; sound, Charles Wilborn; sound re-recording, Theodore Soderberg, Paul Wells, Douglas Williams; sound effects editors, William Hartman, Richard Sperber, David Ice; dialogue editor, Godfrey Marks; special effects, Al Wright, Jr.; camera, Bruno Nuytten; additional camera, Vincent Saizis; editor, Robert Brown.

Robert Redford (Stan Collins [Henry Brubaker]); Yaphet Kotto (Richard "Dickie" Coombes); Jane Alexander (Lillian Gray); Murray Hamilton (John Deach); David Keith (Larry Lee Bullen); Morgan Freeman (Walter); Matt Clark (Purcell); Tim McIntire (Huey Rauch); Richard Ward (Abraham Cook); Jon Van Ness (Zaranska); M. Emmet Walsh (C. P. Woodward); Albert Salmi (Rory Poke); Linda Haynes (Carol); Everett McGill (Caldwell); Val Avery (Wendel); Ronald C. Frazier (Willets); David D. Harris (Duane Spivey); Joe Spinell (Birdwell); James Keane (Pinky); Konrad Sheehan (Glenn Elwood); Roy Poole (Dr. Gregory); Nathan George (Leon Edwards); Lee Richardson (Warden Renfrew); John McMartin (Senator Hite); Harry Groener (Dr. Campbell); John R. Glover (Ackroyd); Alex A. Brown (Fenway Park); John Chappell (Captain Cleaves); Brent N. Jennings (Mr. Clarence); William M. Newman (Dunfield); Noble Willingham (Dr. Fenster); Wilford Brimley (Rogers); Jane Cecil (Bea Williams); Ebbe Roe Smith (Pavitch); Young Hwa Han (Leonard Ng); Vic Polizos (Billy Baylock); Jack O'Leary (Floor Walker); James Dukas (Oafish Rankman); J.C. Quinn, Jerry Mayer (Barbers); Ivy Featherstone (Peterson); Kent Broadhurst (Whitly); Hazen Gifford (Patridge); Elaine Rower Richardson (Mrs. Renfro); Bill

Opposite: **The exercise yard in** *Brothers* **(1977).**

McNulty (Richards); Linda Milligan (Female Reporter); Rob Garrison (Pretty Boy); James E. Fraunfelter, Jr. (Barracks Trusty); E. J. Pearcy (Transfer Guard); Ritch Brinkley (Gate Guard); J. K. Mahle (Bus Driver); Vivian P. Bass (Waitress); Greg Martin (Trusty); Philip E. Combs (Young Reporter); Richard L. Denny (State Trooper); Michael Holiday (Gate Trusty).

Earnest, shocking, prettified, theatrical, are all adjectives properly affixed to *Brubaker,* a strong film by Stuart Rosenberg who had directed another memorable prison study, *Cool Hand Luke* (1967), q.v. As *Brubaker* documents the horrendous treatment of prisoners at Wakefield Prison Farm (somewhere in the South), the viewer's sensibilities are quickly numbed. This cannot be based on reality, or can it? In actuality, yes! *Brubaker* derives from the revelations of Thomas O. Murton, a young, steadfast prison reformer from Oklahoma who, in 1968, was appointed by Governor Winthrop Rockefeller of Arkansas to rectify conditions at two prisons within that state's penal system. The brutal handling of convicts at the notorious Cummins Prison Farm led the enraged Murton to publicly demand penal reforms. When he uncovered several bodies of tortured convicts buried at the farm, the news made national headlines. It also caused tremendous repercussions for many Arkansas politicians. After a brief year on the job, Murton was fired from his post. He then collaborated on telling the facts in a book with Joe Hyams, published in 1969. In 1971 Murton was the controversial subject of a *Playboy* magazine interview detailing more of his revelations and experiences. Murton served as technical adviser for *Brubaker,* which was filmed in Ohio.

The recently appointed warden of Wakefield Prison Farm, Henry Brubaker (Robert Redford), arrives at the facility using the guise of being a new convict named Stan Collins. He experiences first hand the ferocity and squalor of the overcrowded institution. Here an inmate (especially a black man) can be whipped for doing nothing, be punished by being made to stand at attention for hours on cases of bottles in the hot sun, or be subjected to the "phone call" torture, where a prisoner is electrically shocked with voltage from a phone battery pack. The men toil for long hours in the fields, frequently doing hard labor (without pay) for corrupt local contractors who have paid a bribe for the use of their services. There are maggots in the food, the men sleep in overcrowded, filthy dorms. Sodomizing and brutalizing go unchecked at the farm, and in the unsanitary hospital ward, the uncaring doctor only visits occasionally. To help their battle for survival, the men sell their blood. Worst of all, the men accept the dehumanizing conditions as the status quo and have no thought (or hope) of changing the system.

Aghast at what he has witnessed already in his brief stay at the farm, Brubaker makes himself known to the old warden, with the latter telling him as he cleans out his desk, "You want it, you got it." The idealistic Brubaker wastes no time in assembling the men in the yard:

> I figure most of you guys belong here. I figure basically you don't have any respect for other people or yourselves. You want more from me, you're going to have to earn it. We're going to figure out some way to make this run like a twentieth century farm. You're going to stop selling blood to buy decent food. You're going to go out in the fields and plant vegetables which we're going to eat right here.... No more fifteen hour shifts.

While some of the men want to believe that reforms could come to the farm, they have heard it all before from past new wardens. They are too cynical about life to believe that anything really good will come of Brubaker's do-gooder plans.

As Brubaker digs into the ways and means of the sprawling farm, he uncovers more graft and corruption. He learns about local contractors who use the convict labor for their own gain, with prison officials looking the other way. Brubaker's sponsor for his post had been Lillian Gray (Jane Alexander), special assistant to the governor. (He had run a military stockade in Maryland and more recently was teaching penology at a university when she came in contact with him.) She admires Brubaker's honesty and well-meaning, but believes there is a right and wrong way to get reforms accomplished. She insists that all changes must come from *within* the system, which means dealing with and compromising with the likes of the fatuous, corrupt John Deach (Murray Hamilton), chairman of the Prison Board for the past seventeen years. For Brubaker, cowing to the likes of Deach is odious. ("It's one standard for everybody, the way I see it.... I don't see playing politics with the truth.")

One of the major problems at the farm is the discrimination against blacks both by the white and black guards and by the white prisoners. Brubaker has twelve blacks removed from their lengthy solitary lockup and returned to general population, hoping to build trust among this segment of the men. One of those Brubaker can least understand is Richard "Dickie" Coombes (Yaphet Kotto), a black trusty serving a sentence for murder.

BRUBAKER: When you're out in the field and you're sitting on your horse and holdng your gun and holding all the cards, what keeps you from taking off.

COOMBES: I wouldn't turn around and be puttin' a bullet in anyone's head. I mean, one day we could just lay down all our shovels and guns and stop playing the Man's game. Just pick up and run off.

But, as Brubaker realizes, the suspicious Coombes, like the rest of the men, has seemingly given into the system, no matter how cruel and unfair it is.

During a severe rainstorm one of the barracks' roofs cave in and several men are injured. Brubaker discovers that a local contractor (M. Emmet Walsh) has used faulty materials in building the roof and now wants an exorbitant fee to repair it. He offers Brubaker a bribe, which the latter refuses. Brubaker decides he and the men will repair the roof themselves. Later, he finds that a tremendous amount of food provisions purchased for the men has disappeared. He traces it to several corrupt guards who have been selling off the foodstuff for profit. Brubaker puts a stop to this. He also burns the guards'/trusties' hidden-away shacks used to entertain prostitutes. Meanwhile, Brubaker makes realignments among the trusties and staff, trying to bring a semblance of fairness to the farm. He also organizes a prisoners' council.

One day Brubaker encounters elderly Abraham Cook (Richard Ward), a black prisoner who has lost count of his years at the institution. Brubaker finds out that the man, having served his thirty-year sentence, should have been released three years ago. While interviewing the man, who cannot adjust to the concept of freedom on the outside, Brubaker learns that Abraham has been the farm's coffin maker and that he had helped to bury several convicts tortured and killed at the facility. To prevent Brubaker from learning more, the trusties apply the phone box torture to Abraham and he dies. His corpse is hung upside down on the yard flagpole as a warning to Brubaker. Refusing to be intimidated, Brubaker leads the men and trusties to the fields where they begin digging, eventually uncovering several corpses buried in shallow graves.

Robert Redford in *Brubaker* (1980).

When Brubaker brings an assortment of grievances to the pompous, hypocritical Prison Board, which besides Deach includes the doubting Rogers (Wilford Brimley), he realizes finally what he is up against with this unsavory political group and that his own inability to compromise is an equal flaw:

> You know who the real obstacles to prison reform are . . . it's prison reformers. Pseudo-reformers. People who just want to say the right thing, be at the right place at the right time, get themselves in the paper and get nothing done.

Desperately attempting to arouse some feeling in these uncaring, self-serving folk, Brubaker explains:

> For the first time it's occurring to those prisoners that they don't have to take everything that's shoved at them, because they're still human beings. So maybe someday when they get out they won't rape John Deach's daughter or murder his son.

Because Brubaker has refused to diplomatically play the game, the Prison Board has no further use for him. He has proved to be an embarrassment with his too well-publicized discoveries of horrors at Wakefield. (Besides, his reforms are too costly within the budget.) Brubaker resigns, and a new warden takes over. As he prepares to leave the farm, he hears the incoming administrator, a stern disciplinarian, informing the men, "We've all got to get back to the basics at hand." Just before he departs Wakefield, Coombes, long one of Brubaker's sharpest opponents, confronts Brubaker and admits, "You were right" (even though Brubaker's reform efforts have cost the lives of several prisoners who tried to help him). As Brubaker's car pulls out of the grounds, the convicts begin a round of applause for their departing savior.

A postscript to the film acknowledges: "Two years after Henry Brubaker was fired, twenty-four inmates led by Richard "Dickie" Coombes, brought suit against Wakefield Prison. The Court ruled that the treatment of prisoners at Wakefield was unconstitutional and ordered the prison be reformed or closed. The governor was not re-elected."

One of the more unique aspects of *Brubaker* is that it is a prison drama focusing on a good, well-meaning warden, which makes this motion picture a definite novelty in the genre. Charles Champlin (*Los Angeles Times*) observed, "*Brubaker* is cool-handed in its own way, taking no easy stances, working no easy sentimentality although it spares no voltage in its illumination of the horrors. . . . It's an angry and admirable film, impressively uncompromised and hard-edged in a time when you'd have said such a story was impossible to get financed." Vincent Canby (*New York Times*) agreed that the film "looks and sounds authentic, especially when it is seeing prison life through the eyes of the mysteriously self-composed new prisoner." However, added Canby, "As soon as Brubaker identifies himself and takes command of Wakefield to begin his reform program, the film loses all tension and becomes, instead a predictable inventory of the problems faced by all reformers who, like Brubaker, refused to compromise."

For some reviewers, one of the problems with *Brubaker* was socially-conscious Robert Redford, the handsome movie star and box-office magnet who could get such unbankable projects as *Brubaker* made. This led David Ansen (*Newsweek* magazine) to query, "Just what kind of star vehicle is this?" He added, "In the end, the issue of penal reform [in *Brubaker*] gives way to abject hero worship of Redford the reformer. The sentimentality is all the more troubling because the lines between Redford the crusading liberal actor and Brubaker the crusading prison reformer, between political fervor and movie-star narcissism, become hopelessly blurred." For Andrew Sarris (*Village Voice*), "The biggest problem with *Brubaker* is the inherently misleading spectacle provided by the genre itself. Even journalistic articles on 'prison conditions' are dishonest in much the same way. All we see or read about is the plight of 'prisoners' conveniently detached from their crimes and their victims." The old-fashioned prison movies sometimes sentimentalized convict-stars as victims of miscarriage of justice or mob frame-ups. A more anarchic entertainment like *Escape from Alcatraz* revels in the fact that its escaping convicts are hardened felons. *Brubaker* tries to cut it both ways by reminding us that the cheated and oppressed convicts are indeed guilty of crimes, but that the corrupt prison system is even more reprehensible."

Brubaker received an Oscar nomination for Best Screenplay, but lost to *Melvin and Howard*. The film earned $19,300,000 in domestic film rentals paid to the distributor, making it one of the most profitable prison films produced to date. (*Escape from Alcatraz*, 1980, q.v., is another.) Director Stuart Rosenberg was a replacement for Bob Rafelson, who left the production during the early filming due to "creative differences."

42. *Brute Force* (Universal, 1947), 98 min.

Producer, Mark Hellinger; associate producer, Jules Buck; director, Jules Dassin; story, Robert Patterson; screenplay, Richard Brooks; art directors, Bernard Herzbrun, John F. De Cuir; set decorators, Russell A. Gausman, Charles Wyrick; music, Miklos Rosza; assistant director, Fred Frank; technical adviser, Jacques Gordon; sound, Charles Felstead, Robert Pritchard; special camera, David S. Horsley; camera, William Daniels; editor, Edward Curtiss.

Burt Lancaster (Joe Collins); Hume Cronyn (Captain Munsey); Charles Bickford (Gallagher); Yvonne De Carlo (Gina); Ann Blyth (Ruth); Ella Raines (Cora Lister); Anita Colby (Flossie); Sam Levene (Louie); Howard Duff (Soldier [Becker]); Art Smith (Dr. Walters); Roman Bohnen (Warden Barnes); John Hoyt (Spencer); Richard Gaines (McCollum); Frank Puglia (Ferrara); Jeff Corey (Fresh-man); Vince Barnett (Muggsy); James Bell (Crenshaw); Jack Overman (Kid Coy); Whit Bissell (Tom Lister); Sir Lancelot (Calypso [James]); Ray Teal (Jackson); Jay C. Flippen (Hodges); James O'Rear (Wilson); Howland Chamberlain (Gaines); Kenneth Paterson (Bronski); Crane Whitley (Armed Guard in Drain Pipe); Charles McGraw (Andy); John Guy Beach (Convict Foreman); Edmund Cobb (Bradley); Tom Steele (Machine Gunner); Alex Frazer (Chaplain); Will Lee (Kincaid); Rusty Sanderson (Miss Lawrence); Francis McDonald (Regan); Jack S. Lee (Sergeant); Virginia Farmer (Sadie); Billy Wayne (Prisoner); Paul Bryar (Harry); Glenn Strange (Tompkins); Al Hill (Plonski); Peter Virgo, Eddy Chandler, Kenneth MacDonald (Guards); Herbert Heywood (Chef); Rex Lease (Hearse Driver); William Cozzo, Frank Marlo, Rex Dale (Prisoners); Kippee Valez (Visitor).

> As a prison melodrama, *Brute Force* is one of the most powerful, virile pictures of its kind, but as entertainment it is certainly not a picture for the squeamish, for the action is as violent and vicious as anything yet depicted on the screen. Some of the situations are so brutal that chicken-hearted patrons will turn their faces from the screen.
>
> *(Harrison's Reports)*

So intense was *Brute Force*'s depiction of caged humanity governed by corrupt and sadistic keepers, that it set a new standard for prison fare, a benchmark still in force today. Made at a time when Hollywood thought there still needed to be male-female romantic interludes—even in a grim study like this—*Brute Force* utilized flashback sequences to work in subplots involving four of the convicts and the women who caused them to end in prison. *Brute Force*'s graphic representation of a prison hellhole was so ardent that most viewers ignored the genre clichés it embraced or those it created anew.

At West Gate Penitentiary, a sixty-two year old inmate, forced to work on the drainpipe detail, has just died of heart failure. Another convict, Calypso (Sir Lancelot), sings a ditty as the corpse is taken from the facility. "No more aches and no more pains. The good lord he treat Franklin very fine. He let him off before he finished his time." This is a sentiment the convicts can appreciate, especially the tough, sullen Joe Collins (Burt Lancaster), who adds "we're buried, ain't we? The only thing, we ain't dead." Veteran convict Gallagher (Charles Bickford), who runs the prison newspaper, has his own observations about life behind bars, "Those gates only open three times. When you come in, when you've served your time or you're dead."

It is quickly apparent that the weak-willed Warden Barnes (Roman Bohnen) is not really in charge at this penitentiary, nor is his colleague, the alcoholic Dr. Walters (Art Smith), who is stir crazy and needs alcohol to blur his conscience. Rather it is the sadistic and crafty Captain Munsey (Hume Cronyn), a bully who covets Barnes's position, who is the mastermind running the establishment. He thrives on power and his ability to control so many individuals' destinies. He brags to the cowering warden, "You put on a guard's uniform and see how much they love you. You talk to the prisoners over a loudspeaker. You only make the rules, I have to enforce them."

Munsey's authoritarian, harsh methods are closely in line with the desires of the prison board which insists "What this prison needs is discipline, not charity." According to Munsey's theories of mob control:

> Kindness is actually weakness. Weakness is an infection that actually makes a man a follower.... Nature proves that the weak must die so the strong may live. Authority, cleverness, imagination. Those are the real differences between men. I walk among these convicts, these murderers, thieves, alone. But they respect me. They obey me!

In response to this diatribe, the drunken doctor taunts Munsey, "Where else would you find so many helpless flies to stick pins in?" The physician makes a prophetic final retort to the self-inflated guard captain, "Congratulations. Force does make leaders. But you forget one thing. It destroys them."

The many men in the institution include the occcupants of cell R-17. There is Soldier (Howard Duff) who, as a G.I. in Italy during World War II, took the blame when his wife Gina (Yvonne De Carlo) shot her black-marketeering father (Frank Puglia). Bookkeeper Tom Lister (Whit Bissell) embezzled funds so he could buy a fur coat for his grasping wife Cora (Ella Raines). Collins pursued further criminal ways to pay for an operation for his crippled girlfriend (Ann Blyth). Slick con artist Spencer (John Hoyt) recalls how he was outsmarted in Florida by a sharp confidence girl named Flossie (Anita Colby).

Feeling they have nothing to lose, several of the men, including Collins, Soldier and Spencer, decide to make a break. They plan to use their assignments

Sam Levene and Charles Bickford in *Brute Force* (1947).

in the drainpipe-digging project to tunnel to the other side of the guard tower, so they can then force the guards to open the gate and let all of the escaping convicts flee. At first, Gallagher refuses to join them, believing the warden's promise that he will be paroled soon. Later, when this hope is dashed, he joins in the plan, with his news reporter Louie (Sam Levene) assigned to pass messages among the various factions helping with the breakout scheme. Another convict participant is Andy (Charles McGraw), who works in the auto shop and who has amassed an arsenal of guns and fire bombs. Meanwhile, as a result of Munsey's psychological warfare against Lister, the latter has killed himself.

Munsey is warned of the pending breakout plot and tortures Louie into revealing some of the details. Restlessness in the yard increases when the spineless Warden Barnes is forced by the Prison Board to resign and to announce that the arrogant Munsey is his replacement. The escape plan is soon put into operation. Freshman (Jeff Corey), who has proven to be a stoolie, is tied to the front of the drainpipe dirt cart and when the cart comes into the guards' sight, he is shot dead by them. (Earlier, another squealing convict had been forced at the point of blow torches to back into a machine shop press where he was killed.) Casualties mount on both sides as the carnage continues. Kid Coy (Jack Overman) dives at a guard and is shot dead. Gallagher rams the front gate with a delivery truck he has commandeered and dies in the process. Munsey mans the machine gun in the guard turret, but the wounded Collins, before dying himself, reaches the position and throws the man off the tower into the crowd below. Finally the men are subdued with tear gas.

The riot is over. As the camera pans the cell block, several cubicles are empty; their occupants now dead. Calypso is heard singing "Whenever you get men in prison, they want to get out." Dr. Walters has the final words, "Nobody escapes. Nobody really escapes."

Variety decided, "*Brute Force* packs plenty of boxoffice wallop.... *Brute Force* is by no means a man's picture solely. The prisoners, for all their unsavory backgrounds, are personable types with plenty of muscles which will get the femmes.... The aspect of an audience rooting for the prisoners plotting a jailbreak is given a sharp turn-about, at the proper time, to point up that brute force by prisoners is as wrong as the brute force exercised by their keepers." Bosley Crowther (*New York Times*) reviewed "*Brute Force* is faithful to its title — even to taking law and order into its own hands. The moral is: don't go to prison; you meet such vile authorities there." On the other hand, he thought the production was overslanted in the prisoners' favor and noted, "any wonder that the inferential parallel seems to be to a concentration camp, with the prisoners the pitiable victims and the authorities the villains with the clubs?" A minority voice of disdain was issued by James Agee (*The Nation* magazine), "I was astounded to hear that some knowledgeable people think of *Brute Force,* a movie about men in a big jail, as a happy return to the melodramas of the early thirties. Maybe so, in some of the jab-paced, slickly sadistic action sequences. But there isn't a line in it, or a performance, or an idea, or an emotion, that belongs much later than 1915, and cheesy 1915 at that. And terrible as the movie is, that is its considerable charm."

Because the violence and brutality, and to a lesser degree the romantic flashback interludes, captured so much of viewers' attention, little was mentioned about the film's lip service to the need of prison reform, a carryover from such 1930s films where it was felt that orating a social message created a balance and an excuse to exploit gratuitous horrors. It is deliberately ironic that in *Brute Force* the spokesman for changing the prison system is the besotted physician. It is Dr. Walters who says to the Prison Board,

> You put up prisons, thick walls and think your job is over, finished. But is it over? You and your patent medicine remedies. Change the warden, new personnel, absolute discipline. Do you know what the prison is? One big human bomb. And you say kick it and it will be quiet. Smash it and it won't explode... By your methods we send a man back to society a worse criminal than when he was sent to us.... For men like you, there will never be any solution. What we need here is a little more patience and understanding.

In May 1989 it was announced that filmmaker William Luftig had purchased the remake rights to *Brute Force* from the Mark Hellinger estate and that he wanted Burt Lancaster to play the tyrannical Captain Munsey role in the new edition.

43. *Buckstone County Prison* (Film Ventures International, 1977), color, 90 min.

Producer, Earl Owensby; director, Jimmy Huston; screenplay, Tom McIntyre; music, David Allan Coe, Arthur Smith; stunt coordinator, Ed Parker; camera, Darrell

Cathart; editor, Huston.

Earl Owensby (Seabo); David Allan Coe (Rebstock); Don "Red" Barry (Warden Coley); Sunset Carson (Sheriff Deese); Ed Parker (Jimbo); Leonard Dixon (Zack); Holly Conover (Effie); Rod Sacharnoski (Sam); Ron Lampkin (Jess); Craig T. Nelson (Escapee).

When an escaped convict attempts to rape the young daughter of a black man, the father shoots him in the back. However, it is bounty hunter Seabo (Earl Owensby), on the trail of the convict, who takes the blame. Disliked by the local judicial system, Seabo is sent to Buckstone County Prison where he is chained and tortured on orders of the vicious warden (Don "Red" Barry), who blames him for the death of his son. When a bank robbery occurs, Sheriff Deese (Sunset Carson) has Seabo paroled into his custoy so he can track down the thieves, along with Seabo's enemy Rebstock (David Allan Coe), who aided the robbers. When the lawbreakers and Rebstock are killed, Seabo disappears. Meanwhile, the warden has gone insane.

Shot on location in the Great Smoky and Blue Ridge Mountain areas, *Buckstone County Prison* was originally called *Seabo*. Shooting was completed May 21, 1977 in North Carolina. The story takes place in 1957 and shows the harsh environment of fenced rural prisons and their chain gangs. With a cast of 105 speaking parts, *Buckstone County Prison* was advertised as "The Hell Hole of North Carolina!" and grossed $4.4 million in its first four months of release. It was primarily shown in the South and did not receive national viewing until it appeared on cable TV in the mid–1980s.

Producer/star Earl Owensby, whose North Carolina-based EO Corporation had made such cheap fare as *Challenge* (1974), *Wolfman* (1979), *Living Legend* (1980) and *Rottweiler* (1982), is a bland hero in *Buckstone County Prison*. His passive performance is more than offset by the fine work from former "B" Western heroes, Don "Red" Barry and Sunset Carson. The latter is particualrly impressive in his relaxed work as the essentially honest Southern lawman. Overall, this film is a backwoods excuse for plenty of violence. Co-star David Allan Coe also co-wrote the movie's music.

44. *Buried Alive* (Producers Distributing Corp., 1939), 74 min.

Director, Victor Halperin; story, William A. Ullman, Jr.; screenplay, George Bricker; music director, Dave Chudnow; camera, Jack Greenhalgh; editor, Holbrook N. Todd.

Beverly Roberts (Joan Wright); Robert Wilcox (Johnny Martin); George Pembroke (Ernie Mathews); Ted Osborne (Ira Hanes); Paul McVey (Jim Henderson); Alden Chase (Dr. Robert Lee); Don Rowan (Big Billy); Peter Lynn (Gus Barth); Norman Budd (The Kid); and: Joe Coits, Edward Earle, Robert Fiske, Bob McKenzie, James H. McNamara.

Don Miller said it all when he wrote in *B Movies* (1973) of this cheaply-assembled double-bill item, "a prison yarn with all the frayed trimmings; hero (Robert Wilcox) condemned for a crime he didn't commit, prison nurse (Beverly Roberts) who stands by him, trickery to obtain a last-minute confession from the guilty, and other foreseeable plot machinations." *Variety* viewed that "Most obstinate factor in this film's chances is the trite yarn, chief reason for the cast's failure to do better."

Beverly Roberts and Robert Wilcox in *Buried Alive* (1939).

45. *Buy and Cell* (Empire Films, 1989), color, 91 min.

Executive producer, Charles Band; producer, Frank Yablans; associate producers, Louis Pernano, Debra Dion; director, Robert Boris; screenplay, Ken Krauss, Merrin Holt; production designer, Giovanni Natalucci; set decorator, Joe Chevalier; costumes, Robin Lewis; makeup, Giancarlo Del Brocco; music, Mark Shreeve; music supervisor, Jonathan Scott Botgner; music coordinator, Cari Lutz; assistant directors, Gianni Cozzo, Luca Lachin; stunt coordinator, Remo De Angelis; sound, Giuseppe Muratori; ADR editor, Jessica Gallavan; special effects, Giovanni Cappelli; camera, Daniele Nanuzzi; editor, Bert Glastein.

Robert Carradine (Herbie Altman); Michael Winslow (Sly); Malcolm McDowell (Warden Tennant); Lise Cutter (Dr. Ellen Scott); Randall "Tex" Cobb (Wolf); Ben Vereen (Shaka); Tony Plana (Raoul); Roddy Piper (Cowboy); Michael Goodwin (Reggie Forsythe); Imogene Coca (Bit); Fred Travalena (VCR); Mickey Knox (Arthur); West Buchanen (Money); Tony Carroll (Duke); Larry Clark (Ned); Carolyn L. DePonsega, Robert B. Spafford (Board Members); Paul De Domenico (Emilio); Gerella Giancarlo (Mona); Julian Jenkins (Malcolm); Harold Bradley (Detective); Josephine Kalin (Secretary).

"*Buy and Cell* . . . is such a labored prison comedy that watching it is like serving a life sentence on the chain gang without chance of parole" (Kevin Thomas, *Los Angeles Times*). Equally unimpressed was Scott Haller (*People* magazine), "*Buy and Cell* is a one-joke premise predicated on the notion that there's something intrinsically funny about watching hardened prisoners talk about profit shares. . . . *Buy and Cell* tries to lampoon big business but it is, in fact, the movie equivalent of junk bonds."

Robert Carradine (*Revenge of the Nerds,* 1984) stars as Herbie Altman, a yippie clod investment broker on Wall Street, who is framed by his slick boss, Reggie Forsythe (Michael Goodwin), for inside trading/embezzlement. He is sentenced

to a $200,000,000 fine and thirteen years in prison. When he arrives at the
Lewiston Correctional Facility, he is introduced to quirky Warden Tennant
(Malcolm McDowell), a devoted reader of the *Wall Street Journal.* This man, who
has a sign on his wall which reads "It's Fun to Be on the Winning Side," is agog
that his new charge is such a major white collar criminal.

> TENNANT: I'm very impressed.
>
> ALTMAN: I'm very innocent.
>
> TENNANT: *(Mockingly)* "That's the first time anyone ever said that to me.

Tennant then admits (tongue-in-cheek) to Altman:

> I've been sentenced too. I'm doing hard time just like the rest of you. I've been
> judged guilty of being an excellent leader of men and I have been sentenced to a
> cruel life with murderers, rapists, bank robbers. These are the kind of people I have
> to break bread with. Now I meet an inside trader, an embezzler. A man who's reached
> the pinnacle of white collar crime. . . . Maybe we can get together some time and talk
> about the market. I have a unique interest in the world of high finance.

Herbie is soon introduced to his cellmate, Sly (Michael Winslow), a groovy
convict who runs gambling pools, sells contraband items ranging from shoes to
cigarettes. It is Sly who observes of their unique keeper:

> The warden is a killer. He sold all the machines in the machine shop. He sold all
> the wood in the wood shop. All the tools in the tool shop. He figures we're coming
> back in, so why waste money teaching us a trade.

Herbie quickly decides to unite with his fellow prisoners — including Sly,
Shaka (Ben Vereen) and the psychotic VCR (Fred Travalena) — to begin a new corporation, CON, Inc., which plays the stock market. Starting with $300, Altman
parlays the assets into a mega success, with the inmates having an elaborate com-
puter network and phone system to monitor their escalating financial holdings.
With some of their profits, they fix up the prison yard to look like a Club Med setting, install a disco lounge, and accomplish other reforms to make living at
Lewiston approximate the good life. Eventually, Herbie's old boss, Reggie Forsythe, unaware of who owns CON, Inc., arrives at the facility to purchase this hot
investment firm for $12,000,000. However, before Altman and his pals are
through with Forsythe, Reggie and the corrupt Warden (who has been skimming
money from the inmates' food budget) are behind bars.

   In its vain effort to satirize prison films, *Buy and Cell* makes references to the
tyrannical Guard Muncey (of *Brute Force,* 1947, q.v.) and to the "lack of ability
to communicate" theme of *Cool Hand Luke* (1967), q.v.. Within this limp comedy, one crazed convict performs an imitation of James Cagney's berserk prison
eating hall scene from *White Heat* (1949), q.v. There is also a philosophical interchange between Warden Tennant and his new prison psychologist, Dr. Ellen Scott
(Lise Cutter), which is *supposed* to be a satirical play on do-gooder prison reformers:

TENNANT: You're here to watch how absolute power controls crime. Brute force keeps these men in line not Freud.

SCOTT: Do you know what the recidivism rate is. Seven out of ten convicts come back to this prison. Doesn't that bother you?

TENNANT: Of course, it does. It means three of those scumbags are still out on the streets. Doesn't that bother you?

The best ingredient of this unfunny comedy is Michael Winslow (the sound effects-generating cop of the *Police Academy* series) as Robert Carradine's enterprising cellmate. *Variety* pinpointed the movie's major problem as "a flaccid and rarely amusing screenplay."

Buy and Cell was shot in Italy by the now-defunct Empire Films.

46. *Cage Without a Key* (CBS–TV, Oct. 8, 1981), color, 100 min.

Executive producer, Douglas S. Cramer; producer, Buzz Kulik; associate producer, Robert Mintz; director, Kulik; art director, Ross Bellah; set decorator, Audrey Blasdel-Goddard; makeup, Ben Lane, Carl Silvers; music, Michel Legrand; assistant director, Thomas McCrory; camera, Charles F. Wheeler; editor, Roland Gross.

Susan Dey (Valerie Smith); Jonelle Allen (Tommy Washington); Sam Bottoms (Buddy Goleta); Michael Brandon (Ben Holian); Anne Bloom (Joleen); Karen Carlson (Betty Holian); Edith Diaz (Angel Perez); Susie Elene (Suzy Kurosawa); Dawn Frame (Sarah); Katherine Helmond (Mrs. R. C. Little); Vicky Huxtable (Jamie); Karen Morrow (Mrs. Turner); Lani O'Grady (Noreen); Margaret Willock (Wanda Polsky); Marc Alaimo (Workman); Lewis Charles (Liquor Customer); Jerry Crews (Supervisor); Edward Cross (Social Worker); Ann D'Andrea (Mrs. Smith); Joella Deffenbaugh (Girl in Corridor); Al Dunlap (Liquor Counterman); Annette Ensley (Rosie); Carol Carrington (Juvenile Hall Matron); Dan Evanilla (Coach); Harvey J. Goldenberg (Mr. Feiner); Basil Hoffman (Judge); Elizabeth Lane (Miss McGinnes); Carmen Martinez (Miss Marquez); Miko Mayama (Mrs. Little's Secretary); Allan Miller (Phil Kenneally); Tom Newman (Mr. Watkins); Gary Pagett (Station Duty Officer); Andrew Rubin (Russo); R. B. Sorko-Ram (Auto Club Driver); Richard Williams (Booking Officer).

Scarcely six months after NBC–TV's highly-rated *Born Innocent*, q.v., rival network CBS–TV aired *Cage Without a Key*. It was quite derivative of the former and was far more preachy and slower-moving than its predecessor. (*TV Guide* magazine would call the production "overdrawn".) However, it won a healthy viewership, many of whom eagerly tuned in to see Susan Dey, the teleseries star of "The Patridge Family" (1970–74), in such a turnabout acting assignment. Sue Cameron (*Hollywood Reporter*) was very impressed by this exploitive teleplay, calling it "a fabulous movie about how terrible the juvenile justice system is, as well as the appalling conditions in young women's prisons. It will inevitably be compared to last September's *Born Innocent,* but it is really a definitive movie."

Through a flashback, the story is told of how seventeen-year old Valerie Smith (Susan Dey) came to be at the San Marcos School for Girls, an institution within the Department of Youth Authority. Valerie had just graduated from high school and was planning to vacation with cousins in northern California for two weeks before beginning a summer job. When her friend's car breaks down, she accepts a ride with the latter's acquaintance, Buddy Goleta (Sam Bottoms), in his truck. Along the way he harasses her sexually, and when she does not respond, he forces her to join him in a liquor store holdup. A killing occurs during the attempted robbery and both Buddy and Valerie are arrested. The crafty Buddy makes a deal with law enforcers, and to get even with Valerie for not having sex with him, he insists that she was a willing part of the holdup. The bewildered girl is assigned Ben Holian (Michael Brandon) as her public defendant, but try as he does he cannot persuade the judge of her innocence. The judge, who notes that Valerie had previously been detained by the law for being caught smoking pot, sentences her to an indefinite term at the San Marcos School for Girls.

The dazed Valerie arrives at the reformatory at the same time as fourteen-year old Sarah (Dawn Frame), a mixed-up druggie whose mother had turned her in to the authorities and whom a judge has labeled incorrigible. Valerie feels no empathy for the stern facility administrator Mrs. Turner (Karen Morrow), the latter a rigid disciplinarian. The gentle Valerie must cope with a whole new way of life, associating with toughened peers with whom she has little in common beyond their mutual captivity. A black girl, Tommy Washington (Jonelle Allen), and an Oriental girl, Suzy Kurosawa (Susie Elene), both are powerful ring leaders among the teenagers, and each exert power plays over Valerie, wanting to woo her into their entourage. The manipulative Suzy, who takes a dislike to the uncooperative Valerie, steals cigarettes and an ashtray and plants them in Valerie's room to get her in trouble with the authorities. When Noreen (Lani O'Grady) attempts to sexually attack Valerie, Tommy comes to the newcomer's defense.

The vulnerable yet angry-at-the-system Valerie finds it "easier" to communicate with the staff's Mrs. Little (Katherine Helmond), although they do not at all share the same philosophy about the institution.

> VALERIE: I'm not talking about how it looks. I'm talking about what is going on.... Well, I guess what's not going on. There are girls in here for assault and murder and instead of rehabilitating them, dealing with their problems, you're teaching them how to sew and style hair.
>
> MRS. LITTLE: I don't have to defend our programs. We know what we're doing here.
>
> VALERIE: You don't know what's happening here!
>
> MRS. LITTLE: Like what?
>
> VALERIE: Like homosexuality. Like Drugs.
>
> MRS. LITTLE: This is San Marcos, not San Quentin.
>
> VALERIE: You really believe there's a lot of difference. You really think if you put a cute name in front of something, you're going to change the essence of it.... You lock a girl up in her cell for two weeks and you call it 'meditation.' We are completely surrounded by brick walls and guards, but it's called 'a school for girls.' We're not prisoners, we're 'wards.'. . . It's an Alice-in-Wonderland existence, Mrs. Little. Can't you see it?

Valerie's outspokenness earns her the enmity of several peers at San Marcos and one day, while on kitchen duty, another inmate throws a vat of boiling fat at her. Instead, the vat sprays over Sarah, injuring her badly. Another day on the volleyball court, Wanda (Margaret Willock) is deliberately hit on the head with a ball by Suzy. Wanda later dies. Time passes and Valerie becomes hardened to her hellish existence in which she and the other girls are locked in their rooms nightly, sent to solitary confinement for any infractions of the arbitrarily-enforced rules, and must survive the in-fighting among the frustrated, toughened inmates. The sensitive Valerie quickly becomes inured to her negative environment, now nearly accepting it as her new way of life.

Meanwhile, Valerie's one-time attorney, Ben Holian, persuades his wife (Karen Carlson) to pretend to be a reporter doing a story and to entrap Buddy Goleta into confessing that Valerie was innocent of any complicity in the liquor store robbery/killing. With this admission tape recorded, Ben demands that the juvenile authorities release Valerie from San Marcos. Before this can happen, during a ruckus in the reformatory yard, Suzy stabs Tommy with the latter's knife. Tommy dies cradled in Valerie's arms. Valerie has become a hardened witness to the cruelties of life; the traumas of which will never be wiped away.

A voice-over postscript to *Cage Without a Key* states:

> Fourteen billion dollars on alcohol, nine billion dollars on tobacco. Two billion dollars on pets, but on children locked in reform schools, two hundred million dollars. That's ninety percent less than we spend on our dogs and cats.

47. *Caged* (Warner Bros., 1950), 96 min.

Producer, Jerry Wald; director, John Cromwell; screenplay, Virginia Kellogg, Bernard C. Schoenfeld; art director, Charles H. Clarke; set decorator, G. W. Bernsten; costumes, Leah Rhodes; makeup, Perc Westmore, Ed Voight; music, Max Steiner; orchestrator, Murray Cutter; assistant director, Frank Mattison; technical adviser, Doris Whitney; sound, Stanley Jones; camera, Carl Guthrie; editor, Owen Marks.

Eleanor Parker (Marie Allen); Agnes Moorehead (Ruth Benton); Ellen Corby (Emma Varges); Hope Emerson (Evelyn Harper); Betty Garde (Kitty Stark); Jan Sterling (Smoochie [Gita Krosky]); Lee Patrick (Elvira Powell); Olive Deering (June Roberts); Jane Darwell (Isolation Matron); Gertrude Michael (Georgia Harrison); Sheila Stevens (Helen); Joan Miller (Claire Devlon); Marjorie Crossland (Cassie Jenkins); Gertrude Hoffman (Millie); Lynn Sherman (Ann); Queenie Smith (Mrs. Warren); Naomi Robison (Hattie Cassidy); Esther Howard (Grace); Marlo Dwyer (Julie Klein); Wanda Tynan (Meta Minnelli); Peggy Wynne (Lottie Brannigan); Frances Morris (Mrs. Foley); Edith Evanson (Miss Barker); Yvonne Rob (Elaine Mullen); Ann Tyrell (Edna); Eileen Stevens (Infirmary Nurse); June Whipple (Ada); Sandra Gould (Skip); Grace Hayes (Mugging Matron); Taylor Holmes (Senator Donnolly); Don Beddoe (Commissioner Walker); Charles Meredith (Chairman); George Baxter (Jeffries); Guy Beach (Mr. Cooper); Harlan Warde (Dr. Ashton); Bill Hunter (Guard); Barbara Esback, Marjorie Wood, Evelyn Dockson, Hazel Keener, Jane Crowley (Matrons); Gail Bonney, Doris Kemper, Lovyss Bradley; Ezelle Poule, Margaret Lambert, Eva Nelson, Rosemary O'Neil, Jean Calhoun, Nita Talbot, Marie Melish, Pauline Creasman, Joyce Newhard, Helen Eby-Rock, Sheila Stuart, Claudia Cauldwell, Tina Menard, Carole Shanon, Gladys Roach, Virginia Engels (Inmates); Bill Haade (Laundryman); Ruth Warren (Miss Lyons); Davison Clark (Doctor); Pauline Drake (Doctor's Wife); Gracille LaVinder (Visiting Room Matron); Bill Wayne (Ada's Father); Doris Whitney (Woman Visitor); Grace Hampton, Helen Mowery, Helen Spring, Frances Henderson (Women).

"Pile out, you tramps. It's the end of the line."

So begins *Caged*, one of the most remarkable studies of women behind bars ever to be presented onscreen. Not since the late 1930s, with such films as *Condemned Women* (1938), q.v., had Hollywood dealt so starkly with the traumatic existence that female prisoners endure so frequently. This stark cinematic study was produced by Warner Bros., who had released one of the strongest indictments of the prison system ever made, *I Am a Fugitive from a Chain Gang* (1932), q.v. More recently, the same studio had produced *White Heat* (1949), q.v., starring James Cagney as a crazed convict behind bars.

To research her material for *Caged,* veteran scenarist Virginia Kellogg spent more than two months as a special prisoner in four different women's penitentiaries to learn about her subject first hand. Director John Cromwell, noted for his polished women's pictures, had dealt with the genre before in *Ann Vickers* (1933), q.v., and would later treat the subject of parole in *The Company She Keeps* (1951). *Caged* would win three Academy Award nominations: Best Actress (Eleanor Parker), Best Supporting Actress (Hope Emerson) and Best Story-Screenplay. Eleanor Parker was awarded the Volpi Cup at the Venice (International) Film Festival as Best Actress of the Year.

Caged spares the viewer nothing in its impassioned exposé of female penitentiaries. There is the colloquial language (i.e. "freeside" = being outside prison; "booster" = shoplifter; "behind the iron" = being in prison; "pogey" = the infirmary). There is the exploration of the harshness of adjusting to the unnatural regimen in which individuality, decency, normal sexual expression and safety are forgotten human rights. All this is depicted graphically within the movie. The ensemble performances of the cast heighten the production's grittiness and authenticity. If the scripwriters have contrived the scenario for heightened effect—and added perverse jocularity to occasionally lighten the mood of gloom—it nevertheless remains a horrifying reflection of a facet of life that most people will never know first hand, let alone dare to even contemplate.

Among the "fresh meat" at Women's State Prison is nineteen-year old Marie Allen (Eleanor Parker), embarking on a one-to-fifteen year prison term for being an accessory to armed robbery. As she tells a disinterested receiving room worker (Edith Evanson), she had been persuaded to help her husband (now dead) to rob a gas station for $40.00. The lifeless attendant responds, "Five bucks less and it wouldn't be a felony."

Aghast at being in such surroundings, Marie is shunted along with the other new admittees (many of whom have been to the facility before and who treat the siutation like returning home) through the admissions production line. Now convict #93850 and no longer an individual, Marie is embarrassed and humiliated by the impersonal physical examination. Seeing her singularity and femininity stripped from her, layer by layer, she is made to dress in a drab prison outfit. She begs a guard:

> MARIE: Couldn't I have a comb?
>
> FEMALE GUARD: What's the difference. There's no men in here.

Marie is assigned to the isolation ward for two weeks, until her blood test results come back from the lab regarding her pregnancy. (Upon entering that depressing barracks, one inmate cackles at her, "Welcome to Lysol Lane!") Bewildered and vulnerable, Marie is later sent to the office of Superintendent Ruth Benton (Agnes Moorehead) for her indoctrination interview. The efficient and very business-like Benton is a strange mixture of authority and sensitivity, a woman struggling to maintain control of an increasingly troublesome institution. As the chief administrator here, she must cope with the demands and whims of the Prison

Olive Deering and Eleanor Parker in *Caged* (1950).

Board who are unsympathetic to reform, overbudgeting, or anything that might possibly cause repercussions. In her conversation with Marie, one can almost see Benton telling herself, "There but for the grace of God, go I." With so many inmates to deal with, Benton proceeds with her pat speech, nevertheless lacing the comments with understanding smiles.

> I want you to know we're all here to help you. I want you to believe I'd like to be your friend. You'll find all kinds of women in here, just as you would outside. A large institution must have rules and the matrons are here to see the rules are obeyed. You weren't sent here to be punished. Just being here is the punishment. First offenders, like you Marie, are our greatest concern. Unfortunately, they have to be crowded in with more experienced women, simply because we haven't more space and you will be with such women.... No prison is a normal place.... We want to help you so you can start a new life.... Try to keep busy, it's important.

Having been told that it is against the rules for pregnant women to be released to have their babies, Marie is given the pacifier that if her record is good, she will be paroled from the prison in ten months. Her job while at the prison will be in the laundry. With that, she leaves Benton's office, about to start her odyssey into hell.

Once returned to the "bull pen" (the general dormitory), Marie discovers that her sparse existence in the isolation ward was pleasant compared to this. The over-crowded room, with its rows of double-decker bunk beds is filled with a wild assort-ment of humanity of all ages and races, of all backgrounds, and of all levels of meanness and culpability. But nothing compares to the matron-in-charge, the towering bundle of viciousness, Evelyn Harper (Hope Emerson). (Says one inmate, "Don't kid me. Harper's first name is filth.") Harper is a grotesque creature, a tyrant who demands complete allegiance and will brook no insubordination from the prisoners, let alone from her fellow guards. Not only does she treat her charges extremely badly, but she exploits them at every turn. She has drugs for sale, she insists she can pass on "real news" to the inmates' contacts on the outside for a price, and she demands little presents from "my gals." As one inmate jokes about Harper and her crowd, "At least we got honest matrons in here. When I bribe one, they stay bribed."

What makes tough Evelyn Harper even more frightening is her "feminine side," the part of her personality that is drawn to reading romance novels, munch-ing on caramels, having a nip of liquor now and then (from her bottle tucked under her mattress), and dressing up on her days off (in garish outfits that she thinks are fetching) to meet her men friends. As Harper explains to the still-innocent Marie, "I could get you whatever you wanted. Time is money to me. Can't favor every one of sixty girls." When Marie explains she has no money, Harper loses interest in this newcomer. Intent on training Marie from the start who is boss, Harper tells Marie that her first chore is to scrub the floor. "Home sweet home. Just like the big cage in the zoo. Only you clean it up, instead of the keeper. Bucket and brush is in the corner closet."

Marie soon comes into contact with several other inmates in her dorm. There is husband-killer Kitty Stark (Betty Garde), a tough broad who knows all the angles; Smoochie (Jan Sterling), a "c.p." (common prostitute), who yearns for the good life on the outside; the well-bred, check forger Georgia Harrison (Gertrude Michael) whose only way of coping with her hopeless prison life has been to escape into a fantasy world; and scatter-brained Emma Varges (Ellen Corby) who has her own theory why she landed in prison for having finally killed her husband. ("Well, it's that judge. If he'd a'nabbed me the first three times while I was just practicing, I wouldn't be here now for murder. It's all the judge's fault.") And then there is seventy-one year old murderess Millie (Gertrude Hoffman). "I'm a tall weed in the grass and the grapevine is blooming." She is a tough old bird who knows how to survive. When someone gets in her way, she spits back, "Lay a hand on me and I'll put your lights out. I'm in for life and one more like you is just so much vel-vet."

Despite this disparate lot, one thing unites the women: their perpetual desire to be free. The prison is situated near train tracks, and everytime an express train whizzes by, the women stop whatever they are doing, to longingly listen to the sounds of the train speeding away—far, far away. Frequently, the inmates brag about their past and what they will do when they are released. However, all of them (in this era of pre-women's liberation) agree, "if it wasn't for men, we wouldn't be here." On the other hand, as Kitty reflects, "If you stay in here too long you don't think of guys at all. You get out of the habit."

As time passes and the drab routine and harrowing fight for survival becomes the norm, Marie loses her spirit and her hope. She has learned, as one fellow prisoner warned her, "In this cage, you get tough or killed." Wondering what she will do when she does get released, Kitty suggests that when Marie is paroled, she can find her a job as a shoplifter, backed by an important local crime syndicate. June (Olive Deering), whose parole has just been denied, comforts Marie with, "You're lucky your man's dead. He can't turn you into a two-time loser like mine did." Later, June discouraged beyond redemption, hangs herself.

Marie, at eight months, gives birth prematurely to a baby in the prison infirmary. She names the infant Tommy and begs her mother (Queenie Smith) to take the child till she is paroled, but the other is more concerned with the displeasure of her new husband, and the infant is given away for adoption.

While Marie sinks further into despair and listlessness, Harper is having her own battles with the beleaguered Superintendent Benton. The latter wants to re-suspend the matron (who already has three suspensions), but Harper reminds her that she has a good political connection who will certainly bail her out once again. Furious with the do-gooder administrator, Harper insists she knows better—and first-hand at that—how this institution should be operated. In a chilling diatribe, she explains her philosophy:

> Do you know how it ought to be run? With a piece of rubber hose. Break them [the inmates] in two if they talk out of turn. Anyone who doesn't toe the mark sits in solitary for one month on bread and water. One funny move from a girl and I'd clip every hair off her head. That's the way it used to be run, and that's the way it ought to be run. They are a bunch of animals in a cage.

Finally, Marie wins her own moment of truth, her long-awaited interview with the parole board. Whenever it is any inmate's turn to meet with the all powerful board, most all of her dorm mates rally to her cause, helping her to groom herself as nicely as possible, offering bits of advice and encouragement, and hoping mightily that she is given the parole, for if it can happen to one convict, it can happen to others. The intimidating, self-conceited board members easily intimidate Marie. More nervous than she has ever been, she fidgets in her chair, desperate to make the "right" impression on these controllers of her fate.

> I've lived a lifetime in a year in the cage. If I have to fall back in, I'll be like the others and I'm not like them. Oh please, please, give me a chance to prove it! Oh, I've paid my debt. You'll never regret it, I promise.

Marie soon learns that her parole has been (arbitrarily) denied, and this fate-sealing action causes her to break out into an emotional frenzy. She runs through the institutional corridors, heading for the compound walls and desperately anxious to climb the barbed wire fence. With bleeding hands, she is brought back to reality by the pursuing matrons. Marie has become a sullen victim of the system.

Back in the bull pen, Marie witnesses the much-heralded arrival of a new inmate, the infamous Elvira Powell (Lee Patrick). Elvira is the well-publicized vice queen who knows her way around the crime syndicate and jail. The well-groomed, mannish Elvira, a long time rival of Kitty, immediately asserts her authority and sets her sights on removing Kitty from control of the dorm. She also knows how to oil the wheels of the system and confides to Harper that she will pay her $100 weekly to do her bidding. The ever-observant Elvira catches sight of Marie and makes a snap judgment, "She's a cute trick."

More dead time passes and by now, Marie is a seasoned con, aware of the paths of survival. When Kitty teaches a group of women the art of shoplifting, Marie, at first, cannot be bothered to participate, but later proves that has the intelligence and skill to be an expert in the field. Christmas arrives and there is a brief moment of brightness for the women. Elvira, in a play of power, gives all the dorm girls their individual lipsticks. When Harper uses this situation to assert her cruelness by announcing that she will take away this one tie to their past femininity, Superintendent Benton intervenes and announces that as her holiday gift to the inmates she has changed the rules—they may keep and use this cosmetic.

But the holiday spirit soon disappears. Elvira arranges for Kitty to be placed in solitary confinement for instructing the women in shoplifting. Harper uses the occasion to beat Kitty nearly senseless. When Kitty emerges from this isolation she goes to the infirmary for a month. Something has snapped inside the woman; she has lost control of herself and gone "stir crazy." The pathetic Kitty who comes back, a zombie, to the bull pen is such a contrast to her former self that even Elvira is shocked by the change and admits she wishes she had not played this rotten trick on Kitty.

Marie finds a kitten and hides it in the dormitory. When she later refuses to hand it over to Harper, the two women get into a tussle, which leads to a riot in the dormitory. Benton arrives to quell the uprising. When things have quieted down, the animal is found dead, and Marie is sent to solitary confinement for three days. When released, Harper, unbeknownst to Benton, exerts her power by subjecting Marie to the greatest humiliation she can accomplish. She shaves the young inmate's head, leaving her bald. Now stripped of all her dignity, the hysterical, dazed Marie shuts the door on the young woman she once was. She accepts herself as a hardened case, with only one option in life, to survive—no matter how, and no matter how many laws she must break in the future. (She has a brief, pathetic moment of self-realization when she observes a visiting socialite who is making a tour of the prison. It reminds her briefly of what might have been hers, but never will be.) Marie becomes friendly with Elvira, who promises to help her once she is released.

Meanwhile, the crazed Kitty goes berserk and one day stabs Harper repeatedly with a fork. The other inmates cheer Kitty on, chanting "Kill her! Kill her! Kill her!" The animals have turned against their keeper. For this homicide, Kitty is sent to the death house, while Smoochie reveals to the investigating committee all about Harper and her corrupt ways.

Finally, Marie is to be paroled, after 502 days in jail. As a departing "gift," she is to be paid six cents per day for her work at the institution (minus, of course, the ten days' interruption when she had her baby and her three days in solitary confinement). To convince the parole board that she should be released, she has lied to them about a phony cashier's job she has lined up. Actually she has made arrangements to be met by Elvira's syndicate pals, who will introduce her into a new life of crime. Marie has a termination meeting with superintendent Benton, who is fighting her own battle with the Prison Commission to maintain her post due to the irregularities at the prison:

> BENTON: In a couple more months, the parole officer could have found you work. You'd have made some honest money, had self respect and decency.

MARIE: Where did those things ever get me?

BENTON: Why do you give up, now, when you don't need to, when you're free.

MARIE: Free for what? Go to my baby? Sit down to a turkey dinner with a family and kiss my husband? (She lights a cigarette.)

BENTON: I know it's difficult to start over again.

MARIE: From now on, what's in it for me is all that matters. You did your best and where did it land you? You can't lick the system. Well, if you've got nothing more to say....

BENTON: If you ever need any help....

MARIE: Thanks, but I won't. (The two shake hands.) I hope you win. For that $40 I heisted, I certainly got myself an education.

Marie departs, having discarded her wedding ring. As she passes out the front gates of the prison, she is met by members of the syndicate and drives away with them. Benton observes all this from her office window. Turning back to her workload, Benton's thoughts about Marie are interrupted by her secretary:

SECRETARY: What should I do with her [Marie Allen's] file?

BENTON: Keep it alive. She'll be back.

On this desperate, harsh note, *Caged* concludes.

Strangely, at the time, reviewers were not that impressed with the integrity and craftsmanship of *Caged,* which was certainly not the normal product turned out by Hollywood of that period. *Variety* complained, "A grim, unrelieved study of cause and effect, it has exploitation possibilities but still adds up to very drab entertainment, unleavened with any measure of escapism that would brighten its chances in the more general market." Thomas M. Pryor *(New York Times)* assessed, "*Caged* plays awfully hollow. There is a prevailing synthetic atmosphere about the picture which defeats whatever real basis the story might have.... *Caged* is a cliché-ridden account of institutional brutality and depravity." Definitely bothered by the film's stark portrayal, Pryor added, "it does not necessarily follow, as the picture insists, that prisons breed hardened criminals. In this respect we venture to say that the ... [filmmakers] have tipped the scales of justice."

As time passed, and *Caged* was shown repeatedly on television, its reputation as an exceptional motion picture continued to grow. Its study of the transformation of an innocent young woman into a callous criminal by the abusive prison environment would lead to a rash of women's penitentiary pictures in the mid–1950s (*Women's Prison,* q.v.). *Caged* itself would be reshaped/remade in 1962 as *House of Women,* q.v., a far weaker offering than its sturdy predecessor.

One of the finest assessments of *Caged* is offered by Doug McClelland in *Eleanor Parker; Woman of a Thousand Faces* (1989). There McClelland weighed, "*Caged* does indeed remain the definitive dramatic portrait of women behind bars and was directly responsible for the installation of reform programs at many women's penal institutions." Jim Morton, in his essay "Women in Prison Films" for *Re/Search: Incredibly Strange Films* (1986), observed, "*Caged* was successful both critically and financially.... But the film was not perceived for what it was: the first of a new kind of movie. To most people it was just another crime drama. But the exploitational aspects were not lost on Bryan Foy, producer of dozens of exploitation films [including *Women's Prison,* q.v.]."

Originally, Joan Crawford had been considered for the role of Marie Allen in *Caged.* But knowing she was too mature for the part, she brought the script to Eleanor Parker's attention. Parker was immediately drawn to the dramatic challenges of the role, but had to fight to win the assignment against Wanda Hendrix who was the first choice of director John Cromwell and producer Jerry Wald. The previous year, Virginia Kellogg had authored the screen story for James Cagney's *White Heat,* q.v.

48. *Caged Heat* (New World, 1974), color, 83 min.

Executive producer, Samuel Gelfman; producer, Evelyn Purcell; director/screenplay, Jonathan Demme; art director, Eric Thiermann; music, John Cale; assistant director, David Osterhout; sound, Alex Vanderkar; special effects, Charlie Spurgeon; camera, Tak Fujimoto; editor, Johnna Demetrakis, Carolyn Hicks, Michael Goldman.

Juanita Brown (Maggie Cromwell); Roberta Collins (Belle Tyson); Erica Gavin (Jacqueline Wilson); Ella Reid (Pandora Williams); Lynda Gold (Crazy Annie); Warren Miller (Dr. Randolph); Barbara Steele (McQueen); Toby Carr Rafelson (Pinter); and: John Aprea, Carmen Argenziano, George Armitage, Cindy Cale, Mickey Fox, Layla Gallaway, Essie Hayes, Valley Hoffman, Keisha, Gary Littlejohn, Dorothy Love, Hal Marshall, Carol Miller, Leslie Otis, Amy Randall, Bob Reese, Mike Shack, Rainbeaux Smith, Cynthia Songey, Ann Stockdale, Irene Stokes, Joe Viola, Patrick Wright.

Jonathan Demme, who would later direct *Melvin and Howard* (1980), *Swing Shift* (1984) and *Something Wild* (1987) among others, had already scripted the black exploitation feature *Black Mama, White Mama* (1973) when he received his first opportunity to direct a feature. The project was a trash picture produced by Roger Corman's New World Pictures, which combined the then popular women's gang motif with women-behind-bars, the latter an increasingly popular format for softcore pornography filmmakers. In *The Illustrated Guide to Film Directors* (1983), David Quinlan ranks *Caged Heat* favorably for having "a style which transcended its origins. It also had Erica Gavin, just about the most animated actress [softcore pornography filmmaker] Russ Meyer ... ever used, and the extraordinary Barbara Steele as the villainess. Demme made the most of the personalities of the actresses involved...."

Having participated in a robbery, Jacqueline White (Erica Gavin) is sentenced to a term in Connorville women's prison, a harsh institution supervised by the crippled, sadistic McQueen (Barbara Steele), her willing assistant Pinter (Toby Carr Rafelson) and by Dr. Randolph (Warren Miller). Another prisoner, Pandora Williams (Ella Reid) is ordered to solitary confinement on a phony charge, and her pal Belle Tyson (Roberta Collins) is caught, when she attempts to steal food for Pandora. For killing the staff informant, Belle is scheduled to be subjected to an experimental lobotomy surgery at the hands of the unorthodox Dr. Randolph. Sickened by the horror around her, the now hardened and rebellious Jacqueline teams with Maggie Cromwell (Juanita Brown) to escape through the prison orchard. Later, they join with Crazy Annie (Lynda Gold), a massage parlor worker. After robbing a bank, they return to Connorville to save Belle. They succeed in their mission and then take McQueen and Randolph hostage. The girls escape from the pursuing local authorities, but McQueen and Randolph die in the shoot-out.

When shown in England in late 1975 where it was cut to a running time of 79 minutes, Tony Rayns (British *Monthly Film Bulletin*) endorsed the feature as "an indefatigable melodrama in which the variously corrupt, sick and frustrated figures of authority happen to wind up dead, while the rough-talkin', hard-actin' renegade women themselves get their way." Rayns also observed "it's arguably the first film of its kind since [Roger Corman's] *Bloody Mama* [1970] that manages to indulge all the statutory exploitation elements (from shower scenes to depraved medical malpractice) without ever becoming either grautuitous or condescending." In retrospect, Jim Morton, in his essay on "Women in Prison Films" for *Re/Search: Incredibly Strange Films* (1986) observed that in the genre, the "level of corruption varies from film to film. In *Caged Heat,* the entire system is rotten. The warden . . . is a crippled woman, full of anger and sexual repression. We catch bits of information that indicate she wasn't always wheelchair-bound, but director Jonathan Demme never gives us enough to arouse sympathy. As in all of Demme's films, the focus is on the quirky personalities of the social misfits."

A.k.a.: *Renegade Girls.*

49. *Carbine Williams* (Metro-Goldwyn-Mayer, 1952), 90 min.

Producer, Armand Deutsch; director, Richard Thorpe; screenplay, Art Cohn; art directors, Cedric Gibbons, Eddie Imazu; set decorators, Edwin B. Willis, Ralph Hurst; costumes Walter Plunkett; makeup, William Tuttle; music, Conrad Salinger; sound supervisor, Douglas Shearer; special effects, A. Arnold Gillespie, Warren Newcombe; camera, William Mellor; editor, Newell P. Kimlin.

James Stewart (David Marshall "Marsh" Williams); Jean Hagen (Maggie Williams); Wendell Corey (Captain H. T. Peoples); Carl Benton Reid (Claude Williams); Paul Stewart ("Dutch" Kruger); Otto Hulett (Mobley); Rhys Williams (Redwick Karson); Herbert Heyes (Lionel Daniels); James Arness (Leon Williams); Porter Hall (Sam Markley); Fay Roope (District Attorney); Ralph Dumke (Andrew White); Leif Erickson (Feder); Henry Corden (Bill Stockton); Howard Petrie (Sheriff); Frank Richards (Truex); Stuart Randall (Tom Vennar); Dan Riss (Jesse Rimmer); Bobby Hyatt (David Williams); Willis Bouchey (Mitchell); Emile Meyer (Head Guard); Bert LeBaron, Duke York, Richard Reeves (Guards); Robert Foulk (Torchy); Harry Cheshire (Judge); Lillian Culver (Mrs. Laura Williams); Marlene Lyden (Mary Eloise Williams); Norma Jean Cramer (Mary Ruth Williams); Robert Van Orden (Bob Williams); Jordan Corenweth (Will Williams); Harry Macklin (John Williams); Jon Gardner (Mac Williams); Bob Alden (Messenger); Erik Nielsen (Child at Wedding); Sam Flint, Nolan Leary, Marshall Bradford, George Pembroke (Board Members); Fiona O'Shiel (Mrs. Rimmer); James Harrison (Trusty).

A somewhat bewildering combination of personal attributes, some of them exemplary and some of them sinister and gross, is arranged for almost solid admiration by the people of MGM in a picture called *Carbine Williams.* . . .

(Bosley Crowther, *New York Times*)

Here is a distinctly different screen biography, one which traces the life of a noted American who, while incarcerated in prison, used his spare time to creatively devise a repeating firearm (the carbine rifle) which proved very helpful to the Allied forces during World War II. This movie chronicle is a study of a man who may or may not have committed the crime (homicide) for which he was imprisoned. However, like the offbeat film itself, the "hero" of the piece is not bent on exposing penal system abuses. Rather, once he has accepted and adapted to the penitentiary regimen, he wants to get on with life as best he can and to accomplish constructive things. Years later, looking back on his prison stay, he has few bitter memories; rather he concedes that the sojourn was a necessary rehabilitation method and regards the warden and the prison guards as lifelong friends. Clearly this is a very unusual prison drama, one laced with the "nice guy" image that was such a part of Jimmy Stewart's screen persona. As the *New York Times's* Bosley Crowther analyzed it, "a certain degree of sentiment is aroused that may not be entirely supported when the elements are carefully analyzed."

In the present, David Marshall "Marsh" Williams (James Stewart), an executive with the Winchester Repeating Arms Co. and his wife Maggie (Jean Hagen) agree that the recurring moodiness of their eight-year-old son David (Bobby Hyatt) is due to the taunts of his schoolmates that his father is an ex-convict. Marsh takes David to Central Prison at Raleigh, North Carolina to meet with Captain H. T. Peoples (Wendell Corey), the warden. Marsh wants his good friend and mentor to tell his son his story.

As Peoples explains to David of convicts in general, "They're not all bad.... Others have made only one mistake." With that, the narrative flashes back to Prohibition times in the backwoods of North Carolina where Marsh, one of eleven children, has just left the Navy, having served two enlistments. His father (Carl Benton Reid) insists Marsh must work for two years before he receives his four hundred-acre share of the farm. Marsh refuses the offer, wanting to get married now to his girlfriend Maggie. Being a rugged individualist, he soon tires of the menial roadbed laborer job he has on the Atlantic Coastline Railroad. He decides he can better support his wife as a moonshiner. He joins with two pals (Rhys Williams, Porter Hall) in bootlegging, which few in the state—federal agents to one side—consider a wrongful occupation. (As Marsh sees it, "There's a natural right to things and a legal right.") When federal authorities raid Marsh's stills and attempt to arrest him, a gun battle ensues and a government agent is killed. No one is sure who fired the crucial shot, least of all the jury at the trial. A new trial is ordered, but Marsh decides to accept a plea bargaining charge of second degree murder, which should only carry a fifteen-year sentence at worse. However, the strict judges sentences Marsh to a thirty-year term of hard labor. Honor-bound to serve out his sentence graciously, Marsh wants Maggie to divorce him and his relatives to forget him, but they refuse.

In a voice-over, Warden Peoples explains to young David about Marsh's initial time behind bars.

> The first day is the worst. When he realizes he is no longer free, that this is his home, that this would be his world from now on. Every convict takes prison different.... Each man fights it in his own way.

Marsh falls in with hardened convict "Dutch" Kruger (Paul Stewart), who sells contraband tobacco to fellow prisoners. Later a stoolie is killed with a knife, and Marsh, being found with the weapon, is put on a chain gang.

People explains to Williams's son:

> The chain gang is the end of the line. I've seen a lot of men broken on the chain gang.... It breaks a man's body, breaks his spirit or both.

Wendell Corey, James Stewart and Otto Hulett in *Carbine Williams* (1952).

After enduring the harsh rigors of the chain/road gang, Marsh is transferred to Caldonia Prison Farm. Kruger and others try to escape. Marsh refuses to join them, and, in fact, he tries to stop them. At the Prison Farm, Marsh meets his new keeper, Captain Peoples.

Peoples delivers his indoctrination speech.

> I'm the law here. Now if you behave yourself, you'll be treated square. Get out of line, you'll be hose-piped. Try to escape, you'll get drilled through the head.

Marsh proves to be a rebellious individual, causing Peoples to insist, "There's room for only one self-minded man in this camp and that's me." Regarding Marsh's sense of integrity, the warden opines, "You've got strange ideas, Williams, on what's right or wrong. What's fair and not fair.

Slowly, Peoples, a stern but fair man, begins to have an influence on Williams. Eventually, at Peoples's persuasion, Marsh agrees to see his wife and Peoples allows him a special twenty-four hour pass off the farm to be with Maggie, who has been attending college to while away the hours.

Marsh finds it difficult to relate to his wife.

> MARSH: I'm as good as dead.... Convicts don't have wives. One day a year is worse. It just helps keep you alive. That's no good when you can't breathe fresh air. It's just better to be dead. Up there [in heaven] you can't want nothing."
>
> MAGGIE: I'm in prison too, Marsh, without you.... I want a child.
>
> MARSH: No kid would pick a convict for a father.

Later, Maggie finds that she is pregnant and she has their child, David. Meanwhile, Marsh earns a job at the prison camp in the blacksmith shop where he plays around with an idea he has for a new type of rifle. (The notion came to him earlier while serving thirty days in solitary confinement.) He makes the gun out of old parts and over a six-year period perfects it. He eventually convinces Peoples, who has finally discovered the secret project, that though he broke the rules working on the rifle, he has hit upon a good invention. Just as Marsh is about to actually test the new weapon, the newspapers learn of the amazing story. Peoples is called before the aghast Prison Board. He insists that the experiment should continue and that if Marsh should use the testing period to escape, he would personally serve out the rest of the convict's term. The impressed Board allows the experiments to continue. The test is successful and a gun manufacturer offers Marsh a contract for his innovative lightweight rifle. Meanwhile, the Governor of the state, deciding that Marsh has been in prison too long (especially when there was no real proof he had killed anyone), pardons him. The narrative concludes with David, now understanding his father much better, rushing out of the meeting to the arms of his waiting dad.

Variety had reservations about this ninety-minute, black and white feature which was based on a *Reader's Digest* magazine article. "A mild type of interest is developed by the episodic unfoldment of the story, mostly because it is an essentially honest account of a man still living." The trade paper added that the story "comes to the screen with too many obscurities in plotting...."

With a title that sounded more like one belonging to a Western, and a downbeat story (spiked with dollops of saccharine) *Carbine Williams* was not a box office winner; its only allure to moviegoers being the marquee attraction of its star Jimmy Stewart. For many, even though it was based on fact, the story was too glossy to have credence. Even the chain gang sequences seemed too prettified to be as stark or harrowing as intended.

50. *Castle on the Hudson* (Warner Bros., 1940), 76 min.

Executive producer, Hal B. Wallis; associate producer, Sam Bischoff; director, Anatole Litvak; based on the book *20,000 Years in Sing Sing* by Warden Lewis E. Lawes; screenplay, Seton I. Miller, Brown Holmes, Courteney Terrett; art director, John Hughes; gowns, Howard Shoup; makeup, Perc Westmore; music, Adolph Deutsch; orchestrator, Ray Heindorf; music director, Leo F. Forbstein; dialogue director, Irving Rapper; special effects, Byron Haskins, Edwin DuPar; sound, Robert B. Lee; camera, Arthur Edeson; editor, Thomas Richards.

John Garfield (Tommy Gordon); Ann Sheridan (Kay Manners); Pat O'Brien (Warden Walter Long); Burgess Meredith (Steven Rockford); Henry O'Neill (District Attorney); Jerome Cowan (Ed Crowley); Guinn "Big Boy" Williams (Mike Ca-

gle); John Litel (Prison Chaplain); Margot Stevenson (Ann Rockford); Willard Robertson (Ragan); Edard Pawley (Black Jack); Billy Wayne (Pete); Nedda Harrigan (Mrs. Long); Wade Boteler (Principal Keeper); Barbara Pepper (Goldie); Robert Strange (Joe Morris); Grant Mitchell (Dr. Ames); Robert Homans (Clyde Burton); Joseph Downing, Sol Gorss (Gangsters); Charles Sherlock, Mike Lally, Jack Mower, Frank Mayo, Pat O'Malley, Walter Miller (Guards); Pat Flaherty (Stretcher Attendant); Ed Kane (Club Manager); Claude Wisberg, Michael Conroy (Newsboys); Frank Faylen (Guard Who Is Slugged); Nat Carr, William Telark, William Hopper (Reporters); Lee Phelps (Guard in Visitors' Room); James Flavin (Guard in Death Row).

A great deal had changed since Warden Lewis E. Lawes's book *20,000 Years in Sing Sing* (1932) had been turned into the Warner Bros. film (1933), q.v., of the

Burgess Meredith, Ann Sheridan and John Garfield in *Castle on the Hudson* (1940).

same title. The Depression was over, the United States was being drawn into World War II, and Americans had begun adopting a new attitude towards prisons and prisoners. No longer were these cold walls merely a place where a wrongdoer went to serve out his just sentence and where, if anything untoward occurred, it served the lawbreaker damn right. Thanks to a growing enlightenment and a slowly growing reform movement, it was being realized that even the most heinous convict was still a human being who deserved the chance for reformation through rehabilitation. It was a concept easier to accept as a theory than to put into practice.

No one on the Warner Bros. lot in 1940 was better suited to playing the perpetual victim of the Depression than John Garfield and he was chosen to star in *Castle on the Hudson,* a remake of *20,000 Years in Sing Sing.* By now, an established screen figure, he brought a distinct persona to every movie characterization he undertook. In any role he played — no matter how immoral the character — the figure possessed an ingratiating, vulnerable charm and drew sympathy from moviegoers.

While the basic plotline of *20,000 Years in Sing Sing* is retained (as well as assorted stock footage) in *Castle on the Hudson,* the aim of the new version is different (more an action story than a social statement) and the attitude of the scriptwriters has altered (convicts were now victims of a system, not merely receiving their just desserts).

Flippant New Yorker, Tommy Gordon (John Garfield), an experienced criminal, is arrested for assault with a deadly weapon and the intent to kill. He is sentenced to Sing Sing Prison at Ossining, New York. On the train ride to upstate New York, he tells a reporter boastfully about his pending stay at the "castle on the Hudson." "It don't mean a thing to me. Nothing gonna get me down. Once

I'm in the joint, I'll own the place. They'll be lucky to keep me a month.... If I don't like the joint, I'll move out." The cocky man is convinced that his lawyer Ed Crowley (Jerome Cowan) will find some way to get him released. However, once at the facility and transformed into prisoner #68431, Tommy meets his match in Warden Walter Long (Pat O'Brien). The latter is equally as breezy and nonchalant as the newcomer, but is a man who treats his charges with respect and a sense of individuality. (As played by Pat O'Brien, there is always a tender catch to his voice and a sympathetic moistness to his eyes.)

> LONG: I don't suppose you like the food or the hours either. I guess maybe you don't like your cell.
>
> TOMMY: It's rotten.
>
> LONG: No, it isn't rotten. It isn't the best place in the world, but it's clean.
>
> TOMMY: I rate a better joint than that.
>
> LONG: All you're entitled to is food and a place to sleep. Anything else you get, you get from me.

Assuring the conceited Tommy that he will soon change his thinking, Long adds, "You've got to be useful to live." Sure enough, after a month in solitary confinement, Tommy yearns for even the rock pile detail and becomes a more cooperative convict. Once in general population, Tommy meets Steven Rockford (Burgess Meredith), a very erudite prisoner ("I'm a pretty smart bozo myself") and they become pals, both working in the machine shop. Later, Rockford plans a breakout, agreeing to allow the dimwitted Mike Cagle (Guinn "Big Boy" Williams) to be part of the plan. When Tommy realizes that the escape plan is to take place on a Saturday, he refuses to go along, being superstitious that Saturdays always bring him bad luck. The escape scheme is foiled, and when Rockford is cornered, he jumps from the edge of the upper level cell block tier and dies.

Tommy's girlfriend Kay Manners (Ann Sheridan) visits him at Sing Sing and mentions that she has been in contact with Crowley, intending to persuade him to help Tommy's case. Gordon warns her against the lawyer, now realizing he has been double-crossed by his former cohort. Thereafter, because Tommy has become such an improved convict, Warden Long allows him a special pass out of the prison to visit Kay who is hospitalized and not expected to live. Tommy gives Long his word of honor that he will return. At the hospital, Gordon learns from Kay that she was injured jumping out of Crowley's speeding car when he began forcing his attentions on her. Suddenly Crowley arrives, intending to buy off Kay before she can incriminate him with the law. Tommy and Crowley have a scuffle. To protect Tommy, Kay uses her gun to kill Crowley and then urges Gordon to run away. Tommy remains in hiding until he reads about Long's battle with the Prison Board who is demanding his resignation if Gordon is not found. He turns himself in and, despite the protestations of Kay, who has recovered, Tommy is convicted of homicide. Now on death row, Tommy waits for his day of reckoning. His harmonica-playing friend Mike Cagle goes to the electric chair, dragged all the way to meet his fate. Kay comes for a final visit to Tommy. Resigned to his bad luck, he tells her, "I belong to the state of New York and in a few minutes they're going to take me out and burn me." The warden comes for the final visit. During their chat, he lights Tommy's cigarette, having found great respect from this honorable criminal. With the prison chaplain (John Litel) leading the way, Tommy goes forth to meet his destiny. It is a Saturday.

"[I]t is a strong prison melodrama, unpleasant in some respects, but gripping. . . . Most of the comedy is concentrated in the first half; the laughter is provoked by the methods employed by the warden in breaking down the arrogance of the hero. . ." (*Harrison's Reports*). *Variety* was less impressed, "It's a routine prison melodrama, and along familiar lines of former 'big house' pictures turned out by Warners during the past several years." B. R. Cristler (*New York Times*) judged, "The cast is good—so good that a player like Burgess Meredith appears satisfied with fourth billing—but the plot, the dialogue and the scenery are the same as ever."

To be noted is that Grant Mitchell played the prison physician in both versions of *20,000 Years in Sing Sing*.

British release title: *Years Without Days*.

51. *Cell 2455, Death Row* (Columbia, 1955), 77 min.

Producer, Wallace MacDonald; director, Fred F. Sears; based on the autobiography of Caryl Whittier Chessman; screenplay, Jack DeWitt; art director, Robert Peterson; set decorator, Frank Tuttle; music, Mischa Bakaleinikoff; assistant director, Eddie Saeta; technical adviser, Gino Anselmi; sound supervisor, John Livadary; sound, James Speak; camera, Fred Jackson; editor, Henry Batista.

William Campbell (Whit); Robert Campbell (Whit, as a Teenager); Marian Carr (Doll); Kathryn Grant (Jo-Anne); Harvey Stephens (Warden); Vince Edwards (Hamilton); Allen Nourse (Serle); Diane DeLaire (Hallie); Bart Bradley (Whit, as a Young Boy); Paul Dubov (Al); Tyler MacDuff (Nugent); Buck Kartalian (Monk); Eleanor Audley (Blanche); Thom Carney (Hatcheck Charlie); Joe Forte (Lawyer); Howard Wright (Judge); Glenn Gordon (Superior Guard); Jimmy Murphy (Sonny); Jerry Mickelsen (Tom); Bruce Sharpe (Bud); Wayne Taylor (Skipper Adams); Kerwin Mathews (Reporter); Maureen Cassidy (Girl); Joseph Turkel (Curly); Jock Talbot (Boy); Ben Pollock (Mug); Alan Dexter, Greg Kingsford (Plainsclothesmen); John Marshall, John Halloran (Officers).

The amazing life and times of Caryl Whittier Chessman (1912–1960) have long intrigued the public. Some two months after he was released from prison for robbery, he was arrested in January 1948 as a suspect in an armed robbery of a men's clothing store. This led the police to suspecting him of being the "red light" bandit, a man who drove up to parked cars on lovers lane, flashing a red spotlight to make it appear he was driving a police vehicle, then the bandit would rob the couple, and sometimes force the woman to engage in oral sex. Because of circumstantial evidence (a .45 automatic pistol and a penlight found in Chessman's stolen car were close to those used in the crimes) and because he was "identified" by several victims in lineups, he was charged and convicted on several counts of kidnapping/rape/robbery. There began his twelve years of appeals as he campaigned to reverse the original verdict. During his long stay in prison (he arrived at San Quentin Prison's Death Row on July 3, 1948), he helped to finance his cause by writing three books and a novel, with his autobiography *Cell 2455, Death Row* (1954) becoming a national best-seller. His well-publicized battle for freedom created a great furor worldwide among opponents to capital punishment. After eight stays of execution, he died in the gas chamber at San Quentin Prison on May 2, 1960.

In the midst of Chessman's prison stay, Columbia Pictures acquired the rights to the notorious convict's book and produced this hastily assembled, sensationalized

William Campbell (prisoner in cell #2455) in *Cell 2455, Death Row* (1955).

account of the criminal, called here Whit. The story opens in 1954, just before Whit (William Campbell) is to be executed in San Quentin's gas chamber. As he paces in his cell (#2455, Death Row) he tells the warden (Harvey Stephens) how much he wants to live and that he still hopes to obtain another stay of execution.

Via flashback, his life is traced, when as a child (Bart Bradley), he suffers from asthma and his parents (Allen Nourse, Diane DeLaire) bring him to California to improve his health. Things go well until his mother is injured in a car accident, and being crippled permanently, medical expenses escalate. When his father attempts suicide, the embittered fifteen-year-old boy (Robert Campbell) begins stealing groceries to feed his family. Later to impress a blonde moll (Kathryn Grant) he admires, he steals a car and begins a life of crime. He is sent to reform school, but when released he (William Campbell) break parole and reforms his gang. By now he has a new girlfriend (Marian Carr) and leads his group on a series of holdups. When captured, he is sent to San Quentin. Later he learns about the newly-instituted honor farm at Chino and maneuvers his way into being transferred there. He escapes from the farm, but is soon captured and sent to Folsom, a maximum security prison, for four years. With his mother near death, he convinces the parole board to free him and once freed, he organizes a new gang which he decides will prey only on gangsters. It is at this time that Los Angeles is being terrorized by the "Red Light" bandit, and when Whit is captured on one of his robbery forays, the wheels of justice spin against him. The arrogant Whit decides not to use a public defender and handles his own defense. Under the terms of the Little Lindberg Law, he is found guilty and sentenced to death.

Returning to the present, it is dawn and soon Whit will die. He says to himself, "I can't show fear, but I am afraid, God in Heaven forgive me. I have died fifty times in this cell. But I have changed. I know now what brings a man to Death Row. Only the man himself." The warden arrives to tell him that he has won another stay of execution. The jubilant Whit sits down at his typewriter to start a new legal brief for his defense.

Treated as an exploitation feature, *Cell 2455, Death Row* was made as a quick play-off for the action market. *Variety* acknowledged, "Direction of Fred F. Sears, although minimizing the psychological aspects, handles the many action sequences with finesse." However, added the trade journal, "the criminal career of cell 2455's occupant proves to be such a senseless round of car thefts, stickups and hijacking that one wonders what mental quirk was behind all this." Jack Moffett (*Hollywood Reporter*) minced no words, "One cannot look at it [the film] without feeling that someone who decided to make the picture did not care how sensational he got in promoting a fast buck." In retrospect, Clive Hirschhorn (*The Columbia Story*, 1989) judged, "as scripted by Jack De Witt from Chessman's own book, [the film] barely scratched the surface of its subject's personality. Motivation wasn't what motivated Wallace MacDonald's production, and the result was simply a bald narrative depicting a senseless life of crime."

The personable William Campbell did the best he could with a very surface role in *Cell 2455, Death Row;* his brother Robert playing the lawbreaker as a teenager. Twelve years later, NBC–TV telecast *Kill Me If You Can,* q.v., with Alan Alda as Carryl Chessman. It was a far more thoughtful and intense study of the renowned criminal's vain efforts to win his freedom.

52. *Chain Gang* (Columbia, 1950), 70 min.

Producer, Sam Katzman; director, Lew Landers; screenplay, Howard J. Green; art director, Paul Palmentola; set decorator, Sidney Clifford; makeup, Ray Sebastian; music director, Mischa Bakaleinikoff; sound, Josh Westmoreland; camera, Ira H. Morgan; editor, Aaron Stell.

Douglas Kennedy (Cliff Roberts); Marjorie Lord (Rita McKelvey); Emory Parnell (Captain Duncan); William Phillips (Snead); Thurston Hall (John McKelvey); Harry Cheshire (Pop O'Donnell); Don Harvey (Langley); William G. Lechner (Eddie); George Eldredge (Adams); William Tannen (Harry Cleaver); Frank Wilcox (Lloyd Killgallen); Rusty Wescoatt (Yates); George Robotham (Regan); Dorothy Vaughan (Mrs. Briggs); William Fawcett (Zeke).

> The question in the case of this picture is, not that it is a poor entertainment, but whether it should have been produced at all.... [The] story is completely artificial and unbelievable, and the direction and acting amateurish.
>
> *(Harrison's Reports)*

Rita McKelvey (Marjorie Lord) and Cliff Roberts (Douglas Kennedy) rival newspaper reporters, are in love, much to the chagrin of her wealthy, snobbish stepfather John McKelvey (Thurston Hall). Roberts has been writing an exposé of the prison system and to gain additional information, he gains a job as a prison guard. Adopting an assumed name and having a miniature camera (in the shape of a cigarette lighter) he reports for duty to Captain Duncan (Emory Parnell), the sadistic chief of guards at the penitentiary. Soon Cliff amasses evidence of prisoner abuse / torture (muddy slop for food, the use of seatbox, racks and whippings) and

Douglas Kennedy and George Eldredge in *Chain Gang* (1950).

his photos are published. This upsets McKelvey, who, unknown to Rita, has amassed a great deal of fortune through the exploitation of cheap chain gang labor. When she learns the truth, she leaves home and quits her newspaper (which her stepfather owns) to join Cliff's publication. Meanwhile, Cliff's identity is uncovered—thanks to McKelvey's henchman (William Tannen)—and Duncan orders his men to beat up the spy. At that moment, a convict escapes and in the confusion, Cliff flees. He is shot and left for dead. However, he is helped by the escaping prisoner (William Phillips), whom he once befriended, and reaches safety. Cliff's research proves invaluable in the crusade to outlaw chain gangs.

Geared on the lowest level of acceptance, *Chain Gang* won no endorsements from the trade press. "It doesn't contain many surprises storywise," noted *Variety*. "A poor attempt at fashioning a prison escape thriller with journalistic exposure" *(Film Daily)*. "The political angles of the plot seem somewhat contrived..." *(Hollywood Reporter)*.

53. *Chain Gang Women* (Lee Frost Productions, 1971), 85 min.

Producer, Wes Bishop; director, Lee Frost; screenplay, Frost, Bishop; music director, Billy Sprague; music supervisor, Porter Jordan; songs, Jordan, Bob Duncan and Don Lee, Ross Olmsted; assistant director, Mike Mikler; camera/editor, Frost.

Michael Stearns (Mike Weed); Robert Lott (Billy Harris); Barbara Mills (Farmer's Wife); Linda York (Ann); Ralph Campbell (Farmer); Wes Bishop (Coleman); William B. Martin (Willy); Bruce Kemp (Fat Sam); Phil Hoover (Gentry); Chuck Wells (Jones); John Bliss (Prison Guard); "Red" Schryver (Larson); James McLarty (Police Officer); and: Chick Minsker.

Home-movie production values make it impossible to enjoy this muddled film as either a thriller or as sexploitation. Shabbily photographed and punctuated by inappropriate Country-and-Western songs, its only pleasures are two well-constructed multi/split-screen chase sequences, and the indignant girlfriend's post-coital line to the swaggering rapist ('I take it you've finished now?').

Derek Elley (British *Monthly Film Bulletin*)

Billy Harris (Robert Lott) is transfered to a Georgia chain gang to complete his final six months of incarceration for a marijuana offense. On the gang he is forced to cope with Mike Weed (Michael Stearns), a sex killer, with whom he is chained on work detail. When the opportunity arises, Weed clubs a guard (Bruce Kemp) and makes his chained partner Billy join him in escaping. They seek refuge in the apartment of Ann (Linda York), Weed's girlfriend. On one occasion while Weed is away, Billy rapes her. When their attempt to sneak over the state border fails, Billy urges her to leave them. Later the two men break into a farmhouse and take charge, forcing the farmer (Ralph Campbell) to view his young wife (Barbara Mills) being ravaged. An attempt to crash a roadblock fails, and the escapees return to the farmhouse. There the farmer strangles Weed while he sleeps and later he shoots Billy.

One of the ad campaigns for this picture proclaimed, "The road from a chain gang to Hell is very short."

A.k.a.: *The Chain.*

54. *Chained Heat* (Jensen Farley, 1983), color, 95 min.

Executive producers, Ernst Von Theumer, Lou Paciocco; producer, Billy Fine; associate producer, Gerhard Scheurich; director, Paul Nicholas; screenplay, Vincent Mongoi, Nicholas; art director, Bob Ziembicki; wardrobe, Jacqueline Kinnaway, Susie De Santo; music/music conductor, Joseph Conlon; music editor, Dino Moriana; music consultants, Bob Reno, Stephen Metz; creative consultant, Aaron Butler; assistant director, Nancy King; sound, Anna De Lanzo; supervising sound editor, Richard Raderman; special effects, Doug White; camera, Mac Ahlberg; editor, Nono di Marco.

Linda Blair (Carol); John Vernon (Warden Bachman); Sybil Danning (Ericka); Tamara Dobson (Duchess); Stella Stevens (Captain Taylor); Sharon Hughes (Val); Henry Silva (Lester); Jennifer Ashley (Grinder); Edy Williams (Paula); Susan Meschner (Genderson); Diana Rose (Dr. Pascal); Christina Cardan (Miss King); Ann Dane (Harriet); Kelly Lawrence (Carmen); Charles Messenger, Jeff Goodman (Guards); Martha Gallub (Miller); Gloria Fioramonti (PCP Girl); Leala Chrystie (Chana); Aaron Butler (Willy); Nicole Geus, Donna Rizzitello, Annie Davidson, Sharon Hoffman, Chrissie Quinn, Katherine Vernon (Cellmates); and: Greta Blackburn, Michael Callan, Sharon Hughes, Kandal Kaldwell, Jody Medford, Louisa Moritz, Nita Talbot.

In the nearly ten years since Linda Blair had starred in the telefeature *Born Innocent,* q.v. she has become a regular presence in exploitation features. *Chained Heat,* a followup to *The Concrete Jungle* (1982), q.v., exploited Blair's association with *Born Innocent* by casting the still youthful-looking actress as a slightly older version of the innocent girl exposed to the dregs of humanity when imprisoned. Being made in the far more permissive 1980s, *Chained Heat* did its best to provide huge dollops of nudity, perverted sex and disturbed, violent female humanity at every turn. It was geared to fill the fantasies of all those enthusiastic of bondage, torture and vicious language. *Variety* reported that the movie "manages to pack in enough sex tease and violent action to satisfy undiscriminating action fans."

Comparing the results to a similar film of a decade ago, *Caged Heat* (1974), q.v., the trade paper noted that the new picture "is a step down from the modest but fun genre films of a decade ago...."

New inmate Carol (Linda Blair), a student-gone-wrong, arrives at the overcrowded women's correctional facility, an institution meant to hold 1,500 but overstuffed with 2,000 brooding, frustrated, angry convicts. Carol quickly discovers the situation is more than she can handle and that to survive will require all her ingenuity. Her only friend in the walls of hell is Val (Sharon Hughes). There is corrupt prison warden Bachman (John Vernon) who trafficks in drugs, plans robberies and heads a prostitution ring (whisking prisoners in and out of the facility to commit assorted crimes, always with a great alibi for their whereabouts). Sex-driven Bachman revels in orgiastic unions with his "girls" and takes delight in videotaping his athletic hot tub action in his office. Meanwhile, butch Captain Taylor (Stella Stevens), the warden's willing chief helper, makes her own deals with a drug dealer (Henry Silva) and exploits her charges at every avenue. Within the inmate population there is 6' 2" Duchess (Tamara Dobson) who leads the black faction among the convicts. Her opposite number among the white women prisoners is blonde Ericka (Sybil Danning). Each group strives to dominate the action within the big walls. To achieve their goals, they are not above pummeling, knifing and strangling their opponents, whether in the cells, the showers (a favorite site in such pictures), or in the underground passages. The degenerate warden meets a violent end when Captain Taylor drowns him in his hot tub. However, since his videotape camera was running during the whole event, Captain Taylor is soon undone as well.

Chained Heat was made in West Germany in December of 1982 by German director Paul Nicholas. *Variety* argued that Nicholas "displays little feel for the prison genre, emphasizing archaic sex-for-voyeurs scenes, reaching a nadir in the warden's tacky office.... Hard action scenes are in scarce supply, with only Tamara Dobson ... convincing in battle.... Blair displays her new uninhibited image here, but remains an unconvincing performer in dramatic scenes." On the other hand, when a videocassette version of *Caged Heat* was released by Vestron, *Video Review* magazine judged that the film "could be the most entertaining babes-behind-bars flick ever made...."

To be noted in a small role within *Chained Heat* is Edy Williams, the Russ Meyer "starlet" of mostly softcore pornography. Co-star Sybil Danning had been a former *Playboy* magazine cover girl. Statuesque ex-model Tamara Dobson, the black action star of *Cleopatra Jones* (1973) had teamed previously with Stella Stevens in *Cleopatra Jones and the Casino of Gold* (1975).

Linda Blair, having survived this ordeal, would star in another titillating prison escapade, *Red Heat* (1985), q.v. In early 1990 it was announced that *Chained Heat II* was in pre-production. The promotional teaser stated: "The sizzling sequel to the most successful women-in-prison film ever made.... 1500 women. No warden. Out of control."

55. *Circumstantial Evidence* (20th Century–Fox, 1945), 67 min.

Producer, William Girard; director, John Larkin; story, Nat Ferber, Sam Duncan; screenplay, Robert Metzler; adapted by, Samuel Ornitz; art directors, Lyle Wheeler, Richard Irvine; set decorator, Thomas Little, Fred J. Rode; music, David Buttolph; music director, Emil Newman; assistant director, Bill Eckhardt; sound, George

Leverett; camera, Harry Jackson; editor, Norman Colbert.

Michael O'Shea (Joe Reynolds); Lloyd Nolan (Sam Lord); Trudy Marshall (Agnes Hannon); Billy Cummings (Pat Reynolds); Ruth Ford (Mrs. Simms); Reed Hadley (Prosecutor); Roy Roberts (Marty Hannon); Scotty Beckett (Freddy Hanlon); Byron Foulger (Bolger); Dorothy Adams (Bolger's Wife); John Eldredge (Judge White); Eddie Marr (Mike); Selmer Jackson (Warden); William B. Davidson (Chairman); John Hamilton (Governor Hanlon); Ben Welden (Kenny); Ralph Dunn (Cleary); Ray Teal (Policeman); Thomas Jackson (Detective).

A rather preposterous premise governs this 20th Century–Fox programmer; i.e. that a man locked up on death row can slip in and out of prison easily. However, this budget feature benefits from a solid cast, especially the performances of ever-reliable Lloyd Nolan and Michael O'Shea.

Hot-headed parent Joe Reynolds (Michael O'Shea) gets into an argument with a difficult storekeeper who insists that Joe's son (Billy Cummings) return a hatchet he has picked up. In the scuffle, the merchant falls and hits his head and dies. The frightened Joe intends to leave town, but his postman/friend Sam Lord (Lloyd Nolan) convinces him to stay and clear himself. At the trial, several eyewitnesses insist that they saw Joe raising the hatchet to strike the deceased. On such slim evidence, Joe is condemned to die in prison.

Loyal Sam works out a plan to clear his friend. He arranges a boxing competition for young boys and includes in the group both the son (Scotty Beckett) of the governor and the offspring of the judge (John Eldredge) in the case. During the sporting event, which finds the governor, judge and case witnesses in attendance, Sam has the youths reenact the facts in Joe's case. When one of the youths falls to the ground, apparently struck by a hammer, and everyone claims they saw how it happened, Sam reveals his ploy. The governor is so impressed by this lesson that he insists that Joe have a new trial. Meanwhile, Joe has escaped from prison, hoping for a final visit with his son. Hearing the new turn of events, he must now sneak back into prison undetected. He succeeds and later, at the new trial, is freed.

"If 20th–Fox had a commendable idea in pointing out how dangerous circumstantial evidence testimony can be, the obvious way the script went about it destroys all the effect. There's no subtlety or imagination in the telling" (*Variety*).

56. *City of Silent Men* (Paramount, 1921), 6,326'.

Presenter, Jesse L. Lasky; director, Tom Forman; screenplay, Frank Condon; camera, Harry Perry.

Thomas Meighan (Jim Montgomery); Lois Wilson (Molly Bryant); Kate Bruce (Mrs. Montgomery); Paul Everton (Old Bill); George MacQuarrie (Mike Kearney); Guy Oliver (Mr. Bryant).

Two popular Paramount players, Thomas Meighan and Lois Wilson, starred in this crime melodrama which, for part of its unfolding, utilized a Sing Sing Prison backdrop. The title of the film refers to the penitentiary, where men have no voice in their daily lives.

Naïve country youth Jim Montgomery (Thomas Meighan), a mechanic, comes to the city to seek work. He is innocently drawn into criminal activity by crooks. During the robbery, a watchman is killed and Jim is the one caught. He is sentenced to prison for life. At Sing Sing Prison his cellmate is the elderly Old Bill (Paul Everton), a confirmed criminal who has a streak of kindness. Later Bill helps Jim to escape. He relocates to California where he soon falls in love with Molly (Lois Wilson), the daughter of his employer (Guy Oliver). His happness is short lived, for he has been pursued by New York policeman Mike Kearney (George MacQuarrie). When Kearney discovers how desperate his prey is to retain his freedom, he decides to drop the case. Meanwhile, Bill has been released from prison and tracks down the real culprits. At last, Montgomery is a free man.

With its very contrived screenplay, *Variety* found the silent photoplay "disjointed and rambling." Furthermore, the publication argued, "The whole thing is ridiculously theatrical and artificial and an unworthy vehicle for so satisfying a screen player as [Thomas] Meighan."

57. *City Without Men* (Columbia, 1943), 75 min.

Producer, B. P. Schulberg; associate producer, Samuel Bronston; director, Sidney Salkow; story, Budd Schulberg, Martin Berkeley; screenplay, W. L. River, George Skier, Donald Davis; art directors, Lionel Banks, Cary Odell; set decorator, William Kiernan; music, David Raskin; music director, Morris Stoloff; assistant director, Abby Berlin; sound, Lambert Day; camera, Philip Tannura; editor, Al Clark.

Linda Darnell (Nancy Johnson); Edgar Buchanan (Judge Malloy); Michael Duane (Tom Adams); Sara Allgood (Mrs. Barton); Glenda Farrell (Billie LaRue); Leslie Brooks (Gwen); Doris Dudley (Winnie); Margaret Hamilton (Dora); Constance Worth (Elsie); Rosemary DeCamp (Mrs. Salde); Sheldon Leonard (Monk LaRue); Joseph Crehan (Father Burns); Clyde Fillmore (Malloy, Head of the Prison Board); and: Oscar O'Shea.

One aspect of the prison drama that has received scant attention from scenarists is how do the wives and loved ones of prisoners survive while their men are serving out their sentences. *City Without Men* deals with this subject. Unfortunately, the programmer lacked the originality of execution to match its creative topic.

Boat pilot Tom Adams (Michael Duane), on hand to guide an incoming vessel to berth, notices the S.S. *Hanseatic* discharging two Japanese men into a row boat. Adams later rescues them. They, in turn, force him to outmaneuver a pursuing Coast Guard cutter. However, Adams's craft is soon captured. At his trial, he is accused of attempting to smuggle in aliens, especially after the prosecutor establishes that the *Hanseatic* was sunk a year ago. Nancy Johnson (Linda Darnell), Tom's fiancée, follows him to the prison town where she rents a room in a boarding house run by Mrs. Barton (Sara Allgood), whose late husband was a lifer. Other boarders at Mrs. Barton's are Billie LaRue (Glenda Farrell), Gwen (Leslie Brooks), Winnie (Doris Dudley) and Elsie (Constance Worth). Nancy hires Judge Malloy (Edgar Buchanan), a tippling lawyer and the brother of the head of the prison board (Clyde Fillmore), to work on Tom's behalf. Meanwhile, with the advent of Pearl Harbor, Tom and many of the convicts sign a petition asking permission to join the military service. Their request is denied. Several of the convicts' wives plan a prison break, their ploy dependent on Tom's skill at piloting a boat. Nancy discovers their scheme and also learns from the newspapers that there has been a Japanese ship masquerading as the *Hanseatic*. She convinces Judge Malloy to plead the new facts in Tom's case to his brother and the prison board. Malloy delivers a telling defense which impresses the board. Tom learns of his release before the prison break can occur. He and Nancy are reunited.

"[T]he action is slow-moving, the surroundings sordid, and the doings of some of the characters, demoralizing. In spite of the sympathy one feels for the hero ... and for the heroine ... it is not enough to hold one's attention" *(Harrison's Reports)*.

To be noted is that the script was by Budd Schulberg, author of the Hollywood novel *What Makes Sammy Run?* and several screenplays (including *On the Waterfront*, 1954, *The Harder They Fall*, 1956, and *A Face in the Crowd*, 1957). Schulberg's father, B. P., the producer of this double-bill item, had once been the general manager of Paramount Pictures. This was the first loan-out assignment for beautiful Linda Darnell, then a 20th Century–Fox contract star.

58. *The Concrete Jungle* (Pentagon, 1982), color, 99 min.

Executive producers, Jay Schultz, Richard D. Reinberg; producer, Billy Fine; director, Tom DeSimone; screenplay, Alan J. Adler; additional dialogue, Jack Cummins; wardrobe, Sandi Love; makeup, Anne Aulenta-Spira, Lora Bean; music/music director, Joe Conlan; music consultants, Bob Reno, Stephen Matz; music editor, Dino Moriana; assistant directors, Cummins, Nancy King, David Watkinson; stunt coordinator, Alex Plasschaert; sound, Don Sanders; sound re-recording, George R. West, Mel Metcalf, David Hudson; supervising sound editor, Richard Raderman; camera, Andrew W. Friend; editor, Nina Di Marco.

Jill St. John (Warden Fletcher); Tracy Bregman (Elizabeth Demming); Barbara Luna (Cat); June Barrett (Icy); Peter Brown (Danny); Aimee Eccles (Spider); Sondra Currie (Katherine); Susan Meschner (Breaker); Robert Miano (Stone); Niki Dantine (Margo); Nita Talbot (Shelly Meyers); Marcia Karr (Marcy); Sally Julian (Sweets); Justine Lenore (Max); Kendal Kaldwell (Eyes); Carol Ita White (Cheeks); Maria Caso (Blimp); Cynthia Grant (Bill); Karole Le Man (Odette); Camille Keaton (Rita); Mae E. Campbell (Drums); Brianna Clark (Dana); Kimberly Binion (Sister); Millie Baron (Mom); Chris De Rose (Chris); Greg Finley (Detective Parelli); Robert de Simone (Parelli's Assistant); Patrice Bousson (Nurse Miles); Betty Bridges (Officer Pierce); Linda Alznauer (Desk Officer); Angleine Butler (Matron); Joel Redlin (Dr. Zeitlin); Ron Shotola (1st Detective); Debra Louise Morris (Annie); Mary Cowan (2nd Detective); Tiana Pierce (Guard); Greta Blackburn (Lady in Bar); Shanit Keter (Prisoner); Karen Shepard (Kung Fu); Linda Arocha (Officer Wood); Carol Connors (Carol Davies).

The ad campaign for this feature boasted, "Welcome To This Sadistic, Depraved Female Penitentiary." However, Linda Gross *(Los Angeles Times)* was aggravated by her "visit" to this onscreen prison. "This is an exploitation movie of the worst kind because it wallows in sadism, suffering, dominance, drug abuse, degradation and survival by dehumanization.... [It] offers in one terrible package every cliché situation and character and every atrocity that every other prison movie has had." Gross did admit, "What stands out in this film is the ensemble acting, generally of a high caliber."

Danny (Peter Brown) sets up his girlfriend Elizabeth Demming (Tracy Bregman) as an unwitting cocaine courier. She is arrested, and while still believing that Danny will help her out of this scrape, she is sentenced to the Women's Correctional Institution. She quickly discovers that Warden Fletcher (Jill St. John) is a stern taskmaster, and that tough convict Cat (Barbara Luna) not only rules the dormitory with an iron fist, but she has a yen for Elizabeth. Frightened about survival, Elizabeth is a silent observer of the corruption and brutality within the prison system, and even says nothing when she witnesses Cat murdering another prisoner, Margo (Niki Dantine). Meanwhile, Shelly Meyers (Nita Talbot), a crusading administrator, is gathering evidence against Fletcher's nefarious practices. Elizabeth is ordered to solitary confinement when she fights off Cat's henchwomen, and upon returning to the dorm, the women belittle her about Danny's failure to help her. Angered, she gets into another scuffle and this time is sentenced to the hole where she is raped by a guard (Robert Miano), beaten, and almost starved. Eventually, Meyers rescues her and she is placed in the infirmary, where her inmate friend Katherine (Sondra Currie) is recovering from a forced drug overdose. Overwhelmed with anger, Elizabeth confronts Cat and, in their fight, Cat is electrocuted. Fletcher now offers Elizabeth a deal, but instead she goes to Meyers who gains her release in exchange for incriminating evidence against Fletcher and Danny.

Janet Maslin *(New York Times)* judged that this sexploitation feature "Starts off tawdrily and stays that way which gives it a certain cheap momentum, if nothing else." The bemused Maslin also noted, "Never mind the drug operation [within the storyline] — somebody is supplying these inmates with illicit designer jeans." Paul Taylor (British *Monthly Film Bulletin*) decided *The Concrete Jungle* has "neither the zappy energy of the New World [Pictures] cycle of women's prison pics nor the reformist impulse of the docu-drama exposé. Only the most easily pleased voyeur is likely to derive any satisfaction from the sex or sadism reticently represented here; anyone else will be stifling guffaws over the incompetently arty setups with which the affair is peppered."

The following year producer Billy Fine would package *Chained Heat*, q.v., another violent sexploitation drama set in a horrible women's prison.

59. *Condemned* (United Artists, 1929), 91 min. (Also silent version.)

Producer, Samuel Goldwyn; director, Wesley Ruggles; suggested by the book *Condemned to Devil's Island* by Mrs. Blair Niles; screenplay, Sidney Howard; set designer, William Cameron Menzies; song, Jack Meskill and Pete Wendling; dialogue director, Dudley Digges; camera, George Barnes, Gregg Toland; editor, Stuart Heisler.

Ronald Colman (Michel Oban); Ann Harding (Mme. Vidal); Dudley Digges (Warden Jean Vidal); Louis Wolheim (Jacques Duval); William Elmer (Pierre); William Vaughn (Vidal's Orderly); Albert Kingsley (Felix); Henry Ginsberg, Bud Somners, Stephen Selznick, Baldy Biddle, John George, Arturo Kobe, Emil Schwartz, John Schwartz (Inmates); Constantine Romanoff (Brute Convict).

Moviegoers' intrigue with the mystique of the French Foreign Legion is only matched by a similar fascination with the French penal colony in South America known as Devil's Island. This dreaded prison isle has been the setting for an assortment of action pictures (*Escape from Devil's Island*, 1935, *Devil's Island*, 1940, *I Escaped from Devil's Island*, 1973, and *Papillon*, 1973, qq.v.). All of these movies deal with the exploitation and brutalization of convicts and the men's passionate dream to find a way — no matter how dangerous or foolhardy — to escape their tormentors. In *Condemned*, an early sound feature (also released in a silent version), producer Samuel Goldwyn went one step further; he introduced blatant romance into the setting, and to play the lead he assigned his debonair contract star, Ronald Colman. What emerged was an unbelievable melodrama, full of posturing and drawing room artifice, which neither gave a realistic picture of the penal colony nor delved into the psyche of its inhabitants: the keepers, the keepers' families, and the prisoners.

Michel Oban (Ronald Colman), a dapper young bank robber from Paris, and

Jacques Duval (Louis Wolheim) a hardened murderer, are among the prisoners being transported to the dreaded Devil's Island. The reckless, gallant Michel is
unfearful about his future, even when he encounters Jean Vidal (Dudley Digges)
the harsh warden of the compound. The latter enunciates the rules to the
newcomers:

> You will be expected to learn the regulations. You will be severely punished if
> you don't obey them. You have come here filled with ideas of escape. You have
> heard that prisoners here are loosely guarded. That is because this prison lies between
> the jungle and the sea. The jungle is filled with fever and the sea with sharks. There
> is *no* escape from Devil's Island.

It develops that the warden's young wife, Madame Vidal (Ann Harding) is in
need of a domestic helper. Her gruff, authoritarian husband suggests/demands
that she use a convict as a household laborer. The gentle lady replies, "I'm afraid
of your convicts." (One wonders what strange, deep-seated [sub]conscious factors
led this refined woman of breeding to wed this unfeeling elder man and to be exiled
to an isolated existence on a tropical penal isle.)

Eventually, suave Michel comes to work for Madame Vidal and, before long,
the town is gossiping about the suspected relationship between the two. When
Vidal becomes aware of the situation, he confronts both his wife and Michel with
his accusations. She insists that Michel is innocent of any improprieties. The enraged
Vidal orders Michel sent to solitary confinement on the island of St. Joseph. When
Vidal intends to ship his wife back to France, she gets word to Michel, through
Jacques, and they plan an escape together. At the last minute, Vidal shows up at
the steamer, but he is later drowned at the hands of the helpful Jacques who is
himself shot. (As Jacques dies, he urges Michel, "Live respectable. Live respectable.") The gentlemanly Michel surrenders to authorities, but announces his undying love for Madame Vidal. ("We both have got to serve out time. Square with
the law. It won't take long. We'll both still be young. Will you wait for me? . . .
I'll live respectable. . . .") Once he completes his sentence, they are reunited in
France.

Based on a 1928 book, *Condemned* received a great ballyhoo premiere from
the Samuel Goldwyn film factory, opening at Times Square's Selwyn Theatre with
a $2.00 admission tag and a two-a-day-showing policy, including an intermission.
Nevertheless, this very artificial film impressed the *New York Times*'s Mordaunt
Hall, who reported, "It is a talking picture in which every advantage has been taken
of cinematic values." He also noted, "the types selected for some of the prisoners
are almost apt to make one shudder because of their emaciated conditions. There
are men who are but skin and bones." He concluded his (over)laudatory review
with, "It is a melodrama, this *Condemned,* but . . . it would be difficult to think
of another film of its kind that has been produced anything like as well." On the
other hand, *Variety* was far more realistic when it judged, "Film has too many false
notes to make it a standout effort." The trade paper cited many instances of incongruous behavior/dialogue within *Condemned,* including the fact that in the
climax aboard the steamer Michel "repeatedly returns for a last caress [of Madame
Vidal] with pursuers milling all around him. They [the audience] can't and won't
stomach overly sweet love scenes in dialog." A. Scott Berg noted in *Goldwyn*
(1989), "This simplistic melodrama offered little more than a chance for Colman

to display a broader acting range than he had previously shown ... [to make] his character as attractive as possible, several pieces of comedic business were tossed into the production." *Condemned*, according to Berg "netted the Goldwyn Company almost $350,000."

60. *Condemned Women* (RKO, 1938), 77 min.

Producer, Robert F. Sisk; director, Lew Landers; story/screenplay, Lionel Houser; art directors, Van Nest Polglase, Feild M. Gray; music director, Roy Webb; sound, Earl A. Wolcott; montage, Douglas Travers; camera, Nicholas Musuraca; editor, Desmond Marquette.

Sally Eilers (Linda Wilson); Louis Hayward (Dr. Phillip Duncan); Anne Shirley (Millie Anson); Esther Dale (Head Matron Clara Glover); Lee Patrick (Big Annie Barry); Leona Roberts (Kate); George Irving (Warden Edmund Miller); Richard Bond (David); Netta Packer (Sarah); Rita LaRoy (Cora); Florence Lake (Prisoner); Jack Carson, Edmund Cobb (Detectives); Dorothy Adams (Nurse); Edythe Elliott (Dr. Barnes); John Marston (Defense Attorney); Hooper Atchley (Prosecutor); Paul Stanton (Judge); Vivien Oakland (Mrs. Walter Hempstead); Kathryn Sheldon (Matron).

This modest RKO programmer, with its depiction of the brutality and life-deadening regimen of a women's prison was one of the more resilient prison dramas of the 1930s. It also foreshadowed *Caged* (1950), q.v. In fact, actress Lee Patrick who plays Big Annie Barry in *Condemned Women* would return to the genre in *Caged* to handle a similar role as another tough convict. Not to be overlooked in *Condemned Women* is Esther Dale's sinister performance as Head Matron Clara Glover, a seemingly kind-hearted older woman who is actually a dedicated tyrant with no conception of humanity. As in most such genre pieces, (impassioned and or gratuitous) pleas for prison reforms were woven into the narrative. However, in *Condemned Women* it was handled skillfully. To its credit, this motion picture had many sharp observations to make about the psychological effects of incarceration, and not all of them were negative. For example, one wise convict reflects to another about life on the outside: "Sometimes you can run into as much tough luck out there as you can in here. You got food, ain't you? And a place to sleep? And somebody to talk to?"

If one can find fault with this prison drama, it was that the distaff prisoners often looked as if they had just stepped from a beauty shop (despite their drab garb) and that Louis Hayward was too genteel and naïve in his characterization as the romantic lead.

Millie Anson (Anne Shirley), who is taking the blame for an embezzlement charge committed by her law student boyfriend David (Richard Bond) is among the boat passengers heading to the State Penal Institution for Women. Also aboard is Linda Wilson (Sally Eilers), a distraught convict-to-be, who attempts to jump overboard but who is saved by Dr. Phillip Duncan (Louis Hayward) a young psychiatrist headed to join the prison staff.

Once at the prison, no-nonsense head matron Clara Glover (Esther Dale) asserts her authority over the newcomers, issuing commands and making snap judgments. Even after years of penal work, she has no real comprehension of her charges, let alone the psychological makeup of a woman. For this spinster dictator, it is still an amazing fact that "Ninety-nine percent of the women in here are here because of some man, and still they want to keep their pictures."

Millie, serving three years behind bars, is assigned to a cell with Big Annie Barry (Lee Patrick) and Linda as her roommates. The wisecracking Linda is very curious:

BIG ANNIE: What you in for?

LINDA: I needed a rest.

When Big Annie notices Linda is still coveting her cosmetics, she advises: "You can put that stuff in storage. What's the use of making yourself beautiful, when there's no one to see you? It's strictly a hen party." The pessimistic Linda has her own viewpoint about life and the opposite sex. "There are two times you oughtn't to believe a man: daytime and nighttime."

Warden Edmund Miller (George Irving), a gentle administrator with good intentions, but a man overwhelmed with responsibilities, has very contrasting views of rehabilitation than does starchy Matron Glover.

WARDEN: Of course, they're here to be punished. They come here bitter, but we're better off if we don't send them out the same way.

GLOVER: Twenty years ago, we didn't worry about how prisoners felt when they went out.

WARDEN: You're right. But if we had the same women here today in these modern prisons, we'd have less worry.

GLOVER: You're not trying to tell me women are different now.

WARDEN: They *are*. Full of tensions and nerves they never used to have. It's a hundred times harder for a woman to stand imprisonment than it used to be. We must make changes to meet that."

As time passes, Big Annie, who is already making plans to "lam" out of jail, takes a dislike to Linda and to show her contempt sabotages the latter's sewing machine in the vocation plant and causes Linda to lose two weeks of good behavior time. Millie learns first hand the stigma of being a convict, when a visitor (Vivien Oakland) touring the facility turns out to be a woman for whom she once babysat, and not this matron is nervous to even acknowledge she had once known Millie.

The kindly, idealistic Dr. Duncan, whose father was an old friend of the warden, attempts to bring a touch of kindliness and levity to the convicts' lives (he has a lab skeleton he named "Henrietta"). It is Duncan's theory (very advanced for that day) that if the inmates are given psychological testing to learn their personality/vocational dispositions, their prison stays can be far more productive. He meets resistance from Glover, who insists, "We've had three months of these aptitude tests . . . changes of schedule . . . ridiculous! . . ." When Duncan suggests that the scheduling should be changed so prisoners are not locked up from Saturday noon till Monday morning (except for meals), his theories are scoffed at by the administration. When Duncan learns that Linda had been a student nurse (who could not afford her studies and had been arrested for vagrancy and shoplifting), he requisitions her help in the infirmary. She is particularly helpful when there is an outbreak of typhoid among the convicts. Soon she and Duncan are in love and are sharing clandestine meetings in the laboratory and in the boiler room.

An inmate with a heart lesion is pushed to do hard work and dies. Because Glover knew of the person's poor health record, she is brought to task for her complicity in the death. To save her job, Glover tells the warden about Duncan's and Linda's clandestine romance. The warden orders Linda to his office for a chat. Even

Louis Hayward and Sally Eilers in *Condemned Women* (1938).

here, during this very private conversation, a matron closely watches the prisoner, a person granted no privacy. Much like a military officer or parent controlling his charge's fate, the warden informs Linda that she *must* sever her relationship with Duncan. "Scandal will follow you. You've been a convict." Even to this semi-enlightened man, there is no normal future for an ex-prisoner.

Dragged back to stark reality, Linda agrees to go along with Big Annie's jail break. The latter assaults a matron, escapes to the steam room and fills the cell-blocks with smoke. This precipitates a riot, during which Millie and a female doctor (Edythe Elliott) are shot by Big Annie and die. Big Annie and Linda take Glover hostage and force her to drive them out the front gate. But Big Annie's freedom is short-lived for she was wounded during the prison break. No sooner does she reflect, "What a feeling to be able to do anything you want, anything...." then she dies. Linda is later tricked into attending a lecture where Duncan is supposed to be a participant. At her trial, due to Duncan's prompting, the warden comes forth and his testimony provides mitigating circumstances for Linda's action. She is given an added year to her sentence. However, she knows that when she is released, she will be reunited with Duncan who is now on the staff of a metropolitan hospital.

The *New York Times's* B. R. Cristler offered the film a back-handed compliment when he ranked *Condemned Women* as "a first-rate production in the frankly third-rate, or pulp-wood, class. It is one of those dubious achievements of which we can cry 'Well done' to everybody except to the person responsible for doing it at all." *Variety*, for some reason, expected the production should have been more glamorous, more romantic, "Cold, stark and with nary a trace of softness, the picture is of the doubtful kind. Perhaps the studio got all there was out of the kind of story that this is. The settings are not colorful.... It's the usual prison drama, except that the hardened criminals are all women instead of men. Maybe that's a new twist, but it's not very palatable entertainment."

61. *Convicted* (Columbia, 1938), 56 min.

Producer, Kenneth J. Bishop; director, Leon Barsha; based on the story "Face Work" by Cornell Woolrich; screenplay, Edgar Edwards; music director, Morris Stoloff; camera, George Meehan; editor, William Austin.

Charles Quigley (Burns); Rita Hayworth (Jerry Wheeler); Marc Lawrence (Milton Miltis); George McKay (Kane); Doreen MacGregor (Mary Allen); Bill Irving (Cobble-Puss Coley); Eddie Laughton (Berger); Edgar Edwards (Chick Wheeler); Phyllis Clare (Ruby Rose); Bob Rideout (Rocco); Michael Heppell (Pal); Noel Cusack (Aggie); Grant MacDonald (Frankie); Don Douglas (District Attorney).

What does a man do when he is falsely charged with homicide and is locked up in prison? In the case of *Convicted,* he is lucky enough to have shapely Rita Hayworth for a sister. She convinces a detective that her sibling is innocent and together they prove the man's innocence. This was the fifth of six low-budget quickies to star the minor league team of Charles Quigley and Rita Hayworth. *Variety* dismissed it as "Little to recommend it—trite theme and treatment ... so-so performances...."

When her brother Chick Wheeler (Edgar Edwards) is erroneously convicted of a murder charge, his nightclub hoofer sister Jerry (Rita Hayworth) sets out to prove his innocence. She persuades detective Burns (Charles Quigley), the man responsible for the damaging evidence against Chick, that the now-jailed man is not guilty. Together they prove that underworld leader Milton Miltis (Marc Lawrence) is the culprit.

62. *Convicted* (Columbia, 1950), 91 min.

Producer, Jerry Bresler; director, Henry Levin; based on the play *The Criminal Code* by Martin Flavin; screenplay, William Bowers, Fred Niblo, Jr., Seton I. Miller; art director, Carl Anderson; set decorator, James Crowe; makeup, Newt Jones; music, George Duning; music director, Morris Stoloff; assistant director, Frederick Briskin; sound, Lodge Cunningham; camera, Burnett Guffey; editor, Al Clark.

Glenn Ford (Joe Hufford); Broderick Crawford (George Knowland); Millard Mitchell (Malloby); Dorothy Malone (Kay Knowland); Carl Benton Reid (Captain Douglas); Frank Faylen (Ponti); Will Geer (Mapes); Martha Stewart (Bertie Williams); Henry O'Neill (Detective Dorn); Douglas Kennedy (Detective Baley); Ronald Winters (Vernon Bradley); Ed Begley (Mackay); Frank Cady (Eddie); John Doucette (Tex); Ilka Gruning (Martha Lorry); John A. Butler (Curly); Peter Virgo (Luigi); Whit Bissell (Owens); Fred Sears (Fingerprint Man); Fred Graham, Eddie Parker, James Millican, Ray Teal, Robert Malcolm, James Bush, Bill Tannen, Clancy Cooper (Guards); William E. Green (Dr. Masterson); Charles Cane (Sergeant); Wilton Graff (Dr. Agar); Vincent Renno (Freddie); Harry Cording (Brick, 3rd Convict); Griff Barnett (Mr. Hufford); Richard Hale (Judge); William Vedder (Whitey, 2nd Convict); Alphonse Martell (Melreau); Harry Harvey, Marshall Bradford, Bradford Hatten (Patrolmen); Jimmie Dodd (Grant); Benny Burt (Blackie); Thomas Kingston (Conductor); Jay Barney (Nick); Chuck Hamilton, Charles Sherlock (Policemen).

The impressive Broadway penal drama, *The Criminal Code* (1929), had already been transferred to the screen twice: the superior *The Criminal Code*

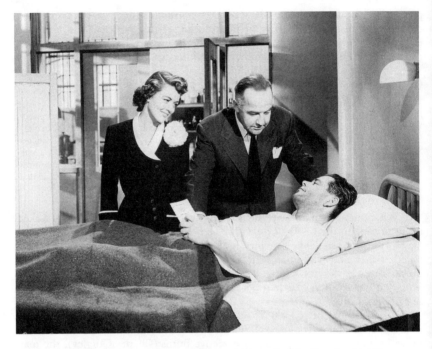

Dorothy Malone, Broderick Crawford and Glenn Ford in *Convicted* (1950).

(1931), q.v., and the less resilient *Penitentiary* (1938), q.v. For its third movie outing, Columbia cast two of its most popular contract leads (Glenn Ford, Broderick Crawford) in the by-now too familiar tale. *Harrison's Reports* rated the results "A fair prison melodrama that rises slightly above the level of program fare.... The fault seems to lie in the incredible plot, which is written loosely and padded considerably. The picture should, however, get by with undiscriminating audiences...."

Stock brokerage worker Joe Hufford (Glenn Ford), an ex–Marine, gets into a barroom scrape which leads to the accidental death of a drunk. Because the dead man had a politician father, the case is well publicized. District Attorney George Knowland (Broderick Crawford) is sympathetic to Joe's plight and even attempts to suggest the legal path his attorney should take at Joe's trial, but the case is bungled. Joe is sentenced to ten years in prison for second degree murder. After serving two years, Joe's parole is denied when the board learns the pedigree of Hufford's victim. Embittered, he joins with his cellmates in an escape plot. However, on the day of the planned break, he learns that his father has died and, in anger, he strikes a guard. He is placed in solitary confinement. Meanwhile, the breakout occurs, but due to the information supplied by a convict stoolie, Ponti (Frank Faylen), the guards are alerted and they shoot the escaping men.

Later, Knowland is appointed the new warden of the prison and one of his first acts is to make Joe his chauffeur. Soon Joe and Knowland's daughter, Kay (Dorothy Malone) fall in love. Meanwhile, Knowland learns of the convicts' emnity to Ponti and to protect him, he puts the man on his staff. On the night before his parole, Joe is a witness to Ponti's murder by another convict, Malloby (Millard Mitchell). Knowland is sure that Joe can identify the killer, but Hufford refuses to violate the criminal code. Joe is placed in solitary confinement where the sadistic chief of guards, Captain Douglas (Carl Benton Reid), tortures him. Malloby learns that a knife has been smuggled to Joe. Fearful that Hufford will ruin his parole by murdering Douglas, Malloby deliberately creates a riot and gets himself placed into solitary with Joe. He gets possession of the knife, publicly admits to having killed Ponti, and then kills Douglas before being mortally wounded himself. Joe gains his freedom. He and Kay are reunited with Knowland's blessing.

Variety was sympathetic to the film's artistic values, "While plotting is essentially a masculine soap opera, scripting supplies plenty of polish and good dialog to see it through and hold the attention."

The ad campaign for *Convicted* insisted "Drama of High Excitement! The code of the convict vs. the code of the law!... A brilliant dramatic triumph for Glenn Ford! Another sensational performance by the Academy Award winning star [Broderick Crawford].... *Willie Stark of All the King's Men!*"

A.k.a.: *One Way Out.*

63. *Convicted* (ABC-TV, May 12, 1986), color, 100 min.

Executive producer, Larry Thompson; producer, Paul Pompian; co-producer, Harriet Brown; director, David Lowell Rich; art director, Jo-Anne Chorney; set decorator, Donna Stamps; costumes, Judie C. Champion; makeup, Kathryn Miles Logan; music, Steve Dorff; sound, John Sutton III; special effects, Ron Trost; camera, Jules Brenner; editors, Argyle Nelson, Barry Gold.

Lindsay Wagner (Martha Forbes); John Larroquette (Douglas Forbes); Carroll O'Connor (Lewis May); Gary Grubbs (Tom Cowan); Jenny Lewis (Shelley Forbes); Gabriel Damon (Joel Forbes); Alyson Craft (Yolanda Forbes); James McEnnan (Lance Forbes); Glenn Morrissey (Klennard Forbes); Charles Bartlett (Porter Forbes);

Patricia Gaul (Norma Forbes); Laurie O'Brien (Audrey Delaney); Caitlin O'Henaey (Carla Larkin); Burton Gilliam (Lieutenant Nance); Paul Comi (Preacher Soames); Peter Jason (Ray Larkin); Clare Halis (Claire); Bert Remsen (Grandfather); and: Nancy Abramson, J. Lee Ballew, Sharon Barr, Stewart Bradley, Josh Cadman, Patrick Culliton, Steven Danton, Michael D'Agosta, Chip Heller, Gloria Hillard, Jeanine Jackson, Christopher Johnson, Barry Laws, Allen Michael Lerner, Michael J. London, Michael Moore, Manny Perry, Peter Rich, Christopher Roberts, Mike Scott, Ronnie Slavis, Tony Swartz, Hank Underwood, Delane Vaughn, Wanda Von Kleist, Grace Weston, Sandy Brown Wyeth, Richard Warlock.

Set in Johnson City, Tennessee, this true-to-life telefeature deals with the account of a respectable mail carrier, Douglas Forbes (John Larroquette) who is wrongly accused of raping two women. As a result of the overzealous prosecutor (Carroll O'Connor), Forbes is sentenced to prison where he undergoes a harrowing, traumatizing set of experiences at the hands of cruel guards and vicious convicts — all the time knowing he has been confined for a crime he did not commit. His loyal wife Martha (Lindsay Wagner) crusades to win his freedom and to keep up her husband's sagging spirits. Even after the real culprit confesses, Douglas's plight is not over. After five years he is finally freed, a nearly broken man. He is awarded $500/month permanent disability for his years behind bars.

Daily Variety noted of this graphic made-for-television movie, "If the first ninety minutes of *Convicted* are marred by an overemphasis on the trauma of the incident, the last thirty minutes are equally marred by a dusting over the scars inflicted by the incident." The trade paper also observed, "Perhaps a less intentional message to the vidpic was that, if prison is such a hell for the falsely accused, perhaps it's also a blot on society's ledger that we tolerate these inhuman conditions for the justifiably convicted." Miles Beller *(Hollywood Reporter)* observed, "Too much message and not enough development make *Convicted* largely ploy and little payoff. Though Lindsay Wagner does have some true moments, there are times she emotes and chokes back so much emotion, one fears she might start hyperventilating."

64. *Convicted: A Mother's Story* (NBC–TV, Feb. 2, 1987), color, 100 min.

Executive producer, Lucy Antek Johnson; producer, Ervin Zavada; director, Richard T. Heffron; story, Elizabeth Gill; teleplay, Ellen Kesend, Katherine Specktor, Gill; production designer, Charles L. Hughes; set decorator, Bill Newman; costumes, Linda Matthew, Bruce Walkup; makeup, John Norin; music, David Shire; sound, Dean Hodges; camera, Steve Larner; editor, Scott C. Eyler.

Ann Jillian (Billie Nickerson); Kiel Martin (Van); Gloria Loring (Janice Huggins); Fred Savage (Matthew Nickerson); Christa Denton (Tiffany Nickerson); Veronica Redd (Odile); Ren Wood (Rayleen); Jenny Gago (Angie); O'Lan Jones (Rhonda); Ray Girardin (Mr. Anderson); Arthur Taxier (Bumgarten); Taliesin Jaffe (Grant); Christian Jacobs (Jeremy); James Handy (Bob Higgins); Frances Bay (Ma Barker); Dana Goldstone (Dana); Lee Kessler (Susan); and: Vivian Bonnell, William Bronder, Lisa Chess, William DeAcutis, Randolph Dreyfuss, Shanee Edward, George Galvan, Sharon Gregg, Ernie Lively, Sandy Martin, John Mahon, Danielle Michonne, Letga Rector, Marji Martin, Ron Soble, Donald Thompson, Ta-Tanisha, Susan Watson.

What might have been a compelling human interest story about the emotional and physical anguish confronting a mother sent to prison emerged a trite TV movie fantasy with too many plot contrivances. Despite the turgid soap opera, Ann Jillian, as the problem-plagued heroine, struggles to surface above the suds.

Billie Nickerson (Ann Jillian), a single mother with two children Matthew (Fred Savage) and Tiffany (Christa Denton), is employed by a taxi company. When her hard-pressed boyfriend, Van (Kiel Martin), pressures her to "borrow" $10,000 from her company she is easily persuaded to do so. After she passes over the stolen funds, he disappears. Shortly thereafter, she is arrested by the police, tried for embezzlement, and sentenced to a prison term. Her sister Janice Higgins (Gloria Loring), already engulfed in her own domestic problems, is forced to take care of her two offspring while game Billie copes with the physical and mental anguish of prison life. In the slammer, Billie must not only deal with the realities of confinement, but she must cope with fellow inmate Angie (Jenny Gago) who rules the convicts.

Even once released, Billie's problems are not solved. There is a question whether she can/will get her children back, for there is a petition that her troublesome son be placed in a foster home. Then her feckless boyfriend reappears, wanting to take up where he and Billie had left off.

Miles Beller *(Hollywood Reporter)* complained, "The movie hopes to break hearts but winds up strangling them. For it's a painfully obvious story, an exercise in mannered down-and-outism, that's about life as lived in TV movies, where strife and despair are never far away and relief is synonymous with The End." *Daily Variety* was equally disappointed with the production. "Telefilm cries out for the touch of Fannie Hurst.... Instead, writers ... have concocted a machine-driven teleplay which begs for melodramatic twists and instead leaves Jillian twisting in the wind in search of substantial script construction."

65. *Convicted Woman* (Columbia, 1940), 65 min.

Producer, Ralph Cohn; associate producer, Wilbur McGaugh; director, Nick Grinde; story, Martin Mooney, Alex Gottlieb; screenplay, Joseph Carole; music, Morris W. Stoloff; camera, Benjamin Kline; editor, James Sweeney.

Rochelle Hudson (Betty Andrews); Frieda Inescort (Mary Ellis); June Lang (Duchess); Lola Lane (Hazel); Glenn Ford (Jim Brent); Iris Meredith (Nita); Lorna Gray (Frankie); Esther Dale (Miss Brackett); William Farnum (Commissioner McNeil); Mary Field (Gracie); Beatrice Blinn (May); June Gittleson (Tubby); Dorothy Appleboy (Daisy); Linda Winters (May); Dorothy Fay (Frances); Marion Pope (Martha); Lucille Raye (Cleo); Evelyn Dockson, Blanche Payson, Marin Sais, Helen Dickson (Matrons); Stanley Andrews (Prosecutor); Bruce Bennett (Reporter); Willis Claire (Floorwalker); Frank Jaquet (Department Store Manager); John Tyrrell (Bart); Ralph Peters (Truck Driver); Nick Copeland (Bus Starter); Walter Sande (Cop); Hal Price (Detective); Roger Haliday (Reporter).

The very contrived, minor *Convicted Woman* was based on a story coauthored by Martin Mooney, a frequent contributor to the prison genre oncamera. Its saccharine presentation was so exaggerated that B. R. Cristler *(New York Times)*, jibed, "Here, at last, is a picture with sufficient courage to come and state flatly what other pictures about women's prisons merely hint at: namely, that the State should provide antique pineapple poster bed . . . a mess-hall like a Madison Avenue tearoom, Thanksgiving and Christmas holidays (on the merit-honor system) and finally an annual spring dance, with a stag line made up of handsome cops and friendly newspaper reporters with dimples."

Young, unemployed Betty Andrews (Rochelle Hudson) is arrested for theft, but she is innocent. Nevertheless, and despite the best efforts of attorney Mary Ellis (Frieda Inescort), Betty is sent to the House of Corrections, a women's reformatory. There conditions are harsh, due to the sternness of administrator Miss Brackett (Esther Dale) and the tight control exerted by inmate Duchess (June Lang) who extorts money from fellow inmates for assorted privileges. Duchess tells Betty that for $50 she can help her escape. Since the newcomer has no funds, she contacts young reporter Jim Brent (Glenn Ford), whom she had met previously, who loans her the money. In payment, Betty provides him with information about the suicide of one of the women prisoners. Later, it proves that Duchess has doublecrossed Betty and her escape plan is foiled. Meanwhile, Jim's story is published and it creates a great public outcry. Miss Brackett is replaced by Mary Ellis as administrator of the Curtiss Home for Girls (as it is now known). Soon the institution has both a new, pleasing physical look, and a policy of tolerance and humanity towards its girls. Betty is one of ten prisoners who is allowed a holiday away from the Home. Duchess plots with Brackett to prevent Betty from returning on schedule. However, Jim rescues her and gets her back on time. At this juncture news comes that Betty's innocence has been proven. She is pardoned and she and Jim continue their romance.

66. *Convict's Code* (Syndicate Pictures, 1930), 65 min.

Director, Harry Revier; story/screenplay, Mabel Z. Carroll, Vincent Valentini; sound, George Luckey, T. Dewhurst; camera, George Peters, Al Harsten.

Cullen Landis (Kenneth Avery); Eloise Taylor (Nan Perry); William Morris

(Theodore Perry); Robert Cummings (Governor Johnson); Lyle Evans (Robert Shannon); Mabel Z. Carroll (Mazie Lawrence); John Irwin (A Lifer); John Burkell (Trustee).

A slapdash, minor effort from the independent Syndicate Pictures, starring silent screen leading man Cullen Landis.

Stockbroker Kenneth Avery (Cullen Landis) is about to be electrocuted for the murder of Mazie Lawrence (Mabel Z. Carroll). His fiancée, Nan Perry (Eloise Taylor) begs the governor (Robert Cummings) for a stay of execution and recites the facts in the case. It seemed that Mazie, a married woman, had taken a liking to Kenneth and lured him to her apartment. Just as he refuses her advances, Nan and attorney Robert Shannon (Lyle Evans) enter the scene. An argument ensues, a shot is fired and Mazie is dead. Nan believes that Kenneth fired the fatal shot and testifies so at his trial. Later, she realizes she may have been wrong. The governor refuses to issue a stay. However, a prison break leads to a riot and the execution is delayed. During the mêlée Shannon, who is on the scene, is wounded. As he dies, he admits to having killed Mazie.

67. *Convicts 4* (Allied Artists, 1962), 105 min.

Producer, A. Ronald Lubin; director, Millard Kaufman; based on the book *Reprieve: The Testament of John Resko* by John Resko; screenplay, Kaufman; art director, Howard Richmond; set decorator, Joseph Kish; wardrobe, Roger J. Weinberg, Wally Harton, Norah Sharpe; makeup, Willie Turner; music/music conductor, Leonard Rosenman; music editor, Eve White; assistant directors, Clark Paylow, Arthur Broidy, Mickey Lewis; technical adviser, Resko; sound, Ralph Butler; special effects, Milt Olsen; camera, Joseph Biroc; editor, George White.

Ben Gazzara (John Resko); Stuart Whitman (Principal Keeper); Ray Walston (Iggy); Vincent Price (Carl Carmer); Rod Steiger (Tiptoes); Broderick Crawford (Warden); Dodie Stevens (Resko's Sister); Jack Kruschen (Resko's Father); Sammy Davis, Jr. (Wino); Naomi Stevens (Resko's Mother); Carmen Phillips (Resko's Wife); Susan Silo (Resko's Daughter); Timothy Carey (Nick Perkoski); Roland LaStarza (Duke); Tom Gilson (Lefty); Arthur Malet (Storekeeper); Lee Krieger (Stanley); Myron Healey (Gunther); Josip Elic (Barber); Jack Albertson (Art Teacher); Robert H. Harris (Commissioner); Andy Albin (Convict); Burt Lange (Gallery Man); John Kellogg, Adam Williams, Robert Christopher, Warren Kemmerling, Kreg Martin, John Close, Billy Varga (Guards); Reggie Nalder (Greer); John Dierkes (Cell Block Guard).

Allied Artists, one of the minor major Hollywood studios, went all out to promote this "prestige" offering. The promotional campaign for *Convicts 4* (initially reviewed as *Reprieve*) promised, "*The Real Story of Killers on Lifers Row.... Cons in Solitary.... Sadistic Guards.... Iron-Fisted Wardens!.... Powerful! Shocking! True!....* Resko's life was counted out by every tick of the prison clock.... He'd given up everything except the hope of *Reprieve!...* Here is the suspense-true story fearlessly told by the man who lived it!"

Based on John Resko's book *Reprieve: The Testament of John Resko* (1956), this black-and-white feature traces the events that led up to his lengthy incarceration for murder. On Christmas Eve, 1930, in New York City during the height of the Depression, John Resko (Ben Gazzara) accidentally kills a storekeeper for attempting to prevent him from taking a $3.95 teddy bear toy for his infant child. As he awaits execution in the electric chair at Sing Sing Prison, his sentence is commuted. He is transferred to Dannemora Prison. Rebellious and surly, he remains a difficult case for both the authorities and his fellow cellmates, which include the jokester/psychotic Iggy (Ray Walston) and Wino (Sammy Davis, Jr.), known as the "Halloween Bandit."

Things do not improve when John learns that his wife (Carmen Phillips) has left him and that his father (Jack Kruschen) has drowned while trying to rescue a child at the beach (an attempt to make amends for his son's crime). There follows for John, two unsuccessful escape attempts ("I want wall to wall freedom") and many long periods in solitary confinement. Then Resko's talent to paint is discovered by the prison's new principal keeper (Stuart Whitman), an enlightened penologist who had dealt with Resko previously at Sing Sing. With prodding (the keeper suggests "Have you ever thought of art as a weapon to get you out of here?"), John finally participates in the prison's art classes, headed by a convict (Jack Albertson). He slowly finds that his drawings/paintings provide him with a therapeutic outlet. ("I took some paints and canvasses and discovered a new world, but I don't know if I belong in it.") This leads to his gradual rehabilitation. When famed art critic Carl Carmer (Vincent Price) happens to visit the prison, he notes John's creative work and later promotes Resko's output to the outside world. Finally, in 1949, after eighteen years in prison, Resko is paroled, thanks to the efforts of the Principal Keeper and Carmer. (Even the widow and two offspring of the man Resko killed signed a petition to have him released.) As he departs Dannemora, he is met by his now-adult daughter (Susan Silo) and his grandchild.

Partially filmed at Folsom Prison, the episodic *Convicts 4* has a tawdry, lean look due to its low production budget. It suffers from an obtrusive quasi-jazz score (by Leonard Rosenman) and a pious, overly reverent tone instilled by Ben Gazzara's self-conscious performance. Obviously, whatever real money was devoted to this film went for its assortment of stars and guest performers, the latter doing some very quirky cameo turns.

There is the paranoid Tiptoes (Rod Steiger), the veteran head keeper at Dannemora Prison. When Resko and the other new convicts arrive at the facility, they are subjected to one of the most bizarre and heavy-handed welcoming speeches in the annals of prison films, heightened by Steiger's blatant overacting:

> There are a few facts I'd like you new fish to understand. You get your keep from the state and I'm your keeper. The state pays me so I'm not interested in philanthropy. I enjoy my work, and I hope you enjoy yours. Now do we understand each other, cause I would not like to create what you would call an "illusion." You see, I used to think I was happy being Officer Good Guy. I attempted to understand every louse that came into the population. I wanted to make life, which is hard enough, easier for all concerned, for which I was rewarded with this. [He points to a scar.] I got knifed in an attempted jail break in 1920. Now wouldn't you think that would sharpen my sense of self-preservation? It did not! In 1926, I was clubbed by a junkie and that was unfortunate for you, because it knocked whatever love I had for my fellow men right out of my head. It was in this painful manner that I learned that the state does not pay me to pamper clowns. Are there any clowns present? Because if there are, I want to tell you what to expect from me. I am *not* friendly. I am *not* sympathetic. I am *not* even neutral....
>
> Now let me tell you what to expect from the state. You get three meals a day. You get ten minutes for breakfast, fifteen minutes for dinner and ten minutes for supper and you get one bath a week that takes five minutes including a shave. Now when I tap with this stick once, that means halt. If I rap twice that means move on. And understand this, moving or standing still, you will, at all times, be lined up, buttoned up and shut up. *At all times!*

THEY'RE LOCKED IN, BUT THEY'RE WAY OUT!

BEN GAZZARA - The Killer was going to bust out or bust!

STUART WHITMAN - The Keeper held the keys to a thousand secrets!

ROD STEIGER - "Mr. Al Capone" trades his tommy gun for a club!

SAMMY DAVIS, JR. matches his great portrayal in "Sergeants 3"!

They'll blow every fuse in the Big House!

Iggy dug a 400 ft. tunnel, but ended up at the warden's feet!

CONVICTS 4

STARRING BEN GAZZARA · STUART WHITMAN · RAY WALSTON

GUEST STARS VINCENT PRICE · ROD STEIGER · BRODERICK CRAWFORD · DODIE STEVENS · JACK KRUSCHEN

AND SAMMY DAVIS, JR.

Written for the screen and Directed by MILLARD KAUFMAN · A. RONALD LUBIN · Based on "Reprieve" the Autobiography of JOHN RESKO · A KAUFMAN-LUBIN Production · An ALLIED ARTISTS Picture

No sooner has Tiptoes disappeared from the storyline than the gruff, overweight warden (Broderick Crawford) of Dannemora Prison comes charging into view. Bearing down on the gentle, sympathetic Principal Keeper, he barks:

> I know your type. You want to change things, make a difference. You want to rehabilitate this dogmeat with painting, writing, carpentry. You're spitting in the face of a penal system that's worked for two hundred years.

The warden dismisses the Principal Keeper's efforts at rehabilitation as "artsy craftsy" and growls, "I'm getting a little old and you're a little long on ambition." With that he vanishes from the proceedings.

Later in *Convicts 4,* Sammy Davis, Jr. waltzes on, à la Las Vegas stage show style, as a flashy criminal from Harlem who has vented his hatred for discrimination and poverty by turning to a life of robbery. ("I'm a walking razor blade.") Vincent Price, a real life art connoisseur is authoritative as the denizen of the art world, but he parades through his brief sequences as if quite anxious to be elsewhere.

A. H. Weiler (*New York Times*) warned, "the producers have only skimmed the surface of a rare and inspiring case history.... [It] is only rarely compelling or memorable.... The excitement and drive of the truth inherent in the career of a strange, exceptional and gifted man only rarely emerge from this dramatization." On the other hand, he noted approvingly, "Since truth is the basis for *Convicts 4,* it is hardly surprising that the drama ... is not made of the pyrotechnics usually associated with prison pictures." *Variety* observed, "Ben Gazzara's delineation of the title character is firm, persuasive and sympathetic, but his success in the role is abbreviated by the lack of character focus and uncompromising honesty...." The trade paper added, "A kind of sub-plot in the film, though not an especially timely one, is the metamorphosis of penal institutions over the two-decade span of the story."

Occasionally within *Convicts 4* there are some intriguing insights into the ways of prison life. As John Resko is awaiting his turn for the electric chair, he discusses this form of death with a death row guard:

> RESKO: In death row I heard guys say the electric chair ain't exactly painless. They say it don't kill you, only stuns. They kill you in the morgue in the autopsy afterwards.
> GUARD: John, believe me it's the most scientific, the most humane [way]. ... You might as well cheer up. Before you know it, your troubles will be over.

The guard then compares the various ways of carrying out the death penalty in other states and countries, offering a provocative commentary on the art of execution.

There is a brief, touching moment within this film when Resko and another convict (Timothy Carey) talk in the exercise yard, finding some privacy on a hillside. "Up here, we got each other, somebody who gives a damn." It says a great deal about convict comradeliness and how isolated they feel from the real world. Then there is the mentally twisted Iggy who has his own philosophy about lawbreakers: "This society we live in has got the criminals it deserves." And there is Resko's

Opposite: Advertisement for *Convicts 4* (1962).

decades-long hope for parole, to be finally free. "I guess I want to be on the other side so much, I don't even care if I go in a box."

A.k.a.: *Reprieve.*

68. *Cool Hand Luke* (Warner Bros.–Seven Arts, 1967), color, 126 min.

Producer, Gordon Carroll; associate producer, Carter DeHaven, Jr.; director, Stuart Rosenberg; based on the novel by Donald Pearce; screenplay, Donn [Donald] Pearce, Frank R. Pierson; art director, Cary Odell; set decorator, Fred Price; costumes, Howard Shoup; makeup, Gordon Bau; music, Lalo Schifrin; assistant director, Hank Moonjean; sound, Larry Jost; camera, Conrad Hall; editor, Sam O'Steen.

Paul Newman (Luke Jackson); George Kennedy (Clarence Dragline); J. D. Cannon (Society Red); Lou Antonio (Koko); Robert Drivas (Loudmouth Steve); Strother Martin (Captain); Jo Van Fleet (Arletta); Clifton James (Carr); Morgan Woodward (Boss Godfrey); Luke Askew (Boss Paul); Marc Cavell (Rabbitt); Richard Davalos (Blind Dick); Robert Donner (Boss Shorty); Warren Finnerty (Tattoo); Dennis Hopper (Babulugats); John McLiam (Boss Kean); Wayne Rogers (Gambler); [Harry] Dean Stanton (Tramp); Charles Tyner (Boss Higgins); Ralph Waite (Alibi); Anthony Zerbe (Dog Boy); Buck Kartalian (Dynamite); Joe Harmon (Girl); James Gammon (Sleepy); Joe Don Baker (Fixer); Donn Pearce (Sailor); Norman Goodwins (Stupid Blondie); Chuck Hicks (Chief); John Pearce (John, Sr.); Eddie Rosson (John, Jr.); Rush Williams (Patrolman); James Jeter (Wickerman); Robert Luster (Jabo); Rance Howard (Sheriff); James Bradley, Jr., Cyril "Chips" Robinson (Black Boys).

Cool Hand Luke is one of the more important feature films of 1960s Hollywood and certainly one of the most popular and well-remembered motion pictures of that decade. Not only is it a resolute study of prison life in the deep South, but it is a film with a strong message. (The script's most oft repeated catchphrase is taken from a pet expression of the prison camp warden, "What we have here is a lack of communciation," and would become part of the American idiom.) With its mythical (almost mystical) folk hero, Cool Hand Luke Jackson, this movie is a resounding plea for the right of individuality in an age when the Establishment and conformity were governing principles.

The same studio's much earlier *I Am a Fugitive from a Chain Gang* (1932), q.v., was a vivid indictment of the road gang penal system in the South. On the other hand, *Cool Hand Luke,* which spares nothing in depicting the harsh treatment of the men, strives to enshrine its focal character as an icon of man's right to be free. In *Cool Hand Luke*, the pitiless, impersonal prison camp organization becomes a symbol of all that is oppressive to man's individuality and self-expression. In doing so, *Cool Hand Luke* sacrifices a degree of realism; but no more so than having handsome box office attraction Paul Newman as the swaggering, good-looking Luke Jackson who cannot help but buck the system and, in the process, dies.

In a small town in the deep South, Luke Jackson (Paul Newman), a former war hero who went through the war as a buck private, is arrested for having removed the heads from parking meters while drunk. For this act of defiance, he is sentenced to two years on the chain gang.

No sooner has the aloof Luke arrived at the Division of Corrections's Road Prison #36 than he encounters the sweet-talking Captain (Strother Martin). This deceptively rigid man informs the strutting Luke: "We got all kinds [here] and you gonna fit in real good.... It's all up to you. I can be a good guy or a real mean son-of-a-bitch. It's all up to you."

Equally direct and autocratic is Carr (Clifton James), the section supervisor of the men in Luke's "dormitory."

> Them clothes got laundry numbers on 'em. You remember your number and always wear 'em.... Any man forgets his number, spends the night in the [sweat]box. These here spoons you keep with ya. Any man who loses his spoon, spends the night in the box. There's no playing grab ass or fightin' in the building. You got a grudge against another man, you fight him Saturday afternoon. Any man caught fighting or playing grab ass, spends the night in the box.
>
> First bell is at five minutes of eight. Last bell is at eight. Anybody not in his bunk at eight spends the night in the box. There's no smokin' in the prone position in bed. You smoke, you must have both legs over the side of your bunk. Any man caught smoking in the prone position, spends the night in the box. You get two sheets. Every Saturday you put the clean sheet on the top, the top sheet on the bottom. The bottom sheet you turn into the laundry, boy. Any man turns in the wrong sheet spends the night in the box. No one will sit in the bunks with duty pants on. Any man with duty pants on, sitting on the bunk, spends the night in the box. Any man don't bring back his empty pop bottle spends the night in the box. Any man not allowed talking, [caught talking] spends the night in the box.
>
> You got questions, you come to me. I'm Carr the floor walker. I'm responsible for order here. Any man who don't keep order, spends the night in the box.

The bunkhouse is filled with a diverse group of convicts, of all ages, races, and levels of toughness. Luke happens to be issued the bunk bed above the burly Clarence Dragline (George Kennedy), the latter suspicious of Luke's charming nature. Dragline, the leader of the chain gang men, is convinced the newcomer is a slick con artist with a gift of gab and a too sure hand at cards, who is out to cheat his unsuspecting fellow convicts of their few possessions. This leads to an epic battle one Saturday afternoon between the two men, with the muscular Dragline convinced he can easily beat the glib, slighter-built Luke. As the fight progresses, with the men cheering their favorites and the guards awaiting the outcome with interest, Dragline knows he could easily kill Luke in this hand-to-hand encounter. "Stay down. You're beat," he begs him. But the flinty Luke refuses to yield, "You're goin' to have to kill me." Because Luke refuses to be ground into submission and because Dragline respects this, the two become fast friends. Soon Dragline is the camp's biggest booster of the defiant Luke, the latter gaining his nickname from a card game in which, while bluffing, he says, "Sometimes, nuthin' can be a real cool hand."

One visiting day Luke's ailing mother Arletta (Jo Van Fleet) is brought to the prison camp by her other son John (John Pearce) who is ashamed to have such a nonconformist, law-breaking brother as Luke. She admits she loves Luke best of all, but adds "You've worn the hell out of all of us." She is philosophical about dying, while Luke is equally philosophical about living.

"Things never, just never, the way they seem Arletta. A man's gotta go his own way.... I just can't seem to find no middle of the road." His brother gives Luke his guitar and later Luke entertains the men in the barracks with his "Plastic Jesus" song, an irreverent ditty so typical of his insurgent nature.

Much of the prisoners' lives at the camp is spent working on the road gang, where "the Man" (the guards) is always watching their every move, rifle in readiness. (The chief symbol of this authority is Boss Godfrey [Morgan Woodward] a cracker-jack shot who wears mirrored sunglasses, does his job, says nothing, but is *always* watching.) It is not long before the rambunctious Luke toys with "the Man" by suddenly going into overdrive speed working on the road, with his loyal followers taking his lead and doubling the pace of their working. Luke's reckless defiance amuses his admiring co-prisoners, but it baffles and frightens the disciplinarian guards. By his deeds and his statements ("Calling it your job, don't make it right boss") he is always questioning their authority. Later in the bunkhouse, there is the big egg-eating contest where Luke's capacity and endurance earns him near folk legend status.

When word comes through that Luke's mother has died of consumption, the Captain has Luke put in the sweatbox, just to insure the convict does not "get rabbit in his blood" and decide to head off to his mother's funeral. Having been so emotionally as well as physically cramped by the torture, Luke is bound to rebel. It is only a matter of time before he escapes, with the camp guards in hot pursuit along with their eager bloodhounds. Luke is brought back in ankle chains and is beaten. The patronizing Captain, who feigns abhorrence of punishing his charges ("I don't like it any more than you men") has chains put on Luke's legs, telling him that discipline will make a better man of him. The still jaunty, undaunted Luke replies "I wish you'd stop being so good to me." Luke escapes again, and is caught again, this time he is shackled with two sets of chains. By now, Luke is a camp hero, but the price of living up to this reputation is an emotional drain on him. (He tells his co-convicts, "Get onto yourselves. Stop feedin' off me!") The sadistic authorities are extremely anxious to break Luke, to set the example for any others who even think of being disobedient nonconformists. Luke is physically punished with brutal work loads on the road gang and the pressure causes even the god-like Luke to nearly break. He begs his tormentors for mercy. "Oh God. I pray to god you don't hit me anymore. I'll do anything you say, but don't hit me anymore."

By this juncture it seems Luke has been broken, that he has become a docile, fetching toady for the prison guards. He is an embarrassment to his followers, especially the bewildered Dragline who feels Luke has betrayed them all by breaking the myth built up around him. Then one day, while out on the gang, Luke steals a camp dump truck, and with Dragline along for the ride, they make their break for freedom. This leads to a very revealing interchange between the two. The jubilant Dragline, with his hero now restored, brags of his friend, "You are *an* original. That's what you are." He lauds Luke for his crafty, well-developed escape plan. Luke bursts his bubble by admitting, "I never planned anything in my life."

Soon Luke and Dragline are only half-a-step ahead of the law. Luke insists the two go their separate ways to better their chances. This frightens Dragline. That evening Luke is drawn to an empty church where he embarks on a confession to God, "I started out pretty strong and fast, but then it got me. . . . Guess I'm pretty tough to deal with. A hard case. Guess I've got to find my own way."

Next the unimaginative Dragline has been caught by the camp authorities and is forced to lead them to Luke at the church. Dragline begs his friend, "All you got to do is give up nice and quiet. Play it cool." But the defiant Luke refuses to be cowed, even in this desperate situation. He remains his own man till the end, and is shot dead by the guards. Dragline goes berserk and attacks the boss man, but is beaten into submission. Dazed, but pleased to have his (dead) hero figure intact, he is soon back on the chain gang telling the other convicts, "Old Luke. He was some boy!"

In analyzing this major film, *Variety* quickly acknowledged that this was another of Paul Newman's "loner" roles (e.g. *The Hustler,* 1961, *Hud,* 1963), that "Newman pix usually do well" and that the production values were "firstrate." The trade paper decided "Versatile & competent cast maintains interest throughout rambling exposition to a downbeat climax." While admitting that the film's theme of rebellion was "commercial," the paper added, "The unsatisfying aspect of such protests is that all the fury goes into the acts of protest, after which the rebels succumb to, or are subdued by, the particular Establishment. Goals represent wasted effort." In reassessing *Cool Hand Luke* from the perspective of time, David Zinman in *Fifty Grand Movies of the 1960s and 1970s* (1986) observed, "despite all ... [its] professionalism, the film fell short of the mark. It had many virtues—it was gripping, lyrical, tragic, and humorous all at once—and it was an ambitious venture. But its hero was not a major one because he lacked a cause." On the other hand, Zinman admitted, "What makes it appealing to so many moviegoers is that its storyline exists on several levels." He added, "*Cool Hand Luke* is a moving story.... All the while, we see visions of sensual, earthy beauty ... and the soft, mellow colors and slow, twangy accents ring true."

Much of the outdoor scenes of *Cool Hand Luke* were filmed in the San Joaquin River Delta near Stockton, California, used to represent the deep South. The picture was produced by actor Jack Lemmon's Jalem Company. Donn [Donald] Pearce, who co-scripted the movie based on his 1965 novel, appears briefly in the film as "Sailor." Originally, Bette Davis was wanted for the role of Newman's mother. However, she rejected the cameo part, insisting her presence would distract from the film's balance. *Cool Hand Luke* earned $7,300,000 in domestic film rentals paid to the distributor. It won an Academy Award for Best Supporting Actor (George Kennedy). It was nominated for three other Oscars: Best Actor (Paul Newman), Best Screenplay-Based on Material from Another Medium, and Best Original Music Score.

69. *Crime of Innocence* (NBC–TV, Oct. 27, 1985), color, 100 min.

Executive producer, Don Ohlmeyer; co-executive producers, Karen Danaher, Paul Radin; co-producers, Michael Berk, Douglas N. Schwartz; associate producer, Christopher Sands; director, Michael Miller; teleplay, Berk, Schwartz; art director, William T. McAllister; set decorator, Dan May; wardrobe, Lynn Bernay; makeup, Kathryn Miles Logan; music, Paul Chihara; assistant director, Mack Bing, Don Eaton; sound, Chris Carpenter; camera, Kees Van Oostrum; editors, Fabien Torjmann, Scott Hancock.

Andy Griffith (Judge Julius Sullivan);

Diane Ladd (Rose Hayward); Steve Inwood (Dennis Specht); Shawnee Smith (Jodi Hayward); Ralph Waite (Frank Hayward); Jordan Charney (Spencer Mulholland); Brent Spiner (Hinnerman); Tammy Lauren (Rene Peterson); Michael Champion (Jailer); Alex McArthur (Cory Yeager); Brian Robbins (Lonnie); Michelle Rogers (Sarah Thompson); Oceana Marr (Mrs. Rodgers); Belita Moreno (Marge Kennedy); Lynne Marta (Lucille); and: Khrystyne Haje, John M. Jackson, Michaelian McNab, Hauanai Minn, Jessica Myerson, Bruce Reed, Steven L. Ross, Megan Wyss.

In the 1980s, Andy Griffith enacted a series of counter-casting TV roles. These roles were designed to show viewers that he could portray more gritty, dimensional characters than the Mayberry, North Carolina, Sheriff Andy Taylor of television's

"The Andy Griffith Show" (1960–68). One of Griffith's most disturbing such characterizations was in *Crime of Innocence* as Julius Sullivan, a juvenile division judge in a southern state. This drama re-emphasized just how much power a member of the judiciary can wield in determining the fate of a minor, since there are no juries in such cases. At the whim of a judge like Sullivan, an underage defendant can find herself relegated to jail and or a reformatory with hardened criminals, where anything can and too frequently does happen. Such an ordeal is the subject of this teleplay.

In a southern town, fifteen-year-old Jodi Hayward (Shawnee Smith), a generally obedient teenager, joins her sixteen-year-old friend Rene Peterson (Tammy Lauren) in a lark. They borrow Rene's boyfriend's car (without his express permission) and go for a drive one evening. Jodi's parents Frank (Ralph Waite) and Rose (Diane Ladd) become concerned when she does not return home on time that evening. They report the matter to the police and are persuaded to list her as a runaway. Having done so, they have temporarily relinquished custody of their child's welfare to law enforcers. Jodi and Rene are stopped by the police and ordered to appear before Judge Julius Sullivan (Andy Griffith) of the Juvenile Division. When the girls appear before him, accompanied by their bewildered parents, the autocratic Sullivan advises the teenagers, "I can put you in jail for anything I decide to." And he does, sentencing them to stay in Millboro County jail until Monday.

Once in lockup, the girls are I.D. photographed and fingerprinted, as if they were common criminals. The antagonistic jailer (Michael Champion) warns them, "In here you do what you're told, when you're told. What you think, don't mean squat." Jodi is shocked to realize that being in jail is no lark.

> JODI: It can't get worse.
>
> JAILER: Yes it can.

His prophecy comes true when narcissistic, young policeman Cory Yeager (Alex McArthur), a one-time jock at the high school Jodi and Rene now attend, takes a special interest in the two attractive girls.

> CORY: I can make your time easy or hard. . . . You're going to like it better easier.

Cory transfers Rene to another cell. He leads Jodi to a private cell where he forces the virgin to have sex with him. The stunned Jodi refuses to talk about the traumatic event.

On Monday, Sullivan visits the jail and because he does not feel the girls are treating the situation properly (they are both hysterically laughing when he arrives; their way of coping with the horror), he places them on probation for six additional days. Ordered to his court again, he warns them that at any time they misbehave, he can and will return them to jail. "You girls are a disgrace and a shame," he insists.

When Jodi confesses to her parents that she has been raped, her father becomes violently upset, demanding revenge on the system and the judge. No matter how Jodi's mother attempts to pacify her daughter ("the nightmares stop when you open your eyes") or her husband, things get worse. Jodi is convinced her father thinks she is trash, while the father feels he has lost grasp of the situation and has failed his daughter. Mr. Hayward hires attorney Dennis Specht (Steve Inwood) to handle the case, and this compassionate lawyer gently leads his young client through the various steps of bringing an action against the tyrannical judge. Tensions mount as Specht gathers evidence to present at the hearing, which necessitates the Haywards reliving the traumatic event. All the while, Jodi feels paranoid about the reaction of family and classmates to this devastating episode and to the fact that her father is holding such tight control over her.

> MR. HAYWARD: Do you want Sullivan to throw you back to jail?.
>
> JODI: What difference does it make. I feel like I'm in jail anyway.

Later, Jodi attempts to explain to her dad why she gave in to Cory without more of a fight. "Have you ever been in jail? You have no idea what it's like. You have to do what they say. I was scared. Oh God, I was so scared!"

At the deposition Sullivan and his attorney do their best to humiliate and discredit Jodi. However, she remains firm, spitting forth, "The only thing I did wrong was stay out all night. But kids shouldn't be put in jail for stuff like that. You [Sullivan] said you wanted to make my cry. You did. Are you happy now?"

Further into the proceedings, the conceited Sullivan trips himself with details about his record of harsh treatment of juveniles, often for no justified reason whatsoever. He admits he had no special training for the juvenile court job, except thirty years of legal practice and raising two kids. "I went to the school of hard knocks." In his tirade he reasons, "Someone has to draw the line and show them that if they cross the line, they have to pay the consequence. . . . They need a strong hand to pull them along the right path. . . . I make kids afraid of me so they don't succumb to peer pressure."

Sullivan has no viable response when Specht asks, "How long do you think they [juveniles] have to stay in jail before they are scarred for life?"

A postscript to the drama states that Jodi's case was settled out of court, Sullivan lost the next election and Cory Yeager received a ten-year jail sentence (but was released after thirty days). After the case, Jodi left Millboro . . . and she still has nightmares.

A more severe than need be *Daily Variety* reviewer decided, "The potential of this film remained locked away, despite some excellent performances, because of a confining script, full of Hollywood heavy-handedness." However, the merit of the telefilm is that its message about the damaging affect of jail to (innocent) teenagers, stays with the viewer.

70. *Crime School* (Warner Bros., 1938), 86 min.

Associate producer, Bryan Foy; director, Lewis Seiler; story, Crane Wilbur; screenplay, Wilbur, Vincent Sherman; art director, Charles Novi; costumes, N'Was McKenzie; music, Max Steiner; orchestrators, Hugo Friedhoffer, George Parish; assistant director, Fred Tyler; dialogue director, Sherman; sound, Francis J. Scheid; camera, Arthur Todd; editor, Terry Morse.

Humphrey Bogart (Mark Braden); Gale Page (Sue Warren); Billy Halop (Frankie Warren); Bobby Jordan (Lester "Squirt" Smith); Huntz Hall (Richard "Goofy" Slade); Leo Gorcey (Charles "Spike" Hawkins); Bernard Punsly (George "Fats" Papadopolos); Gabriel Dell (Timothy "Bugs" Burke); George Offerman, Jr. (Red); Weldon Heyburn (Cooper); Cy Kendall (Superintendent Morgan); Charles Trowbridge (Judge Robert E. Clinton); Milburn Stone (Joe Delaney); Harry

Cording (Guard); Spencer Charters (Old Doctor); Donald Briggs (New Doctor); Frank Jaquet (Commissioner); Helen Mac-Kellar (Mrs. Burke); Al Bridge (Mr. Burke); Sybil Harris (Mrs. Hawkins); Paul Porcasi (Nick Popadopolo); Jack Mower (John Brower); Frank Otto (Junkie the Junkman); Ed Gargan (Officer Hogan); James B. Carson (Schwartz); John Ridgely (Reporter); Harry Cording (Official); Hally Chester (Boy).

As a followup to their impressive screen debut in *Dead End* (1937), Warner Bros. hired "the Dead End Kids" to star in *Crime School*, one of a rash of exposé dramas dealing with the harsh and unfair treatment of juvenile delinquents within reformatories. (Astute filmgoers noted that *Crime School* was a fairly faithful remake of *Mayor of Hell* [1933], q.v., starring James Cagney and Frankie Darro.) Using all the exploitive idioms of the adult prison dramas, these "young convicts" dramas followed a set forumla aimed to win sympathy for the put-upon victims of society who found themselves stuck in reformatories, which were hell-bent on punishing them, *not* rehabitating them. As *Variety* assessed, it is a "tense, melodramatic film with a message of modern penology. It is rough entertainment, sometimes brutal, mostly interesting and exciting, and should do good business where audiences like 'em tough." At this juncture, the Dead End Kids were still a welcome screen novelty and extremely popular. Moreover, for many, it was an interesting change of pace to see perennial screen bad guy Humphrey Bogart in such a do-gooder role.

On the lower east side of Manhattan, a group of mischievous neighborhood youths—Frankie Warren (Billy Halop), Lester "Squirt" Smith (Bobby Jordan), Richard "Goofy" Slade (Huntz Hall), George "Fats" Papadopolos (Bernard Punsly); and Timothy "Bugs" Burke (Gabriel Dell), led by roughneck Charles "Spike" Hawkins (Leo Gorcey)—are involved in selling stolen merchandise to a local fence, Junkie the Junkman (Frank Otto). One night in Junkie's pawn shop, they have an argument and Spike hits him over the head, leading to the gang being brought before Judge Clinton (Charles Trowbridge). Sue (Gale Page), Frankie's sister, begs the judge not to unduly punish these underprivileged youths, insisting about her orphaned brother, "If you send him to reform school, he'll come out hard, mean and bitter." Nevertheless, the six teenagers are ordered to the Cade School for two years.

From the start, things do not auger well at the depressingly stark facility. The fatuous, portly Superintendent Morgan (Cy Kendall) warns the newcomers:

> If you kids behave yourselves, you'll get on all right. Just make up your minds to do what you're told and keep your mouths shut. When you hear the whistle at six in the morning, you'll roll out, make up your beds, get into your school uniforms and leave your own clothes on a neat pile on the cot.

Not only are the youths denied supper (because their train was late), but the hard-hearted Morgan threatens Frankie:

> Don't use that tone with me! You're here because you're petty criminals. But we're going to change all that. Anybody who doesn't like that can apply for a transfer to the penitentiary right now.

To emphasize his point, the bullying Morton slugs Frankie.

The boys are put under the tutelage of Red (George Offerman, Jr.), an old-timer

Harry Cording, Billy Halop, Weldon Heyburn and Cy Kendall in *Crime School* (1938).

who knows the ways and means of surviving the rugged regimen under the corrupt Morgan and his equally ruthless head guard Cooper (Weldon Heyburn). Frankie, rebellious by nature, bridles under Morgan's severe treatment of his charges. When he tries to escape, Morgan whips him. Such corporal punishment fits in with Morgan's theory of teaching "the boys the meaning of law and order."

Meanwhile, Mark Braden (Humphrey Bogart), formerly of the Holloway Settlement House and a zealous social worker, is made the new head commissioner of the territory. He visits the Cade School and suspects a cover-up of the true conditions there. He discovers the strap marks on Frankie's back. Furthermore, he finds that the doctor in charge (Spencer Charters), Morgan's brother-in-law, is a hopeless drunk and that the food served the youths is bilge. Braden fires Morgan and takes charge himself. However, because Cooper puts on a phony act of contrition, he is allowed to remain. As part of his reform program at the School, Braden has the barbed wire fences removed, and adopts a military barracks ambiance at the facility, hoping to instill enthusiasm and pride in the dispirited young inmates. Nevertheless, the cynical, wisecracking youths are suspicious of Braden's real motives. As Spike views it, "Anytime a copper helps you, he's getting something out of it."

Cooper, acting in conjunction with Morgan who still fears an investigation of his past corruptions, works on Spike's suspiciousness to stir up dissent. Cooper, via Spike, convinces Frankie that Braden's romance with Sue is compromising his sister and making a fool of Frankie and the boys. Riled up, Frankie and his pals sneak out of the institution—with Cooper's assistance, which includes a getaway car and a gun—to check up on the situation. Braden alibis for the vanished boys and sets out to convince them he is being fair in all respects. Braden gets his charges back to the School before an investigating committee can verify their absence. As for Morgan, Braden has him arrested for misappropriations of funds. Before Cooper follows his cohort to jail, Braden beats him up. At the finale, the older boys of the group are paroled and sent to trade school, with the younger ones returned to complete their schooling at home. The enthusiastic, if not-so-bright Goofy has his own ambitions and is busily absorbed in reading "How to Break into Society." Braden and Sue pursue their romance.

Even in this period, the subgenre was becoming frozen with contrived, clichéd set pieces. It led Frank S. Nugent (*New York Times*) to observe, "the least effective [segments] are those celebrating warden Bogart's redemption of the junior gunmen, an unconvincing chain of pollyantic. . . ." At least in *Crime School* there is a generous dollop of humorous moments, supplied by the antics of the lovable ruffians, the Dead End Kids.

The Dead End Kids would follow up *Crime School* with another similar study, *Hell's Kitchen* (1939), q.v., also for Warner Bros. Humphrey Bogart, Gale Page and Billy Halop would form a different type of triangle in another genre study from the same studio, *You Can't Get Away with Murder* (1939), q.v.

71. *The Criminal Code* (Columbia, 1931), 96 min.

Producer, Harry Cohn; director, Howard Hawks; based on the play by Martin Flavin; adaptor/additional dialogue, Fred Niblo, Jr., Seton I. Miller; art director, Edward Jewell; sound, Glenn Rominger; camera, Teddy Tetzlaff, James Wong Howe, (uncredited) William O'Connell; editor, Edward Curtis.

Walter Huston (Warden Martin Brady); Phillips Holmes (Robert Graham); Constance Cummings (Mary Brady); Mary Doran (Merwin Fontaine [Gertrude Williams]); DeWitt Jennings (Captain Gleason); John Sheehan (McManus); Boris Karloff (Ned Galloway); Otto Hoffman (Jim Fales); Clark Marshall (Runch); Arthur Hoyt (Leonard Nettleford); Ethel Wales (Katie); John St. Polis (Dr. Rinewulf); Paul Porcasi (Spelvin); James Guilfoyle (Doran); Lee Phelps (Terry Doherty); Hugh Walker (Lew); Jack Vance (Reporter); Andy Devine (Prisoner) and: Nicholas Soussanin.

Two searing stage productions, *The Criminal Code* (1929) and *The Last Mile* (1930), opened within a few months of one another on Broadway. They were both so popular that not only were they each filmed (and later remade) by Hollywood, but they started a fresh wave of screen prison dramas. *The Criminal Code*, starring Arthur Byron, Russell Hardie and Walter Kingsford, ran for 174 performances, giving audiences new (melodramatic) insight into life behind bars where "the criminal code" demands that a convict protect a fellow prisoner. The play's title also referred to the legal set of statutes which sets forth what is right and what is wrong. These two conflicting codes govern the fate of the naïve young hero.

While out celebrating his twentieth birthday, stock brokerage clerk Robert Graham (Phillips Holmes) meets street walker Gertrude Williams (Mary Doran). She takes him to a cafe run by Spelvin (Paul Porcasi). A mug named Parker tries to cut in on Graham while he is dancing with Gertrude. In the course of an argument, Robert hits Parker with a carafe, the man falls, hits his head and dies. Ambitious district attorney Martin Brady (Walter Huston) is in charge of the prosecution. He admits to an associate that if he were handling the defense, he could easily find mitigating circumstances on behalf of the youth. However, the well-publicized episode militates that Brady be ruthless. He tells the bewildered Robert, "Tough luck Bob. That's the way things go sometimes. You've got to take 'em the way it falls." Robert's firm sends their meek corporate counsel (Arthur Hoyt), a man innocent in the ways of criminal law, to discuss matters with the ruthless Brady. The latter insists to the former, "The criminal code is my bible. An eye for an eye.... Somebody's got to pay." As a result of his untutored counsel, Robert ends by pleading guilty to manslaughter and receiving a ten-year sentence in the state prison.

A title card announces "The years go on—drab—empty—hopeless years." Robert's home is cell #170; his cellmates are Jim Fales (Otto Hoffman), a man desperately scheming a breakout, and the forbidding Ned Galloway (Boris Karloff). The latter had previously served eight years of a twenty-year term and was out on parole. One day, he had *one* drink in a bar—which violated the terms of his parole—and he was sent back to prison for twelve years. Galloway vows to revenge himself on the "squealer" who caused this to happen—Captain Gleason (DeWitt Jennings) of the prison's guard staff. The endless, hopeless routine of prison life has badly affected Graham's mental state of being. In despair, he says, "If I could just get one breath of air outside, one good square meal. If I could just see a woman's face again. I dream about these things . . . night after night." Matters get worse for Robert when he receives word that his mother, his one link to the outside, has died. He becomes almost hysterical, but receives no sympathy from the callous Captain Gleason.

Robert has been an inmate for six years when Martin Brady, having lost the political race for the state's governorship, is appointed as the new prison warden. Although this penitentiary is filled with men serving terms for crimes prosecuted by Brady, he remains unfearful. Arriving at his new post, he is greeted by the yard full of convicts "yammering" (muttering repeated "yeahs" loudly), their way of protesting his presence. The unfearful Brady stalks into the exercise yard, cigar in mouth, and stares down the rebellious men. Soon Brady, who has long ago forgotten the Graham case, is brought into contact with Robert, who the facility physician (John St. Polis) insists is having a nervous breakdown. At the doctor's suggestion, Robert is removed from the regimen of working in the prison mill and made the chauffeur to Brady and his attractive daughter Mary (Constance Cummings). Even the doctor is amazed by Robert's recovery. "It's a strange phenomenon. It takes a prison six years to break a man and something mends him in three short months."

As a romance develops between Robert and Mary, he explains to her what prison does to a man:

> Awfully hard to make yourself believe it's worthwhile to try and you've got to do that or otherwise you'll break. They [the convicts] all think they got a rotten deal in there and that's all they talk about. Gets under your skin sometimes and fills you with a bitterness and hate.

Meanwhile, Fales has attempted to escape, but his plan is ruined by a squealer named Runch (Clark Marshall). A deadly silence fills the massive institution of 2,251 convicts, where there is one common thought: to get even with Runch. Gleason explains to Brady about mob control, "No talking, no laughing, that's a bad sign. Of course, I'm not giving them much chance to think it over. The guards have orders to keep 'em moving, but I don't like it." Despite the intensified guard surveillance, the brooding men have their own way of communicating among themselves in the yard (cryptic messages written on the wall, in the dirt, etc.). Brady has put the frightened Runch under special protection, making him a clerk in his office. Galloway warns Robert to "watch your step" and stay out of the brewing trouble. Meanwhile, Runch insists to Robert that he was tricked by the guards into informing on his peers and begs Robert to understand, pointing out the same thing could happen to him. Later, it is Galloway who carries out the execution of Runch.

Because Robert was a witness to the murder but refuses to inform on his fellow convicts, the warden threatens him with solitary confinement ("no ray of light, no human voice, black emptiness, that's all"). However, Robert will not yield, even though this could adversely affect his parole which is due to come through any time now. Once in solitary, the convicts sneak a knife to Robert so he can either kill himself or Gleason—or both. The distraught Mary discusses Graham's fate with her stern father:

> MARY: What good is it to save a man if you destroy him while doing it?... Prisons are full of broken men, broken minds and souls. What good is it to save a man for that when he'd be better dead?
>
> BRADY: The laws must take its course.

The gravely polite Galloway insists to another that "the kid don't take no rap for me." After announcing "I'm going to keep an appointment," he deliberately stages a fight with a guard so he is sent to the dungeon. Once there, he insists, "no rat ever got away from me" and pulls out a pick that has been snuck to him. After confessing publicly that he killed Runch, he engages in a struggle with Gleason. The sadistic keeper is killed while Galloway is himself shot. The bewildered Robert is brought up from the dungeon where Brady tells him his parole has come through. A revitalized Robert tells Mary, "I'm all right. I'm all right now."

This screen adaptation was geared especially to be sympathetic to the plight of prisoners in its exposé of the harsh existence behind bars. The original play was altered to have the hero go free at the end; whereas on stage he is the one who kills the vicious head guard and who, as a result, receives a life sentence. (According to director Howard Hawks he told the play's story to a gathering of convicts who provided him with how they thought the plot should work itself out.) As had been the case with MGM's *The Big House* (1930), q.v., *The Criminal Code* did much to establish requisites for prison stories on screen: the unyielding warden, the brutal guard(s), the comaraderie among the convicts who exist in a twilight zone of a subculture with its own jargon, rules and drab uniforms. Much is made of the endless, boring routine that confronts the convict, who shuffles through his days as a nameless number living in a barred cage. For lower echelon Columbia Pictures, *The Criminal Code* was a major prestige production, which benefitted greatly from having the inestimable Howard Hawks (*The Dawn Patrol*, 1930, *Scarface*, 1932) as director.

While Phillips Holmes (his usual oversensitive self), Walter Huston (his usual overauthoritarian self) and Constance Cummings (in her screen debut) were the official stars of *The Criminal Code*, it was Boris Karloff who proved to be the film's highlight with his quietly menacing performance. He had played the role of Ned Galloway for seven months in the West Coast production of the stage hit and this screen characterization, along with his starring role in *Frankenstein* (1931), did much to consolidate his growing reputation oncamera.

Variety enthused of the production, "Plenty of action all the way, in and out of the prison yard.... Dialog carries no unnecessary frills and has its share of comedy.... [It is] a highly dramatic yarn done by players who can and have been directed to probe for and extract all that it holds." Comparing it to *The Big House,* the trade paper noted, "Some of the prison shots are quite similar ... but on the other hand, also they supply new angles and pieces of business." Somewhat less enthusiastically, Mordaunt Hall *(New York Times)* who focused most of his praise for Walter Huston's performance, reflected, "Granted that Howard Hawks's direction is for the most part intelligent and firm there are occasional sequences which he spoils by extravagant ideas or by leaving too little to the imagination."

The Criminal Code would be remade by Columbia Pictures, to far less results, as *Penitentiary* (1938), q.v. and *Convicted* (1950), q.v. A segment from *The Criminal Code* (featuring Galloway stalking Runch) would be used in Peter Bogdanovich's feature *Targets* (1967), starring Boris Karloff.

72. *The Danger Rider* (Universal, 1928), 60 min.

Director Henry MacRae; story, Wynn James; adaptor/screenplay, Arthur Statter; titles, Harold Tarshis; art director, David S. Garber; camera, Harry Neumann; editor, Gilmore Walker.

Hoot Gibson (Hal Doyle); Eugenia Gilbert (Mollie Dare); Reeves Eason (Tucson Joe); Monty Montague (Scar Bailey); King Zany (Blinky Ben); Frank Beal (Warden Doyle); Milla Davenport (Housekeeper); Bud Osborne (Sheriff).

Popular cowboy star Hoot Gibson provided a pleasing entry with this offbeat, fanciful sagebrush tale. *Variety* approved stating, "Revival in westerns would be assured were they all as good as *The Danger Rider*.... There are some fairly novel angles and a yarn, close knit for a western, that moves at a fast clip."

Hal Doyle (Hoot Gibson), the offspring of a prison warden (Frank Beal), is enamored with attractive Mollie Dare (Eugenia Gilbert) who supervises a reformatory for ex-convicts. To be close to his loved one, he pretends to be Tucson Joe, the infamous outlaw. However, the actual Tucson Joe (Reeves Eason) is inducted into the reformatory and, with the aid of another recalcitrant prisoner (Monty Montague), intends to rob the institution's safe. Doyle prevents the robbery and Tucson Joe is remanded for further punishment. Hal makes his real identity known, and he and Mollie continue their romance.

73. *Dark Holiday* (NBC-TV, May 1, 1989), color, 100 min.

Executive producer, Lou Antonio; producer, Peter Nelson; supervising producers, Pat Finnegan, Bill Finnegan, Sheldon Pinchuk; director, Antonio; based on the book *Never Pass This Way Again* by Gene LePere; teleplay, Rose Leiman Goldenberg; production designer, Richard Sherman; set decorator, Leslie Weir; costumes, Eileen Kennedy; makeup, Lorraine Polak; music, Paul Chihara; music editor, Abby Trelog-gen; assistant directors, Eric Jewett, Tamu Blackwell; stunt coordinator, Fred Lerner; sound, Trevor Black; supervising sound editor, George H. Anderson; camera, Larry Pizer; editor, Gary Griffen.

Lee Remick (Gene LePere); Roy Thinnes (Jimmy); Norma Aleandro (Isha); Shanit Keter (Lufti); Tony Goldwyn (Ken Horton); Suzanne Wouk (Neshe); Jim Antonio (Edwin Gant); Gonca Ondemir (Sara); Sirri

Advertisement for *Dark Holiday* (1989).

Murad (Judge); Pamela Kosh (Connie Devon); John Standing (Charnaud); Kim Lonsdale (Nancy Rust); Anne Marie Gillis (Marie); Ian Abercrombie (Captain); Evangelia Costantakos (Ozgol); Christine Burke (Bea); Yomi Perry (Usemen); Leeza Vinnichenko (German Woman); Vida Ghahremani (Hanifa Hanin); Tracy Kolis (Mother with Baby); Richard Assad (Customs Man); Javad Pishvaie (Court Clerk); Irene Roseen (Travel Agent); Agim Coma (Hotel Clerk); Shaun Toub (Prison Soldier); Avner Garbi (Doctor); Azdine Melitti (Young Soldier); Mary Angela-Shea (Clerk); Reva Rose (American Woman); Apollo Dukakis (Turkish Man); Ray Nazzari (Airport Travel Clerk); Vachik Mangassarian (Customs Chief); Efrat Lavie (Curator); Sharon Barr (Hikmet); Richard Balin (Larry); and: Hildy Brooks, Tuck Milligan.

The advertisement for *Dark Holiday* insisted, "An American in a foreign land. Accused. Imprisoned. There's only one person she can depend on ... herself."

Most every aspect and emotion surrounding the cruel imprisonment of an

American in a stinking Turkish jail was dissected in the superior *Midnight Express* (1978), q.v. Eleven years later, this telefeature aired, based on a true story as recounted in the book *Never Pass This Way Again* (1988) by Gene LePere. It boasted two prime assets. One was the plot twist of an innocent American woman being imprisoned and her circumventing the bureaucratic indifference of her own government to stage her escape. The other was the casting of radiant, talented Lee Remick in the focal acting assignment of a feisty well-bred woman who refused to be cowed by an overwhelming rash of misfortune.

While on a six-week Mediterranean cruise in 1983, American divorcée Gene LePere (Lee Remick), of Mount Hollings, New York, joins the other tourists in exploring the sights of Alanya in Turkey. While off on her own, she purchases three small, seemingly insignificant stone heads from two beggars at an ancient ruin. When she passes through customs to return to her ship, she is stopped. In Turkey it is a criminal offense to "smuggle" antiquities out of the country. (Matters are not helped that her late father had been a wealthy benefactor who endowed an American museum.) Despite her continuing protests of "I am innocent," matters deteriorate. The representative at the American Embassy, Ken Horton (Tony Goldwyn), pompously seeks to pacify her, but he realizes before Gene does, that the Turks intend to make an example of her. He finds an attorney for her, Isha (Norma Aleandro), a very sympathetic lawyer who understands the ways of her country. It soon develops that, despite Gene's innocence, the American embassy will not jeopardize its diplomatic relationship with Turkey by interfering and that the Turkish court is unsympathetic to the defendant's plea of ignorance of the law of the land regarding exporting art objects. While the Turkish court debates what to do, Gene is placed in a dank prison.

Almost immediately this foreigner is engulfed in a maelstrom, not understanding the Turkish ways, let alone the rules for survival in this brutal environment. Lufti (Shanit Keter), a conniving fellow convict who speaks English, attempts to exploit Gene, who, at first, remains passive. As time passes, Gene becomes more incensed at the lack of constructive help from Ken Horton or the usefulness of Edwin Gant (Jim Antonio), an American businessman with supposed influential contacts. She becomes more self-assertive. Isha does the best she can to plead Gene's cause, so that a disposition in the case will occur, but there are countless legal postponements. Growing despondent, Gene hoards the sleeping pills given to prisoners at night, and threatens suicide. She tells Isha, "In the beginning, you wake up every morning and think it must be a dream, but it isn't. It's my real life and I don't want it anymore."

Gene finds renewed inner strength, especially when her ex-husband (Roy Thinnes) flies in to Turkey to see her and to offer his encouragement (although he quickly departs thereafter). Now with a strong will to overcome this nightmare and stirred further by the ineptitudes of the American embassy, Gene announces to Lufti, "I'm not going to die in here. This place is not going to kill me. Nor is the likes of you!" Gene's resiliency again in tact, she develops friends among the inmates as her stay in the dehumanizing fortress continues.

Eventually, the handcuffed Gene is taken to her bail hearing, having been helped by other convicts to freshen her drab appearance. The court allows her to be released on $1,500 bail. Isha suggests that perhaps the court set the bail so low, because they do not know how to deal with the case and are hoping she will escape. Isha also warns Gene that, if found guilty, she could be imprisoned for several years. By now, Gene has fired Gant from her cause. She plans her escape through the airport at Ankora, hoping to bluff her way through customs with her now-returned passport (which has been stamped restricted by the Turkish government). She convinces Horton to provide a small degree of assistance and she boards the plane. It takes off to its German destination. She is, at last, free. A postscript states, "After eight Turkish trials in absentia, Gene LePere was finally judged not guilty."

Daily Variety was unimpressed by the "mechanical adventure." "The drama fusses about her rough time in prison and how she's dragged down by the other inmates into taking her first friend — one of the two women who speak English — on a fight if necessary. . . . Fellow prisoners are surprisingly kind to her. . . . Of course, the women guards stand around looking tough." Miles Beller (*Hollywood Reporter*) rated this "the sort of telefilm that's been done so many times it's wearing thin not just around the edges, but all over. . . . Perhaps there's a built-in audience for this variety of benumbing excursion into genre." Beller also noted, "genre conventions abound, and the movie is sapped by all-too-familiar means used to tell its tale." In the minority was Ray Loynd (*Los Angeles Times*) who felt this entry "brings stature to the lurid genre of the women's prison movie." He championed, "Director Lou Antonio and several Turkish-speaking actresses create broiling prison scenes that suggest festering rats in a nest. Flashes of camaraderie are not sentimental."

Dark Holiday effectively used Roman ruins in Southern France as substitutes for the area where the heroine meets the men selling her the antiquities. Several southern California sites (in Los Angeles, Brentwood, Pasadena and Compton) substituted for other Turkish locations.

74. *Dead Man Out* (HBO–Cable, March 12, 1989), color, 90 min.

Executive producers, Colin Callender, Robert Cooper, David R. Ginsburg; co-executive producer, Michael Cox; co-producers, Forrest Murray, Lorna Soroko; director, Richard Pearce; story, J. D. Maria, Soroko; teleplay, Ron Hutchinson; production designer, Anne Pritchard; set decorator, Gilles Aud; costumes, Francois La Plante; makeup, Louise Mignault; music, Cliff Eidelman; assistant directors, Pierre Houle, Louis Bolduc; stunt coordinator, Ginette D'Amico; sound, Gabor Vadnay; supervising sound editor, Mace Matiosian; camera, Michel Brault; editors, Mia Goldman, Bruce Cannon.

Danny Glover (Dr. Alex Marsh); Ruben Blades (Ben); Larry Block (Kleinfeld); Tom Atkins (Warden); Sam Jackson (Calvin Fredricks); Maria Ricossa (Prison Doctor); Ali Giron (Chairwoman); Sam Stone (Guard Munroe); Val Ford (Security Cage Guard); Jon Cuthbert (Escort Honcho #1); Eric Hoziel (Gate House Guard); Harry Standjofski (Gun Guard Honcho #1); Minor Mustain, Michael Scherer, John Walsh (Extract Team).

Dead Man Out was one of the most publicized of recent prison dramas. It was an original teledrama written for cable television. Despite the project's lofty intentions and gritty reality in presenting ethical dilemmas, "[B]y the telefilm's end, the Philosophy 101 dialogue has given way to a grandly undergraduate gesture of romantic freedom" (Henry Sheehan, *Hollywood Reporter*). From the standpoint of entertainment, Sheehan judged the production a "prison-bound existential talkathon." To some degree, he was correct.

Whatever its structural faults and its theatrical performances (especially by Danny Glover), *Dead Man Out* presents a very provocative genre situation: a man convicted of homicide is on death row; however, he has been displaying psycho-

pathic tendencies and cannot be executed until he is judged sane. The emotional
pressures on the convict and his "judge" (in this case a prison-appointed psychiatrist) form the basis for this strange behind-bars relationship.

Black psychiatrist Dr. Alex Marsh (Danny Glover) has been hired by the
prison to consult on a particularly delicate case. Convicted killer Ben (Ruben
Blades), now on death row for having murdered four people in a diner holdup,
has been behaving strangely. According to the law (as interpreted by the U.S.
Supreme Court in a 1986 ruling), executing an insane prisoner is cruel and unusual
punishment. Marsh's task is to evaluate Ben's "demented" condition. (Due to years
on death row he wavers from periods of near catatonic withdrawal to moments of
outright hysteria.) Thereafter, Marsh must treat the prisoner so that once Ben is
sufficiently mentally healthy, he can be executed.

Marsh, unfamiliar with the peculiar environment of prisons or its dangers, arrives for his first meeting with his patient. He is jolted into reality by the blunt
warden (Tom Atkins) who explains:

> We don't have a hostage policy, which is why we never had a hostage situation
> in this place. But should someone try to make a grab for your ass, this is what hap-
> pens. The gunny [guard] on the rails fires one warning shot, then fires directly into
> the center of the disturbance....

The warden makes no effort to conceal his callous approach to the death
penalty as it affects the men on death row in general or Ben in particular:

> All it takes is twelve seconds to strap them in the chair and thirty seconds after
> the pill drops, nothing is going to bother them anymore.

Marsh's initial visit with Ben quickly convinces him of the complexity of Ben's
mental state and the arduous task ahead to break through this man's psychological
barriers. During Marsh's many return trips, he begins to appreciate the ramifica-
tions of being healer *and* executioner.

Everyone at the prison has a different point of view regarding Ben. The guards
refer to any convict on death row as "dead man walking." On the other hand, Ben's
attorney (Larry Block) who has had contact with his convict client during his many
years of appeals, wonders:

> You tell me how you reach someone who for eight years hasn't been in the
> presence of another human being without iron on his wrists and ankles. You and
> no one here has touched him except with a boot or baton.

As for Ben, a minority product of the slums, his attitude throughout life has
been to avoid taking responsibility for his actions. He is comfortable blaming
others ("the system") for whatever bad luck he has been dealt. He justifies all his
actions with the rationalization "It's the way it goes down." Because he has been
treated badly in prison, he has reacted with violence and bizarre behavior. ("How
else are you going to get noticed?" Ben asks Marsh.) To protect his psyche over the
many years of despair regarding his appeals, he refuses to confront his impending
date with death.

As Marsh's sessions with his patient stabilize the once unhinged man, Ben
shares confidences with his psychiatrist.

> BEN: You think a guy on the [death] row doesn't keep seeing the faces [of his vic-
> tims]? Ain't always hitting replay, which I got out from under, which I put in a box
> somewhere.... I went in mean and I kept getting meaner and no one did it but
> me....

Regarding interpersonal relationships with the men on death row, Ben having witnessed a frightened convict (Sam Jackson) led to the gas chamber asks, "What is the percentage of having lifelong friendships in here?"

As his sanity returns, Ben questions Marsh, "Don't [you] think it's loopy to tell guys like me 'Thou shall not kill' and to rub it in, we'll ice you?"

One of the ironic situations at the prison, where tough reality is such a common stance, is that everyone refers to unpleasant events with euphemisms. Ben calls his pending execution as "the item," the prison authorities reference the matter as "the date."

Time passes and the unfeeling warden pesters Marsh to reach a conclusion, so the matter can be finally settled. As the doctor pushes his patient to take responsibility for the actions of his past and his present, so the convict jibes at his healer to acknowledge his part in bringing about Ben's death. While Marsh has no personal feeling one way or the other regarding the rightness of the death penalty, it is revealed that he has had his own traumatic experience in the past when he took the responsibility for permitting the ending of the cancer-ridden life of a loved one. It had left him an emotional cripple until now.

Finally, it is acknowledged that Ben is mentally competent to face his punishment. One day, while being accompanied from his cell to the visiting room, the chained man makes a break for the yard. He refuses to halt and is shot dead by the tower guards. Marsh has witnessed the events on the monitor and silently acknowledges that Ben has chosen to take control of the end of his life. For the stern warden, the finale is a quick resolution to a bad situation. "Well, he's out of here," is his only comment.

"With a powerful demonstration of existentialism at work, writer Ron Hutchinson has delivered an intense, compact study of two men astride an alien world and facing off. Abetted by a profound underlying irony, *Dead Man Out* pokes around the psyche of a man on death row and of the man bent on relieving his pain. It's a tight look at full-blown incongruity" *(Daily Variety)*. Susan White *(New York Daily News)* decided "Despite the film's emphasis on talk over action, the story is filled with enough suspense to hold almost any viewer's interest." White was especially impressed by the performances of the co-stars in particular that of the Panamanian-born Grammy-winner/singer/actor Ruben Blades. "Glover is very good as the tight-reined psychiatrist, but Blades is truly spectacular as the scarred prisoner.... [When] his naked body lies frail and helpless on the floor of an isolation cell, it's hard to remember that this is an actor, not a real Death Row inmate facing his own execution." Howard Rosenberg *(Los Angeles Times)* weighed, "You may fault its message but not its effectiveness in making you care about its characters or the way it draws you inside their thoughts.... [Director Richard] Pearce artfully conveys the gray, claustrophobic doom of Death Row while expanding on psychological and intellectual levels a movie that probes deeply moral and ethical issues."

Dead Man Out was filmed at Laval and Bordaux prisons in Canada. At the 11th Annual ACE Awards for cable excellence in January 1990, Ruben Blades was named Best Actor in a Drama for his performance in *Dead Men Out*. Blades said that his prior background as a lawyer helped to prepare him for the role. "I was familiar with life in jail." (While writing his thesis for his criminology degree from the University of Panama, he lived on the Panamanian penal island of Coiba, observing the inmates.)

75. *Deathwatch* (Beverly Pictures, 1966), 88 min.

Producers, Leonard Nimoy, Vic Morrow; director, Morrow; based on the play *Haute Surveillance* by Jean Genet; screenplay, Barbara Turner, Morrow; art director, James G. Frieburger; music, Gerald Fried; camera, Vilis Lapenieks; supervising editor, Irving Lerner; editor, Verna Fields.

Leonard Nimoy (Jules LeFranc); Michael Forest (Greeneyes); Paul Mazursky (Maurice); Gavin McLeod (Emil); Robert Ellenstein (Guard).

Co-starring Leonard "Star Trek" Nimoy and directed by actor Vic Morrow, *Deathwatch* is a very arty adaptation of the 1949 Jean Genet French play which, in translated form, appeared on Broadway in 1958 and later in a West Coast presentation. The bulk of the movie, shot for approximately $120,000, is set in a jail cell occupied by three convicts. *Variety* reported of this existential drama, "There is little action in the story which evolves around the development of the three characters—their strong-points and their failings—through a constant stream of dialog, punctuated by facial expressions." Written by a former convict who became a prolific French man of letters, *Deathwatch* had far more success as a stage offering than on the big screen. "This is a slow, static, talky picture, whose protagonists arouse little sympathy or even curiosity. The only interesting thing about it is the losing battle off-screen by a group of plucky young people to make it come alive as a movie" (Howard Thompson, *New York Times*).

Jules LeFranc (Leonard Nimoy), a petty thief who has always felt adrift from and a victim of society, shares a dismal cell in a French prison with Greeneyes (Michael Forest), a notorious killer awaiting the guillotine. The social outcast LeFranc admires the infamous but illiterate Greeneyes, for whom he writes and reads letters. In this manner, LeFranc gains insights into the life of his idol. Meanwhile, a homosexual prisoner, Maurice (Paul Mazursky), is transferred to the cell and he quickly arouses LeFranc's jealousy by pampering the murderer in every possible way. Soon both Jules and Maurice are fierce rivals for Greeneyes's attention, each eager to bask in his identity. To show his "worth," LeFranc strangles Maurice. Instead of winning Greeneyes's admiration, he earns his scorn, for Jules has committed a willful act (instead of one of passion as did Greeneyes). Thus the tormented LeFranc finds himself isolated by the criminal code as an outsider.

Thompson of the *New York Times* concluded, "If Mr. Genet is pointing a finger at a merciless society beyond prison walls, old-hat melodramas like *The Big House* and *The Last Mile* and the powerful, French-made *Night Watch,* have done this before and better."

Even with the use of flashbacks and opening the story up for screen moments in the prison yard, *Deathwatch* remained claustrophobic. To boost its box office appeal, the film was promoted with the campaign "homosexual outlaws on a rampage." It did not help.

To be noted in the case is Paul Mazursky (b. 1930), who later directed such feature films as *Bob and Carol and Ted and Alice* (1979), *An Unmarried Woman* (1978) and *Down and Out in Beverly Hills* (1985). Gavin McLeod went on to co-star in several TV series: "The Mary Tyler Moore Show" (1970–77) and "The Love Boat" (1977–87).

76. *Destroyer* (Moviestore, 1988), color, 94 min.

Executive producer, Joseph Ignat; producers, Peter Garrity, Rex Hauck; director, Robert Kirk; screenplay, Garrity, Hauck; production designer, Paul Staheli; art director, Randy Holland; set decorator, Keith Kalohelant; makeup, Gordy Wein, Sheryl Blume, Judee Guilmette; music, Patrick O'Hearn; assistant directors, Robert King, Greg Babcock; stunt coordinator, Brian D. Veatch; sound, Brent Rogers; special sound effects, Russell Jessum; supervising sound editors, Stacey Foiles, Mike Janescu; special effects, Patrick Ryan Denver, Rex L. Whitney; camera, Chuy Elizondo; second unit camera, Len Aitken; editor, Mark Rosenbaum.

Deborah Foreman (Susan Malone); Clayton Rohner (David Harris); Lyle Alzado (Ivan Moser); Anthony Perkins (Director Edwards); Tobias Andersen (Russell); Lannie Garrett (Sharon Fox); Jim Turner (Rewire); Pat Mahoney (Warden); David Kristin (Fingers); Vanessa Townsell (Bea); Stanley Kirk (Cabbie); Bernie Welch (Officer Callahan); Robert Himber (Len); Eric Meyer (Foley); Kent Hubler (Tommy); Jacqut Claw (Mac); Tim Dornec (Boomer); Margaret Sioberg (Wardrobe Lady); Michael Ford (Actor); Charles Hutchinson, Craig McNeil, Chris Lutz, Dutch Shindler, A. G. Gilliam, John Larsen, Damien Veatch, Joseph Wilkens (Guards); Steve Kelley (Game Show Host); Gary Owens (Game Show Announcer); Cathy Eberhard (Susan Starr); Chuck Henry (Newscaster); Bea Hururty (Woman in Diner); Tom Kanter, Tammy Snyder, Linda Scott, Jay Dee Holland (Film Crew).

Destroyer is among the slew of recent slasher features, more colorful for their special effects than for their slim storylines or surfacy performances. *Destroyer* combines the horror genre with the softcore pornography women-behind-bars motifs, too anxious to be all things to all people: horrific, titillating, and satirical. When released to videocassette in late 1988, Ed Hulse (*Video Review* magazine) weighed it a "cheeky horror-thriller [that] comes as a pleasant if goofy surprise. . . . The tale is told with plenty of deadpan gallows humor, and I can honestly say that former grid star [Lyle] Alzado is, er, electric as the *killer.*"

Ivan Moser (Lyle Alzado), who tortured, raped or killed twenty-four men, women and children is sentenced to die in the electric chair. As this hulking serial killer is being electrocuted, a prison riot occurs with thirteen guards and thirty-seven inmates dead before the uprising is quelled. After that, the prison was closed and now, eighteen months later, film director Edwards (Anthony Perkins) and a crew have arrived to shoot location scenes for a girls-in-prison flick called *Death House Dolls.* The star of the production is curvaceous Sharon Fox (Lannie Garrett). Scriptwriter David Harris (Clayton Rohner) is intrigued by the closed institution and begins investigating that last riot. All this upsets the former Warden (Pat Mahoney) who has returned to his former domain. As the lensing progresses, David's girlfriend Susan Malone (Deborah Foreman), the stuntwoman on this picture, and others of the cast and crew make a frightening discovery—brutish Ivan still haunts the cell blocks with his super-electrically charged body which throws off sizzling rays. It is Susan who proves to be Ivan's most enterprising opponent, managing to re-electrocute him on the cell bars. Meanwhile, among those murdered is the brutal Warden. David, who had been injured falling into the basement sewer hole once constructed as a dungeon containment for Ivan, recuperates at a nearby hospital.

Destroyer is full of all the artifices so favored by the horror genre, including sequences which turn out to be nightmares. In its own absurd way, the picture makes a few telling comments about the thin lines between reality and fantasy, not only in actual life, but in these "real" movies.

Originally, Roddy McDowall was set to have played the film director. It was a shame he did not, as Anthony Perkins appeared most uncomfortable cavorting in this type of low-budget shenanigans.

77. *Devil's Canyon* (RKO, 1953), color, 91 min.

Producer, Edmund Grainger; director, Alfred Werker; story, Bennett R. Cohen, Norton S. Parker; screenplay, Frederick Hazlitt Brennan; adaptor, Harry Essex; art directors, Albert D'Agostino, Jack Okey; set decorators, Darrell Silvera, Jack Mills; makeup, Mel Berns; music, Daniele Amfitheatrof; assistant director, Edward Donahoe; visual consultant, Julien Grinzberg; sound, Earl Wolcott, Clem Portman; camera, Nicholas Musuraca; supervising editor, Frederick Kundston; editor, Gene Palmer.

Virginia Mayo (Abby Nixon); Dale Robertson (Billy Reynolds); Stephen McNally (Jesse Gorman); Arthur Hun-nicutt (Frank Taggert); Robert Keith (Warden Steve Morgan); Jay C. Flippen (Captain Wells); George J. Lewis (Colonel Gomez); Whit Bissell (Virgil Yates); Morris Ankrum (Sheriff); James Bell (Dr. Betts); William Phillips (Red); Earl Holliman (Joe); Irving Bacon (Abby's Guard); Tom Powers (Joe Holbrook); Jim Hayward (Man in Saloon); Fred Coby (Cole Gorman); John Cliff (Bud Gorman); Glenn Strange (Marshall, the Wagon Driver); Murray Alper (Driver-Guard); Harold "Stubby" Kruger (Prisoner); Paul Fix (Gatling Guard); Gregg Martel (Tower Guard); Larry Blake (Hysterical Prisoner).

RKO Pictures was on the fast downhill slide when it produced this economy Western. Sloppily scripted and indifferently acted, the movie boasted an unusual setting for a sagebrush tale — a prison — and it was lensed in the then popular 3-D process. With its rural setting, this tale utilized many of the standard routines and clichéd dialogue interchanges so much a part of the modern penitentiary film. The advertising slogan for *Devil's Canyon* proclaimed, "Like jungle beasts they fight for the love of an Outlaw Queen!" Bosley Crowther (*New York Times*) ranked this picture as "one of those things that come and go."

The preface advises:

> Arizona territory in 1897 was the last of the old frontiers. The story we are about to tell is well known to historians. Names have been changed but the lust and brutality, the love and sacrifice of the people involved remain for the record unchanged. The woman outlaw and her lovers belong now to folklore — in 1897 they lived.

In late nineteenth century Arizona, ex-marshal Billy Reynolds (Dale Robertson) runs afoul of a new territorial law regarding the carrying and use of firearms. He encounters two outlaws, Bud (John Cliff) and Cole Gorman (Fred Coby), who intend to get even with Reynolds for having sent their renegade brother, Jesse (Stephen McNally), to prison. Because he defends himself and kills the two men, Reynolds is sentenced to ten years at hard labor in the territorial prison, an institution reputed for its harsh treatment of inmates.

Warden Steve Morgan (Robert Keith) and his chief guard, Captain Wells (Jay C. Flippen), discuss the state of life at the facility.

WARDEN: I'll bet it's 130° in those cells.

WELLS: Well, anyway it keeps them a little quiet.

WARDEN: Not their minds. You know the feeling of hate is so strong around this place, you could cut it in slices.

WELLS: This always takes care of everything. [He pats a gatling gun.]

WARDEN: [Ominously] So far.

Soon the new inmates, including Reynolds, arrive at the hellhole. Brandishing a club, the warden delivers his "greetings" to the new men.

We had a little trouble here months ago. Some of the boys decided they'd like to get out for a spell and they went to a lot of trouble. Well, they got out all right. They're still outside — in the cemetery. Now if you'd like to know about this prison, it's solid rock. You got the river and quicksand on two sides of you and walls eight feet thick on the other two. We've got a sun here that boils up to 130 in the shade. And if that's not enough to cool your boisterous spirits, we've got solitary cells, plenty of guards and plenty of guns.

Reynolds is placed in a cell with Frank Taggert (Arthur Hunnicutt), Virgil Gates (Whit Bissell) and Colonel Gomez (George J. Lewis). Gates has a fondness for setting fires, which gives his roommates concern. As for the polished Gomez, a cattle rustler who terms himself a "speculator in live stock," he has spent too much time already in this prison cell, an 8' x 7' airless enclosure.

GOMEZ: When the walls start closing in on you, it seems more like 2' x 2'.

REYNOLDS: When they start closing in on me, I'm gonna bust right through.

GOMEZ: You get used to it.

REYNOLDS: Not me. I'll never get used to it.

Before long, the newcomers have taken note that Wells is a very authoritarian man. Wells snarls at the ex-sheriff:

Don't ever sit there and look at me when I tell you to move. . . . [Snapping to orders] that's the way we run things, Reynolds, by jumping when we're told to jump, smiling when we're told to smile, and even giving up our teeth if one of the guards seems to want 'em bad enough.

Taggert, an eccentric critter, has his own philosophy of survival in the new environment, garnered from many past experiences:

I'll be lost in a crowd. It's the only way to get along in any prison. If they can remember your name, they'll always think to call it out if there's any dirty work or any punishment to be given out. You know I've lived through eight prisons and just about the same amount of wives by blending into the background when the noise gets loud.

Before long, the rebellious, individualistic Reynolds, and the taskmaster warden have a meeting, each measuring the other's verve. Reynolds speaks out against the brutal convict treatment at this prison:

HEAT-CRAZED!
HATE-FILLED!

500 desperate men on
the loose with an
Outlaw Queen!

HOWARD HUGHES presents
VIRGINIA MAYO
DALE ROBERTSON
STEPHEN McNALLY
ARTHUR HUNNICUTT
in
DEVIL'S CANYON
Color by TECHNICOLOR
An EDMUND GRAINGER Production

Screenplay by
FREDERICK HAZLITT BRENNAN · Directed by ALFRED WERKER · Produced by EDMUND GRAINGER

Advertisement for *Devil's Canyon* (1953).

WARDEN: Well, I'm not proud of it. But criticizing prison conditions isn't an answer to the question [why the former lawman stubbornly refused to plea bargain for a parole]. . . . Now look Reynolds, there are just two ways for a man like you to go. You can accept your punishment and come back on the right side of the law or you can turn renegade to every decent thing you ever believed in.

Reynolds responds by promising the warden he will break out at the first opportunity.

At the same prison is Reynolds's arch enemy, Jesse Gorman, who shares a cell with Joe (Earl Holliman) and two other underlings. Jesse swears he will get revenge on his brothers' killer. No sooner does one convict leave (killed trying to escape) than a very special new one arrives. It is Abby Nixon (Virginia Mayo), a train robber associate of Jesse whom Reynolds once spared from capture because he was attracted to her. She is so notorious that the court decided to send her to this men's prison, with the warden now forced to make special accommodations for her two-year stay. She is housed in the infirmary and ordered to work out her time assisting the staff physician, Dr. Betts (James Bell). The warden warns the self-sufficient Abby of what to expect here:

WARDEN: These are desperate, dangerous men.

> ABBY: I'll try not to make them any more desperate. And as for being dangerous, I didn't know they made any other kind. . . . Don't worry warden. As for the men, I've taken care of myself even when they've had guns.

When Abby greets several of the convicts by name, ever-vigilant Wells is impressed:

> WELLS: You seem well acquainted here.
>
> ABBY: Yeah, I used to get around quite a bit.

Wells, intrigued by her looks, attempts to make a deal with Abby; offering to do a favor for the comely woman if she will respond to his sexual advances.

> WELLS: I can make it easy for you or I can make it plenty tough. Plenty tough.
>
> ABBY: And you get one thing straight, stupid. You ever threaten me again and I'll really put you in a bind.
>
> WELLS: You? What could you do?
>
> ABBY: Do you want me to give you an idea?
>
> WELLS: Yes. Go ahead.
>
> ABBY: I guess this might be a good time at that. [She screams, intimating that she has been sexually attacked. The warden berates the embarrassed Wells.]

Before long, Reynolds and Jesse fight one another in the dining hall; Jesse throws a knife at Reynolds, injuring his arm. By now, Abby has decided she loves Reynolds more than Jesse and, to save her beau from the other's wrath, she convinces Jesse to break out, promising they will go to Mexico. She has guns smuggled into the prison and Jesse breaks out of his cell with his cronies, taking several guards hostage. Abby releases Reynolds from solitary confinement and hands him a gun. He stops several of the mutineers and then reaches the guard tower which houses the gatling gun. He forces the remaining escaping convicts to return to their cells. For their help in quelling the uprising, the warden promises to have both Reynolds and Abby pardoned.

Variety, being in a generous mood, stated, "Alfred Werker's direction plays it for a rough and ready reaction, stressing the story's grimness, and the playing is in tune. . . . Sometimes motivations and characters are a bit cloudy. . . ."

For the seasoned movie watcher, *Devil's Canyon* is not only a compendium of clichés of the prison genre, but it holds several other statistical delights: one can make the film's running time pass more quickly by counting the number of optical affects geared for the 3-D cameras with objects being tossed front and center; one can wonder constantly where, in this small-set production, the other cells are that supposedly house the rest of the five hundred convicts; and one can list the many veteran performers (Tom Powers, Paul Fix, Murray Alper, et al.) who parade by in the ninety-one minutes.

78. *Devil's Island* (Chadwick, 1926), 6,900′.

Director, Frank O'Connor; story/screenplay, Leah Baird; camera, Andre Barlatier.

Pauline Frederick (Jeanette Picto); Marion Nixon (Rose Marie); George Lewis

(Leon Valyon); Richard Tucker (Jean Valyon); William Dunn (Guillet); Leo White (Chico); John Miljan (Andre Le Fevier); Harry Northrup (The Commandant).

A fanciful drama/romance from the independent Chadwick Pictures Corporation which did its best to romanticize life and times at the horrific penal colony known as Devil's Island. "[T]he story with its heavy drama is pretty old stuff and the burden of its sincere interpretation is almost entirely on Pauline Frederick and Marian Nixon.... *Devil's Island* wasn't a wallop, neither is it a dud" *(Variety)*.

Jean Valyon (Richard Tucker), a formerly highly regarded Paris surgeon who has been wrongly convicted of a serious crime, endures seven years at the French penal colony on Devil's Island where the commandant (Harry Northrup) badly mistreats the prisoners. Surviving the ordeal, Jean is then relocated to the prison city of Cayenne in nearby French Guiana, where he finds his faithful sweetheart, Jeannette Picto (Pauline Frederick), waiting for him. The couple marry and they are given land to cultivate. Later, they become the parents of Leon (George Lewis). When the latter grows up, he too becomes a surgeon. After Jean's death, Jeannette hopes to send her son to Europe where his medical skills will be appreciated. However, he has fallen in love with Rose Marie (Marian Nixon), a dancer, and refused to leave. Jeanette maneuvers to have a Court of Inquiry clear her late husband's name and at the same time clear the reputation of Rose Marie who is in the compromising custody of the sinister commandant. This is granted and news of her release is broadcast over a wireless radio, in time to prevent her seduction. Rose Marie and Leon are reunited.

With its silly premise the silent *Devil's Island* was more in the fanciful tradition of *Condemned* (1929), q.v. than the later gritty *Papillon* (1973), q.v. Its star, Pauline Frederick (1883–1938), made a speciality (e.g. *Madame X,* 1920) of playing noble, suffering mothers who age several decades during the course of any given photoplay.

79. *Devil's Island* (Warner Bros., 1940), 65 min.

Producer, Bryan Foy; director, William Clemens; story, Anthony Coldeway, Raymond Schrock; screenplay, Kenneth Gamet, Don Ryan; art director, Max Parker; dialogue director, John Langan; technical adviser, Louis Van Den Ecker; sound, Robert B. Lee; camera, George Barnes; editor, Frank Magee.

Boris Karloff (Dr. Charles Gaudet); Nedda Harrigan (Mme. Helene Lucien); James Stephenson (Colonel Armand Lucien); Adia Kuznetzoff (Pierre LeRoux); Rolla Gourvitch (Colette Lucien); Will Stanton (Bobo); Edward Keane (Dr. Duval); Robert Warwick (Demontre); Pedro de Cordoba (Marcal); Tom Wilson (Emil); John Harmon (Andre Garon); Richard Bond (Georges); Earl Gunn (Leon); Sidney Bracey (Soupy); George Lloyd (Dogface); Charles Richman (Governor Beaufort); Stuart Holmes (Gustav Le Brun); Leonard Mudie (Advocate General); Egon Brecher (Debriac); Frank Reicher (President of Assize Court); John Hamilton (Ship's Captain); Harry Cording, Al Bridge, Earl Dwire, Dick Rich (Guards).

Warner Bros. was having great success with its rash of contemporary prison pictures (e.g.: *San Quentin,* 1937, *Alcatraz Island,* 1937, *Crime School,* 1938, qq.v.) and decided to further explore the penal system. This time, in the programmer *Devil's Island,* it was the notorious French penal colony, the same locale where Joseph Schildkraut (as the "infamous" Dreyfus) had been shipped for punishment in *The Life of Emile Zola* (1937). To star in this "B" picture, the studio cast Boris Karloff, best known for playing Frankenstein's monster onscreen, but also having provided a chilling and menacing convict in *The Criminal Code* (1931), q.v.

When *Devil's Island* was released initially in early 1939, the French consulate took exception to *Devil's Island*. The picture was immediately withdrawn, for fear of ruining the distribution of studio product in French territories abroad. It was not until mid–1940, after France had fallen to the Nazis and that market was cut off anyway, that this feature was released. The new print was in an edited form and contained a tacked-on conciliatory foreword:

> Devil's Island: scene of martyrdom for Dreyfus, until Zola's fiery crusade won his freedom. An island of death . . . ruled of necessity by an iron regime . . . here the most dangerous enemies of France were herded into exile . . . of purely fictional material, this story pictures that time, now past.
>
> A modern understanding of penal administration has brought a change. Today humanity makes easier the burden of correction. For modern France is committed to the task of remaking men . . . not breaking them.

Because brain surgeon Dr. Charles Gaudent (Boris Karloff) of Paris had operated to save the life of a wounded revolutionist (Stuart Holmes)—who later dies—he is convicted of treason and sentenced to ten years of hard labor on Devil's Island, the hell on earth which its prisoners had dubbed "the dry guillotine" (i.e., living death).

The colony's commander, Colonel Armand Lucien (James Stephenson) is a stern taskmaster, untempered by his caring wife Helene (Nedda Harrigan) or loving little daughter Colette (Rolla Gourvitch).

> LUCIEN: You seem never to understand Helene, that these men are criminals, sent here to be punished.
>
> HELENE: I know, but you actually seem to enjoy exerting your authority over them.
>
> LUCIEN: The more I exert my authority now, the less trouble I'll have later.

The unfeeling Lucien, who is also skimming money from his position, meets the new shipment of unfortunates:

> I know what most of you men are thinking about . . . how to escape. Well, here on this island you'll have a certain amount of liberty. You may try to escape, but I warn you we have two strong guardians. On this side there's the Atlantic and across the channel there's the mainland. You might steal a boat, you might even reach the mainland, but there you'll find a guardian as strong as the ocean itself. The jungle. So you can take your choice. You can either try to swim back through an ocean full of sharks or take your chances with the fever and the black ants in the jungle swamp. Incidentally, the penalty for attempted escape, if you live to incur it, is solitary confinement in the prison.

Now prisoner #46357, one of 3,500 convicts at the dreaded compound, Gaudet suffers from the cruel treatment afforded prisoners and the endless hard toiling cutting timber. He soon loses hope and admits, "We'd all be better off dead." When a fellow convict dies, Gaudet and other prisoner revolt and in the ensuing fight, a guard is killed. Gaudet and several others are sentenced to death. The prideful Lucien agrees to spare Gaudet's life and that of the others, if he can save Colette who has been injured in a carriage accident. The surgery is a success, but the dastardly Lucien revokes his promise and sentences Gaudet to the pits and Pierre LeRoux (Adia Kuznetzoff), who killed the guard, is ordered to be guillotined. Gaudet and some of the others escape with the help of money from Helene. However, they later are rescued by a ship which is heading back to Devil's Island. By now, Helene realizes that her sadistic husband intends to kill Gaudet, because he knows too much about his corrupt regime, so she hastens to the Governor (Leonard Mudie) who returns with her to the compound. They are in time to save Gaudet's life and he is given the news that he has been pardoned, his innocence at last proven. Lucien is arrested for his crimes and in his stead Gaudet agrees to run the facility, using fairness and humanity in treating the prisoners. Helen and Colette leave the island.

Devil's Island certainly dealt with a topical subject, for the horrors of this penal colony bore contemporary parallels to the abhorrent conditions in the concentration camps of the Third Reich. However, even acknowledging the changes made to the film for its re-edited 1940 release, much of *Devil's Island* works at cross purposes. While Boris Karloff is effective in his characterization (avoiding much of the overplaying that he used in other feature films of the day), several of the featured cast are inadequate: James Stephenson postures like a child as the martinet commandant, Rolla Gourvitch is annoyingly precocious and saccharine as his offspring, Nedda Harrigan is bland as the humane wife/mother. At times, the drama is touching in its exposé-style of the burden borne by the prisoners (including the segment where the weary prisoners chant ("The Song of the Doomed Men"), but then the movie's direction switches tempo. Scenes like the riot and Gaudet's escape play like mediocre chapters from a Republic Pictures's cliffhanger.

Granted there are moments of strong social protest as when a knowing black convict tells Helene about the price of freedom at the colony: "Money will buy anything in the island Madame. And it will buy a man's way to the coast and a boat too, with which he might reach the mainland.... The guards at the pits are changed every day but they all can be bribed." But then there are equal, distracting moments of "comic" relief such as the recurring gag about the convict who is constantly given new jobs at the Island. When a fellow inmate asks him how he earned a soft job working on kitchen duty, the other replies, "When they asked my profession, they thought I said cook."

In its day, however, even the abbreviated *Devil's Island* received some favorable reviews. Thomas M. Pryor *(New York Times)* judged, *"Devil's Island* pulls no punches of the barbarous conditions popularly supposed to prevail in the French penal colony.... While the camera probes the brutalities inflicted on the prisoners the drama is savagely realistic." On the other hand, *Variety* weighed it "just another meller of the dreaded isle down in the Caribbean." *Harrison's Reports,* assessing the offering for its box-office potential, observed, "One feels pity for the hero, an innocent victim of political intrigue, who when placed on the island, suffers intensely both physically and mentally; but this is not enough to hold one's interest. There is no romance...."

80. *Devil's Mate* (Monogram, 1933), 65 min.

Producer, Ben Verschleiser; director, Phil Rosen; story/screenplay, Leonard Fields, David Silverstein; sound, John A. Stransky, Jr.; camera, Gill Warrenton.

Peggy Shannon (Nancy Weaver); Preston Foster (Inspector O'Brien); Ray Walker

(Natural); Hobart Cavanaugh (Parkhurst); Barbara Barondess (Gwen); Paul Porcasi (Nick); Harold Waldridge (Joe); Jason Robards (Clinton); Bryant Washburn (District Attorney); Harry Holman (Mc- Gee); George Hayes (Collins); James Durkin (Warden); Gordon DeMaine (Butler); Paul Fix (Maloney); Sam Flint (Prison Doctor); Henry Otho (Witness); Henry Hall (Chaplain).

One of those unfortunate cases where a film just misses classification above and below the line. It's a mystery yarn, with some good, some new, some bad and some stupid angles.

(Variety)

Several witnesses—including the Warden (James Durkin), the prison doctor (Sam Flint) and the chaplain (Henry Hall)—are gathered to observe the electrocution of a convicted killer. Just as the prisoner is about to confess the name of his gang's leader, he is murdered by a poison dart. Police inspector O'Brien (Preston Foster) is assigned to solve the case, and he finds that his girlfriend, Nancy Weaver (Peggy Shannon), a newspaper reporter, is of great assistance in solving the case which sees additional murders, including that of Gwen (Barbara Barondess), the deceased convict's girlfriend.

Harrison's Reports endorsed this minor entry, "The plot occasionally is not logical, but the action is fast and for that reason, the interest is held. The closing scenes are exciting."

The film would be remade by Monogram Pictures in 1941 as *I Killed That Man* starring Ricardo Cortez and Joan Woodbury. The same gambit, setting a screen whodunit in a prison, would also be used in *Murder in the Big House* (1942), q.v.

81. *Doin' Time* (Warner Bros., 1985), color, 80 min.

Executive producers, Ken Sheppard, Carol Mallen; producers, Bruce Mallen, George Mendeluk; director, Mendeluk; story, Franelle Silver, Ron Zwang, Dee Caruso, Mendeluk, Peter Wilson; screenplay, Silver, Zwang; production designer, Jack McAdam; set decorator, Linda Allen; costumes, Arlene Zamiara; makeup, Kathy W. Estocin; music, Charles Fox; song, Max Carl and Andrew Kastner; second unit directors, Robertson, McAdam; assistant director, Robertson; stunt coordinator, Erik Cord; sound, Donald B. Summer; special effects, Bob McCarthy; camera, Ronald V. Garcia; second unit camera, Philip A. Pastuhov, Paul Laufer; editor, Stanford C. Allen.

Jeff Altman (Duke Jarrett); Dey Young (Dr. Vicki Norris); Richard Mulligan (Mongo Mitchell); John Vernon (Big Mac); Coleen Camp (Nancy Catlett); Melanie Chartoff (Linda Libel); Graham Jarvis (Prescott); Pat McCormick (Warden B. J. Fallis); Eddie Velez (Weback); Jimmie Walker (Shaker); Judy Landers (The Bride); Nicolas Worth (Animal); Mike Mazurki (Bruno); Muhammad Ali (Himself); Henry Bal (Guard Kowisski); Gene Bell (Vaudevillian); Big Yank (Bubba Felstein); Simmy Bow (Snake Eyes); Drew Bundini Brown (Himself); David Lee Bynum (Prisoner); Max Carl (Vocalist); Robert Clotworthy (Attorney); Dee Cooper (Truck Driver); Ji-Tu Cumbuka (Bernie Felstein); Robert Czakel (Duke's Trainer); Eugene Davis, Jr. (Prisoner); Nora Denney (Martha); Melinda Fee (Denise); Bambi (Gayle Fox); Irma Gacia (Maid); Stuart Gillard (Senator Hodgkins); Dulcie Jordan (Female Inspector); Lex Landi (KRAT Producer); Lee Robert Laningham (Prisoner); Julius Le Flore (Murray); Frank Lugo (Guard Garcia); Travis McKenna (Slob); Charlie Messenger (Referee); Kitten Natividad (Tessie); Joseph Nipote (Angelo Chrispini); Ron Palillo (Pappion); John Reilly (Governor); Don Richey (William Gibbons); Dennis Robertson (Father O'Brien); Rhonda Shear (Adriane); Dona L. Speir (Card Holder); Paul Stader (Old Man); Duke Stroud (George); Jaynie Sustar (Monique); James Welch (Billy Cox); Peter M. Wilcox (Melvin); Joel Zurlo (Unit Manager); Ron Zwang (Arthur).

[T]his dismal attempt to do for prisoners what *Police Academy* did for the police force has few laughs and little entertainment value.... Jokes, such as they are, are sexist, vulgar and derivative.... Pic is technically sloppy, too....

(Variety)

Because he has been caught (with his pants down) sleeping with the governor's wife, cyrogenics salesman Duke Jarrett (Jeff Altman) is disciplined with a term at the John Dillinger Memorial Penitentiary. When the daffy newcomer arrives at the unusually run prison, quirky Warden B. J. Fallis (Pat McCormick) advises him:

Let me point out . . . this is the first prison in the country with P-TV, our own closed circuit TV operated by the inmates . . . and we're rather proud of the education shorts produced by the men.

Before long, the ineffectual, overly permissive Fallis has been replaced by Warden Mongo Mitchell (Richard Mulligan), a strutting autocrat who emerges as a buffoon version of General George Patton. Mitchell announces to the disrespectful convicts:

You step out of line, I'll chew you up and swallow you. You talk back to me, I'll chew you up and I'll swallow you.... While I'm in charge here, there'll be no milk and cookies at bedtime, no TV, no drugs.... There are two ways of doing things in prison, my way and my way. Take your pick.

Mitchell's reforms spoil much of the fun enjoyed by the eccentric inmate population, such as the men's betting on whether or not Jarrett can bed the sexy new prison psychologist Vicki Norris (Dey Young). Because Mitchell's changes interrupt too many of the men's hedonistic ways, they decide to teach the man a lesson. While Mitchell is busily organizing a boxing match between Jarrett and one of the guards, the convicts concoct a plan involving the warden's libidinous young secretary (Colleen Camp). Transforming a wok into a satellite telecast dish, the men employ the prison's closed-circuit TV station to broadcast Mitchell's sexual coupling with her to the nation at large. This causes Mitchell to be fired and Fallis to be reinstated, much to the convicts' joy. Meanwhile, Jarrett earns a parole.

In between the flat-footed comedy and the strenuous efforts of the cast (many of them unemployed TV sitcom performers), *Doin' Time* is a lame satire. There are occasional moments of amusement, but very few and very far between: There is a sendup of James Cagney's "Top of the world, ma!" speech and going berserk in the mess hall from *White Heat* (1949), q.v. When a convict (Jimmie Walker) attempts a prison escape, a priest attempts to talk him out of the misdeed and, instead of being pacified, the prisoner shoots at the surprised clergyman. At one point, Warden Mitchell issues the command, "I want you to stop whipping as a punishment immediately. They [the convicts] like it. They're lining up for it." Burly inmate Big Mac (John Vernon) announces, "I'm planning to bust out of here so I can screw up my parole." But, generally, in *Doin' Time,* the comedy efforts are misfires. One of the more annoying gimmicks is the use of a M*A*S*H-like public address system in the prison for (supposedly) humorous announcements ("Will those expecting a visit from a criminal lawyer please come to the visiting area immediately. Those expecting honest lawyers can also come.")

TV Guide magazine rated *Doin' Time* a near dud, giving it only one star.

82. *Doing Life* (NBC–TV, Sept. 23, 1986), color, 100 min.

Executive producers, Gene Reynolds, Tony Danza; supervising producer, Burt Metcalfe; director, Reynolds; based on the book by Steve Bello; teleplay, Bello; art director, Gavin Mitchell; set decorator, Enrico Campana; costumes, Mary Jane McCarty; makeup, Inge Klaudi; music, Arthur B. Rubinstein; supervising music editor, Susan Mick, stunt coordinator, Shane Cadwell; assistant directors, Otto Hanus, Jacques Hubert, Jeff Authors; sound, Douglas Ganton; ADR supervisor, Tim Shoemaker; camera, Miklos Lente; editor, Christopher Nelson.

Tony Danza (Jerry Rosenberg); Jon DeVries (Warden Henry Felber); Alvin Epstein (Lou Rosenberg); Mitchell Jason (Judge Samuel S. Leibowitz); Lisa Langlois (Rose Ann Rosenberg); Rocco Sisto (Anthony Portelli); Dawn Greenhalgh (Belle Rosenberg); Dan Lauria (Captain Lubway); Kenneth Pogue (Probst); Allan Royal (Jameson); John Randolph Jones (Benny Stabler); Reginald Vel Johnson (Taylor);

Mara Hobel (Rachel Rosenberg at age fifteen); Frank Pesce (Red Hot Vitale); Angelo Rizacos (Teddy Kemper); Gary Farmer (1st Prisoner); Michael J. Reynolds, Charles Gray (Parole Board Members); Paul Soles (Jake Epstein); Henry Ramer (Edelbaum); Larry Reynolds (Judge Kellog); Peter Jobin (District Attorney Selzer); John Friesen (Dr. Frederick); Warren Davis (Dr. Hampton); Alar Aedma (Cadmore); Guy Sanvido (David Samilson); Neil Dainard (Bennett); James Bearden (Guard); Dee Francis McCafferty (Proctor); Eugene A. Clark (Wiggins); Gene Mack (Freddie); Aaron Schwartz (Murray Auerbach); Robert O'Ree (Luther Greenhouse); Jennifer Gula (Rachel Rosenberg at Age Eight); John Winston Carroll (Editor); David Bolt (District Attorney Coleman); Clark Johnson (TV Reporter); Vito Rezza (Caracio); Tony DeSantis (Sal); Justin Louis (Bobby); Jack Duffy (Jury Foreman); Jorge Montessi (Latino Translator).

Doing Life focuses on a convict sentenced to life imprisonment who educates himself to assert his legal rights and who, in the process, rehabilitates himself. This fact-based drama has a surprising integrity and drive to it, thanks to the compelling performance by Tony Danza, the TV sitcom series star of "Taxi" (1978–82) and "Who's the Boss?" (1984–   ). Danza made his telefeature movie debut here. *Daily Variety* enthused, "it's Danza's energetic, concentrated performance, that pulls the vidpic together; as the centerpiece, he's terrif."

In 1962, a small-time Brooklyn punk, Jerry Rosenberg (Tony Danza), is arrested for the murder of two police detectives during a tobacco warehouse robbery. Claiming he is innocent, the glib Jerry refuses to make a deal with the District Attorney, as his lawyer advises. He is convicted of the homicides and sentenced to be executed at Sing Sing Prison during the week of March 31, 1963. As a guard on death row tells him, "Two thousand volts. The answer to all your problems." Soon another convict on the row, Freddie (Gene Mack), is led to the electric chair and the depressed Jerry awaits his turn, which due to the legal process, stretches onward. To wile away the hours, Jerry, who never got beyond the fourth grade, begins to study law books. His wife Rose Ann (Lisa Langlois), who gave birth to a baby girl during Jerry's trial, visits him, as do his parents (Alvin Epstein, Dawn Greenhalgh). On June 1, 1965 the death penalty is abolished in the state of New York. However, this does not affect Jerry's status since the law exempts those convicted of killing a police officer or a prison guard. Meanwhile, Jerry enrolls in the Stedford College of Law, a correspondence course, believing that he has "got to keep fighting, somehow." With the encouragement of his parents ("my son the lawyer"), the admiration of his bewildered fellow convicts, and the cynicism of the prison administration to egg him on, Jerry pursues his studies. He writes a letter to the governor pointing out an illegality in his case, and the administrator commutes his sentence to life.

Jerry is transferred to Auburn Prison where he meets Warden Henry Felber (Joe DeVries). The latter lectures this "jail house lawyer" whom he fears will inspire too much individuality and rebellion among the prisoners:

> The inmates in this prison are in here for a reason. They act like criminals. They perceive other people as victims to be exploited.... Most of all they need to take responsibility for their prior acts.

The warden bargains with Jerry that he may continue his law studies, *if* he does not loan out his law books or provide free legal advise.

WARDEN: Fair enough?

JERRY: Nuthin' fair in prison.

A trustee in D block, Luther Greenhouse (Robert O'Ree), asks Jerry to give him legal advice regarding his case, and despite the Warden's warnings, Jerry agrees to having a transcript of the case smuggled to him. Rosenberg is caught and, as punishment, he is brutalized by the guards, put in the solitary "box" and loses his books. Later, he writes a letter to the Federal Court which, in turn, decrees that Jerry has a right to help other criminals, although the prison may set strict limitations. This leads to another confrontation between Rosenberg and the warden.

JERRY: Are you scared of the law?

WARDEN: Scared of it falling into the wrong hands.

The dour Captain Lubway (Dan Lauria) makes life exceptionally difficult for Jerry whom he views as a threat to his authority. For any slight infraction of the rules (e.g. wearing sweat shirts instead of regulation garb), he punished Rosenberg. Nevertheless, the regenerated Jerry, eager for knowledge, completes his mail order course and passes the bar examination. His achievement is a first among prison convicts in the United States.

With his new status, Jerry petitions for a hearing in his case, citing several irregularities with the original trial. Judge Leibowitz (Mitchell Jason) rules against him. Back in prison, Rosenberg as negotiator during a bloody prison riot in 1978, helps to bring about a (very) few reforms from the reluctant administrators and cost-conscious prison board.

The story jumps to March 1979 where Jerry is in court defending a fellow inmate at a jury trial who is bringing action against an indifferent prison doctor who failed, it is claimed, to give the plaintiff adequate medical attention. Rosenberg wins the case. It leads to improved medical conditions at the penitentiary and he is a hero to the other convicts. However, the down side to the courtroom episode is that his participation in the trial adversely affects his pending parole application. His bid for freedom is denied and he must wait two more years for his next application. Meanwhile, his fifteen-year-old daughter, Rachel (Mara Hobel), who lives in Texas with her mother, visits her father. She displays no shame about his prisoner status, only admiration for his optimistic nature. She confides that she intends to become a lawyer herself.

Forced to remain in prison, Jerry contents himself with his belatedly discovered purpose on this earth, helping other convicts with their legal problems. A postscript advises that Rosenberg is still in prison.

The virtues of this factual TV movie are that it offers an ebullient performance by Tony Danza and that, unlike so many other prison dramas, it revolves around a relatively positive situation: the maturing and rehabilitation of a minor league hood. Like most such genre pieces, it tries too hard to be realistic in its depiction of life behind bars (and somehow TV movies are never as gritty or impressive as their big screen counterparts). While *Doing Life* is based on real life events, its use of a prolonged riot sequence seemed geared more to open up the telefilm and create distraction with violent action than to further the storyline. Finally, the etching of Jerry's overprotective Jewish parents is too ethnic and cutesy, aimed more at slight comic relief and human interest than in verisimilitude. *Daily Variety* also pointed out another flaw in this made-for-television production, "It fails to make its point, however, when it takes the side invariably of the criminal against the law enforcer.... The deck's stacked so that the prisoners are wronged, human beings being badly treated."

Doing Life was filmed at studios in Toronto, Canada.

83. *Down by Law* (Island, 1986), 107 min.

Producer, Alan Kleinberg; director/ screenplay, Jim Marmusch; costumes, Carol Wood; makeup, Donita Miller; music, John Lurie; songs: Tom Waits; Naomi Neville; camera, Robby Muller; editor, Melody London.

Tom Waits (Zack); John Lurie (Jack); Roberto Benigni (Roberto); Nicoletta Braschi (Nicholetta); Ellen Barkin (Laurette); Billie Neal (Bobbie); Rockets Redglare (Gig); Vernel Bagneris (Preston); Timothea (Julie); L. C. Drane (L. C.); Joy Houck, Jr. (Detective Mandino); Carrie Lindsoe (Young Girl); Ralph Joseph, Richard Boes (Detectives); Dave Petitjean (Cajun Detective); Adam Cohen (Uniformed Cop); Alan Kleinberg (Corpse); Archie Sapier (Prisoner); David Dahlgren, Alex Miller, Elliott Keener, Jay Hilliard (Guards).

Madri Gras is not the only thing that happens in New Orleans. People also go to jail there. Disc jockey Zack (Tom Waits), after fighting with his girlfriend, Laurette (Ellen Barkin), is approached by minor criminal Gig (Rockets Redglare) and told he can make some easy money by driving a stolen car across town. He agrees, only to be later stopped by the police who discover a corpse in the trunk. Meanwhile, a pimp, Jack (John Lurie), makes amends with a fellow pimp and former enemy named Preston (Vernel Bagneris). What Jack does not realize is that Preston has set him up with a very underage girl (only ten years old). Jack is caught by the law and, like Zack, is locked up at the Orleans Parish Prison where they are made cellmates.

These divergent types have little in common with one another and are too engulfed in their own worlds to communicate much beyond exchanging jibes. Before long, the cramped cell has another resident, Roberto (Roberto Benigni), a warm-hearted Italian who has great difficulty with the English language. "Not enough room to swing a cat," insists the foreigner. He later explains in fractured English that he accidentally killed another person by throwing a billiard ball which hit the victim in the forehead.

The three prisoners decide to escape, making their exit through an underground tunnel which leads them to the bayou. With the police and bloodhounds in pursuit, the men locate a boat which they use to navigate through the swamps. Later, they seek refuge in a tiny shack and, further on, angry with one other, split apart. Eventually, they are accidentally reunited and stop at a desolate roadside diner. Roberto risks going inside, while the other two hide in the bushes outside. Finally, after several hours, the two venture inside to find out what has happened to their companion. To their surprise, he is dining with the attractive owner of the restaurant, Nicoletta (Nicholetta Braschi), and announces that he intends to remain with his new-found love. The next day, Zack and Jack say their goodbyes and depart down the road, each man soon going his own way.

Made on a budget of $1,000,000, this arty, black-and-white picture was first screened at the Cannes Film Festival in May 1986. It led *Variety* to report, "The Jarmusch penchant for off-the-wall characters and odd situations is very much in evidence in *Down By Law,* but audiences attuned to his special brand of comedy will have lots of fun with the picture. . . . [The] black and white photography is a major plus, and so is John Lurie's score." Jay Robert Nash and Stanley Ralph Ross noted in *The Motion Picture Guide: 1987 Annual* (1987), "Jarmusch has created a world which lies somewhere between the poetic atmosphere that often characterizes European films and the narrative construction common to American films. His characters are insignificant antiheroes adrift in an America which is both 'said and beautiful.'" *TV Guide* magazine rated this offbeat feature three out of four stars.

Robert Benigni is an Italian actor/director. Tom Waits both wrote and sang several of the songs used on the soundtrack.

84. *Duffy of San Quentin* (Warner Bros., 1954), 76 min.

Producers, Berman Swarttz, Walter Doniger; director, Doniger; based on the book *The San Quentin Story* by Warden Clinton T. Duffy, Dan Jennings; screen story, Swarttz, Doniger; screenplay, Doniger; music, Paul Dunlap; assistant director, Ralph Slosser; camera, John Alton; editors, Edward Sampson, Jr., Chester Schaeffer.

Louis Hayward (Edward Harper); Joanne Dru (Anne Halsey); Paul Kelly (Warden Clinton T. Duffy); Maureen O'Sullivan (Gladys Duffy); George Macready (Winant); Horace McMahon (Pierson); Irving Bacon (Doc); Joel Fluellen (Bill); Joseph Turkel (Frank); Jonathan Hale (Boyd); Michael McHale (Pinto); Peter Brocco (Nealy).

Hollywood was embarking on another cycle of prison yarns in the mid–1950s and found grist for its production mills in the book *The San Quentin Story* (1950) by Clinton T. Duffy, the long-time warden of that maximum security penal institution.

A riot occurs at San Quentin Prison and Clinton T. Duffy (Paul Kelly), chief assistant to the warden, soon finds himself appointed temporary administrator for a thirty-day period. Duffy immediately inaugurates a series of changes: abandons the solitary confinement punishment, rectifies the graft in the kitchen department which improves food conditions, eliminates the stool pigeon system and even orders that the convicts will no longer have shaved heads, but receive hiarcuts. Among those affected by Duffy's reform is Edward Harper (Louis Hayward) who is removed from solitary (the "rat hole") where he was being punished for having an illegal weapon. Harper insists to the warden that he was not fashioning a dagger from a toothbrush handle, as the guards charged, but was carving a ring for a woman friend. He also relates that he was framed by an overzealous prosecutor, Winant (George Macready). Duffy's further overhauling of the system includes a strict rule against any guard using unauthorized punishment weapons. Duffy's wife, Gladys (Maureen O'Sullivan) suggests that he hire a female nurse in the hospital, to give at least one area of prison life a more natural balance. Later, when a riot/prison break is about to explode during the showing of a movie (another first) to the convicts, Harper prevents it.

Duffy becomes the full-fledged warden at San Quentin and he hires Anne Halsey (Joanne Dru) to join the infirmary staff. Harper, now a male nurse there, is stubbornly opposed to Anne being put in charge. However, when she takes the blame for an error that he made in treating a patient, they become friends. Meanwhile, Winant is sent to San Quentin, convicted for bribing a witness. Duffy is fearful that if he leaves the newcomer in general population, he will be murdered by the men who were prosecuted by this lawyer. On the other hand, if he removes the man to the prison farm, observers will insist he is part of a political machine. Duffy chooses the former choice and Winant is almost killed by revengeful inmates. However, he is saved by Harper's intervention. Winant refuses to name his assailants and later, he decides to start a law practice in prison to help remedy the injustices he had heaped on several defendants now at San Quentin. His first case is Harper whom he has freed. Harper and Anne plan to marry.

Bosley Crowther *(New York Times)* carped of this independent programmer released by Warner Bros., the home of prison films, "This sort of romantic impulse within the walls of one of the nation's toughest jails would look just a wee bit fantastic, even if played extremely well. As played by Mr. Hayward ... it looks like the silliest sort of eyewash in the most hackneyed sort of prison film." *Variety* agreed. "It's a slow-moving prison melodrama, developed in ordinary fashion, and there is very little of interest, even for undiscriminating audiences...."

Paul Kelly and Maureen O'Sullivan would recreate their roles of Warden and Mrs. Duffy in *The Steel Cage,* q.v., released by United Artists later in the year. Ironically, Paul Kelly (1899–1956) had been a prisoner at San Quentin Prison in 1927–29 when he was convicted of manslaughter for causing the death of musical comedy performer, Ray Raymond, the mate of actress Dorothy Mackaye with whom Kelly was in love.

British release title: *Men Behind Bars.*

85. *Dust Be My Destiny* (Warner Bros., 1939), 88 min.

Executive producer, Hal B. Wallis; associate producer, Lou Edelman; director, Lewis Seiler; based on the novel by Jerome Odlum; screenplay, Robert Rossen; art director, Hugh Reticker; gowns, Milo Anderson; makeup, Perc Westmore; music, Max Steiner; orchestrator, Hugo Friedhofer; music director, Leo F. Forbstein; sound, Robert B. Lee; special effects, Byron Haskin; camera, James Wong Howe; editor, Warren Low.

John Garfield (Joe Carson [Joe Bell]); Priscilla Lane (Mabel Alden); Alan Hale (Mike Leonard); Frank McHugh (Caruthers); Billy Halop (Hank); Bobby Jordan (Jimmy Glenn); Charley Grapewin (Pop); Henry Armetta (Nick Balucci); Stanley Ridges (Charlie Garrett); John Litel (Prosecutor); Moroni Olsen (Slim Jones); Victor Kilian (Doc Saunders); Frank Jaquet (Ab Connors); Ferike Boros (Delicatessen Proprietor); Marc Lawrence (Veneill); Arthur Aylesworth (Magistrate); William Davidson (Warden); George Irving (Judge); Ward Bond (Drifter).

Warner Bros. was a master at producing slick social protest dramas and one of its leading arbiters of such "entertainment" was John Garfield. The latter was very adept at playing the Depression's stepchild, the victim of social inequality (frequently an unjust legal and penal system), whose only crimes were that he was broke and wanted to work. Garfield has been Oscar-nominated for his co-starring

John Garfield and Priscilla Lane in *Dust Be My Destiny* (1939).

role with Priscilla Lane in the studio's *Four Daughters* (1938). This attractive screen couple were reunited in *Daughters Courageous* (1939) and, that same year, joined together again for *Dust Be My Destiny*. It was a lushly romanticized offering about another good guy tossed around by the law. The gilt-edge production values (including a Max Steiner score) made the glossy movie very palatable to moviegoers, including its message about the unyielding and sometimes exploitive penal system which often does not bother to make exceptions for truth, fairness and justice.

Joe Bell (John Garfield) has served sixteen months, thirteen days, four hours and twenty-three minutes for a robbery he did not commit. Now about to be freed, he is understandably bitter when the warden (William Davidson) bids him farewell:

> WARDEN: I can't say you've been a model prisoner. You've been rebellious and unruly. I want you to know now, I acted in the line of duty, I'm a warden, not a judge. It wasn't my business to determine your guilt or. . . . But you're free. . . . I'm sorry.
>
> JOE: You're sorry. You didn't serve time. I did. I'm sorry I was chump enough to think cops would believe in a nobody like me when I told them I was only trying to help a guy who was shot. I should have kept my nose out of trouble. Don't worry, warden. I'm wised up now, cause no matter what happens or who gets hurt, Joe Bell runs the other way.

Once on the road, with no prospects, Joe seeks employment — anything — to survive, but with no luck. As he hitchhikes from town to town, he joins with two young drifters, the Glenn brothers—Hank (Billy Halop) and Jimmy (Bobby Jordan). When a mean hitcher (Ward Bond), on the run from the law, crosses paths with this trio, he decides to be nasty and is captured by the law. He implicates Joe and the Glenns in his own problems. As a result, the youths are given thirty days sentences on the Rosedale County Work Farm; because Joe talked back at the hearing he is given ninety days.

The farm is operated by the drunken Charlie Garrett (Stanley Ridges), who, after sizing them up like prize work animals, snidely informs his "helpers":

> Most of you are here because you're tramps. You were too dumb to learn when you were kids but you're going to learn here the hard way. You're going to learn one of the wonderful things in the world—farming. . . . First thing you learn here is to keep your mouth shut. . . .

Many of the inmates are put to work in the fields, but Joe, because he has innocently dared to talk with Garrett's fetching stepdaughter, Mabel (Priscilla Lane), is assigned to the more arduous road gang. He has no recourse to such arbitrary decisions. That evening the vindictive Garrett corners Joe and taunts him, "What you've been through today will seem to you tomorrow like a Sunday school strawberry festival if you don't stay away from the girl. Understand me?"

But it is not long before Joe and Mabel are conversing again, their mutual attraction too strong to deny. She tells him about her life on the farm, treated like a servant and mentally abused by her hard-drinking stepfather. Later, when Garrett tries to beat Mabel, Joe hits him. The man falls and hits his head and dies. As a result, Joe and Mabel run away. In a nearby town they get married, but keep moving from place to place, fearful that the law will find them. They find a brief reprieve in one small town where a coffee shop owner (Henry Armetta) gives them work, even after being told of their plight. At one point, Mabel is jailed by the law, but Joe helps her to escape.

In yet another town, Joe, who has a camera and a desire to become a newspaper photographer, happens to take photographs of a bank robbery. He sells the timely photographs to the editor, Mike Leonard (Alan Hale) of the *Doreville Daily Journal*. Leonard hires Joe to his staff and becomes his friend, even after learning of his past. When Joe later saves his boss from the bank robbers, led by Veneill (Marc Lawrence), his picture gets in the paper and this leads to his arrest. At Joe's trial, the prosecutor (John Litel) is articulate in presenting his case. However, Mike Leonard, Mabel and even Joe speak eloquently in his behalf. (The defense attorney [Moroni Olsen] says of Joe and all those like him, that they are "thousands of nobodies seeking a spot in the sun" and "a criminal's grave must *not* be their destiny.") The jury finds that Garrett's death was accidental and Joe is freed. At long last, Joe and Mabel are able to settle down and be respectable. They have "finally found a place to hang our hats."

By now, Frank S. Nugent *(New York Times)* was inured to such screen fare. "John Garfield, official gall-and-wormwood taster for the Warners, is sipping another bitter brew. . . . It's not even fun, anymore, outguessing the script. . . . The moment we met Joe Bell riding a freight car, looking for work, we knew he was going to be sent to a prison camp." *Variety* judged, "Although story is overlong and episodic, these deficiencies, are partially overcome by excellent performances of Garfield and Miss Lane."

Dust Be My Destiny, was quite popular in its day and led to a remake, the far-lesser *I Was Framed* (1942), q.v.

86. *Each Dawn I Die* (Warner Bros., 1939), 92 min.

Executive producer, Hal B. Wallis; associate producer, David Lewis; director, William Keighley; based on the novel by Jerome Odlum; screenplay, Norman Reilly Raine, Warren Duff, Charles Perry; art director, Max Parker; costumes, Howard Shoup; makeup, Perc Westmore; music, Max Steiner; music director, Leo F. Forbstein; technical adviser, William Buckley; sound, E. A. Brown; camera, Arthur Edeson; editor, Thomas Richards.

James Cagney (Frank Ross); George Raft ("Hood" Stacey); Jane Bryan (Joyce Conover); George Bancroft (Warden John Armstrong); Maxie Rosenbloom (Fargo Red); Stanley Ridges (Muller); Alan Baxter (Polecat Carlisle); Victor Jory (W. J. Grayce); Willard Robertson (Guard Lang); Paul Hurst (Garsky); John Wray (Guard Peter Kassock); Louis Jean Heydt (Joe Lassiter); Ed Pawley (Dale); Joe Downing (Limpy Julien); Emma Dunn (Mrs. Ross); Thurston Hall (District Attorney Jesse Hanley); Clay Clement (Attorney Lockhart); William Davidson (Bill Mason); John Ridgely (Jerry Poague, Reporter); John Harron (Lew Keller, Reporter); Selmer Jackson (Patterson); Roger Homans (Mac, the Guard); Harry Cording (Temple); Abner Biberman (Shake Edwards); Napoleon Simpson (Mose); Cliff Saum, Tom Wilson, Al Lloyd, Jack Goodrich, Stuart Holmes, Alice Conners, Fern Barry (Accident Witnesses); Maris Wrixon (Girl in Car); Garland Smith, Arthur Gardner (Men in Car); James Flavin (Policeman); Charles Trowbridge (Judge); Joe Sully (Man Behind); Eddy Chandler (Deputy); John Dilson (Parole Board Member); Max Hoffman, Jr. (Gate Guard); Henry Otho, Lee Phelps, Dick Rich, Jack C. Smith (Guards); Walter Miller (Turnkey); Fred Graham (Guard in Cell); Wilfred Lucas (Bailiff); Vera Lewis (Jury Woman); Emmett Vogan (Prosecutor); Earl Dwire (Judge Crowder); Frank Mayo (*Telegraph* Editor); Mack Gray (Joe); Bob Perry (Bud); Al Hill (Johnny the Hood); Elliott Sullivan (Convict); Chuck Hamilton (Court Officer); John Conte (Narrator); and: Granville Bates, Nat Carr, Wedgewood Nowell, Jack Wise.

In sorting through all the prison pictures Hollywood in general has ever made or Warner Bros. in particular has ever released, *Each Dawn I Die* stands out from all the rest. It remains a top notch entertainment package, unmatched even by James Cagney's later return to the genre in *White Heat* (1949), q.v. *Each Dawn I Die* is only mildly interested in promulgating prison reforms; it is far more intent on being high calibre, rowdy entertainment. With two such tough guy stars as Cagney and George Raft in pivotal roles, this picture develops quickly into a buddy film. Throughout the storyline, these two macho players vie with one another in being more manly; not only in surviving the rugged ordeal of being a prisoner, but also in exerting his authority over others.

By this juncture, Warner Bros. had produced so many prison opuses that the sets (especially the jute mills where the men work at the carding machines), the subordinate players, and many of the situations seem like old friends. However, the attraction of watching hyper-intense Cagney and smolderingly slow-moving Raft play out their drama provides this movie with its primary appeal. As a by-product, *Each Dawn I Die* reveals that, even under the best of circumstances, prison is a horrendous ordeal, where only the fittest in health and the most resolute of spirit can hope to emerge anywhere near intact. The fact that the grueling prison system can (nearly) do in the two virile male leads here, should give anyone pause to believe that lasting out one's penitentiary sentence is "a piece of cake."

Crusading reporter Frank Ross of the *Banton Record* is investigating the link between District Attorney Jesse Hanley (Thurston Hall), crony W. J. Grayce (Victor

Jory), and the criminal underworld, especially as it concerns the Banton Construction Company. To get Ross out of the way, he is kidnapped and knocked out, put behind the wheel of a car, has liquor spilled over his body and his vehicle made to run amok on a crowded street. As a result, three people die in the crackup. Ross is found guilty of manslaughter, sentenced to one-to-twenty years at hard labor at Rocky Point Prison. His friends at the newspaper, including girlfriend Joyce Conover (Jane Bryan), promise to do their best to find new evidence to prove his innocence.

Once in prison, the embittered, hostile Ross encounters notorious guard Peter Kassock (John Wray) who states ominously, "There's a lot of things going to happen around here you won't like." Kassock is a strict disciplinarian, and he relishes each opportunity to order his charges around: "Get off that dirt! What do think this is, a county jail? Fold your arms. Salute when an officer speaks to yeah!"

Frank also meets "Hood" Stacey (George Raft), a big time racketeer who is serving 199 years, one of his several stays to date, in prison. Stacey has been measuring the newcomer's mark and is frankly impressed: "Your first day here and you tangle with Pete Kassock, the toughest screw in the state. You give his prize rat a sock on the noggin and you lose your privileges for a month. Ah, you've got the markings of a swell con!"

Another long-time convict, Muller (Stanley Ridges), advises Ross that prison is no picnic:

> I'd sooner be dead than live in this madhouse. Break your back working all day, sit in your cell till the next morning. Nothing to do but stare at the walls. Screws going by snooping.... First thing you know you're stir nuts. Just making time till you can get out and kill the first creep who gets in your way.... I wonder if the joint is getting to me?

Yet another convict, Fargo Red (Maxie Rosenbloom), alerts Ross about the perils of being in solitary confinement in "the hole": "Handcuffed to the cell bars eight hours a day, bread and water only at noon. No heat in winter. No light...."

Meanwhile, Stacey settles an old grudge with a stoolie, Limpy Julien (Joe Downing), by killing him with a smuggled-in knife. Later, he uses this murder to gain a new trial where he plans to escape from the courthouse. He takes Ross into his confidence, insisting that once freed he will use his connections to get Ross released. When Frank balks at being part of the plan, his pal wants to know, "What's the matter, you've gone stir nuts too?" Ross makes good his escape, but another stool pigeon (Alan Baxter) rats on Ross. This not only ruins any chance for Ross being paroled, but it leads to the sadistic guard Lang (Willard Robertson) putting the prisoner through a brutal inquisition. Lang tells the battered Ross, "You're going to talk if we have to bury you in the hole for twenty years."

Later, Warden John Armstrong (George Bancroft) learns of Ross's torment. He informs his callous guard:

> I will not tolerate brutality in this penitentiary. I've laid [down] punishment rules that are fully adequate. And, as long as I am warden, those rules will be obeyed. And mark this Lang, if there is any more of what went on here this afternoon, you'll all go.

Jane Bryan, James Cagney and George Bancroft in *Each Dawn I Die* (1939).

By now, Ross is an emotionally beaten man, his faith in getting released honestly gone, for W. J. Grayce is now on the prison parole board. The now unruly Ross challenges the warden's authority by telling his keeper, "The rules are off. I'm going to talk when I please and doing what I like. I'm going to be as mean and dirty and hard to handle as the worst con in the joint and I'll skulldrag any rat or screw that gets in my way."

The recalcitrant Ross ends in solitary confinement for five months. As the warden admits, "He's the most troublesome prisoner I've had in thirty-five years of penal work." When Ross is finally released from the hole, he tells the warden:

> When I first came here, I believed in justice. I believed that some day I'd be released. Then I began to figure in weeks and months and now I hate the whole world and everybody in it for lettin' me in for this. Buried in a black filthy hole because I was a good citizen, because I worked my head off to expose crime. And now I'm a convict! I act like a convict, I smell like a convict! I think and hate like a convict! But I'll get out! I'll get out if I have to kill every screw in the joint!

For this attitude, Ross is sent back to the hole for thirty more days.

Finally Ross is brought before the parole board, where his enemy Grayce goads him. The humbled Ross begs the board, "I can't do anymore time. Please turn me out of here!" His parole is denied, with no new hearing scheduled for five years.

Stacey, who has been enjoying the good life on the outside, has not bothered to help Ross because he believed his pal double-crossed him by having press photographers at the courtroom to record his escape. However, Joyce forces a meeting with Stacey and clears up this misunderstanding. Now Stacey snaps into action and forces Grayce's punk associate Shake Edwards (Abner Biberman) to confess that it was Polecat Carlisle, now at Rocky Point Prison, who was responsible for framing Ross. In an act which astounds his cronies as well as himself, Stacey decides he is honor-bound to solve the matter. He gives himself up to the incredulous prison officials. He snaps at them, "What'd've I got to do, fight my way back in?" Later, during a mass prison breakout, the wounded Hood forces Polecat to publicly confess within the warden's hearing. Stacey then dies, and once the riot is over, Ross's parole is arranged.

B. R. Crisler *(New York Times)* could not take this entertainment seriously. "We have no idea how Warner Brothers dispose of the byproducts of their prison pictures, but they must have produced enough jute in *Each Dawn I Die* . . . to have commercial possibilities." Crisler added, "The story . . . is one of the most wildly implausible of the year, but Mr. Cagney almost plays it plausibly, while Mr. Raft ably seconds him. . . ." *Variety* was less jaded: "Fitting into the string of prison vehicles which, of late, have exposed the cruel tactics of the guards, this latest Warner crimer gains strength through the cycle of events." *Harrison's Reports* acknowledged, "There are several situations that tear at the heartstrings. The situation in which the hero's mother [Emma Dunn] visits him at the prison and tries to control her emotions is a memorable one. . . ."

Each Dawn I Die was based on a novel (1938) by Jerome Odlum, whose book *Dust Be My Destiny,* q.v., had been the basis for another Warner Bros. prison (farm) melodrama. Originally, John Garfield was to have played Hood Stacey, and then it was considered a potential vehicle for Fred MacMurray before ex–Paramount Pictures's star George Raft joined the Warner Bros.' lineup. Initially, Ann Sheridan was to have co-starred as Joyce Conover, a part later reassigned to Jane Bryan. For the record, during the recreation hall murder scene, the prisoners are watching *Wings of the Navy* (1939), a Warner Bros. picture, of course. Elements of *Each Dawn I Die* would be combined with fragments from *Dust Be My Destiny* for a tattered Warner Bros.' budget entry, *I Was Framed* (1942), q.v.

87. *Escape* (CBS–TV, Feb. 20, 1980), color, 100 min.

Executive producers, Henry Jaffe, William Beaudine, Jr.; producer, Michael Jaffe; associate producer, Dick Vane; director, Robert Michael Lewis; based on the book by Dwight Worker, Barbara Worker; teleplay, Michael Zagor; art director, Richard Lawrence; music, James DiPasquale; camera, Isidore Mankofsky; editor, Frank Morriss.

Timothy Bottoms (Dwight Worker); Kay Lenz (Barbara Chilcoate); Colleen Dewhurst (Lily Levinson); Miguel Angel Suarez (Fernando Gardener-Pasquel); Sandra Alexander (Gabrielle); Allan Miller (Jack Branch); Antonio Fargas (Jaime Valdez); Vincent Schiavelli (J. W. White); Jorge Cervera (Tierno); Elliott Street (Roger Brody); Louis Giambalvo (Hank); Philip Levien (Steven); William Marquez (Colonel Fuentes); Tina Menard (Lupe); Ernie Guentes (Guard); Rick Garcia (1st Commando); Bert Santos (2nd Commando); Larry Duran (Arturo); Tiger Perez (Alfredo); Luis Lopez Casanova (Little Guard).

Escape was TV's answer to *Midnight Express* (1978), q.v., but warned Gail Williams *(Hollywood Reporter),* "The telefeature is a flaccid exercise in half-baked suspense. . . . This was a story worth telling, and yet the execution renders sadistic, corrupt guards, a shamefully unjust legal system, a love story between Bottoms and Kay Lenz (who marries him in prison) and the carefully devised escape plan with equal superficiality."

The melodrama is based on the true life story of Dwight Worker (Timothy Bottoms) who is jailed in 1975 for attempting to smuggle cocaine out of Mexico. One day a stranger, Barbara Chilcoate (Kay Lenz), visits the prison, wanting to see the jail from which Pancho Villa once escaped. She becomes attracted to Dwight and, before long, this single mother with a young daughter is in love with the victimized American. Lily Levinson (Coleen Dewhurst) is the earthy American woman in Mexico City who first suggests to Barbara, "Did you ever notice how thoroughly they search you when you go in, but when you leave, they hardly give you a second glance?" This leads to the two crafty women devising an escape plan that calls for Dwight to dress as a woman in order to sneak by the guards.

Daily Variety judged, "Suspense is minimal in the production, perhaps because the outcome has been proclaimed or maybe because the hero's smuggling activities aren't fully explained. . . ." Others in the cast included Miguel Angel Suarez as the tyrannical prison authority and Vincent Schiavelli as an enterprising convict scavenger.

It is claimed that Worker's escape from Lecumberri Prison was the first such successful breakout since Pancho Villa was incarcerated there. Some of the production was filmed on location in Puerto Rico.

88. *Escape from Alcatraz* (Paramount, 1979), color, 112 min.

Executive producer, Robert Daley; producer, Don Siegel; associate producer, Fritz Manes; director, Siegel; based on the book by J. Campbell Bruce; screenplay, Richard Tuggle; production designer, Allen Smith; set decorator, Edward J. McDonald; costumes, Glenn Wright; makeup, Joe McKinney; assistant directors, Luigi Alfano, Mark Johnson, Richard Graves; special effects, Chuck Gasper; sound, Bert Hallberg; sound re-recording, John T. Reitz; sound/special effects editors, Alan Robert Murray, Bob Asman; camera, Bruce Surtees; editor, Ferris Webster.

Clint Eastwood (Frank Morris); Patrick McGoohan (Warden); Robert Blossom (Doc [Chester Dalton]); Jack Thibeau (Clarence Anglin); Fred Ward (John Anglin); Paul Benjamin (English); Larry Hankin (Charley Butts); Bruce M. Fischer (Wolf); Frank Ronzio (Litmus); Fred Stuthman (Johnson); David Cryer (Wagner); Madison Arnold (Zimmerman); Blair Burrows (Fight Guard); Bob Balhatchet (Medical Assistant); Matthew J. Locricchio (Exam Guard); Don Michaelian (Beck); Ray K. Goman (Cellblock Captain); Jason Ronard (Bobs); Ed Vasgersian (Cranston); Ron Vernan (Stone); Reggie Baff (Lucy); Hank Brandt (Associate Warden); Candace Bowen (English's Daughter); Joseph Miksak (Police Sergeant); Gary Goodrow (Eston); Ross Reynolds (Helicopter Pilot); Al Dunlap (Visitors' Guard); Donald Siegel (Doctor); Dan Leegant, John Garabedian, Denis Berkefeldt, Jim Haynie, Tony Dario, Fritz Manes, Dana Derfus, Don Cummins, Gordon Handforth, John Scanlon, Don Watters, Lloyd Nelson, George Orrison, Gary F. Warren, Joe Whipp, Terry Wills, Robert Irvine, Joseph Knowland, James Collier, R. J. Ganzert, Robert Hirschfeld (Guards); Dale Alvarez, Sheldon Feldner, Danny Glover, Carl Lumbly, Patrick Valentino, Glenn Wright, Gilbert Thomas, Jr., Eugene W. Jackson (Inmates).

Escape from Alcatraz (1979) marked the first professional reunion of actor Clint Eastwood and director Don Siegel since their highly-successful *Dirty Harry* (1971). To retell the true-life story of Alcatraz's most famous escape, the filmmakers negotiated to utilize the actual prison site, which had become a tourist attraction after its closure. A great deal of expense and effort went into restoring the prison to the way it looked in 1963 when the breakout occurred. As production designer Allen Smith would reveal, "We had to bring absolutely everything over from the mainland, handling every bucket of paint, every piece of plywood—every piece of material that we needed—seven times before it reached the cell-block area where we could use it." After the filming, many of the "improvements" made by the film company were kept intact for the facility's return as a tourist haunt. For many, the restrained, authoritative performance of Clint Eastwood in *Escape from Alcatraz* is his most fully developed performance to date.

On January 18, 1960, Frank Morris (Clint Eastwood), who has attempted many prior escapes from various federal prisons, is relocated from Atlanta to Alcatraz where the stern disciplinarian warden (Patrick McGoogan) warns the taciturn, new convict:

> Alcatraz is not like any other prison in the United States. Here each prisoner is confined alone to an individual cell. Unlike my predecessors, Johnson and Blackwell, I don't have good conduct programs, inmate councils. Inmates here have no say in what they do. In here, they do as they're told. You're not permitted to have newspapers, magazines, or carry-in news. Knowledge of the outside world is what we tell you.
> From this day on, your world will be everything that happens in this building. You will shave once a day, shower twice a week, cut your hair once a month. Now privileges. You can talk, you can work. Other institutions hand out work, but here, it's a privilege. I promise you, it's a privilege you'll want. Visitors. You are allowed two a month. They cannot be former inmates of this or any other federal prison. All mail that you submit will be carefully checked by the FBI.
> We don't make good citizens [here]. Alcatraz was built to keep all the rotten eggs in one basket. I was especially chosen to make sure the stink from the basket does not escape. Since I've been warden, a few people have tried to escape. Most of them have been recaptured; those that haven't been killed or drowned in the bay. No one has ever escaped from Alcatraz and *no one ever will*.

Almost at once, this rugged newcomer to D Block comes into conflict with the brutish Wolf (Bruce M. Fischer) who wants him to be his boy. This leads to a tussle and Morris is sentenced to solitary confinement. Later, Morris returns to the general prison population and begins the deadening routine whereby convicts earn 15 cents an hour for their labor. As one fellow convict observes of the merciless daily pattern, "There are twelve counts a day. Sometimes I think that's all this shit hole is, one long count. We count the hours, the bulls [guards] count us and the king bull [the warden] counts the counts."

Among the prisoners Morris comes to know on his cell block are English (Paul Benjamin), a black convict who received two life sentences for defending himself against bigots back home in Alabama; the aged Doc (Robert Blossom) who has special privileges from the guards to do oil paintings; and the pathetic Litmus (Frank Ronzio), whose best friend is his pet mouse and whose chief passion is consuming pasta. Later, the egalitarian warden inspects the cells and, upon discovering an unflattering portrait of himself by Doc, sadistically suspends the man's hobby rights. The dejected Doc slices off his own fingers and later dies, as does Litmus who has a heart attack. Frank's reaction is to determine to escape. With two friends—Clarence (Jack Thibeau) and John Anglin (Fred Ward)—from the Atlanta penitenitiary, who have just been transferred here, Morris plots their escape.

Advertisement for *Escape from Alcatraz* (1979).

They will dig through the crumbling cell walls, make a passage through the ventilator shafts and cross the cold bay waters on rafts constructed from raincoats. Frank's cell neighbor Charles Butts (Larry Hankin), whose mother is dying, persuades the trio to let him join the scheme. With the help of other inmates they create makeshift tools, fashion dummies of themselves to use in their stead during evening bed checks by the guards, and create false ventilation grilles to hide their excavations. Slowly they dig their way out. At the last minute, Charley drops out of the plan, too frightened to proceed. The remaining three vanish. A full-scale search reveals no trace of the convict trio, although a chrysanthemum flower (a favored symbol in Doc's paintings) is found along the rocky edge of the water. The aghast, meglomaniac warden decrees that the trio *must* have drowned. A year later, in 1963, Alcatraz is closed permanently as a prison facility.

The uncompromisingly grim *Escape from Alcatraz* met with excellent reviews. "This is a first-rate action movie.... There is more evident knowledge of moviemaking in any frame than there are in most other American films around at the moment" (Vincent Canby, *New York Times*). "Neat and suspenseful. Eastwood ... shines with stony cynicism and indomitable self-confidence" (Ernest Leogrande, *New York Daily News*). "Ingenious, precise and exciting. Audiences can rediscover the simple, classic pleasures of moviegoing.... Alcatraz's cool, cinematic grace meshes ideally with the strengths of it.... Eastwood proves that less can be more" (Frank Rich, *Time* magazine). "Eastwood shines. The quieter things are, the more powerful he seems. He always acts a bit more psychotic in his roles than seems necessary, but here, his spooky unreachableness fits right in. His wolfish features seem right at home against a prison wall" (Peter Rainer, *Los Angeles Herald Examiner*).

In studying its social message, Tom Milne (British *Monthly Film Bulletin*) decided that *Escape from Alcatraz* was "Less a film about imprisonment than about the *idea* of imprisonment." He noted, "Reformists might take exception to the Warden's avowed aim of making good prisoners rather than good citizens...." He observed, "Questions of reform are left unraised by the film, which goes rather out of its way to portray an Alcatraz whose warders, disciplinary methods and general conditions seem strikingly decent when compared to the cinematic norm. Latent throughout, however, is the question of imprisonment itself, and the slow, soul-destroying despair it evokes both in those who impose and those who suffer it, because their imagination is confined within four walls with nothing to see and nothing to hope for beyond." Another flaw noted by many in *Escape from Alcatraz* was that the script goes out of its way to paint most of the convicts in a sympathetic if enigmatic light, as if fearful that if they presented the prisoners as antisocial thugs, the story would have lost its edge.

Escape from Alcatraz earned a very healthy $21,500,000 in domestic film rentals paid to the distributor. To be noted in the cast is director Don Siegel playing a doctor. Also appearing in small roles are Fritz Manes (a stunt coordinator and later director on Clint Eastwood projects), as well as emerging actors Danny Glover and Carl Lumbly.

The 1963 escape from Alcatraz would also figure into *Alcatraz: The Whole Shocking Story* (1980), q.v.

89. *Escape from Devil's Island* (Columbia, 1935), 64 min.

Director, Albert Rogell; story, Fred De Gresac; screenplay, Earle Snell, Fred Niblo, Jr.; camera, John Stumar; editor, Otto Meyer.

Victor Jory (Dario); Florence Rice (Jo-hanna); Norman Foster (Andre); Stanley Andrews (Steve); Daniel Haynes (Djikki); Herbert Heywood (Bouillon); Frank Lackteen (Python); Arthur Aylesworth (Commandante); Noble Johnson (Bisco).

> The new film ... contemplates at length the monotonous, soul-crushing existence of the social outcasts that inhabit the French penal colony ... Columbia's casting director deserves credit for peopling it with as motley a crew of cut-throats as we have seen in many a month.
>
> (Thomas M. Pryor, *New York Times*)

Dario (Victor Jory), who had previously been associated with international spy Steve (Stanley Andrews) is sentenced to hard labor on Devil's Island. Life there, under the Commandante (Arthur Aylesworth), is the worst hell on earth. Dario's eventual escape plans rely on his becoming a trustee, since trustees also become the penal colony guards. Making his break with Andre (Norman Foster), the two nearly succeed. Just as they are boarding a boat that will carry them to Venezuela, the long-brewing jealousy (over Steve's daughter Johanna [Florence Rice]) breaks out and ruins their plans. Later, Andre is cleared of the charges which sent him to prison.

Variety reported of this dual-bill entry, "Hopelessness of convict life on the island and the severe discipline imposed is effectively portrayed. A motley group of men have been cast to play the island's penal inhabitants. Some unusual types among them." Among the supporting cast, Frank Lackteen as Python the informer was especially effective.

90. *Escape from San Quentin* (Columbia, 1957), 81 min.

Producer, Sam Katzman; director, Fred F. Sears; screenplay, Raymond T. Marcus [Bernard Gordon]; art director, Paul Palmentola; set decorator, Sidney Clifford; music, Laurindo Almenda; song, Johnny Desmond; assistant director, Leonard Katzman; technical adviser, Hank Coffin; sound, Josh Westmoreland; camera, Benjamin H. Kline; editor, Saul H. Goodkind.

Johnny Desmond (Mike Gilbert); Merry Anders (Robbie); Richard Devon (Roy Gruber); Roy Engel (Hap Graham); William Bryant (Richie); Ken Christy (Curly Gruber); Larry Blake (Mack); Don Devlin (Piggy); Victor Millan (Mendez); John Merrick (Sampson); Norman Fredric (Jerry); Barry Brooks (Georgie); Lennie Smith (Bud); Peggy Maley (Georgia Gilbert).

There are few maximum security prisons in the world as impregnable to escape as the one on Angel's Island in San Francisco Bay. Breaking out from an escape-proof bastion has always challenged its convicts, and in no less, Hollywood. The film industry has had a recurring fascination with this particular penitentiary and those who wished to leave it—the hard way! However, this low-budget entry from the Sam Katzman production units at Columbia Pictures is misleading in its title, for the men who escape are exploding out of a San Quentin prison farm.

Among the several prisoners transferred from San Quentin Prison to an honor farm in the mountains are the rehabilitated Mike Gilbert (Johnny Desmond) a former U.S. Army flyer, and Roy Gruber (Richard Devon), the latter a hardened criminal who intends to use Mike for his escape plan. When Mike receives word that his wife Georgia (Peggy Maley) is asking for a divorce, he has a burning desire to reach Los Angeles to prevent the breakup. Gruber, who has hidden away $119,000 in loot from his last robbery, tells Mike he will share the money with him, *if* he will join in the escape plan. The scheme calls for stealing one of the private piper cub planes which hunters often park in the area near the honor farm.

Meanwhile, the hulking Hap Graham (Roy Engel), another convict, overhears the two men's plot and demands to be taken along. At the last moment, the vicious Gruber beats up Hap and leaves him for dead, confirming for Mike what kind of partner he has. They make good their escape and reach the San Fernando Valley near Los Angeles. Mike gets in touch with Georgia's sister, Robbie (Merry Anders)—who is in love with Mike—and she agrees to attempt to get Georgia to meet Mike. Georgia wants no part of her husband and Robbie returns to Mike's motel. Later, Hap, having recovered and escaped on his own, reaches Los Angeles and stakes out the home of Curly Gruber (Ken Christy), Roy's father, hoping to get a clue where the loot is stashed. However, Mike, Gruber, Robbie and Richie (William Bryant), one of Roy's dishonest pals on the outside, escape from Hap and his friends and flee to Mexico. Still later, after being temporarily put in a Mexican jail for purse-snatching, Gruber kills the wounded Richie and is himself shot by state troopers after they have crossed back into the United States and are holed up at a motel. Because Mike took the initiative of reporting his whereabouts to the troopers and for his efforts in corralling the vicious Gruber, it is suggested that once he returns to San Quentin, his remaining prison term will be slight.

The premise for *Escape from San Quentin* was as diluted as its execution. It led James Powers (*Hollywood Reporter*) to chide, "A number of plot deficiencies undermine the potential strength of the production, including the fact that Desmond is represented as so in love with his wife he risks his life to escape, but when he does get out, he doesn't even see her." For box-office "allure," producer Katzman signed pop vocalist Johnny Desmond for the lead role. (He sang the song "Lonely Lament" in the course of the movie.) The script for *Escape from San Quentin* was actually by Bernard Gordon who used the alias of Raymond T. Marcus because, at the time, he was one of the blacklisted writers (from the Communist witch hunts of the late 1940s) in Hollywood.

91. *The Executioner's Song* (NBC–TV, Nov. 28–29, 1982), color, 200 min.

Supervising producer, John Thomas Lenox; producer, Lawrence Schiller; associate producers, Michael Economou, Mimi Rothman; director, Schiller; based on the book by Norman Mailer; teleplay, Mailer; production designer, Jack McAnelly; art director, Keith Hein; costumes, Andrew Hylton, Pat Tonnema; makeup, Peter Knowlton, Julie Purcell; music, John Cacavas; songs, Waylon Jennings; music coordinator, John Fresco; music editor, John Mick; assistant directors, Tony Brown, Paul Moen; sound, Steve Marlowe, Ken Suesov; sound re-recording, Ray West, David J. Hudson, Robert Glass, Jr.; sound effects, Jim Troutman; special effects, Rick Josephson; camera, Freddie Francis; editors, Richard A. Harris (part one); Tom Rolfe (part two).

Tommy Lee Jones (Gary Gilmore); Rosanna Arquette (Nicole Baker); Christine Lahti (Brenda Nichol); Eli Wallach (Uncle Vern Damico); Jordan Clarke (Johnny Nicol); Steven Keats (Larry Samuels); Richard Venture (Earl Dorius); Jenny Wright (April Baker); Walter Olkewicz (Pete Galovan); Michael LeClair (Rikki Wood); Grace Zabriskie (Kathryne Baker); Pat Corley (Val Conlan); Mary Gregory (Ida Damico); John Dennis Johnston (Jimmy Poker-Game); Norris Church (LuAnn); Kenneth O'Brien (Spencer McGrath); Jim Youngs (Sterling Baker); Rance Howard (Lieutenant Nielsen); John Chappell (Ron Stanger); Charles Cyphers (Noall Wootton); Ray Girardin (Snyder); Grant Gottschall (Mikal Gilmore); Mark Campbell (Benny Bushnell); Kathryn Whitehead (Debbie Bushnell); Bruce Newbold (Max Jensen); Babetta Dick (Chris Caffee); Sharon Lehner (Sue); Angie Sorenson (Sunny); Victoria Jean (Pepper); Greg Soohov (Conlin's Salesman); H.E.D. Redford (Norman Fulmer); Kenneth White (Warden Smith); Judith Ramsey Wolbach (Sue Canfield); Jerry Rodrigues (Correction Officer); Spencer Moody (Kid in Drugstore); Tip Boxell (Toby Bath); Elizabeth Grand (Woman Customer); Duane Hill (Administrator); Stuart McDonald (Biker); John Hansen (1st Detective); Tim Eisenhart (1st Police Officer); Toby Bath (2nd Police Officer); Russ McGinn (1st Patrolman); Oscar Rowland (1st Judge); Walt Field (2nd Judge); Phil L. Hansen (Judge Ritter); Leo Ware (Chairman of the Board); Jeanette D. Young (Matron); Jay Bernard (Prison Official); Harold Ray Dennis (Van Driver); Stephen Boyd (Singing Prison Inmate); Thomas Carlin (1st Speaker); Anthony Leger (2nd Speaker); Dennis L. Boaz, Reverend Thomas J. Meersman, Bob Mood, Ted Peacock, John C. Wood (Themselves).

While much of *The Executioner's Song* deals with Gary Gilmore's life outside the penitentiary, the sections within prison are an integral part of this arresting account of the real-life killer who actually brought suit to have the state carry out the death penalty against him rather than endure a life sentence within prison. This action in itself is a telling commentary of the penal system. Based on Norman Mailer's best-selling book (1979), which many dismissed as specious, well-written commercialism, *The Executioner's Song* is an arresting drama, coming to grips with one condemned prisoner's direct regarding his own doomed future.

In the spring of 1976, thirty-five-year-old Gary Gilmore (Tommy Lee Jones) is released from the Marion, Illinois Penitentiary where he served twelve years for armed robbery. Overjoyed at his freedom ("I'm out, I'm really out!"), he heads for Orem, Utah where he is met by his attractive cousin Brenda Nichol (Christine Lahti), for whom he still has a romantic crush, and her husband Johnny (Jordan Clarke). Brenda's parents, Vern (Eli Wallach) and Ida Damico (Mary Ethel Gregory), take Gary in, giving him a job in Vern's shoe repair shop. Having spent so much of his life imprisoned, Gary is ripe for the company of women ("Half my life I've been looking at pictures of naked women in *Playboy* magazine. You bet I'm hard up!"), and all the material items those around him have. Thus he takes a better-paying job at Spencer McGrath's (Kenneth O'Brien) recycling business and purchases his first car.

Gary meets the bizarre, nineteen-year-old Nicole Baker (Rosanna Arquette), who has been married several times already and who has two young children. There is an immediate rapport between the two (he calls her "my guardian angel") as they each believe in reincarnation, and they decide to live together. She finds herself constantly apologizing for his outbursts of hostility to others. ("The guy's been locked up for a long time. It takes a while to get used to being really out. . . . Love is the only way to really help a situation.") However, friction develops between the two immature people. (He says of himself, "I'm just an iron boat. I bang along from rock to rock.") To acquire more money, he takes to petty thievery, and later steals several guns. Nicole eventually leaves Gary.

One evening, while he is driving around town in his new truck with Nicole's drug-dosed sister, April (Jenny Wright), he robs a gas station and kills the attendant. The next night he shoots a motel manager and is himself wounded. He calls Brenda for help, but she in turn summons the police. Found guilty of homicide, Gilmore demands that he be executed by a firing squad. When an effort is made by do-gooders to commute his sentence, he hires new attorneys to plead his right for the death sentence. ("The noise is too much for me," he explains. "I don't want to live another thirty years. I want silence.")

He and Nicole get back into contact. In one letter, he writes to Nicole: "I truly belong in a place this dank and dirty. I want my debt paid, whatever it may takes. . . . What do I do? Rot in prison and eat my heart out for the wondrous love you gave me which I threw away cause I was so spoiled." They attempt a suicide pact, but fail. Media coverage of Gilmore's unusual death plea causes public repercussion over the state's death penalty. He remains firm that he wants to die, even offering to pay for the execution himself. "I accept the sentence given me. . . . I thought you were supposed to take . . . [it] seriously . . . and not a joke." With all the hoopla over his case, Gary becomes perhaps the best known convict in U.S. history. There is talk of making a movie of his life and there is much discussion over the film rights to his story. (He wants Warren Oates to play him onscreen.) Finally, after several more delays, at dawn on January 17, 1977, he is led into the warehouse room where, seated and blindfolded, he is executed. It takes two minutes for Gilmore to die, after four bullets from .30-caliber rifles hit his chest.

The true story of Gary Gilmore's final nine months, from a prison parole to the murders that put him on Death Row!

TOMMY LEE JONES
ROSANNA ARQUETTE
ELI WALLACH

KTLA PREMIERE!   8pm **5**

Advertisement for *The Executioner's Song* (1982).

A postscript to *The Executioner's Song* stated that Vern's wife, Ida, had a stroke; Vern had to sell his shoe shop to care for her; Nicole's mother left Provo, Utah, and became a waitress in Reno, Nevada; Gary's mother remained in her trailer (in Portland, Oregon) and died there alone; and Nicole moved away from Provo and set out to remake her life.

The ads for *The Executioner's Song* promoted: "The true story of Gary Gilmore's final nine months, from a prison parole to the murders that put him on Death Row!..." *Daily Variety* was both fascinated and repelled by this filmed project, labeling the major project "a production so slick and convincing it's like a walk through Hell and . . . [it creates] a sense of wonderment at the callousness in which everyone has joined to portray the disintegration of a psychopathic killer. It's like watching a untended wound fester." Richard Combs (British *Monthly Film Bulletin*) noted, "What one misses here is even so basic a structure as Richard Brooks' deterministic cutting between victims and approaching killers in his adaptation of *In Cold Blood* [1967, q.v.,], the first instance of crimewriting as factual novel. . . . [The] film improves immeasurably when it ceases to be a character study and, in the last half, focuses instead on the media and interest-group furore occasioned by Gilmore's execution (and which in turn occasioned [director Lawrence] Schiller's contracting first for Mailer's book and then this film."

Tommy Lee Jones won an Emmy Award as Outstanding Actor in a Drama

Special for his compelling performance in *The Executioner's Song*. Other Emmy nominees included: Outstanding Supporting Actress (Rosanna Arquette), Best Teleplay (Norman Mailer), Best Sound and Best Sound Mixer. When released theatrically in England, the two-part telefeature was condensed to a 135-minute format.

92. *Experiment Alcatraz* (RKO, 1950), 58 min.

Producer/director, Edward L. Cahn; based on a screenplay by George W. George, George F. Slavin; new screenplay, Orville H. Hampton; art director, Boris Leven; set decorator, Otto Siegel; wardrobe, Frank Tait, Esther Krebbs; makeup, Ted Larsen; music/music director, Irving Gertz; assistant director, Frank Fox; sound, John R. Carter; camera, Jackson J. Rose; editor, Philip Cahn.

John Howard (Dr. Ross Williams); Joan Dixon (Joan McKenna); Walter Kingsford (Dr. Finley); Lynne Carter (Ethel Ganz); Robert Shayne (Barry Morgan); Kim Spalding (Duke Shaw); Sam Scar (Eddie Ganz); Kenneth MacDonald (Colonel Harris); Dick Cogan (Dan Staley); Frank Cady (Max Henry); Byron Foulger (Jim Carlton, the Realtor); Ralph Peters (Bartender); Lewis Martin (Assistant District Attorney Walton); Harry Lauter (Richard McKenna); Raymond Largay (Warden Keaton).

A bizarre programmer from RKO Pictures which relied on a plot device from an earlier prison entry, *Millionaires in Prison* (1940), q.v., to promulgate its fanciful storyline.

Experiment Alcatraz opens with a stark preface:

> The rock: a little iron curtain world of lost souls sitting in the shadow of the Golden Gate. Its inmates are felons the other prisons didn't want. That little stretch of water between Alcatraz and San Francisco is wider than the Pacific as far as the prisoners are concerned. They're not going to cross it unless they die or serve their time. But modern science performs many wonders. To five Alcatraz convicts the scientific experiment brought the greatest miracle of all. A chance to get off the rock.

Five convicts at Alcatraz—including Dan Staley (Dick Cogan), Eddie Ganz (Sam Scar) and Barry Morgan (Robert Shayne)—are offered a special deal by the Warden (Raymond Largay). The U.S. government is conducting a research experiment and if they agree to participate, they will be freed, no matter what happens during the testing. They are taken to the mainland to a U.S. Military Hospital where they are told, "You have a chance to do great service to humanity." They are subjected to radioactive isotopes, after having been injected with a special salt solution. The experimenters hope to develop a cure for leukemia. Meanwhile, one of the convicts, Morgan, stabs another (Ganz) while under the treatment, and it causes an abrupt halt to the vital experiment. Nurse Joan McKenna (Joan Dixon), whose own brother (Harry Lauter) is a leukemia victim at the base hospital is anxious to assist Dr. Finley (Walter Kingsford) and Dr. Ross Williams (John Howard) unravel the mystery over Ganz's death, so that the medical experiment can continue. While investigating the background of the dead convict, they visit Alcatraz where convict Max Henry (Frank Cady) gives them a clue that Morgan was actually tied into Ganz in their pre-prison life. The trail leads to Lake Tahoe where they visit Ganz's stepdaughter Ethel (Lynne Carter). It develops that Ganz had participated in a robbery and hid away $250,000 in loot. Morgan had caused himself to be jailed to get close to Ganz and learn the whereabouts of the money, working in cooperation with Ethel, his wife. In wrapping up the case, Williams is killed, but Kingsford traps Morgan into confessing his crime. The experiments for a cure are to continue.

Variety rightly reacted adversely to this hokey entry. "Edward L. Cahn's direction lacks pace but his production achieves okay values for the limited budget. Script was ineptly written and the dialog unconvincing."

RKO had purchased the distribution rights to *Experiment Alcatraz* from Crystal Productions for $100,000.

93. *Fast-Walking* (Pickman Film, 1982), color, 115 min.

Executive producer, Joseph Harris; producer, James B. Harris; associate producer, Richard McWhorter; director, James B. Harris; based on the novel *The Rap* by Ernest Brawley; screenplay, James B. Harris; art director, Richard Haman; set decorator, Edward J. McDonald; men's costumes, Ron Archer; women's costumes, Michele Dittrick; makeup, Michael Moschella; music, Lalo Schifrin; music editor, Dan Carlin; technical adviser, James G. Bodgett, Sr.; second unit director, George Robotman; assistant directors, Fred L. Miller, Stephen Dunn; stunt coordinator, Roger Creed; sound editors, Douglas Gundstaff, Marvin I. Kosberg; special effects, Bill Balles; camera, King Baggot; editor, Douglas Stewart.

James Woods (Frank "Fast-Walking" Miniver); Tim McIntire (Wasco); Kay Lenz (Moke); Robert Hooks (William Galliot); M. Emmet Walsh (Sergeant Sanger); Timothy Agoglia Carey (Bullet); Susan Tyrrell (Evie); Charles Weldon (Officer Jackson); John Friedrich (Squeeze); Sandy Ward (Warden Riker); Lance Le Gault (Lieutenant Barnes); Deborah White (Elaine Schecter); Helen Page Camp (Lady in Visitor's Room); Sydney Lassick (Ted); K. Callan (Motel Manager); Ernie Fuentes (Straw Boss); Barbara Eaton, Connye Brown (Hookers); Roger Creed (Guard on Gun Walk); Jack Tyree, Hugh Gillin (Heavies); Reggie Valencia (Guitar Player); Jerry Dickson, A. W. Sterling, Robert Dischner, Skip Kellicut (Guards).

Fast-Walking is a very unorthodox prison drama starring the very intense, idiosyncratic James Woods in another of his unusual characterizations. While the movie's pretentious declamations on life offer little to further the viewer's education, *Fast-Walking*'s shock value lies in its casual but effective demonstration that prison guards are frequently as hardened and corrupt as the men over whom they keep guard. While this is not a startling revelation by any means, it is one that is given cogency by Woods's mesmerizing character delineation.

Long-inured to his boring routine as a prison guard, lackadaisical Frank "Fast-Walking Miniver" (James Woods) spends much of his on/off time duty at the penitentiary smoking pot. This redneck dreams of some day escaping the tedium of guard duty. He fantasizes about relocating to Oregon where he imagines an easy, albeit illicit, life of fun and easy money. The fact that he never goes is another indication of his overall indecisiveness. His fellow keeper, the tough Sergeant Sanger (M. Emmett Walsh) is a corrupt bigot, who plays off one convict against another for financial gains.

Among the convict population at this overcrowded, ethnic-split institution, somewhere in the southwest, is the sinister Wasco (Tim McIntire), an enterprising grafter who insists:

> This joint offers undetermined opportunity to those who can change adversity into fortune.... God, I love it here in this joint! Really love it! There's no place like it in the whole damn world. There's nothing you can't do in here, if you've got the brains. It's as simple as that. If you just believe in yourself, follow your star, it leads you right to opportunity.

With his henchmen, including Squeeze (John Friedrich), available to help carry out his orders, Wasco offers a variety of contraband goods (from drugs to weapons) to the prisoners, all for a very high price. One of Wasco's prime contacts on the outside is the tough Evie (Susan Tyrrell) who runs a general store and who operates a whore house on the side. Both she and Wasco try to persuade their cousin, Miniver, into becoming their new courier. He refuses.

The racial unrest in the prison soon reaches a peak: already one Mexican convict has been dumped to his death over the side of a cell tier. The militant black convict segment is aroused to near frenzy because William Galliot (Robert Hooks), a leading figure in the black movement, is being transferred to the prison the next day—and there is a contract out for his life.

Meanwhile, motorcycle-riding Moke (Kay Lenz) appears on the scene, claiming she wants to be one of Evie's girls. She quickly draws Miniver's sexual interest and he becomes so passionately attached to her that he does not appreciate how easily she is drawing him into her scheme. Before long, the conniving Wasco is offering Miniver a lifetime of pleasure with Moke—his girlfriend—if Frank will cooperate in the plan to shoot Galliot in the prison exercise yard. At about the same time, Elaine Schecter (Deborah White) encounters Miniver on the outside and, claiming to be an advocate for Galliot's cause, offers him $50,000 to assist the black convict in escaping.

Galliot arrives at the prison and is immediately made aware of the danger to his life. He figures his adversaries will stage a phony race war among the prisoners to get him accidentally killed. Sergeant Sanger does his bit to enflame the situation when he plants a weapon in Galliot's cell to discredit the man. Later, aided by Moke's convincing arguments, Miniver agrees to help in the escape plot, which also includes Officer Jackson (Charles Weldon). The escape goes as designed, but no sooner is Galliot on the outside than he is shot. From the guard tower Miniver spots that it was Moke who killed the man. As she rides away on her motorcycle, he realizes how duped he had been. Now, further disillusioned about life, Miniver and Jackson decide to do civilization a good turn. They go to Wasco's cell where he is bragging about his success in the Galliot affair and about his political connections that will see him soon pardoned. The two guards nonchalantly grab Wasco and toss him off the cell tier. He falls to his death with the guards feigning ignorance of the matter.

Little-seen in theatres, although a frequent TV offering, *Fast-Walking* received poor critical reviews. "[S]eems overly contrived to appeal not only at the drive-in (the repeated shots of Evie's girls being soaped and showered) but at the art house, as Frank monologizes about his existential choice or as Wasco delivers [John] Barrymore orotundities on the nature of blood ties" (Alex Keneas, *Newsday*). Archer Winsten *(New York Post)* reviewed that filmmaker James B. Harris "has not spared any of the prison-melodrama horses in whipping this one up to a froth of dirty dealings, drugs, femme fatales and men without a trace of decency." *Variety* had negative reaction to the picture which it felt "reeks of a sort of late–1960s, counter-culture existentialism, pic seems oddly out of time and place at this point, even if the bare bones of the action could just as plausibly take place now as then."

Fast-Walking was made in late 1980 and went through several potential releasers before Pickman Film acquired distribution rights. Multi-task filmmaker James B. Harris had previously been a producer for Stanley Kubrick and had later directed such features as *The Bedford Incident* (1965) and *Some Call It Loving* (1973).

Danny Freedman and Michael Greer in *Fortune and Men's Eyes* (1971).

94. *Fortune and Men's Eyes* (Metro-Goldwyn-Mayer, 1971), color, 102 min

Producers, Lester Persky, Lewis M. Allen; co-producer, Donald Ginsberg; director, Harvey Hart; based on the play by John Herbert; screenplay, Herbert; production designer, Earl G. Preston; costumes, Marcel Carpenter; music, Galt MacDermot; songs, MacDermot; MacDermot and William Dumaresq; choreographer, Jill Courtney; songs: Michael Greer; MacDermot and William Dumaresq; assistant director, Arthur Voronka; technical adviser, Stanley Sommerville; sound, Joseph Champagne; camera, George Dufaux; editor, Douglas Robertson.

Wendell Burton (Smitty); Michael Greer (Queenie); Zooey Hall (Rocky); Danny Freedman (Mona); Larry Perkins (Screwdriver); James Barron (Holyface Peters); Lazaro Perez (Catso); Jon Granik (Sergeant Gritt); Tom Harvey (Warden Gasher); Hugh Webster (Rabbit); Kirk McColl (Guard Gasher); Vance Davis (Sailor); Robert Goodlier (Doctor); Cathy Wiele (Cathy); Georges Allard (Fiddler); Modesto (One-Eye); Michel Gilbert (Young Prisoner); Robert Saab (Drummer); A. Zeytounian (Pianist).

John Herbert's graphic drama of life in a dormitory cell inside a Canadian penal reformatory for young male convicts was first presented Off Broadway in February 1967 and lasted 383 performances. It was later revived in a more exploitive version (complete with on-stage nudity and simulated sexual acts), also Off Broadway, in October 1969, directed by Sal Mineo. It ran for 231 performances and, later, went on tour. What made the drama so popular, beyond its searing account of a young farm boy/prisoner being corrupted by his new environment, was the vivid, no-holds-barred depiction of homosexuality in jail. In 1971, MGM released a toned-down version of the play. It was filmed in Canada and starred Wendell Burton (who had made such a hit in the movie *The Sterile Cuckoo,* 1969, opposite Liza Minelli) and Michael Greer. The latter, a very talented impressionist/comic, recreated the oversized role of Queenie, a high camp trustee prisoner who disguises his brutal nature with comic jibes and outrageous drag outfits.

For a relatively minor drug offense, nineteen-year-old Smitty (Wendell Burton) is sentenced to six months detention in a Canadian jail for young men. His cellmates are the strong, tacit Rocky (Zooey Hall); the woeful, effeminate Mona (Danny Freedman); and Queenie (Michael Greer), an outrageously flamboyant homosexual. When Queenie makes sexual advances, the rigid Smitty rejects him, despite warnings from the cross-dresser that he had better watch out for the others in prison. Later, just as Smitty is about to be gang-raped by his fellow convicts, he is saved by Rocky. The naïve Smitty is grateful, until he realizes that Rocky is now his "old man" and that protocol requires him to submit to Rocky's sodomizing at will. Rather than risk the alternative, Smitty becomes Rocky's boy. However, because the envious Queenie taunts him, Smitty engages Rocky in a fight and beats him. He is now a free agent. This causes the humiliated Rocky to commit suicide. The distraught Queenie, upset by Rocky's death, causes a furor when he strips off all his own clothes at a Christmas entertainment attended by the warden and his wife.

Now intending to prove himself cock of the walk, Smitty pressures the gentle Mona to become his boy; the latter rejects the offer. Mona explains that being humiliated by people you care nothing for is meaningless, but to be dehumanized by one you love (i.e. Mona's feelings for Smitty) is agonizing. Smitty suddenly awakens to the negative transformation going on within him. He is horrified.

Addison Verrill *(Variety)* was not impressed by the proceedings. "What emerges is ineptly filmed soap opera centering around the latest cinematic 'fate worse than death': homosexual rape.... [The filmmakers] have floundered in attempting to chart a middle course between valid social commentary and outright sensationalism.... One brief genital flash and two 'demure sodomy sequences' are remarkably restrained, but the dialog makes up for those 'lapses.'" Verrill perceived, "The horror of the U.S. penal system has been well documented by others, but *Fortune*'s soap opera approach (will he or won't he) sparks laughter." Tom Milne (British *Monthly Film Bulletin*) agreed that it was "a hopelessly compromised and unconvincing film, uncertain whether it means to be a reform tract or a tabloid sensation."

After nine weeks of filming at Quebec Prison, director Jules Schwerin was replaced by Harvey Hart.

95. *Front Page Woman* (Warner Bros., 1935), 80 min.

Producer, Samuel Bischoff; director, Michael Curtiz; based on the story "Women Are Bum Newspapermen" by Richard Macaulay; screenplay, Laird Doyle, Lillie Hayward, Roy Chanslor; art director, John Hughes; music, Heinz Roemheld; music director, Leo F. Forbstein; dialogue director, Frank McDonald; camera, Tony Gaudio; editor, Terry Morse.

Bette Davis (Ellen Garfield); George Brent (Curt Devlin); Roscoe Karns (Toots O'Grady); Winifred Shaw (Inez Cordova); Joseph Crehan (Spike Kiley); Joseph King (Hartnett); J. Farrell MacDonald (Hallo-

han); Addison Richards (District Attor-
ney); Dorothy Dare, June Martel (Show
Girls); Gordon Westcott (Maitland Colter);
J. Carrol Naish (Mr. Roberts); Walter
Walker (Judge Rickard); DeWitt Jennings
(Lieutenant); Huntley Gordon (Marvin
Stone); Adrian Rosley (Tailor); Georges
Renavent (Chinad); Miki Morita (Fumi);
Jack Norton, Edward Keane (Reporters);
Dick Winslow (Copy Boy); Charles Moore
(Black Boy); Lester Dorr, Jerry Mandy
(Waiters); Wade Boteler (Cop); Mary
Treen (Nurse); Torben Meyer (Janitor);
Frank DuFrane (Assistant District Attor-
ney).

Front Page Woman was one of five pictures Bette Davis made in 1935 for
Warner Bros., including her Oscar-winning performance in *Dangerous*. *Front
Page Woman* is a pleasant, fast-paced nonsense continuance of the screen teaming
of Davis and George Brent. Its brittle, facile newspaper story is primarily dealing
with the romancing and competing of rival reporters Davis and Brent. However,
sandwiched into the pell-mell proceedings is a sequence which occurs at the State
Prison. It is a telling commentary on the public's viewpoint of the penal system
and the way many regarded executions as a public three-ring circus.

Ace reporter Curt Devlin (George Brent) of *The Daily Express* adores Ellen
Garfield (Bette Davis), sob sister reporter for the rival *The Daily Star*. However,
he is convinced that women are not emotionally equipped to be roughneck, on-
the-spot reporters (or as he so chauvinistically opines, "Women make bum
newspapermen!"). At the moment, the big news in town is the pending execution
of Mabel Gaye, glamorous Broadway notable who became a notorious killer. She
is scheduled to be electrocuted at North Prison at midnight. All the local
newspaper reporters are arriving for the newsworthy event, treating the occasion
as a big clambake. For many of these hard-boiled men, the electrocution is a test
of their manliness, to demonstrate their ability to endure observing the gruesome
occurrence without flinching. Much is made of the newsmen's tough demeanors
as they wisecrack about the pending demise of the convicted murderess.

REPORTER #1: You don't think this Gaye dame will take on, do ya?

REPORTER #2: Oh, probably. The last one I saw screamed all the way to the chair.

REPORTER #3: That's what I hate about dames. They always dramatize everything.

REPORTER #4: Hey. Wouldn't it have been a good idea if that dame had committed suicide before she got to the dance hall.

REPORTER #5: No such luck!

And for glib news photographer Toots O'Grady (Roscoe Karns), who cannot worm
his way into the by-invitation-only proceedings, he wishes his conferrers bad luck,
"I hope when the dame sits down, she blows a fuse."

The camera then focuses on the sole distaff reporter, Ellen, sitting in the
prison waiting room, delicately munching on a sandwich. As her oversized, darting
eyes reveal, she is far from calm. Curt Devlin breezes into the packed room and
salutes his pals, "Hello everybody! And how is everyone on this festive occasion?"
He greets "Little Miss Front Page" and then, enjoying his macho bravery, proceeds
to dramatize for her just how the electrocution will be handled, hoping to scare
her off.

CURT: It's okay for you to shag fires and ambulances, but a burning is different.
It does something to you. It chews you up inside. Look at those guys, they've seen

it before and, believe me, they're really tough. Ah, don't go through with it kid. You don't have to. I'll cover the story for you.

ELLEN: No.... If you can take it, I can.

CURT: Well, I guess it's about time for the slow music.

As they proceed into the observation area outside the death room, a seemingly jovial reporter recalls, "Remember the last time we came through here, I couldn't sleep for a week."

The execution (unseen by moviegoers) proceeds as scheduled. Thereafter, the reporters pour out to rush to the telephones, anxious to call in the big story. Ellen promptly faints and Curt must cover for her with her newspaper.

The remainder of movie deals with the efforts of both Ellen and Curt to solve the murder of Marvin Q. Stone (Huntley Gordon). Although Maitland Coulter (Gordon Westcott) is arrested for the crime, both reporters discover that the mysterious Inez Cordova (Winifred Shaw) knows who the real murderer is.

In reviewing this light-hearted newspaper yarn, Frank Nugent (*New York Times*) judged, "If you keep in mind that this portrayal of newspaper work is a bit on the whimsey side, then *Front Page Woman* can be recommended as a downright amusing photoplay.... Add to that a cast with a neat sense of comedy and you have an excellent tonic for the mid–July doldrums."

96. *Fugitive from a Prison Camp* (Columbia, 1940), 58 min.

Producer, Larry Darmour; director, Lewis D. Collins; screenplay, Albert DeMond, Stanley Roberts; assistant director, Carl Hiecke; camera, James S. Brown, Jr.; editor, Dwight Caldwell.

Jack Holt (Sheriff Lawson); Marian Marsh (Ann Baldwin); Robert Barrat (Chester Russell); Philip Terry (Bill Harding); Dennis Moore (Slugger Martin); Jack LaRue (Red Nelson); George Offerman, Jr. (Ted Baldwin); Frankie Burke (Sobby Taylor); Donald Haines (Burly Bascomb); Alan Baldwin (Jerome Davis); Frank LaRue (Robert O'Brien); Ernest Morrison (Chuckles).

To help his fiancée, Ann Baldwin (Marian Marsh), Bill Harding (Philip Terry) goes to the hideout of criminal Red Nelson (Jack LaRue) where he hopes to convince Ann's brother, Ted (George Offerman, Jr.), to abandon his life of crime. The police arrive at the scene and all are arrested. Because Nelson believes Bill is a stool pigeon, he orders his men not to say anything in Harding's defense. Bill and the others are sentenced to prison. Small town Sheriff Lawson (Jack Holt), who takes a liking to Bill and believes in his innocence, insists he will help the young man win a new trial. He asks him to be patient. Meanwhile, Lawson arranges to send Bill and other convicts to work at a road camp. There, engineer Chester Russell (Robert Barrat) does his best to sabotage operations, because he and a contractor friend had hoped to get the road-building job for themselves. When his case review is not forthcoming, the discouraged Bill escapes; at the same time three other convicts—from the Nelson gang—break out. Lawson tracks Harding to Ann's apartment where, after subduing the violent Bill, he tells the man that Nelson's confederates (whose escape bid failed) have cleared his name.

Shot on the cheap by Larry Darmour's budget unit at Columbia Pictures, *Fugitive from a Prison Camp* was penny dreadful. "[A]ttempting platitudinously to point up prison reforms on the theory that first offenders are not such bad guys at heart if given a chance, the story is of the most hackneyed character. The dialog is banal, action tedious and performances for the most part stilted" *(Variety)*.

Working title: *Offenders of the Law.*

97. *Fugitives* (Fox, 1929), 57 min. (Also silent version, 5,331'.)

Presenter, William Fox; supervisor, Kenneth Hawks; director, William Beaudine; based on the story by Richard Harding Davis; screenplay, John Stone; titles, Malcolm Stuart Boyland; assistant director, Thomas Held; camera, Chester Lyons.

Madge Bellamy (Alice Carroll); Don Terry (Dick Starr); Arthur Stone (Jimmy); Earle Foxe (Al Barrow); Matthew Betz (Earl Rand); Lumsden Hare (Uncle Ned); Edith Yorke (Mrs. Carroll); Jean Laverty (Mame); Hap Ward (Scal, the Rat).

A minor league part talkie made during Hollywood's rush to transfer to sound movies. *Variety* found *Fugitives* "mechanical, routine" and that "Effort for story speed makes players routine in their performances." Its prison setting was no more realistic than the rest of the pedestrian plot.

When nightclub owner Barrow (Earle Fox) is killed and the murder weapon is found on chorine Alice Carroll (Madge Bellamy) she is the likely suspect. Her fate is sealed when another co-worker testifies that she heard Barrow proposition Alice and the latter had said she would rather kill him than yield her reputation. Novice district attorney Dick Starr (Don Terry) prosecutes the case and Alice is sentenced to Sing Sing Prison. Her friend Jimmy (Arthur Stone) helps her to escape from the penitentiary. Later, while rescuing Starr from the wrath of a criminal gang, she proves her innocence and finds love with her former prosecutor.

98. *Gideon's Trumpet* (CBS–TV, April 30, 1980), color, 100 min.

Executive producer, John Houseman; producer, David W. Rintels; associate producers, Myron L. Slobadien, Philip J. Grosz; director, Robert Collins; based on the book by Anthony Lewis; teleplay, Rintels; production designer, Edward G. Carfagno; set decorator, Don Sullivan; wardrobe, Thom Baxter; makeup, Fred B. Phillips; music/music conductor, Joseph Weiss; music supervisor, Harry V. Lojewski; music editor, Scott Peery, Jr.; assistant directors, James Nicholson; sound, James Pilcher, Michael J. Kohlit; sound editor, John Delbis; camera, Don H. Birnkrant; editor, Frank Bracht.

Henry Fonda (Clarence Earl Gideon); Jose Ferrer (Abe Fortas); John Houseman (Chief Justice); Fay Wray (Edna Curtis); Sam Jaffe (1st Justice); Dean Jagger (6th Justice); Nicholas Pryor (Jacob); William Prince (5th Justice); Lane Smith (Fred Turner); Richard McKenzie (Judge Robert

McCrary); Dolph Sweet (Charlie); Ford Rainey (2nd Justice); David Sheiner (Abe Krash); Pat McNamara (Harris); Les Lannom (Bobby Earle); Malcolm Groom (John Ely); Allan Rich (Tobias Simon); Richard Lineback (Lester Wade); David Clennon (James Fitzpatrick); Michael Cavanaugh (Stocker); Paul Benjamin (Artis); Cliff Pellow (Justin Pike); Jerry Hardin (Sheriff Mel Cobb); Frederic Cook (Leo Stafford); Steven Peterman (Arthur Vitale); James O'Connell (Warden); Jon Locke (Supervisor); Gary Grubbs (Deputy Hamilton); Seamon Glass (Prison Guard); Gwen Van Dam (Mrs. Lawrence); James E. Brodhead (Court Crier); Edmund H. North (3rd Justice); Emmett Lavery, Sr. (7th Justice); Liam O'Brien (4th Justice); Herb Benkman (8th Justice); Don Draper (Bailiff); Henry Porach (Guard); Anthony Lewis (Reporter); Timothy Scott (Toby Block).

In one of his final acting assignments, Academy Award-winning actor Henry Fonda (1905–1982) lent dignity and an understated performance to this factually based TV movie. *Daily Variety* reported approvingly, "The course of Gideon's life has been shaped into a satisfying TV form, and Fonda works the character into a believable personality of several dimensions."

In Bay Harbor, Florida, a poolroom is robbed and Clarence Earl Gideon (Henry Fonda), an impoverished middle-aged man, is accused of having committed petty larceny. Having no funds for an attorney and because Florida state law stated that *only* in capital offense cases can the state appoint a lawyer, Gideon must defend himself. The semi-literate man fumbles in the process. Because he has a record of minor crimes and due to circumstantial evidence, he is convicted of the charge and sent to Rayford Prison for five years.

For the low-keyed Gideon, returning to prison is not a traumatic situation, something the matter-of-fact man adjusts to relatively easily. He is comfortable enough in this structured environment to give newcomers advise on how best to survive their time. He has taken a job in the prison garage and suggests to his pupils, "Don't get a job in the hot sun." He also points out, "Then it's out to the yard where the old boys look over the fish [the new men]. That's when you really got to hold your mud together."

Before long, word gets around the prison that Gideon has a knowledge of the law, and several prisoners come to him for advice regarding their cases. As one guard observes, "A couple of months in this place, they all think you're Moses leading them to the promised land."

In browsing through the prison library, especially when reading the legal volumes, it occurs to Gideon that his fundamental constitutional right to have defense provided for him was denied by the Florida law. He learns that he can make application to the U.S. Supreme Court for a review of the situation and he does so, writing his plea with pencil and paper, not even knowing how to use a typewriter. The Chief Justice (John Houseman) of the Supreme Court is intrigued by the legal question posed by Gideon's application. As the review process proceeds, famed attorney Abe Fortas (Jose Ferrer), without even having met Gideon, takes on his case. Fortas realizes that it could develop into a milestone case and his advocacy in the matter will not go unnoticed. The process of the law takes its slow time, with Gideon forced to pass through his daily prison routine, always hoping for some word from Washington, D.C. Eventually, the Supreme Court decides in his favor (a 9–0 vote). The judgment of the original Florida court is put aside after a new state trial. The unassuming Gideon, meanwhile, has helped another convict, the black Artis (Paul Benjamin), who has been imprisoned for twenty years, to appeal his conviction and to be released.

Although Gideon is now a prison hero and a national figure, his plans upon release are simple. He hopes to take more responsibility for his own life and resolves to track down his children whom he has not seen in years. He also intends to visit the poolroom where all his troubles began.

As a postscript to this narrative, on November 1, 1963, Attorney General Robert F. Kennedy issued the following statement:

> If an obscure Florida convict named Clarence Earl Gideon had not sat down in prison with a pencil and paper to write a letter to the Supreme Court and, if the Supreme Court had not taken the trouble to look to the merit in that one crude petition, among all the bundles of mail it must receive everyday, the vast machinery of the American law would have gone on functioning undisturbed.... The whole course of the American legal history has been changed.

While Henry Fonda offered a very self-effacing performance, the same cannot be said of much of the supporting cast, especially those playing Supreme Court

Justices. The weight of the judicial robes seemed to have instilled a need for pomposity and overstated purpose in all of them, including John Houseman who was executive producer of the production. Fonda was Emmy-nominated for his characterization. Also Emmy-nominated was the script by producer David W. Rintels. Fay Wray, whose greatest movie fame was as the screaming heroine of *King Kong* (1933), made a rare TV appearance as Gideon's landlady who never lost faith in his innocence.

99. *The Girl Called Hatter Fox* (CBS–TV, Oct. 12, 1977), color, 100 min.

Executive producer, Roger Gimbel; producer/director, George Schaefer; based on the novel *Hatter Fox* by Marilyn Harris; teleplay, Darryl Ponicsan; art director, Herman Zimmerman; set decorator, Raymond Molyneaux; costumes, Dell Hayden, Tony Faso; makeup, Louis Lane; music, Fred Karlin; music editor, La Da Productions, Inc.; assistant director, Michael J. Kane; sound, Jeff Wexler; sound editor, Horta Editorial; camera, Howard R. Schwartz; editor, Sidney M. Katz.

Ronny Cox (Dr. Teague Summer); Conchata Ferrell (Nurse Rhinehart); John Durren (Claude); Joanelle Nadine Romero (Hatter Fox); Donald Hotton (Dr. Levering); S. John Launer (Mr. Winton); Mira Santera (Mango); Danny Villaneueva (1st Policeman); William Farrington (Bartender); Jeanne Stein (Belle); Jack Maguire (Reverend); Mona Lawrence (Indian Nurse); Robert L. Jones, Arthur Wagner, Hardy Phelps (Men in Bar); David Leyba (2nd Policeman); Denise Montoya (Nurse); Sabra Wilson (Matron); Virginia Bird (Old Indian Woman); Caroline Rackley (Waitress); Biff Yeager (Cabbie); Billy Beck (Man from Orphanage); Adam Williams (Guard); Renn Durren (1st Mango Girl); Deborah Brown (2nd Mango Girl).

> It takes a long time to get there, and the way seems at time overly tortuous, but the journey has its rewards. Its power can't be denied.
>
> *(Daily Variety)*

In operating any institution, those who vary too extremely from the norm always suffer. Such is the case with Hatter Fox (Joanelle Nadine Romero) an Indian girl who is incarcerated, along with two hundred other girls, at the Ranfield Reformatory for Girls in New Mexico. She has a long record of minor criminal offenses and is currently causing a great disciplinary problem for her keepers. Dr. Teague Summer (Ronny Cox), a physician with the Bureau of Indian Affairs, is requested to come to the Reformatory immediately for a consultation about this "incorrigible."

No sooner does he arrive at Ranfield than he is informed by staff physician Dr. Levering (Donald Hotton), "The administrator here is a dedicated man. He believes that discipline can accomplish all things. Each case is a challenge and he hates to lose." According to the reformatory, the only way to discipline the unfathomable, aggressive Hattie is to cage her in an oversized doghouse where she cannot attack anyone. In Summer's first encounter with Hattie, she attempts to stab him and he is so cowed by her violent outburst of anger that he wants no further part of the case. However, those at Ranfield are adamant that he handle the situation. As the self-pleased Ranfield administrator insists, "There is a psychological key to every difficult inmate.... We believe there is *no* such thing as a bad girl, only an unhappy one. Our goal is to create a *supervisable* individual."

Summer is reassigned to the institution, a facility filled with strange individuals, including the dim-witted guard Claude (John Durren), who is happiest when he is playing his harmonica. The free-spirited Summer is aghast at many of the strict procedures at Ranfield, especially those concerning Hattie, whom he feels is being reduced to a cowering animal. His questioning of such rigidness leads Dr. Levering to reply, "I'd like to see you run an institution like this without rules." Through many arduous, tense conferences with Hattie (who is freqeuntly tied to a bed for his protection) the psychiatrist begins to break through her emotional wall. With the help of no-nonsense Nurse Rhinehart (Conchata Ferrell), he uncovers that the Indian girl, who was sexually abused at an Indian mission school as a child, believes she has been cursed with ancient witchcraft. He helps Hattie to overcome her superstitions and to build confidence in herself as a human being of worth. Eventually, she is released from Ranfield into his custody.

This telefeature was filmed on location in Santa Fe and Albuquerque, New Mexico, as well as at the Los Angeles County Juvenile Detention Center in Saugus, California. The best performance in this grim, gray study is provided by the ebullient Conchata Ferrell, who admits to the doctor newcomer how she retains her optimism in the face of such depressing odds: "We've never lost one [a girl prisoner] to the state hospital. It's like a sport, like rival basketball teams."

100. *Girl on a Chain Gang* (Jerry Gross Productions, 1966), 96 min.

Presenter/producer, Jerry Gross; associate producer, Nicholas Demetroules; director, Gross; story, Don Olsen; screenplay, Gross.
With: William Watson, Julie Ange, R. K. Charles.

A very low-grade independent production about a young woman (Julie Ange) who, along with a white man (William Watson) and a black man (R. K. Charles), runs amiss of redneck law enforcers in a southern small town. After being arrested and abused, they are placed on a chain gang. Made a year after the young Civil Rights workers were murdered in Mississippi, this black-and-white exploitation movie received minimum distribution but maximum promotion with its lurid ad campaign:

The film that uncovers the lid of small town hate!

1) When you come back from the fields tonight, I'm going to give you the beating of your life!

2) They said I could go off with her to Perkin's Motel and she'd be real cooperative!

3) Nellie—the town's plaything. She passed for white and they loved it.

101. *Girls in Chains* (Producers Releasing Corp., 1943), 72 min.

Producer, Peter Van Duinen; director/story, Edgar G. Ulmer; screenplay, Albert Reich; set decorator, Fred Preble; music, Leo Erdody; assistant director, Melville DeLay; sound, Paul Schmutz; camera, Ira Morgan; editor, Charles Henkel, Jr.
Arline Judge (Helen); Roger Clark (Frank Donovan); Robin Raymond (Rita); Barbara Pepper (Ruth); Dorothy Burgess (Mrs. Peters); Clancy Cooper (Marcus); Allan Byron (Johnny Moon); Patricia Knox (Jean); Sidney Melton (Pinkhead); Russell Gaige (Dalvers); Emmett Lynn (Lionel Cleeter); Richard Clarke (Tom Haver-

shield); Betty Blythe (Mrs. Grey); Peggy Stewart (Jerry); Beverly Boyd (George); Bob Hill (Dr. Orchard); Henry Hall (Judge Coolidge); Mrs. Gardener Crane (Mrs. McCarthy); Crane Whitley (Reverend Greene); Francis Ford (Jury Foreman).

The world may have been engulfed in World War II, but in Hollywood it was business as usual. The recurrent, titillating theme of girls-behind-bars was the focus of this thrifty production, tossed out by poverty row's PRC, hoping to capture filmgoers' interest with the film's lurid title and an entry which mixed its genres: gangster/detective/prison.

Because her gangster brother-in-law Johnny Moon (Allan Byron) has caused great notoriety by his recent trial/acquittal, high school teacher/psychiatrist, Helen (Arline Judge) is ordered to resign by the school board who feels she may have a bad influence on her students. Thanks to her friend/detective Frank Donovan (Roger Clark), she obtains a post as teacher at a girls' reformatory. The liberal newcomer is aghast at the conditions there, but her efforts for reform are stymied by Superintendent Marcus (Clancy Cooper) and Mrs. Peters (Dorothy Burgess), the head matron. Later, Helen uncovers that Marcus is a stooge for Johnny Moon and that there is a great deal of corruption at the institution. She and Donovan gather evidence to present to the governor. Meanwhile, Rita (Robin Raymond), a former girlfriend of Moon's is sentenced to a term at the reformatory. Thanks to Helen's influence, she changes her ways. To discredit Helen, Marcus and Moon kidnap Rita from the reformatory and kill her. In the interim, Helen is held responsible for the girl's disappearance. The murder was observed by a drunkard (Emmett Lynn) who passes on the information to Donovan. Moon dies while trying to avoid arrest and Marcus is jailed. Helen is appointed the new head of the reformatory.

Harrison's Reports was not impressed, stating, "neither the story nor the background is particularly novel, and it lacks freshness in dialogue, as well as in action." *Variety* noted, "A handful of tough-looking gals put on the leer effectively."

102. *Girls in Prison* (American International, 1956), 86 min.

Producer, Alex Gordon; director, Edward L. Cahn; screenplay, Lou Rusoff; art director, Don Ament; music/song, Ronald Stein; camera, Frederick E. West; editor, Ronald Sinclair.

Richard Denning (Reverend Fulton); Joan Taylor (Anne Carson); Adele Jergens (Jenny); Helen Gilbert (Melanee); Lance Fuller (Paul Anderson); Jane Darwell (Matron Jamieson); Raymond Hatton (Pop Carson); Phyllis Coates (Dorothy); Diana Darrin (Meg); Mae Marsh (Grandma); Laurie Mitchell (Phyllis); Diane Richards (Nightclub Singer); Luana Walters, Riza Royce (Female Guards).

Independent producing company American International Pictures was already making a big dent in the teenage moviegoing market with its science-fiction and horror entries. *Girls in Prison* was one of the studio's many exploitable items, geared to drawing in youths with its mixture of cheesecake, bondage and "tough" action.

Convicted of having participated in a bank robbery with Paul Anderson (Lance Fuller), Anne Carson (Joan Taylor) is sentenced to five years in prison, in particular because she has always refused to reveal where the $38,000 loot was hidden. At first, Anne believes she can cope with her time behind bars and then, once released, enjoy her ill-gotten gains. However, she is horrified at the overwhelming oppressiveness of her new environment. Moreover, she is ill-equipped to deal with her hard-boiled fellow inmates, including cellmates Jenny (Adele Jergens), Melanee (Helen Gilbert) and the deranged Dorothy (Phyllis Coates). Jenny and Melanee do their best to cajole Anne into revealing the whereabouts of her robbery bounty. At the prison, Catholic chaplain the Reverend Fulton (Richard Denning), seeing worth in the young prisoner, attempts to rehabilitate Anne. Meanwhile, Anderson, still at large, attempts to coerce Anne's ex-convict father Pop Carson (Raymond Hatton) into revealing what he knows about the buried money. Pop knows nothing, but greedy for the funds himself, visits Anne in prison and attempts to trick her into revealing its whereabouts. She refuses to tell him.

During an earthquake, Adele and Helen escape and make Anne join them. Before they are free, Helen is killed and Anne, who is beginning to reform, feels responsible. The chase leads to Pop's house where Adele, gun in hand, makes Anne turn over the money. Anderson arrives and, after killing Adele, is himself bested in a tussle with the Reverend Fulton. Anne—with money in hand—and Fulton return to the prison, with the hope that she may soon be paroled.

"*Girls in Prison* is as routine as its title, an overlength jail yarn with telegraphic situations which reduce movement to a walk" *(Variety)*.

This was one of the final screen roles for Academy Award-winning actress Jane Darwell (1879–1967), who appears here as a prison matron. Another veteran actress in the cast was Mae Marsh (1895–1968) as the convict Grandma. Marsh was a leading lady of the silent screen who had co-starred in D. W. Griffith's *The Birth of a Nation* (1915) and *Intolerance* (1916). Director Edward L. Cahn (1899–1963) who had directed the earlier genre piece, *Experiment Alcatraz* (1950), q.v., would also helm *Riot in Juvenile Prison* (1959), q.v.

103. *Girls of the Big House* (Republic, 1945), 68 min.

Associate producer, Rudolph E. Abel; director, George Archainbaud; screenplay, Houston Branch; art director, Gano Chittenden; set decorator, Earl B. Wooden; music, Joseph Dubin; music director, Morton Scott; songs: Jack Elliott; Sanford Green and June Carroll; assistant director, George Webster; sound, Victor Appel; special effects, Howard Lydecker, Theodore Lydecker; camera, John Alton; editor, Arthur Roberts.

Lynne Roberts (Jeanne Crail); Virginia Christine (Bernice); Marian Martin (Dixie); Adele Mara (Harriet); Richard Powers (Barton Sturgis); Geraldine Wall (Head Matron); Tala Birell (Alma Vlasek); Norma Varden (Mrs. Thelma Holt); Stephen Barclay (Smiley Vlasek); Mary Newton (Dr. Gale Warren); Erskin Sanford (Professor O'Neill); Sarah Edwards (Dormitory Matron); Ida Moore (Mother Fielding); William Forrest (District Attorney); Verna Felton (Agnes).

Rather than involve her father (Erskin Sanford), a college president, Jeanne Crail (Lynne Roberts), an innocent small town girl lost in the big city, admits to the theft of a wallet. As a result, she is convicted and sent to prison. Among the other inmates there are Bernice (Virginia Christine), a hardened criminal, Dixie (Marian Martin) and Alma Vlasek (Tala Birell). The latter is in prison for homicide, having killed the wrong man while waiting in ambush for her husband and his then girlfriend. Alma does not realize that Bernice was that other woman. Homesick for her father and fearful of sending him letters (which would bear the prison postmark) she sneaks out of jail. She returns home to be with her dad and with her boyfriend, attorney Barton Sturgis (Richard Powers), telling neither one of the true situation. Returning to prison, she is punished for her breakout. Meanwhile,

Bernice sends word to Sturgis of her plight. When Alma's husband (Stephen Barclay) visits his wife at the prison, he expresses an interest in Jeanne which causes Bernice to attack her. This leads to Alma discovering Bernice's background and she kills Bernice. By now, Braton has investigated the situation and, having proven Jeanne's innocence, arranges her prison release.

There was not very much novel about this pedestrian, implausible entry, with its contrived, coincident-filled plot. One offbeat item was having two songs ("There's a Man in My Life" and "Alma Mater") sung by the inmates in a prison recreational hall sequence, as well as other musical interludes in the film's opening nightclub scene. *Variety* observed, "[L]ack of top names and locale of modestly budgeted story limit its appeal...."

104. *Girls on Probation* (Warner Bros., 1938), 63 min.

Producer, Bryan Foy; directors, William McGann, Harry Seymour; screenplay, Crane Wilbur; art director, Hugh Reticker; costumes, Howard Shoup; camera, Arthur Todd; editor, Frederick Richards.

Jane Bryan (Connie Heath); Ronald Reagan (Neil Dillon); Sheila Bromley (Hilda Engstrom); Anthony Averill (Tony Rand); Henry O'Neill (Judge); Elisabeth Risdon (Kate Heath); Sig Rumann (Roger Heath); Dorothy Peterson (Jane Lennox); Susan Hayward (Gloria Adams); Larry Williams (Terry Mason); James Nolan (Dave Warren);

Esther Dale (Mrs. Engstrom); Arthur Hoyt (Mr. Engstrom); Lenita Lane (Marge); Peggy Shannon (Ruth); Janet Shaw (Inmate); Brenda Fowler (Head Matron); Joseph Crehan (Todd); James Spottswood (Public Defender); Pierre Watkin (Prosecuting Attorney); Maud Lambert, Kate Lawson (Matrons); Jan Holm (Girl Clerk); Fern Barry, Sally Sage, Marian Alden, Paulette Evans, Clara Horton (Prisoners); Glen Cavender (Cop); Reid Kilpatrick (Police Broadcaster); Nat Carr (Pawnbroker).

Any film boasting a cast that includes Susan Hayward, Ronald Reagan, Jane Bryan and Esther Dale cannot be all bad. This lean entry from Warner Bros.' "B" unit had the good sense to be concise (sixty-three minutes) and to the point. "The story ... moves along swiftly and contains the desired plot situations.... Prison scenes strike a note of authenticity and afford some comedy relief. Small part of a hoosegow matron, played by Kate Lawson, has punch" *(Variety)*.

Bridling against her stern father (Sig Rumann) young Connie Heath (Jane Bryan) agrees to sneak away on an evening out with her friend Hilda Engstrom (Sheila Bromley). She borrows one of Hilda's gowns, which gets torn, and only later discovers that Hilda had "borrowed" it without permission from the cleaning establishment where she works. When an investigation is demanded by the owner (Susan Hayward) of the dress, Hilda disappears from town. Connie is arrested for this episode, but later is released when she pays for the dress. Several months later she encounters Hilda and, innocently joining her in conversation, becomes implicated in a bank robbery that Hilda and her cohort, Tony Rand (Anthony Averill), are undertaking. The three of them are caught and sentenced to prison. Soon thereafter, Connie wins the confidence of a parole officer (Dorothy Peterson) who arranges her parole. She finds work for assistant district attorney Neil Dillon (Ronald Reagan) and, soon, they are in love. In the midst of this, Hilda, now released from prison, appears on the scene and threatens to spoil Connie's happiness. With the help of the understanding Neil, Connie is responsible for turning over Hilda and Rand—he having escaped from jail—to law authorities.

105. *Girls Town* (Metro-Goldwyn-Mayer, 1959), 92 min.

Producer, Albert Zugsmith; director, Charles Haas; story, Robert Hardy Andrews; screenplay, Robert Smith; music, Van Alexander; camera, John L. Russell; editor, Leon Barsha.

Mamie Van Doren (Silver Morgan); Mel Torme (Fred Alger); Paul Anka (Jimmy Parlow); Ray Anthony (Dick Culdane); Maggie Hayes (Mother Veronica); Cathy Crosby (Singer); Gigi Perreau (Serafina Garcia); Elinor Donahue (Mary Lee Morgan); Gloria Talbot (Vida); Sheilah Graham (Sister Grace); Jim Mitchum (Charley Boy); Dick Contino (Stan Joyce); Harold Lloyd, Jr. (Chip Gardner); Charles Chaplin, Jr. (Joe Cates); The Platters (Themselves); Peggy Moffitt (Flo); Jody Fair (Gloria Barker); Peter Leeds (Michael Clyde); Nan Peterson (Carhop); Grabowski ("Skin").

This is merely another badly-executed, cheaply made (in black-and-white) exploitation item from Albert Zugsmith (b. 1910), the filmmaker responsible for such cinematic embarrassments as *High School Confidential* (1960), *The Private Life of Adam and Eve* (1961) and *The Incredible Sex Revolution* (1967). The inane plot and grade "Z" (for Zugsmith) acting is compensated for by the unusual array of personalities trapped into this misadventure. The range includes singers Paul Anka and Mel Torme, the sons (Charles Chaplin, Jr., Harold Lloyd, Jr.) of two famous silent cinema clowns and on to fading British-born Hollywood columnist Sheilah Graham. Not to be overlooked, of course, is overly curvacious Mamie Van Doren, yet another contender in the Marilyn Monroe-Jayne Mansfield-Sheree North buxom blonde marathon. *Variety* dismissed this shabby offering as "blatantly crude and vulgar. There is a patina of fake piety spread over some of the proceedings...."

Because she has a record of being rebellious, and, in fact, is on probation for a past misdeed, Silver Morgan (Mamie Van Doren) is blamed for the accidental death of a young man who was supposed to be her date. Rather than be sent to a reformatory, she is shipped to Girls Town, an institution operated by Catholic nuns. The resentful newcomer finds it difficult to adjust, despite the guidance of Mother Veronica (Maggie Hayes). Thanks to another "inmate," Serafina Garcia (Gigi Perreau), an emotionally disturbed girl who is herself helped by friendly Jimmy Parlow (Paul Anka), Silver eventually calms down and adjusts to her surroundings. Meanwhile, her sister Mary Lee (Elinor Donahue), is arrested for participating in a drag strip race with friend Fred Alger (Mel Torme). Mary Lee finds herself at Girls Town where she later admits to her sister that it was she, not Silver, who was accidentally responsible for the ne'er-do-well's death when he attempted to attack her. Eventually, matters are straightened out. The now-reformed Silver completes her stay at the quasi-reformatory.

Since juvenile delinquency in the U.S. was a growing concern at the time of this picture's release, it was assumed that would give this movie some legitimacy. *Variety* was not fooled. "The party scene which opens the film, for instance, is clearly intended to be as stimulating carnally as is possible. Scenes of Miss Van Doren in the tightest of costumes exchanging badinage with nuns are in dubious taste.... The large cast has been chosen chiefly for its exploitation value."

It was a sad sight to have the once mighty Metro-Goldwyn-Mayer, who had once produced *Boys Town* (1938), q.v., release this stinker.

106. *The Glass House* (CBS-TV, Feb. 4, 1972), color, 100 min.

Executive producer, Roger Gimbel; producers, Robert W. Christiansen, Rich Rosenberg; director, Tom Gries; story, Truman Capote, Wyatt Cooper; teleplay,

Tracy Keenan Wynn; wardrobe, Bruce Walkup; makeup, Robert Stein; music, Billy Goldenberg; supervising music editor, Gene Feldman; technical adviser, Gene Logan; assistant director, Mike R. Moder; sound, Herman Lewis; camera, Jules Brenner; editor, Gene Fowler, Jr.

Vic Morrow (Hugo Slocum); Clu Gulager (Brian Courtland); Billy Dee Williams (Lennox Beach); Kristoffer Tabori (Allan Campbell); Dean Jagger (Warden Auerbach); Alan Alda (Jonathan Paige); Luke Askew (Bibleback); Scott Hylands (Ajax); Edward Bell (Sinclair); Tony Mancini (Steve Berino); G. Wood (Pagonis); Roy Jenson (Officer Brown); Alan Vint (Bree).

In the early 1970s, television was still several quantum leaps behind theatrical films in presenting daring topics in a "realistic" manner. At the time *The Glass House* premiered on TV, it was considered a hard-hitting drama, high on realism (it was shot at the Utah State Prison with real convicts used as extras) and very true-to-life with its pessimistic tone and blatant exhibition of brutal behavior. "Without a doubt, this movie will have more effect in bringing about prison reform than any number of riots or demonstrations around the country" (Sue Cameron, *Hollywood Reporter*). Because the literary darling, Truman Capote (author of *In Cold Blood,* q.v.), had co-authored the story, the telefeature received a great deal of critical attention.

Several newcomers arrive at a Utah prison. There is Jonathan Paige (Alan Alda), a college professor serving a short term for manslaughter (he had attacked a reckless driver who had injured his wife), and seventeen-year-old Allan Campbell (Kristoffer Tabori), who had been caught selling drugs and must spend five years or more behind bars. Also aboard the bus pulling into the prison compound is Brian Courtland (Clu Gulager), a disgruntled former Navy man who has served in Vietnam and who has just joined the prison staff as a guard. Courtland (a "fish bull") is quickly advised by the experienced Officer Brown (Roy Jenson) that "this joint is a can of worms" and "Don't let yourself get too soft. This bunch of animals in here will eat you alive." Courtland quickly finds out that the aged Warden Auerback (Dean Jagger) is more anxious to attain a smooth retirement than to cure any ills in the prison system. Courtland observes that the penitentiary is really under the control of tough convict Hugo Slocum (Vic Morrow), and that Brown and the other administrators look the other way at Hugo's victimizing of the other prisoners.

The well-educated, left wing liberal Jonathan is an enigma to the prison population who view him suspiciuosly. Jonathan warns the know-it-all Allan not to become involved with the sinister Slocum, but the teenager soon begins running errands for the gang leader. Only later does he realize the price he must pay for Hugo's favors is becoming Slocum's "boy." When he refuses, the angered Slocum has his henchman gang rape Allan. The teenager later commits suicide by jumping from a cell tier.

The righteous Jonathan is assigned to working in the pharmacy, replacing Slocum's contact man Sinclair (Edward Bell). The straight-lace Jonathan daringly refuses to cooperate with Slocum, thus cutting off Hugo's drug supply. Sinclair, still fearful of the cocaine-snorting Slocum but wanting to help Jonathan, gives him a notebook which details Slocum's illegal activities. The general population observes the brewing battle and waits for the outcome. Meanwhile, Courtland reports this activity to the warden who patronizingly tells him to ignore it. The mock-pious warden insists, "We've learned through experience that sometimes it's better to let certain given situations adjust themselves." After Sinclair is killed,

Jonathan begs Lennox (Billy Dee Williams), the leader of the black faction, to help smuggle the notebook out of the prison. The politically-minded Lennox refuses, explaining he wants a major overthrow of the whole system, not a small scandal exposed. That night Officer Brown leaves the cell doors open so Slocum and his gang can retrieve the notebook from Jonathan. With a gun that Lennox provides him, the desperate Jonathan guns down Slocum. Later, in the confusion, Courtland accidentally shoots Jonathan. Courtland takes the notebook to the warden who insists, "Our duty is to keep things from bubbling over, from exploding. . . . I'm not in love with the system, but it's all we've got." For the ineffectual warden, the matter is closed. Courtland, who has refused to sign a phony confession as to what happened, leaves the prison in disgust.

In retrospect, there is far less to *The Glass House* than appeared at the time, even if the downbeat ending gives the story an "uncompromised" tone. The film is rife with genre clichés: Slocum insists to Jonathan, "There are two kinds of time you can do in here, good and bad." Lennox advises Jonathan, "There are no secrets in here. . . . It's too bad. You could have done easy time." The brutalities are expected set pieces: a hot cauldron of soup is poured over a convict who has held out tribute to Slocum; Allan being sodomized; the ongoing tug-of-war between the black and white convicts and between them and the guards; the corrupt and indifferent prison keepers. Most of all, there is the too obviously structural parallel of the two new convicts and the fledgling guard becoming hardened to their heinous environment and the tragic results for all three of them.

Daily Variety acknowledged that "Prison dramas do not offer much opportunity for variations on the basic facts of life about men in enforced confinement." While lauding *The Glass House* as "engrossing TV fare," the trade paper noted the plot contained "a few contrivances that did not ring true — the absence of any prison authority for Alda to turn to, the need for the dope to pass through Alda's hands. . . ." In retrospect, Tom Milne (British *Monthly Film Bulletin*) decided, "the script is much too busy with melodrama to explore its themes. . . . The fact that the film was shot on location . . . merely underlines the stock characterisations and grotesquely rigged plot. Less outrageous than *Fortune and Men's Eyes* [1971, q.v.], it is even less convincing, and light years behind *Riot in Cell Block 11* [1954]."

Tom Gries received an Emmy for his direction, and Gene Fowler, Jr. was Emmy-nominated for his editing. The teleplay was by Tracy Lee Wynn (the son and grandson respectively of Keenan Wynn and Ed Wynn), who would write the screenplay for *The Longest Yard* (1974), q.v.

A.k.a.: *Truman Capote's the Glass House.*

107. *The Godless Girl* (Pathé, 1929), 90 min. (Also silent version: 9,019′.)

Director, Cecil B. DeMille; story/continuity/dialogue, Jeanie Macpherson; titles, Beulah Marie Dix, Macpherson; art director, Mitchell Leisen; costumes, Adrian; assistant directors, Frank Urson, Curt Rehfeld; technical engineer, Paul Sprunck; camera, Peverell Marley; additional camera, J. F. Westerberg, Franklin

McBride; editor, Anne Bauchens.

Lina Basquette (Judith Craig); Marie Prevost (Mame); George Duryea (Bob Hathaway); Noah Beery (Head Guard); Eddie Quillan ("Goat"); Mary Jane Irving (Grace); Clarence Burton, Dick Alexander (Guards); Kate Price, Hedwig Reicher (Matrons); Julia Faye, Viola Louie, Emily

Barrye (Inmates); and: Jimmy Aldine, Vivian Bay, Elaine Bennett, Wade Boteler, Betty Boyd, Julia Brown, Archie Burke, Colin Chase, Cameron Coffey, Cecilia DeMille, Jacqueline Dyris, George Ellis, Anielka Elter, James Farley, Larry Fisher, Evelyn Francisco, May Giraci, Grace Gordon, Milton Holmes, William Humphrey, George Irving, Peaches Jackson, Dolores Johnson, Jane Kelcey, Nora Kildare, Richard Lapan, Ida McKenzie, Don Marion, Edith May, Mary Mayberry, Colette Merton, Buddy Messinger, Pat Moore, Jack Murphy, Pat Palmer, Janice Peters, Hortense Petra, Gertrude Quality, Rae Randall, Billy Van Avery, Dorothy Wax.

As Hollywood converted to sound films, Cecil B. DeMille added talking sequences to this silent feature to make it more commercially viable. Unfortunately, the drama was handled in such a heavy-handed way that it had very little credibility with audiences. Despite the fact that DeMille ballyhooed that this photoplay exposed prison conditions as they really were, it was actually a very prettified picture he offered of life in a reformatory.

In her high school, Judith Craig (Lina Basquette), the daughter of an atheist, organizes The Godless Society and avidly begins recruiting members. On the other hand, Bob Hathaway (George Duryea), a fervent Christian youth, arouses his fellow students to oppose the atheists. There is a riot and Grace (Mary Jane Irving) is killed when a stairway collapses. As a result, Judith, Bob and another youth, "Goat" Johnson (Eddie Quillan) are sentenced to the state reformatory, where, among others, they encounter a hardened convict named Mame (Marie Prevost). Also, the vicious head guard (Noah Beery) treats them badly. Bob and Judith escape in a grocery wagon, but are soon recaptured. When a fire breaks out in the prison, Bob rescues both Judith and the head guard. As a reward for his heroism, Bob and Judith are pardoned with Judith gaining new faith.

Variety insisted, "Cecil B. DeMille had his tongue in his cheek when he directed this hack yarn with religious undercurrents.... *Godless Girl* is formula preachment of obvious sort.... Story is not only haphazardly conceived but lacks the careful knitting of incident that constitutes expert narrative.... Reform school stuff has been done much better before." The *New York Times* jibed that *The Godless Girl* was "A surprising piece of romantic evangelism ... which stretches from unexpected ludicrous slapstick through scenes in a burning reformatory...."

108. *The Great Imposter* (Universal, 1961), 112 min.

Producer, Robert Arthur; director, Robert Mulligan; based on the book by Robert Crichton; screenplay, Liam O'Brien; art directors, Alexander Golitzen, Henry Bumstead, Robert Luthardt; set decorator, Julia Heron; makeup, Bud Westmore; music, Henry Mancini; music supervisor, Joseph Gershenson; assistant directors, Joseph Kenny, Charles Scott, Jr.; technical adviser, Commodore James Plomer (Commander, RCN); sound, Waldon O. Watson, Frank H. Wilkinson; camera, Robert Burks; editor, Frederic Knudtson.

Tony Curtis (Ferdinand Waldo Demara, Jr.); Karl Malden (Father Devlin); Edmond O'Brien (Captain Glover); Arthur O'Connell (Warden Chandler); Gary Merrill (Pa Demara); Joan Blackman (Catherine Lacey); Raymond Massey (Abbot Donner); Robert Middleton (Prison Lieutenant R. C. Brown); Jeanette Nolan (Ma Demara); Sue Ane Langdon (Eulalie Chandler); Larry Gates (Cardinal); Mike Kellin (Clifford Thompson); Frank Gorshin (Barney); Cindi Wood (WAC Lieutenant); Dick Sargent (Seaman Hotchkiss); Robert Crawford, Jr. (Fred Demara, Jr., as a Boy); Doodles Weaver (Farmer); Ward Ramsey (Executive Officer Howard); David White (Dr. Hammond); Philip Ahn (Hun Kim); Herbert Rudley (Senior Officer); Jerry Paris (Defense Lieutenant); Harry Carey, Jr. (Dr. Joseph C. Mornay); Willard Sage (Lieutenant Thornton); Harry Townes (Warden Ben W. Stone); Lloyd Bochner (Royal Canadian Navy Physician).

The Great Imposter is one of the most infectiously delightful escapade films, benefitting not only from its amazing but true-life basis, but from a wonderfully tongue-in-cheek performance by Tony Curtis, then at the peak of his box-office power. The picture is based on the 1959 book recounting, as the foreword advises, "the facts of the many amazing careers of Ferdinand Waldo Demara, Jr. — who is still very much alive and continuing to prove that 'truth is stranger than fiction.'" As Demara explains his bizarre career to his long-time priest friend/confessor/adversary (Karl Malden), "Waiting for people to get wise to you is part of the fun."

Among the many highlights of this multi-episode narrative, is a penitentiary segment in which the con artist/hero delights in posing as a southern-accented penal authority and testing his self-evolved theory on dealing with convicts.

In the film's opening, Ferdinand Waldo Demara, Jr. (Tony Curtis) has just been arrested by state troopers on an isle off the Maine coast. As a boat takes him back to the mainland, he reflects on his life.

As a Depression youth, Demara learned early that necessity is the mother of invention. After being drafted into the Army and going AWOL (he does not have the proper educational credentials to become an officer), he assumes the identity of a college professor and wins a commission in the Marines. Later, fearing his ruse will be discovered, he fakes a suicide and vanishes. He tricks his way into a Trappist Order supervised by Abbott Donner (Raymond Massey), but soon leaves due to the rigid regimen. The miltiary police capture Ferdinand and he is sent to a detention barracks where he works on the prison's newspaper. Having served his time, Demara uses another's credentials to be hired by Warden Chandler (Arthur O'Connell), the head of the largest penitentiary in the southwest. Demara quickly persuades Chandler that he should devote his innovative penal methods to the maximum security cellblock supervised by R. C. Brown (Robert Middleton). Using common sense, charm and a big dose of nerve, he calms the tough bunch of criminals, including agitated Clifford Thompson (Mike Kellin). While enjoying his success — and the advances of the warden's sex-starved daughter (Sue Ane Langdon) — a former prison mate (Frank Gorshin) arrives and threatens to blackmail him. Later, Demara masquerades as a Canadian Navy physician and romances a young nurse (Joan Blackman). They plan to marry but he is shipped to the Korean war zone. Aboard the Allied vessel, he extracts an impacted tooth from his commanding officer (Edmond O'Brien) and performs several emergency operations. His successes generate tremendous publicity which brings his background to light. When threatened with a court-martial, he persuades the embarrassed naval authorities to drop the matter. Still later, he becomes a school teacher.

The boat docks and the troopers discover that Demara has vanished. Learning that the State Department is hunting him and has summoned one of the troopers to spearhead the search, Demara assumes his latest identity — that of the trooper. As the film concludes a title card says "The End" and Demara emphatically shakes his head no.

Variety analyzed that the picture's flippant tone militated against dimensional characterizations. However, it agreed that "[Robert] Mulligan's otherwise slick direction, along with some stickout performing by several gifted veterans of the screen, is responsible for some memorably humorous passages." A. H. Weiler (*New York Times*) summarized, "Mr. Curtis, as well as his many associates, may not make *The Great Imposter* great as a film, but it does evolve as an engrossing and funny look at a life that certainly has been larger than most."

109. *Hell on Devil's Island* (20th Century–Fox, 1957), 73 min.

Producers, Leon Chooluck, Laurence Stewart; director, Christian Nyby; story, Arndt Giusti, Ethel Giusti; screenplay, Steven Ritch; art director, Frank Sylos; makeup, Ted Coodley; men's wardrobe, Frank Roberts; women's wardrobe, Sabine Manela; music/music director, Irving Gertz; assistant directors, Frank Fox, Nat Merman; sound, Joe Edmondson; camera effects, Jack Rabin, Louis DeWitt; camera, Ernest Haller; editor, Warren Adams.

Helmut Dantine (Paul Rigaud); William Talman (Bayard); Donna Martell (Giselle Reault); Jean Willes (Suzanne); Rex Ingram (Lulu); Robert Cornthwaite (Governor Pierre Renault); Jay Adler (Toto); Peter Adams (Jacques Boucher); Edward Colmans (Jean Robert); Mel Welles (Felix Molyneaux); Charles Bohbot (Marcel); Alan Lee (Leon Philippe); Henry Rowland (Guard #1); Edward Coch (Gendarme); Paul Bringegar (Armeaux); Allen Pinson (Bruiser #2); Roy Jenson (Bruiser #1); Elena Da Vinci (Gina); Edwin [Ed] Nelson (Guard #2); Paul MacWilliams (Chauvin).

This cheaply-assembled trash was shot in widescreen (Regalscope) and black-and-white. The performances and contrived theatrics were no more convincing than the threadbare soundstage settings.

Paul Rigaud (Helmut Dantine) is sentenced to many years on Devil's Island for daring to write against the French collaborators during World War II. His ire is aroused by the brutal treatment afforded him and the other prisoners by the sadistic overseer, Bayard (William Talman). Unable to bear the oppression anymore, he attacks Bayard and, in turn, is almost killed by a lashing. However, the toughened Rigaud survives and is finally released. Like the other ex-convicts (the "libertees") on the penal island (who even after being released from the compound can never leave the isle), he finds himself at the mercy of an opportunistic plantation owner Jacques Boucher (Peter Adams), a greedy banker (Mel Wells) and the cynical police chief Jean Robert (Edward Colmans). This corrupt trio has set up a system of having Suzanne (Jean Willes), who owns a run-down island cafe, extending credit to the libertees. Jean Robert then arrests them for being in debt and sentencing them to work on Boucher's plantation where no worker ever survives the unbearable regimen.

A new and humane governor (Robert Cornthwaite) takes charge of the penal colony. He persuades Rigaud to assist him in righting the wrongs. With the assistance of the governor's daughter, Giselle (Donna Martell), they uncover the fact that the past administration had been operating a gold mine using convict labor and that they had never paid taxes on their profits. Paul finds the mine and in a confrontation kills both Bayard and Boucher. Having the evidence he requires, the governor puts his reforms into motion, aiming to close down the dreaded penal colony. Paul is granted a full pardon and chooses to remain on the isle as assistant administrator. He and Giselle continue their romance. Meanwhile, as of April 10, 1946, the prison at St. Laurent is abolished and 2,800 men are given every chance for a pardon.

Within its seventy-three minutes, this programmer abounds in clichés. The sinister Bayard says of a man he has nearly tortured to death, "He'll live. A man doesn't break his favorite toy." (Later Bayard sighs when a convict escapes his control by dying: "He's dead and we only got a week's worth out of him.") The idealistic governor insists, "Men are more than just facts and figures to me." One lusty convict says to another of a nearby comely woman, "There's only one thing more beautiful to me than this pardon."

For *Variety,* this lackluster production was "long on brutality and short on entertainment." The best performance, relatively, in *Hell on Devil's Island* is offered by Rex Ingram as a black convict cohort of Helmut Dantine.

110. *Hellgate* (Lippert, 1952), color, 87 min.

Producer, John C. Champion; director, Charles Marquis Warren; story, Champion, Warren; screenplay, Warren; music, Paul Dunlap; camera, Ernest W. Miller; editor, Elmo Williams.

Sterling Hayden (Gil Hanley); Joan Leslie (Ellen Hanley); Ward Bond (Lieutenant Tod Vorhees); Jim [James] Arness (George Redfield) Marshall Bradford (Dr. Pelham); Peter Coe (Jumper Hall); Richard Paxton (George Nye); John Pickard (Gundy Boyd); Pat Coleman (Hunchy); Bob Wilke (Sergeant Major Kearn); Sheb Wooley (Neill Price); Richard Emory (Dan Mott); Kyle James (Vern Brechene); Rory Mallinson (Banta); Ed Hinton (Ault); Timothy Carey (Wyand); William Hamel (Lieutenant Colonel Woods); Stanley Price (Colonel Telsen); Rod Redwing (Pima).

Like the later *Devil's Canyon* (1953), q.v. and *There Was a Crooked Man* (1970), q.v., *Hellgate* was one of the few Hollywood Westerns to concern itself with prison life on the old frontier. *Newsweek* magazine endorsed, "*Hellgate* ... is part Western, part prison story, with enough difference from both classic film forms to make for an unusual and grimly effective melodrama.... While the plot is unrelieved in its toughness, the author rarely goes out of his way for gratuitous cruelty." *Newsweek* lauded the movie's "realistic impact" and especially praised "[director/scriptor Charles Marquis] Warren—a specialist in the Southwest's history by way of the New York Public Library—for uncovering a forgotten chapter in U.S. penal procedure."

This modest picture deals with the infamous Hellgate Prison located in the hot, arid deserts near Yuma, Arizona. It was here, amid underground caverns and rock walls, that the U.S. Government herded the incorrigibles from both sides of the recent Civil War. Because of the unbearable living conditions—and the horrendous treatment of its prisoner population—the facility was nicknamed "America's Devil's Island." The government finally abandoned the notorious prison in 1871.

In 1867, guerrilla raider Vern Brechene (Kyle James) and his henchmen are on the run after making a daring escape from a vigilante mob in Brandon, Kansas. They make a hasty stop at the home of ex–Confederate soldier Gil (Sterling Hayden) and Ellen Hanley (Joan Leslie), forcing them to provide fresh horses and food. When a government patrol discovers Brechene's tired mounts and saddlebags at the Hanleys, Gil is accused of being an accomplice to the guerrillas. For his sedition, he is sent to the infamous Hellgate Prison near the Mexican border which is supervised by Army Lieutenant Tod Vorhees (Ward Bond). Vorhees, whose own family was massacred by guerrillas, is particularly vicious to Gil and subjects him to extra punishment. (The authorities have ordered that Gil not be killed, because they hope he will one day lead them to Brechene and his men.) Although Gil attempts to escape, he is soon recaptured. A typhus epidemic hits the prison and the compound's physician (Marshall Bradford) orders that all contaminated water at Hellgate be dumped. The nearby villagers, fearful of contracting the disease, refuse to bring fresh water. Vorhees finds himself forced to ask Gil to trek across the desert to seek out a new water supply. Gil agrees, on condition that

Vorhees pursue leads that could prove Gil's innocence. Gil goes to the villagers and convinces them to ship fresh water to the prison (reasoning that if the men at Hellgate are cured, it will end the contagion danger). Grateful for his efforts, Vorhees obtains the evidence necessary to free Gil. Hanley returns to Ellen, who has been waiting patiently for his release.

Variety noted approvingly, "Picture . . . is a lesson in production economics, achieving creditable values within a tight budget without costly location treks or expensively stage settings." *Boxoffice* magazine judged "Gory and grim, but gripping nonetheless, is this uncompromising picture of one of the most shameful situations in America's history."

Some of the location work was done at Bronson Canyon in the Hollywood Hills. Giving a very effective account of himself was James Arness (of later "Gunsmoke" fame) as a rough-and-ready convict. In actuality, *Hellgate* is an unofficial remake of *The Prisoner of Shark Island* (1936), q.v., John Ford's well-regarded study of Dr. Samuel Mudd's incarceration at Fort Jefferson in the 1860s.

111. *Hell's Highway* (RKO, 1932), 62 min.

Executive producer, David O. Selznick; director, Rowland Brown; screenplay, Samuel Ornitz, Robert Tasker, Brown; art directors, Van Nest Polglase, Carroll Clark; music director, Max Steiner; sound, John Tribby; camera, Edward Cronjager; editor, William Hamilton.

Richard Dix (Frank "Duke" Ellis); Tom Brown (Johnny Ellis); Rochelle Hudson (Mary Ellen); C. Henry Gordon (Blacksnake Skinner); Warner Richmond (Pop-Eye Jackson); Sandy Roth (Blind Maxie); Charles Middleton (Matthew, the Hermit); Louise Carter (Mrs. Ellis); Clarence Muse (Rascal); Stanley Fields (Whiteside); Jed Kiley (Romeo Schultz); Fuzzy Knight (Society Red); Bert Starkey (Hype); Bob Perry (Spike); Harry Smith (Buzzard); Oscar Apfel (Billings); Edward Hart (Turkey Neck); John Arledge (Carter); and: Louise Beavers, John Lester Johnson.

Two months before Warner Bros. released its heavily-promoted and subsequently much-acclaimed *I Am a Fugitive from a Chain Gang*, q.v., RKO distributed *Hell's Highway*, its own vigorous indictment of the infamous chain gang system in the deep South. *Hell's Highway* was conceived by the talented Rowland Brown (1901–1963), whose sparse output as a director included only two other feature films, both gangster pieces: *Quick Millions* (1931) and *Blood Money* (1933). Brown's co-writers on this bleak study of hell on earth were an ex-convict (Robert Tasker) and a former social worker (Samuel Ornitz).

In analyzing this film from the perspective of time, Stephen Zito (in program notes prepared for an American Film Institute screening of the film in 1972) observed, "The details of life on a chain gang are used for a triple purpose: to construct a melodramatic plot, to argue against the injustice and severity of the chain gang system, and to comment on society by mirroring the larger ills of Depression America in the small world of prison life."

The film opens with the placard:

> Dedicated to an early end of the conditions portrayed herein—which, though a throwback to the Middle Ages, actually exist today.

Among those prisoners toiling at a certain prison camp in the deep South are Frank "Duke" Ellis (Richard Dix), a confirmed bank robber, and Matthew, the Hermit (Charles Middleton), a bigamist. The convicts are assigned forced labor to complete the Liberty Road County Highway and their overseers are determined to finish the construction at any costs, so that contractor Billings (Oscar Apfel) will make a sizeable profit. How little the prisoners' welfare means to their pitiless keepers is reflected in a telling interchange between a snarling guard and Rascal (Clarence Muse), a black prisoner:

GUARD: Don't you know better than to leave them mules out in the sun?

RASCAL: Yes, sir, boss. Mules cost $4.00 a head, convicts cost nothing.

One of the less hardy new inmates (John Arledge), who cannot keep up with the pace of the labor detail, is punished by being placed in a sweat box, an innovation introduced by Billings. The youth dies from the torture, choking on the leather strap binding his neck within the small baking tin enclosure. The guards report that his death was a suicide. Meanwhile, dictatorial overseer Blacksnake Skinner (C. Henry Gordon), angered that a convict dared to steal a spoon, is determined to find the culprit no matter how much he must torment his powerless charges. Opposing his tyranny is jaunty Duke, who prides himself on being able to endure the cruel regimen. Duke stirs up his fellow inmates, leading them in a chant "No food, no work!"

Duke is preparing to escape the camp when he notices the arrival of a new shipment of convicts. Among them is his admiring, younger brother Johnny (Tom Brown), who has been convicted of assault with a deadly weapon. (Johnny was attempting to shoot the man who had squealed on Duke.) Duke decides to remain on the premises to watch out for his idealistic sibling. Meanwhile, the other convicts who attempted to escape are hunted down and killed. During the mêlée, guard Pop-Eye Jackson (Warner Richmond) murders his cheating wife and blames the homicide on the fleeing prisoners. Later, Johnny, unable to keep up the pace on the road construction is put in the sweat box. ("I don't believe in coddling prisoners," explains Skinner.) Duke uses his knowledge of Jackson's wife-killing to gain better consideration for his brother, who is given a soft clerical job. Duke swears that he will make the men work faster on the road work.

When Johnny learns that Duke is about to be extradited to Michigan where he will probably be given a life sentence for crimes committed in that state, he plots a new escape. Duke tries to prevent his brother (who only has three months more time to serve) from joining him, but Johnny goes along. When their presence is missed, the guards—with baying bloodhounds in readiness—pursue.

SHERIFF: $50 a head for every convict you bring back.

POSSE MAN: How much if they're dead? [Laughter].

During their flight, Johnny is wounded and Duke elects to return with him to the camp to obtain medical help. There they find that much of the compound is in flames, and that Skinner has been stabbed to death. Soon the governor, alerted to the irregularities at the camp by his investigator, Whiteside (Stanley Fields), arrives, determined to halt the corruption and the tortuous treatment of the inmates.

BILLINGS: Governor, I hope this is not going to affect my contract.

GOVERNOR: It's going to affect your treatment of human beings in the state.

Billings is arrested on charges of corruption. As for Johnny, who before escaping saved the locked-up guards from being burned, wins his freedom. As for Duke, for the time being, he remains incarcerated.

Mordaunt Hall *(New York Times)* judged that in *Hell's Highway*, "The glimpses of the convict at work on a highway are not without a certain impressiveness." However, he criticized, "The producers fail by being overeager to horrify audiences by depicting the cruel treatment of the chain-gang convicts. . . ." *Variety* reported, "Productionally the direction is remarkably good at most points. Some handsome scenic backgrounds are created during the hunt for the convicts." The trade paper then warned exhibitors, "It is not entertainment, and to be questioned whether a sufficient number of persons will feel an interest in the convict, despite the famous 'sweat box' trial of recent date, on which the story appears to have been founded."

There are several artistic factors which prevented *Hell's Highway* from being as powerful a social document as *I Am a Fugitive from a Chain Gang*. Handsome, rugged Richard Dix was much too theatrical a star to abandon his flamboyant stage mannerisms for this role and he played Duke Ellis for grand heroics rather than with understated realism. Moreover, RKO executives were fearful that Rowland Brown's searing production was too desolate in tone. As such, several scenes were cut, restructured and re-arranged, as well as additional sequences being added by other creative talent. (The original ending for the picture, as screened in Los Angeles, found Duke making a last, futile attempt for freedom, knowing full well he will be shot on the spot. The picture originally ran at 78 minutes.)

Part of the potent message of *Hell's Highway* was vitiated by making a few characters (Billings, et al.) the scapegoats for villainy rather than broadly attacking local customs and state governments. Moreover, a distracting saccharin tone is added by introducing idealistic Johnny Ellis's sweetheart, Mary Ellen (Rochelle Hudson) into the story. Her brief appearances—visiting the camp—lend a Pollyanna unreality to the grim settings. Finally, as a leavening influence, *Hell's Highway* resorts to the (then traditional) use of comic relief to soften the bleak mood. (For example, at the finale, the eccentric, multi-married Matthew the Hermit admits to Duke, "Brother a man can escape from the strongest jail. But can you tell me how he can possibly get away from three wives. Prison is a pleasure.")

Among the other later Hollywood features that would deal with exposing the horror of life on the chain gang would be: *Blackmail* (1939), *Chain Gang* (1950) and *Cool Hand Luke* (1967), qq.v.

112. *Hell's House* (Capital Films Exchange, 1932), 80 min.

Producer, Benjamin F. Zeidman; director, Howard Higgin; story, Higgin; screenplay, Paul Gangelin, B. Harrison Orkow; camera, Allen S. Siegel; editor, Edward Schroeder.

Junior Durkin (Jimmy Mason); Pat O'Brien (Kelly); Bette Davis (Peggy Gardner); [Frank] Junior Coghlan (Shorty); Charley Grapewin (Uncle Henry); Emma Dunn (Aunt Emma); Morgan Wallace (Frank Gebhardt); Hooper Atchley (Captain of the Guards); Wallis Clark (Judge Robinson); James Marcus (Superintendent Thompson); Mary Alden (Mrs. Mason).

> This could have been made into a real first-run, class A Feature. . . . The theme, which lent itself excellently to being a *Big House* of a boys' state reformatory, projects as having been put together in a slipshod manner.
>
> *Variety*

Orphaned young Jimmy Mason (Junior Durkin) is persuaded to work for bootlegger Matt Kelly (Pat O'Brien), a man he much admires. The police raid Kelly's headquarters and Mason, the only one there, is caught and sentenced to three years at the State Industrial School for Boys, a reformatory. The horror-ridden institution is mismanaged by corrupt Superintendent Thompson (James Marcus) and his chief accomplice, the sadistic guard captain (Hooper Atchley). Jimmy quickly becomes friends with Shorty ([Frank] Junior Coughlan). The latter dies of heart failure due to mistreatment in solitary confinement (he had been trying to help Jimmy smuggle a letter out of the establishment). The boy's death leads newspaper publisher Frank Gebhardt (Morgan Wallace) to crusade for reforms at the institution. However, his campaign is temporarily thwarted when the staff learns of a "surprise" inspection.

When Jimmy learns from his aunt (Emma Dunn) that Kelly has been dating his girlfriend Peggy (Bette Davis), he escapes and confronts Peggy. She confesses she was being friendly to the gangster hoping to convince the braggart to maneuver Jimmy's release from reform school. Meanwhile, the police track Jimmy to the apartment where they overhear Kelly's confession. Jimmy is cleared.

Mordaunt Hall *(New York Times)* judged, "The direction of the film is old-fashioned," and reasoned, "The attempt to pillory reform schools in *Hell's House* is hardly adult in its attack, but it has a few moderately interesting interludes. There is, however, insufficient detail on the institutions that appeals to the spectators as being presented without prejudice...."

Because this independently-made muckracking feature co-starred the fast-rising Bette Davis and Pat O'Brien it would be re-issued frequently over the years and would become a staple in the videocassette marketplace. Its crude production values have not improved over the decades.

113. *Hell's Island* (Columbia, 1930), 77 min.

Producer, Harry Cohn; director, Edward Sloman; story, Tom Buckingham; screenplay, Jo Swerling; art director, Harrison Wiley; assistant director, C. C. Coleman; sound, G. R. Cooper, John Livadary; camera, Ted Tetzlaff; editor, Swerling.

Jack Holt (Mac); Ralph Graves (Griff); Dorothy Sebastian (Marie); Richard Cramer (Sergeant Klotz); Harry Allen (Bert the Cockney); Lionel Belmore (Monsieur Dupont); Otto Lang (German Legionnaire); Carl Stockdale (Colonel).

One of the many films which sought to emulate the boisterous comradeship of the buddy army heros in *What Price Glory?* (1926). As delineated here, the Devil Island's setting is a mere contrivance to further the exploits of the swaggering adventurers.

Americans Mac (Jack Holt) and Griff (Ralph Graves) are members of the French Foreign Legion whose friendship falters when they become rivals for cabaret performer Marie (Dorothy Sebastian). When Mac is shot during a desert skirmish with the Riffs, he believes Griff is responsible. (Actually an enemy sniper had fired the telltale shot.) Griff refuses to obey orders and leave his friend to die. For his insubordination he is sentenced to Devil's Island. Later, when Mac has recovered and has left the service, he and Marie wed and she convinces him to become a guard at Devil's Island so they can be near Griff. Mac still wants revenge on Griff and pretends to go along with her plan, including helping Griff to escape confinement. At the last minute he learns that Griff had not been responsible for his long-ago injury and, disguised as Griff, he diverts the prison guards from the real escape and is killed. Marie and Griff make good on their escape to a better life.

Of this fanciful, macho escapism, *Variety* recorded, "General outline of story suggests it was written to order or from memory. It has borrowed liberally from many, but . . . there is something substantial to the picture, and it remains a good talker. . . ."

114. *Hell's Kitchen* (Warner Bros., 1939), 81 min.

Producers, Mark Hellinger, Bryan Foy; directors, Lewis Seiler, E. A. Dupont; story, Crane Wilbur; screenplay, Wilbur, Fred Niblo; art director, Hugh Reticker; costumes, Milo Anderson; dialogue director, Hugh Cummings; sound, Dolph Thomas; camera, Charles Rosher; editor, Clarence Kolster.

Billy Halop (Tony Marco); Leo Gorcey (Gyp Haller); Bobby Jordan (Joey Richards); Huntz Hall (Bongo); Gabriel Dell (Ace); Bernard Punsly (Patrick Henry "Ouch" Rosenbloom); Stanley Fields (Buck Caesar); Ronald Reagan (Jim Donahue); Margaret Lindsay (Beth Avery); Grant Mitchell (Hiram Krispan); Frankie Burke (Soap); Fred Tozere (Mike Garvey); Arthur Loft (Elmer Krispan); Vera Lewis (Sarah Krispan); Robert Homans (Hardy); Charley Foy (Floogie); Raymond Bailey (Whitey); Robert Strange (Johnnie Callahan); Clem Bevans (Mr. Quill); George Irving (Judge Chandler); Lee Phelps (Bailiff); Jimmy O'Gatty (Mug); Ila Rhodes (Maizie); Don Turner (Chick); Joe A. Devlin (Nails); Jimmie Lucas (Roll Mop); Jack Kenney (Pants); Sol Gorss (Sweet Al); Cliff Saum (Guard); Charles Sullivan, Jack Gardner (Henchmen); Max Hoffman, Jr., Dick Rich, Tom Wilson (Guards); Reid Kilpatrick (Announcer); George O'Hanlon (Usher); Jack Mower (Detective); Ruth Robinson (Mrs. Margaret Chandler); George Offerman, Jr. (Jury Foreman).

Hell's Kitchen is a derivative follow-up to Warner Bros.' *Crime School* (1938), q.v. It also shares a few plot ingredients of James Cagney's *Mayor of Hell* (1933), q.v., which was remade as *Crime School*. In *Hell's Kitchen* the rowdy Dead End Kids are once again the highlights of this contrived exposé of corrupt reform school practices. The film's title derives from the name the young charges have given to the reformatory. As one young inmate (Billy Halop) explains, "We call it 'Hell's Kitchen' and, sometimes, we leave off the kitchen."

When gangster Buck Caesar (Stanley Fields) is given a suspended sentence for smuggling and defrauding the government, the judge (George Irving) states that if Caesar can prove during the next year that he has been rehabilitated and has become an asset to society, the sentence will be removed. The boisterous Buck, upon the advise of his nephew/attorney Jim Donahue (Ronald Reagan), decides to reform one hundred percent. ("I could have got 150 years, maybe life," he sighs.) Buck abandons all his former rackets. This upsets his former cohorts, particularly Mike Garvey (Fred Tozere).

With time to spare, the restless Buck takes an interest in the Hudson Shelter for Homeless Boys, a reform school to which he has made sizeable contributions in the past. The institution's corrupt head, Hiram Krispan (Grant Mitchell)— along with his conniving sister Sarah (Vera Lewis) and his nephew Elmer (Arthur Loft) is distraught when Buck arrives full of enthusiasm. Upon seeing the actual conditions there, the ex-gangster demands reforms. Jim, with the assistance of Beth Avery (Margaret Lindsay) at the school forms a hockey team for the youths. The proud Buck arranges for a big play-off match at the New York Ice Palace and to show his faith in the boys, places a large bet on their winning against the young inmates of the Gladstone Home. When Caesar finds that Garvey, in connivance

Billy Halop, Bernard Punsly, Bobby Jordan, Huntz Hall, Leo Gorcey and Gabriel Dell in
Hell's Kitchen (1939).

with Krispan hired professionals to play on the opposing ice squad, Caesar knocks
Garvey down. Because this violates his parole rules, Caesar goes into hiding. Meanwhile, Krispan takes control of the school again, countermanding the inmate self-
ruling group headed by Tony Marco (Billy Halop) and his chief aid, Gyp Haller
(Leo Gorcey). During his new regime of terror, Krispan punishes Joey Richards
(Bobby Jordan) by locking him in a freezer and Joey dies. The youths rebel, chanting about their tyrannical administrator, "He killed Joey! He killed Joey!" They
hold a mock trial and find Krispan guilty. Buck arrives in time to prevent the boys
from harming Krispan. Once again, he sets the school in order and then willingly
gives himself up to serve his term. Jim and Beth take charge of the school.

At the time of its release, *Hell's Kitchen* was just one more entry in the overcrowded marketplace of reformatory exposés. Like its many predecessors it was
filled with the standard litany of abusive authoritarian figures, innocent young
victims—including a martyred teenager—and a denouement of optimistic reform.
What gave the production any spirit was the presence of the raucous Dead End
Kids, whose boisterous antics and flavorful vernacular added verisimilitude to any
story of downtrodden youths. *Variety* evaluated, "Production starts off auspiciously

and then gets tangled in the final reels when devious and absurd counterplots assert themselves. It never completely untracks itself. Results are not satisfactory...."

David Hayes and Brent Walker noted in retrospect in *The Films of the Bowery Boys* (1984), "*Hell's Kitchen* is intense melodrama. With a setting that is perfect for the Dead End Kids ... it is an uprising tale told with vigor.... Ironically, *Hell's Kitchen* has comic moments, delivered by Stanley Fields.... It may be said that Buck handles the comedy while the Dead End Kids perpetrate the melodrama."

When *Hell's Kitchen* was released in England the censors rated it "H" for "Horrific" because of its graphic illustrations of youths being abused.

115. *Hold 'em Jail* (RKO, 1932), 65 min.

Associate producer, Harry Joe Brown; director, Norman Taurog; story, Tim Whelan, Lou Lipton; screenplay, S. J. Perelman, Walter DeLeon, Mark Sandrich, Albert Ray; radio dialogue, John P. Medbury; art director, Carroll Clark; music, Max Steiner; camera, Len Smith; editor, Artie Roberts.

Bert Wheeler (Curly Harris); Robert Woolsey (Spider Robbins); Edna May Oliver (Violet Jones); Roscoe Ates (Slippery Sam Brown); Edgar Kennedy (Warden Elmer Jones); Betty Grable (Barbara Jones); Paul Hurst (Coach); Warren Hymer (Steele); Robert Armstrong (Sports Announcer); John Sheehan (Mike Maloney); Jed Prouty (Warden Charles Clark); Spencer Charters (Governor); Monty Banks (Timekeeper); Lee Phelps (Spike); Ernie Adams, Monte Collins (Referees); Ben Taggart (Doorman); G. Pat Collins (Whitey); Stanley Blystone (Kravette).

If Stan Laurel and Oliver Hardy could parody the prison genre in MGM's *Pardon Us* (1931), q.v., RKO's prime comedy team, Bert Wheeler and Robert Woolsey could do the same in *Hold 'em Jail*. Here they spoofed the movie form that had gained so much viewer interest since the release of *The Big House* (1930) and *The Criminal Code* (1931), qq.v. *Hold 'em Jail*, which also lampooned the rah-rah college football movies, was the buffoon duo's tenth of twenty studio comedy features.

Harassed Warden Elmer Jones (Edgar Kennedy) of the Bridemore State Penitentiary is determined to have a winning football squad this year when he competes against rival institutions. His coach (Paul Hurst) advises him, "We ain't gettin' the material we used to. You oughta make more inducements to get people to come here." Jones heeds the advise and turned to an alumnus, Mike Maloney (John Sheehan), to recruit new squad members. By coincidence, novelty salesman Curly Harris (Bert Wheeler) and Spider Robbins (Robert Woolsey) arrive at Maloney's club on a sales call. He sizes up the intruders as potential gridiron material.

> MALONEY: Is he an all–American?
>
> SPIDER: He's [Curly] half Scotch and half ginger ale, but I wouldn't have it any other way.

Appreciating that he has two fools on hand, Maloney tricks them into staging a holdup of the club and he has them arrested. Before they know it, the two ex-salesmen are inmates of Jones's penal institution.

Curly and Spider are brought into the warden's office where they create havoc both before and after meeting Jones's angular, matronly sister Violet (Edna May

Oliver) and the warden's curvacious blond offspring, Barbara (Betty Grable). Violet is attracted to Spider, while Barbara takes a liking to boyish Curly. Soon the exasperated warden agrees to let Curly and Spider become trustees helping out in his home—anything to get these zany nitwits out of his office. When it is discovered that Curly has talents as a quarterback, the two newcomers receive royal treatment, with Spider acting as his agent/intermediary. In the big game against Lynwood Prison, chloroformed handkerchiefs are introduced to sabotage the players, but the winning points are scored when the football is accidentally attached to the star's spike and he unknowingly walks across the goal line. Bridemore wins the big game 18–12! Thus Jones has the last laugh on his counterpart, Warden Charles Clark (Jed Prouty), and wins the $1,000 wager. Meanwhile, the boys prove their innocence and are freed.

Mordaunt Hall *(New York Times)* admitted, "There is little rhyme or reason to the incidents, which are always set forth in a bludgeon-like fashion." He acknowledged, however, that there was humor in such situations as when the numbskull convict Steele (Warren Hymer) comes to the blacksmith shop where the boys work to have his ball and chain removed, since the warden lost the key. *Variety* thought *Hold 'em Jail* left a lot to be desired, "the general effect is slow and some of the better gags are lost through not being put over smartly.... [The] photography and sound are not good."

On the other hand, there are virtues to *Hold 'em Jail*. Not only are Wheeler and Woolsey at their daffiest, they also broadly tease the conventions of the prison film. They create mayhem in their interaction with the hardened convict types they encounter at Bridemore in the cell block, at the rock quarry, during a nightime breakout, etc. Then there are contretemps with the easily-perturbed Warden Jones. Additionally, this screen comedy offers a relatively early example of starlet Betty Grable's work, and presents acerbic comedienne Edna May Oliver in rare form. Whether Oliver is warbling (dreadfully) at the piano or sitting atop the warden's desk and accidentally generating a variety of alarm bells, she is always a constant delight.

116. *Hold Your Man* (Metro-Goldwyn-Mayer, 1933), 88 min.

Producer/director, Sam Wood; story, Anita Loos; screenplay, Loos, Howard Emmett Rogers; art directors, Cedric Gibbons, Merrill Pye; set decorator, Edwin B. Willis; costumes, Adrian; song, Arthur Freed and Nacio Herb Brown; camera, Harold G. Rosson; editor, Frank Sullivan.

Jean Harlow (Ruby Adams); Clark Gable (Edward "Eddy" Huntington Hall); Stuart Erwin (Al Simpson); Dorothy Burgess (Gypsy); Muriel Kirkland (Bertha Dillon); Garry Owen (Slim); Barbara Barondess (Sadie Kline); Paul Hurst (Aubrey C. Mitchell); Elizabeth Patterson (Miss Tuttle); Theresa Harris (Lily Mae Crippen); Inez Courtney (Maizie); Blanche Friderici (Mrs. Wagner); Helen Freeman (Miss Davis); George Reed (Reverend Crippen); Louise Beavers (Elite Club Rest Room Maid); Jack Cheatham, Frank Hagney (Cops); Jack Randall (Dance Extra); G. Pat Collins (Phil Dunn); Harry Semels (Neighbor); Nora Cecil (Miss Campbell, the Sewing Instructress); Eva McKenzie (Cooking Teacher).

Clark Gable and Jean Harlow, two of MGM's (and Hollywood's) most popular stars in the 1930s, had already made two successful features together (*The Secret Six,* 1931, *Red Dust,* 1932) when the studio reunited them for *Hold Your Man.* (The ad copy proclaimed "Together Again in Another Man and Female Drama.") On one level, this romantic comedy, provides a marvelous illustration of how well the chemistry worked between these two box office luminaries; they spar, they

Theresa Harris, Dorothy Burgess, Jean Harlow, Elizabeth Patterson, Muriel Kirkland and Barbara Barondess in *Hold Your Man* (1933).

clinch, they spat, they make-up, they become noble, they reunite. On another level, *Hold Your Man* is a superb contemporary illustration of how Hollywood and moviegoers sometimes viewed the regenerative effects of prison.

Unlike either *Ladies of the Big House* (1932) or *Ladies They Talk About* (1933), qq.v., in *Hold Your Man* the criminals are not downtrodden and bitter when they are caught by the law and sentenced to jail. Instead, they regard it as an occupational risk and an inconvenient obstacle to get around or endure. For some, such as the heroine, the reformatory environment provides a near mystical experience, transforming both she and her boyfriend into decent, law-abiding citizens. Thus the social reform message in *Hold Your Man* is not an indictment of the inhumane prison system, but rather a testament to the positive results it can have on reshaping misguided individuals. It was a refreshing change for Hollywood and another reason why this upbeat comedy, boasting superior production values, was so well-received by filmgoers.

In Brooklyn, scam artist Eddy Hall (Clark Gable) beats a hasty retreat from his latest victim. He rushes into an apartment building and finding an unlocked door, darts into the apartment. Ruby Adams (Jean Harlow) has just gotten out of her bubble bath; Eddy jumps in and with soap suds disguising his features manages to elude the pursuing police. The attractive couple quickly take each other's measure:

> EDDY: You know all the answers.
>
> RUBY: To the right questions.

Eddy learns that "sweet meat" (his pet name for her) has "been around" and that this brassy hooker's latest boyfriend is Al Simpson (Stuart Erwin), a traveling salesman from Cincinnati. According to Ruby, "Anything he's got, belongs to me." This tart young woman also explains, "I've got two rules when I'm out visiting. Keep away from couches and stay on your feet." She knows her way around the outer fringes of the underworld and is suspicious of the glib-talking Eddy, "You ain't flirting with jail are ya? . . . All I can say is, if you got a safe racket, you're crazy to fool around with another one. They tell me that jail food is terrible."

Before long, Eddy becomes enamored with Ruby and ditches his current girlfriend, Gypsy (Dorothy Burgess). When Eddy is sentenced to ninety days in jail for participating in a robbery, Ruby visits him. The day he is released, December 18th, he makes two decisions: to marry Ruby and to execute a sting on Aubrey Mitchell (Paul Hurst), her married gentleman friend from Pittsburgh. In the midst of the scam, however, Ruby has a change of heart and the now-alerted Mitchell becomes abusive. In the ensuing mêlée, Eddy knocks the victim down. The man hits his head and dies. Eddy makes his getaway before the police arrive at Ruby's flat, but she is caught. She is sentenced to three years at a state institution.

Wise-cracking Ruby is no stranger to tough breaks and she is quite prepared to accept her "medicine." However, she is miserable because she misses Eddy and because she is expecting his baby. She is assigned to Room D, cottage #3 where her roommates are Bertha Dillon (Muriel Kirkland), Sadie Kline (Barbara Barondess) *and* Gypsy. Even for the very flexible Ruby, it requires an immense adjustment on her part to cope with her new environment. As one sober matron reminds her, "We have rules. This is a reformatory, not a hotel." The status-conscious Sadie points out, "Do you ever hear of society girls being sent up? It's the system!" To give these lawbreakers a new set of values (in this era of pre-women's liberation), the inmates have classes in sewing, cleaning and cooking. This situation leads one amused convict to observe, "A strange place to make an angel cake." Each Sunday, the inmates attend church services and sing hymns:

MATRON: You don't seem to like the hymn.

INMATE: It was a 'him' that got me in here.

Affected by her new surroundings, Ruby reevaluates her shady life. She is encouraged by the kindly matrons to start leading a decent, clean life, especially now that she is about to become a mother. Al Simpson visits and, despite knowing all the sordid circumstances, still wants to marry her. It would mean an early parole for Ruby. However, she refuses, reasoning, "He's too good for me." Obviously she still loves the vanished Eddy Hall.

On Easter Sunday, Gypsy, now paroled and no longer angry with Ruby, returns to the reformatory to tell her that Eddy is outside and intends to see her, even if it should bring him trouble. Once they are reunited, they reconfirm their love and their hopes for their forthcoming child. Next, they ask a black preacher, Reverend Crippen (George Reed), there visiting his wayward daughter (Theresa Harris), to marry them. There is a slight delay when the matrons, sensing something amiss, lock Ruby and others of the girls in solitary confinement. Nevertheless, Ruby finds a way to sneak to the chapel where she and Eddy wed. The police arrive and Eddy is taken away. Time passes. Ruby has given birth to her baby boy and has been released. Mother and son arrive at the train depot to meet Eddy who has just finished serving his time. The happy couple resolve to go straight and, with their son, board a train for Cincinnati where Al Simpson has found Eddy a legitimate job.

Variety enthused of this slickly-concocted entry, "[Scriptwriter] Anita Loos knows her fans.... She ladles out the sentiment in heavy portions, mixes in a generous flavoring of bristling fast dialog of comedy drama purpose, and the results are eminently satisfactory...." The less enthusiastic Frank S. Nugent (*New York Times*), while acknowledging the popularity of the starring team, noted, "the sudden transition from hard-boiled wise-cracking romance to sentimental penitence provides a jolt."

Clark Gable and Jean Harlow would make three additional pictures together: *China Seas* (1935), *Wife Versus Secretary* (1936) and *Saratoga* (1937). It was during the making of the last-named feature that twenty-six-year-old Jean Harlow died on June 7, 1937.

117. *The Hoodlum Priest* (United Artists, 1961), 101 min.

Producers, Don Murray, Walter Wood; director, Irvin Kershner; screenplay, Don Deer [Don Murray], Joseph Landon; art director, Jack Polin; set decorator, Karl Brainard; costumes, Alexis Davidoff; makeup, Ted Coodley; music, Richard Markowitz; camera, Haskell Wexler; editor, Maurice Wright.

Don Murray (Reverend Charles Dismas Clark, S.J.); Larry Gates (Louis Rosen); Cindi Wood (Ellen Henley); Keir Dullea (Billy Lee Jackson); Logan Ramsey (George Hale); Don Joslyn (Pio Gentile); Sam Capuano (Mario Mazziotti); Vincent O'Brien (Assistant District Attorney); Alan Jack (Judge Garrity); Lou Martini (Angelo Mazziotti); Norman MacKaye (Father Dunne); Joseph Cusanelli (Hector Sterne); Bill Atwood (Weasel); Roger Ray (Detective Shattuck); Kelley Stephens (Genny); William Wardord (District Attorney's Aide); Ralph Peterson (Governor); Jack Eigen (A Prisoner); Walter L. Wiedmer (Father David Michaels); Warren Parker (Warden); Joseph Hamilton (Prison Chaplain).

This low-budget biographical entry was based on the endeavors of Reverend Charles Dismas Clark, a slum-born Jesuit priest in St. Louis. He gained acclaim for his spectacular rehabilitation efforts with ex-convicts and who founded Dismas (Halfway) House, which opened on May 16, 1959. Actor Don Murray, who co-produced this venture, filmed largely on location in (East) St. Louis, also co-wrote the picture under the nom-de-plume of Don Deer. Because of its gripping prison scenes, with its implicit anti-capital punishment theme, this well-intentioned film is included in this volume of prison movies.

Father Charles Dismas Clark (Don Murray) of St. Louis has dedicated himself to rehabilitating delinquents and ex-convicts, trying to meet the men on their own terms. One of Clark's focal cases is that of confused Billy Lee Jackson (Keir Dullea), a young thief recently released from the Missouri State Penitentiary. Father Clark not only clears the youth of erroneous, new criminal charges, but he arranges a job for the young man in the local produce market working for Mario Mazziotti (Sam Capuano) and his brother Angelo (Lou Martini). When Billy meets and falls in love with well-bred Ellen Henley (Cindi Wood), he is further motivated to "going straight." Simultaneously, Father Clark joins with criminal lawyer Louis Rosen (Larry Gates) to raise funds for Halfway House, a shelter devoted to helping ex-criminals adapt to civilian life.

When his employer fires him for a theft he did not commit, the embittered Billy and his pal Pio Gentile (Don Joslyn) rob the produce market's safe.

Larry Gates, Keir Dullea and Don Murray in *The Hoodlum Priest* (1961).

During the robbery, Billy defends himself from one of the owners by using a gun he has grabbed. After killing the man, Billy flees. Father Clark tracks Billy to an abandoned slum building where he persuades the young man to surrender. Tried and sentenced to die, Billy is comforted by Father Clark before he is taken to the gas chamber. The priest tells Billy of Dismas, the thief who died on the cross and of how Jesus Christ pledged him eternal life thereafter. After the execution, Father Clark finds Pio awaiting him at the Halfway House, willing to repent.

Admitting that this motion picture has fuzzy character motivation and sketchy plotting, Bosley Crowther *(New York Times)* recognized the film's virtues: "[I]t evolves, through an unpretentious, documentary treatment, as tough and persuasive, if disquieting, drama.... [It] makes its plea, dedication and story strongly felt." *Variety* noted, "Irvin Kershner's direction sustains a flow of excitement and expectation, and is particularly effective in its technique of handling transition without dialog." For many, the harrowing gas chamber scene has had no equal save for the penitentiary death sequence in *I Want to Live!* (1958), q.v.

The Hoodlum Priest was promoted with such advertising teasers as: "He spent his time with thieves and killers.... This man who wore a priest's garb and lived in a white-hot world of violence!... The true story of the strangest name in the world of crime.... A city howled for his scalp!" *The Hoodlum Priest* was the feature film debut of Keir Dullea (b. 1936). Cindi Wood, wife of producer Walter Wood (a former advertising executive), also made her film bow in this production.

118. *The House Across the Bay* (United Artists, 1940), 88 min.

Producer, Walter Wanger; director, Archie Mayo; story, Myles Connolly; screenplay, Kathryn Scola; art directors, Alexander Golitzen, Richard Irvine; set decorator, Julien Heron; costumes, Irene; music/music director, Werner Janssen; choreographer, Sammy Lee; songs: Sidney Clare, Nick Castle and Jule Styne; Al Siegel; George R. Brown and Irving Actman; assistant director, Charles Kerr; sound, Fred Lau; special effects, Ray Singer; camera, Merritt Gerstad; editor, Dorothy Spencer.

George Raft (Steve Larwitt); Joan Bennett (Brenda "Lucky" Bentley); Lloyd Nolan (Slant Kolma); Walter Pidgeon (Tim Nolan); Gladys George (Mary Bogale); William "Billy" Wayne (Barney the Bartender); June Knight (Babe Davis); Peggy Shannon (Alice); Cy Kendall (Crawley); Max Wagner (Jim the Chauffeur); Frank Bruno (Jerry the Henchman); Joseph Sawyer (Charlie); William Halligan, Kenneth Harlan (Men in Nightclub); Mack Gray (Doorman/Lookout); Sam Finn (Head Waiter); Marcelle Corday (French Maid); Sam Ash (Broker); Norman Willis, Eddie Marr (Taresca's Henchmen); Frances Morris (Slant's Secretary); Freeman Wood (Mr. Hanson); Elsa Petersen (Mrs. Hanson); Joseph Crehan, Charles Griffin (Federal Men); Edward Fielding (Federal Judge); Paul Phillips, John Bohn (Reporters); Virginia Brissac (Landlady); Franklyn Farnum, James Farley, Martin Cichy, Al Ferguson, Pat O'Malley (Prison Guards); Dorothy Vaughn, Ruth Warren, Maxine Leslie, Helen Shipman, Kitty McHugh (Prisoners' Wives on Ferry Boat); Etta McDaniel (Lydia, the Maid); Miki Morita (Tim's Japanese House Boy); Peter Camlin (French Pilot); Georges Renevant, Jean Del Val (French Officials); Emmett Vogan (U.S. Official); Armand "Curly" Wright (Barber); Harrison Greene (Irate Customer); Allen Wood (Newsboy); Herbert Ashley (Man in Park); Sam Wren (Draughtsman); Harry Tyler (Fur Peddler); Victoria Vinton, Jean O'Donnell, Edith Haskins, Mitzi Uehlein, Lurline Uller, Kay Gordon, Pearlie Norton (Chorus Girls); Donald Kerr, Max Hoffman, Jr. (Drivers); Harry Harvey, Isabelle Withers (Club Couple); James Craig, Jack Lubell (Brenda's Boy Friends); Kit Guard (Taresca's Driver); Cy Ring (Dance Extra); Dick Rush (Bailiff).

There have been many fanciful Hollywood feature films concerning that maximum of maximum security prisons, Alcatraz. However, *none* have been so fantastic and so romantic as this whimsical picture. The title refers to the nickname given to the penal institution by San Franciscans.

Suave, successful nightclub owner Steve Larwitt (George Raft) falls in love with Brenda "Lucky" Bentley (Joan Bennett) an Indiana farm girl who has come to the big city to make good. She quickly wins a songstress job at Larwitt's establishment. Next, the in-love couple marry. Three years of luxurious bliss follow. Then, she learns that a gangland faction is determined to eliminate Larwitt, who has grown ambitious and wants to expand his activities into other areas. She alerts the federal government to her spouse's shady income tax activities, believing that if he is safely stashed in prison — say, for a year — he will be safe from outside criminal elements. However, she did not count on lawyer Slant Kolma (Lloyd Nolan). His amorous interest in Brenda leads him to undermining Larwitt's courtroom defense. As a result, Steve is sentenced to ten years at Alcatraz Prison.

Brenda rents living quarters in San Francisco, so she can be close to her spouse. She is among the wives, sweethearts and relatives, who pay weekly visits to their loved ones on the "big rock." When she refuses Kolma's advances, he angrily tells Steve of her past actions which landed him in jail. Larwitt escapes from prison, intending to kill his wife. He swims (!) to the mainland, learns the truth of Kilma from Brenda and disposes of the crooked lawyer. Realizing that he has no future, Steve allows himself to be shot down by the pursuing police. The saddened Brenda is now free to accept the honorable advances of wealthy, pipe-smoking airplane manufacturer Tim Nolan (Walter Pidgeon).

For some reviewers—like Howard Barnes *(New York Herald-Tribune)*— couturier Irene deserved the most plaudits in *The House Across the Bay* for having designed Joan Bennett's array of extravagant, sensational costumes. According to *Harrison's Reports*, "This drama has two strikes against it—one, an artificial plot, and the other, slow-moving action." More annoyed was Frank S. Nugent *(New York Times)*, "Prison pictures are bad at best, so familiar have they become, and we regard as a singularly wasteful business practice that of chartering a gilded barge to carry coals to Newcastle. Although Miss Bennett is awesomely gowned, her film is old hat and scarcely worth its maker's bother—or yours."

For the record, in the nightclub sequences, Joan Bennett sings "I'll Be a Fool Again" and "A Hundred Kisses from Now." Bennett and Raft had previously co-starred in *Hush Money* (1931) and *She Couldn't Take It* (1935) and would be reunited for another tale of San Francisco, the period-set *Nob Hill* (1945). The best characterizations in *The House Across the Bay* were of the "rock widows" with whom the heroine comes into contact on her recurrent pilgrimages to Alcatraz. Among them, Gladys George, June Knight and Peggy Shannon gave the film a much needed boost of reality.

119. *House of Numbers* (Metro-Goldwyn-Mayer, 1957), 90 min.

Producer, Charles Schnee; associate producer, James E. Newcom; director, Russell Rouse; based on the novel by Jack Finney; screenplay, Don Mankiewicz, Rouse; art directors, William A. Horning, Edward Carfagno; set decorators, Edwin B. Willis, Otto Siegel; makeup, William Tuttle; music, Andre Previn; assistant director, George Rhein; sound supervisor, Dr. Wesley C. Miller; special effects, A. Arnold Gillespie, Lee LeBlanc; camera, George J. Folsey; editor, John McSweeney, Jr.

Jack Palance (Bill Judlow/Arne Judlow); Barbara Lang (Ruth Judlow); Harold J. Stone (Henry Nova); Edward Platt (Warden).

A great many prison films had paraded in and out of release since Metro-Goldwyn-Mayer produced the trend-setting, remarkable *The Big House* (1930), q.v. Twenty-seven years later, MGM distributed *House of Numbers*, a low-budget entry filmed in black-and-white. It had the distinction of being the first prison yarn to be lensed in the widescreen CinemaScope process. The ad lines for this movie boasted, "Actually filmed within the escape-proof walls of San Quentin!... The most amazing getaway ever ... and the blonde he did it for!"

A stentorian voice-over announces: "San Quentin.... The authorities used to believe there were only two ways out. The main gate after you served your time, or the side gate when you died. Then two men and a girl found a third way out."

Arne Judlow (Jack Palance) is serving a life sentence in San Quentin Prison, having murdered the man who was dating his girlfriend, Ruth (Barbara Lang). Now Barbara, who only knew Arne twelve days before she married him, is helping her husband execute a breakout. The plan is being activated because hot-tempered Arne recently assaulted a prison guard who is hospitalized, still in a coma. If the keeper should recover and identify Arne, he will go to the gas chamber.

Helping Barbara with the scheme is Arne's near-identical older brother Bill (Jack Palance), a gentle man governed by a need to always help out his erring sibling. Bill enthuses to Barbara about the beauty of the plan, "Their whole system is set up to try to prevent men from breaking out of prison. They'll never even

Barbara Lang and Jack Palance in *House of Numbers* (1957).

dream that anyone wants to break in.... Leave it to Arne to figure out the one plan they haven't guarded against!"

Bill and Barbara, posing as man and wife, have rented a cottage adjacent to the prison. They gather the supplies necessary for the plan. One day, they encounter their next-door neighbor. It develops that Henry Nova (Harold J. Stone) is a "correctional officer" (the new term for prison guard) at San Quentin. Nova is a nosy man, who enjoys his work. He tells them that San Quentin used to be called the pastel penitentiary. "Really pretty sight from the outside. The building is painted in pastel colors. Supposed to be good for the morale of the cons ... er ... inmates, we have to call them now."

The meticulous escape plan requires Bill to climb over an unguarded wall one night and to change places with Arne, while the latter prepares the way for an escape from a secluded corner of the exercise yard. In the process, Bill climbs in and out of the prison twice. Nova becomes suspicious and blackmails his neighbors. They pay him hush money and break Arne out of San Quentin. Once freed, the hot-headed Arne quickly realizes that his wife now loves Bill. The angered escapee leaves both of them, planning to hide out on Arcadia Street in San Francisco. Through an anonymous tip from Nova, the escape is traced to Bill and Barbara, who are later convinced by the prison's warden (Edward Platt) that the mentally-disturbed Arne, a human time bomb, must be returned to the penitentiary for the public's safety. A reluctant Bill and Barbara tell the authorities of Arne's whereabouts.

"Anybody who believes *House of Numbers* ... will believe anything.... This ... drama is so blandly absurd ... and so standard on practically every count that some customers may wonder why Metro even bothered to make it" (Howard Thompson, *New York Times*). *Variety* opined, [Russell] Rouse's direction permits the players to indulge in some unrestrained histrionics but Palance effectively delineates the difference between the two brothers in a frequently incredible dual role."

For many movie watchers, one Jack Palance performance per film is more than sufficient. In *House of Numbers* his efforts to present a contrast between the two brothers provides a welcome distraction from the implausible proceedings. Why no guard would become suspicious of the awkward fumbling of the good brother posing as his hardened convict brother is beyond this author. The efforts to give this production an authentic, almost documentary look by lensing on location at San Quentin and using real life convicts as extras are very awkward. So are the vain attempts at humor.

ONE CONVICT: Been to any other colleges?

ANOTHER CONVICT: I spent six years in Alcatraz and four years in Joliet. I'm thinking of a post-graduate course.

Rarely in a prison drama, not even in the PRC efforts of the 1940s, has a movie employed such a small cast of paid performers. Seemingly, in *House of Numbers,* a euphemistic name given to San Quentin, there are very few guards (except in the location footage) and administrators; none of them seem wise to the ways of the convicts. The scenes lensed at the prison factory and in the chow lines are self-conscious. Everyone was obviously given strict orders to steer clear of star Palance as he postured here and there as one of the other Judlow brothers.

As for Barbara Lang, the then latest new imitation Marilyn Monroe who was introduced to movie audiences in this film, her movie career never accelerated after this inauspicious debut.

120. *House of Women* (Warner Bros., 1962), 85 min.

Producer, Bryan Foy; directors, Walter Doniger, (uncredited) Crane Wilbur; screenplay, Wilbur; art director, Leo K. Kuter; set decorator, John P. Austin; costumes, Alexis Davidoff, Florence Hackett; makeup, Gordon Bau, Louis La Cava; music, Howard Jackson; assistant directors, Russell Saunders, Al Alleborn; sound, Robert B. Lee; camera, Harold Sline; editor, Leo H. Shreve.

Shirley Knight (Erica Hayden); Andrew Duggan (Warden Frank Cole); Constance Ford (Sophie Brice); Barbara Nichols (Candy Kane); Margaret Hayes (Zoe Stoughton); Jeanne Cooper (Helen Jennings); Virginia Gregg (Mrs. Hunter); Patricia Huston (Doris); Jason Evers (Dr. F. M. Conrad); Jennifer Howard (Addie Gates); Caroline Richter (Clemens); Gayla Graves (Jackie Lynch); Colette Jackson (Aggie); Jacqueline Scott (Mrs. Stevens); Paul Lambert (Mr. Richard Dunn); Carolyn Komant (Nan); Virginia Capers (Sarah); Drew Vigen (Tommy Brice); Laurie Sheridan (Robin Hayden).

For any astute moviegoer, it was no coincidence that there were so many similarities between Warner Bros.' excellent *Caged* (1950), q.v. and the studio's *House of Women* (1962). While officially *not* a remake of the former, *House of Women* is definitely a distillation of its predecessor. However, it is by *no* means in the same league as that earlier genre classic. Robert A. Nowlan and Gwendolyn Wright Nowlan decided in *Cinema Sequels and Remakes, 1903–1987* (1989):

Although derived from different screenplays, these two women's prison stories are very similar, dealing with an innocent girl brutalized by the conditions and lack of hope that accompany being placed behind bars at the mercy of dangerous fellow inmates and cruel guards.... This [new] version of the story doesn't have the chilling impact of *Caged*. In some ways the fact that the setting is a prison seems almost incidental.

In spite of protestations of innocence, five-month pregnant Erica Hayden (Shirley Knight), a first-time offender, is convicted of robbing a supermarket and sentenced to a five-year term at the State Penal Institution for Women. Stunned by her plight, Erica is aghast to be locked in prison and shudders at the stigma it will place on her unborn child. (In fact, she admits, "I'd rather lose it than have it in here.") The rules of the institution permit her to keep her expected baby with her for three years; thereafter, the child must be placed for adoption if no guardian is found to care for the youngster until the mother is paroled. Having had her baby, Erica is assigned as a domestic in the private residence of the cold, sadistic Warden Frank Cole (Andrew Duggan). He is a self-reliant soul, a taciturn man who is amazingly unempathetic to his charges.

WARDEN: I'm sorry. I have no use for them [i.e. the inmates].

DR. CONRAD: They're still human beings.

WARDEN: I'm not even sure of that.

A variation of this same attitude is echoed by Helen Jennings (Jeanne Cooper), a staff member at the penitentiary. She says of the female inmates, "I can't afford to let myself care."

Cole soon falls in love with Erica, and he begins to soften, displaying greater consideration for his charges. He confides to Erica that some of his hardness was a result of his former wife having talked him into helping a certain convict to be paroled at which point she then ran off with him. Cole displays a rare compassion when he tells Erica, "That's the trouble with prison. There's a big wall between the inmates and the officials. A wall of fear. I guess none of us does anything to break it down."

Time passes. Erica's daughter's third birthday and her own parole hearing arrive almost simultaneously. The warden, fearful of losing Erica, has another severe mood change and blocks her parole. He also institutes an order that all prison children must be separated from their mothers. The welfare authorities take little Robin (Laurie Sheridan) away from Erica.

Shortly thereafter, the son (Drew Vigen) of hard-hearted convict Sophie Brice (Constance Ford) is killed accidentally in a fall from a prison roof. This mentally unhinges Sophie who incites a riot. She takes several guards and a parole board member, Mrs. Hunter (Virginia Gregg), hostage, intending to hurl the woman from the same roof ledge from which her son plunged. However, Erica and the prison's young Dr. Cooper (Jason Evers) restrain her and rescue Mrs. Hunter. Because of the publicity-generating event, Warden Cole is fired and a new replacement, Zoe Stoughton (Margaret Hayes) is installed in his stead. Erica wins her parole and is reunited with her youngster.

Howard Thompson justifiably criticized that *House of Women* "is a lopsided remake of *Caged*, soggily afloat in a bar-enclosed tub of soap-opera suds."

Variety reported, "Only new wrinkle in a film liberally crammed with the clichés of the prison pic is the residential presence in the pen of the offsprings of the lady inmates.... How [Andrew] Duggan ever got the job [as warden] is one of the mysteries of a very mysterious picture in which the inmates generally seem far more sensible, likable and well-adjusted than the staff.... Walter Doniger's direction tends to be rather stilted and theatrical."

Because *House of Women* has such a flat, unrealistic look throughout, it is difficult to take any of the film's faint premises seriously. The pokey does not look *that* unwholesome, the treatment of the female convicts (except by the maladjusted, fluctuating warden) *that* severe or unfair, and because so much of the picture focuses on the filial union between mothers and young children behind bars, the ambiance does not have *that* sterile, frightening aroma of many such prison melodramas.

The uncharismatic Shirley Knight, always a difficult person to cast properly in motion pictures, does not generate much sympathy in *House of Women,* unlike her counterpart (Eleanor Parker) in *Caged.* There is no menace in *House of Women* to equal the nightmarish qualities of the Herculean Hope Emerson of *Caged.* And the sympathetic assistant warden, Margaret Hayes of *House of Women* is no equal to her parallel (Agnes Moorehead) in *Caged.* While Constance Ford is always a solid performer, her role in *House of Women* is so contradictory and shallow that it leaves little impression on the viewer. The one bright acting spot in *House of Women* is brassy Barbara Nichols, who is always interesting to watch oncamera. She shines as Candy Kane, the ex-stripper-now-convict. Candy is the bouncy optimistic sort; with a nasal twang, a perpetual smile, and a swivel to her hips that would make Mae West envious. Having been in and out of jail since the age of eleven, she has her own unique philosophy about prison life and the matter of parole, "Me, I am out on parole and can't drink or mingle with ex-cons. Gotta get permission to marry or die.... I think it [parole] stinks!"

Partway through the filming of *House of Women,* scripter Crane Wilbur (a veteran at prison genre pieces) assumed direction of the movie. When he was denied full directorial credit for the production, he refused billing as co-director. One amusing bit of "in" business in *House of Women* has one of the women prisoners drooling over a framed photograph of Troy Donahue. Donahue was then a Warner Bros. contract star.

A.k.a.: *Ladies of the Mob.*

121. *I Am a Fugitive from a Chain Gang* (Warner Bros., 1932), 93 min.

Executive producer, William Koenig; producer, Hal B. Wallis; director, Mervyn LeRoy; based on the book *I Am a Fugitive from a Georgia Chain Gang* by Robert E. Burns; screenplay, Howard J. Green, Brown Holmes, Sheridan Gibney; art director, Jack Okey; costumes, Orry-Kelly; makeup, Ray Romero; music director, Leo F. Forbstein; technical director, S. H. Sullivan; assistant directors, Al Alborn, Chuck Hansen; technical advisers, Sullivan, Jack Miller, Burns; sound, Al Riggs; camera, Sol Polito; editor, William Holmes.

Paul Muni (Allen James [James Allen]); Glenda Farrell (Marie Woods); Helen Vinson (Helen); Noel Francis (Linda); Preston Foster (Pete); Allen Jenkins (Barney Sykes); Edward Ellis (Bomber Wells); John Wray (Nordine); Hale Hamilton (Reverend Robert Clinton Allen); Harry Woods (Guard); David Landau (Warden); Edward J. McNamara (2nd Warden); Robert McWade (F. E. Ramsey); Willard Robertson

(Prison Commissioner); Louise Carter (Mrs. Allen); Berton Churchill (Judge); Sheila Terry (Allen's Secretary); Sally Blane (Alice); James Bell (Red); Edward LeSaint (Chairman, Chamber of Commerce); Douglass Dumbrille (District Attorney); Robert Warwick (Fuller); Charles Middleton (Train Conductor); Reginald Barlow (Parker); Jack LaRue (Ackerman); Charles Sellon (Hot Dog Stand Owner); Erville Alderson (Chief of Police); George Pat Collins (Wilson); William Pawley (Doggy); Lew Kelly (Mike, Proprietor of Diner); Everett Brown (Sebastian T. Yale); William LeMaire (Texan); George Cooper (Vaudevillian); Wallis Clark (Lawyer); Walter Long (Blacksmith); Frederick Burton (Georgia Prison Official); Irving Bacon (Barber Bill); Lee Shumway, J. Frank Glendon (Arresting Officers); Bud Flannagan [Dennis O'Keefe] (Dance Extra).

I Am a Fugitive from a Chain Gang is not only the ultimate prison story, but it remains one of the most remarkable studies of social injustice ever produced by Hollywood. Jerry Vermilye, in *The Films of the Thirties* (1982), assessed:

> *I Am a Fugitive from a Chain Gang* hit Depression-era audiences with the power of a sledgehammer. Powerful and uncompromising in its indictment of the law (especially with regard to carefully unnamed Southern communities), it was given a realistic, unvarnished production ... and naturalistic, understated acting by its star Paul Muni.... Largely because of his fine performance, this movie remains a powerful statement of social injustice.

Demobilized from World War I military service, American doughboy James Allen (Paul Muni) is frustrated by his return to his hometown and his drab shipping department job at the Parker Shoe Factory. He soon quits to become an itinerant construction worker. His sympathetic mother (Louise Carter) is understanding of his restlessness, while his stuffy clergyman brother (Hale Hamilton) is aghast at his lack of responsibility. Later, finding himself out of work in a southern town, he is duped by fellow hobo Pete (Preston Foster) into participating in a lunch wagon holdup. Pete is killed by the police, while James is sentenced to ten years of hard labor on a chain gang.

For well over a year, James endures the brutality and privation of the chain gang at County Camp #2. Then he escapes. After being sheltered by ex-convict Barney Sykes (Allen Jenkins), he makes his way to Chicago. Using the alias of Allen James, he finds work with a construction firm. Over the years he works his way into a senior management position. By reading a letter from his brother, his youngish landlady, Marie Woods (Glenda Farrell), discovers that he is an escaped convict. As the price of his freedom, she blackmails him into an intolerable marriage and an ever-increasing allowance. Later, James falls in love with the well-bred Helen (Helen Vinson) and attempts to break free of Marie. She refuses a divorce and vengefully informs the police about him.

Initially, the Chicago authorities bar extradition and a nationwide civic campaign is launched on Allen's behalf. While in detention, Allen writes an exposé of the horrendous conditions he experienced on the chain gang. Thereafter, representatives of the southern state where he was jailed trick Allen. They promise him a pardon if he will serve an additional ninety days of his sentence. When he returns down south, Allen is sent to the Tuttle County Prison Camp. (As one guard says of this dreaded site, "It's the last word, it is.") Later, the parole board indefinitely suspends their consideration of his case. This causes the embittered James to escape the camp by truck, joined by an older prisoner, Bomber Wells (Edward Ellis), who is killed by the pursuing guards.

Time passes. Late one night in Chicago, Helen is confronted by a haggard James. She asks the hunted man how he survives.

ALLEN: I hide in rooms all day and travel by night. No friends, no rest, no peace. Keep moving. That's all there's left for me. . . . Forgive me.

HELEN: How do you live?

ALLEN: [He hisses from the shadows] I steal!

There are many factors which make *I Am a Fugitive from a Chain Gang* an astounding document of man's inhumanity to man. Robert E. Burns (the assumed name of the author of the 1932 book on which the film was based) came to Hollywood and spent four weeks working as technical adviser on the project. Paul Muni, having done a great deal of research himself on the subject, threw himself into the role with such dedication that his characterization is solidly authentic. The fateful circumstances which first put the hero into custody lend an atmosphere of cumulative oppression, giving the movie a harrowing tone.

The chain gang scenes themselves are understated, but always grim and effectively create a vivid picture for the viewer of the abominable life on a chain gang. The nerve-wracking plight of the oppressed convicts, shuffling along with leg irons, chained to their cots at nights, being fed slop that pigs would not eat, and expected to do a hard day's work on the rock quarries, is unforgettable. The fact that this deadening routine continues day after day makes it all the more frightening. That these slaves are frequently tortured with whippings or chained in the open yard to sizzle under the blazing sun, adds further impact. As one convict observes, "There are two ways to get out of here. Walk out or ride out [in a hearse]." The one dream that keeps many of these men alive is the fantasy hope of escape. However, the odds of succeeding are slim indeed. ("You got to beat the chains, the bloodhounds and a bunch of guards who'd just as soon bring you back dead.") One of the few concessions that Warner Bros. made in filming this prison story was not referring to Georgia as the state where the hero endured the dreaded chain gang.

RKO's *Hell's Highway,* q.v., a far less effective study of southern chain gangs, had been rushed into release two months earlier than Warner Bros.' ballyhooed production. However, the former film did little to diminish the impact of the new entry. Mordaunt Hall *(New York Times)* approved strongly of *I Am a Fugitive from a Chain Gang:* "The producers do not mince matters in this melodrama, and even at the close there is none of the usual bowing to popular appeal. . . . The scenes of the convicts using picks, shovels and sledge-hammers in the quarries and elsewhere are set forth realistically." *Variety* termed the Warner Bros. production "a picture with guts . . . . That it's a man's picture essentially is apparent from the title. The women will shudder at its gruesome realism but they'll not be bored. . . . For fear of any censorial or other captiousness by civic fathers, the Warners actually have leaned backward in the celluloid version. . . ." *Harrison's Reports* judged it "A powerful drama for adult audiences. It is relentless in its exposure of the brutality and inhumanness of chain gangs; sensitive people will be unable to watch the squalid surroundings, the messy food, and the punishment meted out to the men. . . ."

Years later, in retrospect Tom Pulleine (British *Monthly Film Bulletin*)

Paul Muni in *I Am a Fugitive from a Chain Gang* (1932).

argued that *I Am a Fugitive from a Chain Gang* is remarkable for "direct confrontation of hideous penal practices (an honesty which makes it still frequently painful to watch) but also by a sobriety of tone and unobtrusive rigour of construction which forestalls any charge of glib sensationalism." In *The International Dictionary of Films and Filmmakers, Vol. 1* (1984), Daniel J. Leab ranks this movie high as a "powerful indictment and pungent commentary on social ills . . . thanks to a thoughtful script, taut direction, and vibrant central performances."

  I Am a Fugitive from a Chain Gang was nominated for two Academy Awards: Best Actor (Paul Muni lost to Charles Laughton of *The Private Life of Henry VIII*) and Best Picture (*Cavalcade* won). While the movie is credited with inciting prison reform, that remains speculation. It certainly altered the shape of prison films and remained a benchmark by which any future genre study would be judged. Fifty-five years later, the harrowing account of prisoner/fugitive Robert E. Burns would form the basis of the telefeature *The Man Who Broke 1,000 Chains*, q.v. However, the deficient new production is no match for the sterling 1932 Warner Bros. opus.

  Reissue title: *I Am a Fugitive.*

  British release title: *I Am a Fugitive from the Chain Gang.*

Jim Brown *(left)* and Christopher George *(center)* in *I Escaped from Devil's Island* (1973).

122. *I Escaped from Devil's Island* (United Artists, 1973), color, 87 min.

Producers, Roger Corman, Gene Corman; director, William Witney; screenplay, Richard L. Adams; art director, Robert Silva; set decorator, Jose Gonzalez; music, Les Baxter; assistant directors, Jaime Contreras, Cliff Bush; sound, Jose Carlos; camera, Rosalio Solano; editors, Alan Collins, Tom Walls, Barbara Pokras.

Jim Brown (Le Bras); Christopher George (Davert); Rick Ely (Jo-Jo); James Luis (Dazzas); Paul Richards (Major Marteau); Richard Rust (Sergeant Zamoora); Roland "Bob" Harris (Barber); Jan Merlin (Roenquist); Rosas Lopez (Sergeant Brescano); Jonathan Dodge (Lieutenant Duplis); Quintin Bulnes (Sergeant Grissoni); Gabriella Rios (Indian Girl); Ana de Sade (Bedalia); Max Kerlow (Pelliserre); Aubert Knight (The Dealer); Enrique Lucero (Esteban); Aurora Nunez (Whore); Gaston Melo (Police Captain).

"*I Escaped from Devil's Island* . . . won't drain audiences from the forthcoming film version of the best-selling books *Papillon* [q.v.] to which it bears such obvious resemblance" (Allan R. Holward, *Hollywood Reporter*). *Variety* dismissed the production as "a slovenly, gamy potboiler, far below the standards of producers Roger and Gene Corman. . . ." Made during the wanning days of Jim Brown's success as the premier star of black exploitation features, *I Escaped from Devil's Island* was promoted with "He's the Devil they Named the Island for! . . . No man ever broke this prison! . . . No prison ever broke this man!" The R-rated film, despite its exploitive, sadistic bent, was not a commercial success.

In 1918, black convict Le Bras (Jim Brown) finds that his death sentence at the guillotine has been commuted to life. Nevertheless, he is determined to escape from the French penal colony based on Devil's Island. Joined by two other convicts, Dazzas (James Luisi) and his semi-transvestite lover Jo-Jo (Rick Ely)—the trio prepare for their breakout. Always fearful of being detected by their warders or betrayed by fellow convicts, they secretly build a raft of animal skins. The three men make good their escape, joined unenthusiastically by the pacifist Davert (Christopher George) a political prisoner who was indirectly responsible for saving Le Bras's life. They are promptly pursued by Major Marteau (Paul Richards) and his men. En route to the mainland, Dazzas is killed by a shark. When they reach the shore, they are captured by Amazon Indians after Le Bras murders one of them. Their captors prove to be relatively hospitable, but the men still flee in a stolen canoe, later encountering a leper colony. At the village of St. Thereafter, Jo-Jo is arrested for pickpocketing. He hangs himself before he can be questioned/tortured. Still later, Le Bras is injured by the persistent police. Rather than continue, Le Bras holds off the pursuers while Davert escapes aboard a ship.

In comparing *I Escaped from Devil's Island* with *Papillon,* David McGillivray (British *Monthly Film Bulletin*) remarked, "The element of parody is missing, but the sense of comic-book imitation is very strong.... Once again the four escapees from the penal colony represent brawn, brains, homosexuality and expendability.... True, the film then contributes some ideas of its own, but these amount to staking out the heroes in the sand, involving Le Bras in a sexy tribal ritual and generally wallowing in inimitable Hollywood-style fantasy." In panning *I Escaped from Devil's Island,* McGillivray also noted the film's "unappealing production values," "the language and the violence are gratuitously crude" and that the script is "piecemeal."

123. *I Want to Live!* (United Artists, 1958), 120 min.

Producer, Walter Wanger; director, Robert Wise; based on newspaper articles by Ed Montgomery and the letters of Barbara Graham; screenplay, Nelson Gidding, Don M. Mankiewicz; art director, Edward Haworth; set decorator, Victor Gangelin; costumes, Wesley Jeffries, Angela Alexander; makeup, Tom Tuttle, Jack Stone; music/music conductor, John Mandel; assistant director, George Vietria; sound, Fred Lau; camera, Lionel Lindon; editor, William Hornbeck.

Susan Hayward (Bonnie "Barbara" Wood Graham); Simon Oakland (Ed Montgomery); Virginia Vincent (Peg); Theodore Bikel (Carl Palmberg); Wesley Lau (Henry Graham); Philip Coolidge (Emmett Perkins); Lou Krugman (Jack R. Santo); James Philbrook (Bruce King); Bartlett Robinson (District Attorney);

Gage Clark (Richard Tibrow); Joe De Santis (Al Matthews); John Marley (Father Devers); Dabbs Greer (San Quentin Captain); Raymond Bailey (Warden); Alice Backes (Nurse); Gertrude Flynn (Matron); Russell Thorson, Stafford Repp (Sergeants); Gavin MacLeod (Lieutenant); Peter Breck (Ben Miranda); Marion Marshall (Rita); Olive Blakeney (Corona Warden); Lorna Tyler (Corona Guard); Evelyn Scott (Personal Effects Clerk); Jack Weston (Non Commissioned Officer); Leonard Bell (San Francisco Hood); George Putnam (Himself); Bill Stout (Newsman); Jason Johnson (Bixel); Rusty Lane (Judge); S. John Launer (San Quentin Officer); Dan Sheridan (Police Broadcaster); Wendell Holmes (Detective); Gerry Mulligan, Art Farmer, Bud Shank, Frank Rosolino, Pete Jolly, "Red" Mitchell, Shelly Manne (Musicians).

Twenty-nine-year-old Barbara Graham, a former prostitute and convicted perjurer, was sentenced to die in the gas chamber at California's San Quentin Prison for her alleged participation in the murder of a sixty-two-year-old woman in

Susan Hayward in *I Want to Live!* (1958).

1953. After two stays of execution – one only ninety seconds before she was to enter the death chamber – she was executed on June 3, 1955. The graphic details of this highly-publicized case were still fresh in the public's mind when Susan Hayward starred in *I Want to Live!,* a telescoped dramatization of the Barbara Graham story. For her gutsy, frequently moving performance, veteran actress Hayward received a Best Actress Academy Award. (She had four previous Oscar nominations for Best Actress.) The movie, for which producer Walter Wanger received much opposition in pre-production, earned over $3,000,000.

In San Francisco's tenderloin, brassy good-time gal Barbara Wood (Susan Hayward) leads a promiscuous life. To assist a friend in avoiding conviction on a robbery charge, she perjures herself in court and is later sentenced to a year in jail. Upon her release, she joins forces with two eminently unsavory characters – Emmett Perkins (Philip Coolidge) and Jack Santo (Lou Krugman) – helping them in their con games. Now having a bankroll, she marries bartender Henry Graham (Wesley Lau). She soon discovers that Henry is a confirmed drug addict. Shortly after their baby boy is born, she and Henry break up. Desperately needing money for food and a place for she and her child to live, she becomes reinvolved with Perkins and Santo. She does not know they are on the lam, having just brutally murdered an elderly widow. When the three of them are caught, another criminal, Bruce King (James Philbrook), whose advances she had rejected and who is also involved in the homicide, turns state's evidence. He names Barbara as an accessory to the crime. Panicked at her inability to prove her innocence, she acquires an alibi from Ben Miranda (Peter Breck), the supposed boyfriend of a prison mate. Thereafter, at her trial, Barbara learns that Miranda is actually a police officer who is now a witness for the prosecution. Because this cop insists that she told him in confidence that she was at the scene of the crime, her defense collapses. She is sentenced to die.

Meanwhile, her case generates a great deal of publicity. Many liberal forces (opposed to the death penalty) believe her story that she was tricked into a confession by the Los Angeles police. Among those rallying to her aid is eminent psychologist Carl Palmberg (Theodore Bikel), who insists that she does not have the emotional makeup of a killer. A convert to her cause is *San Francisco Examiner* reporter Ed Montgomery (Simon Oakland), who does a turnabout from his smear campaign. He now crusades for her release. Meanwhile, the endless waiting on death row during the legal maneuvers and the faint hope of freedom, wears down the once spirited Barbara. Despite two last-minute appeals, she dies in the gas chamber, a few minutes before Perkins and Santo are similarly executed.

I Want to Live! concludes with the postscript:

> You have just seen a *factual story*. It is based on articles I wrote, other newspaper and magazine articles, court records, legal and private correspondence, investigative reports, personal interviews — and the letters of Barbara Graham.
>
> (Signed) Edward S. Montgomery

According to Bosley Crowther *(New York Times),* Susan Hayward has "never done anything so vivid or so shattering to an audience's nerves as she does in . . . *I Want to Live.* . . . [The] deathhouse phase of this is a harrowing synthesis of drama and cold documentary detail. . . . Anyone who can sit through this ordeal without shivering and shuddering is made of stone." *Variety* opined that the movie was "overwhelming in its compulsion and power" and registered, "The final 30 to 40 minutes of the film are as harrowing as anything ever done in pictures. It is a purposely understated account of the mechanics involved in the state's legal destruction of life, and its effects is to raise serious thoughts about what constitutes 'cruel and unusual punishment.'"

Boasting a John(ny) Mandel jazz score, *I Want to Live!* is very typical of 1950s Hollywood biographical movies which encompassed exploitive "mature" material. Like Hayward's own earlier *I'll Cry Tomorrow* (1955) which focues on actress/alcholic Lillian Roth, *I Want to Live!* is a series of stark dramatic set pieces. There is very little bridging material nor any sustained psychological probing of the enigmatic lead character. However, thanks to the pungent direction of Robert Wise and his clinical approach to the adult subject matter, veteran trooper Hayward performs the role to the hilt and from the hip, nurturing a chip on her shoulder and fiery look in her eyes throughout. Only occasionally does this very vulnerable dame allow her tough demeanor to crack.

Early in the narrative. Graham, the prostitute, has a sharp interchange with one of her clients:

MAN: Life is a funny thing.

BARBARA: Compared to what?

Later, she and a fellow crook compare notes:

CROOK: What do you do?

BARBARA: The best I can.

Further into the high-voltage chronicle, she encounters the slimy minor criminal Bruce King (James Philbrook):

KING: I heard there was no such thing as not your type.

BARBARA: Until I met you. And believe me, it's purely personal.

Even after she is jailed on the murder charge and everything appears hopeless, she finds a morbid humor to her plight: "All the stuff I read, and I could never read the handwriting on the wall."

When a bullheaded matron acts rough with Barbara, she snaps back to the insensitive keeper, "What can anyone threaten me with now!"

Finally, in the film's most remembered moment (and one of filmdom's most famous dialogue scenes), Graham is strapped into the death chamber chair. A guard places an eye mask on her face.

GUARD: When you hear the pellets drop, count to ten. Take a deep breath. It's easier that way.

BARBARA: How do you know?

I Want to Live! garnered Oscar nominations for Best Director, Screenplay — Based on Material from Another Medium, Cinematography — Black-and-White, Sound, and Editing. It would lead to a respectable telefeature remake (1983), q.v., starring Lindsay Wagner and to a rip-off budget distillation, *Why Must I Die?* (1960), q.v., featuring Terry Moore. Despite all this, no Hollywood deathhouse scene has ever matched the intensity and impact of Barbara Graham's twitching, gasping finale in *I Want to Live!*

124. *I Want to Live* (ABC–TV, May 9, 1983), color, 100 min.

Producer, Paul Pompian; associate producer, Barbara Costaperaria; director, David Lowell Rich; based on newspaper articles by Ed Montgomery, the letters by Barbara Graham and the screenplay by Nelson Gidding, Don M. Mankiewicz; teleplay, Mankiewicz, Gordon Cotler; art director, George B. Chan; set decorators, Sam Gross, Garrett Lewis; costumes, Patrick Cummings; makeup, Robert Ryan, Don Cash; music, Lee Holdridge; music supervisor, Harry V. Lojewski; music editor, Scott Stambler; assistant directors, Jerry Ballew, Ken Collins; sound, Bob Miller; sound editor, Paul Hockman; camera, Charles F. Wheeler; editor, David Finfer.

Lindsay Wagner (Barbara Graham); Martin Balsam (Jack Brady); Pamela Reed

(Edie Bannister); Harry Dean Stanton (Emmett Perkins); Michael Alldredge (Mr. Cooley); Kent Broadhurst (District Attorney); Seymour Cassel (Jack R. Santo); Jon Cedar (Jim Stockard); Dana Elcar (Warden); Ellen Geer (Mrs. Cooley); Robert Ginty (Henry Graham); Barry Primus (Al Matthews); Don Stroud (Jon True); Ken Swofford (Sergeant Black); William Bogert (Prosecution Judge); Vincent Bufano (Sergeant Russo); Darlene Conley (Miss Bain); Pat Corley (Bartender); Michael Currie (Doctor); Cliff Emmich (Saxon); Robert Englund (Sam Cooper); Gerry Gibson (Perjury Judge); Pat McNamara (Captain Polk); William Phipps (Police Lieutenant); Dean Santoro (1st Federal Agent); Rebecca Stanley (Nurse); Peter White (Jerry Charles Fricke); Pamela Baker (Lissa); Ned Bellamy (Jerry Henderson); Steve Burton (2nd Federal Agent); Daniel Chodos (News Editor); Ian Foster (Eric); Lance Gordon (Mr. Wallace); Bert Hinchman (Technician); Dewitt Kirk (Court Clerk); Larry Marko (Reporter); Will Nye (Sailor); Anne Ramsey (Matron); Woody Skaggs (Reporter); Jon Slade (Father Charles); Ed Williams (Minister).

Fifteen years after Susan Hayward's Oscar-winning performance as condemned murderess Barbara Graham, Lindsay Wagner starred in a well-mounted telefeature remake of the acclaimed motion picture, *I Want to Live!* Relying on the 1958 screenplay, among other sources, original co-scripter Don M. Mankiewicz co-authored a new rendition with Gordon Cotler. The new edition is some twenty minutes shorter than the original and is in color. It also a far more informative, full-bodied account of the life and bad times of Barbara Graham, whose complicity or innocence in the 1953 Burbank, California, homicide has never been completely resolved.

For Lindsay Wagner, noted primarily for her TV series "Bionic Woman" (1976–77), this major dramatic assignment proved to be an acting coup, displaying her range of talents as an actress with dimension. The critics, awed by the legend of the big screen original version and the artistic reputation of the late Susan Hayward, were mixed in their reactions. "Graham is used, abused, framed and gassed, but Wagner's performance . . . casts an awe of dignity around the production" insisted Gail Williams of the *Hollywood Reporter*. On the other hand, *Daily Variety* ruled, "[Susan] Hayward's vitality and vibrant personality made Graham a creature not only of sympathy but of awe; Wagner can't find the edge." The reader is invited to make his own comparison, but for this author the remake and its leading player are far more realistic, sympathetic, and mesmerizing than Susan Hayward in the 1958 feature, q.v.

In 1955, as the San Quentin executioner prepares the sulfuric acid and cyanide to be mixed for the gas chamber execution of Barbara Graham (Lindsay Wagner), the nervous condemned woman awaits her end. She fusses with her makeup and wardrobe, wondering if she will have another stay of execution.

> BARBARA: I don't get you people [i.e. the prison nurse]. You're getting ready to kill me, and you need music.

The warden (Dana Elcar) confesses to Graham, "I'm sorry about the uncertainty. I hate last minute stays." Fighting to retain her courage, Barbara reflects back on her troubled life.

As a wayward girl reared in California without any family to take responsibility, she ends in a reformatory. Having served her time, the authorities release her to face the real world. They caution her, "Don't go looking for the fun you missed." She finds work in Oxnard, California, with the Cooleys who have three children. Before long, the randy husband (Michael Alldredge) makes sexual advances to her.

Dana Elcar, Lindsay Wagner and Jon Slade in *I Want to Live* (1983).

To escape the bad situation, she marries young Jerry Henderson (Ned Bellamy), who is being inducted into the U.S. Navy during World War II. She has his child, which she soon leaves with her mother-in-law.

Unshackled of responsibility. Barbara becomes a B-girl, hustling drinks at the Poop Deck Bar. She continues her penchant for taking up with the wrong men. On one occasion she drives to Tijuana with a pick-up, Jim Stockard (Jon Cedar), who, it develops, is smuggling illegal government ration books. The good-natured Barbara takes the rap to save her friend and she is sentenced to one year in the county jail. When paroled, the authorities scold her, "I hope that this experience will cause you to equip yourself to seek legitimate, respectable employment." It does not! She reencounters Stockard in San Francisco and agrees to provide an alibi for the minor league criminal who is now under suspicion on a robbery charge. However, her perjury is found out and she is sentenced to one year in jail with a five year subsequent probationary period.

Time passes. Once again a free woman, the ex-convict relocates to Hollywood where she promptly engages in minor scams. Bartender Henry Graham (Robert Ginty) comes to her rescue when cops spot her plying her con games and these two losers-in-life soon marry. To bankroll their life together, he suggests they team with Emmett Perkins (Harry Dean Stanton) and Jack Santo (Seymour Cassel) for "one last hustle" in which she acts as a shill in a well-staked poker game. Later, she and Graham have a child and split up when he returns to being a drug addict. Adrift and in need of money, the desperate Barbara seeks assistance from Perkins and Santo, not knowing they have recently murdered a Burbank, California, widow and invalid. After she, Perkins and Santo are captured by the police, Jon True (Don Stroud), a confederate of the two men on their deadly caper, implicates Barbara in the crime. It allows him to make a deal with the law.

Jack Brady (Martin Balsam) is the volunteer lawyer assigned to Barbara's case which takes a turn for the worse when she is tricked by undercover cop Sam Cooper (Robert Englund) into implicating herself at the scene of the crime. Cooper testifies of this at her trial and the verdict is guilty. She is incarcerated at San Quentin Prison to await her execution. Among those rallying to her cause are reporters Edie Bannister (Pamela Reed), who develops a special empathy with the accused. As her stay on death row evolves, the flinty Barbara becomes more agitated, especially when she receives a nerve-shattering last minute stay of execution. She tells the warden, "I don't want to be alive. I want to live! This isn't living, is it?"

Finally on June 3, 1955, she is led into the gas chamber and prepared for her execution. There are no more appeals. A guard tells her to "Take deep breaths, it's easier," and the frazzled woman responds, "How would you know?" Graham's body is buried at Mt. Olivet Cemetery in San Rafael, California.

A postscript advises: "Since Barbara Graham's execution, changes have been instituted regarding rules of evidence and self-incrimination."

125. *I Was a Prisoner on Devil's Island* (Columbia, 1941), 71 min.

Producer, Wallace MacDonald; director, Lew Landers; story, Otto Van Eyss, Edgar Van Eyss; screenplay, Karl Brown; camera, John Stumar; editor, Richard Fantl.

Sally Eilers (Claire Martel); Donald Woods (Joel Grant); Edward [Eduardo] Ciannelli (Dr. Martel); Victor Kilian (Guissart); Charles Halton (Commandant); Dick Curtis (Jules); John Tyrrell (Gerault); Eddie Laughton (Brisson); Edmund Cobb (Quarry Guard); Robert Warwick (Governor).

> If the audience doesn't laugh at the wrong times, or claim (as they did at this theatre) 'what a story!' at the conclusion, it may get by as a mild programmer . . . overdone dramatics and slipshod yarn. . . .
>
> *(Variety)*

Carefree American Joel Grant (Donald Woods), first mate on a vessel bound for New York, disembarks when his ship stops at a tiny French port during carnival time. He encounters a weeping young woman, Claire Martel (Sally Eilers), who explains that she had been married to a cruel husband, but that she intends to get divorced. The two quickly fall in love and Grant decides to abandon his nautical career to remain with Claire. However, in an argument with his captain, the latter falls, hits his head and dies. As a result, Joel is sentenced to three years on Devil's Island.

Meanwhile, Claire's husband, Dr. Martel (Edward [Eduardo] Cianneli), has been named as physician at the penal colony and demands that his spouse join him there. She agrees, hoping to be near Grant. Once there, Martel teams with the compound's malevolent commandant (Charles Halton) in corrupt practices, including msiappropriating the prison's annual medical supplies. Later, an epidemic breaks out at Devil's Island and there is no medicine. Martel is himself stricken and, while delirious, confesses his misdeeds. Grant, joined by a friendly guard, speed to the mainland, where they force the drug dealer to return the stolen medicines. The epidemic is stopped and Martel is saved. Thereafter, the governor

(Robert Warwick) is told of the corruption. Martel is jailed, but he is killed while trying to escape. Joel is pardoned, allowing he and Claire to wed.

126. *I Was Framed* (Warner Bros., 1942), 61 min.

Associate producer, William Jacobs; director, D. Ross Lederman; based on the idea within the book *Dust Be My Destiny* by Jerome Odlum; screenplay, Robert E. Kent; assistant director, Bill Kessel; camera, Ted McCord; editor, Frank Magee.

Michael Ames (Ken Marshall); Julie Bishop (Ruth Marshall); Regis Toomey (Bob Leeds); Patty Hale (Penny Marshall); John Harmon (Clubby Blake); Aldrich Bowker (Dr. Phillip Black); Roland Drew (Gordon Locke); Oscar O'Shea (Cal Beamish); Wade Boteler (Ben Belden); Howard Hickman (Stuart Gaines); Norman Willis (Paul Brenner); Hobart Bosworth (D. L. Wallace); Guy Usher (Police Chief Taylor); Sam McDaniel (Kit Carson); Joan Winfield (Nurse); Dick Chandlee (Copy Boy); Sol Gorss (Mills); Don Turner (Tabor); Eddy Chandler (Cop); Frank Mayo, Jack Mower (Guards); Cliff Saum (Fleck); Lee Powell (Policeman); Harry Strang, Ed Hearn (Officers).

Using bits and pieces of Jerome Odlum's writings that had formed the basis of *Dust Be My Destiny* (1939) and *Each Dawn I Die* (1939), qq.v., this hack "B" picture had little to recommend it. "Action is spotty and the whole thing is too difficult to believe to make much of an audience imprint" (*Variety*). Particularly annoying was Patty Hale, the precocious young actress portraying the hero's coy little offspring.

Crusading reporter Ken Marshall (Michael Ames), who is about to expose major corruption in the state, is framed on a vehicular manslaughter charge in which three victims die. Sentenced to prison, Ken frets about his pregnant wife Ruth (Julie Bishop). His experienced cellmate Clubby Blake (John Harmon) suggests that they break out as he has already devised an escape route. Marshall gets out, but Blake is left behind. Later, Ken, Ruth and their baby girl Penny (Patty Hale) settle in a small community where he joins a local newspaper under an alias. Within five years, he has become editor of the paper. However, the now-released Clubby passes through town one day and recognizes Ken. He blackmails Ruth who pays him $1,000. When he demands more, he and Marshall get into a tussle. Ken is wounded and Blake is killed, shot by the summoned police. By the time Marshall recovers, he is overjoyed to learn he has been cleared of all the charges which led to his earlier conviction.

The *Hollywood Reporter* judged, it "doesn't make the grade as entertainment. Reminiscent of a dozen other plots, the screenplay . . . borrows heavily from stock situations. . . ."

127. *If I Had a Million* (Paramount, 1932), 88 min.

Producer, Louis D. Lighton; directors, Ernst Lubitsch, Norman Taurog, Stephen S. Roberts, Norman McLeod, James Cruze, William A. Seiter, H. Bruce Humberstone, (uncredited) Lothar Mendes; based on the novel *Windfall* by Robert D. Andrews; screenplay, Claude Binyon, Whitney Bolton, Malcolm Stuart Boyland, John Bright, Sidney Buchanan, Lester Cole, Isabel Dawn, Boyce De Gaw, Walter DeLeon, Oliver H. P. Garrett, Harvey Gates, Grover Jones, Lubitsch, Lawton Mackall, Joseph L. Mankiewicz, William Slavens McNutt, Seton I. Miller, Robert Sparks, Tiffany Thayer; sound, Frank Grenzbach, Phil S. Wisdom.

Gary Cooper (Gallagher); George Raft (Eddie Jackson); Charles Laughton (The Clerk); Jack Oakie (Mulligan); Frances Dee (Mary Wallace); Wynne Gibson (Violet Smith); Charles Ruggles (Henry Peabody); Alison Skipworth (Emily); W. C. Fields

(Rollo La Rue); Mary Boland (Mrs. Peabody); Roscoe Karns (O'Brien); May Robson (Mrs. Walker); Gene Raymond (John Wallace); Lucien Littlefield (Zeb); Richard Bennett (John Glidden); Grant Mitchell (The Prison Priest); Joyce Compton (Marie); Cecil Cunningham (Agnes); Irving Bacon (Chinaware Salesman); Blanche Friderici (Head Nurse at Old Ladies' Home); Dewey Robinson (Cook at Old Ladies' Home); Gail Patrick (Secretary); Fred Kelsey, Willard Robertson (Doctors); Kent Taylor (Bank Clerk); Jack Pennick (Sailor); Berton Churchill (Warden); James Burtis (Jailer); Edwin Stanley (Mr. Galloway); Gertrude Norman (Idylwood Resident); Ernest Truex (Mr. Brown); Emma Tansey (Idylwood Resident); William V. Mong (Harry the Fence); Margaret Seddo (Mrs. Small); Wallis Clark (Mr. Monroe); Tom Kennedy (Officer/Joe, a Carnival Tough); Frank Hagney (Mike, a Carnival Tough); Charles McMurphy (Mike, a Bank Guard); Henry C. Bradley (Bank Guard); Lew Kelly (Prison Attendant); Samuel S. Hinds (Attorney); Reginald Barlow (Glidden Employee); Clarence Muse (Prisoner); Walter C. Percival (Carnival Attendant); Russ Powell (Bartender); Morgan Wallace (Mike, a Mobster); Hooper Atchley (Hotel Desk Clerk); Margaret Mann, Lydia Knott, Clair Bracy, Bangy Bilby (Idylwood Residents); Robert [Emmett] Homans (Detective); Eddie Baker (Desk Clerk); Joe Winthrop (Idylwood Resident); Larry Steers, John St. Polis, Frederick Santley, Herbert Moulton (Glidden Employees); Marc Lawrence (Hoodlum); James Bush (Teller); Tom Ricketts (Elderly Man); Bess Flowers (Customer); Fred Holmes (Store Clerk); Syd Saylor (Driver); Rolfe Sedan (Salesman); Lester Dorr (Pedestrian).

Paramount Pictures contrived this omnibus production to utilize a variety of its contract stars in short segments directed by a host of directors. With such an impressive assortment of personalities and acting styles, *If I Had a Million* is an engaging curiosity. To maintain audience interest, most of the segments rely on a surprise ending, which impels the viewer on to the next episode. One of the most ironic of the mini-stories is the "Condemned Man's Episode."

Ailing tycoon John Glidden (Richard Bennett) confounds his physicians (Fred Kelsey, Willard Robertson) by arising from his deathbed with a new purpose. He plans to dispose of his sizeable fortune. His plan is to give unsuspecting strangers, picked from the phone book, checks for $1,000,000 each. The experience is so exhilarating to Glidden, that he makes a complete recovery. Among the recipients are: henpecked china shop worker Henry Peabody (Charlie Ruggles), a prostitute (Wynne Gibson), a forger (George Raft), landlady Emily La Rue (Alison Skipworth) and her spouse (W. C. Fields), meek officer clerk Phineas Lambert (Charles Laughton), a marine (Gary Cooper), an elderly lady (May Robson), and John Wallace (Gene Raymond) of 3360 Bellevue Avenue.

Wallace is now on death row for having executed a holdup in which a victim died. His rationale for the crime was, "You can't think when you're hungry." A death row guard observes, "This is the toughest death watch I ever had." The prison chaplain (Grant Mitchell) attempts to provide spiritual consolation. However, the near hysterical Wallace screams to the priest, "Why don't you stop them instead? I don't want to have my soul saved. I want to live! I'm going to be killed because I didn't have money enough to have a good lawyer."

The prisoner's distraught wife (Frances Dee) arrives and he asks the priest for advise:

JOHN: What can I tell her, so she'll want to go on living?

PRIEST: Talk about living.

Thereafter, the tycoon's associate delivers Wallace's $1,000,000 check to the prison. Grasping at straws, John reasons that with this money he can buy his freedom. He shouts at the warden (Berton Churchill), "Warden, you can't kill me now! A million dollars now! I've got to live!... I'm not going to burn! A new deal for me now! I can get a right lawyer."

However, the execution is to take place as scheduled. John is dragged from his cell, screaming "You can't do it!" Unlike the condemned hero of *The Last Mile* (1932), q.v., there is no reprieve for John Wallace, proving once again that money cannot buy everything.

Mordaunt Hall *(New York Times)* applauded *If I Had a Million* as "an unusually good entertainment worked out with true imagination and originality...." However, there was one segment it found wanting. "The dramatic episode of a murderer about to be electrocuted is not so interesting, nor is it worked out with the subtlety of expression with which the other sequences are endowed." *Variety* judged, "[T]he diversity of the topics makes for the best box office appeal the picture possesses."

When *If I Had a Million* was initially released in England, two episodes were deleted by the censors as unsuitable: the prostitute's and the condemned man's, the latter directed by H. Bruce Humberstone. Viewing the restored feature in 1978, John Pym (British *Monthly Film Bulletin*) judged, "Least satisfactory in this respect [i.e., actor's performance] is Gene Raymond, as the condemned man attended in his last moments by his wife, Frances Dee, and facing the electric chair with frustrated hysteria. (His 'realistic' demeanour—clearly box-office anathema— can be compared, incidentally, to that of other Hollywood killers of the decade who faced the same fate with what now seems such chilling equanimity.)"

The gimmick of giving away $1,000,000 checks to unsuspecting recipients would be utilized for the teleseries "The Millionaire" (CBS–TV, 1955–60).

128. *In Cold Blood* (Columbia, 1967), 134 min.

Producer/director, Richard Brooks; based on the book by Truman Capote; screenplay, Brooks; art director, Robert Boyle; set decorator, Jack Ahern; costumes, Jack Martell; makeup, Gary Morris; music, Quincy Jones; orchestrators, Leo Shuken, Jack Haynes; assistant directors, Tom Shaw, Carl Beringer, John Anderson, Jr.; sound, William Randall, Jr., Dick Tyler, A. Plantadosi; sound effects, John Newman, Joe Henrie; special effects, Geza Gaspar; camera, Conrad Hall; editor, Peter Zinner.

Robert Blake (Perry Edward Smith); Scott Wilson (Dick Eugene Hickock); John Forsythe (Alvin Dewey); Paul Stewart (Reporter); Gerald S. O'Loughlin (Harold Nye); Jeff Corey (Hickock's Father); John Gallaudet (Roy Church); James Flavin (Clarence Duntz); Charles McGraw (Tex Smith); Jim Lantz (Officer Rohleder); Will Geer (Prosecuting Attorney); John McLiam (Herbert Clutter); Ruth Storey (Bonnie Clutter); Brenda C. Currin (Nancy Clutter); Paul Hough (Kenyon Clutter); Vaughn Taylor ("Good Samaritan"); Duke Hobbie (Young Reporter); Sheldon Allman (Reverend Post); Sammy Thurman (Mr. Smith); Sadie Truitt (Herself); Myrtle Clare (Herself); Teddy Eccles (Young Hitchhiker); Raymond Hatton (Elderly Hitchhiker); Mary-Linda Rapelye (Susan Kidwell); Ronda Fultz (Nancy's Friend); Al Christy (Sheriff); Don Sollars (Store Salesman); Harriet Levitt (Mrs. Hartman); Stan Levitt (Insurance Man).

Truman Capote's "non-fiction novel," *In Cold Blood* (1966), is an absorbing case study of two killers on death row. The sensational murder of the Clutter family by Perry Smith and Dick Hickock in 1959 had received nationwide publicity.

Capote's best-selling account of these two enigmatic individuals, and the factors that transformed them into murderers, was no less sensational for its romanticizing and subjective approach to factual data. (A side issue of the book was a debate on capital punishment.) A year after the controversial book appeared, director Richard Brook (who also produced and wrote the screenplay) brought this grisly project to the screen. As Douglas Brode (*The Films of the Sixties,* 1980) explained, "*In Cold Blood* was one of the last significant pictures to be filmed in black and white, in order that it might convey the quality of a 1950s documentary.... Straightforward and simple in terms of its visual imagery, it did nonetheless feature a complex storytelling technique — with numerous flashbacks and disorienting jumps in time — in order to restructure events it depicted...."

On November 15, 1959, Perry Smith (Robert Blake) and Dick Hickock (Scott Wilson), both ex-convicts, murdered four members of the Herbert Clutter family (John McLiam, Ruth Storey, Brenda C. Currin, Paul Hough) at their home in Holcomb, Kansas, a farming community four hundred miles west of Kansas City. The killers had the misguided notion that Clutter had $10,000 stashed in a safe in his house; Clutter did not, and the killers found only $43.00. The police, led by the relentless Alvin Dewey (John Forsythe) of the Kansas Bureau of Investigation, are determined to solve the heinous crime. Meanwhile, the two small-minded fugitives head to Mexico where Perry has fantasies of becoming a gold prospector. They later return to the States at Dick's insistence. Thinking they have not left a trail of clues, they continue to cash bad checks. They have no idea that Hickock's prison chum has already informed on them. With the police closing in, the killers are captured in Las Vegas. During interrogation, in which they are separated and pitted against one another, their alibis are broken. Brought to trial and convicted, they are sentenced to be hanged at the Kansas State Penitentiary in Lansing. Despite appeals and several stays of execution, they died on the gallows on April 14, 1965.

The final twenty-three minutes of *In Cold Blood* deals with the trial, appeal and eventual execution of these two notorious, arrogant killers.. They are housed in the penitentiary's security-and-isolation building, on the second floor of which is death row. The cold-blooded killers, who each insist that a lack of a real childhood or home contributed to his waywardness, remain complex to the end. Perry recalls of his victims, "I thought Mr. Clutter was a real nice gentleman. I thought so right up to the time I cut his throat." To wile away the hours, Smith begins sketching in his cell. The more practical Dick debates the actual death process with another death row inmate:

DICK: Does it say in the books what happens when you make the big drop?

CONVICT: It says your neck breaks and you crap in your pants.

As the inevitable, bleak end draws near, there is a voice-over narration by a sanctimonious reporter (Paul Stewart):

Death row has its own routine. Shower, one man at a time, once a week. Shave, twice a week. No radio, no movies, no TV, no cards.... No mirrors, no bottles, no glasses.... No suicide allowed. They could eat, sleep, write, read, dream. They could pray, but mostly they just wait.

Hickock is taken to the prison warehouse, where the gallows have been erected. His final words are "You're sending me to a better world than this ever was." Perry Smith's prime concern, as he prepares to die, is that he will mess himself. Always the daydreamer, the former guitar strummer reflects, "You know there was a time once when we almost had it made." As the gum-chewing Perry is led up the steps to the gallows he pauses to say, "I think maybe I'd like to apologize, but who to?"

Filmmaker Brooks provides a very surprising, graphic finale to this stark production. In the (flashback) scenes depicting the Clutters's messy deaths, Brooks carefully avoids showing any gory sights. This tricks the viewer into believing that the same will hold true of the prison executions. However, the final moments of Perry Smith's life are revealed vividly, with the sounds of his heart beating (and stopping) heard on the soundtrack as he falls through the gallows' trap door.

Bosley Crowther *(New York Times)* rated *In Cold Blood* an "excellent quasidocumentary, which sends shivers down the spine." Crowther observed, "[T]he excitement generated in the viewers is not over who committed the murders, but why.... The final scene of the hanging, which is realistically done, is like some medieval rite of retribution. It leaves one helplessly, hopelessly chilled." *Variety* lauded, "Film has the look and sound of reality, in part from use of actual locales in six states and non-pros as atmosphere players.... [By] Shrewd story-telling and unplaying of climactic events, [Richard Brooks] appeals to the viewer's intellect as well as his senses, never to excess."

In Cold Blood received four Academy Award nominations: Best Direction, Screenplay, Cinematography and Score. Made at a cost of $2,300,000, *In Cold Blood* earned $6,000,000 in domestic film rentals paid to the distributor.

129. *In the Custody of Strangers* (ABC–TV, May 26, 1982), color, 100 min.

Producer, Frank Von Zerneck; associate producer, William Beaudine, Jr.; director, Robert Greenwald; teleplay, Jennifer Miller; production designer, Norm Baron; music, Matthew McCauley; sound, Barry Thomas; camera, Isidore Mankofsky; editor, Robert Florio.

Martin Sheen (Frank Caldwell); Jane Alexander (Sandy Caldwell); Emilio Estevez (Danny Caldwell); Kenneth McMillan (Al Caruso); Ed Lauter (Judge Halloran); Matt Clark (Mike Raines); John Hancock (Judge Bennett); Virginia Kiser (Dr. Foreman); Jon Van Ness (Corky); Judyann Elder (Marni Blake); Deborah Foreman (Karen); Susan Peretz (Big Faye); Peter Jurasik (Barnes); Pat McNamara (Quinn); Henry Tomaszewski (Roach); Ramon Estevez (Pick); Ross Harris (Rusty); J. P. Bumstead (Doctor); W. T. Zacha (Foreman); David Moses (Cop); Bill Smillie (Sergeant); Liz Sheridan (Caseworker); Art LaFleur (Clifford); David Faustino (David); Sonny Davis (Store Clerk); Anthony Davis, Cheryl Francis, Sharon Barr (Inmates).

A grippingly real study of the painful repercussions a teenager can undergo when placed in jail with hardened convicts. "Powerful indictment of judicial and economic systems in the U.S. should bring shudders as a young man goes to prison for 40 days' hell.... [D]elivers a powerful wallop" *(Daily Variety)*.

When his vehicle hits a policeman's car, restive teenager Danny Caldwell (Emilio Estevez), with no driver's license on him, is arrested for drunk driving. Rather than bail him out, the boy's out-of-work father (Martin Sheen) tells the police to keep him in jail overnight. The blue collar worker thinks this will snap his son back into line. The police lock Danny in the tank with several hardened criminals and, during the night, the hot-tempered youth must defend himself from his vicious cellmates. One of the men attempts to sexually molest him. He fights back. As a result, he is charged with assault and it takes forty days for his distraught father and frightened mother (Jane Alexander) to get their traumatized son freed. During one point he is segregated in an isolation cell and the youth becomes catatonic for a spell. Thankfully an observant senior police officer (Kenneth McMillan) steps into the breach created by the arguing lawyers and social workers. Danny is released. However, when his father gets a new job and the family moves to a new town and home, it is clear that his recent experience has left Danny alienated and scarred.

Daily Variety praised Estevez's pivotal acting. [He] conveys the lostness, the awareness of the defeat of Danny in a performance of depth and intelligence." Others in the cast included Kenneth McMillan as the chief jailer, John Van Ness as a probation officer and Deborah Foreman as the youth's girlfriend. Some of this made-for-television feature was shot at the San Pedro (California) city jail. This was the first of several occasions in which Estevez and his real-life father would act together oncamera.

130. *Inmates: A Love Story* (ABC–TV, Feb. 13, 1981), color, 100 min.

Executive producers, James S. Henerson, James G. Hirsch; producer, Bill Finnegan; associate producer, E. Darrell Hallenbeck; director, Guy Green; story, Delia Jordan; teleplay, Hirsch, Jordan; art director, Joe Aubel; music, Dana Kaproff; assistant directors, Nick Marck, Michael Green, Mary Ellen Canniff; sound, Pat Mitchell; camera, Al Francis; editor, Paul LaMastra.

Kate Jackson (Jane Mount); Perry King (Roy Matson); Pamela Reed (Sunny); Paul Koslo (Harold Virgil); Fay Hauser (Grace); Penelope Allen (Gloria); Craig T. Nelson (Daniels); Tony King (John); Paul Lieber (Thomas P. Eliot); Judith Chapman (Leslie Matson); Shirley Jones (Superintendent E. F. Crown); Tony Curtis (Flanagan); Maxayn Lewis (Shawna); Virginia Capers (Agnes); Ted Noose (Lieutenant Hodges); Arva Holt (Marty); Norma Donaldson (Lila); Peggy Walton-Walker (Clair); Duke Stroud (Sheriff); Rita Taggart (Salt); Cynthia Avila (Pepper); Randal Johnson (Tony); Ron Spivey (Mac); Janet Lee Parker (Bennett); S. John Launer (Chairman).

There was so much potential in the "high" concept of this unusual prison story, set in a co-ed facility, that it is maddening how inane and unbelievable the results were. The two capable, attractive lead performers (Kate Jackson and Perry King) are obviously ill-at-ease with the trite dialogue and hack direction, while guest stars Shirley Jones (as a corrupt administrator) and Tony Curtis (as an aging, flamboyant con artist convict) overact embarrassingly. *Daily Variety* dismissed the sloppy project as "a rambling, trite collection of characters trying to be outrageous in a co-ed prison."

Affluent white collar executive Roy Matson (Perry King), an accountant, is pressured by the corporate hierarchy at a major insurance firm to assume the full burden of guilt for financial misconduct regarding company funds. He is sentenced to a term at Greenleaf. As he is inducted into the sprawling, grassy-lawned prison, he is advised:

> You are now entering the Greenleaf State Co-Correctional Institution. Participation in this rehabilitation program of men and women together is a privilege. Failure to follow the rules of the facility will lead to disciplinary action.

You may fraternize with members of your own or the opposite sex, but overt, clandestine sexual acts are illegal. A sexual act is defined as anything beyond hand holding or a closed-mouthed kiss. This will lead to disciplinary action.

The well-bred, but officious Superintendent E. F. Crown (Shirley Jones) quickly warns Roy and another new inmate, Harold Virgil (Paul Koslo):

You'll do your time with them [the women]: work time, meal time, rec[reational] time. But I want to make one thing clear. Any man who molests a woman in any way, shape or form, will be shipped instantly to Briarton [Penitentiary]. No hearings, no nothing. That's the way it is!

At first, the arrogant, elitist Roy is convinced that his stay at Greenleaf will be exceedingly short; he mistakenly believes that his company's attorney (Craig T. Nelson) will arrange his release. He also thinks "doing time" at this experimental, minimum security institution will be a breeze. However, his theories prove to be misconceptions. Adding to his woes, he is assaulted and beaten in the shower by a gang of unruly convicts, including John (Tony King) and the sinister Virgil. A wise old-timer, Flanagan (Tony Curtis) comes to Roy's rescue, as does Flanagan's inmate friend, Jane Mount (Kate Jackson).

Time passes and the angry Matson realizes he is stuck in this prison and better make the best of it. With his own marriage failing, he turns for sympathy and romance to Jane, but this young but veteran cat burglar has a chip on her shoulder. Men have always gotten her into trouble (including the one who fathered her nine-year-old daughter who is living with a foster family) and Jane intends to finish her sentence on her own. Meanwhile, two lesbians (Rita Taggart, Cynthia Avila) ask Roy to father a child by one of them; he refuses, which only wins him more enemies among the general population.

Roy is jolted out of his work routine in the kitchen when Crown demands that he study the prison's accounting books and repair any irregularities in the ledgers. The alternative, if he refuses, is to have his approaching parole denied. He reluctantly agrees, meanwhile pursuing his interest in the embittered Jane (a pessimistic gal who insists "There is no happily ever after.") During his stay at this supposedly liberal facility, Roy observes all types of corruptions: the brutal Lieutenant Hodges (Ted Noose) consorts with the female inmates and allows marijuana to be grown in the greenhouse (which he later sells); the tougher convicts prey on the weaker ones, while the keepers turn the other way; and manipulative Superintendent Crown encourages all sorts of staff abuses of the system in order to keep the facility operating. Later, Roy is paroled when he threatens to expose Crown if she prevents his official release from Greenleaf. However, she has Hodges stir up a female inmate who attempts to knife Matson. Jane saves Roy's life, but for fighting with another convict, she is placed in solitary confinement. When she is released from isolation, she learns that Crown has been dismissed and Thomas P. Eliot (Paul Lieber) is now in charge, intending to make Greenleaf a forward-looking, honest penitentiary. Roy, true to his promise, returns to see Jane. He brings her daughter to the visit.

Apparently, the failure of this shallow telefeature has temporarily dissuaded other filmmakers from tackling the potentially intriguing topic of co-ed prisons.

131. *An Innocent Man* (Buena Vista, 1989), color, 113 min.

Executive producer, Scott Kroopf; producer, Ted Field; co-producer, Neil Machlis; associate producer, Larry Brothers; director, Peter Yates; screenplay, Brothers; production designer, Stuart Wurtzel; art director, Frank Richwood; set decorator, Chris A. Butler; costumes, Rita Ryack; music, Howard Shore; assistant directors, Paul Deason, Kelly Wimberly; sound, Dan Sable; camera, William A. Fraker; editors,

Stephen A. Rotter, William S. Schart.

Tom Selleck (Jimmie Rainwood); F. Murray Abraham (Virgil Cane); Laila Robins (Kate Rainwood); David Rache (Mike Parnell); Richard Young (Danny Scalise); Badja Djola (John Fitzgerald); Todd Graff (Robby); M. C. Gainey (Malcolm); Peter Van Norden (Peter Feldman); Bruce A. Young (Jingles).

> Even Tom Selleck's residual appeal from his baby sitting days [i.e. *Three Men and a Baby*, 1988] will be hard-pressed to overcome this collection of clichés, which accomplishes the almost unthinkable by bringing the prison genre to a new low. Theatrical sentence should quickly be commuted to life in homevideo.
>
> *(Variety)*

By error, two crazy narcotic policemen, Mike Parnell (David Rasche) and Danny Scalise (Richard Young) violently break into the house owned by southern California airline mechanic Jimmie Rainwood (Tom Selleck) and his wife, Kate (Laila Robins). Jimmie, brandishing a hair dryer, is shot by the two smirking policemen. After discovering their major blunder, the hopped-up law enforcers quickly decide to plant a gun and drugs on the unconscious Rainwood, who is soon railroaded into Oroville Prison for six years.

While the off-the-wall Scalise and Parnell are threatening Kate on the outside, the embittered Jimmie is attempting to cope with his hellhole life inside the walls. He is raped by a gang of black convicts. Traumatized, he seeks counsel from a rugged, rough old inmate, Virgil Cane (F. Murray Abraham), who is serving a life sentence. Jimmie revenges his masculinity by killing the ringleader, Jingles (Bruce A. Young) in the bathroom, using a cell-honed shiv. Later, after three years in prison, Rainwood, now accepted as a man among (prison) men, gets out of the penitentiary and returns to his loyal, patient wife. He brutally seeks retribution against the two bad cops, which he accomplishes by setting them up against the Mafia.

The critics rushed to pan this mediocre feature film directed by Peter Yates, best known for action movies like *Bullitt* (1968). *Variety* criticized, "The prison scenes have some initial bite but soon squander any sense of reality or tension through sheer excess, paling next to memorable productions such as TV's *The Glass House....*" Duayne Byrge (*Hollywood Reporter*) found it, "A prototypical clone of just about every prison movie.... It's just plain colorless, with about as much personality as a kitchen applicance.... One needn't have dozed off at more than a half-dozen late-night prison movies to know what will happen next, and next, and next." Michael Wilmington *(Los Angeles Times)* argued of the badly-conceived hero, "Rainwood is a standard big-movie-star part, drained of moral flaws, a generic innocent man. Selleck plays him without agony, without reflection, with the stoicism of a born camera subject. He learns the moves of murder and jail-yard *machismo* as if it were another basketball game."

The ad lines for *An Innocent Man* insisted: "Falsely accused. Unjustly convicted. Struggling to survive on the inside. Determined to find justice on the outside." Made on an estimated negative cost of $17,000,000 (plus another estimated

$9,000,000 for promotion and advertising), *An Innocent Man* only earned $8,972,000 in domestic film rentals paid to the distributor. Like Sylvester Stallone's equally unsatisfying (and even more preposterous *Lock Up* (1989), q.v., *An Innocent Man* had learned nothing from the decades of previous prison films about what qualities make a drama credible, entertaining and sometimes edifying. It was another box-office failure for Tom Selleck, the ex-star of the detective teleseries "Magnum, P.I." (1980–88).

132. *Inside the Walls of Folsom Prison* (Warner Bros., 1951), 87 min.

Producer, Bryan Foy; director, Crane Wilbur; based on the story "Folsom Story" by Wilbur; screenplay, Wilbur; art director, Douglas Bacon; music, William Lava; camera, Edwin DuPar; editor, Owen Marks.

Steve Cochran (Chuck Daniels); David Brian (Mark Benson); Philip Carey (Red Pardue); Ted de Corsia (Warden Rickey); Scott Forbes (Frazier); Lawrence Tolan (Leo Daly); Dick Wesson (Tinker); Paul Picerni (Jeff Riordan); William Campbell (Farretti); Prisoner #07321 (Murder); Prisoner #04327 (Forgery); Prisoner #06752 (Kidnapper); Prisoner #08438 (Arson); Ed Norris (Sergeant Hart); Dorothy Hart (Pardue's Wife); and: Matt Willis.

> For all its clichés, this production . . . is vigorous, fast moving, frequently exciting entertainment . . . written with an eye for grandiose dramatic impact in its device of having the prison itself serve as the narrator. . . . The scenes of brutality have force, and the onlooker breathes a sigh of relief when the old order passes and a new, more hopeful regime is achieved.
>
> *(Hollywood Reporter)*

In a flashback, crusading new warden (David Brian) recalls a time thirty years ago when sadistic Warden Rickey (Ted de Corsia) ruled California's Folsom Prison with an iron hand. Under Rickey's regime, for each and every infraction of the rules, the convicts are dealt severe punishments usually meted out by tough Sergeant Hart (Ed Norris). Because of the horrendous conditions (brutality, terrible food, bad sanitation), a prison break is attempted, but it fails as well as leading to the death of three guards and two convicts. The ringleaders are placed in solitary confinement and all privileges are cancelled. When Mark Benson (David Brian) is assigned to the penitentiary as captain of the guards, he requests permission from the warden to initiate positive changes feeling that brains and understanding are more useful tools than brawn in handling prisoners. Rickey agrees, reasoning that Benson will soon discredit himself with his "soft" humane methods.

Meanwhile, soured convict Chuck Daniels (Steve Cochran), employed in the prison quarry, steals several sticks of dynamite, intending to use them as part of his long-planned prison break. Another convict, Red Pardue (Philip Carey), due soon for parole, is sent to town in a prison truck for supplies. He discovers a fellow convict hidden under the seat. Rather than jeopardize his parole, he tips off the guards. Fearing reprisals, Benson suggests the warden isolate Pardue from the other convicts. Rickey refuses and, as a result, Red is killed "accidentally" the day before his release. This leads to a confrontation between the warden and his chief keeper, with Rickey revoking all of Benson's reforms and firing Mark. Later, Daniels executes his escape plan and holds a guard as hostage. The gutsy Rickey enters the cellblock disguised as a convict and opens fire on the prisoners. He, in turn, is shot by Daniels. The compassionate Benson assumes charge, negotiating

Bud Wolfe, Steve Cochran, Richard Benedict and Philip Carey in *Inside the Walls of Folsom Prison* (1951).

a truce between the non-escaping convicts and the guards. As for the fugitive prisoners who appreciate the futility of their situation, they detonate a dynamite blast which kills them all. A new regime emerges at Folsom Prison, strict but humane.

A. H. Weiler *(New York Times)* reported of this vigorous action yarn, "Warner Brothers, those inveterate cinema penologists, are 'in stir' again, and the old place, which never was grimmer, is still the same." As for the originality of the piece, Weiler weighed, "all he [producer Bryan Foy] captures is another prison picture indistinguishable from those uninspired melodramas that have come regularly from the West.... [M]ost of the footage is standard and unimaginative and, the performances are never above standard." *Variety* approved of the "excitement and pace" and found the actioner "comes over smartly because of the lensing on the actual locale of the story." D. Smith *(Los Angeles Daily News)* decided, "Nobody out there at Burbank has forgotten a thing about how they made the predecessors to this one. All the tricks are here."

As Hollywood had done so many times before, in the name of presenting a case history (Folsom Prison) and advocating prison reform, *Inside the Walls of Folsom Prison* smugly trotted forth the full spectrum of prison abuses for the voyeuristic delight of moviegoers.

133. *Island of Doomed Men* (Columbia, 1940), 67 min.

Producer, Wallace MacDonald; director, Charles Barton; screenplay, Robert D. Andrews; art director, Lionel Banks; costumes, Robert Kalloch; music director, Morris W. Stoloff; assistant director, Thomas Flood; camera, Benjamin Kline; editor, James Sweeney.

Peter Lorre (Stephen Danel); Rochelle Hudson (Lorraine Danel); Robert Wilcox (Mark Sheldon); Don Beddoe (Brand); George E. Stone (Siggy); Kenneth McDonald (Doctor); Charles Middleton (Captain Cort); Stanley Brown (Eddie); Earl Gunn (Mitchell); Don Douglas (Official); Bruce Bennett (Hazen, a Guard); Sam Ash (Ames); Eddie Laughton (Borgo); John Tyrrell (Durkin); Richard Fiske (Hale); Al Hill (Clinton); Trevor Bardette (District Attorney); Howard Hickman (Judge); Addison Richards (Jackson); Ray Bailey (Mystery Man); Lee Prather (Warden); Forbes Murray (Parole Board Chairman); George McKay (Bookkeeper); Bernie Breakston (Townsend); Walter Miller (Detective); Harry Strang, Charles Hamilton (Cops).

Columbia Pictures had a penchant for churning out low-budget, exploitive potboilers about the horrors of Devil's Island (e.g. *Escape from Devil's Island*, 1935, *I Was a Prisoner on Devil's Island*, 1941, qq.v.). To mine additional box-office gold from the same theme, producer Wallace MacDonald packaged this quasi–Devil's Island tale starring the talented, quirky Peter Lorre. As Stephen D. Youngkin, James Bigwood and Raymond Cabana Jr. point out in *The Films of Peter Lorre* (1982), "*Island of Doomed Men* contains the stereotypes and clichés indigenous to penal-colony motion pictures. The characters and situations are invariably the same and depend on the directing and acting for any semblance of originality."

Mark Sheldon (Robert Wilcox), a U.S. Secret Service member, innocently involved in the death of a man (Addison Richards), is tried and convicted. He is sentenced to twenty years in prison. Meanwhile, Stephen Danel (Peter Lorre), a sinister brute who owns a Pacific island (Dead Man's Isle) where paroled men are used as expendable slave labor for his diamond mine, hires a new shipment of ex-prisoners, including Sheldon. Because Sheldon had been involved in investigating Danel's activities and may know too much, he is immediately in disfavor with the tyrant. Danel attempts to torture information from Mark, but he refuses to talk. Danel's wife, Lorraine (Rochelle Hudson), herself a captive on the island, is sympathetic to Mark and attempts to help him. However, Danel puts a stop to this. Mark stirs the oppressed prisoners and disgruntled guards — including chief keeper Captain Cord (Charles Middleton) — into revolting. Just as the suspicious Danel is about to kill Sheldon, Siggy (George E. Stone), Danel's house servant, stabs his master. He had wanted revenge for Danel having killed his pet monkey. Having gathered the needed information, Sheldon flies to Washington, accompanied by Lorraine.

Theodore Strauss *(New York Times)* judged, "Always the gentle fiend, Peter Lorre again is offering a study in sadism in his latest film . . . under the likely title of *Island of Doomed Men*. For psychopathic malevolence is his forte and within the routine dimensions of the script, Mr. Lorre et al. provide enough vicarious excitement to satisfy the most bloodthirsty of . . . patrons." *Variety* criticized Charles Barton's direction "which fails to charge up the tempo in order to catch up the loose ends of the story." *Harrison's Reports* insisted, "Its appeal will be directed mostly to men, for it is doubtful whether women will enjoy the cruelty, beatings, and misery suffered by the men on an island dominated by the villain."

The ad lines for *Island of Doomed Men* read: "Women shuddering at his cruel caress! . . . Men dying under his torturing lash!"

134. *Isle of Missing Men* (Monogram, 1942), 67 min.

Producer, Richard Oswald; associate producer, Louis Berkof; director, Richard Oswald; based on the story "White Lady" by Gina Kaus, Ladislas Fodor; screenplay, Gerd Oswald, Robert Chapin; art director, Frank Paul Sylos; music director, Edward Kay; assistant director, Gerd Oswald; dialogue director, Don Brodie; camera, Paul Ivano; editor, Jack Dennis.

John Howard (Governor Merrill Hammond); Helen Gilbert (Diana Bryce);

Gilbert Roland (Dan Curtis); Alan Mowbray (Doc Brown); Bradley Page (Lieutenant Governor George Kent); Ernie Adams (Captain Sanchez); George Chandler (Steward); Geraldine Gray (Sally); Egon Brecher (Richard Heller); Kitty O'Neil (Nurse Pauline); Kenne Duncan (Bob Henderson); Charles Williams (Jo-Jo); Alex Havier (Native); Dewey Robinson (Burly).

> An indifferent program melodrama, with a poorly constructed plot; it is never convincing. The action is slow and long drawn out. In addition, the direction is poor and so is the acting, except for Alan Mowbray's performance as a drunken doctor. . . .
>
> *(Harrison's Reports)*

Aboard the *S.S. Bombay,* Diana Bryce (Helen Gilbert) is introduced to Merrill Hammond (John Howard), the governor of the penal island of Caruba. He invites her to the isle where she meets the compound's drunken physician, Doc Brown (Alan Mowbray) and George Kent (Bradley Page), the Lieutenant Governor. One of the prisoners, Dan Curtis (Gilbert Roland), who is actually Diane's husband, is planning an escape, against his wife's best advise. When Dan is caught in the midst of his planning, Diana convinces Dr. Brown to assist her husband's cause. Pretending that the man is dying of typhus, the physician arranges for Curtis to escape during his burial. The plan is discovered by Kent, but Merrill refuses to pursue the fleeing inmate, wanting Dan and his wife—whom Merrill now loves—to have a fresh start. He resigns his post. Meanwhile, Diana refuses to join Dan on the awaiting freighter. He goes on alone, has a dispute with the captain (Ernie Adams) and is killed. She returns to Merrill and admits her love for him.

In *B Movies* (1973), Don Miller evaluated, "One of the stronger cast in Monogram films was gathered for *Isle of Missing Men* . . . an American effort by the respected pioneer German, Richard Oswald. The plot of passion and sacrifice in a tropic penal colony sufficed, and for Monogram was above the usual run. But the players made it seem better than it was, with . . . [the cast] giving the stale tale a touch of dignity."

135. *Jackson County Jail* (New World, 1976), color, 89 min.

Executive producer, Roger Corman; producer, Jeff Begun; associate producer, Paul Gonsky; director, Michael Miller; screenplay, Donald Stewart; art director, Michael McCloskey; costumes, Cornelia McNamara; music, Loren Newkirk; second unit director, Jan Kiesser; assistant directors, Richard Schor, Gary Dorf; stunt coordinator, James Arnett; sound, Bill Kaplan; sound re-recording, Ryder Sound; camera, Bruce Logan; second unit camera, Kiesser; editor, Caroline Ferriol.

Yvette Mimieux (Dinah Hunter); Tommy

Lee Jones (Coley Blake); Robert Carradine (Bobby Ray); Frederic Cook (Deputy Hobie); Severn Darden (Sheriff Dempsey); Howard Hesseman (David); John Lawlor (Deputy Burt); Britt Leach (Dan Oldum, the Bartender); Nan Martin (Allison); Nancy Noble (Lola); Lisa Copeland (Girl in Commercial); Clifford Emmich (Mr. Bigelow); Michael Ashe (Mr. Cooper); Edward Marshall (Mr. Blight); Marcie Drake (Candy, David's Girlfriend); Betty Thomas (Waitress); Ken Lawrence (Paulie); Arthur Wong (Cook); Marci Barkin (Girl in Restaurant);

Yvette Mimieux in *Jackson County Jail* (1976).

Michael Hilkene (Vincent Lepardo); Roy David Hagle (Ambulance Driver); William Molloy (Deputy Lyle Peters); Ira Miller (Drunk Man); Jackie Robin (Drunk Woman); Gus Peters (Melon Man Shaw); Patrice Rohmer (Cassie Anne); Amparo Mimieux (Poquita); Mary Woronov (Pearl); Richard Lockmiller (Officer Jessie); Jack O'Leary (Officer Blake); Duffy Hambleton (Sam Hayes); Mark Carllton, Don Hinz, James Arnett (Highway Patrolmen); Norma Moye (Mayor of Fallsburg); Hal Needham (Chief of Fallsburg Police).

Jackson County Jail smartly exploited one of contemporary society's more prevalent paranoias: that the biggest obstacle to surviving life in prison is *not* an inmate's hardened peers, but the brutalizing keepers. This glib actioner was promoted with the catch phrases: "What they do to her in the Jackson County jail is a crime! The cops are there to protect her. But who will protect her from the cops?"

Successful executive Dinah Hunter (Yvette Mimieux) is disgusted with the crass working environment at her Los Angeles advertising agency. Making matters worse, she has a spat with her boyfriend (Howard Hesseman). She decides to relocate to New York to accept a new position. Driving across country, she gives a ride to two unsavory hitchhikers, Bobby Ray (Robert Carradine) and the pregnant

Cassie Anne (Patrice Rohmer). This drug-addicted duo soon commandeer the car at gunpoint and knock her out. They steal the vehicle and her identification. Dinah awakens by a roadside somewhere in southern Arizona and walks into town. There she encounters law enforcers who are suspicious of her dazed account of a car theft. They take her into custody, insisting she will have no problem "if you are who you say you are." The other prisoner in Sheriff Dempsey's (Severn Darden) jail is Coley Blake (Tommy Lee Jones), a truck hijacker who is awaiting extradiction to Texas on a murder charge.

That night, the bullying deputy jailer Hobie (Frederic Cook) rapes Dinah and she, in turn, hysterically assaults the lawman with a nearby wooden stool. He dies. The rowdy but sympathetic Coley assists her in fleeing, convincing Dinah that no one will believe her story if she remains. Dempsey pursues, but dies in a highway accident. Dinah and Coley continue onward, with the law always one step behind. They spend the night at an abandoned farmhouse where the disillusioned Coley ("the whole country is a rip-off. . . . I was born dead anyway") works at persuading her to "drop out" and go underground. The next day, in the town of Fallsburg, Dinah is injured and captured in an ambush, while reckless Coley is shot dead after smashing into a local bicentennial parade. Dinah's uncertain future looks bleak.

Vincent Canby *(New York Times)* endorsed this production as "film making of relentless energy and harrowing excitement that recalls the agit-prop melodramas of the 30's. It's not exactly in a class with [Fritz] Lang's *You Only Live Once* [1937, q.v.], but it possesses the kind of fury that can breathe life into a melodrama even when the point of view is simple-minded. . . . The film manages to stay clear of sentimentality of the conventional sort. . . . Miss Mimieux is excellent in a role that subjects her to as many bruises, humiliations and indignities as she might get in the boxing ring." Richard Combs (British *Monthly Film Bulletin*) applauded director Michael Miller because he "etches the pain of his characters much deeper than the cursory script manages to suggest." However, Combs warned, "Miller still settles for a structure so monotonously signposted that it provides anticipatory glimpses of every event about to befall our heroine — in a manner more than fleetingly reminiscent of *The Perils of Pauline.*" *Variety* thought the picture "annonyingly superficial" and that it "succeeds in futhering the kind of redneck paranoia and shotgun-pickup truck madness firmly espoused in the B-pic tradition. . . ." In retrospect, Bruce Crowther (*Captured on Film: The Prison Movie,* 1989) championed, "Very well made and acted, *Jackson County Jail* is a film which deserves attention; even its explicit rape scene has the notable, and unusual, merit of being depicted from the viewpoint of the victim."

New World Pictures was so enamored with this popular box-office entry (which has gained minor cult status over the years for its feminist point of view) that two years later, it remade the property as the telefeature *Outside Chance,* q.v. Yvette Mimieux and several others of the cast, including Severn Darden and Frederic Cook, repeated their original assignments to far less advantage.

136. *Jacktown* (Pictorial International, 1962), 62 min.

Producer/director/screenplay, William Martin; art director, Jerry Kay; music/music director, Aldo Provenzano; sound, John Feddermack; camera, Arthur J. Ornitz; editor, Ralph Rosenblum.

Patty McCormack (Warden's Daughter); Richard Meade (Thief); Douglas Rutherford (Warden); and: Johanna Douglas, John Anthony, Alice Gordon, Gordon Grant, Harry Newman, Russ Paquette, George F. Taylor, Mike Tancredi.

This seldom seen, economically-made prison (melo)drama starred Patty Mc-Cormack, the child star of *The Bad Seed* (1956).

A young thief (Richard Meade), a juvenile delinquent, is accused of statutory rape. He is sentenced to two-and-one-half to five years at Southern Michigan Prison. There the rebellious youth comes under the sympathetic guidance of the warden (Douglas Rutherford) who permits him to tend his gardens. When the administrator observes his daughter (Patty McCormack) falling in love with the teenager, he transfers the convict to chauffeuring duties outside the penitentiary. Subsequently, there is a prison riot. Later, the young inmate finds himself in a position to escape and he does. However, he is drawn back to the warden's daughter who convinces him to return to prison. She promises to wait for him.

This film was shot on location at Southern Michigan Prison in Jackson ("Jacktown"), Michigan. It also incorporated newsreel footage of the riots (in 1952) at the penitentiary.

137. *Jacobo Timerman: Prisoner Without a Name, Cell Without a Number* (NBC–TV, May 22, 1983), color, 100 min.

Executive producers, Terry Ellis, Richard Dorso; producer, Linda Yellen; associate producer, Jonathan Platnick; director, Yellen; based on the book by Jacobo Timerman; story adaptation, Oliver P. Drexell, Jr., Stan Silverman; teleplay, Yellen, Platnick, Drexell; art director, Ben Edwards; music, Brad Fiedel; sound, Kim Ornitz; camera, Arthur J. Ornitz; editor, Jay Freund.

Roy Scheider (Jacobo Timerman); Liv Ullmann (Risha Timerman); Terance O'Quinn (Colonel Thomas Rhodes); Sam Robards (Daniel Timerman); Zach Galligan (Hector Timerman); Trini Alvarado (Lisa Castello); Paul Collins (General); Kaiulani Lee (Patricia Derian); Christopher Murney (Colonel Rossi); Michael Pearlman (Javier Timerman); David Cryer (Ernesto Keaton); Castulo Guerra (Enrique Vega); Lee Wilkof (Edgardo Sajon); Marcia Jean Kurtz (Dona Maria); Camille Saviola (Estela Rossi); and: Roy Brocksmith, Frances Conroy, Joe Costa, Richard Cottrell, Charles Felder, Ken Gray, Barbara Hanna, Ed Herlihy, Bryce Holman, Leslie Lyles, Michael Medeiros, Joanna Merlin, Natalija Nogulich, David Orange, Carl Pistilli, Richard Russell Ramos, Leland Schwantes, Roco Sisto, Robert Stattel, Art Vasil, J. T. Walsh, Stephen Zettler.

No matter what the crime, being imprisoned is a ghastly experience, and only more so when the victim is an innocent political victim of a tyrannical police regime.

In Argentina, Jewish newspaper publisher Jacobo Timerman (Roy Scheider) becomes incensed by the mistreatment of his son's (Sam Robards) girlfriend (Trini Alvarado). When he attempts to intervene, he unleases a nightmare which finds him branded an enemy of the totalitarian government. Over a period of several years he is threatened, tortured, and placed under house arrest. Eventually, the Timermans, including his wife Rish (Liv Ullmann), escape to the United States.

Daily Variety branded the production "lumbering" and complained, "Teleplay drags awkwardly through party scenes with stilted dialog making a stab at colloquial translations from Buenos Aires patois, and changes tone for Timerman's incarceration to become impassioned."

Much of the location work for this project was accomplished in New York and New Jersey which substituted for Buenos Aires. Many felt the casting of American Roy Scheider and Swedish Liv Ullmann militated against the success of this telefeature. Script writer Budd Schulberg left the production midstream over "creative differences."

138. *Jail Busters* (Allied Artists, 1955), 61 min.

Producer, Ben Schwalb; director, William Beaudine; screenplay, Edward Bernds, Elwood Ullman; art director, David Milton; set decorator, Joseph Kish; costumes, Bert Henrickson; makeup, Emile LaVigne; music director, Marlin Skiles; production supervisor, Allan K. Wood; special effects, Ray Mercer; sound, Ralph Butler; sound effects editor, Charles Schelling; camera, Carl Guthrie; supervising editor, Lester A. Sansom; editor, William Austin.

Leo Gorcey (#41326 [Terrence Aloysius "Slip" Mahoney]); Huntz Hall (#41328 [Horace Debussy "Sach" Jones]); Bennie Bartlett (#41327 [Butch Williams]); David Condon (Charles "Chuck" Anderson); Bernard Gorcey (Louie Dumbrowski); Percy Helton (Warden B. W. Oswald); Barton MacLane (Guard Jenkins); Anthony Caruso (Ed Lannigan); Murray Alper (Gus); Michael Ross (Big Greenie); Fritz Feld (Dr. Fernando F. Fordyce); Lyle Talbot (Cy Bowman); Henry Kulky (Marty); Emil Sitka (Mug, the Photographer); John Harmon (Tomcyk); Henry Tyler (#12784 [Hank]).

It had been five years since the indomitable Bowery Boys had used a jail setting (*Triple Trouble*, 1950, q.v.) for one of their economy comedies at Allied Artists. *Jail Busters*, with its mild genre satire, was no improvement over the earlier entry. However, this time around, the budget screenplay called for no females in the cast, a first for a Bowery Boys series picture.

When their pal Chuck (David Condon), a newspaper reporter at the *New York Blade*, is injured while doing undercover research in prison, the Bowery Boys—Slip Mahoney (Leo Gorcey), Sach Jones (Huntz Hall) and Butch Williams (Bennie Bartlett)—investigate the situation. With the cooperation of Chuck's newspaper superior, reporter Cy Bowman (Lyle Talbot) they stage a fake robbery for which they receive a supposedly-short prison sentence. (However, Bowman, in need of funds, keeps the jewelry from the robbery and later denies knowing anything about the boys' bizarre plan.) Soon the troublesome threesome are in jail, and the State Prison will never be the same.

Daffy Slip thinks the entire matter is a lark. During induction, he advises a scornful prison guard: "I'd like my coat narrow and form fitting, not too broad in the shoulders and, if it's not too much trouble, a belt in the back."

When a guard dares to shout orders at the feckless Slip, he retorts: "Who are you yelling at? You only work here. I happen to be a guest."

Square-jawed Slip also refuses to be cowed by his intimidating surroundings. When he has his mug shots taken, he cavalierly orders the photographer (Emil Sitka) to "Send about twelve copies up to my suite!"

The Bowery stooges are soon ushered before the weasely Warden B. W. Oswald (Percy Helton). The ambivalent administrator, who has been on the job only two weeks, advises the newcomers of the house rules:

> Now men, um ... ehrr ... gentlemen. You'll be treated fairly, but firmly. After all, this is not a country club. We have our rules and you're expected to obey them. If you don't make trouble for us, we won't make trouble for you. It's as simple as that. In due time, I may recommend you for parole and, then again, I may not.

When the convicts inquire what the warden's middle initials stand for, Oswald snaps back, "bread and water!"

From the start, it is clear this trio cannot cope with the strict prison regimen. The institution's psychiatrist, Dr. Fernando F. Fordyce (Fritz Feld), is bewildered by their low mental acumen and sets them to work weaving baskets. When on kitchen duty, Sach finds a worthy adversary in the toaster, which gets the better of him. (When the misused utensil short-circuits the prison's current and the building's lights dim off and on, the curious warden asks, "Who are we frying today?")

Dopey Sach, who lives in his own private world, refuses to be cowed by the bizarre prison routine. As he tells Slip, "So they gave us hard bread. But, at least, the water is soft!"

The boys soon encounter a convict more simple-minded than Sach. It is old-time inmate Hank, who has gone stir crazy. He informs the Bowery gang, "The parole board will turn me loose any time I want. But not me! For twenty-two years, I've been digging a tunnel that will take me right out of this place. Why leave when I've got it almost finished?"

Having adjusted to the new environment, the boys uncover that the prison is controlled by a tough hood named Ed Lannigan (Anthony Caruso). He has a customized cell and enjoys all the luxuries money can buy; he also has gruff Guard Jenkins (Barton MacLane) under his thumb. He brags to the newcomers that he also runs a bookie operation from inside the prison. (An impressed Sach replies, "A convict's work is never done.") Soon the Bowery sleuths uncover that Lannigan was responsible for roughing up Chuck when he was getting too close to the truth. Eventually the boys, who have tried to escape through Hank's tunnel only to end up in the warden's office, uncover the needed evidence from Lannigan's safe. Later the boys help corral Lannigan and his henchmen who attempt a jailbreak.

Demanding to know when they will be released, the warden tells the three cellmates to be patient. The scene fades to show the boys still in prison, so long that they each have long whiskers!

As with all of the mid–1950s Bowery Boys series pictures, the shoestring production was a toss-up as to which was flimsier, the sets or the script.

139. *Jail House Blues* (Universal, 1942), 62 min.

Associate producer, Ken Goldsmith; director, Albert S. Rogell; based on the story "Rhapsody in Stripes" by Harold Tarshis; screenplay, Paul Gerard Smith, Tarshis; art director, Jack Otterson; costumes, Vera West; choreography, Larry Ceballos; sound supervisor, Bernard B. Brown; assistant director, Howard Christie; sound, William Hedgcock; camera, Elwood Bredell; editor, Fran Gross.

Nat Pendleton (Sonny McGann); Anne Gwynne (Doris Daniels); Robert Paige (Cliff Bailey); Horace MacMahon (Swifty); Elisabeth Risdon (Mrs. Aloysius McGonigle McGann); Warren Hymer (Big Foot Louie); Samuel S. Hinds (Thomas Daniels); Cliff Clark (Warden Boswell); John Kelly (Snork); Reed Hadley (Boston); Paul Fix (Danny); Dewey Robinson (Liver Lips); Ralf Harolde (Charlie the Chopper); Hal K. Dawson (Talent Scout); Ralph Dunn (Toddy); Billy Wayne (Blind Beggar); Nora Cecil (Matron); Emmett Vogan (Columnist); William Ruhl (Cripple); Walter Sande (Fudge); Bud Jamison, Kernan Crips, Ed Peil, Sr. (Guards); David Gorcey (Bellboy); Duke York (Man); Ethel Sykes (Winnie); Pat Costello (Flute Player); Jack Herrick, Al Seymour, Kit Guard, Blackie Whiteford, Dave Wengren, Jack Roper (Convicts); Charles Sullivan (Truck Driver).

Universal blended two popular genres—prison dramas and musicals—for this pleasant spoof. "Utterly fantastic in its farce premise, *Jail House Blues* gets a fair share of laughs from the efforts of a hard-working cast and the hard-hitting direction...." (*Hollywood Reporter*). The *Motion Picture Herald* championed it as "A novelty among penitentiary pictures and among comedies...."

Mrs. Aloysius McGonigle McGann (Elisabeth Risdon) remains undaunted in her efforts to break her boy, Sonny (Nat Pendleton), out of jail. She needs him

Nat Pendleton, Warren Hymer and Robert Paige in *Jail House Blues* (1942).

for a new racket she is planning. She is unaware that Sonny has been pardoned, or that he has hidden the document and is remaining in stir to produce the institution's musical show, *Stick 'em Up*. When Charlie the Chopper (Ralf Harolde) breaks out of prison, Sonny loses his "leading lady." Desperate to get Charlie back, Sonny makes a deal with the warden (Cliff Clark). If he leaves his pardon with the administrator, can he go out in search of the Chopper? The warden agrees reluctantly, fearful of the bad publicity about Charlie's too-perfect escape. On the outside, Sonny encounters Doris Daniels (Anne Gwynne) and her boyfriend, Cliff Bailey (Robert Paige), the latter who operates a hotdog stand and is an ambitious tenor singer.

Sonny visits his mother and learns she has organized the area's panhandlers into the A.A.P. (Amalgamated Association of Panhandlers) and, with Cliff's assistance, he helps her defeat the rival C.B.H.G. (Charity Begins at Home Guild) run by Danny (Paul Fix) and his mob. To reward Cliff, he takes him to prison where he convinces the warden to allow Bailey to perform in the big show.

Meanwhile, Sonny has his boys on the outside kidnap several of New York's leading drama critics who are "escorted" to the prison to preview the show. The musical is a hit and the reviews are favorable to Cliff who is hired for a Broadway production. Now he and Doris can wed.

140. *The Jailbird* (Paramount, 1920), 4,988'.

Presenter/supervisor, Thomas H. Ince; director, Lloyd Ingraham, story/screenplay, Julien Josephson; art director/architecture/decorations, Charles H. Kyson; art director/technical, Harvey C. Leavitt; titles, F. J. Van Halle, Carl Schneider, Leo H. Braun; camera, Bert Cann; editor, William H. Marker.

Douglas MacLean (Shakespeare Clancy); Doris May (Alice Whitney); Lew Morrison (Skeeter Burns); William Courtright (Noah Gibbs); Wilbur Higby (Joel Harvey); Otto Hoffman (Elkemah Pardee); Monty Collins (Asa Grider); Bert Woodruff (Grandpa Binney); Edith Yorke (Mrs. Whitney); Joe Hazelton (Alva Finch).

A lighthearted comedy drama which used its prison setting *not* for sensationalism or social reform, but as change-of-pace scenery to further its fanciful storyline.

Shakespeare Clancy (Douglas MacLean) is a restless convict who escapes prison one day by mingling with a crowd of departing visitors. He and Skeeter Burns (Lew Morrison), who has been recently paroled, join forces and head to the small Western town of Dodson where Clancy is to collect a legacy. However, Shakespeare discovers he has inherited an impoverished newspaper and a plot of useless land. He and Skeeter plot to foist the property into unsuspecting purchasers by claiming there is oil on the land. Meanwhile, Clancy falls in love with Alice Whitney (Doris May), the society editor of the paper. Later, fearful of being caught in their oil swindle, the two ex-prisoners prepare to leave town, only to discover that oil has been discovered there. Buoyed by his good luck, Shakespeare decides to complete his prison term. Joining a crowd of visitors, he slips back into the prison and returns to his daily chores as if *nothing* had happened.

Variety assessed of this property, which was one of several vehicles co-starring Douglas MacLean and Doris May, "Pictorially, the picture contains nothing that is away from the commonplace, and in direction there are spots that are rather jumpy, but on the whole the production gets by."

141. *Jailbird Rock* (Continental Motion Pictures, 1985), color, 92 min.

Executive producers, Helen Sarlui, Eduard Sarlui; producer, J.C. Crespo; associate producer, Dennison Rawles; story, Edward Sarlui; screenplay, Carole Stanley, Edward Kovach; costumes, Gloria van Hartenstein; makeup, Alice Adamson; music, Rick Nowels; songs: Tommy Dunear and Charles Judge; George Black and Howard Huntsberry; Nowels and Black; Nowels and Terry Abrahamson; Nowels, Judge and Black; assistant director, George Gunchin; sound effects, Robert Archangeli, Daniele Guadroli; camera, Leonard Soles; editor, Peter Tescher; additional editor, Earl Watson.

Robin Antin (Jessie Harris); Ron Lacey (Warden Bauman); Rhonda Aldrich (Max [Maxine Farmer]); Valerie Gene Richards (Peggy Birch); Jacqueline Houston (Sam [Samantha Edison]); Robin Cleaver (Echo [Esther Herrea]); Debra Laws (Lisa [Elizabeth Strong]); Anne Livingstone (Mouse [Joyce Lafer]); Erica Jordan (Judy Intorre); Perry Lange (Denny); Victoria Lustig (Dr. Victoria Lundee); Marie Noel (Mary the Guard); Sebastian Larreta (Lamonc); Perla Cristal (Jessie's Mother); Ted McNaeney (Stepfather); Maria Carmen

Douglas MacLean and Doris May in *The Jailbird* **(1920).**

(Woman in Store); James Murray (Denny's Friend); Yolanda Pedigza (Max's Friend); Frank Cano (Governor); George Baza (Congressman Knowles).

Just when you thought it was safe to step back into a prison exercise yard, along comes *Jailbird Rock*. This bizarre, low-budget entry is, believe it or not, a mixture of *Cage Without a Key* (1975), q.v., *Flashdance* (1983), and *Fame* (1980). If you can visualize the old Judy Garland-Mickey Rooney MGM gambit of "gee let's put on a show!" but the performers all happen to be inmates at a woman's reformatory, then you can appreciate the creative bent of *Jailbird Rock*. As is typical of so many of these independent, homemade productions, many of the performers are atrocious amateurs, the photography is grainy, and the staged action is unconvincing.

High school student Jessie Harris (Robin Antin), who excels at modern dance, arrives home one day to witness her stepfather (Ted McNaeney) beating up her mother (Perla Cristal) yet again. Jessie reacts by pulling a shotgun from the kitchen closet and shooting the aggressor dead. She is sentenced to five years at the Andrew Cameron Facility for Girls. On the jail bus to the reformatory she talks with Peggy Birch (Valerie Gene Richards), an orphaned teenager who was convicted for being an accessory to murder, having helped her boyfriend with a grocery store robbery in which a clerk was killed. The two youngsters discuss their bleak future:

PEGGY: We're going to prison. Aren't you scared?

JESSIE: Sure I'm scared. But I got a feeling that once we get inside those walls, the last thing we should do is show them we're scared.

PEGGY: We've got to stick together.

JESSIE: Like the buddy system?

PEGGY: Yeah, the buddy system.

While the newcomers are being inducted into the facility, staff psychiatrist Dr. Victoria Lundee (Victoria Lustig) discusses the fresh arrivals with unsympathetic, redneck Warden Bauman (Ron Lacey).

LUNDEE: It's about Jessie Harris, the new girl who's coming in today. She's a dancer. She's been on television. This could be just what the girls need. Maybe she could hold some dance classes or jazz exercise....

BAUMAN: Well, what an idea! Now is this before or after we set up the tanning salon and the sauna? And while we're at it, why don't we really surprise them and bring in some male strippers.... We're dealing with convicted felons, Dr. Lundee ... and your job is to teach them discipline, not dancing. Do you understand?

Bauman is equally abrupt and crude when he interviews Jessie and Peggy: "Remember, you ladies have been sent here to learn to show respect for society and its rules. Only when you have learned that respect will you be worthy of the respect of others. Keep out of trouble and get Mary to give you the list of 'no-nos.'"

When Jessie and Peggy go upstairs to their rooms, they encounter Max [Maxine Farmer] (Rhonda Aldrich), who is serving six years for attempted murder. She is the toughest bird in the institution, whose blonde good looks belie her evil interior. Her chief helper is a black teenager, Echo [Esther Herrea] (Robin Cleaver), who is doing two years for breaking and entering. Max takes an immediate dislike to the self-reliant Jessie, labeling her "Hot Legs," since word has spread through the building that the newcomer is an excellent dancer. Jessie's roommate is Lisa [Elisabeth Strong] (Debra Laws), who is serving one year for shoplifting. Peggy is assigned to room with Mouse [Joyce Lafer] (Anne Livingstone), who is doing one year for grand theft auto.

Lisa quickly explains to Jessie the house rules, pointing out that Max, not Warden Bauman nor Guard Mary (Marie Noel) reigns supreme here: "Max is the barn boss. You know, the big wheel in this shit wagon. You should see how she has Mary, the head guard, eating out of her hands ... and her pants."

Inmates are allowed visitors and Jessie's boyfriend, Denny (Perry Lange) visits her, hoping to keep her spirits buoyant. When she turns pessimistic, even suggesting she no longer cares about dancing, he insists, "The biggest crime you could ever commit would be to forget how good you are [at dancing]. The best!"

But Jessie has more important problems on her mind, namely keeping Peggy and herself in one piece and avoiding contact as much as possible with the vicious Max and her pals.

Later, when Max attacks Sam [Samantha Edison] (Jacqueline Houston) Jessie comes to her rescue. Because Max is having sexual relations with Guard Mary, she is saved from punishment. However, Sam and Jessie are disciplined by serving time in solitary confinement. As they are escorted to their rat-infested chambers, the experienced Sam warns Jessie:

> Just one thing with you in isolation, your imagination. Alone in the dark. . . .
> That's what isolation is all about, surviving your imagination. Keep working, babe,
> keep busy! Cause once you start thinking, you ain't got a chance. One thing about
> isolation, Jessie. It can make you or break you.

By the time the girls are released from isolation, Dr. Lustig has convinced the warden to permit Jessie to organize and star in a big talent show. Realizing he can get good publicity from the event, Bauman agrees. Before long, the governor (Frank Cano) has agreed to attend the event to be held in a large auditorium.

After much rehearsal, the talent show is produced. During the program, Max, who has previously killed one of her peers, is shot to death while attempting to escape. The dance and song revue is a big success and the approving Denny congratulates Jessie on her fine performance.

A postscript (in the mock serious style of *American Graffiti*) advises that Jessie and Denny married and live in Los Angeles where he is a cinematographer. Warden Bauman was appointed to the State Correctional Board, but after six months was fired for incompetency. Dr. Lustig replaced Bauman as head of the Andrew Cameron Facility and instituted many reforms.

The subgenre of teenager girls-behind-bars had developed quite a bit since the days of *Reform School Girl* (1957), q.v., and *Born Innocent* (1974), q.v. By the time of *Jailbird Rock* in the mid-1980s, it was standard procedure to show graphically, even in a non-pornography film, a great deal of nudity as well as lesbian and heterosexual couplings. *Jailbird Rock* does all this, but stops short of the raunch of *Caged Heat* (1974), q.v., or *Reform School Girls* (1986), q.v. Occasionally there is a wry line of dialogue in the film as when Max tells one of her lusting bed partners, "You don't love me, you just love the good parts." But at heart, *Jailbird Rock* is a standard reformatory melodrama, with the callous inmates ruling the roost and even the well-meaning girls who want to go right, admitting, "This place in here is one long nightmare. It's no place for dreams." As for the several dance and rock numbers performed in *Jailbird Rock,* they are enthusiastic if undistinguished.

142. *Jailbreak* (Warner Bros., 1936), 60 min.

Producer, Bryan Foy; director, Nick Grinde; based on the story "Murder in Sing Sing" by Jonathan Finn; screenplay, Robert D. Andrews, Joseph Hoffman; camera, Arthur Todd; editor, Harold McLernon.

June Travis (Jane Rogers); Craig Reynolds (Ken Williams); Barton MacLane (Detective Captain Rourke); Richard Purcell (Ed Slayden); Addison Richards (Dan Varner); George E. Stone (Weeper); Eddie Acuff (Sig Patton); Joseph King (Big Mike Egan); Joseph Crehan (Warden); Mary Treen (Gladys Joy); Henry Hall (Pop Anderson); Charles Middleton (Dan Stone); Robert Emmett Keane (City Editor).

Ex-convict Big Mike Egan (Joseph King) has gone straight. However, gangster Ed Slayden (Richard Purcell) pressures the onetime criminal to participate in new crimes, including robberies and murder. Thinking he might be safer in prison, Egan assaults a cop and is sentenced to two years in the state penitentiary. While he is out of circulation, he leaves his business affairs for his secretary Jane Rogers (June Travis) to handle. Jane confides these facts to her reporter friend Ken Williams (Craig Reynolds), who then explains the situation to a police associate, Detective Captain Rourke (Barton MacLane). This leads to the arrest of Slayden and his hoods who end up being sentenced to the same prison. Believing that Big Mike has squealed on them, Slayden's men vow to kill him. When Egan is found murdered, Williams turns sleuth and, posing as a prisoner, proves that a prison guard (Addison Richards) had murdered Egan and another convict as well. The motive was Egan's revelation to his killer about a $300,000 cache of money. Having scooped the big story, Williams proposes to Jane.

"The fact that the murders take place at a prison gives the picture a novel twist but the plot in itself is routine.... An incidental romance, not connected with the story, is worked into the plot" (*Harrison's Reports*). *Variety* was less impressed, criticizing the whodunit for being "loaded with absurdities only partly camouflaged by a certain speediness" and noted "Fantastic liberties are taken with the realities of penitentiary life and discipline."

While this budget entry suffered from many other inadequacies (e.g. stilted performances by the two leads), Warner Bros. saw fit to remake the property as *Smashing the Money Ring* (1939), q.v., one of Ronald Reagan's four Brass Bancroft entries. Still squeezing mileage from Jonathan Finn's concept, the studio remade the property yet again as *Murder in the Big House* (1942), q.v., this time with screen newcomer Van Johnson in the lead assignment.

British release title: *Murder in the Big House*.

143. *Jailhouse Rock* (Metro-Goldwyn-Mayer, 1957), 96 min.

Producer, Pandro S. Berman; associate producer, Kathryn Hereford; director, Richard Thorpe; story, Ned Young; screenplay, Guy Trosper; art directors, William A. Horning, Randell Duell; set decorators, Henry Grace, Keogh Gleason; makeup, William Tuttle; music supervisor, Jeff Alexander; songs: Mike Stoller and Jerry Lieber; Roy C. Bennett, Abner Silver, Ben Weisman, Aaron Schroeder, Sid Tepper; assistant director, Robert Relyea; technical adviser, Colonel Tom Parker; sound supervisor, Dr. Wesley C. Miller; special effects, A. Arnold Gillespie; camera, Robert Bronner; editor, Ralph E. Winters.

Elvis Presley (Vince Everett); Judy Tyler (Peggy Van Alden); Mickey Shaughnessy (Hunk Houghton); Jennifer Holden (Sherry Wilson); Dean Jones (Teddy Talbot); Ann Neyland (Laury Jackson); Hugh Sanders (Warden); Vaughn Taylor (Mr. Shores); Mike Stoller (Pianist); Grandon Rhodes (Professor August Van Alden); Katherine Warren (Mrs. Van Alden); Don Burnett (Mickey Alba); George Cisar (Jake, the Bartender); Glenn Strange (Simpson, a Convict); John Indrisano (Convict); Robert Bice (Barderman, TV Studio Manager); Percy Helton (Sam Brewster); Peter Adams (Jack Lease); William Forrest (Studio Head); Dan White (Paymaster); Robin Raymond (Dotty); John Day (Ken); S. John Launer (Judge); Dick Rich (Guard); Elizabeth Slifer (Cleaning Woman); Gloria Pall (Stripteaser); Fred Doby (Bartender); Walter Johnson (Shorty); Frank Kreig (Drunk); William Tannen (Record Distributor); Wilson Wood (Record Engineer); Tom McKee (TV Director); Donald Kerr (Photographer); Carl Milletaire (Drummond); Francis DeSales (Surgeon); Harry Hines (Hotel Clerk); Dorothy Abbott (Woman in Café); The Jordanaires (Musicians).

Jailhouse Rock has the distinction of being the only prison film to date to boast a commerative collector's plate. But then again, how many jail movies star the king of rock 'n' roll, Elvis Presley? How many such genre pieces can boast such an extravagantly stylized production number as "Jailhouse Rock," a surrealistic gyration conceived by Presley himself? There may be little reality to *Jailhouse Rock*, especially in its romanticized prison sequences, but it remains an entertaining picture. It exploits Presley in a James Dean-rebel type role and uses a plotline which has parallels to Andy Griffith's *A Face in the Crowd* (1957).

Hot-tempered country boy Vince Everett (Elvis Presley) is a well-paid construction worker with very basic ideas of how to spend his salary. ("Gonna buy me a herd of chorus girls and make them dance on my bed.") One evening at a local redneck bar, he buys a drink for a young woman which causes her boyfriend to turn rowdy. In the ensuing brawl, Vince knocks the man down, who hits his head and dies. Everett is sentenced to one-to-ten years in the state penitentiary for manslaughter.

The warden (Hugh Sanders) is quite prepared to knock the chip off the shoulder of this new young inmate:

> Tough woodchuck, huh? Well, that's what we're here for, to teach you hooligans. It says here, you killed a man with your bare hands. We don't use hands here, we use guns. Oh and I'll tell you another thing we use for cons who don't tow the mark, the whip. Understand?

Vince's cellmate is rough-and-tumble Hunk Houghton (Mickey Shaughnessy), a former country-western singer, who still likes to strum his guitar. He is also particular about his living quarters. ("I live here. I'm touchy about everything!") The veteran convict teaches the naïve Vince the special ways of prison life.

> HUNK: Cigarettes. These here is the coin of the realm.
>
> VINCE: Where do you get the cigarettes?
>
> HUNK: You trade with guys who don't smoke 'em. You buy 'em, you steal 'em, you cheat for 'em, you fight for 'em, just like you do on the outside.

Hunk explains to this "new fish" that their manual labor in prison earns them eighteen cents a day and that until he can make his own way in the can, Houghton will help out: "I'll stake you. I can't have my roommate walkin' around like a bum. I've got a reputation to hold up!"

Ending this indoctrination session, Hunk adds, "You just do what I say, when I say it. That's the basis of my organization."

Vince is among the convicts who labors in the coal yard, in contrast to Hunk who has wangled a soft position in the print shop. Meanwhile, Hunk, the one-time professional musician, assesses that his cellmate, who enjoys singing and strumming chords on the guitar, "will never make a guitar player. You got no rhythm in your bones." Nevertheless, when the warden authorizes a coast-to-coast TV talent show, "Breath of a Nation," to originate from the prison and to use convict talent, Vince is one of the program's singers. Later, when there is an avalanche of fan mail for Vince, Hunk leaves it with the warden, not wanting Everett to get a swelled head. The manipulative Hunk has decided this raw backswoodsman has potential to be a big performing star and he intends to sign him to a management contract. Meanwhile, the unruly Vince becomes involved in a mess hall riot over poor food. He is among the prisoners whipped for his participation. The beating only makes him more bitter: "I'm an animal in a jungle and I got a motto: 'Do unto others what they would do unto you, only do it first.' It's the same on the outside, only worse."

Finally, Vince gets paroled from prison, with the grand sum of $4.00 in his pocket. His final meeting with the dictatorial warden has its own wry humor:

VINCE: How come I didn't see these [his sacks of letters] before?

WARDEN: Because I didn't want you to.

VINCE: That's against the law.

WARDEN: Have me arrested.

Once on the outside, Vince sings in a small bar where he comes to the attention of a fledgling record executive, Peggy Van Alden (Judy Tyler). She advises the raw performer, "Sing it differently, how you feel it. Put your own emotions in it. Make it fit you."

Eventually, they become partners and an on-again, off-again romance begins. While Vince's career is skyrocketing, Hunk is released from prison and is hired by his former cellmate to be a high-priced flunky. On a nationwide TV variety show, Vince performs his tribute to his prison years by singing "Jailhouse Rock." Hollywood beckons Vince and, while making motion pictures, he becomes the West Coast's newest playboy Romeo. He and Hunk argue and, in a scuffle, Vince's throat is injured. The doctors are uncertain if he will ever sing again. However, he recovers and, having learned humility, is reconciled with both Peggy and Hunk.

Jailhouse Rock was Elvis Presley's third motion picture. While not of the same caliber as *King Creole* (1958) or *Flaming Star* (1960), it is an enjoyable musical with such songs as: "Treat Me Nice," "I Wanna Be Free" and "One More Day." As Douglas Brode (*The Films of the Fifties*, 1976) assessed, "His third film, *Jailhouse Rock*, perfected the 'Presley vehicle.' His role was ideally suited to him: a romanticized version of his own image.... Dozens of second-rate rock 'n' roll films soon followed, but only Presley enjoyed the distinction of having such movies tailored to his own personality."

The ad campaign for *Jailhouse Rock* proclaimed, "*Elvis Presley* at his greatest! His first big dramatic singing role!... Singing!... Fighting!... Dancing!... Romancing!"

Judy Tyler, Presley's co-star in *Jailhouse Rock*, was best known for her appearances as Princess Summer-Fall-Winter-Spring on TV's "Howdy Doody Show" (1952–57). She died in a car crash on July 4, 1957, at age twenty-four.

144. *The Jericho Mile* (ABC–TV, March 18, 1979), color, 97 min.

Producer, Tim Zinnerman; director, Michael Mann; story, Patrick J. Nolan; teleplay, Nolan, Mann; art director, Stephen Berger; set decorator, William K. Jolley; costumes, John Perry; makeup, Del Accevedo; music, Jimmie Haskell; additional music, James DiPasquale; assistant directors, Frank Beetson, John R. Kittleson; sound, Jim Webb; sound re-recording, David Dockendorff; sound editor, Michael Hilkene; camera, Rexford Metz; editor, Arthur Schmidt.

Peter Strauss (Larry "Rain" Murphy);

Richard Lawson (R. C. Stiles); Roger E. Mosley ("Cotton" Crown); Brian Dennehy ("Dr. D."); Billy Green Bush (Warden Earl Gulliver); Ed Lauter (Jerry Beloit); Geoffrey Lewis (Dr. Bill Janowski); Beverly Todd (Wylene Stiles); William Prince (OAU Chairman); Miguel Pinero (Rubio); Richard Moll (Jocker Gibb); Edmund Penney (OAU Official); Burton Gilliam (Jimmy-Jack); Ji-Tu Cumbuka (Brother Lateef); Wilmore Thomas ("Moo-Moo"); Leroy Haskins ("Too-Cool"); Gladdis Franklin, Jr. (Sahib Wahib); John M.

Jackson (Boogaloo); Robert L. Jones ("Abba Dabba"); Gilbert Tweksbury (Panfilo David); Benny L. Rapisura ("Kiki" Pardo); Eluterio Rodarte ("Lord Hueva"); Steven White (Charlie Loon); Thomas K. Abihai (Abihai); Jimmy Coppola ("Action Man");

Terry Lee Dawson ("Foghorn"); Marcus R. Colburn IV (Nomoto); Robert Edward Collins (Conway); Harold D. Kuykendall (1st Guard); Ed Morris (2nd Guard); Joe Campoy (Associate Warden).

The Jericho Mile is one of the most effective of all telefeatures ever revolving around prison life. In its relatively unassuming way it is very realistic, full of authentic locales, actual jargon, and real situations. The contemporary penitentiary of this production is a far cry from the institution depicted in 1930s–1950s feature films. As seen here, modern prisons are vastly overcrowded institutions, steaming with racial strife. For today's overworked penal administrators who struggle with inadequate budgets and facilities, the practical policies of maintenance and survival have replaced the concepts of retribution or rehabilitation. As displayed in *The Jericho Mile,* prisoners no longer wear drab conformist uniforms or march to a prison schuffle. These are men who watch TV, have radios in their cells, and enjoy conjugal visiting rights with their wives who visit with them in trailers housed within the prison yard.

As this telefeature sharply reflects, the range of activities, attitudes and corruptions within this diverse social microcosm is staggering. But *The Jericho Mile* shows that a few items have not changed: prison still means a tremendous constraint of personal freedom; the strong still rule the weak; and there is still great hatred between the keepers and the kept.

Larry "Rain" Murphy (Peter Strauss) is serving a life sentence at Folsom Prison in California for murder. This prisoner (#102491) is a loner, who is amazingly resigned about being incarcerated. He believes in the maxim: "If you can't do time, don't do crime. That's the price for rehabilitation." He has no family or friends who visit him. He has refused any job at the prison and watches no TV. His one obsession is running and every day he paces himself on his laps around the exercise yard ball field. In great physical shape, he has honed his athletic abilities so that now he is running close to a four-minute mile, and this without proper running shoes or a decent track.

The prison psychologist (Geoffrey Lewis) attempts to break through Murphy's rigid emotional shell:

JANOWSKI: When you run, where are you?

MURPHY: I'm here. I belong here in this place. I am convicted of murder one. I did it. Now I am doing my own time. I mess with no one, no one messes with me. I did what I did. That's it.

While other convicts such as Murphy's black next-door neighbor, R. C. Stiles (Richard Lawson), are worrying about their next conjugal visit with their wives, or dealing/using drugs, or getting involved in the vicious ethnic tugs-of-war between the blacks, the Chicanos and the whites (the latter led by Dr. D. [Brian Dennehy]), Murphy's modus operandi is to shut himself off from his prison mates. He and the restless Stiles exchange philosophies:

MURPHY: I am into *nothing*. That's how I do my time.

STILES: You don't need nobody. You run until you can't walk. Then you zone out like a glue sniffer till you can't talk, and then maybe you be tired enough to get some sleep. Until the next day when you got to go through the whole thing again. *Now* Mr. Murphy, you don't need nobody ... no stuff.... You got to be the *luckiest* man alive!

Later, Stiles is pressured into helping with a drug shipment being brought into the prison. When the deal goes bad, he is knifed by one of Dr. D's men. Meanwhile, Jerry Beloit (Ed Lauter), a track coach from Sacramento State University learns of Murphy's running talent and asks Warden Earl Gulliver (Billy Green Bush) if he can train Murphy and perhaps enter him in the upcoming Olympic competition. Murphy reluctantly agrees, on condition that he be given a few minutes alone — unsupervised by guards — in the metals industry shop. It is part of his plan to revenge Stiles's murderer. Once in the shop, he uncovers a stash of Dr. D's drug money and burns it in the yard. He also destroys a vat of bootleg liquor. The convict crimelord threatens to kill Murphy, who remains unfrightened.

Dr. Janowski hopes that the athletic training will break down Murphy's emotional barriers. He gives him a stop watch which is inscribed: "To the Jericho Mile." The words refers to Murphy's emotional walls of Jericho. The warden has his own strong reasons for supporting this unorthodox situation:

> Murphy is a model for connecting to the outside. Backing him means a lot. It's not connecting which means staying into the games in that [exercise] yard. Then they [the ex-convicts] hit the streets, they cop out into their comic book fantasies, screw up an armed robbery, kill a few people and then they're right back in here. That's why one Murphy who can play into street values instead of jailhouse values and score is worth so much. Because he breaks down the games they play. And that's why he's got to run.

As part of his revenge on Murphy, Dr. D and his thugs force the other convict factions to picket the building of a regulation track in the exercise yard for Murphy's daily workouts. However, after Murphy, whom some of the black convicts call "Lickity Split" fights it out with the much stronger "Cotton" Crown (Roger E. Mosley), the leader of the blacks, the two become friends. Cotton persuades the Chicano convicts to join with the blacks in breaking through Dr. D's picket line in a bloody brawl. The track is built.

While Murphy continues to enhance his running skills, Janowski experiences a breakthrough with the uptight convict. Murphy finally is ready to deal with the facts of his crime, that he killed his father, a man he also loved. The psychiatrist slowly rips down the man's emotional defenses, which until now have resulted in his stock responses: "What went down went down.... This is where I belong." He begins to accept that a man can have mixed emotions, i.e., loving his father but nevertheless hating this drunkard who used to bash Murphy's stepsister.

The big emotional testing ground is when Murphy must be interviewed by the Olympic Committee to determine if he, despite his convict's status, is worthy of representing the United States in the competition. The autocratic OAU Chairman (William Prince) needles the applicant, bent on finding out whether he is really sorry for having committed murder. In a burst of anger and self-realization, Murphy responds:

I hate what happened, but I will not repudiate what happened and I won't repudiate myself because all I've got is my name and my face. In the same place, and in the same time and in the same conditions, I would blow him away all over again. Man, you are a sneak! You wouldn't last ten minutes in the yard.

Thereafter, disqualified from the Olympics, Rain continues his solitary running. When he learns that one of his would-be opponents ran a three minute, fifty-second mile, Murphy runs a solo race and clocks a faster time. He tosses the stop watch given to him by Janowski at the prison wall. In his own mind he knows that even if he ran in the Olympics, he would still return to Folsom and would always be a prisoner.

The Jericho Mile, not only enjoyed a high viewership when telecast, but it received solid reviews. *Daily Variety* praised the production as an "energetic, often moving, purposeful telefilm" and acknowledged that it "shows shrewd use of the characters and action to tell what might have been only a routine story." *TV Guide* magazine rated the drama four stars, its highest praise. On the other hand, John Pym (British *Monthly Film Bulletin*) had a different perspective: "This made-for-TV feature seems intent on restating the old moral that, for the unreformable individual in an American prison, survival depends on a readiness to kill or maim. In the end, however, the film . . . stops short of a blanket condemnation of the system . . . and focuses instead on a sentimental portrait of the stocial Murphy . . . who wishes only to be left to serve his time in his own way." In *Captured on Film: The Prison Movies* (1989), Bruce Crowther pointed out, "*The Jericho Mile* has a raw vitality and powerful verisimilitude in many areas, not least in its crackling dialogue, which in turn baffled audiences and gave them a new form of slang to use in real life."

For his intense, driven performance in *The Jericho Mile*, Peter Strauss won the Emmy Award as Best Actor in a Drama. Other Emmy winners from this made-for-television movie were: Patrick J. Nolan and Michael Mann (scripters) and Arthur Schmidt (editor). The film was Emmy-nominated as the year's outstanding drama. To be noted in the cast is Miguel Pineo, the author of *Short Eyes* (1977), q.v.

145. *Johnny Apollo* (20th Century–Fox, 1940), 93 min.

Producer, Darryl F. Zanuck; associate producer, Harry Joe Brown; director, Henry Hathaway; story, Samuel G. Engel, Hal Long; screenplay, Philip Dunne, Rowland Brown; art directors, Richard Day, Wiard B. Ihnen; set decorator, Thomas Little; costumes, Gwen Wakeling; music, Frank Loesser, Lionel Newman, Alfred Newman, Mack Gordon; songs: Alfred Newman and Loesser; Loesser and Alfred Newman; Gordon; music director, Cyril J. Mockridge; sound, E. Clayton Ward, Roger Heman; camera, Arthur Miller; editor, Robert Bischoff.

Tyrone Power (Johnny Apollo/Robert Thomas [Bob] Cain); Dorothy Lamour (Mabel "Lucky" DuBarry); Lloyd Nolan (Mickey Dwyer); Edward Arnold (Robert Cain, Sr.); Charley Grapewin (Judge Em-

mett T. Brennan); Lionel Atwill (Jim McLaughlin); Marc Lawrence (John Bates); Jonathan Hale (Dr. Brown); Russell Hicks (District Attorney); Fuzzy Knight (Cell-mate); Charles Lane (Assistant District Attorney); Selmer Jackson (Warden); Charles Trowbridge (Judge Penrose); George Irving (Mr. Ives); Eddie Marr (Harry the Henchman); Anthony Caruso (Joe the Henchman); Harry Rosenthal (Piano Player); Eric Wilton (Butler); Harry Tyler (Trusty); Stanley Andrews (Welfare Secretary); Wally Albright (Office Boy); Charles Tannen, Milburn Stone (Reporters); Tom Dugan (Tom the Prisoner); James Flavin (Guard); Walter Miller (Guard in Solitary); Robert Shaw (Clerk); Ed Gargan (Detective); Gary Breckner (Announcer); Bess Flowers (Secretary); Geneva Sawyer ("La

Contga" Dancer); William Pawley (Paul);
Charles Williams (Photographer); Phil
Tead (Reporter); Jim Pierce, William
Haade, Louis Jean Heydt, Stanley Blystone,
Don Rowan, James Blain (Guards); Em-
mett Vogan (Guard/Announcer); Charles
D. Brown (Detective).

One of rising star Tyrone Power's three major releases of 1940 was *Johnny Apollo*. It was an adroitly contrived gangster melodrama that focused more on romantic conventions than realism, even in its extensive prison segment. This was the type of glossy production that has an attorney (Lionel Atwill) ominously telling his white collar criminal client (Edward Arnold), "They never sent a millionaire to prison as long as I can remember" and the prison-bound millionaire later confiding to his son, "The prison term doesn't mean anything to me. I can do that standing on my head. It was you."

Earnest Ivy League college student Bob Cain (Tyrone Power) is dismayed to learn that his wealthy Wall Street broker father (Edward Arnold) has been jailed for embezzlement. Bob returns home and confronts his father; they part after a bitter quarrel. Cain Sr. is sent to prison for a five-year term. Meanwhile, Bob regrets his negative response to his father in his time of need and plans to work to obtain his release. However, he cannot find a job with any of his dad's former "friends." During a visit to an unsavory attorney, Judge Emmett T. Brennan (Charley Grapewin) — renowned for his ability to get convicts paroled — Bob meets Lucky DuBarry (Dorothy Lamour), the girlfriend of gangster kingpin Mickey Dwyer (Lloyd Nolan). Through Lucky, who is attracted to Bob, he meets Dwyer and soon they become good acquaintances and partners in crime. As part of his new personage, Bob adopts the name of Johnny Apollo. His exploits come to the attention of the imprisoned Cain, Sr. ("There are no secrets in jail" he explains) who refuses to see his son when he visits the prison.

Time passes and both Dwyer and Bob are arrested and sent to the same prison where Cain, Sr. is housed. Mickey and Bob plan a jailbreak. Lucky tells Cain, Sr. of the intended breakout and warns him that the unscrupulous Dwyer would not hesitate to kill Bob if necessary. Cain, Sr. attempts to stop his son from participating in the escape scheme, but he is shot by Mickey. Dwyer then knocks out Bob and leaves the incriminating weapon by his side. The comatose Cain, Sr. is taken to the prison hospital while Bob is held for possible homicide. The prison authorities refuse to believe his relationship to the victim until Cain, Sr. recovers and clears his son's name. Eventually both father and son, who have reconciled are paroled. Lucky is there to welcome Bob on his release.

Variety noted of this popular film that "It's a slight switch on the usual pattern" but criticized its fanciful plotline: "Murder with an icepick; plotting a prison-break; absence of the guard during visiting hours; free access to daily newspapers while in prison, and the like...." B.R. Crisler *(New York Times)* judged this well-mounted picture to be "surprisingly pat." In detailing various plot discrepancies, Crisler appraised the film as "one prolonged symphony of socks in the jaw, subpoenas in night clubs, jail breaks and one flash of a penitentiary newspaper with a gossip column heading which we shall never forget: 'Stir-Tistics.'"

Besides Tyrone Power's well-meaning, if awkward, interpretation of the confused hero, there was excellent support from blustering Edward Arnold as the upper crust swindler who can take this punishment unflinchingly and even rejoice in doing manual labor in the prisoner's boiler shop, Lloyd Nolan as the breezy, disloyal hood, and Charley Grapewin as a sinister, corrupt lawyer. Not to be

Edward Arnold and Tyrone Power in *Johnny Apollo* (1940).

overlooked was Dorothy Lamour — borrowed from Paramount Pictures — who was featured as an old-fashioned gangster's moll. She managed to look wistful, display her shapely legs, model several unchic outfits and sing two downbeat tunes: "This Is the Beginning of the End" and "Dancing for Nickels and Dimes."

One of the more amusing moments of the farfetched prison sequences occurs when a recidivist criminal, Tom (Tom Dugan), is returning to prison yet again. An induction guard questions him as to his previous occupation and his plans once he is released. The non-plussed convict replies, "Thief. . . . Don't worry, I'll get my old job back again."

146. *Johnny Holiday* (United Artists, 1949), 94 min.

Producer, R.W. Alcorn; associate producer, Frederick Stephani; director, Willis Goldbeck; story, Alcorn; screenplay, Jack Andrews, Stephani, Goldbeck; costumes, Robert Martien; makeup, Nicholas Vehr; music, Franz Waxman; assistant director, William Forsyth; sound, Garry Harris, Stanley Cooley; process camera, Mario Castegnaro; camera, Hal Mohr; editor, Richard Fritch.

William Bendix (Sergeant Walker); Allen Martin, Jr. (Johnny Holiday); Stanley Clements (Eddie Duggan); Jack Hagen (Jackson); Herbert Newcomb (Dr. Piper); Donald Gallagher (Superintendent); Lang); Greta Grandstedt (Mrs. Holiday); George Cisar (Barney Duggan); Leo Cleary (Trimble); Alma Platt (Miss Kelly); Jeanne Juvelier (Mrs. Bellni); Governor Henry F. Schricker (Himself); Hoagy Carmichael (Himself); Buddy Cole (Himself); and: The Staff and Boys of the Indiana Boys' School.

Johnny Holiday is very reminiscent of Allied Artists's *Bad Boy* (1949), q.v., another study of the regenerative affect of a boys' reformatory. The latter film received a box office boast by casting World War II hero Audie Murphy in the lead role. On the other hand, *Johnny Holiday* had to ride on its own merits, as well as with the modest attraction of having William Bendix and songwriter/actor Hoagy Carmichael as its only "names."

When his mother (Greta Grandstedt) is hospitalized, Johnny Holiday (Allen Martin, Jr.) comes under the negative influence of a young thief, Eddie Dugan (Stanley Clements). As a result of being caught stealing, Johnny is sentenced to the Indiana Boys' School, where he is detailed to work in the stables under the guidance of roughneck Sergeant Walker (William Bendix), an ex-cavalry, non-commissioned Army officer. The sympathetic Walker observes Johnny's rapport with animals and places the mare Nellie in his care. Just as Holiday is improving his attitude, Dugan arrives at the school to serve a sentence. Now Johnny is divided in his loyalties to Walker and Eddie. Hoping to woo the youth back to the right path, Walker arranges for Holiday to visit his mother. Later, Walker catches Johnny with cigarettes which he purchased from Eddie. When Walker confiscates the smokes, Dugan swears revenge. He tries to kill Walker in a staged accident, but Johnny saves his mentor's life.

Walker is forced to shoot the mare Nellie in order to save her foal. Johnny misunderstands this action and becomes embittered. He agrees to join Dugan in an escape attempt on Christmas Eve. Eddie steals Walker's gun and demands the keys to the Sergeant's car. Johnny has a change of heart and manages to alert the front office of Dugan's latest exploit. Officials arrive in time to capture Eddie and to treat Walker who has been shot. Soon thereafter, the rehabilitated Johnny is released and returns home to his mother.

Variety endorsed, "[This] film, besides carrying a semi-documentary motif, has a surefire combo of the kid's return to the straight and narrow and his love for animals." Thomas M. Pryor *(New York Times)* noted how the school depicted in *Johnny Holiday* differed from the typical institution of a decade earlier (e.g. *Crime School,* 1938, q.v.). "A model reform school, the institution sprawls over acres of rolling, green country. It has no high walled fence, there are no bars on the windows and occupational therapy is liberally and wisely employed." But, observed Pryor, "there also is some question about the wisdom of making reform school life too attractive." The near–Pollyanna qualities of *Johnny Holiday* would stand in stark contrast to such 1980s depictions of juvenile reformatories as seen in *Bad Boys* (1983), q.v.

For the record, guest performer Hoagy Carmichael appeared as himself at the School's Christmas Eve show and sang "My Christmas Song for You." The plot basis for *Johnny Holiday* derived from the early life of independent producer R.W. Alcorn who devised the film's storyline. Indiana's Governor Henry F. Schricker appeared as himself delivering a brief address to the boys at the reformatory. Much of the location filming was accomplished at the Indiana Boys' School at Plainfield, Indiana.

147. *Kill Me If You Can* (NBC–TV, Sept. 25, 1977), color, 100 min.

Producer, Peter Katz; associate producer, Bert Gold; director, Buzz Kulik; teleplay, John Gay; art directors, Ross Bellah, Carl Brauner; set decorators, Audrey Blasdel-Goddard, Richard C. Goddard; makeup, Ben Lane; music, Bill Conti; music editor, Shinichi Yamazaki; technical consultant, Rosalie Asher; sound editors, Douglas H. Grandstaff, Bob G. Human; camera, Gerald Perry Finnerman; editor, Les Green.

Alan Alda (Caryl Whittier Chessman); Talia Shire (Rosalie Asher); John Hillerman (George Davis); Barnard Hughes (Judge Fricke); Virginia Kiser (Virginia Gibbons); Edward Mallory (Warden Teets); Walter McGinn (J. Miller Leavy); Ben Piazza (Bill Edmunds); John Randolph (Judge Lewis Goodman); Herb Vigran (Hart, the Jury Foreman); Maxine Stuart (Mrs. Asher); Rose Portillo (Sara Loper); John P. Ryan (Johnson); Brian Byers (Harris); James B. Sikking (Mr. Lea); George Sperdakos (Court Clerk); Joe E. Tata (Kelton); M. P. Murphy (Sergeant Grant); James Keach (1st Officer); Carmen Argenziano (Lieutenant); Conrad Bachmann (Warden); Arnold Soboloff (Dr. Graves); James E. Brodhead (Judge Carter); Bill Morey (Judge Rexford); Tony Burton (Ben Price); Jack Schultz (Redlight Bandit); Philip Baker Hall (Phillips); Ann D'Andrea (Mrs. Loper); Tom Greenaway (Mr. Perry); F. William Parker (Judge); Sari Price (Irene); Donald Bishop (Reporter); and: Mary Margaret Amato, Anne Bellamy, Vivian Brown, Mward Cumbuka, Danny Dayton, Gary Epper, Loutz Gage, Rori Gwynne, Patrick Hawley, Jim Henaghan, Billy Jackson, Jason Johnson, Joe Linton, Vincent Lucchesi, Jim Malinda, Paul Napier, Charles Picerni, Mark Regis, Leonard Simon, Richard Smedley, Richard Stobie, Gil Stuart, Tom Tarpey, Clint Young.

In 1955 Columbia Pictures had produced *Cell 2455, Death Row,* q.v., a stridently dramatic account of Caryl Whittier Chessman (1912–1960), the convicted "Redlight Bandit." The movie was based on Chessman's best-selling autobiography (1954) written during the several years he was on San Quentin Prison's death row. That film concluded its narrative on an upbeat note, with the condemned murderer receiving yet another reprieve. Twelve years later, NBC–TV telecast its stark version of the full story—including Chessman's execution—based on a script by John Gay, which unlike the former movie, focused only on Chessman the condemned adult. It featured politically liberal actor Alan Alda (then starring in the teleseries "M*A*S*H") as the egotistical convict whose insistence on handling his own defense at his initial trial probably cost him his life. Its treatment of the Chessman case is very anti-capital punishment.

Caryl Whittier Chessman (Alan Alda) has been in and out of prison since he was sixteen, including stretches at Folsom and San Quentin. He has been a free man only a few months when he is picked up in January 1948 by the Los Angeles police on suspicion of armed robbery. This coincidence leads him to being implicated in the series of "redlight bandit" rapes/kidnappings then plaguing the metropolitan area. Chessman claims he is innocent. ("I have my standards too, you know. I'm a pro. Not some red light bum!") Despite the offer of public council Bill Edmunds (Ben Piazza) to defend him at his trial, the arrogant Chessman insists on being his own attorney (with Edmunds as his legal adviser). The foolhardy Caryl unsuccessfully matches wits with the tough prosecuting attorney (Walter McGinn) and a biased judge (Barnard Hughes) who has a reputation for sending a great many convicted killers to the death house. Despite several irregularities in the trial proceedings, Chessman is found guilty on several counts and sentenced to die in the gas chamber at San Quentin Prison. Thus begins his twelve-year ordeal on Death Row, where he is granted several (last minute) stays of execution as he seeks the right to a new trial.

Attorney Rosalie Asher (Talia Shire) is brought into the case when the belligerent Chessman realizes he really needs professional assistance. ("I thought I did pretty good. My client is a fool," he tells her.) Still pugnacious, the extremely bright prisoner can joke about his plight, which includes two death sentences and a total of 167 years of imprisonment. ("I haven't figured out how they're going to kill me twice. I'll let them work on it.") Slowly, the flippant convict allows

Rosalie to take over his complex defense, although he insists upon assisting her and pressures the warden to permit him to have a typewriter, legal books and files in his cell. Time passes and the constant death threat hangs heavily on Chessman. ("Dying in a gas chamber just doesn't make sense. Why should I apologize to society for fighting for my existence?") Meanwhile, to pay some of his legal expenses, Chessman writes his autobiography, sells the property to Hollywood, and authors three additional books, including a novel.

More time passes; more appeals and more notoriety for Chessman, whose extraordinary long stay on Death Row is exploited by anti-capital punishment advocates as cruel and inhuman treatment. Joining Rosalie's crusade to save Chessman are attorneys Ben Price (Tony Burton) and, later, George Davis (John Hillerman). At one point, the California Supreme Court takes away Caryl's cell privileges to help in his own defense, but later decides he was being denied due process. Obsessed by his life-and-death struggle, Chessman becomes paranoid, insisting of the court system "These people are out to kill me! These people want me dead!" At one juncture, Rosalie and Davis suggest he alter his strategy and ask the court for clemency and mercy. This affronts the smug Chessman: "I'm not begging for clemency. It's the same as admitting guilt!" Finally, anxiety overcomes Chessman's last shreds of optimism. He sends Rosalie to pick out his coffin. Meanwhile, Davis submits a plea for clemency to the courts.

At a press conference, the world-renowned Chessman articulates his heartfelt thoughts about prison life in general and existence on death row in particular:

> What you ladies and gentlemen don't realize, perhaps, is you take a situation where you have about thirty men and you put them in a special place behind bars and feed them ... and let them get together once a day. They get to know each other. About once a month you take them out and kill them one by one. But each time, though, you replace the one who's been killed. I've seen about ninety men go that way.
>
> You call this place 'Death Row.' I call it limbo or a monument to futility. You see, I think it is essential to jettison, to throw out, this concept of retributive justice or the idea that good citizenship can be coerced, which I think is extremely wrong. I think I've demonstrated conclusively in my own case it wasn't possible to punish me, to coerce me, to force me to do good. What you need is an affirmative, more creative approach. Before you point to a man what is wrong with him find out what is right with him, what he can do, what he can contribute.
>
> But still you have the righteous calling for vengeance.

On May 2, 1960, the California Supreme Court met at 8 A.M., two hours before Caryl's ninth scheduled execution. At 9:15 A.M. his lawyers learned the court had denied the writ with a four to three vote. Caryl's attorneys hurried to the federal courthouse where Judge Lewis Goodman (John Randolph) was prepared to hear yet another last-minute plea. Shortly after 10 A.M. Randolph advised the lawyers he would give them a thirty-minute stay while he studied the petition. His secretary was asked to call San Quentin officials with the news, but she dialed the wrong number. By the time the judge reached the warden, he was told that the execution was already underway. At 10:12 A.M. Caryl Chessman was declared dead. It was also the end of an ordeal for Rosalie Asher who had been twenty-eight when she began the appeal and was now forty years old.

Daily Variety observed, "Scripter John Gay has blended fact and fiction to deliver an indictment of the death penalty in the name of Caryl Chessman, and the message certainly comes across loud and clear. Chessman's remarkable achievement in postponing his own execution for twelve years makes strong telefare, but has been so weighed in favor of Chessman, it's inconceivable he got the gas chamber." For his central performance as the strong-willed Chessman, Alan Alda was Emmy-nominated.

148. *Ladies of the Big House* (Paramount, 1932), 76 min.

Director, Marion Gering; story Ernest Booth; screenplay, Louis Weitzenkorn; camera, David Abel.

Sylvia Sidney (Kathleen Storm); Gene Raymond (Standish McNeil); Wynne Gibson (Susie Thompson); Rockliffe Fellowes (Martin Doremus); Earle Foxe (Kid Athens); Frank Sheridan (Warden Hecker); Edna Bennett (The Countess); Fritzi Ridgeway (Reno Maggie); Louise Beavers (Ivory); Miriam Goldina (The Mexican Woman); Purnell Prat (John Hartman); Esther Howard (Clara Newman); Ruth Lyons (Gertie); Hilda Vaughn (Millie); Jane Darwell (Mrs. Turner); Mary Foy (Mrs. Lowry); Noel Francis (Thelma); Theodore von Eltz (Frazer); Evelyn Preer (Black Woman).

The very talented Sylvia Sidney, of the large soulful eyes, made a specialty of playing fortune's fool in a long series of Depression era screen dramas. Her home studio, Paramount Pictures, cast her in this "realistic" drama of women-behind-bars. It was one of the first of many that Hollywood would release over the decades. Because this was produced in the pre-censorship code days of the early 1930s, both the dialogue and situations could be more mature and blatant than later would be the case.

Kathleen Storm (Sylvia Sidney) is employed in a flower shop and comes to the attention of handsome mining engineer Standish McNeil (Gene Raymond), recently returned from Mexico. At first she thinks him flippant, but soon they fall in love. All the while, Kathleen is fearful that her sordid past may catch up with her. She had previously been the object of interest to gangster Kid Athens (Earle Foxe), a passionately jealous hoodlum who swore he would kill any other man with whom she became involved. Standish, who is considering a new assignment in Russia, convinces the nervous Kathleen to marry him. On their wedding day, Athens arrives at her apartment. When a policeman appears to question her about Athens's whereabouts, Athens shoots the cop, leaving the telltale gun behind. This leads to the arrest of Kathleen and Standish. Based on circumstantial evidence, McNeil is sentenced to be executed and Kathleen, as an "accessory," is sent to prison for life.

Once inside the "big house," Kathleen convinces sympathetic Warden Hecker (Frank Sheridan) to review the facts in her case. He arranges for her to meet with the assistant district attorney (Rockliffe Fellowes), who turns out to be a stooge working with Athens. Thus, the corrupt prosecutor refuses to "believe" her case. Meanwhile, Kathleen encounters a variety of convict types: the hardbitten Susie Thompson (Wynne Gibson), a pregnant Mexican woman (Miriam Goldina), the aristocratic The Countess (Edna Bennett), the black Ivory (Louise Beavers) and the sniveling snitch Reno Maggie (Fritzi Ridgeway).

Life is difficult at best for the sensitive Kathleen, not only coping with the bleak ways of prison and the strict matrons, but in figuring out some way to help her condemned husband. Discouraged and desperate, she participates in a breakout attempt, hoping the attendant publicity will draw attention to her situation. The escape fails, but the case is publicized by the newspapers. One of

Sylvia Sidney in *Ladies of the Big House* (1932).

Kathleen's co-convicts recognizes a news picture of the murder weapon, a gun she had given Athens. With her testimony and the later confession of the culprit, Kathleen and Standish are soon freed and reunited.

Ernest Booth had authored several stories with prison settings, and being a prisoner himself, his fiction had the ring of authenticity. *Variety* applauded the production as "Superlatively made and faultlessly played," adding that it was "A picture with intense human appeal that abundantly compensates for its depressing atmosphere within a jail." Regarding the penitentiary ambiance, the trade paper judged, "It conveys the sense of grim monotony, but still it has human highlights that give it compelling interest." Andre Sennwald *(New York Times)* noted, "For the normal citizen the routine lives of the men and women, with numbers instead of names, have a cold and rather terrifying fascination. The new film manages to convey this terror with a fair measure of success. An atmosphere of shadows and desolation clings even to those scenes in which love is mostly plainly seen to be finding a way." *Harrison's Reports* observed, "There is some comedy in the prison caused by the bickering of the women prisoners, but for the most part it is depressing and morbid...." From the perspective of time, Bruce Crowther wrote in *Captured on Film: The Prison Movie* (1989), "[T]he movie's chief merits lie in its unflinching (for its day) look at conditions in a penitentiary for women. Even the prison stereotypes: a blowzy gangster's moll, an upper-class dame, the hard-faced muscular matron, are done with panache."

Gene Raymond would play another condemned man in Paramount's *If I Had a Million,* q.v., later in 1932 and Sylvia Sidney would be involved in several dramas in which she and/or her boyfriend was just going in or out of prison (e.g. *You Only Live Once,* 1937, q.v.). The ever-candid Miss Sidney, in discussing her screen career in a December 1989 conversation with *Interview* magazine, recalled that many of her early movies had bad scripts which made acting in them quite difficult:

> Oh, lots of times it was. It's like that line in *Ladies of the Big House*: I say, "You can't kill a man with kindness," and then I faint. What kind of a line is that? Extremely thin. I got through it. There's no other way to end the scene—and also everybody else thinks that's the greatest line that was ever written.

149. *Ladies They Talk About* (Warner Bros., 1933), 68 min.

Producer, Ray Griffith; directors, Howard Bretherton, William Keighley; based on the play *Women in Prison* by Dorothy Mackaye, Carlton Miles; screenplay, Sidney Sutherland, Brown Holmes, William McGrath; art director, Esdras Hartley; costumes, Orry-Kelly; music director, Leo F. Forbstein; camera, John Seitz; editor, Basil Wrangel.

Barbara Stanwyck (Nan Taylor); Preston S. Foster (David Slade); Lyle Talbot (Don); Dorothy Burgess (Susie); Lillian Roth (Linda); Maude Eburne (Aunt Maggie); Harold Huber (Lefty); Ruth Donnelly (Noonan); Robert Warwick (The Warden); Helen Ware (Miss Johnson); DeWitt Jennings (Tracy); Robert McWade (District Attorney); Cecil Cunningham (Mrs. Arlington); Helen Mann (Blondie); Grace Cunard (Marie); Madame Sul-Te-Wan (Mustard); Harold Healy (Dutch); Harry Gribbon (Bank Guard); Snowball (Parrot); William Keighley (Man Getting a Shoeshine); Isabel Withers (Convict); Harry C. Bradley (Reformer); Davison Clark (Chief at Jail); Ferris Taylor (Reformer on Stage); Helen Dickson (Matron with Cigar).

A year after *Ladies of the Big House,* q.v., Warner Bros. released its own variation on the theme. *Ladies They Talk About* featured contract star Barbara

Stanwyck as a small town deacon's daughter who, after enduring reform school, goes from bad to worse—before she reforms. The scenario may have been ludicrous, but the versatile cast was game and the ribald dialogue received excellent handling from the tough dames behind bars.

Nan Taylor (Barbara Stanwyck) is arrested on suspicion of having been an accomplice in a bank holdup. Evangelist David Slade (Preston Foster), who knew Nan when they were children, believes her protestations of innocence. Just as she is about to be released into his custody, she admits to him that she was actually guilty of the crime. She adds that, thanks to his influence, she wants to begin life anew. Now disgusted with her, David refuses to sign her parole papers. As a result, the embittered young woman confesses to the district attorney (Robert McWade) of her complicity in the robbery. She is sentenced to the women's section of San Quentin Prison for three years. During that period, and against her will, David keeps in touch with her, through visits and letters. He even stymies a jailbreak Nan is involved in, which costs the lives of two co-prisoners. When she is finally released, she visits Slade at his revival meetings headquarters and shoots him. Only then does she realize she actually loves the man and is thankful that the wound is superficial.

What gave this contrived melodramatic plotline its bite, was the dialogue among the women prisoners, which ranged from the tough-as-nails Susie (Dorothy Burgess) to the more friendly Linda (Lillian Roth) and including such exotic types as Mustard (Madame Sul-Te-Wan) and the wise-cracking, ex-madam, Aunt Maggie (Maude Eburne).

> SUSIE: Say, there isn't any punishment bad enough for you.
>
> NAN: Yeah. Well, being penned up here with a daffodil like you comes awful close.

Later, Linda provides newcomer Nan with a tour of the drab establishment:

> LINDA: And here, we find the dining room, connected with the morgue.
>
> NAN: Is the food that bad?
>
> LINDA: Well, it's cooked by three dames up here for poisoning.
>
> NAN: What did they use on ya?
>
> LINDA: Beans, mostly.

In reviewing the picture, *Variety* observed that the goings-on in the women's quarters of the prison—with its snappy dialogue—gave the movie its zest. "In *Ladies They Talk About*, San Quentin is a great retreat, the sort of a place where a lot of gals might like to spend a vacation until something or other blew over.... Warners made prison life for men not half bad in *20,000 Years in Sing Sing* [q.v.]. They've give the girls an even better break here." Andre Sennwald (*New York Times*) reported, "*Ladies They Talk About* is effective when it is describing the behavior of the prisoners, the variety of their misdemeanors, their positions in the social whirl outside, their ingenuity in giving an intimate domestic tough to the prison, and their frequently picturesque way of exhibiting pride, jealousy, vanity and other untrammeled feminine emotions."

In retrospect, Ella Smith (*Starring Miss Barbara Stanwyck,* 1974) pointed out about this motion picture:

> While it may not sound like it, the film was attempting to make a serious state-ment. These women were not having the "jolly time of it" that reviewers thought. They were trying to keep from going nuts. Denied the two things they wanted most—"freedom and men"—they used laughs defensively. And the treatment was authentic.... The attitude of the film's characters—as well as the fancied-up decor of the cells that nobody believed either—was meant to give a true picture of prison life.

Ladies They Talk About was based on a stage play that had been produced in Los Angeles starring Dorothy Mackaye, who had co-authored the drama. In the course of the film melodrama, Lillian Roth (as Linda) sings a bluesy number, while starring at a picture of Joe E. Brown (then a studio contract comedian). Co-director William Keighley makes a brief appearance in the movie as a man having a shoe-shine. The compact movie was shot in a brief twenty-four days.

A.k.a.: *Women in Prison.*

150. *Lady in the Death House* (Producers Releasing Corp., 1944), 56 min.

Producer, Jack Schwarz; director, Steve Sekely; story, Fred C. Davis; screenplay, Harry O. Hoyt; art director, Frank Sylos; music, Jan Gray; camera, Gus Peterson; editor, Robert O. Crandall.

Jean Parker (Mary); Lionel Atwill (Finch); Douglas Fowley (Brad); Marcia Mae Jones (Suzy); Robert Middlemass (State's Attorney); Cy Kendall (Detective); John Maxwell (Snell); George Irving (Gregory); Forrest Taylor (Warden).

One of the few Hollywood films, besides *The Traveling Executioner* (1970), q.v., to deal with the occupation of a prisoner executioner. In this budget whodunit, the executioner is even the hero!

Much of the story is told in flashback. State executioner Brad (Douglas Fowley)—who is also a scientist studying the possibilities of reviving the dead—and criminologist Finch (Lionel Atwill) save Mary (Jean Parker) when her dress catches on fire in a cafe. Brad becomes enamored of Mary, but she refuses his mar-riage proposal because of his abhorrent vocation. Neither man knows that Mary has a troublesome past, which includes being blackmailed by a racketeer (George Irving) who threatens to expose her father's criminal past to her employer. Moreover, Mary is plagued by her rebellious younger sister, Suzy (Marcia Mae Jones), who insists on a relationship with the shady Snell (John Maxwell). When the hoodlum is murdered mysteriously in Mary's apartment, she seems the likely suspect. She is tried and convicted on circumstantial evidence and is sentenced to die in the electric chair.

Finch investigates the case and begins unraveling the jigsaw puzzle of clues. He finds a car key on the floor at Mary's apartment. Suzy admits it belongs to Snell. Suzy joins with the criminologist to capture Snell who, in turn, confesses he murdered the man for a large roll of money he had. Finch and Suzy rush their evidence to the warden (Forrest Taylor). However, the governor cannot be reached and the warden demands that Brad carry out the electrocution. Mary is made to walk the last mile to the death chair. At the last minute, Brad locks himself in the room where the switch is. Meanwhile, the governor is located and he grants a timely reprieve.

Variety complained that *"Lady in the Death House* is an overcharged meller that's short on credibility and dated in its dramatic motif." A more kindly reviewer *(Hollywood Reporter)* suggested, "The combination of good performances, excellent direction and effective editing serve to lift the picture above the plane of mediocrity.... The manner of treating the story also has the faculty of removing the oppressive gloom which permeates most prison films."

Working title: *Her Last Mile.*

151. *The Last Mile* (World Wide, 1932), 75 min.

Producer, E. W. Hammons; director, Sam Bischoff, based on the play by John Wexley and the book *The Law Takes Its Toll* by Robert Blake; screenplay, Seton I. Miller; set designer, Ralph DeLacy; music director, Val Burton; camera, Arthur Edeson; editors, Martin G. Cohn, Rose Loewinger.

Preston S. Foster ("Killer" John Mears); Howard Phillips (Richard Walters); George E. Stone (Berg); Noel Madison (D'Amoro); Alan Roscoe (Kirby); Paul Fix (Eddie Werner); Al Hill (Fred Mayer); Daniel L. Haynes (Sonny Jackson); Alec B. Francis (Father O'Connor); Edward Van Sloan (Rabbi); Louise Carter (Mrs. Walters); Ralph Theodore (Pat Callahan, the Principal Keeper); Frank Sheridan (Warden Frank Lewis); Albert J. Smith (Drake); Kenneth MacDonald (Harris); Walter Walker (Governor Blaine); Francis McDonald (Holdup Man); William Scott (Peddie, the Guard); Jack Kennedy (O'Flaherty, the Guard).

On February 13, 1930, four months after *The Criminal Code* debuted on Broadway, *The Last Mile* premiered at New York's Sam H. Harris Theatre. Like *The Criminal Code*, *The Last Mile* was set in a (Oklahoma) prison and its stark drama examined the psychology of men-behind-bars pushed to their utmost limits. In the cast of *The Last Mile*, John Wexley's stage piece was a hard-hitting argument against capital punishment. Directed by Chester Erskine and featuring James Bell, Joseph Calleia, Henry O'Neill, Howard Phillips, Bruce MacFarlane and Hale Norcross, the show piece starred Spencer Tracy. The focal role of the anti-hero Killer John Mears made a Broadway star of Tracy, who, along with the play, received glowing notices.

The critical and public response to *The Criminal Code* and *The Last Mile* led Hollywood to refocus on prison dramas as a likely subject for future films. The first of the cycle was MGM's *The Big House* (1930), q.v., followed by Fox's *Up The River* (1930), q.v., a prison comedy/drama featuring Spencer Tracy in his screen debut. While *The Criminal Code*, q.v., reached the screen in 1931, *The Last Mile* did not make the transition to the film medium until 1932. By then, while still a powerful subject, it was not considered as trendsetting as had been the stage adaptation.

The action of *The Last Mile* is set on a prison's Death Row, where an assortment of convicted men await their executions. A new inmate on the row is Richard Walters (Howard Phillips), scheduled to die on September 13th for murder in the first degree. As his cell neighbor, Killer John Mears (Preston Foster), advises the newcomer, "We call 'em by numbers here, names don't mean much from now on." With each man penned in his cell, Walters soon feels like the other caged animals, all hoping against hope for a stay of execution or a miraculous pardon. Among Walters's other neighbors are Sonny Jackson (Daniel L. Haynes), a black man who sings spiritual songs. There is Eddie Werner (Paul Fix), in cell #8, who has been judged temporarily insane (stir crazy) and has received a stay of execution. Berg

(George E. Stone), in cell #1, is preparing to walk "the last mile" tonight. Nervous about his pending execution, the condemned man asks, "Why do I have to die?" and receives comfort from a rabbi (Edward Van Sloan). Managing bravado at the end, Berg sings "My Blue Heaven" as he is led by the guards on his final walk. "So long everybody. Goodbye. . . . Goodbye." Soon the lights dim, indicating Berg has been executed. One of the survivors on the row blurts out, "You've gotta give him [Berg] credit. He had nerve!" For these men, that is the finest compliment.

There are other occupants on the row besides prisoners. Among the guards there is the sadistic Drake (Albert J. Smith) who delights in taunting these now defenseless men, all of whom are under his control. When their yammering gets too much, he blasts his radio at the guard desk to drown out their complaints and pleas. An occasional visitor to the row is Warden Frank Lewis (Frank Sheridan), whose presence always foreshadows another inmate going to his death. The administrator is unsure that capital punishment is really effective: "One after the other, they stop breathing. I wonder if it is of any use? I wonder afterwards if they know they've been punished?"

Meanwhile, stunned by his situation, young Walters thinks back on the events that led to his being imprisoned. He and his partner had owned a gas station but had not been getting along. Their business had been robbed by several gangsters and, in the mêlée, the partner had been killed. Through circumstantial evidence, Walters had been convicted of the crime and sentenced to die. His mother has valiantly been applying to the governor for a stay of execution, insisting her son is innocent.

Father O' Connor (Alec B. Francis) is a frequent guest on the row, trying to comfort these lost souls. His toughest "customer" is Mears who insists he is not afraid to die and who claims he has no use for religion. However, his pending demise weighs heavily on the killer and when the opportunity arises—on the night of Walters's scheduled execution—he grabs hold of Drake the guard and yanks away his keys. Soon all the men on the row are unlocked from their cells, although crazed Eddie Werner remains cowered. "I'm out. I'm not #5 any more. I'm free!" Walters enthuses. Mears takes several guards hostage and makes demands of the warden, threatening to kill the keepers if his conditions are not met.

The warden, refusing to be intimidated, instructs his guards:

> Get those cons into the dungeons dead or alive. Turn those machine guns loose on all the empty cells. Pour lead into every spot that you can reach. Get bombs on the walks and, if the machine guns don't stop them, we'll blow in the side of the cell block.

The undaunted Mears kills Drake, who at the end turns into a snivelling coward. Among the guards left alive is Pat Callahan (Ralph Theodore), the principal keeper and the warden's brother-in-law. Mears forces Callahan and the other survivors to talk on the phone with the warden, wanting the administrator to realize he means business. The captured priest, brave throughout, attempts to calm the frightened Callahan, reminding him that such dangerous situations are part of his duty. The agitated principal keeper responds, "Who cares about duty when it means our life?"

After several more barrages of machine gun bullets from the guard towers, many of the convicts on death row are dead. By now, Mears realizes that the situation is hopeless. "They'll try to get all of us. We're just a lot of animals. A lot of monkeys in a cage." Knowing that the end is near, Mears no longer can hide his fears or that fact that, beneath his tough exterior, he has normal emotions: "Don't you think I want to live? Don't you think I want to be free. I want to walk in the sun. I want to see an ocean. I want to see a woman again."

As the battle continues, Walters is injured by the rampaging Mears, but the latter realizes that "the kid" has a chance, especially if a last minute reprieve from the governor should arrive. To save the young man, Mears, the last holdout, announces "I think I'll go get a little air." He walks towards the gaping hole in the prison wall, heading to the exercise yard. A volley of machine gun bullets quickly kill him. The riot is over. News comes through that Walters's petition for a pardon has been granted by the governor. One of the actual killers of the boy's partner has confessed the full details, thus clearing Walters.

Mordaunt Hall *(New York Times)* judged *The Last Mile* "grim and gruesome" and that "most of the roles are acted with the necessary vehemence and realism." However, he pointed out that "the diluted screen adaptation" did not have the impact of the Broadway play, even with Howard Phillips recreating his role of Richard Walters (which had been enlarged for the screen). For Hall, many of the artifices which had worked so well on stage, seemed overexaggerated on the big screen. He indicated that the character of Drake the guard "is scarcely true to life, for the man is far too vicious to be credible."

Variety was more direct in analyzing the flaws of this diminished screen adaptation which found the character of Richard Walters not dying as in the original play for the murder of his sweetheart, but surviving his persecution as an innocent victim of circumstantial evidence. *Variety* noted that when *The Last Mile* had been a Broadway hit, the public's consciousness about the penal system was at a peak due to recent riots at Auburn and Dannemora Prisons. The trade paper assessed that a rash of prison dramas had weakened the potential impact of *The Last Mile* as a movie and that the adaptation "compromises with the stage original in many ways, toning down its grim realism . . . and sugar-coating the finale with a happy release of a youth unjustly convicted of murder." Additionally, *Variety* observed, "The searing earnestness of the play is missing here, the play having been manipulated in its vital points to make it endurable as a picture." On the other hand, *Variety* agreed, "Acting is excellent, especially commendable, being the restraint. . . . Indeed, there are times when the acting is too good for comfort, as these players make a living reality of the doom that lies behind the steel portal through which one or the other of them is soon to walk."

The Last Mile was not a box office success, already considered something of a museum piece in the film industry which was developing its own special idiom for the prison movie genre. Nevertheless, just as *The Criminal Code* would be resurrected several times by Hollywood, so too would *The Last Mile* be remade. See *infra*.

When *The Last Mile* was first distributed in 1932 it contained a special anti-capital punishment foreword by Warden Lewis E. Lawes of Sing Sing Prison. It was Lawes who authored *20,000 Years in Sing Sing* (1932) which was turned into a drama by Warner Bros. in 1933, q.v., starring Spencer Tracy.

152. *The Last Mile* (United Artists, 1959), 81 min.

Producers, Max J. Rosenberg, Milton Subotsky; associate producers, Roberta Hodes, Herman Kappert; director, Howard W. Koch; based on the play by John

Ford Rainey and Mickey Rooney in *The Last Mile* (1959).

Wexley and the book *The Law Takes Its Course* by Robert Blake; screenplay, Subotsky, Seton I. Miller; production designer, Paul Barnes; set decorator, Jack Wright, Jr.; costumes, Frank Thompson; makeup, Robert Jiras; music, Van Alexander; assistant director, Charles Maguire; sound, Dick Gramablia; special effects, Milton Olson, Vincent Brady; camera, Joseph Brun; editors, Robert Brockman, Patricia Jaffe.

Mickey Rooney ("Killer" John Mears); Alan Bunce (Stanley F. Stone, the Warden); Frank Conroy (O'Flaherty, the Guard); Leon Janney (Callahan, the Guard); Frank Overton (Father O'Connors); Clifford David (Convict Richard Walters); Harry Millard (Convict Fred Mayor); John McCurry (Convict Vince Jackson); Ford Rainey (Convict Red Kirby); John Seven (Convict Tom D'Amoro); Michael Constantine (Convict Ed Werner); John Vari (Convict Jimmy Martin); Donald Barry (Drake, the Guard); Clifton James (Harris, the Guard); Milton Selzer (Peddie, the Guard); George Marcy (Convict Peter Rodriguez).

If the 1932 edition of *The Last Mile,* see *supra,* is strident and near hysterical, it is a masterpiece compared to this trashy, updated version also shot in economical black-and-white. Whatever integrity was inherent in the original stage drama was vitiated by the blatant hamming of star Mickey Rooney, the fumbling of the supporting cast, the intrusive jazz score of Van Alexander, and the tackiness of the sets. The movie is filled with supposedly meaningful pregnant pauses and several arty blackouts/fadeouts to smooth the transitions from scene to scene. The gimmick of this production was having America's one-time favorite screen teenager, Mickey Rooney (of Andy Hardy movie series fame), play the tough-as-nails Killer Mears. His performance is compelling, but for the wrong reasons (i.e. its awfulness).

A gratuitous prologue advises:

> The picture you are about to see is based on an actual incident which occurred in a prison in the American southwest some time ago.
> Since that time the treatment of prisoners and the choice, selection and training of prison guards and prison personnel has been improved enormously through the more humane methods of modern scientific penology.
> The characters in the film, however, are fictitious and are not to be considered as typical of either the American penal system or the people who carry it out.

Richard Walters (Clifford Davis) is a new prisoner on death row, sentenced to die in the electric chair on the 15th of the month of first degree murder. As he introduces himself to the other condemned men on the row, sadistic guard Drake (Donald Barry) delights in telling the bewildered Walters, "You got here just in time kid to watch the big parade, to watch #2 go through that door." The pugnacious Killer John Mears (Mickey Rooney) advises the newcomer, "Nobody has nerve when they walk through that door. Nerve.... Huh!" Another inmate (John Seven) insists, "It takes twice as much juice if you're head's not shaved."

As the days pass on death row, Walters shares his memories and fears with his cellblock neighbors, all of them hoping for a last-minute reprieve to extend their lives. Each in his own way expresses his hatred and humiliation for being caged like animals waiting to be slaughtered by the minions of the state. Father O'Connors (Frank Overton), a frequent visitor to the row, tries to instill religious belief in the men, particularly Mears. However, the tough Mears refuses to yield to the clergyman: "What are you asking me to do, believe in another world.... Faith. I've got two lousy weeks left and you're asking me to have faith."

On the night that Walters is to be executed, Mears is taunted once too often by Drake. Mears reaches out through the cell bars and grabs Drake, nearly strangling him and grabbing his keys. Freeing the other men, except for the crazy Ed Werner (Michael Constantine) who remains in his cell, the convicts rush to the guard room where they take the keepers hostage. Before long the enraged Mears has shot and threatens to kill the remaining keepers if the warden (Alan Bunce) does not accede to his demands. As Mears reasons, it does not matter to the convicts if they get a bullet through the head or go through that green door to be electrocuted. Later, Mears allows O'Flaherty the guard (Frank Conroy), the warden's brother-in-law, to leave the block to tell the warden personally just how much the rioting convicts mean business. When Mears selects Father O'Connors to be his next victim, Walters objects and while struggling with Mears, Walters is injured. A contrite Mears decides to surrender so that Walters can be treated at the prison hospital. However, Walters begs him to shoot him so he will not have to be the next victim in the electric chair. Mears obliges. He then walks into the open court and is shot dead by the guards.

The new *The Last Mile* suffers from a very draggy first half. However, it added lots of bloody violence to the finale to whet the moviegoers' appetites. But reasoned Howard Thompson *(New York Times),* "[T]hirty years of prison films make the climactic commotion seem all too familiar...." As for Mickey Rooney's focal performance as the brutal killer, Thompson decided, "But to watch his rather youthful countenance shifting expressions like gears as he snarls battle orders to his towering colleagues doesn't quite cut ice — for all the gore and gunfire." *Variety* characterized the production as "A throwback to the 'prison break' cycle of pictures" and observed that it "picks up speed in the second half and ends up with enough mayhem to keep the action crowd happy." In examining the subject matter, the trade paper reasoned, "If one accepts the theory that films like *The Last Mile* make for good entertainment, this picture certainly packs quite a wallop. Inevitably, the audience must identify with the men waiting for the hour of execution, and it's a fairly sickening sensation that produces both tension and terror."

The 1959 *The Last Mile* was shot in New York. The advertising campaign for *The Last Mile* insisted, "The Man. . . . The Role. . . . The Story That Sent a Million Volts Across the Broadway Stage! . . . The One in Front Is Killer Mears . . . Who Led a Pack of Lifers Out of Death Row. . . . and Dared the World to Stop Him! . . . Caught . . . caged like an animal condemned to die—and now he shouted his defiance to the world. . . . 'No one's gonna burn me . . . no one's gonna drag me down The Last Mile—alive!'"

153. *Leadbelly* (Paramount, 1976), color, 126 min.

Executive producer, David Frost; producer, Marc Merson; associate producer, Jack Grossberg; director, Gordon Parks; screenplay, Ernest Kinoy; production designer, Robert Boyle; set decorator, John Kuri; music/music director, Fred Karlin; music technical adviser, John Oliver; choreography, Dana Manno; stunt coordinator, Harold Jones; assistant director, Reuben Watt; sound, Doc Wilkinson, Gene Cantamessa; special effects, Pat Patterson; camera, Bruce Surtees; editor, Harry Howard.

Roger E. Mosley (Huddie Ledbetter); Paul Benjamin (Wes Ledbetter); Madge Sinclair (Miss Eula); Alan Manson (Captain Freeman); Albert P. Hall (Dicklicker); Art Evans (Blind Lemon Jefferson); James E. Brodhead (John Lomax); John Henry Faulk (Governor Neff); Vivian Bonnell (Old Lady); Dana Manno (Margaret Judd); Timothy Pickard (Gray Man); Lynn Hamilton (Sally Ledbetter); Loretta Greene (Lethe); Valerie Odell (Amy); Rozaa Jean (Sugar Tit); Nat Williams (Albert); George Williams (Shorty); Timothy Pickard (Gray Man); William Creamer (Conductor); Dearl Croft (Frank); John C. Johnson (Will); Bill Woodard (Alex); Robert C. Farrow (Blacksmith); Peter Harrell (Ally George); B. T. Henderson (1st Boss); Denny Arnold (2nd Boss); James Taylor (Dog Boy); Drew Thomason (Sharecropper); Robert Keith, Leonard Wrentz (Guards).

The legendary Leadbelly (Huddie Ledbetter: 1888–1949) was one of the first southern black folk singers to gain a national reputation in the United States. He was an expert with the 12-string guitar and was a major factor in reviving interest in folk music, with his versions of such landmark folk songs as "Rock Island Line," "Goodnight Irene," "The Midnight Special" and "On Top of Old Smoky." This affectionate, poignant biography focuses on the musician's rugged life up through 1933, during which time he served two terms in southern prisons for homicide (1918–1925) and for attempted murder (1930–1934). For black film director/still photographer Gordon Parks, who made his biggest impact in motion pictures with the black action pictures *Shaft* (1971) and *Shaft's Big Score* (1972), *Leadbelly* was a return to the lyrical nostalgia provided by his debut feature film, *The Learning Tree* (1968). For muscular star Roger E. Mosley, who provides a thoughtful sensitive characterization in the lead role, it was a change-of-pace role from his earlier action films (e.g. *Terminal Island*, 1973, q.v.) and his later work as T.C. in the long-running teleseries "Magnum, P.I." (1980–88).

In 1933 two musicologists, John (James E. Brodhead) and Alan Lomax come to Louisiana's Angola Prison where they record the songs and life story of the ageing Huddie Ledbetter (Roger E. Mosley). In flashback, Huddie recalls his turbulent life. He relates how he fled his hometown after getting involved in a fight over Margaret Judd (Dana Manno) whom he leaves pregnant, and how he then drifted to Shreveport. There he becomes associated with the madam Miss Eula (Madge Sinclair). It is she who names him Leadbelly, buys him clothes and gives him a guitar which he soon plays in the saloon run by Shorty (George Williams). Soon Leadbelly becomes a leading attraction of Fannin' Street in the red light district. However, as a result of a police raid, he leaves town, hopping a freight train bound for Texas. There he picks cotton and becomes involved with Lethe (Loretta Greene). But the restless man is too full of wanderlust to settle down.

Once again on the road, Leadbelly encounters Blind Lemon Jefferson (Art Evans) and the two musicians become friends and agree to play music together. On one occasion, when they are denied payment at a white dance, a fight breaks out. As a result, Leadbelly is imprisoned. He escapes and drifts back to Lethe.

Still later, Leadbelly attends a dance where he quarrels with a friend, Alex (Bill Woodard), and shoots him in self defense. He is sentenced to thirty years' imprisonment. Thereafter, he escapes from a Texas chain gang, pursued by the guards and their dogs, and is shot in the arm during his recapture. His aged father (Paul Benjamin) attempts to buy his release, but to no avail. Leadbelly learns to play an ethnic type of music style and performs a song which he sings for the patronizing Governor Pat Neff (John Henry Faulk) at a party. As a result he earns a pardon. He returns to Fannin' Street, saddened to learn that everything is now run down. He meets his illegitimate daughter (Valerie Odell) and later is attacked by three white sharecroppers. Because he kills one of the rednecks in self-defense he finds himself back on the chain gang. It is at this time that he is found by the Lomaxes who plan to take his songs to the Library of Congress. With his parole due in six months, Huddie plans to devote the remainder of his life to crossing the country and singing his songs.

In examining the structure of *Leadbelly*, Vincent Canby (*New York Times*) judged, "It's done in bold strokes of incident and color. . . . This Leadbelly is bigger than life — and serenely removed from it. Which is why, I think, one attends to the film carefully and is never very moved." Michael Grossbard (British *Monthly Film Bulletin*) had reservations about the production, "*Leadbelly* emerges as little more than the traditional biopic molasses." Regarding Leadbelly's musical renditions, Grossbard judged, "The songs used . . . are among the finest popular poetry of our century. . . . Unfortunately, they are rendered in an adequate but less than inspired fasion by HiTide Harris, while the film as a whole seems to have little sense of the idiom and style of the songs. . . ." *Variety* was much more impressed by this screen biography: "The odyssey becomes vivid and constantly intriguing through the fine development and characterizations of the featured players." *Variety* approved of Roger E. Mosley's characterization, "As depicted here, Leadbelly emerges as a whole human being — sometimes willful, sometimes selfish, sometimes generous to a fault, etc. — which is still a rarity in pop-arts dramaturgy."

While making *Leadbelly*, filmmaker Gordon Parks remarked that the subject's life "had actually been far more brutal than we could show it in the film." This hesitancy to reflect the facts more accurately was a major flaw of the production. Reviewing the picture in retrospect, Donald Bogle (*Blacks in American Films and Television*, 1988) decided, "Leadbelly's various scrapes with the law and the violence that were so much a part of his existence have been softened and left

unexplained. That same softening is true of the other characters and incidents in the film. . . . The lush, bright cinematography of Bruce Surtees simply adds to the inappropriate lush romanticism of *Leadbelly*."

Whatever its faults, *Leadbelly* offers a compelling picture of the hell of prison life, especially in the deep south of pre-civil rights days, when black prisoners were even more persecuted than their white incarcerated brethren. The scenes of the bigoted chief prison guard (Alan Manson) dealing harshly with black inmates, like so many rambunctious unfortunates who need stern reprimanding, are chilling. Equally effective is the moment when a fellow chain gang prisoner (Albert P. Hall) tells Leadbelly about survival under these brutal conditions, "when they're out to kill ya, living is winning." Like other earlier films dealing with life on the chain gang — *I Am a Fugitive from a Chain Gang* (1932), *Hell's Highway* (1932) and *Cool Hand Luke* (1967), qq.v. — *Leadbelly* is a telling reflection of the price paid by convicts treated like enslaved animals.

At the time of its release, there was a much-publicized contretemps between Gordon Parks and the film's distributor, Paramount Pictures. Parks claimed that not only did the company fail to give the production its promised big New York opening, but that it mispromoted the thoughtful feature as yet another black exploitation action entry. *Leadbelly* was a financial flop.

154. *Let Us Live* (Columbia, 1939), 66 min.

Producer, William Perlberg; director, John Brahm; based on the book *Murder in Massachusetts* by Joseph F. Dineen; screenplay, Anthony Veiller, Allen Rivkin; art director, Lionel Banks; music, Karol Rathaus; music director, Morris W. Stoloff; camera, Lucien Ballard; editor, Al Clark.

Maureen O'Sullivan (Mary Roberts); Henry Fonda ("Brick" Tennant); Ralph Bellamy (Lieutenant Everett); Alan Baxter (Joe Lindon); Stanley Ridges (District Attorney); Henry Kolker (Chief of Police); Peter Lynn (Joe Taylor); George Douglas (Ed Walsh); Philip Trent (Frank Burke); Martin Spellman (Jimmy Dugan); Charles Trowbrige (Judge); Dick Elliott (Rotarian Juror); Alec Craig (Bookkeeper Juror); Byron Foulger (Defense Attorney); Harry Holman (Businessman Juror); Emmett Bradley (Driver); Betty Farrington (Mother Juror); Al Herman (Garage Attendant Juror); Jessie Perry (Head of P.T.A. Juror); Bill Lee (Public Accountant Juror); Harry Bailey (Drug Clerk Juror); Phil Dunham (Nervous Man Juror); John Qualen (Dan); William Mong (Joe Taylor, Sr.); Ian Maclaren (Priest); Clarence Wilson (Lunchroom Proprietor); Ray Walker (Fred Robinson); Beatrice Curtis (Waitress); Eddie Laughton (Cab Driver); Ann Doran (Secretary Juror); Dick Curtis (Cellmate); Jim Blaine, Monte Vandergrift, Ted Oliver (Detectives); Herbert Heywood (Theatre Watchman); William Royle (Prison Guard); Edmund Cobb (Blair); Tom London (Police Sergeant); George Chesebro (Jail Guard); Lee Shumway (Warden's Attendant); Bess Wade (Woman); Philip Morris, Eric Alden, Lee Phelps (Cops).

That prison can break a man's spirit instead of reforming his soul has long been well recognized. Within *Let Us Live*, Henry Fonda, prototype "Everyman" of the 1930s, is reduced to a shattered shell when his character is convicted erroneously of first degree murder and sentenced to die in the electric chair. His screen persona's harrowing plight is depicted graphically in this motion picture, although the impact is vitiated by a pat scenario and the overuse of stereotypical characterizations by the supporting cast. The premise of *Let Us Live* was based on actual events in 1934 when two Boston cab drivers were pointed out by witnesses

Opposite: Roger E. Mosley *(in chains)* in *Leadbelly* (1976).

as having been those who robbed a Lynn, Massachusetts, cinema, killing one victim in the process. During the defendants' trial, three men were arrested in New York who confessed to the crime. The cab drivers were freed, while the criminals were later executed. Because the Commonwealth of Massachusetts was extremely sensitive about this near miscarriage of justice, Columbia Pictures was pressured to alter/disguise the facts of the original case when making *Let Us Live*.

Acknowledging that *Let Us Live* did not present a really new theme, Frank S. Nugent *(New York Times)* nevertheless approved of director John Brahm's efforts to balance action sequences with probing psychological motivations. "What, after all must happen to a man who finds himself victimized by a legal machine which he always had regarded as his protector? That is the essence of Mr. Brahm's drama, the quality which raises it above the death-house thriller class and gives it dignity and maturity." The more jaded *Variety* complained, "As a preachment, it serves a purpose, but falls short of providing sufficient audience appeal for general entertainment. . . . Story is slow and rather ponderous, with ending obvious as soon as Fonda is picked up as a suspect."

Taxi cab driver Brick Tennant (Henry Fonda) drives his girlfriend Mary Roberts (Maureen O'Sullivan) to church. While she is inside he remains in the car. Meanwhile, around the corner, three crooks rob a movie theatre, killing a guard in the process. The criminals then escape in a cab. Later, the police bring in all the taxi drivers who operated such a cab, including Brick and his cab driver-roommate Joe Lindon (Alan Baxter). Based on circumstantial evidence, the two men — who protest their innocence as does Mary — are sentenced to die in the electric chair. The frantic Mary researches the case and uncovers new evidence which she presents to police Lieutenant Everett (Ralph Bellamy). He believes her story and even resigns his post so he can continue the investigation. Finally, on the day the two prisoners are to be electrocuted, Mary and Everett ferret out the actual killers. Joined by the police, they corral the lawbreakers and recover the stolen money. Upon re-examination, the theatre employees who witnessed the robbery now corroborate that the newly-captured men are the real culprits. Brick and Joe are finally released. The emotionally tattered Brick leaves prison a near-broken man, having lost faith in mankind except for Everett.

Henry Fonda made two other mistaken identity films on a similar theme: *You Only Live Once* (1937), q.v. and Alfred Hitchcock's *The Wrong Man* (1956).

155. *The Little Red Schoolhouse* (Chesterfield, 1936), 66 min.

Producer, George R. Batcheller; director, Charles Lamont; screenplay, Paul Peez; camera, M. A. Anderson; editor, Rowland Reed.

Frank "Junior" Coghlan, Jr. (Frank Burke); Dickie Moore (Dickie Burke); Ann Doran (Mary Burke); Lloyd Hughes (Roger Owen); Richard Carle (The Professor); Ralf Harolde (Pete Scardoni); Frank Sheridan (Warden Gail); Matthew Betz (Bill); Kenneth Howell (Schuyler Tree); Sidney Miller (Sidney Levy); Gloria Browne (Shirley); Don Brodie (Ed); Lou Davis (Mac); Corky (The Dog).

The Little Red Schoolhouse, with its misleading title, was a modest, independently-produced programmer that unsuccessfully attempted to cram three divergent motifs into its brief running time. *Variety* quickly dismissed this hokey, contrived melodrama, adding, "Dialog is strictly rudimentary, and in keeping with story."

Frank Burke (Frank "Junior" Coghlan, Jr.) is embarrassed that his school teacher Roger Owen (Lloyd Hughes) is engaged to his sister (Mary). Moreover, he feels that Roger is unnecessarily picking on him in the classroom. As a result, he runs away from home. Once on the road he meets a hobo (Richard Carle) who later takes him to New York City to meet some of his criminal pals. When the gang commits a robbery/murder, Frank is implicated and as a result is sent to a reformatory. Owen learns of Frank's whereabouts and, without telling Mary of her brother's troubles, visits Frank. During their meeting, Frank escapes and Roger is blamed for the escape. He is sentenced to prison himself. Upon learning this, Frank returns and confesses the truth to the warden (Frank Sheridan). Meanwhile, the gang is caught and admits to Frank's innocence. Both he and Roger are released and they head back to their small hometown. After his bad experiences, Frank is content to return to his school regimen.

Whatever impact *The Little Red Schoolhouse* made with its "realistic" treatment of life in a reformatory/prison was diminished by its abrupt, saccharine finale. The best performance in the picture was offered by Corky the Dog. Frank Coghlan, Jr. would make something of a specialty appearing in reformatory exposé dramas: e.g. *Hell's House* (1932), *Boys' Reformatory* (1939), qq.v. Dickie Moore, of "Our Gang" comedy shorts fame, co-starred here as a precocious youngster who sings a song at the rural school's Easter festivities. Actor Frank Sheridan had also played a warden in the far superior genre piece, *The Last Mile* (1932), q.v.

156. *Lock Up* (Jericho Films, 1984), color, 95 min.

Executive producer, Michael Checkik; producers, Christian Bruyers, Tom Shandel; associate producer, Tom Braidwood; director, Shandel; screenplay, Bruyers; production designer, Graeme Murray; set decorator, Rose Marie McSherry; costumes, Trish Keding; music, J. Douglas Dood, Michael Oczko; assistant director, Bob Akester; sound editors, Jane Morrison, Ingrid Rosen; camera, Douglas McKay; additional camera, Tobias Schliessler, Trig Singer; editor, Barbara Evans.

Winston Rikert (Danny Baker); Andree Pelletier (Joan Tremblay); Alan Scarfe (Ron Simmons); John Lord (Louis Martin); Lloyd Berry (Warden Gallagher); Howard Storey (Hiller, a Guard); Antony Holland (Frank McIntyre, a Guard); Elizabeth Leigh-Milne (Karen); Perry Long (Ben Nelson); Dale Wilson (Jim Connors); Tony Morelli (Guard Hostage); Jacques Hubert (Frenchie); Raimund Stamm (The Bug); Ron Sauve (Terry); Bill Mancuma, Denis Nouveau, Kent Barrett, Christopher Haddock (Community Awareness Group); Hagan Beggs (TV Spokesman); Judith Berlin (TV Reporter); Mike Winslow (TV Announcer); Lon Katzman (Entrance Guard); Cam Lane (Solitary Keeper); John Warclow (Medic); Ted Stidver (Prison Cleaner).

In 1984–85, the Canadian Broadcasting System produced two intriguing TV dramas dealing with the deadening effects of the contemporary penal system on its victims. Besides the superior *Turning to Stone* (1985), q.v., there was *Lock Up*, which has had frequent showings on U.S. television. Although *Lock Up* is often crude in its histrionics and amateurish in its technical aspects, its raw approach provides welcome verisimilitude. In its impassioned earnestness, the telefilm owes a great deal to the social protest movies of 1930s Hollywood, which in the name of entertainment cried out for penal reforms. The inelegant but nevertheless effective *Lock Up* is a lineal descendent of such protest films. It is worth the patience required in viewing this telefeature to appreciate the cumulative affect.

At Western Penitentiary, three convicts are attempting an escape. One of the embittered men is Danny Baker (Winston Rikert), who is serving two life sentences for murder. He has spent the last five of seven years in solitary confinement. Liberal attorney Ron Simmons (Alan Scarfe) is on hand to bargain with the escapees. (He has been representing some of this prison's inmates in a class action suit against the institution for cruel and unusual punishment.) By now, the frustrated, explosive Danny has lost all patience with the slow moving legal machinery. He wants action—now! "Screw the courts! No judge is going to know the meaning of 'cruel' until he's been made to do some time in this place. No court is going to call something 'unusual' when its been going on since time began...."

Peace negotiations at Western Penitentiary have collapsed into a screaming match between the rebellious inmates and the hostile guards. Both sides are armed and willing to fight it out to the finish. As one pessimistic keeper assesses the perilous situation, "They've written themselves off." Another guard insists that if capital punishment was still in effect, they would not have this containment problem now.

A flashback details how dedicated social worker Joan Tremblay (Andree Pelletier) began moderating an experimental prisoner rehabilitation program at the penitentiary several months earlier. In her group therapy sessions with convicts, she attempts to break through Danny's hostilities. In her interchanges with Danny and other convicts she pushes the men to perceive life through the values of law-abiding people. Her do-gooder efforts are not made easier by the hard-line Warden Gallagher (Lloyd Berry) who, despite having been a prisoner for an extended period during the Korean War, cannot relate his past situation to that experienced by the men now locked up under his charge.

Just as Joan's efforts are showing positive results, everything turns sour. Frenchie (Jacques Hubert), a hallucinating convict on drug withdrawal, loses his bid for freedom with the parole board. Depressed, he strangles himself in his cell. This causes the already angry Danny to become more unmanageable. Meanwhile, an antagonistic guard sneaks a razor blade into Baker's cell, and as he hoped, Danny slits his wrists. However, he is found in time and saved. The trauma causes Danny to cooperate with Joan as well as with attorney Simmons's legal action to better prison conditions. By now, Danny feels sufficiently comfortable with Joan to confide his innermost thoughts to her. He explains how he "does his time":

> It's like going to a university, right? After five years you earn some kind of degree. I earned my masters in astro projection. I learned how to project myself into whatever time or space I wanted to be in.... If I ever told them [the prison authorities] where I went, they'd try to get me there.

Buoyed by Danny's progress, Joan selects him to deliver a keynote speech at the banquet she has arranged to introduce the prisoners in the experimental therapy group to the public officials responsible for endorsing the program. The proud Joan and benign Warden Gallagher look on, as Danny, painfully nervous but equally full of sudden self-worth, speaks candidly to the invited audience. Each heartfelt word is carefully selected. He is acutely aware that he may never have another such opportunity to champion the cause of prisoners:

> None of you know what goes on in here in the name of justice. It's time you started to realize you can't force us to abide by your laws when you subject us to torture. This only makes us angrier. It gives us more reason to fight back, no matter what the cost. We've got nothing to lose, right.

Danny's impassioned speech is respectfully received and the banquet is a great success. Or so it seems. But the self-serving guards are resentful of their prisoners suddenly having a voice in their own future. They maliciously place drugs in several of the convicts' cells. This causes the inmates to go on a rampage, which brings the narrative back to the present. The rioting inmates, who have taken hostages — including Joan — demand more narcotics. When these are delivered, they prove to be bad drugs. Feeling more betrayed than ever, the three paranoid convicts shoot it out with the trigger-happy guards. In the crossfire Joan is killed.

Soon the revolt is quelled. The rampaging convicts are locked back into solitary confinement. The guards and administration have triumphed. Everything has returned to the status quo before the reform movement.

A.k.a.: *Walls*.

157. *Lock Up* (Tri-Star, 1989), color, 103 min.

Executive producer, Michael S. Glick; producers, Lawrence Gordon, Charles Gordon; co-producers, Lloyd Levin, Adam Simon; director, John Flynn; screenplay, Richard Smith, Jeb Stuart, Henry Rosenbaum; production designer, Bill Kenney; art directors, William Ladd Skinner, Bill Groom; set decorators, Jerry Adams, Tim Galvin; costumes, Bernie Pollack; makeup, Gary Liddiard; music, Bill Conti; orchestrator, Jack Eskew; music editor, Stephen A. Hope; assistant directors, Newt Arnold, David Sosna; second unit director, David Lux; stunt coordinator, Frank Orsatti; prison adviser, Robert Vazuqez; sound, Charles Wilborn; supervising sound editor, David B. Cohn; supervising ADR editor, James Beshlars; special effects coordinator, Joe Digaetano; camera, Donald E. Thorin;

editor, Michael N. Knue, Donald Brochu.

Sylvester Stallone (Frank Leone); Donald Sutherland (Warden Drumgoole); John Amos (Captain Meissner); Sonny Landham (Chink); Tom Sizemore (Dallas); Frank McRae (Eclipse); Darlanne Fleugel (Melissa); William Allen Young (Braden); Larry Romano (First Base); Jordan Lund (Manly); John Lilla (Wiley); Dean Duval (Ernie); Jerry Strivelli (Louie Munsfo); David Anthony Marshall (Mastrone); Kurek Ashley, Micahel Petroni, Danny Trejo (Chink's Gang); Frank D'Annibale, Tony Lip, Clarence Movie, Joe Pentamgello, Eli Rick, Bo Bucker, Randy Sandkumi (Guards); Robert Vasquez (Officer Vasquez); Tony Manapo (Prisoner); Frank Pesce (Johnson); Troy Curvey, Jr. (Prison Receptionist).

For well over a decade, moviegoers had applauded the macho fantasies provided by Sylvester Stallone's Rocky and Rambo action movie series. With their crafty combination of machismo, a victorious blue collar underdog, blood and gore, and a dash of patriotism, these R & R entries made bundles of money at the box office and in videocassette / laser disc distribution. It seemed a logical extension for multitalented Stallone to next tackle the prison genre. By following the tradition of feisty James Cagney (*Each Dawn I Die*, 1939, and *White Heat*, 1949, qq.v.), the equally short Stallone's (jailed) hero could triumph once again over the towering, brutal enemy (here vicious prison guards). Unfortunately, what emerged on screen in *Lock Up* was a comic book-style caper, so ludicrously contrived and artificial in its efforts to be a triumph of the human spirit that only the most diehard Stallone fan could relish the self-indulgent ego flexing. As Sean Plottner (*US* magazine) analyzed, "Mildly entertaining at best, the movie is mostly cruel-and-unusual punishment." Or as Kyle Counts (*Movieline* magazine) moaned, "By the time you stumble out of *Lock Up*, you'll feel like you've done hard time yourself — it's that torturous."

Frank Leone (Sylvester Stallone) is in New Jersey's Treadmore Prison for having

Sylvester Stallone in *Lock Up* (1989).

defended an old man being beaten up by punks. For his violent, retributive assault and battery he was given an eighteen month sentence. It was nothing he could not handle. He had been a model prisoner, except for one indiscretion when he escaped from the low security facility to visit his dying foster father. Then he returned voluntarily to incarceration, with additional time (five years) added to his sentence. Now he has only six months left to serve before he is to be paroled. He looks forward to returning to his car repair shop and to his beautiful, loyal girlfriend, Melissa (Darlanne Fleugel).

Suddenly, everything turns to hell. Late one night, guards drag him from his cell and without explanation cart him off to the dreaded Gateway Prison, a maximum security penitentiary run by the notoriously sadistic Warden Drumgoole

(Donald Sutherland). This is the same demented person who once supervised Treadmore Prison, the very same unfeeling brute who denied Leone a good conduct pass to see his expiring foster father. Although Leone was in the wrong and Drumgoole in his right for bringing the prisoner back to prison, public sympathy went out to Frank and Drumgoole's career was severely damaged.

The perplexed, handcuffed Leone is dragged into the confines of the foreboding new facility. He is advised:

> You will be issued one bar of soap, two rolls of toilet paper per month. Somebody steals them or you lose them, you will be wiping yourself. You have one uniform. Your number is 510 — remember it! This is C wing. You will eat, shower and take yard time with your wing. There are six counts a day. Miss one, you're in the hole, miss two and I'll personally put you in the house of pain.

His teacher then introduces himself as Captain Meissner (John Amos): "Two things. One. I am Meissner. Two. Never fuck with Meissner."

Before long, staunch Leone is brought in to meet his persecutor, Warden Drumgoole. Drumgoole delights in displaying for his bemused prisoner the recently restored prison electric chair where 120 men were electrocuted over the years. The pleased administrator fondles the death weapon, murmuring that the restoration was accomplished "to remind me of how things ought to be." The vengeful Drumgoole whines he has a score to settle with Frank, "Making a criminal into a hero and the warden into a criminal. You took my future away from me. You and those bleeding heart politicians. . . ."

With satanical delight, Drumgoole spells out the punishment he has in mind for his captive victim: "In Gateway, six months could be a lifetime. Anything could happen. . . . You have no rights unless I give them to you. You feel no pleasure unless I tell you, you can. This is hell. I'm going to give you the guided tour."

Accepting that the next months will be full of unpleasant surprises, Frank elects to work in the prison auto repair shop under the supervision of Eclipse (Frank McRae), another convict. Yet another inmate, the obsequious, garrulous Dallas (Tom Sizemore) does his best to ingratiate himself with non-responsive Frank.

Meanwhile, Frank, the experienced prisoner, shares with his fellow convicts some of the wisdom he has accumulated over the years while serving time.

On being on the offensive:
You always got to be ready to move first. That's the only way to get to first base in this place.

On being optimistic:
A mind set. Your body has to be in here, but your brain doesn't.

On keeping sane:
In here, you gotta respect something. You don't get much, but what you got, you got to protect.

The unfearful Frank quickly earns the hatred of convict Chink (Sonny Landham) and his thugs who go out of their way to pulverize Leone in the exercise yard football game. The hulking Eclipse comes to Frank's rescue. Later, the heinous Drumgoole begins paying surprise visits to Leone's cell to jumble his captive's nerves. However, the latter remains calm, insisting, "You won't break me."

In the auto shop, Frank and the others reconstruct a red 1964 Mustang into a sporty road killer. Then off-the-wall Dallas insists on taking the vehicle for a joy ride in the exercise yard, not only wrecking the car but causing problems for Leone who comes to his rescue. Frank is shoved into the hole for six weeks. There he is tortured with beatings, lack of food and no peace of mind. He is tormented by a constantly repeated buzzer which prevents him from having any decent interval of rest. He survives the ordeal and returns to the general prison population only to learn that one of his pals, First Base (Larry Romano), has been killed by Chink and his men. Frank goes berserk and fights it out with the vicious man, emerging victorious, although wounded severely.

Melissa visits Frank in the prison hospital. No sooner does she leave than Frank is told that his enemies in the joint plan to have their friends on the outside rape Melissa as a reprisal against smug Leone. This causes Frank to join with Dallas in hatching an escape plan. However, Dallas makes a deal with the double-crossing warden and plans to lead Frank into an ambush. Dallas is later killed by a brutish guard. As for Leone, the guards chase him down and torture him with forced steam. However, he overwhelms them and, in a table-turning action, grabs Drumgoole as a hostage. He forces the warden into the electric chair and threatens to pull the switch. This causes the now deranged administrator to confess a variety of crimes he has committed. Frank then admits the electric chair has been deprogrammed. As for the warden, whose confession was heard by the now-sympathetic Meissner, he is led off to a jail cell. Frank is released and, when he reaches the outer gate, Melissa is waiting for him with open arms.

Variety was properly disenchanted with the finished results. "For those who don't care if their warrior is ever more charmless, violent and glum, *Lock Up* meets most expectations. . . . A weak attempt to film a Rocky-esque car-fixing scene in the prison shop . . . to the tune of the upbeat song 'Vehicle' elicits unintentional laughter instead. . . . This is macho posturing at its nadir. . . ." Duane Byrge (*Hollywood Reporter*), who found some merit to the production, noted that East Jersey State Prison (Rahway Prison), where much of the film was shot on location was the movie's real star. "With its rusted pipe innards and twisted steel stairwells, [it] is the most gut-twisting opponent Stallone has faced since Clubber Lang (Mr. T). Kyle Counts (*Movieline* magazine) perceived why Stallone's latest escapist entertainment failed to impress most viewers: "There's a hollow ring to his victory this time; Drumgoole is so thoroughly, unbelievably evil that his undoing is like putting a mad dog out of its misery." Paying the film a backhanded compliment, *Los Angeles Reader* assessed *Lock Up* as "Astonishing bit of sadomasochistic fetishism. . . . [The] film is original in its quasi-pornographic fascination with the unbroken series of beatings and humiliations that Stallone endures before he can finally start dishing it out himself in the final two reels."

Made at an estimated negative cost of $17,000,000, *Lock Up* earned $8,015,150 in domestic film rentals paid to the distributor.

Like the more sluggish *An Innocent Man* (1989), q.v., *Lock Up* set back the cause of the prison genre several light years.

158. *The Longest Yard* (Paramount, 1974), color, 121 min.

Producer, Albert S. Ruddy; associate producer, Alan P. Horowitz; director, Robert Aldrich; story, Ruddy; screenplay, Tracy Keenan Wynn; production designer, James S. Vance; wardrobe, Charles James; makeup, Tom Ellingwood; music, Frank

DeVol; second unit director, Hal Needham; assistant directors, Clifford Coleman, Ron Wright; dialogue supervisor, Robert Sherman; prison technical adviser, Warden Joe S. Hopper; football technical adviser, Patrick Studstill; sound effects, Gordon Daniel, Jim Fritch, Howard Beals; re-recording, John Wilkinson; montage, Steve Orfanos; camera, Joseph Biroc; editors, Michael Luciano, Frank Capacchione, Allan Jacobs, George Hively.

Burt Reynolds (Paul Crewe); Eddie Albert (Warden Rudolph Hazen); Ed Lauter (Captain Knauer); Michael Conrad (Nate Scarboro); Jim Hampton (James "Caretaker" Farrell); Harry Caesar (Granville); John Steadman (Pop); Charles Tyner (Unger); Mike Henry (Lieutenant Rasmeusen); Bernadette Peters (Warden's Secretary); Pervis Arkins (Mawabe); Tony Cacciotti (Rotka); Anitra Ford (Melissa); Michael Ford (Announcer); Joe Kapp (Walking Boss); Richard Kiel (George Samson); Pepper Martin (Shop Steward); Mort Marshall (Assistant Warden); Ray Nitschke (Bogdanski); Sonny Sixkiller (Indian); Dino Washington (Mason); Ernie Wheelwright (Spooner); Joseph Dorsey (Bartender); Dr. Gus Carlucci (Team Doctor); Jack Rockwell (Trainer); Sonny Shroyer (Tannen); Roy Ogden (Schmidt); Don Ferguson (Referee); Chuck Hayward, Alfie Wise (Troopers); Robert Tessier (Shokner); Tony Reese (Levitt); Steve Wilder (J. J.); George Jones (Big George); Wilbur Gillan (Big Wilbur); Wilson Warren (Buttercup); Joe Jackson (Little Joe); Howard Silverstein (Howie); Donald Hixon (Donny); Jim Nicholson (Ice Man).

The Longest Yard is one of the most fondly recalled of all prison pictures. Not only is it an enjoyable celebration of over exaggerated macho pride but, in its childish fantasy way, it depicts the regenerative effects life behind bars can have on a once unscrupulous soul. Pauline Kael notes in *5001 Nights at the Movies* (1984), "The picture is a brutal bash, but the laughter at the brutality has no meanness in it; everybody knows that the blood isn't real.... [I]t's almost irresistibly good-natured and funny."

One of the highlights of this ole boys picture is the characterization of the dictatorial Warden Hazen by Eddie Albert. The frightening depths of this man's life-and-death control over his convict population is made bearable only because the movie is a deliberate comic farce. Nevertheless, when in the course of *The Longest Yard,* the warden expresses his theory of fear and violence as his greatest weapon in controlling the inmates, one can only shudder at the real-life examples from which this expertly-executed caricature was drawn.

One-time professional football star Paul Crewe (Burt Reynolds), known affectionately as the "wrecking Crewe" until he began throwing gridiron games for payoffs, has a new career as a stud gigolo. When he runs off one morning with a wealthy woman's sports car, the police of a southeastern state give pursuit and he is captured after driving the car into the river. As a result, he is sent to the state prison run by the megalomanic Warden Rudolph Hazen (Eddie Albert). If Hazen lacks compassion for his prisoners, he has great enthusiasm for the game of football. In welcoming smart-mouthed Crewe to the facility, it is clear that the obsessed Hazen has something specifically in mind for the cocky newcomer:

> It's good to have you here. Young people can learn a great deal from a skillfully played football game: offense, defense, spirit of achievement. Teamwork, you might say. The game embodies what made our country great. It's a great game played by great men.

Hazen's greatest pride is his prison guard's football squad. For the past five years they have been runners-up as national champions in the southeast league. However, this year he wants greatness from his men. He wants the championship.

As such, he has decided that Crewe should coach a pick-up team of inmates to play against the guards and help to hone the latter into winning shape. The blasé prisoner insists that he has not touched a football in eight years and rejects the post. The offended Hazen retorts that he pulled a lot of political strings to get Paul assigned to his prison, and that *if* Crewe helps to win the championship for him, he will make his eighteen-month stay at the penitentiary far more agreeable. At first, Crewe remains recalcitrant. However, the Warden has persuasive methods: Crewe is assigned to the grueling swamp work detail (digging up mud and shoving it back in), shoved into the sweat box, etc. He finally accepts the task of whipping the prisoners into a starring guard.

Crewe chooses veteran convict Nate Scarboro (Michael Conrad) as his chief coach and they select the most vicious bruisers in the general population for their players, including hulking George Samson (Richard Kiel). At first, the black convicts refuse to join the white squad, but Paul convinced them—Granville (Harry Caesar) in particular—that this is an excellent opportunity to even the score with the brutal guards. He advises them that the first game will be against the prison keepers, coached by the sadistic Captain Knauer (Ed Lauter). The black brothers quickly volunteer. Next, Paul and his inmate spies learn every vulnerable point on the guards' team (i.e. who has prior bone injuries, etc.); anything that will help them on the field. By now, the once blasé Crewe, who had no respect for anyone—including himself—has gained self-esteem. He is determined that his team not only survive the match against the guards, but win. He has begun to appreciate what a morale booster it will be for the inmates to have their self-worth restored. He learned this lesson from Nate:

> [Y]ou spend fourteen years in this tank and you begin to understand that you've only got two things left they can't sweat out of you or beat out of you. Your balls! And you better hang on to 'em, because they're about the only thing you're going to have left when you get out of here.

By now, Paul is as possessed as the warden to win the game. He assigns himself as the team's quarterback and tells his co-players, "We have one chance in a million to humiliate those bastards!" Already, Hazen is suspicious of Crewe's ultimate loyalty, especially after Paul snidely advises him, "I'm just trying to give you a football team, Warden. And along the way, maybe give the men some pride and dignity. Of course, only for a little while."

The warden has obviously underestimated the crafty Crewe. The latter seduces Hazen's randy secretary (Bernadette Peters) who, in turn, provides him with access to the warden's home movies of past football games, so the convicts can study their opponents' gridiron techniques. The enterprising prisoners "borrow" some of Knauer's new football uniforms and assemble an amazing array of weapons (brass knuckles, hardened plaster of Paris, etc.) to employ in the no-holds barred big game. Meanwhile, the brutal Knauer causes the death of James "Caretaker" Farrell (Jim Hampton), a convict who has been overhelpful to the prisoners' team. Now, Crewe and his men are seething for vengeance in the big game.

By this juncture Hazen has gone over the top emotionally. He issues a final warning to Crewe that if he does not insure that the convicts lose the game with at least a twenty-one point spread, he will see to it that Paul is implicated in

Burt Reynolds in *The Longest Yard* (1974).

Caretaker's death and spends the rest of his life in prison. The enraged warden then demands of the cowering Knauer, "Before the game is over, I want every prisoner in this institution to know what I mean by power."

Game day arrives and the convicts, who call themselves the "mean machine," not only survive the brutal onslaught, but emerge the victors with a score of 36–35. Having won the competition, Crewe strides off the field, seemingly intent on escaping with the departing crowd. The fuming warden orders Knauer to shoot the prisoner. The guard captain refuses, which is fortuitous, for Crewe was only retrieving the victory football. As he passes by the storming warden, Crewe jabs, "Stick this in your trophy case!"

Thus the warden's power has been broken.

Variety rated *The Longest Yard* "an outstanding action drama" in which "the metaphysics of football . . . are neatly interwoven with the politics and bestialities of totalitarian authority." The trade paper enthused at the combination of "the brutish excitement of football competition with the brutalities of contemporary prison life." Far less impressed was Vincent Canby *(New York Times)*, "Though *The Yard* is a terrible picture, I'll admit to having unwillingly enjoyed some of the football practice and parts of the final game—even though it's much too long." As for Burt Reynolds's star turn here, Canby judged, "Mr. Reynolds departs from mimicry [i.e. aping Marlon Brando's performance in *On the Waterfront,* 1954] only in his style of wearing clothes: he manages to make even the prison chains look like fashionable men's wear, as though he were modeling the latest in metal accessories." For many critics, there was a direct parallel between director Robert Aldrich's earlier *The Dirty Dozen* (1967) and the equally violent *The Longest Yard;* both were tributes to machismo and both showed the regeneration of life's losers. Other reviewers noted the intriguing parallel between the sinister guards and sadistic convicts, a trade-off in baser instincts, who are battling it out to the finish.

The Longest Yard was an enormous crowd pleaser, earning $23,017,000 in domestic film rentals paid to the distributor. The film received an Oscar nomination for Best Film Editing. *The Longest Yard* was shot on location at the Georgia State Prison at Raidsville. Warden Joe S. Hopper served as prison technical adviser. *The Longest Yard* was scripted by Tracy Keenan Wynn, who had written the teleplay for an earlier—far more sober—prison study, *The Glass House* (1972), q.v. In 1990 it was announced that Wynn was scripting *The Longest Yard II.*

159. *Love Child* (Warner Bros., 1982), color, 97 min.

Producer, Paul Maslansky; director, Larry Peerce; story, Anne Gerard; screenplay, Gerard, Katherine Specktor; art director, Don Ivey; set decorator, Richard A. Helfritz; makeup, Marie Del Russo; music, Charles Fox; orchestrator, Miles Goodman; song, Fox and Carly Simon; music editor, Dan Carlin; assistant directors, David Whorf, Paul Rose; technical adviser, Terry Jean Moore; sound, Howard Warren; ADR system, Tally Paulos; special effects, J. B. Jones; camera, James Pergola; editor, Bob Wyman.

Amy Madigan (Terry Jean Moore); Beau Bridges (Jack Hansen); Mackenzie Phillips (J. J.); Albert Salmi (Captain Mark Ellis); Joanna Merline (Superintendent Helen Sturgis); Margaret Whitton (Jacki Steinberg); Lewis Smith (Jesse Chaney); Dennis Lipscomb (Arthur Brady); Anna Maria Horsford (Mara); Michael Shane (Judge Hare); Randy Dreyfuss (Jeff Striker); Rhea Pearlman (June Burns); Juanita Mahone (Cecily); Raymond Peters, Al Kiggins (Correctional Officers); Annette Fosaner (Woman in Yard); Norma Davids (Bonnie);

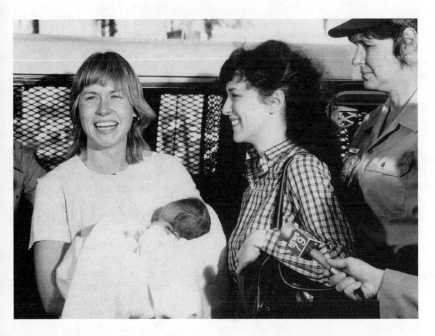

Amy Madigan and Margaret Whitton *(center)* **in** *Love Child* **(1982).**

Ronnie Mickey (Faith); Tame Connelly (Norma); Liba Carole May (Vicki); Lynn Lathan (Claudia); Sterling Swanson (Officer); Thomas Monshan (Broward Correctional Institution Officer); Alan Minor (County Jail Guard); Terry Jean Moore (Inmate).

> With its miraculously happy, upbeat ending, its condescending moral tone, and its swarm of prison-movie clichés, *Love Child* is strictly formula TV Movie of the Week fodder—best appreciated with a box of Twinkies on the living room sofa, and preferably with enough commercial interruptions to allow plenty of time for crossword puzzles.
>
> Rex Reed *(New York Post)*

Love Child deals with a nineteen-year-old inmate who gives birth to a baby fathered by a prison guard. This low-budget movie was based on an amazing but actual Florida case, one which came to national prominence and even rated a segment on television's "60 Minutes." However, cautioned Janet Maslin *(New York Times)*, who panned the low-keyed feature, this film is "the latest bit of evidence that a film's being based on a true story need not guarantee it an authentic air.... [Director] Larry Peerce ... tries for as much prison-movie stridency as the material will bear, but his portrait of Terry is so mild that the film's harsher touches seem gratuitous.... All of the film's characters have a tendency to come on too strong and then wear out their welcome."

In August 1977, nineteen-year-old Terry Jean Moore (Amy Madigan), of Orlando, Florida, who has been mostly on her own for the past few years, decides to hitchhike to New Orleans with her irresponsible young cousin Jesse Chaney (Lewis Smith). En route, he impulsively robs at gunpoint the driver who has picked them up. The youths are soon caught and Jesse turns state's evidence. He is placed on juvenile probation, while Terry, who could be convicted of armed robbery (which has a life sentence penalty) is convinced by her lawyer (Randy Dreyfuss) to accept a lesser charge of robbery. The harsh judge sentences her to a fifteen-year term; half of which is to be served behind bars, the rest on probation. For the confused, embittered Terry, this is just another example of life's inequities. She immediately proves to be a troublesome prisoner and, for causing a fire in a prison building, has five years added to her sentence. She is later relocated to the Broward Correctional Institution, a facility with no barbed wire and no armed guards. However, as Superintendent Helen Sturgis (Joanna Merlin) and guard Captain Mark Ellis (Alber Salmi) quickly advise the newcomer, there are strict rules and regulations. For missing any of the daily inmate checks, the penalty is thirty days in solitary confinement; there is also a tough policy for any escape attempts.

Terry quickly learns the ropes of survival at Broward. One fellow prisoner tells her: "It ain't goin' be your stuff unless you put your number on it. . . . The trick is to figure who's on your side and who ain't."

Terry meets the lesbian J.J. (Mackenzie Phillips) who, after failing to convert her into a lover, decides to become Terry's friend/mentor. Meanwhile, the rebellious Terry gets into a fight with another inmate and spends two weeks in solitary. When sympathetic guard Jack Hansen (Beau Bridges) first meets Terry, he wonders, "What's a nice kid like you doing in a place like this?" Seeing that she refuses to tow the disciplinary line, he warns her, "You better learn the rules around here and learn quick." As time passes, and the insubordinate Terry passes in and out of solitary, she begins on the Broward work program, gardening in the prison yard, performing mess hall duty, and working in the prison library with June Burns (Rhea Perlman). Terry constantly encounters Hansen and soon they are having trysts in a deserted warehouse on the grounds. Time passes and she discovers she is pregnant. When she confronts Jack with the facts, she learns that he is married and has two children already. (He later resigns his position at Broward.)

By now, rumors have spread that Terry may be pregnant, but she refuses to submit to medical tests demanded by the facility authorities. (Her plan is to keep the pregnancy a secret until an abortion is no longer medically safe.) For her insubordination, she is placed in solitary/medical confinement. Meanwhile, she contacts legal aid attorney Jacki Steinberg (Margaret Whitton) who agrees to take her case, not only working for her release but also to insure that her rights are protected once her pregnancy is revealed.

Once the superintendent confirms Terry's pending motherhood, she insists that the child-to-be not be allowed to remain at Broward, claiming it would be dangerous and would upset routine. However, Jacki cites a Florida statute, which states an inmate mother may keep her baby with her in prison, until the child is eighteen months old. This leads to a court contest, where Terry, full of new purpose in life, tells the judge, "For the first time in my life I got a responsibility. . . . It's all up to me and I need to keep this baby . . . we belong together."

The judge rules in her favor. Terry gives birth to her baby (a girl). On August 21, 1979, after spending 741 days in prison, Terry and her baby Precious are paroled. A voice-over postscript advises that she is serving her probation in Orlando "and you know what, it really is a free world."

According to Carrie Rickey *(Village Voice)*, "I don't like *Love Child* much, but it contains one gem: Amy Madigan's raw-nerve performance as the shiftless, cussin' Florida 19-year-old.... *Love Child* is soggy with right-to-life sentiment that's mystifyingly combined with a feminist self-determination polemic." Alex Keneas *(Newsday)* complained, "*Love Child* ... seems not to know what to do with its material. On the one hand it aims for a documentary-like ambience of authenticity; it even subtitles its segments, Iranian-hostage style ('Day 220' etc.). On the other hand, it's evasive. For example, it glosses over the apparent reluctance of prison authorities to investigate Terry's pregnancy. The guard (a laconic Beau Bridges) simply 'resigns.' ... [It's] all more a lifeless diorama than a successful recreation of grit.... *Love Child* aches for television, what with its endless closeups of talking heads and its sanitized-for-the-home portrait of prison life." The box office minded *Variety* observed, "The well-made Paul Maslansky production eschews the exploitation film excesses common to the 'women in prison' genre, but that means trouble with it comes to 'exploiting' this little picture...."

The uncommercial *Love Child* was shot on location at the Broward Correctional Institution. Terry Jean Moore who served as technical adviser for this movie, also played a small role as an inmate.

160. *Love, Mary* (CBS–TV, Oct. 8, 1985), color, 100 min.

Supervising producer, Stan Hough; producer, Ellis A. Cohen; director, Robert Day; teleplay, Clifford Campion; art director, Michael Bolton; set decorator, Jim Erickson; costumes, Frances Harrison Hays; makeup, Phyllis Newman; music, Robert Drasnin; music editor, Robert Takgi; assistant directors, Peter Schindler, Lee Knippleberg; technical advisers, Dr. Mary Groda-Lewis, Dr. Ellen Wiebe, Dr. George Price; stunt coordinator, Jacob Ruff; sound, Ralph Parker; sound editor, Sam Horta; camera, Frank Stanley; editor, Ray Daniels.

Kristy McNichol (Mary Groda-Lewis); Matt Clark (Fennie Groda); David Paymer (David Lewis); Rachel Ticotin (Rachel Martin); Piper Laurie (Christine Groda); Leslie Wing (Jill); Wayne Robson (Dr. Sitton); Dorothy Dells (Beatrice Symes); David Sage (Dr. Miller); Romy Windsor (Jean); Lycia Naff (Delia); David Faustino (Christopher); Sarah Partridge (Barbara); Ron Recasner (Bernard Fuller); Tamu Blackwell (Eugenia); Shana Lane-Block (Iris); Jackson Davies (Mr. Yates); Tom Heaton (Gerald Crowhurst); Kate Robbins (Jan); Sheila Moore (Dr. Hofflund); Todd Duckworth (Dr. Grovner); Tom McBeath (Dr. Pearl); Christianne Hirt (Natalie); Lossen Chambers (Tanya); Twyla Dawn Vokins (Beth); Sharon Wahl (Secretary); Gabrielle Rose (Julie Trenton); Karen Austin (Proper Lady); Peter Yunker (Richard); Pam Dangelmeier (SDS Teenager); Stephen Chang (Karate Instructor); Frances Flanagan (Nurse Osco); Ruby Montgomery (Nurse Curtis); Joseph Golland (Dr. McWright); Dr. David Mitchell (Optometrist).

Another of those amazing but true docudramas that shows the resourcefulness of the human spirit once aroused. While the reformatory setting forms a backdrop for only part of this story, the cumulative effects of Mary's four years at the institution play a strong role in shaping her future. The fact that Mary's learning disability was not diagnosed early in her life leads to repercussions (drugs, booze, promiscuous sex) that she and her family find difficult to overcome. It is another illustration of how the mass processing of incarcerated human beings can lead to severe negative consequences.

Teenager Mary Groda (Kristy McNichol) has run away yet again from the Hollyridge Reformatory. This time she and a male friend have stolen a car. The police return her to Hollyridge where sympathetic counselor Rachel Martin (Rachel Ticotin) attempts to break through the emotional barrier the girl has established. Rachel interviews Mary's parents, Christine (Piper Laurie) who is a nurse and blue collar worker Fennie (Matt Clark) who is more concerned with his other five children at home than in pursuing the continuing problems of rebellious Mary. Eventually, it is discovered that part of Mary's problems is that she suffers from dyslexia. Once diagnosed and treated, her scholastic advancement is remarkable and the reformatory enters her as one of five students to embark on the experimental Upward Bound program which allows inmates to leave the institution and live on campus at a nearby college. However, because the other girls break the regulations, they are all shipped back to Hollyridge.

By now, Mary is determined to pursue her education and she manages to secure a permanent job which means she can be paroled and attend college. Finally encouraged by her parents, she continues her college studies. However, the recurring defiant side of her causes Mary to be promiscuous and, in the next years, she has two illegitimate children, each by a different man. The second delivery is very difficult and she suffers a heart seizure; for a time she is partially paralyzed. She not only overcomes this disability, but decides to become a physician, no matter the obstacles. (It has taken her eleven years to complete college.) David Lewis (David Paymer) enters her life and, after a see-sawing relationship, they marry.

A postscript advises that Mary is a family practice resident at Youngstown Hospital Association in Youngstown, Ohio.

Daily Variety endorsed, "One of the remarkable assets of the telefilm is the manner in which young Gloria's sordid life is suggested without baring all." A bespectacled Kristy McNichol offers a low-keyed, very effective performance.

The title of this made-for-television movie refers to Mary, who while working as a part-time supplies packer, signed rolls of toilet tissues being sent to troops in Vietnam with her personal greetings: "Love, Mary."

161. *The Lullaby* (Film Booking Offices of America, 1924), 72 min.

Director, Charles Bennett; story, Lillian Ducey; screenplay, Hope Loring, Louis D. Lighton; camera, Jack MacKenzie.

Jane Novak (Felipa/Antoinette); Robert Anderson (Tony); Fred Malatesta (Pietro); Dorothy Brock (Baby Antoinette); Cleo Madison (Mrs. Marvin); Otis Harlan (Thomas Elliott); Peter Burke (Thomas, Jr.); Lydia Yeamans Titus (Mary); Pat Moore (Elliott, Jr. at age six); Mickey Moore (Elliott, Jr. at age eight).

> [Although] the picture has been produced artistically, directed intelligently and acted capably, being thus made deeply appealing almost all the way through, it may not be construed by the masses as a good entertainment.
>
> *(Harrison's Reports)*

Newly married Felipa (Jane Novak) and Tony (Robert Anderson), reach New York and begin their new life in the Italian ghetto. Pietro (Fred Malatesta), a bachelor friend of the couple, shares their apartment. When Tony returns home one evening and witnesses Pietro attempting to seduce Felipa, a fight ensues and Pietro is killed. Tony is found guilty of first-degree murder and Felipa of second-degree murder. Tony is hung while Felipa begins serving a twenty-year prison term. She gives birth to a child, Antoinette (Dorothy Brock), which, at age three, is placed in an orphanage. Later, the child is adopted by the state's governor (Otis Harlan)—who had been the judge at her trial—and his wife. Years later, having served her sentence, the much-altered Felipa goes in search of her adult daughter

(Jane Novak). She arrives on the day of her offspring's coming out party and is soon made part of the household.

There were many implausibilities in this independent production, including the railroading of the hero and heroine to prison. *Variety* carped, "the story is full of illogical episodes, but none more violent to the conventions than the picking of the blonde and blue-eyed Jane Novak as an Italian bride. . . . The picture is full of heavy, sombre emotional scenes such as . . . the hanging, indicated by the close-up of a swinging rope, and the prison scenes."

162. *The Man Who Broke 1,000 Chains* (HBO–Cable, Oct. 31, 1987), 115 min.

Executive producer, Michael Campus; producer, Yoram Ben-Ami; director, Daniel Mann; based on the book by Vincent Godfrey Burns; teleplay, Campus, David Wyles; production designer, Vincent J. Cresciman; set decorator, Cecilia Rodarte; costumes, Jack Buehler; makeup, Pamela S. Westmore; music, Charles Bernstein; supervising music editor, Allan K. Rosen; assistant director, Robert J. Koster; stunt coordinator, Randy "Fife"; sound, Ed Novick; supervising sound editor, Kevin Spears; camera, Mikael Salomon; editor, Walter A. Hannemann.

Val Kilmer (Elliot Burns [Robert Elliot Burns]); Charles Durning (Warden Hardy); Sonia Braga (Emily); Kyra Sedgewick (Lillian Saylo); William Sanderson (Trump); James Keach (Vincent Godfrey Burns); Elisha Cook (Pappy Glue); Clancy Brown (Flagg); Taj Majal (Bones); Taylor Presnell (Seales); Daniel Mann (Store Owner); Bill Bolender (Rayford); Esther Benson (Mother Burns); Burt Conway (Father Burns); Charles Carroll (Hobo #1); Ransom Andrews (Hobo #2); Stan Sturning (Burns's Atlanta Lawyer); John Mitchum (Atlanta Judge); Roy Morgan (Deebo); Bert Williams (Police Chief); Lawrence Parks (Merle McBain); Chris Mulkey (Burns's Chicago Lawyer); Billy Kadie (Burley); Jerry Anderson (Speech Chairman); Rony Clanton (Cowboy); Warren Vanders (Stuckey); Tommy Bush (Chicago Judge); Bill Gratton (Parole Board Officer); Michael Clark (Detective #1); George Auld (Detective #2); Helen Hall (Bookstore Owner); Pat Minter (Trustee #1); Joe McCaig (Trustee #2); Harlan Jordan (Backwoodsman); Julius Tennon (Nub); Desmond Dhooge (Dog Handler); Dennis Pace, Charles Floyd, Richard Nelson, Stephen Ham, Glynn Bradley, Robert Callander, Tim Hicks, Page Doyle, Mitch Smith, Kenneth Cooks, Clyde Hutchinson, Jr., L.B. Jernigan, Edward C. Langston, Charles McClelland (Georgia Chain Gang Prisoners).

The hauntingly graphic *I Am a Fugitive from a Chain Gang* (1932), q.v., has long been regarded as the epitome of Hollywood exposés of the horrors of life on the American chain gang. In 1987, the Home Box Office (HBO) Cable Network chose to recount that film's poignant story in *The Man Who Broke 1,000 Chains*. *TV Guide* magazine rated the new rendition only two stars, insisting, "Justice isn't served with this cable remake about a fugitive from a Georgia chain gang, casting Val Kilmer in the Paul Muni role." In actuality, *The Man Who Broke 1,000 Chains* is *not* a remake, but a retelling of the facts in the tormented life of Robert Elliot Burns, based on the account by Burns's brother Vincent.

After serving in World War I combat in France, Robert Elliot Burns (Val Kilmer) returns to the United States. The scene shifts to 1921 and to New York City where Burns, a shell shock victim of the war, has recovered and is now a protestor for civil reforms. Deciding to try his luck job searching in Florida, he takes to the road. Six months later he is a hobo wandering the countryside. He becomes involved with another drifter who robs a grocery store. Burns is caught and sentenced to six to ten years of hard labor on a Georgia chain gang.

Arriving at Fulton County Camp #9, he is informed by one sinister official: "Chains give you a short step. But you'll get used to it. Count on it. . . . Prison is for punishment, where they expiate your sins. . . . The sooner you feel guilty, the better off you'll be."

Burns soon meets veteran convict Pappy Glue (Elisha Cook), who admits: "Half the cons in here didn't do. But I done it!"

Pappy also advises the newcomer about how to handle eating the horrendous gruel (a mixture of pig fat, corn pone, soy beans and molasses for breakfast; red beans and mush for dinner) that the men are served seven days a week: "Don't get no better looking at it."

In a voice-over Burns expresses the horror of his situation: "Chained next to animals, insane people, murderers and victims like me. Full of plans of escape, what they'll do when they get out, what they did to get in. Nobody wants to die here."

The brutal physical regimen of working fifteen hours a day in which each man is expected to swing his pick axe fifteen licks a minute, nine hundred an hour, wears down Burns's will to live. Because he is a Yankee, he receives rougher treatment than many of the other men and ends in the tortuous sweat box. As one sadistic guard tells him, "We're going to squeeze you like a grape till you burst in the sun." Finally, when he can endure no more, Burns chances an escape, getting another convict to break his chain. He flees to Marietta, Georgia, and then on to Tennessee.

It is now 1923 and Burns arrives in Chicago where he rents a room and begins working, using the alias Elliot Burns. His landlady Emily (Sonia Braga) takes a romantic interest in him and helps him to start a left wing-oriented magazine. When she demands he marry her, the disinterested Burns is forced into compliance by her threat of revealing his background. By 1929 Burns has become a civic leader and he begins dating waitress Lillian Saylo (Kyra Sedgwick). When the vindictive Emily learns of the liaison she informs on her husband. The Georgia authorities demand his return. There is a public protest in Burns's favor, but he decides to serve out his time, promised that if he returns for forty-five to ninety days, he will be freed.

No sooner does Burns return to Georgia than he is sentenced to chain gang life again. He is warned, "You're just convict meat again. The flies are going to be over you real quick this time." Because he had flaunted the prison system, Burns is treated far more severely than the others and is frequently whipped. Lillian visits and finds him embittered and desperate. When the parole board denies his promised release, he is shattered. He wills himself to "hold on" and with the assistance of his brother (James Keach) he escapes again. Thereafter, he writes a book dealing with the medieval tortures utilized in the chain gang system. Film rights to this book are purchased by Hollywood and transferred into a movie starring Paul Muni. Burns, still a hunted fugitive, sneaks into a theatre to see his life portrayed on the screen. He has a last meeting with Lillian, who has since married.

A postscript, revealing a deserted chain gang camp, states:

> After an enormous struggle, Robert Elliot Burns was finally pardoned on November 1, 1944. . . . The furor he created greatly contributed to abolishing the Georgia chain gangs.

While the facts of Robert Burns's trouble-plagued existence are still gripping, there is a bland haze permeating this production, making every incident seem unreal. The prison camp scenes have a stagey look to them and one never senses the stark horror that fills each waking moment of a convict's life. Then too, because this adaptation views the inhumanity to man by man from a perspective of time, it loses most of the pertinency that *I Am a Fugitive from a Chain Gang* possessed.

For some reason it was decided to have Val Kilmer's Robert Burns speak with an accent, which makes much of his dialogue sound as if he is talking with a mouth full of marbles. The less said about the overstated performances of Sonia Braga and Kyra Sedgewick the better.

Obviously, director Daniel Mann (who also appears in the telefeature as the store owner) was dissatisfied with the final (re)assembling of the feature. A notice on the screen credits reads, "After director completed director's cut, final version was supervised by production company."

163. *Manslaughter* (Paramount, 1922), 9,061'.

Presenter, Jesse L. Lasky; director, Cecil B. DeMille; based on the novel by Alice Duer Miller; adaptor/screenplay, Jeanie Macpherson; art director/costumes, Paul Iribe; choreography, Theodore Kosloff; camera, Alvin Wyckoff, Guy Wilky.

Thomas Meighan (Daniel J. O'Bannon); Leatrice Joy (Lydia Thorne); Lois Wilson (Evans, her maid); John Miltern (Governor Stephen Albee); George Fawcett (Judge Homans); Julia Faye (Mrs. Drummond); Edythe Chapman (Adeline Bennett); Jack Mower (Jim Drummond, a Policeman); Dorothy Cumming (Eleanor Bellington); Casson Ferguson (Bobby Dorset); Mickey Moore (Dicky Evans); James Neill (Butler); Sylvia Ashton (Prison Matron); Raymond Hatton (Brown); "Teddy" (Gloomy Gus); Mabel Van Buren, Ethel Wales, Dale Fuller (Prisoners); Edward Martindel (Wiley); Charles Ogle (Doctor); Guy Oliver (Musician); Shannon Day (Miss Santa Claus); Lucien Littlefield (Witness); and: Spottiswoode Aitken, Sidney Bracy, William Boyd, Clarence Burton, Nora Cecil, Fred Kelsey, Emmett King, J. Farrell MacDonald, Madame Sul-Te-Wan, Theodore von Eltz, Charles West.

In the "unenlightened era" of the roaring 1920s it was the general consensus that the penal system meted out the eye-for-an-eye punishment a criminal rightfully deserved. However, once a prisoner served his time, that was that. If he happened to reform, so much the better. It was also believed, often with good foundation, that the spoiled rich were a law unto themselves and, even more than a working class criminal, a wealthy lawbreaker would benefit greatly from the kick-in-the-pants trauma of penitence behind bars. All this is encompassed in Cecil B. DeMille's silent photoplay, *Manslaughter*. Besides being a self-serving moral essay, DeMille craftily interwove flashbacks into the proceedings, allegedly for historical comparisons. However, it was just an excuse to introduce lavish Biblical settings, risqué costuming and debauched behavior. (In this case it was a feast of Bacchus.)

Wealthy Lydia Thorne (Leatrice Joy) is a spoiled playgirl, who delights in fast living and faster driving. When she is stopped by a motorcycle cop (Jack Mower) for exceeding the speed limit, she bribes him with the gift of a diamond bracelet. Later, when her maid Evans (Lois Wilson) begs her for the loan of money to move her sickly child to a warmer climate, Lydia is too preoccupied to pay attention. The desperate Evans robs Lydia's jewelry box of a valuable ring. Assistant district attorney Daniel O'Bannon (Thomas Meighan), who is in love with the reckless Lydia, investigates and uncovers the culprit. He confronts Lydia about the situation (detailed in title cards in this silent photoplay):

O'BANNON: Lydia, don't you think this is a case for mercy—rather than justice?

Thomas Meighan, Leatrice Joy and John Miltern in *Manslaughter* **(1922).**

LYDIA: I've no sympathy for thieves—a crime's a crime! But in her case the law seems to be not only merciful—but affectionate!

When Lydia forgets to appear in court, as arranged, to ask for clemency for the defendant, Evans is sentenced to Auburn Prison for three-and-a-half to five years. Later, she is repentant and actually tries to help Evans's son. While on one of her errands of mercy, the motorcycle policeman spots Lydia's car and follows her, wanting to return the bracelet. She misinterprets his pursuit and begins speeding. He follows at a faster clip and an accident ensues, in which he dies. In the court-room, her attorney begs the court for a lenient verdict on her manslaughter charge, explaining, "[B]ecause to a woman of her sheltered upbringing, a prison sentence is a more severe punishment than the law contemplated."

The court is unsympathetic to the defense plea and Lydia is sentenced to three to seven years at Auburn Prison. Suddenly, the aristocratic socialite is tossed into harsh surroundings where she is no longer a prominent citizen, but merely prisoner #149. Her humiliation is completed during the induction process when she is ordered to take a disinfectant bath.

A title card informs further of Lydia's plight:

In prison—there is little need for a good coiffure or a good bridge-player. Nor have all the expensive machines Lydia has driven—helped her in the least with a washing machine.

Meanwhile, O'Bannon, guilt-striken at having prosecuted his true love, has resigned from office. He visits Lydia in prison, but she misinterprets the reason for his coming: "I've supposed you come to gloat over my humiliation? To see a woman turned into an animal."

She slowly adjusts to the stark prison routine and learns to handle her various manual labor duties. However, she cannot rid herself of bitterness towards O'Bannon. She becomes ill and, while delirious in the infirmary, dreams of killing the man.

Another title card advises:

> After two long years—under the warmth of Evans's patient kindness—Lydia comes to learn that the worth-while things in life are Life and Service.

By now Lydia and Evans are friends, both regenerated by their prison experiences. Evans tells her prison mate, "Doesn't this doughnut remind you of a life preserver? That's just what prison has meant to most of us—a *life* preserver."

Eventually, both Lydia and Evans are paroled. Lydia has a new purpose in life. She confides to Evans, "I had to come to prison to learn the meaning of freedom. To be locked in a cell, to know that I had a soul.... And now, my time and my effort and money are all going to help those who taught me."

Later, Lydia has a reunion with her rich friends and surprises them with her transformation. She tells the aghast bluebloods, "In prison—I learned that keeping time to human heartbeats, is far more important than keeping time to a saxophone."

While performing charitable work, Lydia chances upon O'Bannon, now a skid row bum, who has come to her soup kitchen for a free meal. With Lydia's support, he regains his self-esteem and runs in the election for governor against the incumbent, Stephen Albee (John Miltern). However, he withdraws his candidacy when he decides to wed Lydia, understanding that her criminal record would be a deficit to his political life.

The *New York Times* judged of *Manslaughter,* "It is a decidedly good picture, although parts of it have been considerably exaggerated to make a director's holiday.... When ... [the author's] pampered heroine gets inside prison walls the story is gripping." *Variety* was more overawed by the lavish trappings than by the film's contents. "The photography is excellent. The entire picture has been staged with a liberal hand and a technical expertness that makes the romantic story a gripping series of events." Laurence Reid (*Motion Picture News*) approved, "[W]e must give him [DeMille] credit for building the most direct action which has graced the screen in many a day."

To its credit, *Manslaughter* presented a rather barren picture of prison life with an assortment of inmates one would prefer not meeting—ever!

164. *Manslaughter* (Paramount, 1930), 82 min.

Director, George Abbott; based on the novel by Alice Duer Miller; adaptor, Abbott; sound, Earl Hayman; camera, Archie J. Stout; editor, Otto Levering.

Claudette Colbert (Lydia Thorne); Fredric March (Dan O'Bannon); Emma Dunn (Miss Bennett); Natalie Moorhead (Eleanor); Richard Tucker (Albee); Hilda

Vaughn (Evans); G. Pat Collins (Drum- Ivan Simpson (Morton); Irving Mitchell
mond); Gaylord [Steve] Pendleton (Bobby); (Foster).
Stanley Fields (Peters); Arnold Lucy (Piers);

When Paramount decided to remake *Manslaughter* (1922), q.v., as a talkie at its Astoria, Long Island, studio, it became a vehicle for contract stars Claudette Colbert and Fredric March. Much of the cloying sentimentality was removed from this updated version.

In the new *Manslaughter* wealthy Long Island playgirl Lydia Thorne (Claudette Colbert) is found guilty of manslaughter in the vehicular death of a motorcycle cop. The poor but dedicated district attorney, Dan O'Bannon (Frederic March), who had been romantically intrigued with Lydia, prosecutes the case. He is determined that an example be made of this pampered socialite. He contends there should be one law for all classes. She is sentenced to prison where she encounters her former maid, Evans (Hilda Vaughn) who had once committed a petty theft against Lydia. Although Lydia is supposed to serve a long prison term, she manages to be paroled in two years. Meanwhile, O'Bannon, remorseful at his severe treatment of Lydia, has resigned his position and has led an aimless life. Later, he has regained his self-worth and it is at this juncture that Lydia intends to carry out her vengeance on her persecutor. She goes to O'Bannon's employer, demanding he fire Dan. He learns of her action and, in a confrontation, he admits that he really still loves her. This revelation causes her to realize that her life in prison has altered her approach to life. She has a new perspective on the worthwhile things in life, including Dan's love. She admits that she loves him.

The *New York Times* found the new version both antiquated and implausible. In recounting the fabrications offered, the reporter recited — tongue-in-cheek — some of the more incredible plotline,

> When Lydia Thorn [sic] arrived at the prison she was undoubtedly a bit stand-offish. Her hands, for example, hadn't been used to rough work. During the first day another prisoner shoved them into hot water and that started a riot. But in two years she had changed. The beginning was when she said to her former maid ... 'Evans, what's your first name?' And the climax was when the girls were having a spelling bee in the prison school. Told to choose sides, both at once called 'Lydia.'

Variety's Abel Green was blasé about the remake. "As a completed product it will stand up for the average fans because it holds a competent admixture of acting, production and action. It is also susceptible to the usual ballyhoo of 'sending his own sweetheart to prison for manslaughter' and that routine." In retrospect, Lawrence J. Quirk (*Claudette Colbert: An Illustrated Biography*, 1985) gave a positive assessment of this remake: "[I]t's rather outlandish, sentimental, and frankly claptrappish situations were considerably modernized by famed theater director George Abbott.... Abbott did an excellent job in making the tale something 1930 audiences could understand and relate to."

The new *Manslaughter*, more interested in being chic and entertaining than realistic, gave scant heed to the grueling conditions that frequently made up life in contemporary prisons. Instead, it presented a storybook version of distaff convict life, more on the order of MGM's *Hold Your Man* (1933), q.v., than of Paramount's own hard-boiled *Ladies of the Big House* (1932), q.v., or Warner Bros.' abrasive portrayal of *Ladies They Talk About* (1932), q.v.

165. *Marie* (Metro-Goldwyn-Mayer/United Artists, 1985), color, 112 min.

Executive producer, Elliot Schick; producer, Frank Capra, Jr.; director, Roger Donaldson; based on the book *Marie: A True Story* by Peter Maas; screenplay, John Briley; art director, Ron Foreman; set decorator, Tantar Leviseur; costumes, Joe I. Tompkins; makeup, Massimo DeRossi; music, Francis Lai; supervising music editor, Dan C. Garde; assistant directors, Bob Howard, Michele Panelli; stunt coordinator, Julius Leflore; sound, David Hildyard; sound re-recording, William McCaughey, Ray O'Reilly, Aaron Rochin; supervising sound editor, Don Warner; camera, Chris Menges; editor, Neil Travis; additional editor, Tony Lawson.

Sissy Spacek (Marie Ragghianti); Jeff Daniels (Eddie Sisk); Keith Szarabajka (Kevin McCormack); Morgan Freeman (Charles Traughber); Lisa Banes (Toni Greer); Fred Thompson (Himself); Trey Wilson (FBI Agent); John Collum (Deputy Attorney General); Don Hood (Governor Ray Blanton); Graham Beckel (Charlie Benson); Macon McCalman (Murray Henderson); Collin Wilcox Paxton (Virginia); Robert Green Benson, III (Dante Ragghianti); Dawn Carmen (Therese Ragghianti); Shane Wexel (Ricky Ragghianti); Vincent Irizarry (Dave Ragghianti); Michael P. Moran (Roundtree [Bill Thompson]); Clarence Felder (Jack Lowery); Lisa Foster (Sherry Lomax); Charles Kahlenberg (Arnold Hurst); Joe Sun (Tommy Prater); R. Pickett Bugg (Bernie Weinthal); David Eddings, Tom Story (Detectives); Leon Rippy (Gary Gerbitz); George Gray, Mac Pirkle (Doctors); Timothy Carhart (Clayton Dawson); Fia Porter (Rape Victim); Phil Markert (Judge); Ivan Green (Jury Foreman); Sarah Hunley (Court Stenographer); Edwrd Carr (George Edwards); Ruby L. Wilson (Rose Lee Cooper); Stephen Henderson (Cooper's Husband); Lorenzo Allen (Prisoner); Herb Harton (Polygraph Operator); Jane Powell (Singer at Rally); John-Michael Maas (Chris); Alan Sader (Professor); J. Michael Hunger (Bartender at "Villa"); Carla Cantrelle (Marilyn); Jeff Marcum (Motorcycle Cop); James Fields (Death Row Prisoner); Billy McIntyre (Death Row Guard); Jerry Rushing (Gas Station Attendant); Larry Brinton, Drue Smith, Dwight Lewis, Chip Arnold (Reporters).

In recent years there has developed a sub-genre of films dealing with courageous young country women who triumph over adversities, especially evils engendered by the Establishment. There was *Norma Rae* (1979), *Silkwood* (1983), *Country* (1984), *Places in the Heart* (1984) and *The River* (1984). Then came *Marie*, a true story of a woman who combatted the state political machinery in Tennessee where the governor and several subordinates and associates were selling pardons. "In most respects," argued Michael Wilmington *(Los Angeles Times)*, "*Marie* is a fine movie.... In today's atmosphere of hopped-up hoke, prurient adolescence and stylized sadism, it comes across as a breath of fresh air. Yet, somehow, it doesn't leave you with enough—neither the rich satisfaction of seeing justice triumph nor the acid clarity of understanding evil."

In 1968 Marietta, Georgia Marie Ragghianti (Sissy Spacek) is a battered wife. She flees with her three children to Nashville, Tennessee, where she moves in with her paraplegic mother (Collin Wilcox Paxton). She waits on tables in a restaurant bar to support her family while she earns degrees in English and psychology at Vanderbilt University. The narrative jumps to 1973. Her problem in finding a position are solved when Eddie Sisk (Jeff Daniels), a long time friend, is appointed legal advisor to the newly elected Democratic Governor Ray Blanton (Don Hood). Eddie maneuvers Marie a position as state extradition officer. To indoctrinate her into her new career work, he takes her to the state prison, flippantly inquiring, "Have you ever visited Disneyland?" The tour continues through the cell blocks where Marie is subjected to a volley of enthusiastic cat calls from the horny men.

When she is escorted onto death row and shown the electric chair, a callous guard explains, "Some folk call it The Chair. Some folk call it Old Smokey. No one makes friends with it. We have to use our own generator. They won't let us use TVA [Tennessee Valley Authority] power for it."

Marie takes her work seriously, but she finds the glib Eddie pressuring her to expedite parole requests and clemencies for several particularly unsavory prisoners. She soon realizes that both the governor and his associate, the shady Bill Thompson (Michael P. Moran), are tied into the irregularities as is Charles Traughber (Morgan Freeman), the chairman of the parole board. Meanwhile, Marie attempts to be a responsible mother, coping with the ailments of her youngest child, Ricky (Shane Wexel), whose severe health problems are eventually traced to a pistachio shell lodged in one of his lungs.

To pacify the ever-inquiring, bothersome Marie, Eddie arranges for her to become a parole board member and eventually she is appointed chairwoman. In her new post, she uncovers evidence which links Eddie and Bill Thompson to the selling of paroles. The duplistic governor repeatedly denies knowledge of corruption on the board and, to prove his alleged good faith, he insists that Marie make decisions as she sees fit. Thus she rejects parole petitions arranged by Thompson and refuses to be cowed, even when the angered Eddie threatens to have her fired. However, when a police witness (R. Picket Bugg) against Thompson's misdeeds is murdered, Marie goes to the FBI. They begin a thorough investigation. The indignant governor and Sisk demand Marie's resignation, but she refuses. She is later arrested on a falsified drunk driving charge, giving Blanton an excuse to fire her. He also charges her with professional misconduct. Marie fights back by hiring lawyer Fred Thompson (himself), of Watergate prosecution fame, to handle her defense. Meanwhile, her friend and associate, Kevin McCormack (Keith Szarabaika), is killed before he can testify in her behalf. This act gives Marie the courage to proceed with the case. At the trial she is cleared of any misdeeds. The case brings forth evidence of misconduct by Sisk and Thompson.

A closing title card states:

> In 1981, Eddie Sisk and Bill Thompson went to prison for selling clemencies.... Governor Blanton was ousted from office for clemency abuses before the end of his term. In 1983 he went to prison on related corruption charges.... Marie now lectures and writes on the criminal justice system.

"*Marie* . . . opens with a legend emblazoned across the screen: 'Marie Ragghianti is a real person. This is a true story.' . . . Beware of any movie that begins with such bald claims on truth. Almost inevitably they serve as apologia, as a warning that the upcoming truth is going to be somewhat duller than fiction.... For much of the movie Marie is a cupcake, and when she finally gets around to reacting, it seems more the fury of a woman fired than one responding to any nobler cause" Richard Corliss (*Time* magazine). He pinpointed the movie's inherent problem. "As in *Missing* and *The River*, Spacek here is in danger of being strangled by a halo that is a bit too large for the character she plays." *Marie* was not a popular box-office entry.

Although it is central to this screen drama, very few scenes in *Marie* deal directly with the hopes, prayers (and sometimes machinations) of prisoners seeking to be paroled from prison. However, this subtext is always present as Marie

Sissy Spacek in *Marie* (1985).

uncovers the graft demanded by some people in power who hold the carrot of potential freedom up to confined criminals who want to beat the system.

For the record, the performer Jane Powell, who appears as a singer at the rally within *Marie*, is not the MGM singing star of the 1940s–50s, but a contemporary black gospel performer.

166. *Mayor of Hell* (Warner Bros., 1933), 85 min.

Producer, Lucien Hubbard; director, Archie Mayo; story, Islin Auster; screenplay, Edward Chodorov; art director, Esdras Hartley; costumes, Orry-Kelly; makeup,

Perc Westmore; music director, Leo F. Forbstein; assistant director, Frank Shaw; camera, Barney McGill; editor, Jack Killifer.

James Cagney (Patsy Gargan); Madge Evans (Dorothy Griffith); Frankie Darro (Jimmy Smith); Allen Jenkins (Mike); Dudley Digges (Superintendent Thompson); Sheila Terry (The Girl); Robert Barrat (Mr. Smith); Farina (Smoke Hemingway); Harold Huber (Joe); Dorothy Peterson (Mrs. Smith); George Pat Collins (Brandon); Edwin Maxwell (Louis Johnston); John Marston (Hopkins); Mickey Bennett

(Butch Kilgore); Sidney Miller (Izzy Horowitz); Hobart Cavanaugh (Tommy's Father); George Humbert (Tony's Father); Raymond Borzage (Johnny Stone); George Offerman, Jr. (Charlie Burns); Charles Cane (Tommy Gorman); Charles Wilson (Guard); Arthur Byron (Judge Gilbert); William V. Mong (Walters); Wallace MacDonald (Johnson's Assistant); Adrian Morris (Car Owner); Fred "Snowflake" Toone (Hemingway); Wilfred Lucas (Guard); Bob Perry, Charles Sullivan (Collectors); Ben Taggart (Sheriff).

> Deeply appealing. The story is an indictment against the inhuman system of punishment and the poor care given to young boys in reformatory schools, and although brutal in some of the situations it is realistic and touching at all times.
>
> *(Harrison's Reports)*

When they are caught stealing from a variety shop, young Jimmy Smith (Frankie Darro) and several members of his hooligan gang are sent to the State Reformatory where Mr. Thompson (Dudley Digges) is the abusive superintendent. From the start, the authoritarian Thompson strikes fears into the newcomers:

> I want you boys to get this straight from the start. You're here because you're petty criminals. If you behave yourselves, you'll get along all right. Do as you're told and don't ask questions. Before you stay one night here, make up your minds you're going to work hard and keep your mouth shut. Now anybody that doesn't like the idea can apply for a transfer to the penitentiary.

Because rebellious Jimmy refuses to conform to the strict rules, he is severely punished and is frequently beaten. Among the other complaints the youthful offenders have is the poor quality and quantity of food provided at the institution. It develops that Thompson has been channeling much of the allotted food budget into his own pocket by purchasing cheap foodstuff.

Meanwhile, cocky ward heeler Patsy Gargan (James Cagney), as a reward for loyal political party work, is appointed deputy commissioner and arrives at the school to investigate the abuses of power. He observes first hand the brutalities the young inmates have endured and learns from the school nurse, Dorothy Griffith (Madge Evans), more about Thompson's heartless treatment of his charges. It is the idealistic Dorothy who counsels Patsy: "[A] reform school is supposed to be where they're shown the right things. It's implied they can learn that better here than in their own homes. But that's not true, not least at this school at any rate."

Later, the former ward heeler, a reformed man with a purpose to life, is given charge of the school. Patsy and Dorothy bring about tremendous reforms, giving the boys democratic control of their lives at the institution. They set up a miniature city government with Jimmy Smith as Mayor and the rough-and-tumble Butch Kigore as chief of police.

One night Gargan is called back to his district to deal with Joe (Harold Huber), an unruly subordinate who is attempting to take over Patsy's territory. In the course of an argument, he injures the man. Fearing Joe may die and he will be held accountable by the law, Patsy hides out until he learns where he stands. Meanwhile, the domineering Thompson regains control of the school and reinstitutes his cruel methods. (As he tells his subordinates, "This is no boy scout camp. This is a reformatory.") He persuades Charlie Burns (George Offerman) to convince Jimmy Smith to run away from the reformatory, hoping it will throw Gargan's programs into turmoil. (Jimmy later returns to the institution.) Dorothy is made to resign. She finds Patsy and tells him of Thompson's new regime. More concerned with the boys' welfare than his own well being, he rushes to the school and finds it in chaos. One of the youngsters, Johnny Stone (Raymond Borzage) has died of tuberculosis as a result of harsh punishment enforced by the unfeeling Thompson. Now Jimmy and his pals are demanding revenge, having already set fire to the superintendent's barricaded retreat. After the sniveling Thompson dies trying to escape, Patsy calms the boys and restores order. A later investigation clears the young inmates of any criminal charges. Patsy, having resolved his own problems, decides to marry Dorothy. They plan to stay on at the school to continue their reform work.

Andre Sennwald (*New York Times*) was very enthusiastic about this film which he likened to *I Am a Fugitive from a Chain Gang* (1932), q.v., insisting that Warner Bros. "have nearly produced its equal." Approving of the picture's social protest theme, he cited "the impact of its mounting bitterness and resentment against the penal system at the reform school. . . . The wild fury of the boys in the closing scenes becomes contagious. . . . As the leader of the boys inmates, Frankie Darrow [sic] gives a hard-faced performance that is genuinely disturbing." *Variety* found flaws in the film, "The big item which customers have to swallow is that while reforming kids, Cagney sticks to his trade as a gang leader. . . . While having the framework of a junior *Big House* — it's only the framework. Story isn't so strong."

Always anxious for grist for its social protest cycle of movies, Warner Bros. would remake *Mayor of Hell* as *Crime School* (1938), q.v., a vehicle for the Dead End Kids with Humphrey Bogart inheriting the whitewashed James Cagney bad-good guy role. A great deal of the rawness and verve that made *The Mayor of Hell* such a solid vehicle were toned down for the remake. Moreover, audience identity with the Dead End Kids in *Crime School* greatly softened the impacted of the 1938 edition.

Despite the strong performance by Frankie Darro and its sober theme, *Mayor of Hell* was basically a James Cagney vehicle. Thus it was promoted by the studio as another of the popular star's glib, slambang action slug fests. "With Jimmy setting new standards of male behavior, no maiden's jaw is safe. When he notices them, their hearts beat pitter-patter and their teeth rattle." The film's title refers to the position of authority Frankie Darro's character holds in the student government at the reformatory, which had been a hellhole.

167. *Me, Gangster* (Fox, 1928), 70 min.

Presenter, William Fox; director, Raoul Walsh; based on the novel *Me – Gangster* by Charles Francis Coe; screenplay, Coe, Walsh; titles, William Kernell; assistant director, Archibald Buchanan; camera, Arthur Edeson; editor, Louis Loeffler.

June Collyer (Mary Regan); Don Terry (Jimmy Williams); Anders Randolf (Russ Williams); Stella Adams (Lizzie Williams); Burr McIntosh (Bill Lane); Walter James (Captain Dodds); Gustav von Seyffertitz (Factory Owner); Al Hill (Danny); Herbert Ashton (Sucker); Bob Perry (Tuxedo George); Harry Castle (Philly Kid); Carol

[Carole] Lombard (Blonde Rosie); Joe   (Danish Looie); Arthur Stone (Dan the
Brown (Joe Brown); Nigel De Brulier   Dude).

Me, Gangster was an underworld melodrama based on a popular novel (1927), itself supposedly derived from fact. It is told in diary fashion from the point-of-view of a gradually repentent hoodlum. It benefitted from the direction of Raoul Walsh, famed for his *What Price Glory?* (1926). In addition, it had the added box office attraction of having a synchronized recorded music score on the soundtrack, then still a novelty as Hollywood was transferring from silent photoplays to talkies.

A victim of his environment, slum dweller Jimmy Williams (Don Terry) escalates from petty crimes to armed robbery. His latest crime is robbing a factory of $50,000. He is caught by the police but refuses to disclose where he has hidden the loot. He is sentenced to prison. During his stay behind bars, whether working in the rock quarry or meditating in his cell, he has plenty of time to think about his criminal ways. Helping in his transformation are the traumatic death of his mother (Stella Adams) and the influence of the good-natured Mary Regan (June Collyer). Once released on early parole, he intends to return the $50,000 to its owner, but his old gang, learning of his plan, try to grab the money for themselves. He and Mary manage to outwit the hoodlums and to return the funds. Now, with a clear conscience, Jimmy and Mary start a new life together.

Variety found pros and con to this movie, noting negatively that "after a repetition or two of the same formula of dodging the gendarmes, planning and executing a larceny or stick-up the routine becomes tiresome...." On the other hand, the trade paper was impressed by a moment in the prison segment "with a fellow-inmate deterred from passing a chocolate bar to his baby.... The guard comes over when signalled, and ... passes the harmless confection to the baby, creating one of the all too few heart-throb moments...." Mordaunt Hall *(New York Times)* also cited the penitentiary scenes positively. "The admirable prison sequences depict Williams being finger-printed and locked in a cell. He is seen at his prison work and, sometimes later, going out to a big room to talk to his mother and Mary. Here Mr. Walsh gives an excellent idea of the manner in which the keepers watch the convicts and the visitors.... [There] sits the keeper on a high chair. Nothing can pass from the visitors to the prisoners without his seeing it."

To be noted in a small role as a gangster's moll was future star Carol(e) Lombard.

168. *Mean Dog Blues* (American International, 1978), color, 108 min.

Producers, Charles A. Pratt, George Lefferts; director, Mel Stuart; screenplay, Lefferts; art director, J. S. Poplin; set decorator, Don Sullivan; costumes, Bill Milton, Chris Zamiara; makeup, Michael Moschella; music, Fred Karlin; assistant directors, Kenneth Swor, Richard Luke Rothschild; stunt coordinator, Bill Couch; dog trainers, Cindy James, Carl Spitz; sound, Dwight Mobley; sound editor, James J. Klinger; camera, Robert B. Hauser; editor, Houseley Stevenson.

Gregg Henry (Paul Ramsey); Kay Lenz (Linda Ramsey); George Kennedy (Captain Omar Kinsman); Scatman Crothers (Mudcat); Tina Louise (Donna Lacey); Felton Perry (Jake Turner); Gregory Sierra (Jesus Gonzales); James Wainwright (Sergeant Hubbell Wacker); William Windom (Victor Lacey); John Daniels (Yakima Jones); Marc Alaimo (Guard); Edith Atwater (Linda's Mother); James Boyd (Sonny); Edward Call (Road Gang Guard); Christina Hart (Gloria Kinsman); Chris Hubbell

(Elroy Smith); Stephen Johnson ("Mary" Emerson); Logan Ramsey (Edmund Oberlin); Gene Silva (Tonto); Lee Weaver (Cheatem); Ian Wolfe (Judge); David Lewis (Dr. Caleb Odum); Billy Beck (Deadman); Herb Armstrong (Bailiff); James Bacon (Court Clerk); Hunter van Leer (Guard at Conjugal Barracks); Kimberly Allan (Max); Andy Albin (Truck Driver); Georgie Paul (Masseuse); John Dennis (Deputy Sheriff); Bill Catching (Mr. Vogel).

The promotional campaign for this entry from Bing Crosby Productions read, "No One Ever Escaped from Prison Camp #4. . . . But the Kid Is Going to Try!" The *Independent Film Journal* judged of the results, "Some of the acting raises the plot a few notches above the routine and accounts for most of its effectiveness."

After his car breaks down, country and western musician Paul Ramsey (Gregg Henry) has to hitchhike to Nashville. He is given a ride by corrupt politician Victor Lacey (William Windom) and his wife Donna (Tina Louise). When they stop at a roadside cafe, high-drinking Victor gets drunk but insists on driving. He later runs down a little girl, but claims that Ramsey was driving at the time. Lacey arranges to have Paul charged with driving while under the influence of drugs. Lacey's lawyer convinces the young man to plea bargain. As a result he is sentenced to one to five years on a prison work farm. The camp is run by the brutal Captain Omar Kinsman (George Kennedy) and his equally sadistic subordinate, the ex–Marine, Sergeant Hubbell Wacker (James Wainright). Among his fellow inmates are Jesus Gonzales (Gregory Sierra) and Mudcat (Scatman Crothers). When the latter is killed by an unmuzzled doberman, Paul inherits his job of helping to train the pursuit dogs, which takes him away from the unfriendly other inmates. Meanwhile, Ramsey's wife, Linda (Kay Lenz), pushes after the Laceys to admit the truth and get her husband freed. When Wacker nearly rapes Linda, after one of her visits to Paul, he gets into a fight with the guard and nearly kills him.

Life at the prison farm is hell for Ramsey, who is pursued sexually by both fellow inmates and guards and the commandant's randy sixteen-year-old daughter (Christina Hart). When not being overworked or bullwhipped by the ruthless Kinsman and his minions, Paul is thinking of ways to escape. Finally, when Donna Lacey learns that Linda is pregnant, she persuades her husband to use his connections to have the governor pardon Paul. A pardon is dispatched to the prison, but meanwhile, Kinsman finds Paul in a compromising position with his daughter and assumes Ramsey is to blame. Holding back information about the pardon, the enraged Kinsman orders that Paul engage in a race to the bitter end with the killer doberman, Rattler. Paul survives the ordeal by killing the animal with a stone. The berserk commandant demands that Ramsey then be killed, but the other prisoners protest in Paul's favor. Paul is released and reunited with his wife.

Variety found *Mean Dog Blues* acceptable action fare, rating it "an effective, if predictable, meller." It noted, "Only the open acceptance of prison homosexuality . . . distinguishes *Mean Dog Blues* from a bunch of similarly-themed pix, and provides the plot angle that leads to Henry's inevitable escape attempt." Far less sympathetic was Paul Taylor (British *Monthly Film Bulletin*): "This warmed-over stew of every prison-farm picture from *I Am a Fugitive from a Chain Gang* to *Cool Hand Luke,* crudely packaged yet played with inapposite conviction by its leads, makes for rudimentary, tediously predictable melodrama. The AIP stockpot can rarely have been so flavourless."

Gregg Henry had previously starred in the mini-series, "Rich Man, Poor

Man—II" (1976–77). For George Kennedy who won a Best Supporting Actor's Academy Award for *Cool Hand Luke* (1967), q.v., *Mean Dog Blues* was a return to the genre. However, this time around, he was on the other side of the coin, dishing out the punishment to the chain gang prisoners, and pampering the two loves of his life: his killer dog and his sexually precocious daughter.

169. *Men of Boys Town* (Metro-Goldwyn-Mayer, 1941), 106 min.

Producer, John Considine, Jr.; director, Norman Taurog; screenplay, James Kevin McGuinness; art directors, Cedric Gibbons, Henry McAfee; set decorator, Edwin B. Willis; music, Herbert Stothart; camera, Harold Rosson; editor, Frederick Y. Smith.

Spencer Tracy (Father Edward Joseph Flanagan); Mickey Rooney (Whitey Marsh); Bobs Watson (Pee Wee); Larry Nunn (Ted Martley); Darryl Hickman (Flip); Henry O'Neill (Mr. Maitland); Mary Nash (Mrs. Maitland); Lee J. Cobb (Dave Morris); Sidney Miller (Mo Kahn); Addison Richards (The Judge); Lloyd Corrigan (Roger Gorton); George Lessey (Bradford Stone); Robert Emmett Keane (Burton); Arthur Hohl (Guard); Ben Welden (Superintendent); Anne Revere (Mrs. Fenely).

> Those who enjoyed *Boys Town* should enjoy also this follow-up, even though it is not as powerful as the first picture. It nevertheless has human interest, comedy, and sentimental appeal; as a matter of fact, it is sometimes a little too sentimental.
>
> *(Harrison's Reports)*

Unable to resist the financial reward of a sequel to its blockbuster *Boys Town* (1938), q.v., MGM reteamed Spencer Tracy, Mickey Rooney and several of the original cast for this derivative follow-up. Norman Taurog again directed.

Inspired by his success, Father Flanagan (Spencer Tracy) intends to expand the facilities at Boys Town. However, he meets with obstacles in raising the necessary funds. Once again, he turns to his friend Dave Morris (Lee J. Cobb), who scolds the priest for not being content with his present buildings. Nevertheless, Dave agrees to help with the building program.

Young Ted Martley (Larry Nunn) comes to the priest's attention. He has been charged with killing a guard in a reformatory. The youth admits to Father Flanagan he did so because the man had beat him so severely that he had become a cripple. The court places Ted under the clergyman's care. Whitey Marsh (Mickey Rooney), mayor of Boys Town, and his followers attempt to help the embittered Ted adjust, but he remains unresponsive. Later, Father Flanagan informs the youth that he has obtained the services of a noted surgeon who can cure his physical disability.

The wealthy Mr. and Mrs. Maitland (Henry O'Neill, Mary Nash) want to adopt Whitey. Father Flanagan has come to depend on Whitey a great deal and hates the idea of losing this boy for whom he has come to care. However, he does not wish to stand in the youth's way. On his part, Whitey is saddened to leave this home. Later, while delivering a message to a friend of Ted's at the reformatory, Whitey gets involved with Flip (Darryl Hickman), a tough runaway from the institution. Both boys are arrested and placed in solitary confinement at the reformatory. Father Flanagan rushes to Whitey's help and he obtains the release of both youths whom he takes back to Boys Town. Ted's surgery is successful and the Maitlands, who take an emotional interest in the boy, make a sizeable donation to Boys Town's building program.

Variety decided, "Tracy again presents a sincere and human portrayal of the priest, Father Flanagan, while Rooney displays plenty of restraint in handling the assignment of the completely-reformed boy.... Peak comedy episode is a slow motion wrestling match staged by Rooney and Sidney Miller. Throat lump-erupter is the accidental death of the crippled boy's dog, burial on the grounds and the kid's miraculous walk, after the operation, to his pet's grave." Bosley Crowther *(New York Times)* was not easily pleased, citing that the new picture "matches its predecessor only in theme." He found this follow-up "an obvious and maudlin reassembly of clichés out of the cabinet marked Pathos, lacking completely the sincerity which did distinguish the first, and so frequently punctuated by close-ups of blubbering boys that one finally feels an embarrassed inclination to look away." Crowther concluded, "There have been a great many motion pictures about the sad plight of underprivileged boys, and, except for the excellent performance of Spencer Tracy as Father Flanagan, this one is just another of those."

This sequel to *Boys Town* earned no Academy Award nominations and ended the screen saga of Father Edward Joseph Flanagan. However, MGM would distribute the lurid *Girls Town* (1959), q.v., an independent production which deals with a church-run correctional facility for wayward girls. It had nowhere near the quality of either *Boys Town* features. In 1986, Robert Conrad would star in *North Beach and Rawhide*, a made-for-television movie which used a *Boys Town* concept, this time focusing on the operator (Conrad) of a cattle ranch/reformatory for delinquent city youths.

170. *Men of San Quentin* (Producers Releasing Corp., 1942), 80 min.

Producers, Martin Mooney, Max M. King; director, William Beaudine; story, Mooney; screenplay, Ernest Booth; camera, Clark Ramsey; editor, Dan Miller.

J. Anthony Hughes (Guard Sergeant Jack Holden); Eleanor Stewart (Anne Holden); Dick Curtis (Butch Mason); Charles Middleton (Deputy Warden Saunderson); Jeffrey Sayre (Jimmy); George Breakston (Louis); Art Mills (Big Al); John Ince (Board Chairman); Michael Mark (Convict in Ravine); Joe Whitehead (Joe Williams); Skins Miller (Himself); Jack Shay (Phone Guard); Jack Cheatham (Court Gate Guard); Drew Demarest (Guard Gaines); Nancy Evans (Mrs. Doakes).

One of the unique features of this poverty row feature dealing with penal reform was its on-location filming at San Quentin Prison. In fact, even the penitentiary's band provided the music for the movie's credits. *Harrison's Reports* found other virtues to this economy genre piece. "Void of the triteness of so many prison stories, it is an effective drama depicting two schools of thought in the disciplinary treatment of convicts by their keepers—the one that is hardened in its handling of criminals, and the other that believes in humanitarianism." Within eighty minutes, *Men of San Quentin* jams a great deal of plotline into the narrative.

Having just married, guard Sergeant Jack Holden (J. Anthony Hughes) returns with his bride Anne (Eleanor Stewart) to San Quentin Prison where he resumes his supervisory duties. Meanwhile, convict Louis (George Breakston) is being framed by the warped Deputy Warden Saunderson (Charles Middleton) for the killing of a guard. Later, when inmate Butch Mason (Dick Curtis) kills a guard (Drew Demarest) while trying to escape, Saunderson, envious of Holden, forces testimony from a subordinate that Holden had ordered the now dead guard to shoot two escaping convicts. (Actually they had been killed by Butch.) At the hearing, Butch is pressured into admitting the truth.

Meanwhile, prisoner Jimmy (Jeffrey Sayre), who had been assigned as houseboy to the Holdens so he could spy on them for Saunderson, has a change of heart and tells Anne the facts. Later, Jimmy shoots the manipulative Saunderson and then commits suicide. Jack is thereafter appointed warden to replace the ailing chief administrator and he is able to quell an attempted jail break. Holden introduces humanitarian reforms at San Quentin which cause the inmates to respond favorably.

Focusing on the complicated, contrived scenario, *Variety* reported, "Incoherent story and poor direction are keys to the poor b.o. [box office] prospects."

Shot over a two-week period at a cost of $25,000 ($4,000 over the usual PRC budget), *Men of San Quentin* had its premiere at the famed prison. The scenario for the film was by Ernest Booth, who was serving time in San Quentin for a bank robbery. The picture was dedicated to the then warden of the institution, Clinton T. Duffy.

171. *Men Without Souls* (Columbia, 1940), 62 min.

Director, Nick Grinde; story, Harvey Gates; screenplay, Robert D. Andrews, Joseph Carole; music, Morris W. Stoloff; camera, Benjamin Kline; editor, James Sweeney.

John Litel (Reverend Thomas Storm); Barton MacLane (Blackie Drew); Rochelle Hudson (Suzan Leonard); Glenn Ford (Johnny Adams); Don Beddoe (Warden Schaefer); Cy Kendall (Captain White); Eddie Laughton (Lefty); Dick Curtis (Duke); Richard Fiske (Crowley); Walter Soderling (Old Mack).

Sterling character actor John Litel (1895–1972) had been a regenerated gangster in *Alcatraz Island* (1937), q.v., and a priest in *Over the Wall* (1938), q.v. He returned to the cloth for *Men Without Souls,* a feeble genre piece. The predictable double-bill item featured another much-in-demand character player, Barton MacLane (1900–1969), who was adept as portraying a snarling guard (*San Quentin,* 1937, q.v.) as he was a growling convict (*Mutiny in the Big House,* 1939, q.v.). *Men Without Souls* also showcased a rising young star, Glenn Ford (b. 1916), who would reappear in several prison dramas, including *Convicted Woman* (1940) and *Convicted* (1950), qq.v. The reviewers found little satisfaction to *Men Without Souls:* "It is a rehash of the typical prison story; the surroundings are sordid since all the action takes place in the prison.... The plot is so familiar that is doubtful if the average picture-goer will have the patience to sit throughout the entire picture. Two attempted prison breaks are the only exciting occurrences...." *(Harrison's Reports).*

Reverend Thomas Storm (John Litel) has recently been appointed as chaplain at a badly run prison where he attempts to win the respect of the embittered inmates. His task is made harder because on his first day at the penitentiary, he foils an escape attempt by Blackie Drew (Barton MacLane) and several other convicts. Among the other prisoners is Johnny Adams (Glenn Ford). He has contrived (by embezzlement of funds at the bank where he worked) to be sent to prison so that he could revenge the death of his convict father, who died at the hands of a sadistic guard, Captain White (Cy Kendall). Both Storm and Suzan Leonard (Rochelle Hudson), Johnny's girlfriend, work to convince Adams that his retribution plan is self-defeating.

Meanwhile, Blackie stages another breakout and insists that Johnny go with him. When Adams refuses, Drew thinks that the young man is a stool pigeon. As such, he kills Captain White and puts the blame on Johnny. Johnny is tried for the crime and sentenced to death. On the day Adams is to die, Blackie undertakes his breakout, which calls for blowing up the boiler room. In the process he is badly injured and before he dies, he confesses to Storm that it was he who killed White.

Variety summarized: "Whole thing follows formula, with prison color and violence invariably the expected. John Litel gives a capable performance. . . . Barton MacLane is the toughest of the cons. Don Beddoe is convincing as the shaggy-haired warden and Cy Kendall is a realistically cruel guard captain."

172. *Midnight Express* (Columbia, 1978), color, 121 min.

Executive producer, Peter Guber; producer, Alan Marshall, David Puttnam; director, Alan Parker; based on the book by Billy Hayes with William Hoffer; screenplay, Oliver Stone; production designer, Geoffrey Kirkland; art director, Evan Hercules; costumes, Milena Canonero; makeup, Mary Hillman, Penny Steyne; music, Giorgio Moroder; song, David Castle; fight arranger, Roy Scammell; sound, Clive Winter; sound re-recording, Bill Rowe; sound editor, Rusty Coppleman; camera, Michael Seresin; editor, Gerry Hambling.

Brad Davis (Billy Hayes); Randy Quaid (Jimmy Booth); John Hurt (Max); Irene Miracle (Susan); Bo Hopkins (Tex); Mike Kellin (Mr. Hayes); Franco Diogene (Yesil); Michael Ensign (Stanley Daniels); Gigi Ballista (Chief Judge); Kevork Malikyan (Prosecutor); Peter Jeffrey (Ahmet); Zanninos Zanninou (Turkish Detective); Tony Boyd (Aslan); Michael Yannatos (Translator); Abmed El Shenawi (Negdir); Dimos Starenios (Ticket Seller); and: Yasfar Adem, Joe Zammit Cordina, Vic Tablkian, Raad Rawi.

Midnight Express is certainly one of the most graphic accounts of a man's survival through five years of hellish confinement. During his imprisonment, the hero is subjected to a full range of brutalities at the hands of heinous guards and equally violent fellow prisoners. That he survives the overwhelming ordeal is amazing enough, but that he escapes to freedom gives this true-life adventure a welcome, optimistic tone. Even more a popular than a critical hit, this award-winning drama, once seen, leaves an indelible impression. Years after its initial release, *The Cable Guide* magazine would say of this still powerful drama: "The physical and emotional brutality . . . [the hero] endures and his unflagging desire to escape pack an unforgettable emotional wallop."

On October 6, 1970, at the Istanbul airport, American college student Billy Hayes (Brad Davis) is returning to the United States with his girlfriend Susan (Irene Miracle). During the customs search, he is detained for possessing two kilos of hashish which he was attempting to smuggle on his person out of the country. The innocent Susan is allowed to go free, while Billy is arrested. When he later attempts to escape, he is dragged to Sagamilcar, a prison fortress. There he is beaten and sodomized by Hamidou (Paul Smith), the brutish chief guard. Billy's distraught father (Mike Kellin) visits him at the prison and his fearful son begs, "Dad, get me out of here!" However, there is nothing Mr. Hayes can do.

Billy is sentenced to four years and two months. He is forced to adapt to the routine of his dilapidated prison, filled with cutthroats, deranged souls and a variety of other unsavory types. Among the other prisoners are the dissolute Britisher, Max (John Hurt), who has been in jail for seven years already, and Erich (Norbert

Mike Kellin and Brad Davis in *Midnight Express* (1978).

Weisser), a young Swede, who makes homosexual advances to Billy, which the latter rejects. Billy also meets another American, the quirky Jimmy Booth (Randy
Quaid):

> JIMMY: We're all crazy here.
>
> BILLY: I'm Billy Hayes, or I used to be.

It is Jimmy who first tells Hayes of the "midnight express," the prison expression
for escape.

Time passes and Billy keeps his sanity by writing letters to his family and to
his girlfriend. He confides to Susan, "You can drift in here and never know you're
gone. You can fade so far out you don't know where you are any more or anything
else is. I find loneliness a physical pain which hurts all over. You can't isolate it
in one part of your body."

Two years have passed since his incarceration. Billy passes up an opportunity to join in an escape plan, convinced that his lawyer Yesil (Franco Diogene) will finally be able to purchase his release. However, the appeal court in Ankara decrees that he serve a life sentence (later reduced to thirty years). Having lost all hope, he defiantly shouts out to the judges who do not understand his English:

> I just wish you could be standing where I'm standing right now and feel what that feels like, because then you would know something that you don't know, Mr. Prosecutor, mercy. You would know that a concept of a society is based on the quality of that mercy, its sense of fair play, its sense of justice. But I guess that's like asking a bear to shit in a toilet.
>
> For a nation of pigs, it sure is funny you don't eat 'em. Jesus Christ forgave the bastards, but I can't. I hate you! I hate your nation! And I hate your people!

Feeling anything is better than remaining in this hellhole, Billy joins the hotheaded Jimmy and the deranged Max in an escape scheme that will take them through the catacombs beneath the fort. However, the prisoner Rifti (Paolo Bonacelli) informs on the men and Jimmy is taken away to be punished. In reprisal, Billy and Max steal Rifki's hidden hoard of money and, in turn, Rifki frames Max. The enraged Billy attacks Rifki, gouging the man's only good eye and biting out the betrayer's tongue. As a result, Billy is transferred to cell block 13, the section for the criminally insane. Meanwhile, Susan arranges a visit to the prison. Her physical presence helps Billy to maintain his sanity. She also smuggles money to him which he uses to bribe his way out of the prison. His attempted transaction is noted by the guards and he is taken to a private interrogation room where Hamidou begins to attack him. Fighting back, Billy accidentally kills his tormentor. He quickly dresses in the dead man's guard uniform and escapes. A postscript notes: "On the night of October 4, 1975, Billy Hayes successfully crossed the border to Greece. He arrived home at Kennedy Airport three weeks later."

While admitting that "cast, direction and production are all very good," *Variety*'s reporter duly noted, "[I]t's difficult to sort out the proper empathies from the muddled and moralizing screenplay which, in true Anglo-American fashion, wrings hands over alien cultures as though our civilization is absolutely perfect." The trade paper further reasoned, "Acceptance of the film depends a lot on forgetting several things: He [Billy Hayes] was smuggling hash; Turkey is entitled to its laws, and is no more guilty of penal corruption and brutality, than, say, the U.S., U.K., France, Germany, etc...." Judith Crist (*5001 Nights at the Movies*, 1984) claimed, "[T]he film is like a porno fantasy about the sacrifice of a virgin. It rushes from torment to torment, treating Billy's ordeals hypnotically in soft colors—muted squalor—with a disco beat in the background. The prison itself is more like a brothel than a prison. All of this is packaged as social protest." ·

Midnight Express won two Academy Awards: Best Screenplay (Oliver Stone), Best Original Score (Giorgio Moroder). It received four Academy Award nominations: Best Picture, Best Director, Best Supporting Actor (John Hurt) and Best Editing. The picture earned $15,065,000 in domestic film rentals paid to the distributor. The Award-winning soundtrack album was exceedingly popular. In recent years there has been talk of making *Midnight Express II*. A TV movie, *Dark Holiday* (1989), q.v., also based on a real life experience, provides a distaff version of an American tourist (Lee Remick) imprisoned in Turkey. *Midnight Express* was shot on location in Malta.

173. *Millionaires in Prison* (RKO, 1940), 63 min.

Executive producer, Lee Marcus; producer, Howard Benedict; director, Ray McCarey; story, Martin Mooney; screenplay, Lynn Root, Frank Fenton; art director, Van Nest Polglase; wardrobe, Renie; music, Roy Webb; sound, Richard van Hessen; special effects, Vernon L. Walker; camera, Harry Wild; editor, Theron B. Warth.

Lee Tracy (Nick Burton); Linda Hayes (Helen Hewitt); Raymond Walburn (Bruce Vander); Morgan Conway (James Brent); Truman Bradley (Dr. William Collins); Virginia Vale (May Thomas); Cliff Edwards (Happy); Paul Guilfoyle (Ox); Thurston Hall (Harold Kellogg); Chester Clute (Sidney Keats); Shemp Howard (The Professor); Horace MacMahon (S.O.S. [Sylvester Ogden Scofield]); Thomas E. Jackson (Warden Tom Hammond); Elliott Sullivan (Brody); Selmer Jackson (Dr. Harry Lindsay); Jack Arnold [Vinton Haworth] (Windsor); Frank O'Connor (Guard in Warden's Office); Grady Sutton (Jock); Anthony Warde (Max); Robert Emmett Keane (Editor); Charles C. Wilson (R.J. Reynolds, Sunday Editor); Dell Henderson, Leo Cleary, John Sheehan (Deputies); Dick Cramer (Dick, the Guard); Chester Tallman, Larry McGrath, Roger Laswell (Guards); Bruce Mitchell (Conductor); John Dilson (Spectator); Sammy Stein (Guard in Mess Hall); Kenneth Harlan (Jerry Connell); Joe Devlin (Vince Connell); Charles Hall (British Convict); Sam Lufkin (Convict); George Magrill (Yard Guard); Donald Kerr (Librarian); Carol Tevis (Mabel); Carol Wayne (S.O.S.'s Wife); Grace Leonard (Marie Brody); Al Seymour (Red Vernon); Frank Mills (Dominic, the Chef); Brooks Benedict, Eddie Hart, Hal K. Dawson, Don McNamee (Reporters).

A mild little confection depicting how the upper crust fumbles and then buckles down to survive in a "rugged" prison environment. The comedy relief is derived from having blue bloods forced to mingle with the hoi polloi and getting their comeuppance. The story was by Martin Mooney, who made a specialty of prison stories.

Rich, young Dr. William Collins (Truman Bradley) must serve a prison term for manslaughter committed while drunk driving. His girlfriend Helen Hewitt (Linda Hayes) comes to the train station to wish Collins well. Others heading to Longley State Prison that day are: millionaires Bruce Vander (Raymond Walburn) and Harold Kellogg (Thurston Hall) who innocently became involved in a crooked deal, and wealthy, dishonest stockbrokers Sidney Keats (Chester Clute) and James Brent (Morgan Conway).

The addled Vander and the blustering Kellogg think this (mis)adventure is a lark and Harold, used to having his own way, insists, "I see no reason why the warden should object to uniforms by our own tailor." However, once confined to drab prison garb and forced to conform to the daily regimen, the benign twosome are no longer so amused. They are assigned to a cell, already inhabited by S.O.S. (Horace MacMahon) and The Professor (Shemp Howard). Used to haute cuisine, this duo have to make a great adjustment to the mess hall grub.

> VANDER: [To a guard]. See here, my good man. I can't eat beans. It just so happens they don't agree with me.

> KELLOGG: We haven't been supplied with either knives or forks and there's no butter for the bread. Would it be possible to eat in the cell? We'll pay to have the food brought in.

Meanwhile, the newcomers learn that convict Nick Burton (Lee Tracy), a tough egg who insists, "I'm strictly a believer in percentages," runs the prison population. Actually, Nick has a healthy perspective on life and it is he who encourages Collins to work in the prison hospital. At first, it appears that Nick is going to help the conniving Keats and Brent fleece their fellow prisoners, but later he forces the con artists to make good their phony stock offerings to their fellow inmates. Collins becomes engrossed in an experiment to cure Malta fever and he turns to Nick to solve the problem of financing his work. (Nick pressures Vander and Kellogg into contributing to the cause.) Four convicts volunteer to be injected with the experimental serum. The experiment proves a success and received great coverage in the press. For his efforts Collins is due to be paroled in two months; he puts in a good word for Nick to accelerate his new friend's release.

It was hard to fault this agreeable minor offering. Bosley Crowther *(New York Times)* commended, "[A] more comfortable and congenial jail-house has certainly never been seen on the screen. Not only are most of the inmates the most chummy chaps one ever met but they also have Convict Lee Tracy to direct their uncertain steps and to intercede for them with the warden whenever necessity compels. And of course, the warden submits." *Variety* reported, "Picture is different in that it fails to make prison life gloomy, and there is not a single jail break."

One of the more engaging scenes in this likeable fable occurs when Bruce Vander's insipid nephew, Jock (Grady Sutton) comes for a visit and is counseled by his uncle and Harold Kellogg on the proper menu for his crucial bachelor's dinner.

Prisoners being used as experimental guinea pigs would also be a plot gimmick of a later RKO release, the murder mystery, *Experiment Alcatraz* (1950), q.v.

174. *Mrs. Soffel* (Metro-Goldwyn-Mayer/United Artists, 1984), color, 111 min.

Producers, Edgar J. Scherick, Scott Rudin, David A. Nicksay; associate producer, Dennis Jones; director, Gillian Armstrong; screenplay, Ron Nyswaner; production designer, Luciana Arrighi; art directors, Roy Forge Smith, Ed Pisoni; set decorators, Jacques Bradette, Hilton Rosemarin, Dan Conley; associate costume designer, Shay Cunlifee; makeup, Patric Green, Linda Gill; music, Mark Isham; music supervisor, Todd Boekelheide; second unit directors, Glenn H. Randall, Jr., Ron Bozman; assistant directors, Mark Egerton, Scott Maitland, Richard Flower, Rocco Gismondi, Bozman, Anthony H. Gittelson; stunt coordinator, Randall, Jr.; sound, David Lee; sound re-recording, Jay M. Harding, Ray O'Reilly, David J. Kimball; sound effects editors, Dennis Drumond, George Anderson; supervising sound editor, Bob Grieve; foley editor, Joanne D'Antonio; special effects, Neil Trifunovich, Kevin Pike; camera, Russell Boyd, Peter Norman, Darwin Dean; editor, Nicholas Beauman.

Diane Keaton (Kate Soffel); Mel Gibson (Ed Biddle); Matthew Modine (Jack Biddle); Edward Herrmann (Peter Soffel); Trini Alvarado (Irene Soffel); Jennie Dundas (Margaret Soffel); Danny Corkill (Eddie Soffel); Harley Cross (Clarence Soffel); Terry O'Quinn (Buck McGovern); Pippa Pearthree (Maggie); William Youmans (Guard Koslow); Maury Chaykin (Guard Reynolds); Joyce Ebert (Matron Garvey); John W. Carroll (Guard McGarey); Dana Wheeler-Nicholson (Jessie Bodyne); Wayne Robson (Halliday); Les Rubie (Mr. Stevenson); Paula Trueman (Mrs. Stevenson); David Huckvale (1st Russian Twin); Douglas Huckvale (2nd Russian Twin); Ralph Zeldin (Russian); Nancy Chesney (Mrs. Fitzgerald); Samantha Follows (Becky Knotts); Katie McCombs (Rachel Garvey); Linda Cabler (Leota Yoeders); Eric Hebert (Paperboy); Alar Aedma (Guard); Tom Harvey (Attorney Burke); Jack Jessop (Attorney Watson); Lou Pitoscia (Prisoner); John Dee (Old Prisoner); William Duell (Lenny); Len Doncheff (Polish Guard); David Fox (McNeil); Fred Booker (Trustee); Valerie Buhagiar (Alice); Jane Foster (Elsie); Phillip Craig (Sketch Artist); John Innes (2nd Reporter); Norma Dell'Agnese (Woman Reporter); Al Kozlik (3rd Reporter); Derek Keurvorst (Reporter); Kay Hawtrey (Peter's Secretary); Brian Young (McNeil's Secretary); Frank Adamson (Swinehart); Don Granberry (Roach); Gerald Tucker (Policeman); Heather Graham, Linda Carola (Factory Girls); George Belskey (Mr. Bodyne); Marushka Stankova (Mrs. Bodyne); James Bradford (Minister); Charles Jolliffe (Sheriff Hoon); Rodger Barton (Deputy Hoon); Jack Mather (Mr. Watson); Lee-Max Walton (Harry); Sean Sullivan, Warren Van Evera, Clay Pollett (Farmers); Chris Cummings (Boy); Dan Lett (Young Man); Don McManus (6th Reporter); Dorothy Phelan (Old Aunt); Walter Massey (Mr. Robinson).

There are so many flaws in this arty motion picture that it is hard to decide which elements were most damaging to the final results. Although the story is based on fact, the truth seems so preposterous as presented, that the viewer soon stops caring. Much of the film is so murkily photographed that the meticulously recreated/refurbished historical settings are frequently lost in the gloom. The chemistry between the two leads (Diane Keaton, Mel Gibson) is nearly non-existent and both stars squirm so uncomfortably with their ambiguous characterizations that the watcher's mind quickly begins to drift. Thus, it is little wonder that *Mrs. Soffel*, with its bizarre prison tale, was such a box office disaster. Made at an estimated negative cost of $14,000,000, the movie earned a paltry $1,700,000 in domestic rentals paid to the distributor.

In 1901 Pittsburgh, Kate (Diane Keaton), the bored wife of stuffy Warden Peter Soffel (Edward Herrmann) of Allegheny County jail, has been ill for several months. Recently, she has returned to her charitable duties dispensing words of Christian hope to the inmates. Among the housed convicts are two condemned killers, Ed (Mel Gibson) and Jack Biddle (Matthew Modine). These handsome young murderers, who robbed a grocery shop and killed the owner, are awaiting execution. Kate is drawn to the older brother Ed and she makes excuses to visit the Biddles frequently. After the depressed Ed nearly kills himself in a fire in his cell, the emotionally-drawn Kate agrees to help the brothers break free.

On the evening of their escape, Ed, against Jack's advice, goes to the warden's house (which is within the prison structure) and convinces Kate to abandon her family to join them in flight. The affair creates a scandal in turn-of-the-century Pittsburgh society. The trio head for Canada, but Kate's poor health slows down their progress. Near the Canadian border, an old couple provides them shelter. During their night of lovemaking Ed confesses that it was he who had killed the victim and not his brother. When their identity is discovered by their hosts, the three fugitives flee, with a posse in pursuit. Knowing they cannot escape, Kate forces Ed to keep his promise (of not letting her be taken alive), and he shoots her. Thereafter, the brothers are killed by the posse. Kate, however, survives and is brought back to Pittsburgh to be imprisoned for participating in the escape. Still adoring her lost lover, the rebellious Kate has a picture of Ed smuggled into her cell.

"The movie is so quiet that it doesn't seem to be taking place in America. The crude humor, the violence and energy of the big young country are missing. And even after the Biddles and Mrs. Soffel have escaped, the movie remains forbiddingly dark.... Despite all the talent at work in it, one still has to fight off the enfolding arms of sleep" (David Denby, *New York* magazine). For Richard Schickel (*Time* magazine), "*Mrs. Soffel* (rhymes with woeful) is *Bonnie and Clyde* with the emotional lights turned down, *Tristan and Isolde* without the saving soaring music." According to Leo Seligsohn (*Newsday*), "The movie gets off to a slow start trying,

Mel Gibson and Matthew Modine in *Mrs. Soffel* (1984).

unsuccessfully, to establish the characters and the relationship. It doesn't help that many of the early scenes were shot in the still-operational Allegheny County Jail, where the actual events occurred. It is a dark fortress whose gloomy interior intensifies a soddenness and lack of movement in the early scenes."

On the other hand, Rex Reed *(New York Post)* found that "It is still pretty shocking, although it happened 83 years ago, which makes it all the more timely.... The story, pieced together through prison records and love letters, is far from complete.... But it's vital. It's the stuff of tales and legends." For Sheila Benson *(Los Angeles Times)*, "*Mrs. Soffel* manages to be as romantic in spirit ... as it is realistic in context.... [The] fact that [director Gillian] Armstrong is a woman has got to be a plus. Particularly impressive is her ability to depict relationships; taking us into the increasingly stultifying world of Mrs. Soffel with its domestic routines and, most important, her depiction of Mrs. Soffel's relationship with her eldest daughter...."

175. *Murder in the Big House* (Warner Bros., 1942), 59 min.

Producer, William Jacobs; director, B. Reeves Eason; based on the story "Murder in the Death House" by Jerome Chodorov; screenplay, Raymond L. Schrock; art director, Hugh Reticker; costumes, Orry-Kelly; camera, Ted McCord; editor, Terry Morse.

Faye Emerson (Gladys Wayne); Van Johnson (Bert Bell); George Meeker ("Scoop" Conner); Frank Wilcox (Randall); Michael Ames ("Dapper Dan" Malloy); Roland Drew ("Mile-Away" Gordon); Ruth Ford (Mrs. Gordon); Joseph Crehan (Jim

"Pop" Ainslee); William Gould (Warden John Bevins); Douglas Wood (Bill Burgen); John Maxwell (Prison Doctor); Pat McVeigh [McVey] (Chief Electrician); Dick Rich (Guard); Fred Kelsey (Keeper); Bill Phillips (Mike); Jack Mower (Ramstead); Creighton Hale (Ritter); Henry Hall (Chaplain).

Not only is *Murder in the Big House* a remake of sorts of the studio's earlier *Jailbreak* (1936), q.v., and *Smashing the Money Ring* (1939), q.v., but it was the first movie leading role for actor Van Johnson, who had made his screen debut in RKO's *Too Many Girls* (1940). Like its predecessors, it was a mixture of the whodunit and the prison yarn, with the jigsaw puzzle of clues solved by a cub reporter anxious for that big scoop.

"Dapper Dan" Malloy (Michael Ames) is reassured by his crooked attorney Bill Burgen (Douglas Wood) that the governor will not only commute Malloy's death sentence, but that he will announce it on the radio one hour before the scheduled electrocution. Malloy agrees to listen to the broadcast using the radio set and earphones in his cell. Meanwhile, "Scoop" Conner of the *Morning News* is too intoxicated to cover the execution. (It is the first one he will miss in eight years!) Therefore, earnest newspaper worker Gladys Wayne (Faye Emerson) impulsively takes fledgling reporter Bert Bell (Van Johnson) with her to cover the story. Arriving at the prison, the news media convene in the press room. There is a major electrical storm that night and soon the news is brought to the reporters that Malloy has died ahead of schedule, a victim of a flash of lighting.

Back at the paper, the enthusiastic Bert discusses the strange death with the now-sobered Conner and the latter agrees that something is amiss. They set out to gain the needed evidence to substantiate their suspicions. Returning to the prison, Bell uncovers that "Mile-Away" Gordon (Roland Drew), a death row pal of Malloy, has (also) been told by lawyer Burgen that his sentence will be commuted and that he should listen on the radio for the news. This leads the now suspicious Bell to contacting Gordon's wife (Ruth Ford) and providing her with information that could save her husband's life. On the night of his execution, Gordon feigns death in his cell just as the switch on the electric chair is tested. Bert traces special wiring from the electric chair to the headphones in Malloy's cells. It develops that the crooked warden (William Gould), the culprit, was tied into the mouthpiece Burgen and his mob. Mile Away's sentence is commuted to life and, as for Bert and Gladys, they decide to marry and honeymoon in Miami Beach.

Variety found some virtue in this unassuming programmer. "Pleasant relief from general prison picture display is total elimination of large cellblock settings and parade of prisoners around the big house and grounds. Prison sequences are thus confined to the death cells and the electrocution chamber." The more critical Thomas M. Pryor *(New York Times)* argued, "Nobody expects an air-tight script in this type of potboiler fare, but a dash of suspense is not too much to ask. Or is it?"

After boyish, freckle-faced Van Johnson became a major star at Metro-Goldwyn-Mayer, Warner Bros. reissued this "B" picture in 1945 as *Born for Trouble*. This time around, Johnson received prominent top billing.

British release title: *Human Sabotage*.

176. *Mutiny in the Big House* (Monogram, 1939), 83 min.

Associate producer, Grant Withers; director, William Nigh; story, Martin Mooney; screenplay, Robert D. Andrews; art director, E.R. Hickson; wardrobe, Louis

Brown; music director, Edward Kay; assistant director, W.B. Eason; sound, Karl Zint; camera, Harry Neumann; editor, Russell F. Schoengarth.

Charles Bickford (Father Joe Collins); Barton MacLane (Red Manson); Pat Moriarity (Warden Pat); Dennis Moore (Johnny Gates); William Royle (Captain

Ed Samson); Charles Foy (Bitsy); George Cleveland (Dad Schultz); Nigel de Brulier (Mike); Ed Foster (Duke); Richard Austin (Singing Jim); Russell Hopton (Frankie); Jeffrey Sayre (Milo); Jack Daley (Evans); Dave O'Brien (Daniels, the Guard); Wheeler Oakman (Benson); and: Charles King, Merrill McCormick.

Take the name "Monogram" out of the introductory title and put in its place "Paramount," "RKO," or the name of any other major company, and you will think that this is one of their very good "B" prison-theme pictures. Although the thrills are not as plentiful as those in big prison pictures of major companies, there are thrills, just the same, and one is held in pretty tense suspense throughout.

(Harrison's Reports)

The foreword to this film states:

In every prison, devoted men of every creed work every day, seldom paid and seldom honored, to save the souls and rebuild the lives of broken men.

This is the story of a prison chaplain. The story is fiction and the characters are invented. Yet the story is based on fact.

This picture is presented in honor of all prison chaplains, and in tribute to Father Patrick O'Neil of the Order of Saint Benedict, who risked his own life to save men from death in the Canon City, Colorado prison riot, October 3, 1929, in which seven guards and five convicts were killed — and who was awarded the Carnegie Medal for heroism.

Father Joe Collins (Charles Bickford) is chaplain of an overcrowded state prison, built for 1,280, but now holding 3,296 inmates. He has turned down offers of wealthy parishes, joking to the prison staff, "Where else could I be assured of a congregation that size?"

Among the new arrivals at Westview Penitentiary is Johnny Gates (Dennis Moore), who has been sentenced to one to fourteen years for forging a $10 check, which he used to buy medication for his ailing mother. Father Joe, who prides himself on his ability to judge a man's character, has faith that Gates is a basically decent individual. Not even the fact that once in prison Gates begins acting tough deters Collins's belief in him.

Gates becomes acclimated to the drudgery and severeness of prison life. His tough cellmate, Red Manson (Barton MacLane) warns him: "You think it's just printed on there [your prison number] and you can leave it behind with your coat when you get out of here. Well, you can't kid, cause it's branded right on your skin."

As for Johnny's hopes of an early parole, the cynical Manson crushes those dreams: "You better plan on seven [years]. The board don't know any smaller number."

When Mike (Nigel de Brulier) is scheduled to be executed, another convict, Singing Jim (Richard Austin), offers consolation in song. Father Joe tries to console the condemned man who begs, "Tell me how to pray." The sardonic Manson comments after Mike dies, "Well, he got out."

Meanwhile, the hyperactive Bitsy (Charles Foy) is agog at his responsibilities in choreographing the upcoming prison variety show, *Westview Preview of 1940*.

It is a major project for him to audition actors as he is convinced that his own talent outshines anyone else's. Johnny is transferred to working in the library where Dad Schultz (George Cleveland) is in charge, although the latter is soon to be released after serving twenty years.

Always eager to help his flock in any way, Father Joe helps Bitsy conduct his auditions. Later, he attends a prison board meeting where he learns the committee has decided to cut expenses further. This leads to a confrontation between the clergyman and the supercilious board members.

> BOARD MEMBER: When a man has completed his debt to society, he is free.

> FATHER JOE: Free to go mad, to steal, to starve. . . . An ex-convict with every door of opportunity closed to him. Has this man any citizenship privileges? Will the government give him a job? No, my friends, there is not one employer in a hundred who'll give him a chance. And what happens? He gets hungry. He gets bitter. He gets desperate and back he comes. That's why prison expenses are high and why crime goes on!

Time passes, and when rumors spread that a breakout is planned, the staff focus on Johnny who supposedly has information of the scheme. When he refuses to admit anything, he is put in the hole. Later, Red and his pals in the machine shop start a riot to cover their breakout attempt. Several guards are taken hostage and soon several convicts and other keepers are killed in the exchange of gunfire. Father Joe braves going into the shop to confront Red. With the help of Johnny, he quells the revolters.

As the prisoners are led back to their cells, Father Joe and the warden (Pat Moriarity) discuss Red Manson's bleak future.

> WARDEN: You don't think you can save him?

> FATHER JOE: I've got till they hang him.

The film concludes with the title card:

> Greater love has no man than this that he may lay down his life for his friends.

Between all the clichés of *Mutiny in the Big House* there are a few outstanding moments. When Dad Schultz is released from prison the scene shifts to the city where the elderly man is befuddled by the moving traffic around him. Confused and frightened he returns to the prison and begs to be allowed to return, to have a cell again and to be allowed to tend the flower gardens in the exercise yards. George Cleveland makes this a very poignant, thought provoking interlude. There are also some wry observations on prison routine. When guards are killed during the riot, the captain of the guards says offhandedly, "That's the chance they took when they signed up." It is a somber reflection on this dangerous occupation. There are also moments of humor, mostly provided by the frenetic Bitsy (played by Charley Foy, a one time member of the Seven Little Foys and a frequent participant in prison screen dramas).

BITSY: Can you do a time step?

JOHNNY: What's that? Some kind of convict march?

In appraising its box office potential, *Variety* noted of *Mutiny in the Big House*, "The picture deals wholly with the work of a prison chaplain ... and in those communities predominantly Catholic, it lends every natural angle for tieup and recommendation because it honors one of the heroes of the church."

This was the first producing assignment for actor Grant Withers. Charles Bickford would later play a convict in the prison genre classic *Brute Force* (1947), q.v. The ad copy for *Mutiny in the Big House* promised:

> *Conflict* as a man of mercy and a man of murder face each other across machine-gun battlements!

> *Conflict* as a thousand caged convicts riot for one last, desperate grab at freedom!

> *Conflict* blasts the screen wide open with thrills when there's *Mutiny in the Big House*.

177. *My Six Convicts* (Columbia, 1952), 104 min.

Producer, Stanley Kramer; associate producers, Edna Anhalt, Edward Anhalt; director, Hugo Fregonese; based on the book by Donald Powell Wilson; screenplay, Michael Blankfort; art director, Edward Ilou; music, Dimitri Tiomkin; assistant director, James Casey; camera, Guy Roe; editor, Gene Havlick.

Millard Mitchell (James Connie); Gilbert Roland (Punch Pinero); John Beal (Doc); Marshall Thompson (Blivens Scott); Alf Kjellin (Clem Randall); Henry [Harry] Morgan (Dawson); Jay Adler (Steve Kopac); Regis Toomey (Doctor Gordon); Fay Roope (Warden Potter); Carlton Young (Captain Haggerty); John Marley (Knotty Johnson); Russ Conway (Dr. Hughes); Byron Foulger (Doc Brint); Charles Buckinsky [Bronson] (Jocko); Peter Virgo, George Eldredge, Paul Hoffman, Dick Cogan, Allen Mathews, H. George Stern (Convicts); Jack Carr (Higgins); Carol Savage (Mrs. Randall); Danny Jackson (Convict #1538); Joe Haworth (Convict #9670); Chester Jones (Convict #7546); Vincent Renno (Convict #9919); Frank Mitchell (Convict #3007); Joe McTurk (Big Benny); Harry Stanton (Banker); Fred Kelsey (Store Detective); Edwin Parker (Guard on Dump Truck); Joe Palma (Convict Driver); Barney Phillips (Baker Foreman); Dick Curtis, John Monaghan (Guards).

Based on the best selling book by Donald Powell Wilson about his experiences as a visiting psychologist at Levinworth prison, *My Six Convicts* is an engaging blend of comedy, heartwarming drama and occasional thrills.

A psychologist, Doc (John Beal), arrives at Harbor State Prison to conduct an experiment with the prison population. His aim is to create a valid test for determining the aptitudes and attitudes of convicts so a more realistic rehabilitation program can be devised. The warden (Fay Roope) is antagonistic towards the concept, but is pressured to go along with the project. Fearful that the convicts may reveal too much about prison life, Doc is made to agree that he will keep confidential anything the inmates divulge to him. At his initial testing session, the wary convicts are uncooperative and behave in an obstreperous manner. Because Doc does not squeal on them, he gains the respect of the men, especially flippant convict James Connie (Millard Mitchell), a one-time safecracker.

Connie becomes Doc's assistant, acting as intermediary with the other inmates. Soon five other prisoners become Doc's aides: Punch Pinero (Gilbert

Marshall Thompson, Jay Adler, Gilbert Roland, Alf Kjellin and Millard Mitchell in *My Six Convicts* (1952).

Roland), a mobster and killer; the well educated, psychopathic killer Dawson (Henry Morgan), embezzler Steve Kopac (Jay Adler), alcoholic Blivens Scott (Marshall Thompson), and robber Clem Randall (Alf Kjellin). All goes well with Doc's testing till one day, in a drunken stupor, Scott destroys Doc's laboriously gathered records. As a result, Scott is not allowed to pitch on the prison ball team. The inmates rebel until they learn the full story from Doc; then they see the fairness of Scott's punishment. Later, the crazed Dawson hatches an escape plan, using Doc as his hostage to make his breakout. Thanks to the enterprising efforts of Doc's other assistants, the situation is resolved positively.

Variety endorsed *My Six Convicts.* "As did the tome, the film makes humans of the imprisoned men, and deals with them with whimsical humor and intelligent understanding.... It's no regular prison drama of the common type. There's some screen license evident in the treatment of several situations, but nothing that prevents the story from playing with a compelling plausibility...." A. H. Weiler *(New York Times)* agreed, "[P]enology, psychology and crime have been blended into a compassionate, thoughtful, incisive and, above all, genuinely humorous account of life behind prison walls." In retrospect, Clive Hirshhorn *(The Columbia Story,* 1989) would judge, "Eschewing melodrama for genuine character development, the film offered a series of well-observed case-histories all of which were socially relevant."

For many viewers, the highlight of this remembrance of a psychologist's two-year experiment behind prison walls was the segment in which Connie, the wise-

The Naked Cage 297

mouthed safecracker, is briefly escorted out of prison so he can open a troublesome bank safe for authorities. It is also the philosophical Connie who tells Doc that the conflict between convicts and everyday citizens is "a war between the ins and outs." Not to be overlooked is the episode in which Clem Randall has his wife (Carol Savage) snuck *into* prison, leading to expected complications.

On location filming was accomplished at the recently renovated San Quentin Prison. Several of the walk-ons and extras were real life convicts. To be noted in the cast, billed fourteenth, is Charles Buchinsky [Bronson] as Jocko the convict. He would later appear in several prison-oriented features, including: *The Valachi Papers* (1972) and *Breakout* (1975), qq.v.

178. *The Naked Cage* (Cannon, 1985), color, 97 min.

Executive producers, Menahem Golan, Yoram Globus; producer, Chris D. Nebe; director/screenplay, Paul Nicholas; art director, Alex Hajdu; set decorator, Marlene McCormick; wardrobe, Shelly Komarov; makeup, Lily Benyair; music, Christopher Stone; assistant director, Bradley Gross; stunt coordinator, Al Jones; sound, Morteza Rezvani; sound effects supervisor, Glenn Gebhard; ADR editor, Jim Bogardt; foley editor, Steve Mann; dialogue editor, Frank McKelevey; camera, Hal Trussell; editors, Warren Chadwick, Nino DeMarco.

Shari Shattuck (Michelle); Angel Tompkins (Warden Wallace); Lucinda Crosby (Rhonda); Christina Whitaker (Rita Morani); Faith Minton (Sheila); Stacey Shaffer (Amy); Nick Benedict (Smiley); Lisa London (Abbey); John Terlesky (Willy); Aude Charles (Brenda Williams); Angela Gibbs (Vonna); Leslie Huntly (Peaches); Carole Ita White (Trouble); Seth Kaufman (Randy); Larry Gelman (Doc); Susie London (Martha); Valerie McIntosh (Ruby); Flo Gerrish (Mother); James Ingersoll (Father); William Bassett (Jordan); Nora Niesen (Bigfoot); Jennifer Anne Thomas (Mock); Chris Anders (Miller); Al Jones (Bartender); Sheila Stephenson (Bank Teller); Bob Saurman (Motorcycle Cop); Rick Avery (Security Officer); Christopher Doyle (Police Officer); Gretchen Davis, Beryl Jones, Michael Kerr (Prison Guards).

By the early 1980s, with such commercially successful entries as *The Concrete Jungle* (1982) and *Chained Heat* (1983), qq.v., the softcore pornography women-behind-bars formula had frozen into expected conventions. Within its confines, most variations on the theme had been explored. Therefore, new entries were judged on more whimsical standards: how attractive were the "canned tomatoes," how many shower room scenes were there, and did the cast get down and dirty in the assorted rumble, rape and reprisal sequences. If the dialogue was occasionally amusing or wry (whether deliberate or not), so much the better. If the technical aspects were above par, that made the going a lot easier. On such criteria, *The Naked Cage* rates a B+. After all, *any* picture that co-stars action film queen Angel Tompkins cannot be all bad! Moreover, *The Naked Cage* was directed by Paul Nicholas, who had proven his expertise with the subgenre in *Chained Heat.*

Michelle (Shari Shattuck) is content with her life. She lives on a ranch with her parents (Flo Gerrish, James Ingersoll), enjoys riding her horse Misty and has a decent job at the local bank. But then her no-good ex-husband Willy (John Terlesky) comes back into her life. He has stolen a red Corvette and, having met up with no nonsense Rita Morani (Christina Whitaker), an escaped convict, decides to rob a bank—the same one where Michelle works. In the getaway, Willy is killed and the cops arrest Rita *and* Michelle. The law assumes Michelle must have been part of her ex-spouse's plan and sulky Rita does not dissuade them of this theory. Before she can blink her eyes, Michelle is sentenced to a three-year prison term, and she finds herself carted off in tandem with tough-as-nails Rita.

Arriving at the prison, a guard immediately warns the very innocent Michelle, "Don't mess with the warden! Whatever she wants, give it to her."

Once settled in the cellblock dormitory, Michelle makes friends with Amy (Stacey Shaffer), who sleeps in the bunk under hers. Amy tells Michelle that her bed used to be occupied by an inmate who died of a drug overdose provided by roughneck convict Sheila (Faith Minton), who dictatorially controls the inmates. Wanting to gain points with Amy, the fast-learning Michelle brags about her criminal record:

> MICHELLE: I robbed a bank.
>
> AMY: God, that's great!

Despite the above par decor, Michelle learns about the unpleasant aspects of life in this prison. There is the randy guard Smiley (Nick Benedict), who has a penchant for raping inmates. If his victims are indisposed, like the marijuana-smoking Ruby (Valerie McIntosh), a patient in the prison infirmary, so much the better. Then there is the bitch guard Martha (Susie London), whom wise prisoners avoid. When Michelle is summoned to meet Warden Wallace (Angel Tompkins), she is easily intimidated. At first, the administrator appears to be a pleasant, outgoing sort, but her mood abruptly changes:

> You know they call this place, the cage. . . . And the longer I work here I think they're god damn right. The guards are the zoo keepers and you are the animals. As long as you stay loyal to me, I'll protect you and you'll have certain privileges.

It is not long before Michelle appreciates the full meanings to the warden's inferences. She learns that Wallace delights in inviting the more attractive inmates to her art deco apartment for conversation, to watch the fish in her beloved aquarium, and for whatever else may develop.

However, Warden Wallace does not believe in equality among the staff, as demonstrated in her interrogation of Smiley about Ruby's death (she committed suicide) and his possible role in the affair.

> SMILEY: I'm entitled to have a little fun on the job.
>
> WARDEN: Keep your hands off the girls.
>
> SMILEY: What about you, Warden?

Matters take a troublesome turn at the prison when Brenda Williams (Aude Charles), the spokeswoman for the black convicts, protests Ruby's death and the lack of a proper investigation by the warden. (It did not help to smooth over the situation that Wallace's response to Brenda's demand for action was met with, "This is a prison, not a suicide prevention center.")

By now, Michelle's life is spiraling towards deep trouble. The warden pressures her to become a stool pigeon for the staff. There is the constant danger of beatings or worse from the guards, and many of the inmates would just as soon kill the newcomer as not. Michelle is aghast.

MICHELLE: God, it's so strange here.

AMY: The first few weeks are tough.

Rita, who has remained antagonistic to Michelle, attacks her with a screwdriver and stabs her through the hand. Later, inmate boss Sheila takes umbrage at Michelle's lack of respect, warning her and the others, "I said I'm in charge here or do I have to beat that into your dumb skulls." Soon Michelle is suffering from nightmares of being attacked/slashed in the shower, or raped in the deserted corridors. One night she awakens terrified from these bad dreams:

AMY: [Trying to calm her friend.] It's just a nightmare. It's all over.

MICHELLE: Oh my god, it's just begun.

Later, the fast-adapting Michelle knows enough to stand clear as Rita beats Sheila in a rough-and-tumble power fight. Thereafter, Michelle, pushed to her limits, gets into trouble with the staff and is punished with solitary confinement. Smiley pays a visit to her isolation cell and attempts to rape her. In defending herself, Michelle breaks her attacker's nose. Finally, a real friend comes to her rescue. Rhonda (Lucinda Crosby) the guard admits she is really an undercover law enforcer assigned to unearth the corruption at the prison. During the forthcoming riot, the black prisoner contingent get their revenge on Smiley. Rhonda is on hand when Michelle tricks a confession out of Rita, the latter electrocuted when she falls against exposed wires in the basement. With the convict rebellion quelled, Warden Wallace's regime comes to an end. (She sighs nostalgically, "This used to be such a nice place.") As for Michelle, she is soon freed and is back on the farm riding Misty. It is as if it were all a bad dream.

Variety refused to take this ritualistic nonsense seriously. "Though they call it *The Naked Cage*, a woman's prison is actually kind of a nice place, with lots of showers and beds and they don't make the ladies wear brassieres or very long dresses or much of anything if they don't want to. If the menfolk don't believe they'll just have to go see for themselves."

179. *Nameless Men* (Tiffany-Stahl, 1928), 60 min.

Director, Christy Cabanne; story, E. Morton Hough; screenplay, John Francis Natteford; titles, Viola Brothers Shore; set designer, Burgess Beal; camera, Chester Lyons; editor, Martin G. Cohn. Claire Windsor (Mary Cameron); Antonio Moreno (Robert Strong); Eddie Gribbon (Blackie); Ray Hallor (Hughie Cameron); Charles Clary (Mac); Carolynne Snowden (Maid); and: Stepin Fetchit, Sally Rand.

A modest underworld melodrama that relied on a prison setting to propel its storyline. *Variety* rated *Nameless Men* "a good neighborhood picture with an excellent cast fine direction and story rendered interesting through treatment."

To learn information from convict Hugh Cameron (Ray Hallor), detective Robert Strong (Antonio Moreno) goes undercover and arranges a six-month prison term for himself. He is hopeful of persuading the young inmate to reveal where he hid the loot from a bank robbery. The naïve Hugh, who is soon to be paroled, reveals to Strong the name of his partner, Blackie (Eddie Gribbon), who had escaped capture. Later, on the outside, Strong meets with Hugh and Blackie.

However, they now suspect he is a lawman and tie him up while they rush off to claim their hidden loot. Strong escapes and goes off in pursuit. By now, Hugh has turned good guy and doublecrosses Blackie. The latter kidnaps Hugh's sister Mary (Claire Windsor), who has fallen in love with Strong, and flees in a speedboat. Strong follows and, in a subsequent shootout, saves Mary. For his good services, Hugh is forgiven by the law.

To be noted in the cast is Sally Rand (1904–1979) more famed for her trademark rendition of the fan dance than for her screen appearances: *Getting Gertie's Garter* (1927), *The King of Kings* (1927), *Bolero* (1934), etc.

180. *Nevada Smith* (Par., 1966), color, 128 min.

Executive producer, Joseph E. Levine; producer/director, Henry Hathaway; based on a character in *The Carpetbaggers* by Harold Robbins; story/screenplay, John Michael Hayes; art directors, Hal Pereira, Tambi Larsen, Al Roelofs; set decorator, Robert F. Benton; costumes, Frank Beetson, Jr.; makeup, Del Acevedo; music, Alfred Newman; orchestrators, Leo Shuken, Jack Hayes; assistant directors, Daniel J. McCauley, Joseph Lenzi; sound, Harold Lewis, Charles Grenzbach; special effects, George C. Thompson, Paul K. Lerpae; camera, Lucien Ballard; editor, Frank Bracht.

Steve McQueen (Max Sand [Nevada Smith]); Karl Malden (Tom Fitch); Brian Keith (Jonas Cord); Arthur Kennedy (Bill Bowdre); Suzanne Pleshette (Pilar); Raf Vallone (Father Zaccardi); Janet Margolin (Neesa); Pat Hingle (Big Foot); Howard Da Silva (Warden); Martin Landau (Jesse Coe); Paul Fix (Sheriff Bonnell); Gene Evans (Sam Sand); Josephine Hutchinson (Mrs. Elvira McCanles); John Doucette (Uncle Ben McCanles); Val Avery (Buck Mason); Sheldon Allman (Sheriff); Lyle Bettger (Jack Rudabaugh); Bert Freed (Quince); David McLean (Romero); Steve Mitchell (Buckshot); Merritt Bohn (River Boat Pilot); Sandy Kenyon (Bank Clerk); Ricardo [Ric] Roman (Cipriano); John Lawrence (Hogg); Stanley Adams (Storekeeper); George Mitchell (Paymaster); John Litel (Doctor); Ted de Corsia (Hudson, the Bartender); Joanna Moore (Jesse Coe's Wife).

Harold Robbins' smashingly successful novel, *The Carpetbaggers* (1961) had been turned into a movie mega-hit (1964) by independent filmmaker Joseph E. Levine, earning $15,500,000 in domestic film rentals for the distributor. One of the characters to gain most attention in that blockbuster trash film about 1920s–30s Hollywood was Nevada Smith (Alan Ladd), the mysterious cowboy friend of multimillionaire/movie mogul Jonas Cord (George Peppard). Hoping to tap more gold from the same source, Levine filmed a prequel to *The Carpetbaggers* in which he traced the earlier life of the intriguing Nevada Smith. Alan Ladd, even had he not died before the release of *The Carpetbaggers,* would have been too mature to play the young Nevada Smith. Thus, Levine turned to younger, very popular Steve McQueen to handle the pivotal role in *Nevada Smith.*

In the 1890s, young half-breed Max Sand (Steve McQueen) lives in the desert/mountain West. After three gunslingers torture and kill his parents, the naïve Max swears revenge. En route, he meets traveling gunsmith Jonas Cord (Brian Keith) who teaches him how to handle a gun. As his persistent quest continues, Max encounters Jesse Coe (Martin Landau), one of the murderers, and kills him in a showdown knife fight in a western town. The wounded Max is cared for by Neesa (Janet Margolin), a Kiowa maiden.

Although Neesa asks Max to remain with her and her tribe, the restless man pushes onward, determined to find the other murderers. The chase leads to Louisiana where Sand learns that another of the killers, Bill Bowdre (Arthur Kennedy), is serving a prison sentence on a chain gang. Max robs a bank in order to maneuver himself into the prison camp. Arriving there in chains, he is brought in to meet the disheveled warden (Howard Da Silva). Examining his latest victim, the ruffian sneers:

> Two years hard labor. That's the only kind we got here. Starting with me, everything in this place is mean and miserable. The heat, mosquitos, the food, the life. There's nothing to do all day but work. Nothing to do at night, but sleep.
> We don't have any walls or fences. The swamp is our wall. Miles and miles of it, filled with dirty water, quicksand, moccasins [snakes] and malaria. . . . Just one more thing. Don't ever make me mad. [He slugs Max who falls to the ground.]

Recovering from this "interview," he is led by Big Foot (Pat Hingle) to the prisoner shack. Along the way, he is given new instructions:

> Don't be lookin' at this gun, boy. They want you to go for it. In case you're wonderin', I'm a prisoner. I'm a trustee.
> You don't get to keep anything, boy, except a blanket and your clothes. You get a bath and shave once a week, one razor for the whole batch. This is your bunk. It belonged to a fella named Miller. He died.

Max is dismayed to learn that Bowdre has recently escaped from the camp. However, the guards and bloodhounds soon return with the nearly-unconscious escapee. Bowdre is strung up and whipped severely in front of the other men, with the warden announcing that he will not only finish out his sentence but additionally that of the man who died attempting to escape with him. Max befriends Bowdre and soon they become pals. Max suggests they escape, this time getting outside help. The opportunity arises when both of them are among the convicts loaned to planters for the planting season. It is tradition that once a month the slave labor have visitation rights from the Cajun women working on the farm.

Max meets Pilar (Suzanne Pleshette), who quickly falls in love with him. He urges her to help them break out, promising that she can flee with them. They make good their escape in the boat provided by Pilar. However, she is bitten by a snake and soon dies. Before gunning down Bowdre (with the gun Max stole from Big Foot), Max reveals his identity.

Max learns that the third villain is in California, mining in the gold fields. He locates his final prey, Tom Fitch (Karl Malden). Max shoots his opponent in both legs, but cannot complete the job, having found new faith from a traveling padre (Raf Vallone). The hardened gunslinger throws away his firearms and departs. Later, calling himself Nevada Smith, he asks munition maker Cord for a job.

For Vincent Canby *(New York Times)*, "[T]he principal problem with *Nevada Smith* is that it is just too long. It also is too episodic. . . . This kind of narrative construction only works to the extent that tension and suspense mount with the progression of events. Unfortunately . . . [here] they do the reverse." *Variety* agreed that the project was "stifled by uneven acting, often lethargic direction, and awkward sensation-shock values. Overlength serves to dull the often spectacular production values."

There was much that stultified this ambitious, banal oater, including several bizarre cameo guest appearances (such as Suzanne Pleshette as a Cajun swamp guide!). More creditable but too theatrical were the cast in the bayou prison camp sequence: Howard Da Silva as the brutal warden and Pat Hingle as the (very man-nered) genial trustee. The glossy environs of this southern prison compound were a far cry from the gritty realism of *I Am a Fugitive from a Chain Gang* (1932), q.v. Never once did Steve McQueen look as if he were an impounded slave, rather he was his usual squeaky-clean, squinty-eyed self, with chest bared (for added box office allure).

Despite all its hoopla, the overblown *Nevada Smith* earned a relatively unspectacular $5,500,000 in domestic film rentals paid to the distributor. A projected TV series spin-off never happened, although a pilot film was lensed.

181. *Nightmare in Badham County* (ABC–TV, Nov. 5, 1976), color, 100 min.

Executive producer, Douglas S. Cramer; producer, Wilford Lloyd Baumes; associate producer, Herb Wallerstein; director, John Llewellyn Moxey; teleplay, Jo Heims; production designer, Jan Scott; set decorator, Fred R. Simpson, costumes, John S. Perry; makeup, Dee Manges; music, Charles Bernstein; music editor, John Harris; sound editor, John Kline; camera, Frank Stanley; editor, Carroll Sax.

Deborah Raffin (Cathy Phillips); Lynne Moody (Diane Emery); Chuck Connors (Sheriff Dannen); Fionnuala Flanagan (Dulcie); Tina Louise (Greer); Robert Reed (Superintendent Deaner); Della Reese (Sarah); Lana Wood (Smitty); Ralph Bellamy (Judge); Kim Wilson (Emiline); Leslie Albers (Waitress); Simpson Hemphill (Governor's Aide); Annette Henley (1st White Inmate); Tom Keith (Gas Station Attendant); John Malloy (Mr. Phillips); John Clyde Rober, Jr. (Restaurant Manager); Essex Smith (George); Tommie Stewart (Alma).

If the big screen *Jackson County Jail* (1976), q.v., could portray the hellish odyssey of one fetching female crossing the U.S., then *Nightmare in Badham County* could outdo that: there were two females in distress in this telefeature.

College girls Cathy Phillips (Deborah Raffin) and Diane Emery (Lynne Moody) take vacation drive across the United States. While in the deep South, they encounter fascist Sheriff Dannen (Chuck Connors) a lecherous bastard who not only sexually attacks one of them, but carts both of the beaten, humiliated young women off to a corrupt prison farm overseen by Superintendent Deaner (Robert Reed). They are trapped there, with no way to let relatives or loved ones know their whereabouts. Among the inmates they encounter are the pitiful Sarah (Della Reese), a prisoner with no hope, and a trustee named Dulcie (Fionnuala Flanagan).

Despite the clichés of the genre, characters and dialogue, *Nightmare in Badham County* was effective small screen fare. "It is a brutal story because many of its people are brutal, but it is illuminated by a belief in love, respect and courage that raises it to a high level of dramatic experience" (Moina Murphy, *Hollywood Reporter*).

A.k.a.: *Nightmare*.

182. *The Noose* (First National, 1928), 75 min.

Presenter, Richard A. Rowland, producer, Henry Hobart; director, John Francis Dillon; based on the play by Willard Mack; screenplay, H. H. Van Loan, Mack; adaptor/continuity, James T. O'Donohoe; titles, Garrett Graham; camera, James C. Van Trees; editor, Jack Dennis.

Richard Barthelmess (Nickie Elkins); Montagu Love (Buck Gordon); Robert Emmett O'Connor (Jim Conley); Jay Eaton (Tommy); Lina Basquette (Dot); Thelma Todd (Phyllis); Ed Brady (Seth McMillan);

Fred Warren (Dave); Charles Giblyn (Bill Chase); Alice Joyce (Mrs. Bancroft); William Walling (Warden); Robert T. Haines (Governor Bancroft); Ernest Hilliard (Craig); Emile Chautard (Priest); Romaine Fielding (Judge); Yola D'Avril, Corliss Palmer, Kay English, Cecil Brunner, Janice Peters, Ruth Lord, May Atwood (Cabaret Girls).

Hijacker Nickie Elkins (Richard Barthelmess) has been reared by gangster Buck Gordon (Montagu Love). Romantically he is intrigued by society girl Phyllis (Thelma Todd), but his heart belongs to cabaret performer Dot (Lina Basquette). One day Buck reveals that Nickie's mother is actually Mrs. Bancroft (Alice Terry), the wife of the state's governor (Robert T. Haines). Buck admits that he has asked Nickie's mother to have him pardoned. When Elkins refuses, Buck insists he will then confront Mrs. Bancroft himself to obtain his freedom as well as money. In a moment of passion, the angered Nickie shoots Buck. As a result he is tried and sentenced to die. On the day he is to be executed, his mother telephones the warden (William Walling) to order the hanging halted. The prisoner is later brought before the governor, who is expected to pardon him.

Variety enthused of this improbable silent photoplay based on a 1925 Broadway play, "It's an extremely well directed and played drama, with meller tendencies, a touch of the underworld with a real cabaret scene one of the standouts." The more reality-prone *New York Times* rated the photoplay, "a curious blend of the sublime and the ridiculous.... It has its moments, however. there is a little touch near the end, when The Girl [Lina Basquette] comes to see the Governor and wants to get the young man's body in order to bury it.... Mr. Barthelmess is not always at his best in the picture, being designed by nature less for a bootlegger and more for a football hero."

Richard Barthelmess received an Academy Award nomination for his work in *The Noose* and *The Patent Leather Kid* (1927 — a far bigger hit). He lost the Oscar to Emil Jannings (who won for *The Last Command* and *The Way of All Flesh*). Barthelemess would return to the prison genre in *Weary River* (1929), q.v., a part-talkie production made for First National.

183. *Numbered Men* (First National, 1930), 65 min.

Director, Mervyn LeRoy; based on the play *Jailbreak* by Dwight Taylor; screenplay, Al Cohn, Henry McCarthy; art director, Jack Okey; camera, Sol Polito; editor, Terrill Morse.

Conrad Nagel (Bertie Gray); Bernice Claire (Mary Dane); Raymond Hackett (Bud Leonard); Ralph Ince (King Callahan); Tully Marshall (Lemuel Barnes); Maurice Black (Lou Rinaldo); William Holden (Warden Lansing); George Cooper (Happy Howard); Blanche Friderici (Mrs. Miller); Ivan Linow (Pollack); Frederick Howard (Jimmy Martin).

A highly fictional treatise on penal life about as accurate as the average theme dealing with colleges. Melodrama of the old school, spotted with seedy dialog.... Other than a prison riot and two killings, which require but a few minutes, the convicts are either playing cards, listening to the radio or eating cookies at a near-by farmhouse.

(Variety)

Bertie Gray (Conrad Nagel) learns from fellow prisoner Bud Leonard (Raymond Hackett) — who is serving an erroneous ten-year stretch for counterfeiting — that the latter has a sweetheart named Mary Dane (Bernice Claire). On the outside, Lou Rinaldo (Maurice Black) the blackguard who framed Bud, attempts to win

Mary's attention. Meanwhile, Mary finds employment at Mrs. Miller's [Blanche Friderici] farmhouse near the prison, hoping that she will thus be able to see Bud who works on a road gang that stops there frequently for meals. The persistent Rinaldo devises a scheme to get rid of Bud and the brutal King Callahan (Ralph Ince), yet another man he framed. He intends to have them captured by the law while attempting to escape. Mary learns of the scheme and prevents Bud's breakout to freedom. As for Rinaldo, he is murdered by a vengeful Callahan, who is himself shot down. The ever-helpful Bertie gets himself into further trouble with prison officials, covering for Bud who is due soon to be paroled.

There was no comparison between the grim prison life depicted in the Award-winning *The Big House* (1930), q.v., and the fantasy jailhouse environs reflected in *Numbered Men*. For Mordaunt Hall *(New York Times)*, the prison scenes in *Numbered Men* "call to mind a club of the free." He explained, "The good-conduct room [in the prison] has its members who may read, play music, listen to the world outside over the radio and spend relatively pleasant hours.... Then there is also the envied job of the road gang felons, who pay visits to Mrs. Miller's nearby farm and enjoy freshly cooked doughnuts and cookies."

First National Pictures/Warner Bros.' contractee Bernice Claire, the heroine of *Numbered Men*, had gained a degree of fame in early talkies singing in several musical comedies and operettas: *No, No Nanette* (1930), *Song of the Flame* (1930), etc.

184. *On the Yard* (Midwest Film, 1979), color, 103 min.

Producer, Joan Micklin Silver; associate producer, Mike Haley; director, Raphael D. Silver; based on the novel by Malcolm Braly; screenplay, Braly; art director, Leon Harris; costumes, Robert Harris; music, Charles Gross; assistant director, Haley; camera, Alan Metzer; editor, Evan Lottmann.

John Heard (Juleson); Thomas Waites (Chilly); Mike Kellin (Red); Richard Bright (Nunn); Joe Grifasi (Morris); Lane Smith (Captain Blake); Richard Hayes (Stick); Hector Troy (Gasoline); Richard Jamieson (Lieutenant Carpenter); Thomas Toner (Warden); Ron Faber (Manning); David Clennon (Psychiatrist); Don Blakely (Tate); J. C. Quinn (Luther); Dominic Chianese (Mendoza); Eddie Jones (Lieutenant Olson); Ben Slack (Clemmons); James Remar (Larson); Dave McCalley (Redmond); Ludwick Villani (Candy); John Taylor (Schulte); Ivan Yount (Inmate); Ralph Hobbs (Zeke); David Berman (Caterpillar); Joseph Mazurkiewicz, Lowell Manfall, Peg French (Parole Board); Ralph Basalla (Processor); Walter Sanders (Cool Breeze); Roland Jackson (Cadillac); Leon J. Cassady, Frank Conrad, Leroy Newsome (Bakery Workers); Robert Johnson (Mechanic); Fred Jones, James Johnson, George Gamble, John Demmitt (Therapy Session); John Kephart, Alan Gramley, Jan Chawie (Prison Squad); John Berhosky (Bus Guard); William Carver (Night Guard); Morris Pratt (Office Guard).

The husband-wife filmmaking team of Raphael D. Silver and Joan Micklin Silver had already released *Hester Street* (1976) and *Between the Lines* (1978). Their *Crossing Delancey* (1989) was in the future when they prepared *On the Yard*, directed by Raphael D. Silver. Based on Malcolm Braly's novel (1977), which Braly adapted for the screen, *On the Yard* never received the proper attention this independent production deserved. Vincent Canby *(New York Times)* endorsed that "*On the Yard* neither exploits prison life nor sentimentalizes it. The film is brutal at times, but what we respond to is its surprising humanity. It's a movie that finds decency in the most unlikely of hosts."

Several convicts stand out among the ethnically diverse inmates at the state prison run by an unsympathetic warden (Thomas Toner) and his insensitive guards, headed by Captain Blake (Lane Smith) and Lieutenant Carpenter (Richard Jamieson). There is Chilly (Thomas Waites), a seasoned convict who has spent most of his life behind bars, and who now controls life in the prison among the inmates, operating a black market in cigarettes and drugs and running a gambling racket. There is the intellectual Juleson (John Heard), a confirmed loner whose crime on the outside was killing his wife and who now is nearing a nervous breakdown. (He is also deeply in financial debt to Chilly for a pricey carton of cigarettes, and there is the danger that Chilly's enforcer, Gasoline [Hector Troy], will do him in.) Middle-aged Morris (Joe Grifasi), the prison yard gofer who is an excellent stitcher, sews together a hot air balloon, an escape vehicle created for his cellmate. There is also the aging Red (Mike Kellin), who has devoted more time to life in prison than out and whose vain efforts to convince the parole board that he is a good candidate for release causes him to perceive how institutionalized he has really become.

In the course of *On the Yard,* the articulate Juleson deliberately starts a fight with Gasoline, hoping that the guards will intervene — they do — and that this ploy will save his hide. The wounded enforcer later drinks some gasoline and dies. Later, Chilly orders the vicious Stick (Richard Hayes) to beat up Juleson, but the latter is killed before he can. While the black convicts are engaging in a prizefight exhibition, Stick attempts a wild escape in the balloon fashioned by his cellmate, Morris. When Red's parole is denied, Waites helps the convict break out to freedom. Meanwhile, tough con Nunn (Don Blakely), a power figure in the prisoner hierarchy, switches allegiance from Chilly to black contender Tate (Don Blakely). By the time Red is back in the general population six months later, Tate is running the inmates. As for the enterprising Chilly, he is already hatching new devious plans.

Kevin Thomas *(Los Angeles Times)* responded favorably to *On the Yard.* "It's a resolutely low-key film, and is all the more devastating for being so." For Tom Allen *(Village Voice),* "*On the Yard* is not a genre prison movie *(Brute Force),* not topical *(Riot in Cell Block 11),* not biographical *(Brothers),* not contemporary ethnic *(Short Eyes)* — not anything, really, but an old-fashioned story that happens to have a prison setting. As in most reactionary films, the acting is good." On the down side, *Variety* pinpointed several reasons why the picture proved "uncommercial": "Its makers have tried too hard to capture the total picture of prison life and have ended up with a series of vignettes that never add up to much of a story.... There are just too many situations to follow here.... *On the Yard* is too superficial to attract the intellectuals and too tame to appeal to the blood and guts crowd." David Ansen (*Newsweek* magazine) agreed: "He [Raphael Silver] has taken a novel bursting with harrowing ironies and turned it into a bland, curiously respectable movie. It's a strangley self-defeating accomplishment."

On the Yard was filmed on location at Rockview State Correctional facility near State College, Pennsylvania. It was a medium-security prison with a 1,000 inmates. Scripter Malcolm Braly had spent twenty years in prison himself. The film was promoted with the advertising tag line, *All That Counts Is Surviving!*" In the book original, the character of the effeminate Candy, Chilly's cellmate and lover, was a plant of the keepers, intended to smash Chilly's control of the convicts.

185. One-Way Ticket (Columbia, 1935), 72 min.

Producer, B. P. Schulberg; director, Herbert Biberman; based on the novel by Ethel Turner; screenplay, Vincent Lawrence, Joseph Anthony, Oliver H. P. Garrett, Grover Jones; camera, Henry Freulich; editor, John Rawlins.

Lloyd Nolan (Jerry); Peggy Conklin (Ronnie Bourne); Walter Connolly (Captain Bourne); Edith Fellows (Ellen); Gloria Shea (Willa); Nana Bryant (Mrs. Bourne); Thurston Hall (Mr. Ritchie); George McKay (Martin); Robert Middlemass (Bender); Willie Fung (Wing); Jack Clifford (Charlie); James Flavin (Ed).

When a bank is financially gutted by its unprincipled executive, angry depositor Jerry (Lloyd Nolan) takes it upon himself to rob the restructured institution of the exact sum ($4,643.87) his father had lost. This is an immediate tip-off to the law and he is soon apprehended, and sent on a one-way ticket to the state penitentiary. There he suffers under the abusive treatment of prison Captain Bourne (Walter Connolly) and falls in love with the man's wholesome daughter, Ronnie (Peggy Conklin). While some other prisoners die—along with several hostage guards—in a futile breakout attempt, Jerry is more crafty. He has Ronnie help in his escape scheme. Later, while on the lam, they are married. When the law closes in on their honeymoon apartment and she realizes that he would be safer back in prison, she shoots him. As the wounded Jerry is taken back to the slammer he agrees that Ronnie made the right decision. Now, as soon as both he and she (an accessory to his escape) complete their jail sentences, they can be reunited and go straight.

Andre Sennwald (New York Times) was pleasantly surprised by this modest production: "[It] possesses a really skillful physical production, has freshness and individual style, and emerges as a considerably more likable photoplay than you might suspect from a brief digest of its story." Variety noted, "Actually, the story unfolds a preachment not that the law is fair or just but that jails are tough places to get out of."

186. The Onion Field (Avco Embassy, 1979), color, 122 min.

Producer, Walter Coblenz; director, Harold Becker; based on the book by Joseph Wambaugh; screenplay, Wambaugh; production designer, Brian Eatwell; set designer, Joe Hubbard; set decorator, Dick Goddard; costumes, Ken Harvey; makeup, Robert J. Mills; music, Eumir Deodato; assistant directors, Tom Mack, D. Scott Easton; technical advisers (courtroom), Phillip Halpin, Dino Fulgoni; technical adviser (police procedures), Richard Falk; sound, Jim Webb; sound editor, Keith Stafford; camera, Charles Rosher; editor, John W. Wheeler.

John Savage (Karl Francis Hettinger); James Woods (Gregory Ulas Powell); Franklyn Seales (Jimmy "Youngblood" Smith); Ted Danson (Ian Campbell); Ronny Cox (Pierce Brooks); David Huffman (District Attorney Phil Halpin); Christopher Lloyd (Jailhouse Lawyer); Diane Hull (Helen Hettinger); Priscilla Pointer (Chrissie Campbell); Beege Barkett (Greg's Woman); Richard Herd (Beat Cop); Lee Tari (Emmanuel McFadden); Richard Venture (Glenn Bates); Lee Weaver (Billy); Phillip R. Allen (District Attorney Marshall Schulman); Pat Corley (Jimmy's 1st Lawyer); K. Callan (Mrs. Powell); Sandy McPeak (Mr. Powell); Lillian Randolph (Nana); Ned Wilson (Los Angeles Police Department Captain); Jack Rader (Internal Affairs Division Captain); Raleigh Bond (2nd Judge); Brad English (Red-Haired Cop); Stanley Grover (Greg's 2nd Lawyer); Michael Pataki (District Attorney Dino Fulgoni); Steve Conte (1st Prison Guard).

Joseph Wambaugh's well-regarded "non-fiction" book, The Onion Field (1973), dramatically examined the issue of whether the American legal system protects the guilty at the expense of the innocent. The film adaptation, like the book, meticulously traces the traumatic effects on the surviving partner of a murdered policeman. It also focuses on the brutalizing aftermath in which he must repeatedly endure testifying—and reliving the nightmarish horrors—at the defendants' several protracted courtroom trials and retrials over the years. Melded into this compelling police drama are the repercussions on the two killers of the landmark Escobedo, Dorado and Miranda court decisions as well as California's later (temporary) abolition of capital punishment. Within this emotionally draining chronicle, several scenes depict the two murderers as they pass through years of imprisonment.

On the night of March 9, 1963, in Hollywood, California, patrolmen Ian Campbell (Ted Danson) and Karl Francis Hettinger (John Savage) stop parolees Gregory Powell (James Woods) and Jimmy "Youngblood" Smith (Franklyn Seales). The ex-convicts are en route to commit their latest in a series of liquor store holdups. The frightened suspects kidnap the two officers. At a vegetable farm near Bakersfield, Campbell is shot and killed, while Hettinger escapes through an onion field. The two kidnappers are caught, and both initially promise to cooperate at their trial. However, police investigator Pierce Brooks (Ronny Cox) cannot determine which of the two defendants actually fired the killing shots. Soon, the two criminals—charismatic, psychotic Powell and slum-poor, subservient black man Smith—turn against one another. Thanks to a series of precedent-altering Supreme Court decisions dealing with suspects'/prisoners' civil rights, their attorneys parlay the trials, mistrials, appeals, etc. into several years of activity on behalf of their clients (making it one of the longest cases in the state's legal history). Meanwhile, the suicide-prone Hettinger, driven by guilt that he survived the ordeal while his partner died, suffers from terrible nightmares, kleptomania, and impotency in his marriage. Through the many years of legal maneuvering by the defendants' lawyers, Hettinger's life is turned topsy-turvy as he becomes a prime victim of the engulfing legal system. Some of the attorneys in the case use their high visibility to bolster their careers, while another one quits the legal profession altogether in frustration at the system. Karl Hettinger survives—barely.

As *The Onion Field* mingles its narrative of Hettinger's post-trauma existence with the continuous trial life of the defendants, the devious, posturing Powell is shown serving as his own wheeler-dealer attorney and, at the finale, is seen pompously giving legal advice to another prisoner in the penitentiary. The cocky Powell is confident he will be back on the streets in the near future. (To date, he is still in prison.) On the other hand, Smith, who has matured emotionally and intellectually during his recent stays in prison, remains fatalistic about his future. He tells an old guard, "My man. I was born for a prison yard." (Since his parole in 1982 at age fifty-one, Smith has been arrested five times and sent back to prison on several occasions. His latest clash with the law occurred in June 1989 when he was arrested in West Covina, California, for abduction, attempted rape, assault with a deadly weapon and false imprisonment.)

Janet Maslin *(New York Times)* assesed, "This is a strong, affecting story but it's also a straggly one, populated by tangential figures and parallel plotlines; the criminals' histories are every bit as convoluted and fascinating as those of the policemen they abducted. Even the courtroom drama is unusually complicated." Roger Ebert, in *Movie Home Companion, 1990* (1989), decided, "This is a movie that, once seen, cannot be set aside." Regarding the two hoods, Ebert noted, *"The*

Onion Field makes these two characters startlingly convincing: It paints their manners, their speech, their environment, their indecisions in such a way that we can almost understand them as they blunder stupidly into their crimes."

The Onion Field earned $4,317,617 in domestic film rentals for the distributor. Joseph Wambaugh and director Harold Becker would reunite to bring Wambaugh's *The Black Marble* (1980) to the screen.

187. *The Ordeal of Dr. Mudd* (CBS–TV, March 25, 1980), color, 143 min.

Executive producer, Paul Radin; producers, Michael Berk, Douglas N. Schwartz; director, Paul Wendkos; teleplay, Berk, Schwartz; production designer, Jack DeShields; music, Gerald Fried; sound, Ray Barons; camera, Hector Figueroa; editor, Ken Zemke.

Dennis Weaver (Dr. Samuel A. Mudd); Susan Sullivan (Francis Mudd); Richard Dysart (Edwin Stanton); Michael McGuire (Captain Murdock); Nigel Davenport (Colonel George Grenfell); Arthur Hill (General Thomas Ewing); Mary Nell Santacroce (Ellen Stanton); Larry Lason (Riggins Thorpe); Teddy Milford (Andrew Mudd, at age six); Angela Tully (Sissy Mudd, at age four); Ryan Grady (Thomas Mudd, at age three); Panos Eli Karatassos (Sam, Jr., at age one); Bill Gribble (Tyler [John Wilkes Booth]); Luke Halpin (Tyson [David Herold]); Terry Beaver (Union Sergeant); Sean Ahern (1st Union Soldier); Roy Tatum (Lieutenant Lovett); Don Kovacs (Officer Lloyd); Lawrence Montaigne (Judge Holt); Harold Bergman (Undersecretary); Fred Covington (Attorney Lake); Joe Dorsey (General Edward Trafe); Jim Peck (General Harris); Gregg Oliver (Louis Weichman); Bill Eudally (Daniel Thomas); Don Devendorf (George Mudd); Tony Kish (William Watson); Wallace Wilkinson (D.C. Prison Guard); Anthony Edenfield (1st Prisoner); Jere Beery (3rd Guard); Kent Stephens (Zachary); Stuart Culpepper (Boone); Mark Rand (Andrew Mudd, at age nine); Melonie Martin (Sissy Mudd at age seven); Earl Miller (Thomas Mudd, at age six); David Hamilton (Sam, Jr., at age four); Richard Andrew (Anthony Ellis); Dan Chandler (Master Sergeant); Richard Reiner (6th Guard); J. Don Ferguson (4th Soldier); Jack Norhanian (5th Guard); Pat Hurley (1st Patient); Skip Foster (Decampo); Charles Kaufman (Jones); Tommy Lane (Captain Longheart); Bill Hindman (President Andrew Johnson); George DeVries (Waters); Ilse Earl (Screaming Woman); Richard Andrew (Orator).

The tragedy that befell Dr. Samuel Mudd (1833–1883) for innocently attending to John Wilkes Booth, the wounded assassin of President Abraham Lincoln, was well documented in John Ford's feature film *The Prisoner of Shark Island* (1936), q.v. The new edition was not notable. "Directed by Paul Wendkos to the point of distinguished tedium, telefilm boils down to a slow, handsome study of a basically dull man" *(Daily Variety)*. Bruce Crowther *(Captured on Film: The Prison Movie,* 1989) pointed out a major difference between the 1980 and the 1936 version: "When the story of Samuel Mudd was retold in 1980 ... the racism that damaged the earlier version was removed. The doctor was also changed from being the epitome of white Southern aristocracy ... to a down-to-earth, hard-working, small-town physician.... [The] deliberately middle-of-the-road liberal stance the movie adopts causes it to fall behind the emphatic stature of the earlier version."

After chief executive Abraham Lincoln is shot in 1865 at Ford's Theater in Washington, D.C., fleeing assassin John Wilkes Booth (Bill Gribble), posing as a man named Tyler, requires treatment of his broken leg. He receives medical attention from Maryland physician Dr. Samuel A. Mudd (Dennis Weaver) who has no idea whom his patient really is. Later, Mudd is accused and sentenced for helping the hunted assassin. He is sentenced to rot at Fort Jefferson, a prison in the Dry

Tortugas, where sharks infest the surrounding waters, and disease-carrying mosquitos fill the air. After years of hardship, the dedicated physician proves his mettle by helping to stamp out an outbreak of yellow fever in the prison. For his noble efforts, he is pardoned by President Andrew Johnson (Bill Hindman). All through the years of ordeal, Dr. Mudd's loyal wife, Francis (Susan Sullivan), and their children remain steadfast.

Fort Pulaski on Cockspin Island was used as a substitute for Fort Jefferson. Locations in Springfield, Georgia, was employed to represent Dr. Mudd's Maryland home. Among the supporting cast in this overlong production, Larry Larson (as a young sympathetic guard), Arthur Hill (as a Union general lawyer) and Nigel Davenport (as the curious Colonel George Grenfell) provided some needed vitality. Within the frequently bland proceedings, star Dennis Weaver and the filmmakers were overly respectful to the historical import of the drama. At least, the sense of the horrendous living conditions thrust on prisoners both during and after the Civil War was successfully portrayed.

188. *Outside Chance* (CBS–TV, Dec. 2, 1978), color, 100 min.

Executive producer, Roger Corman; producer, Jeff Begun; associate producer, Richard Schor; director, Michael Miller; teleplay, Ralph Gaby Wilson, Miller; art director, John Carter; music, Lou Levy, Murphy Dunne; song, Royce D. Applegate; camera, Willy Kurant; additional camera, Ron Johnson; editor, Bruce Logan.

Yvette Mimieux (Dinah Hunter); Royce D. Applegate (Larry O'Brien); Beverly Hope Atkinson (Clair); Susan Batson (Mavis); Babs Bram (Miss Hopkins); Frederic Cook (Deputy Hobie); Severn Darden (Sheriff Dempsey); Howard Hesseman (David); Lee Fergus (Doctor); John Lawlor (Bill Hill); Betty Thomas (Katherine); Britt Leach (Alfred); Charles Young (Luther); Kim Owens (Mirror Glasses); Ira Miller (Dale); Nancy Noble (Lola); Robin Sherwood (Tottie); Dick Armstrong (Arnold Bradfield); Janina T. White (Matron); Jerry Hamlin (Jimmy, the Diesel Driver); Nan Martin (Allison); William Malloy (Deputy Lyle Peters); Larry Hankin (Deputy in Van); Amparo Mimieux (Woman Who Bit Off Nose); John Ross (Bailiff); Allen Wood (Judge); Peter Vedro (O'Brien's Aide); Dorothy Dells (O'Brien's Secretary); Janice Hamlin (Nurse); John Abbott (Coroner); Marge Levine, Jean Francois Ferriol (Bar Regulars); H. Curley Moore (Sheriff).

Less than two years after the surprisingly popular *Jackson County Jail* (1976), q.v., the same producers (Roger Corman, Jeff Begun), director (Michael Miller) and stars (Yvette Mimieux, Frederic Cook, Severn Darden) reunited to do *Outside Chance,* a remake of the big screen feature. A good deal of telescoped footage from *Jackson County Jail* (including scenes showing boyfriend Howard Hesseman) was employed as establishment shots for the new version, although later the story veered off into new directions.

Deciding to go East to accept a new position, Los Angeles advertising executive Dinah Hunter (Yvette Mimieux) drives cross country. She innocently picks up two hitchhikers, the manipulative Bobby Ray (Robert Carradine) and the pregnant Lola (Nancy Noble). Before long her young passengers have stolen her car and identification and left her stranded on the roadside. She is jailed by the dogmatic Sheriff Dempsey (Severn Darden) who is suspicious of this stranger and that night she is raped by the randy Deputy Hobie (Frederic Cook). The hysterical Dinah lashes out at her attacker and in a fight kills the rapist with a handy stool. She and jailmate Larry O'Brien (Royce D. Applegate) flee. Their misadventures continue as they become involved with a motley crew of hillbillies operating a black market bearskin rug ring. While escaping the pursuing lawmen, the duo help deliver a baby and inadvertently become accessories to a robbery.

Gail Williams *(Hollywood Reporter)* was not impressed by this hack, economical rehash. She pointed out that *Outside Chance* was "sloppily constructed and full of non sequitur dialogue and chains of events." *TV Guide* magazine rated this lurid (by television standards) odyssey only one star.

189. *Outside Woman* (CBS–TV, Feb. 12, 1989), color, 100 min.

Executive producers, Jim Green, Allen Epstein; producer, Lou Antonio; co-producer, Leigh Murray; supervising producer, Albert J. Salzer; director, Antonio; teleplay, William Blinn; production designer, Charles Bennett; art director, Roger Pancake; costumes, Dianne Anthony-Kennedy; makeup, Hallie Damore; music, Jerrold Immel; music editor, Tom Villano; second unit director/stunt coordinator, Fred Lerner; sound, Richard Birnbaum; camera, Paul Lohmann; editor, Craig Holt.

Sharon Gless (Joyce Mattox); Scott Glenn (Jesse Glen Smith); Max Gail (Billy Ballew); Kyle Secor (Jimmy Leonard); Peter Michael Goetz (Everett Madison); Ken Jenkins (Junior Miller); Lenore Banks (Delia); Taylor Simpson (Bonnie); Barbara Chaney (Mrs. Forrester); Peter Gabb (Chaplain Wicks); David Dahlgren (Pilot); Roger Thomas (Prison Guard); Leigh Murray (Television Reporter); Lane Trippe (Mindy Kaufman); Ray Spruell (Emmett); Robert Kearney (Clanton); Eliot Keener (Mecom); Carol Sutton (Guard); David E. Dossey (Burly Man); Dean Cochran (Trustee); Rod Masterson (Guard); Danny Hanemann (Plainclothes Officer); Stanley Zareff (Bass Singer); James Michael Bailey (State Trooper); Lon Bondreaux (Crowd Control Officer); Robert Pfeiffer (Prison Guard); Leslie Carde (Television Reporter); Dekki Moate (Mrs. Jesse); Harold Evans (Dwayne); Patrick Baldauff (Highway Lieutenant); John Wilmot (State Trooper); Barbara Tasker (Matron); Ralph Joseph (Bailiff); B. J. Hopper (Judge).

Over the decades, an undercurrent in prison dramas has been the strange fascination that convicts have for people on the outside. Likewise, there are those civilians who fantasize about the mysterious crimes committed that lead a person into incarceration and of the appealing inner fortitude required to withstand the rigors of restrictive prison life. *The Outside Woman* examines this strange attraction (which can lead to a strong sexual chemistry) in a compelling straightforward narrative. As *Daily Variety* lauded, "This superb drama had everything going for it—sex, a prison break, real-life inspiration—and features terrific principal performances by Sharon Gless and Scott Glenn."

In back country Louisiana, divorcee Joyce Mattox (Sharon Gless) is bored with her mundane factory job. She fears that her drab existence could lead to her growing old before her time and falling over dead at her workplace, just as a co-worker had done recently. While she wants much more out of life, Joyce is unsure just what that may be. A friend warns her that life "can't be all fireworks and French vanilla," and her redneck boyfriend, Junior Miller (Ken Jenkins), is baffled by her dissatisfaction with the status quo. When the fellowship group at Grace Baptist Church organizes a Bible study group at the Louisiana State Penitentiary, Joyce initially cannot see the value of such a program. Mrs. Forrester (Barbara Chaney), the patronizing group leader, feels differently:

> MRS. FORRESTER: Well, who would need Bible study more, I'd like to know? Nobody on this earth, that's who. And there's a certain civilizing influence in letting those poor men know they are not cut off.
>
> ANOTHER MEMBER: But they are cut off. That's why they call it prison.

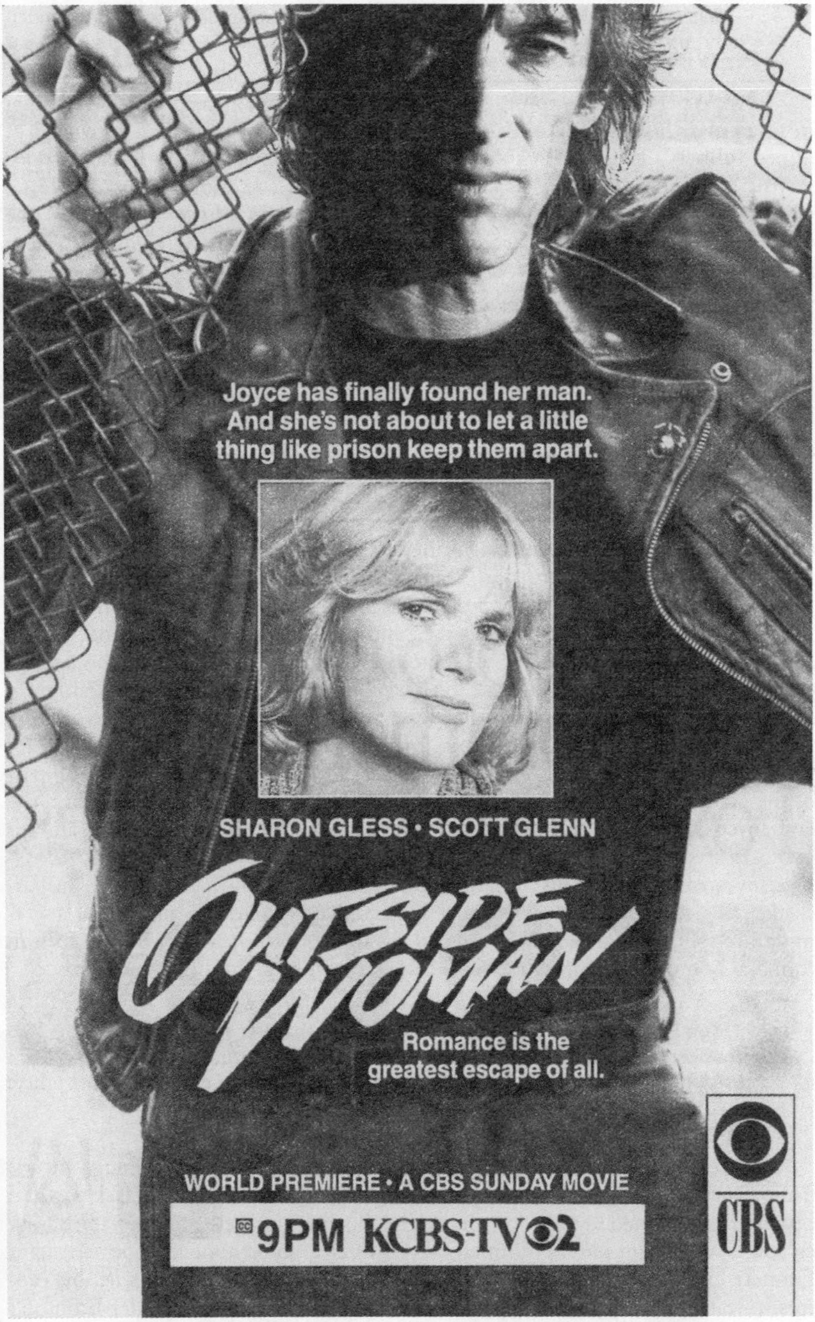

Advertisement for *Outside Woman* (1989).

MRS. FORRESTER: Certainly not cut off from Christian compassion and understanding, for heaven's sake.

Joyce is persuaded to volunteer and soon finds herself attracted to one prisoner
in particular, Jesse Glen Smith (Scott Glenn), a middle-aged man convicted of
armed robbery, assault with a deadly weapon and attempted murder and who is
serving a fifteen to twenty year term. She is drawn to the oddly charismatic Jesse,
who warns her enticingly, "I'm bad Joyce and more than a little dangerous." She
finds herself visiting him every Saturday. Soon they are exchanging audiocassette
letters and Joyce, yanked from her humdrum existence, thinks she is in love. The
crafty Jesse knows exactly how to present himself as a romanticized underdog, telling her, "What wears you down is being forgotten."

Smith cunningly leads her on. He tells her, "Having somebody like you in my
life is making me crazy. You got so much energy and vitality. When I'm about
you, I see how it can be between you and me."

Having baited his prey, he throws out the hook, "How much are you willing
to put on the line to get us the kind of life we ought to have?... I need me an
outside woman."

Realizing that she is getting herself into a dangerous situation, Joyce ra-
tionalizes to the perplexed Junior Miller why she needs a drastic change in her
everyday existence: "I'm in prison. Every time I think of leaving, something happens.... I'm going to be here the rest of my life unless I do something."

That something is helping Jesse escape from the prison compound. As instructed by the mesmerizing Jesse, she orders a gun by mail, gathers the needed
equipment and rents a helicopter. She has the bewildered pilot (David Dahlgren)
land in the prison confines and soon Jesse, along with two other convicts—Billy
Ballew (Max Gail) and Jimmy Leonard (Kyle Secor)—have made their dash for
freedom. Amazed at her own resourcefulness, Joyce adapts quickly to being part
of the getaway gang which steals new vehicles in their continuing flight from the
law. Joyce is distressed to discover that Jesse is already married and that he and his
two bizarre cohorts delight so much in their new found notoriety.

Joyce comes to understand a prisoner's mentality much more fully. In particular, she learns a great deal from the hyperactive, immature Jimmy, who is serving a life sentence for having murdered his high school teacher who forced him
to make homosexual pornographic films. According to Jimmy, in prison:

> You learn that you don't waste time on stuff that free men waste time on. You
> don't let little hurt feelings keep you from getting something you want. You don't
> waste time on that kinda junk, cause in this kind of life [i.e. convict/crook] there
> isn't that much time to waste.

As they continue their flight, Joyce is reassured by Jesse that although he was
using her at first, he really loves her now. As a disguise, she buys a black wig and
becomes as intrigued her co-conspirators in following the media blitz on the daring
escape. The quartet kidnap Emmett (Ray Spruell), an orthopedic shoe salesman.
Emmett finds his (mis)adventure exciting and willingly cooperates with his captors. (He relates the wild experience to a movie he once saw, Charles Bronson's
Breakout [1975], q.v.) As Billy tells Emmett, "If you play it right, it's kinda a kick."
When the quartet leave Emmett, they extract a promise of his further help in

throwing the law enforcers off their trail. Happily watching *It's a Wonderful Life* on the motel room's TV, Emmett bids goodbye to his new friends:

EMMETT: A deal is a deal.

JESSE: Boy, you'd make a good con!

The group flees into Alabama where they are caught. The men are sent back to prison and Joyce is jailed, pending trial. Sobered by her new environment, but still loving Jesse, Joyce confers with public defender Mindy Kaufman (Lane Trippe).

JOYCE: Men have been taking me in and out of things most of my life.

When her meeting ends, Joyce looks directly at her lawyer, saying, "Honey, it's tough here."

At the trial, Jesse speaks up for Joyce, insisting, "We are who we are and what we are and I don't expect it's going to change. But Joyce is different. She's just a woman who got involved."

Jesse, Billy and Jimmy receive forty years tacked onto their existing sentences while Joyce is given a thirty-seven year sentence, to be served at the prison in Mt. Pleasanton, California. (The prison authorities are fearful of having Joyce in the same penal system with Jesse.)

As she is being led out of the courtroom, the nonplussed Joyce demands to speak to Jesse, wanting to thank him for his kind words at the trial.

JESSE: I love you pretty lady.

JOYCE: I had me five days of life like most women won't see in fifteen.

REPORTER: Was it worth it?

JOYCE: I guess it will have to be.

As she is police-escorted to the airport, Joyce expresses excitement about her pending plane flight.

According to Lynne Heffley *(Los Angeles Times)*, "The melodrama may brew nostalgia for the days when [Sharon] Gless [of TV's "Cagney & Lacey"] was on the right side of the law, but the clichés are mitigated by humor and a dash of the unexpected.... [The filmmakers] mostly skim the motivational surface, taking viewers on an ingenuous, easy ride. There are a few quiet, telling moments, however, and Gless, soft-eyed and wistful, makes the most of them." Miles Beller *(Hollywood Reporter)* appreciated the director's "steady control" and thought the leads were "top-notch." However, he decided that *"The Outside Woman* doesn't get inside its subjects with the conviction required to capture what's most vital, the subtextual intensity of love in flight."

Lou Antonio, the resourceful producer/director of *The Outside Woman* would next helm another telefeature genre piece, *Dark Holiday* (1989), q.v. Location work for *The Outside Woman* was accomplished at Louisiana State Prison.

190. *Over the Wall* (Warner Bros., 1938), 72 min.

Executive producer, Hal B. Wallis; producer, Bryan Foy; director, Frank McDonald; based on the story "One More Tomorrow" from the book *20,000 Years in Sing Sing* by Warden Lewis E. Lawes; screenplay, Crane Wilbur, George Bricker; art director, Esdras Hartley; gowns, Howard Shoup; songs, M. K. Jerome and Jack Scholl; assistant director, Jesse Hibbs; dialogue director, Frank Beckwith; sound, Stanley Jones; camera, James Van Trees; editor, Frank Magee.

Dick Foran (Jerry Davis); June Travis (Kay Norton); John Litel (Father Connor); Dick Purcell (Ace Scanlon); Veda Ann Borg (Maxine); George E. Stone (Gyp); Ward Bond (Eddie Edwards); John Hamilton (Warden); Jonathan Hale (Governor); Tommy Bupp (Jimmy Davis); Robert E. Homans (John Davis); Mabel Hart (Mrs. Davis); Raymond Hatton (Convict); Alan Davis (Joe); Eddie Chandler, Wilfred Lucas (Keepers); Henry Otho (Bruiser); Frank Shannon (Duke); Priscilla Lyon (Little Girl); Cliff Saum (Officer); Carole Landis, Eleanor Bailey, Sandra Ramoy (Girls); Jimmy Conlin (Jerry's Handler); Sam Flint (Judge); Stuart Holmes (Foreman); Kernan Kripps, Lane Chandler, Galan Galt (Guards); Sol Gorss (Hospital Trusty); Edgar Washington (Black Man); Dick Wessel (Convict Trusty); William Marceau (Prison Doctor).

> *Over the Wall* . . . is the lightest stretch we ever did in a Warner Brothers prison picture. It's the quietest, too; no screaming sirens, chattering machine-guns, playing searchlights—not even . . . a wall. It's rather nice for a change after a succession of [prison] films . . . which have almost driven us stir-crazy. . . .
>
> B.R. Cristler *(New York Times)*

Arrogant Truck driver Jerry Davis (Dick Foran) is hopeful of becoming a prizefighter and has his manager, Eddie Edwards (Ward Bond), arrange a match with a boxer managed by gangster Ace Scanlon (Dick Purcell). Edwards, in league with Scanlon, causes Jerry to be knocked out in the first round by having a piece of lead placed in his opponent's gloves. Later, at Edwards's apartment, Davis confronts his manager about this trickery and, after knocking him out he leaves. Scanlon arrives on the scene and kills the manager, arranging the evidence to throw blame on Jerry. Davis is arrested and sentenced to prison for five years on a manslaughter charge. He becomes a unruly inmate, constantly protesting that he was framed. Meanwhile, Father Connor (John Litel), the prison chaplain, takes an interest in the rebellious Jerry, councils him to get rid of the chip on his shoulder, and persuades him to pursue his singing hobby. Soon Davis is singing on the clergyman's prison-based radio program. Later, when convict Gyp (George E. Stone) is dying he tells Jerry that it was Scanlon who really killed Edwards. Jerry has his girlfriend, Kay Norton (June Travis), take a job with Ace to gather information. She does and then appeals to Father Connor to use the newly-found evidence to gain Jerry's freedom. Scanlon is arrested and Jerry is pardoned. He and Kay plan to wed and he intends to pursue his singing career professionally.

While approving of the picture's entertainment values, *Variety* questioned the production's box office appeal due to the lack of strong marquee names. Moreover, the trade paper warned exhibitors, "There is the additional handicap of hitting theatres at a time when prison yarns are surfeiting the market."

For the record, tenor Dick Foran had been singing in sagebrush and non-Western features for a few years. In *Over the Wall* he sang such numbers as "One More Tomorrow" and "Ave Maria." As for the promise of the film's title, the hero's escape attempt actually occurs when he is outside the prison on special duty. The story was from the pen of Lewis E. Lawes, warden of Sing Sing Prison.

John Litel and Dick Foran in *Over the Wall* (1938).

191. *Paid* (Metro-Goldwyn-Mayer, 1930), 83 min.

Director, Sam Wood; based on the play *Within the Law* by Bayard Veiller; screenplay, Lucien Hubbard, Charles MacArthur; art director, Cedric Gibbons; costumes, Adrian; camera, Charles Rosher; editor, Hugh Wynn.

Joan Crawford (Mary Turner); Robert Armstrong (Joe Garson); Marie Prevost (Agnes Lynch); Kent Douglass [Douglass Montgomery] (Bob Gilder); John Miljan (Inspector Burke); Purnell B. Pratt (Edward Gilder); Hale Hamilton (District Attorney Demarest); Polly Moran (Polly); Robert Emmett O'Connor (Cassidy); Tyrell Davis (Eddie Griggs); William Bakewell (Carney); George Cooper (Red); Gwen Lee (Bertha); Isabel Withers (Helen Morris).

Emerging superstar Joan Crawford was in her shop girl heroine period when she starred in *Paid*, based on a 1912 play that had previously been brought to the screen in 1917 (with Alice Joyce) and in 1923 (with Norma Talmadge). In the course of this glossy soap opera—did MGM make any other kind?—Crawford's Mary Turner endures years behind bars, emerging not rehabilitated, but with vengeance on her mind.

Through a series of bad luck events, innocent department store clerk Mary Turner (Joan Crawford) is wrongly sentenced to prison for a crime she did not

Joan Crawford and Marie Prevost in *Paid* (1930).

commit. In court she insists she will get even with the law for this miscarriage of justice. (She vows to her opponents, "You're going to pay for everything I'm losing in life.") In prison she becomes #4922 and serves her time doing menial work within the gray walls. Among her fellow inmates is the resilient Agnes Lynch (Marie Prevost). After serving three years, Mary is released. Once on the outside, she teams with three criminals: Joe Garson (Robert Armstrong), Red (George Cooper) and Agnes. With them she undertakes a variety of underhanded activities (ranging from near embezzlement to almost larceny), but always staying within the law. To have revenge on her former employer, Edward Gilder (Purnell B. Pratt), she marries his son Bob (Kent Douglass [Douglass Montgomery]). As time passes, she comes to love him. Meanwhile, the senior Gilder attempts to have his son's marriage annulled and when that fails, he collaborates with a stool pigeon, Eddie Griggs (Tyrrell Davis), to persuade Joe and Red to rob Bob's home (and put the blame on Mary). She learns of the plan which leads to Joe murdering Eddie. The police initially accuse Mary of the crime, but when Joe is captured and confesses, she is freed. She and Bob are reunited.

Mordaunt Hall *(New York Times)* was duly impressed with this prestigious MGM production, labeling it "a vigorous talking picture, with unusually competent performances from all its players." *Variety* endorsed, "Crook meller with a strong dramatic tug. An underworld idea that sidesteps the beaten path...." In retrospect, Alexander Walker, in *Joan Crawford: The Ultimate Star* (1983), noted of the star's performance in *Paid*, "Her prison scenes are brief. Yet they allow her to empty trash cans, battle for a place in the communal showers and outface a segment of tough female society that was much more commonplace in the 'Big House' melodramas of a male-oriented studio like Warners. It was a thrill for her fans to see her literally stripped of her finery, though she gets it back swiftly enough on release from prison...."

Originally the role of Mary Turner was assigned to studio star Norma Shearer, but when she became pregnant, Crawford crusaded with studio head Louis B. Mayer for the dramatic assignment. In 1939 MGM remade the film with far lesser results as *Within the Law,* a programmer starring Ruth Hussey.

British release title: *Within the Law.*

192. *Papillon* (Allied Artists, 1973), color, 150 min.

Executive producer, Ted Richmond; producers, Robert Dorfman, Franklin J. Schaffner; associate producer, Robert O. Kaplan; director, Schaffner; based on the novel by Henri Carriere; screenplay, Dalton Trumbo, Lorenzo Semple, Jr.; production designer, Anthony Masters; art director, Jack Maxsted; set decorator, Hugh Scaife; costumes, Anthony Powell; makeup, Charles Schram; music, Jerry Goldsmith; assistant directors, Jose Lopez Rodero, Juan Lopez Rodero; technical adviser, Lucien LaMontagne; stunt coordinator, Joe Canutt; sound, Deek Ball; sound re-recording, Richard Portman; sound editor, Gordon Daniel; special effects, Alex Weldon; camera, Fred Koenekamp; editor, Robert Swink.

Steve McQueen (Papillon [Henri Charrierel]); Dustin Hoffman (Louis Dega); Victor Jory (Indian Chief); Don Gordon (Julot); Anthony Zerbe (Toussaint, the Leper Colony Chief); Robert Deman (Maturette); Woodrow Parfrey (Clusiot); Bill Mumy (Lariot); George Coulouris (Dr. Chatal); Ratna Assan (Zoraima); William Smithers (Warden Barrot); Gregory Sierra (Antonio); Barbara Morrison (Mother Superior); Ellen Moss (Nun); Don Hammer (Butterfly Trader); Dalton Trumbo (Commandant); Val Avery (Pascal); Victor [Vic] Tayback (Sergeant); Dar Robinson (McQueen's Cliff Stunt); Mills Watson (Guard); Ron Soble (Santini); E. J. Andre

(Old Con); Richard Angarola (Comman-
dant); Jack Denbo (Classification Officer);
Len Lesser (Guard); John Quade (Masked
Breton); Fred Sadoff (Deputy Warden);

Allen Jaffe (Turnkey); Liam Dunn (Old
Trustee); Anne Byrne Hoffman (Mrs.
Dega).

Papillon is perhaps the ultimate tale of the infamous Devil's Island, the
cesspool prison that had so long fascinated Hollywood filmmakers. It was based on
Papillon (1929), the international best-seller by the late Henri Carriere, which
recounted — in somewhat romanticized terms — his years of hell at that French
Guiana confine. Allied Artists spent a whopping $13,000,000 on this widescreen
adaptation filmed in Jamaica. To insure audience interest in this spectacular prison
movie, Steve McQueen and Dustin Hoffman were cast in the lead roles. For
McQueen, it was a return of sorts to the genre, since he had enjoyed one of his
biggest box office hits starring in the World War prisoner-of-war adventure, *The
Great Escape* (1963).

In 1931 France, as convicts board a prison ship destined for the penal compound at French Guiana, they are instructed:

> As of this moment you are the property of the penal administration of French
> Guiana. After serving your full term in prison, those of you with sentences of eight
> years or more will remain in Guiana as workers and colonists for a period equal to
> that of your original sentence. As for France, the nation has disposed of you. France
> has rid herself of you altogether. Forget France and put your [prison] clothes on.

Aboard the vessel is a Parisian safecracker nicknamed Papillon (Steve Mc-
Queen), a man wrongly sentenced to a life term for a homicide (the murder of a
small-time pimp) he did not commit. Another prisoner is the nervous, bespectacled
Louis Dega (Dustin Hoffman), a well known forger/stock market swindler reputed
to be carrying a lot of (ill-gotten) money with him. The enterprising Papillon suggests to the urbane Dega that he will become his bodyguard in exchange for financial assistance with his pending escape plan. Before they reach Devil's Island, the
self-sufficient Papillon saves Dega's life when another convict attacks him.

Once ashore, this mean assortment of convicts are greeted with a stern
reminder of their dire fate:

> Welcome to the penal colony of French Guiana whose prisoners you are and from
> which there is no escape. First attempts to escape add two years in solitary to existing
> sentences. Second attempts add five more. Of course, more serious offenses are dealt
> with in this fashion. [He points to the guillotine standing ready in the courtyard.]
> Make the best of what we offer you and you will suffer less than you deserve.
> Dismissed.

The two men are sent to a jungle work camp where the resourceful Papillon
buys a boat from a butterfly trader. After preventing a sadistic guard from beating
the defenseless Dega, Papillon bolts from the camp. However, he is given a leaky
boat by the double-crossing trader and is soon captured. As punishment, Papillon
is locked into solitary confinement. The strict warden (William Smithers) advises
the rebellious inmate:

> We process dangerous men into harmless ones. This we accomplish by breaking
> you, breaking you physically, spiritually and . . . [mentally]. Put all hope out of your

mind and masturbate as little as possible. It drains the strength. Take him away.

Later, when the imprisoned Papillon refuses to admit who has been smuggling him supplementary rations (it was Dega), he is restricted to half-rations and locked in full darkness. Two years later he is released, much weathered from his ordeal. While recovering in the compound's hospital, he concocts his next escape plan, this time teaming with a homosexual trustee/orderly, Maturette (Robert Deman), and an older prisoner, Clusiot (Woodrow Parfrey). At first, Dega, who has manipulated himself into a "comfortable" existence at the facility, does not want to join the breakout attempt. However, after Clusiot is killed by a guard, Dega is dragged into the flight. While climbing the prison wall, Dega breaks his ankle, but he is helped along by Papillon and Maturette. Later, thanks to the assistance of those they encounter at a leper colony, they obtain a boat to sail for Colombia. Once there, they are stopped by an army search patrol, with only Papillon escaping to the jungle. He is wounded by Indian trackers and nursed back to health by a tribe of compassionate Indians led by their aged chief (Victor Jory) who offers the fugitive the pleasures of one of his maidens (Ratna Assan). Still later, while hiding at a convent, he is betrayed by a Mother Superior (Barbara Morrison) and taken back to the penal colony where he is placed in solitary confinement for five years. When released, the much aged, white haired Papillon is allowed to become a prison colonist on the island. He encounters Dega busily tending to his nearby plot of land. (The fuss budget Dega says, "Funny you and me ending up here. We're the only ones left.") Still unbroken, Papillon conceives a new escape plan. At first, Dega appears to go along with the scheme, but finally tells his friend to escape alone. Papillon tosses a raft made of coconuts into the ocean and then jumps after it from the high cliffs. As Papillon disappears over the horizon (shouting heavenward, "Hey you bastards! I'm still here!"), Dega looks on wistfully. A postscript advises that not only did Papillon survive out his life as a free man, but that he outlasted the prison at Devil's Island.

While appreciating the breathtaking visual spectacle of *Papillon* and acknowledging that it "is the escapist movie we used to go see," Vincent Canby *(New York Times)* perceived that the film "fills the screen with information designed to convince us that because the setting is real, so must be the people in it. . . . [The] screenplay . . . defines its characters less in terms of what they feel or think than in terms of extravagant incidents and superhuman heroics." Regarding the lengthy drama, *Variety* added, "The oppressive atmosphere is so absolutely established within the first hour of the film that, in a sense it has nowhere to go. . . ."

Variety attested that *Papillon* "is expert in all creative and technical areas," but thought emotionally the drawn out epic was a "downer." The trade paper reasoned, "[T]he atmosphere bores into the brain like it does to its victims, leaving them as well as an audience stunned, disoriented, incredulous and nearly catatonic. . . . The script is very good within its limitations, but there is insufficient identification with the main characters." For Richard Combs (British *Monthly Film Bulletin*), "[W]hat is missing is any of the book's anger at the outrageous hypocrisy, injustice and inhumanity of the system, any of the passion which feeds Papillon's compulsion to escape." Combs was not impressed by the film's contrived structure: "documentary in the first part, larger-than-life adventure in the second

Steve McQueen and Dustin Hoffman in *Papillon* (1973).

and doddering whimsicality for the scenes of the two men as premature dotards
on Devil's Island at the end."

In retrospect, Douglas Brode *(The Films of Dustin Hoffman,* 1983) would
judge, "In just about all superficial respects . . . *Papillon* represented a return to
the colossal adventure movies of the past. . . . But in just about every respect that
really matters, *Papillon* was actually a strikingly small movie: short on intelligence,
on taste, and on imagination. . . . *Papillon* . . . aped all the obvious, barren trappings of genuine epics, while missing entirely the basic ingredients which made
them great." For Casey St. Charnez, in *The Films of Steve McQueen* (1984),
Papillon "has all the clichés of the prison film, but endows them with a new

ugliness overlying the clichés to make it something new.... The disgusting is italicized; a prisoner's decapitated head splashes blood on the camera lens, a rifle wound pumps blood arterially, a centipede is sectioned with a spoon edge and dumped into a vomitous soup in solitary.... Overall, a depressing collection of details ... [the filmmakers] find necessary to liven things up."

Despite the mixed reviews and the inordinate length of this motion picture (which had an intermission), *Papillon* earned $22,500,000 in domestic film rentals paid to the distributor. It was Oscar-nominated for Best Original Dramatic Score, but lost the Academy Award to *The Way We Were*. When initially reviewed by the Motion Picture Association of America, it was rated R, but upon appeal the rating was changed to PG (parental guidance suggested). Dalton Trumbo, the once blacklisted writer who scripted *Papillon,* has an unbilled role in the picture as the commandant at the film's opening who addresses the lineup of naked prisoners.

With its overindulgent length, gore and "realism," *Papillon* was the ultimate of the Devil Island movies. Having reached such verisimilitude, there seemed nothing left for future filmmakers to say about this dreaded penal colony.

The word "papillon" in French means butterfly. The criminal/hero of this work was known by this nickname among the Paris underworld, in deference to the butterfly tattoo he had on his chest.

193. *Pardon My Stripes* (Republic, 1942), 64 min.

Associate producer, Albert J. Cohen; director, John H. Auer; screenplay, Lawrence Kimble, Stuart Palmer; art director, John Victor MacKay; music director, Cy Feuer; camera, John Alton; editor, Howard O'Neill.

Bill Henry (Henry Platt); Sheila Ryan (Ruth Stevens); Edgar Kennedy (Warden Bingham); Harold Huber (Big George Kilraine); Paul Hurst (Feets); Cliff Nazarro (Nutsy [Nuttington]); Tom Kennedy (Casino); Edwin Stanley (Andrews); Dorothy Granger (Peaches); George McKay (Old Timer [Joe]); Maxine Leslie (Myrtle).

This goofy little comedy really required a Damon Runyon to bolster its sagging storyline. "Story is far from clever either in itself or in its presentation, for all its sequences have been seen in one version or another before.... Situations are drained to the last inch to gain a laugh...." *(Variety).*

College football player Henry Platt (Bill Henry) is not well coordinated on the gridiron. When he runs the wrong way on the field, the opponent scores the winning touchdown. Meanwhile, gangster Big George Kilraine (Harold Huber), who made a killing ($17,000) on the game, hires the feckless Henry to bring the gambling winnings from California to Chicago. Because of an interfering reporter, Ruth Stevens (Sheila Ryan), Platt must charter his own craft. In flight, he accidentally drops the cash-laden, black briefcase overboard, and it tumbles into the courtyard of the state prison. Henry next maneuvers himself into becoming a prisoner at Rockford State Penitentiary, setting himself up on an embezzlement charge. There, the harassed warden (Edgar Kennedy) advises the newcomer, "I make a specialty of cracking tough nuts like you."

Platt is assigned to a cell with Old Timer (George McKay), who has already been incarcerated for twenty years, and Nutsy (Cliff Nazarro), a crazed man with a split personality. Before long, everyone at the prison is aware of the missing money. This leads to a confrontation between the aggravated warden and interfering Ruth:

WARDEN: I ain't gong to start a treasure hunt here in my prison. You don't know what kind of boys I have.

RUTH: What do you care if they have a little fun in their own home?

Wanting the inmates to help locate the cash, Ruth announces details of the missing briefcase over the prison's loudspeaker. Soon there is pandemonium as the greedy convicts rush hither and thither seeking the loot. To avoid the angry warden, Ruth disguises herself as a prisoner and is on hand as the convicts start to dig up the prison exercise yard. Before long there is a mad scramble football game with the coveted money as the booty. Big George is watching the shenanigans from a nearby telephone pole and later drives away, thinking he finally has the bag full of cash. However, he is mistaken, for Nutsy—who is really Nuttington of the Internal Revenue Service—has grabbed the dough as back payments owed by the criminal.

Among the weak gags used to spoof the prison genre are such side-splitters as one convict (Paul Hurst) receiving a care package which contains files in a pile of shirts and explosives in a box of fudge.

194. *Pardon Us* (Metro-Goldwyn-Mayer, 1931), 56 min.

Producer, Hal Roach; director, James Parrott; screenplay, H. M. Walker; songs: LeRoy Shield, Edward Kilenyi, Arthur J. Lamb, H. W. Petrie, Will Marion Cook, Irving Berlin, Cole and Johnston, Abe Olman, M. Ewing, Frederic Van Norman, L. E. de Francesco, J. S. Zamecnik, Freita Shaw, Marvin Hatley; sound, Elmer Raguse; camera, Jack Stevens; editor, Richard Currier.

Stan Laurel (Himself); Oliver Hardy (Himself); Walter Long (The Tiger); James Finlayson (School Teacher); June Marlowe (Arden's Daughter); Charlie Hall (Dental Assistant/Deliveryman); Sam Lufkin, Silas D. Wilcox, George Miller (Prison Guards); Wilfred Lucas (The Warden); Frank Holliday (Officer in Classroom); Harry Bernard (Warren, the Desk Sergeant); Stanley J. "Tiny" Sandford (Officer LeRoy Shields); Robert "Bobby" Burns (Prone Dental Patient); Frank Austin (Dental Patient in Waiting Room); Otto Fries (Dentist); Robert Kortman, Leo Willis (Pals of The Tiger); Jerry Mandy (Convict Who Cannot Add); Bobby Dunn, Eddie Dunn, Eddie Cooke, Charles Dorety, Dick Gilbert, Will Stanton, Jack Herrick, Jack Hill, Gene Morgan, Charles A. Bachman, John "Blackie" Whiteford, Charley Rogers (Insurgent Convicts); Gordon Douglas (Typist at Desk); James Parrott, Hal Roach (Prisoners Marching Next to Laurel and Hardy); Eddie Baker (Plantation Overseer on Horseback); The Etude Ethiopian Chorus (Cotton Pickers); Belle (The Bloodhound).

For their feature film debut, Stan Laurel and Oliver Hardy appeared in *Pardon Us,* a broad spoof of *The Big House* (1930), q.v., MGM's Academy Award-winning drama that had started Hollywood on its new cycle of prison movies. Originally, this burlesque project, which lampoons most of the genre's emerging conventions, was to have been a two-reel comedy using the still standing prison set at MGM. However, producer Hal Roach demanded more autonomy than MGM was willing to allow, so he constructed his own prison interior/exterior. To justify the cost of the set construction, he expanded the two-reeler into a feature film. It began production on June 24, 1930, with the movie, previously known as *The Rap,* gaining a new working title, *Their First Mistake.* Finally, in mid–August 1931, after much editing and reworking, the feature debuted. Mordaunt Hall *(New York Times)* judged, "Although it has some good gags, which are unfailing in eliciting laughter, it seems a pity that the clever acting of this team was not rewarded by a keener and less robust variety of humor."

During Prohibition, Stan Laurel and Oliver Hardy (themselves) hit on a scheme to make some easy money. They manufacture home beer and decide to sell what they cannot drink. They accidentally sell a bottle of the home brew to a policeman, whom they have mistaken for a streetcar conductor. As a result they are arrested and sent to prison.

The imposing warden (Wilfred Lucas) greets his latest charges, #44634 (Stan Laurel) and #44633 (Oliver Hardy):

> My, my. And still they come. Keep one thing in mind. It all depends on you yourselves, how you are going to fare here. Never forget that this is a prison and in a prison all rules must be obeyed. Discipline is the one thing that must be observed. If you are good prisoners, everything will be okay. But if not, if you break the rules, it will be just plain hell on earth.

Life is not made easier for the wide-eyed newcomers because of Stan's wobbly molar which causes him to make unexpected "razzberry" sounds. Some listeners mistake this for a sign of disrespect. When the warden asks the boys if they understand the import of his speech, Stan responds with a "Yes sir," plus a razzberry.

The irate warden screams, "Get them out of here before I lose my temper." He assigns them to cell #14 and as they leave he mutters, "The idea. Talking to a warden like that!"

In their six-person quarters, one of Stan and Oliver's cellmates is the hulking The Tiger (Walter Long) who asks what the boys did for a living on the outside. Ollie proudly replies, "We're a couple of beer barons." The Tiger soon is calling Stan "Squirt" and admires him for his nerve (i.e. making the razzberry sound). That night, Stan and Laurie decide to share the same upper bunk and in trying to get comfortable in their new surroundings, end up with the bed crashing to the floor.

In the prison classroom, the teacher (Jimmy Finlayson)—dressed in cap and gown—has a strict regimen. He demands that his rough flock of students always start the day with a docile rendition of the song "Good Morning Dear Teacher" which blends into an overly solicitous "Good Morning Dear Playmates...." To insure that his audience always pays attention, the teacher carries a big stick he uses to prod the recalcitrant pupils to rise or sit down. He is full of questions, leading to a display of Stan's I.Q.:

TEACHER: What is a blizzard?

STAN: The inside of a buzzard.

When prankish Ollie tosses an ink ball at the teacher, this leads to both Laurel and Hardy being sent to solitary confinement for a long period of contemplation. While wiling away the hours, they think of what life would be like living on a farm.

Meanwhile, The Tiger stages a breakout. While he is captured, the two boys escape. Bloodhounds are put on their trail and a $500 reward is offered. The troublesome twosome come across cotton pickers (the Etude Ethiopian Chorus) singing spirituals in the field and quickly decide to don blackface and pass themselves off as members of the group. Stan wisely puts chewing gum on his troublesome tooth so it will not buzz anymore. Feeling more confident that their disguise is working, Hardy provides a cotton field solo of "Lazy Moon" while Stan does a soft shoe dance.

When the car driven by the warden's daughter (June Marlowe) breaks down on the road adjacent to the cotton field, gallant Oliver and Hardy attempt to repair it. During the process the bloodhounds return and before the vehicle is working again, one of the dogs has licked half the blackening off of Ollie's face. Things take a turn for the worse, when Stan, the gum now gone from his mouth, accidentally makes one of his razzberry sounds. The game is up and the two escapees are taken back to prison, where in the prison yard, the convicts sing "I Want to Go Back."

Deciding enough is enough, a guard forces Stan to go to the penitentiary dentist (Otto Fries) to have that tooth pulled. Oliver ends up in the dentist's chair as well and has an unneeded tooth extraction. Then the dentist moves on to Stan, but removes the wrong tooth. Stan still makes the buzzing sound! (Laurel and Hardy had done their tooth pulling routine on stage and also in their silent comedy short, *Leave 'em Laughing,* 1928.)

One day in the mess hall, The Tiger has a machine gun snuck in and it is passed along from one convict to another. The innocent Stan pulls the contraband weapon above the table and it starts blasting a volley of bullets. This forces The Tiger to start his latest prison break earlier than planned. A riot occurs and it takes a regiment of soldiers to quell the uprising. For their (accidental) help in quelling the mayhem, Stan and Ollie are pardoned. The avuncular warden tells them, "My boys and you are my boys. . . . Let this episode be a hiatus to be obliterated from your memory."

The boys take this advice to heart, for no sooner does the warden complete his speech than the single-minded Stan Laurel wants to take the administrator's order for a couple of cases of beer. And his tooth starts buzzing again!

Variety was critical of *Pardon Us.* "Just another stretch of a two-reel idea on a six-reel frame with the usual strain resulting. . . . First 20-odd minutes are brimming with solid laughs. . . . What's in its seems funny because it isn't late enough for implausibility to take effect."

Regardless of the critical reaction, Laurel and Hardy were exceedingly popular with the public and this picture was a general crowd pleaser. It led to several more features for the comedy team and, over the years, thanks to the legion of Laurel and Hardy admirers (including their still very active global appreciation club, The Sons of the Desert) *Pardon Us* continues to be seen and appreciated.

During production and after previews, several sequences were deleted from *Pardon Us,* including a scene in which Stan and Ollie rescue the warden's daughter from a prison fire and an exercise yard encounter between the boys and some pugnacious convicts. As was typical procedure in this period, there were four foreign language versions made of *Pardon Us,* parallel scenes shot simultaneously with the English language version and frequently utilizing a different supporting cast. (E.g. in the French version, Boris Karloff had the role of The Tiger.) The foreign language versions were: *Sous les Verrous* (French), *Hinter Schloss und Riegel* (German), *Muraglie* (Italian) and *De Bote en Bote* (Spanish).

The very broad satire of *Pardon Us,* which had as many misses as on target barbs, doubtlessly inspired another screen comedy team, Bert Wheeler and Robert Woolsey, to make their own mockery of the conventions of the emerging prison films, *Hold 'em Jail* (1932), q.v. Decades later, in *They Went That-a-Way and*

That-a-Way (1978), Tim Conway and Chuck McCann starred as two fumbling cops who go undercover in the "big house" to trace the whereabouts of stolen money and then must pursue escaping prisoners. Allegedly, the misguided antics of Conway and McCann were inspired by the greatness of Laurel and Hardy, but it was difficult to discern from the misfire onscreen.

British release title: *Gaol Birds.*

A.k.a.: *Jail Birds.*

195. *The Penal Code* (Frueler, 1932), 62 min.

Director, George Melford; story, Edward T. Lowe; screenplay, F. H. Herbert; camera, Edward Kull; editor, Fred Bain.

Regis Toomey (University Smith [Bob Palmer]); Helen Cohan (Marguerite Shannon); Pat O'Malley (Sergeant Detective Bender); Robert Ellis (James Forrester); Virginia True Boardman (Mrs. Palmer); Henry Hall (Mr. Shannon); Leander De Cordova (Isaac Lewin); John Ince (War-den); Murdock MacQuarrie (Lefty, a Convict); Olin Francis (McCarthy, a Convict); Jack Cheatham (Detective Black); Barney Furey (Gambler); James Eagles (Newsdealer); Julia Griffith (Friend of Mrs. Shannon); Dorothy Sinclair (Girl on Train); Elizabeth Poule (Telephone Operator); Jean Porter (Office Girl); Albert Richman (Postman); Henry Henna (The Boy); Jack Grant (Ice Man).

Small town bank clerk Bob Palmer (Regis Toomey), despite the devotion of his overprotective mother (Virginia True Boardman), gets involved with a criminal element and ends in prison. To avoid letting his mother know the bad news, he takes advantage of a business which remails letters from convicts, using an Australia postmark. Bob is unaware that this firm uses its wealth of information to later blackmail paroled customers. When Bob returns home and regains his bank position, James Forrester (Robert Ellis) from the bureau soon appears, intending to blackmail Palmer. This leads to another cashier at the bank learning of Bob's checkered past and then trying to thrust the blame for another robbery he commits onto Bob. Thanks to the assistance of Sergeant Detective Bender (Pat O'Malley), a New York policeman, the situation is salvaged and Bob's reputation cleared.

Variety dismissed the independently produced vehicle: "Not much to offer as novelty in this combination of stressed drama and some rather mawkish attempts at mother love and young romance. . . . [It] is amateurish in plot, development and appeal." Others in the cast were John Ince (the warden), Helen Cohan (the ingenue in love with Bob), and Murdock MacQuarrie and Olin Francis as two knowing convicts.

196. *Penitentiary* (Columbia, 1938), 74 min.

Producer, Robert North; director, John Brahm; based on the play *The Criminal Code* by Martin Flavin; screenplay, Seton I. Miller, Fred Niblo, Jr.; music director, Morris Stoloff; camera, Lucien Ballard; editor, Viola Lawrence.

Walter Connolly (Thomas Mathews); John Howard (William Jordan); Jean Parker (Elizabeth Mathews); Robert Barrat (Captain Grady); Marc Lawrence (Jack Hawkins); Arthur Hohl (Finch); Dick Cur-tis (Tex); Paul Fix (Runch); Marjorie Main (Katie Mathews); John Gallaudet (State's Attorney); Edward Van Sloan (Dr. Reinewulf); Ann Doran (Blanche Williams); Dick Elliott (McNaulty); Charles Halton (Leonard Nettleford); Ward Bond (Prison Barber); James Flavin (Doran); Stanley Andrews (Captain Dorn); Robert Allen (Doctor); Jack Dougherty, Ethan Laidlaw, Frank Mayo, Harry Hollingworth, Frank Meredith (Cops); Lee Shumway (Guard); Lester

326 *Penitentiary*

Dorr (Reporter); Thurston Hall (Judge); Louise Stanley, Bess Flowers (Women); Perry Ivins (Lou); Billy Arnold (Fingerprint Man); Eric Wilton (Butler); Lee Prather (Sergeant).

By 1938 Hollywood was embarked on a new cycle of prison dramas, following in the wake of a highly publicized breakout attempt from Alcatraz Prison. Columbia Pictures decided to remake its pathfinding 1931 feature *The Criminal Code,* q.v., itself based on the 1929 hit Broadway play by Martin Flavin. In comparing the two versions, *Harrison's Reports* found faults with the new edition: "For one thing, the background and action are not as novel now as they were in 1931, owing to the fact that many prison melodramas have been produced since then. For another, the tempo seems to be slower here."

While drunk, William Jordan (John Howard) becomes enmeshed in a nightclub quarrel and his opponent dies in the brawl. He is sentenced to ten years in prison for manslaughter. Before the end of his sixth year behind bars, he is verging on a nervous breakdown, his morale shattered. At this juncture, Thomas Mathews (Walter Connolly) the crusading district attorney responsible for his conviction, is made the new warden of the prison. Dr. Reinewulf (Edward Van Sloan), the prison physician, brings Jordan's condition to the warden's attention. At Reinewulf's suggestion Jordan is removed from his work in the penitentiary's jute mill and becomes Mathews's chauffeur. In his new job, which renews his spirit, he meets and falls in love with the Mathews's daughter, Elizabeth (Jean Parker). Just as Jordan is about to be paroled, he witnesses the murder of a squealer (Paul Fix) by another inmate Jack Hawkins (Marc Lawrence). Because he refuses to break the criminal code of not telling on a fellow prisoner, he is placed in solitary confinement. Fearful that Jordan will seek revenge on the sadistic Captain Grady (Robert Barrat), Hawkins arranges to be placed in solitary. There he admits that he killed the stool pigeon and then murders Grady, against whom he had a long standing grudge. Hawkins, in turn, is killed by the guards. Jordan's parole is imminent and Mathews gives his blessings to Elizabeth and William marrying.

Variety agreed that this "B" film was surprisingly sturdy ("One of the best of the penal yarns"), but it warned exhibitors, "It is doubtful, however, that the remake will click as did its predecessor.... Walter Connolly, who works hard and well, isn't as adaptable to the hot spot as was Huston. He's not the rough type." Even the *New York Times*'s B. R. Cristler who gave no indication that he realized he was watching a remake, wrote, "You've seen it all before, of course."

Columbia Pictures would remake *The Criminal Code* yet again, this time entitled *Convicted* (1950), q.v., and starring Glenn Ford.

197. *Penitentiary* (Jerry Gross, 1979), color, 99 min.

Producer, Jamaa Fanaka; co-producers, Alicia Dhanifu, Al Shepard; associate producers, Irving Parham, Leon Isaac Kennedy, Lynette Stansell; director/screenplay, Fanaka; art director, Adel Mazen; set decorator, Beverly Green Etheredge; costumes, Debra Bradford, Deirdre Naughton; makeup, Gregory Lewis; music, Frank Gaye; song, Mark Gaillard and the Slim and Trim Band; stunt coordinator, John Sherrod; boxing adviser, Charles Young; second unit director, Sherrod; assistant directors, Jovon Gilloham, Yance Hamlett, Sergio Mimms; sound, Ed White; sound editor, Jim Nownes; camera, Marty Ollstein; additional camera, Stephen Posey; editor, Betsy Blankett.

Leon Isaac Kennedy (Martel "Too Sweet" Gordone); Thommy Pollard (Eugene T. Lawson); Hazel Spears (Linda); Donovan Womack (Jesse Amos); Floyd Chatman (Hezzikia "Seldom Seen" Jackson); Wilbur

"Hi-Fi" White (Sweet Pea); Gloria Delaney (Peaches); Badja Djola ("Half Dead" Johnson); Chuck Mitchell (Lieutenant Arnsworth); Cepheus Jaxon (Poindexter); Dwaine Fobbs ("Lying" Latney Winborn); Ernest Wilson ("Cheese"); Will Richardson (Magilla Gorilla); Elijah Mitchell, Darrell Harris, Lonnie Kirtz (Nuts); Tony Andrea (Moon); Ray Wolfe ("A" Block Night Guard); Charles Young ("Tough Tony," Manager and Referee); Michael Melvin, Steve Eddy (Bikers); Bill Murry ("Rappin'" Larry); Terri Hayden (Counter Lady); Herman Cole (Cook); Carl Erwin (Sam Cunningham); Irving Parham ("A" Block Day Guard); Warren Bryant (Gay Boxing Spectator); Lorri Gay (Second Girl in Rest Room); Thomas Earl Stiratt ("Wolf"); Walter Gordon (Second Male in Rest Room); Joaquin Leal (Rubin); David Carter, Hassan Abdul-Ali, Marcus Guttierrez (Guards); Zee Howard (Female Lieutenant); Cardella Demilo, Onia Fenee, Deloris Figueroa, Ann Hutcherson, Gwynn Pineda, Irene Stokes, Beverly Wallace (Female Guards); Renee Armanlin, Zeola Gaye, Brenda Joy Griffin, Shelli Hughes, Sarah Jaxon, Jackie Shaw, Irene Terrell, Barbara Torres, Lisa Visco (Female Inmates); William Bey, Robert Wayne Cornelius, Shawn Davis, Quitman Gates, Dominic Giusto, Johnny Jones, Casey J. Littlejohn, Sam Olden, Tony Rapisarda, Tyrone S. B. Thompson, Edgardo Williams, Roderic Williams (Male Inmates).

See summary under *Penitentiary III*.

198. *Penitentiary II* (Metro-Goldwyn-Mayer/United Artists, 1982), color, 103 min.

Producer/director/screenplay, Jamaa Fanakia; music, Jack W. Wheaton; camera, Steve Posey; editor, James E. Nownes.

Leon Isaac Kennedy (Martel "Too Sweet" Gordone); Ernie Hudson ("Half-Dead" Johnson); Mr. T (Himself); Glynn Turman (Charles); Peggy Blow (Ellen); Cepheus Jaxon (Do Dirty); Marvin Jones (Simp); Donovan Womack (Jesse "The Bull" Amos); Ebony Wright (Sugar); Eugenia Wright (Clarisse); Rene Wood (Nikki); Marci Thomas (Evelyn); Dennis Libscomb, Gerald Berns (Announcers); Joe Anthony Cox (Midget); Sephton Moody (Charles, Jr.); Malik Carter ("Seldom Seen" Jackson); Stan Kamber (Sam).

See summary under *Penitentiary III*.

199. *Penitentiary III* (Cannon, 1987), color, 91 min.

Producers, Jamaa Fanaka, Leon Isaac Kennedy; director/screenplay, Fanaka; production designer, Marshall Toomey; art director, Craig Freitag; set decorator, Beverly Etheredge; makeup/special effects, Mike Spatola; music, Garry Schyman; music editor, John Elizalde; second unit director, John Sherrod; assistant director, Brent Sellstorm, Pat Kirck; martial arts advisers, Hugh Van Patton, Glen Eaton; sound, Oliver Moss; supervising sound/foley editor, John Post; camera, Marty Ollstein; second unit camera, Joseph W. Calloway; editor, Ed Harker.

Leon Isaac Kennedy (Martel "Too Sweet" Gordone); Anthony Geary (Serenghetti); Steven Antin (Roscoe); Ric Mancini (Warden); Marie Burrell Fanaka (Chelsea Remington); Raymond "The Haiti Kid" Kessler (Midnight Thud Jessup); Rick Zumwalt (Joshua); Magic Schwarz (Hugo); Jim Bailey (Cleopatra); Big Bull Bates (Simp); Big Yank (Rock); Bert Williams (Tim Shoah); Mark Kemble (Rufus); Jack Rader (Fred); Madiso Campudoni (El Cid); Mike Payne (Jess); Drew Bundini Brown (Sugg); Ty Randolph (Sugar); J. J. Johnson, Earl Garnes (Announcers); Jim Phillips (Suited Gentleman); Faith Minton, Marcella Ross, Ray Hollitt (Female Boxer); Danny Trejo (Sam Veer); Mary O'Connor, Cardella Demilo (Female Guards); "Dr. De" Ron Demps (Referee).

There seems to be little middle ground in viewers' reactions to the *Penitentiary* series. All three films (1979, 1982, 1987) were directed by Jamaa Fanaka and each starred Leon Isaac Kennedy. While this trio of gritty action movies progressed

Leon Isaac Kennedy in *Penitentiary III* (1987).

from the crude to the absurd, from the underbudgeted to the overindulged, there is no denying the intensity of experience that each of these pictures offers. Taken together, they represent a unique chapterplay about prison life as well as a documentation of the changing content of black action features in 1970s–1980s Hollywood.

The *Penitentiary* series owes a great deal to the success of Sylvester Stallone's *Rocky* series which began in 1976 (and continued through 1990). The fantastic box office profits of *Rocky* paved the way for many other cinematic studies of athletes emerging from underdog to champion. While *Rocky* dealt with the white world in which blacks intermingled, the *Penitentiary* entries do the reverse. Its prominent black director, Jamaa Fanaka, was a graduate of the U.C.L.A. Film School and had already been responsible for two coarse but emotion-charged films, *Welcome Home Brother Charles* (1975) and *Emma Mae* (1976), each dealing with black people fighting for their rights in an oppressive white world. The star of the Penitentiary series was Leon Isaac [Kennedy], a handsome black actor and former disc jockey from the midwest who had already appeared in several black exploitation features before marrying actress/model/sportscaster Jayne Kennedy (and adding on her surname).

For the *Penitentiary* canon, Fanaka and Kennedy created a resilient fantasy figure, Martel "Too Sweet" Gordone, who continually finds himself back in stir, a mean institution where the black inmates have it even tougher. In the dank confines of the *Penitentiary* episodes, if a man is to survive, he must fight hard for his rights. Too Sweet uses or is forced to utilize his skills as a boxer to champion his survival and the rights of his downtrodden fellow convicts. The down and dirty prisons depicted in the *Penitentiary* series make Jim Brown's *Riot* (1969), q.v., seem tame by comparison. One can only wonder how such past celluloid veterans of the prison genre as James Cagney, Spencer Tracy or John Garfield would have survived in the sewers that Too Sweet inhabits in his stretch behind bars.

Young and restless black hitchhiker Martel Gordone (Leon Isaac Kennedy) finds himself fighting two belligerent bikers over a fickle prostitute, Linda (Hazel Spear), who promptly disappears. One of the bikers is killed in the skirmish and Martel is unjustly sentenced to a state prison. There his fondness for candy (especially Mr. Goodbars) earns him the nickname "Too Sweet." In his foreboding cell block, tough Jesse Amos (Donovan Womack) is boss and his prime henchman is the savage "Half Dead" Johnson (Badja Djola). The latter goads Gordone into a fistfight, and, to everyone's surprise except Too Sweet's, Martel punches hell out of his opponent.

Later Too Sweet comes to the rescue of Jesse's sexually harassed cellmate, Eugene T. Lawson (Thommy Pollard). This leads to Gordone and Jesse battling it out, and as a result, both convicts are ordered to solitary confinement. Later, they are offered the opportunity to settle their grudge in the prison boxing tournament, *if* they promise no further trouble. As added inducement, champions in the several matches are promised connubial visits, and the top victor might have the chance to be handled by the warden's brother-in-law, a fight promoter.

By now, Too Sweet is sharing a cell with veteran convict Hezzikia "Seldom Seen" Jackson (Floyd Chatman), himself a former boxing trainer. He gives Gordone the benefit of his experience. Martel wins the championship match and finds time for sexual relaxation with Linda. She is now serving time for her part in the biker's death and is one of the female prison inmates brought in from a neighboring facility to watch the boxing contest. Later, the disgruntled Amos and Johnson seek reprisals against Gordone, and when Lawson comes to Martel's assistance, he is murdered. This leads to Too Sweet fighting Amos in another match. His new victory paves the way for his release and as he leaves the penitentiary, he convinces Seldom Seen to become his professional trainer.

There is much that is graphically frightening about the energetic *Penitentiary*. The prison is shown as overcrowded, bursting with racial tension, full of corruption on both sides of the bars, and the sexually deprived men taking out their frustrations in mayhem, murder and homosexual rape. (This is a far cry from the brutal but sanitized prisons depicted in prior generations of genre entries.) In other ways, *Penitentiary* follows the traditional formula. The relatively controlled hero has to adapt to his hellish surroundings, once inside the prison gates. He tells a downtrodden brother, "Don't nobody have to be nobody's property!" And he means it. If his fists are his only salvation at hand, so be it. ("I'm no boxer," he says. "I fight to protect myself.") Before the storyline is completed, he has been seasoned into a tough survivor, who knows how to fight in and out of the ring to keep on living.

Besides its blunt, close-up look at bigotry and homosexuality in prison, *Penitentiary* offers a touching portrayal of a convict who has become so institutionalized, that he is afraid of any other type of life. Seldom Seen Jackson has been incarcerated for fifty of his sixty-five years and is scared to face the outside world. (This is very similar to George Cleveland's character in *Mutiny in the Big House* [1939], q.v.) This leads to a touching, insightful dialogue between the elder convict and his young protégé:

> SELDOM SEEN: I'm afraid of the streets.... It just scares me going out there and being a nobody. What can I do? Who wants me? Who even will pay attention to an old out-of-date fool like me. Here I am somebody. I got my own TV, my own stereo, my own home. I mean somethin' in here. I got respect.
>
> TOO SWEET: There's only one thing wrong. You ain't got no hope.... We can make it out there.... We can at least try!

Kevin Thomas *(Los Angeles Times)* judged, "Filled with vividly drawn larger-than-life characters and loaded with action, *Penitentiary* bursts with energy and emotion. It's operating in the best, bravura sense.... Fanaka is too vital and personal to be a copy of anything." Tom Allen *(Village Voice)* endorsed, "*Penitentiary* in its angled photography is one of the most expressive American movies of the year and much more accomplished in its visuals than its acting.... Even as Fanaka makes us squirm by drowning us in raw sex and violence, he transcends the primitivism." Martyn Auty (British *Monthly Film Bulletin*) was more disturbed by the viewing experience, "What makes *Penitentiary* an even more debased experience is that the prison's all-black population is made to embody every racist stereotype—the 'wild man' Half-Dead, the sullen fixer Jesse, the elderly man of wisdom Seldom Seen and, most dubious of the bunch, the Caucasian-looking 'good' black Too Sweet.... [Too Sweet's] final victory is nothing more than a corrupt evasion of corrupt justice, made possible by the subjugation of fellow blacks already brutalised within a redneck-run prison. For all its posturing, this is a film that ideologically enslaves blacks."

Made on an estimated budget of $250,000, *Penitentiary* grossed $13,120,235 in ticket sales. It seemed almost inevitable, by Hollywood tradition, that a sequel would follow. However, whereas *Penitentiary* had been a gutsy independent production held together with determination and bursting emotions, *Penitentiary II* (1982) was a disappointing follow-up. This time Metro-Goldwyn-Mayer/United Artists financed the production, giving the filmmaker and his star a $1,000,000 major studio production budget. For this second entry in the *Rocky*-inspired series, Fanaka-Kennedy borrowed an actual performer from that series, Mr. T, who does a guest starring cameo in Penitentiary II. With money not an object for the filmmaker, the creative hurdle for scenarist Fanaka in the sequel was to dream up a "convincing" reason to land Too Sweet behind bars—again!

An elaborate title card prologue to *Penitentiary II* explains that Too Sweet (Leon Isaac Kennedy) is now living with his sister, Ellen (Peggy Blow), and her family and that he works as a roller-skating messenger(!) for his brother-in-law, Charles (Glynn Turman). Gordone, we are told, must fulfill his obligations to his fight promoter, the warden's brother-in-law, or lose his parole. Meanwhile, his worst enemy, "Half Dead" Johnson (Ernie Hudson) has escaped from prison, along with Do Dirty (Cepheus Jaxon) and Simp (Marvin Jones) and is screaming for Too Sweet's blood.

Too Sweet's romance with Clarisse (Eugenia Wright) ends tragically when Half Dead kills her. This trauma causes the rehabilitated Gordone to spring to life. He reasons, "I was dead. But now I'm going to box. I'm goin' to be someone. I'm gonna get respect!" This new ambition leads Too Sweet back to prison to contest Jesse "The Bull" Amos (Donovan Womack) in the ring, while his brother-in-law sets about rescuing his kidnapped family from Do Dirty and Simp. Ellen and Charles rush to ringside to prove to Too Sweet that they are fine, which causes the badly pummeled Martel to have a burst of new energy and he knocks out the champ.

The overinflated, clichéd *Penitentiary II* was a creative disappointment to fans of the original, although the film allegedly grossed several million dollars in global distribution. According to *Variety,* "Still wearing three hats . . . Fanaka winds up with a cheap, exploitive, preposterously dumb mess. Life does have its reverses." Vincent Canby *(New York Times)* admitted the picture has "a self-assurance that is so brazen that it almost persuades you that the film's ineptitude is its chosen style." However, he cautioned, "The boxing sequences are so lethargic that the movie keeps cutting away from the ring during crucial fights, as if embarrassed. The plot, pacing action and especially, the violence are absurd."

Both Jamaa Fanaka and Leon Isaac Kennedy struggled to crash out of their *Penitentiary* career rut. However, by 1987, the two talents, in search of a winning property, agreed to making *Penitentiary III,* packaged by Cannon Pictures for approximately $2,000,000, which was eight times the cost of the original entry.

What emerged onscreen in the third installment of the Martel Gordone saga was incredible flim-flam. It led *Variety* to querying rhetorically, "Are cartoons and professional wrestling matches fun? If you answer yes to the second question then this movie definitely is for you."

Prissy penitentiary kingpin Serenghetti (Anthony Geary) wants Too Sweet (Leon Isaac Kennedy) back in prison so he can promote him for an upcoming jailhouse match. To accomplish this, he arranges for Gordone to be drugged during a boxing match which causes him to go berserk and pummel his opponent to death. Now imprisoned, Too Sweet has again sworn off fighting, fearful of his lethal fists. However, almost immediately, Martel is drawn into the conflict between two local opposing forces: the boxing teams sponsored on the one hand by the warden (Ric Mancini) and on the other that controlled by Serenghetti, the king of the cellblock. When Gordone proves uncooperative, Serenghetti exerts a little persuasion. He arranges for the Midnight Thud (Raymond "The Haiti Kid" Kessler), a murderous midget boxer convict, to attack the newcomer. When Too Sweet wins out over this little person, he is punished by electro-shock treatment. Later, he and Midnight Thud form a truce and become pals. Meanwhile, the shock of seeing his convict friend Roscoe (Steve Antin) almost killed in the ring inspires Too Sweet to fight once again. Midnight Thud serves as his trainer and instructs him in various martial arts skills. For the big match, Too Sweet is to fight the hulking Hugo (Magic Schwarz) who has been dosed with the same drug that previously turned Gordone into a frenzied monster. Nevertheless, Gordone emerges victorious and Serenghetti's reign is broken.

Amazingly, the overwrought *Penitentiary III* received several decent reviews. Kevin Thomas (*Los Angeles Times*) noted, "*Penitentiary III* . . . is pure action fantasy, but Fanaka pushes its possibilities to the limit. Too Sweet, so well played by the wiry and talented Kennedy, is a mythical figure, the wronged, oppressed black man who overcomes injustice not merely by his fists but by strength of character, spirit and discipline." For Duayne Byrge *(Hollywood Reporter)*, "While *Pen III* is sensibly roped off into a tight strong ring — good guys vs. bad guy in the championship bout — there's a bevy of weird and bizarre between-story-round stuff that spruces up the formula. . . . Despite some expositional deliveries that clank against the action, *Penitentiary III* is a lean and mean entertainment." Jonathan Gold *(LA Weekly)* neatly summarized this entry with, "Jamaa Fanaka brings us yet another poorly shot, abysmally lighted and thoroughly entertaining trip through his surrealistic pen, where S & M guards hang out in medieval dungeons and nasty mobmen run the joint from their plushy appointed cells. The picture isn't good, but it sure is fun. . . . This is fast-paced cartoon violence, and, as in *Road Runner* cartoons, almost nobody gets hurt."

To be noted in the cast of *Penitentiary III,* in an almost throwaway role (at least in the final editing), is famed impressionist Jim Bailey as Serenghetti's "girlfriend" Cleopatra, who parades through the movie in a series of drag outfits looking elegant and dramatic but saying little.

Despite the surprisingly favorable reviews for *Penitentiary III,* it was not a box office winner. Its distributor, Cannon Films, was in the midst of corporate chaos and thus its release pattern was ineffectually handled.

Having borrowed so heavily from Sylvester Stallone's *Rocky* series, Stallone returned the "favor" when he created his own fantasy macho excursion through prison in *Lock Up* (1989), q.v. Unlike the *Penitentiary* entries, *Lock Up* took itself seriously, was too wildly absurd, and was not half as decadent or "enjoyable."

200. *Pennies from Heaven* (Columbia, 1936), 80 min.

Producer, Emmanuel Cohen; director, Norman Z. McLeod; based on the story "The Peacock's Feather" by Katherine Leslie Moore, William Rankin; adaptor, screenplay, Jo Swerling; art director, Stephen Goosson; music, Arthur Johnston; music director, George Stoll; orchestrator, John Scott Trotter; songs, Johnny Burke and Johnston; technical adviser, Norman Blackburn; camera, Robert Pittack; editor, John Rawlins.

Bing Crosby (Larry Poole); Madge Evans (Susan Sprague); Edith Fellows (Sarge [Patsy Smith]); Donald Meek (Gramps Smith);

John Gallaudet (J. C. Hart); Louis Armstrong (Henry); Tom Dugan (Crowbar Miller); Nana Bryant (Miss Howard); Charles Wilson (Warden); Harry Tyler (Concessionaire); William Stack (Carmichael); Tom Ricketts (Briggs); Nydia Westman (Landlady); George Chandler (Waiter); and: The Louis Armstrong Band, Lionel Hampton.

If Bing Crosby's singing is enough to satisfy his fans, then this picture will go over, for he sings several good numbers in his customary style, and looks better than he looked in his last few pictures.

(Harrison's Reports)

If that "singing fool" Al Jolson could go to jail during the course of *Say It with Songs* (1929), q.v., then so could Bing Crosby in *Pennies from Heaven*. There was certainly nothing realistic about the crooner's stay in prison, for rarely in real life does a wandering troubadour get to sing a solo requested by a condemned man. But this was 1930s Hollywood!

Larry Poole (Bing Crosby) who had been raised in an orphanage, had grown up to become a wandering singer. He had been a stowaway on a freighter. When crew members of the vessel were seized for being part of a smuggling operation, Larry had been arrested as well. The judge had not believed he was innocent and he landed in prison. His cell is down the row from J. C. Hart (John Galludet), a condemned killer. As the warden (Charles Wilson) prepares Hart for the last walk to his execution, the prisoner has a few requests. He explains to the warden, "You can't be too technical at a time like this."

Hart tells Larry, who is strumming on his lute, "Many's the time I heard you out in the yard. It kinda took my mind off things."

Larry sings a song for him, and then Hart has another request. Would Larry, due to be paroled soon, deliver a letter to a family named Smith who live near Middleton, New Jersey. Hart explains why he has selected the good-natured Larry on this important errand: "Because you're the only guy around here I can trust. Anybody that can sing sappy sentimental songs in prison wouldn't double cross a guy taking his last walk."

When released from prison, Larry goes in search of the Smiths and finds two members of the family, Patsy (Edith Fellows) and her grandfather (Donald Meek). It develops that Hart has deeded a home in New Jersey to the Smiths, to make up for having killed Patsy's father in an argument. Meanwhile, a strict social worker, Susan Sprague (Madge Evans), warns Larry that unless he could demonstrate some visible means of being able to support the youngster, she will be placed in an orphanage. Driven to ingenuity, Larry barters with local merchants to turn the house into a nightclub, the Haunted House Cafe (featuring home cooked chicken dinners). However, opening night is a financial disaster for the audience is filled with his "partners." The discouraged but still resilient Larry goes away to earn money doing death defying stunts in a circus sideshow. He is injured and hospitalized. During his absence, Patsy is taken to the orphanage. His efforts to rescue her fail and, later, when encountering Susan, he berates her for her unfeeling behavior. She explains she had been against the board's decision and had in fact quit her job. Larry and Susan reconcile and decide to marry, planning to adopt the precocious Patsy.

Variety was not enthused about the final results. "Story hops disconcertingly from realism to hoke farce with pauses for Crosby to sing. . . . Picture opens with a condemned man on his last walk to the electric chair. A gruesome start for a comedy."

Frank S. Nugent *(New York Times)* was kinder in his critical reaction. "Mr. Crosby invests his familiar crooning with a certain philosophic romanticism...." However, noted Nugent, "[T]he chief honors properly belong to little Miss Fellows. Hers really is an exceptional performance for a youngster, skirting the perils of bathos in her scenes and playing her rebellious ones with comic impertinence."

The best songs in this unpretentious musical were the title tune (which was nominated for an Academy Award), "One, Two, Button Your Shoe" sung by Crosby, and a duet ("Skeleton in the Closet") between Crosby and the infectiously bubbly Louis Armstrong. One of the nicest ingredients in *Pennies from Heaven* is the opportunity to watch the energetic Louis Armstrong Band performing at their peak.

Finally, it should be noted that there is no relationship between this 1936 release and the 1981 Steve Martin-Bernadette Peters musical of the same title.

201. *Prison* (Empire, 1988), color, 102 min.

Executive producer, Charles Band; producer, Irwin Yablans; director, Renny Harlin; story, Yablans; screenplay, C. Courtney Joyner; art director, Phillip Duffin; set decorator, Patti Garrity; costumes, Stephen Chudel; makeup, Suzanne Sanders; music, Richard Band, Christopher L. Stone; music editor, Dan Johnson; music co-ordinator, Cari Lutz; assistant director, Matthew Carlisle; stunt coordinator, Kane Hodder; supervising sound editors, Harry Ryatt, Robert Fitzgerald; effects editors, Fred Wasser, Allen Hartz, Sach Enoy Davis; camera, Mac Ahlberg; editor, Ted Nicholaou.

Lane Smith (Ethan Sharpe); Viggo Mortensen (Burke); Chelsea Field (Katherine); Andre De Shields (Sandor); Lincoln Kilpatrick (Cresus); Ivan Kane (Lasagna); Steven Little (Rhino); Mickey Yablans (Brian Young); Tom "Tiny" Lister, Jr. (Big Sam); Tom Everett (Rabbitt).

The R-rated *Prison* is a potentially intriguing blend of the prison and horror genres that never reaches its potential. Thankfully, it is boosted by superior special effects. Similar to several recent entries, it carried the horrors of prison life one step beyond reality, invoking the supernatural for an added dose of blood-and-gore. Unfortunately, there were too many mundane ingredients in the creative process to make *Prison* outstanding.

At Creedmore Prison at Rawlins, Arizona, guard Ethan Sharpe (Lane Smith) is responsible for the death of a prisoner and, then, placing the blame on another convict who is electrocuted. In 1968, the crumbling prison fortress, built at the turn-of-the-century, is closed. Meanwhile, Sharpe moves up the penal system's professional ladder elsewhere. In addition, he continues to have severe nightmares about his gross misdeed.

Twenty years later, it is announced that, because of overcrowded prison conditions and budget cuts, the dilapidated Creedmore will reopen. Young penal psychologist Katherine Walker (Chelsea Field) is against the appointment of veteran Sharpe to the post of Creedmore's warden. She warns the prison board, "The man is a dinosaur. All he knows is chain gangs and tommy guns. Is that your solution?"

It is not long before the dictatorial, old-line Sharpe and the progressive Katherine have their first major confrontation. Sharpe instructs her on his views of rehabilitation: "I will not have you interfere with our primary purpose.... Punishing criminals, keeping them away from the public at large. All the rest.... So much window dressing."

Prisoners are bused in from other facilities and the cruel Sharpe immediately embarks on a power game to show the seasoned convicts that he means business. He launches many hard-nosed policies. For the bulk of the convicts, this is nothing new, for they have endured the same or worse at other institutions. However, for young and handsome short-timer Connie Burke (Viggo Mortensen), the warden's disgusting scare tactics are a challenge he will not overlook. Meanwhile, Sharpe has some of the convicts excavate the basement execution chamber that had been bricked up years ago. This activity unleashes the spirit of the wrongly killed prisoner and this blue spirit begins a rampage of revenge. It develops that one aging black inmate, Cresus (Lincoln Kilpatrick) shares the warden's secret from years ago. Another black convict attempts using voodoo to summon forth the spirit so it can be confronted. After a riot engulfs the prison and several more guards and convicts are killed by the rampaging ghost, the frightened Sharpe escapes in his car. Outside the prison gates, he is electrocuted by the vengeful spirit. Justice has been served.

Occasionally, in the middle of the special effects and the rampaging spirits and convicts, *Prison* has an astute commentary to make on the life of a prisoner, such as when one black convict waxes philosophically, "I've been dong time for thirteen years and all I learned is to cut my meat with a spoon and to call my best friend 'mother fucker.'"

Variety had mixed feelings about this budget-conscious effort. "A veritable *Poltergeist Penitentiary*. *Prison* should be a breeze to market because of the clear-cut audiences out there for both rough penal pix and special effects-laden horror stories. This rare amalgam should guarantee strong initial business, but the routine lensing, acting and ending foreshadow's a short theatrical run." Less tolerant was Leonard Klady *(Los Angeles Times),* "It's not that this yarn of a spirit loose in a maximum security lockup is without merit. But the premise has been stretched beyond any reasonable expectation. Ideally, and thematically, the film fits snugly into a 'Twilight Zone' slot.... Technically, and on a performance level, *Prison* ... earns time off for good behavior. However, the story feels as if it was conceived by someone working with an expired artistic license."

Prison was lensed at the Wyoming State Penitentiary at Rawlins, closed since 1981.

202. *Prison Break* (Universal, 1938), 68 min.

Producer, Trem Carr; director, Arthur Lubin; based on the story "The Walls of San Quentin" by Norton S. Parker; screenplay, Parker, Dorothy Reid; camera, Harry Neumann; editor, Jack Ogilvie.

Barton MacLane (Joaquin Shannon); Glenda Farrell (Jean Fenderson); Paul Hurst (Soapy); Constance Moore (Maria); Ward Bond (Red Kincaid); Edward Pawley (Joe Fenderson); Edmund MacDonald (Chris); John Russell (Jackie); Frank Darien (Cappy); Victor Kilian (Fenderson); Glenn Strange, Edmond O'Brien (Prisoners).

> Unlike most of our modestly-budgeted melodramas dealing with the parole system, *Prison Break* ... omits the jubilant finale in which the boss-racketeer controlling the parole board is exposed and the warden-in-cahoots is sent further up the river.
>
> (Frank S. Nugent, *New York Times*)

When a slug-happy crook, Red Kincaid (Ward Bond) kills a seaman for his money, California tuna fisherman Joaquin Shannon (Barton MacLane) takes the blame, believing his brother-in-law committed the crime. The innocent Shannon is sent to prison on a manslaughter charge where he soon encounters the vicious Kincaid, arrested on a different charge. Red makes Joaquin's difficult life behind bars more difficult which leads the penitentiary guards into believing that Shannon is incorrigible. When Joaquin is finally released, he discovers his torment is not over. Because of the conditions of his parole, he cannot pursue his career as a fisherman (he is forbidden to go beyond the twelve-mile limit) and he cannot marry his sweetheart, Jean (Glenda Farrell). Later events have Joaquin's sister Maria (Constance Moore) and her husband drowned and, in the finale, Joaquin and Jean are held prisoners by the vengeful Red. Eventually, the hoodlum is overcome with Joaquin intending to turn the killer over to the police.

Variety was resistant to this preachy double-bill item. "Story of undying sacrifice, with over-emphasis of prison background, never quite arouses the sympathy or interest intended. The material for an intriguing yarn is visibile, but it doesn't pan out."

203. *Prison Farm* (Paramount, 1938), 67 min.

Presenter, Adolph Zukor; director, Louis King; story, Edwin V. Westrate; screenplay, Eddie Welch, Robert Yost, Stuart Anthony; art directors, Hans Dreier, Earle Hedrick; set decorator, A. E. Freudeman; music director, Boris Morros; sound, Harold Lewis, John Cope; camera, Harry Fischbeck; editor, Edward Dmytryk.

Shirley Ross (Jean Forest); Lloyd Nolan (Larry Harrison); John Howard (Dr. Roi Conrad); J. Carrol Naish (Noel Haskins); Porter Hall (Superintendent Chiston R. Bradby); Esther Dale (Cora Waxley); May Boley ("Shifty" Sue); Marjorie Main (Matron Brand); Anna Q. Nilsson (Matron Ames); John Hart ("Texas" Jack); Diana R. Wood (Dolly); Howard Mitchell, Carl Harbaugh, Jack Hubbard (Guards); Mae Busch (Trixie); Ruth Warren (Josie); Robert Brister (Joe Easy); Virginia Dabney (Maizie); Phillip Warren (Injured Prisoner); Blanche Rose (Woman Trusty); Betty Mack (Meg); Jimmy Conlin (Dave the Grocery Store Clerk); Dick Elliott (Judge); Ethel May Hall, Cecil Weston (Matrons); Bosy Roth (Waitress); Archie Twitchell (Telegraph Operator); Pat West (Station Agent); Edwin J. Carlie (Mailman); Charles C. Wilson (Reardon); Gloria Williams (Woman); William Holden (Inmate).

Loving the wrong man can lead a young woman to heartache and disaster. Such is the message of *Prison Farm*, a wonderfully compact love story featuring the background of a prison farm where corruption, torture and general malaise are the unpleasant order of the day.

Despite the warning of her good friend Cora Waxley (Esther Dale), who owns a coffee shop, wide-eyed, twenty-one-year-old Jean Forest (Shirley Ross) loves no-good Larry Harrison. Unknown to Jean, Harrison has just robbed an armored truck at the Southern Grain Company's warehouse, killing the guard in the process and stealing $9,000. He informs the naïve Jean he has just negotiated a good job in Winnipeg, Canada, and that they are to relocate there to marry and live. On her way to meet him at the train station in nearby Glenby, her car runs out of gas and she is given a ride by Noel Haskins (J. Carrol Naish), a guard at the nearby Sunny Grove Prison Farm. At the station, Haskins tries to force her into a sexual situation with him and the angered Larry battles it out with Haskins. Haskins arrests both Larry and Jean, and, as a result, they are sentenced to six months at Sunny Grove. Meanwhile, Harrison sews his stolen money into the lining of his coat, which is placed in storage at the prison, until his release.

Sunny Grove Prison Farm is not an ideal rehabilitation spot for any type of prisoner. Idealistic Dr. Roi Conrad (John Howard) has learned that the hard way

Shirley Ross, Marjorie Main and Blanche Rose in *Prison Farm* (1938).

during his tenure at the work camp. He remains at the facility thinking he can do more good for the inmates if he is there rather than quitting. However, he and Superintendent Chiston R. Bradby (Porter Hall) definitely have opposing points of views regarding their charges. Conrad informs Bradby that several men who suffered from food poisoning at the camp should remain in the infirmary. The money-minded Bradby thinks differently.

> BRADBY: [A] little fresh air and exercise might do the boys some good.... I'm afraid I'll have to do a little prescribing myself, I have a contract to deliver a large shipment of lumber. It must be cut.
>
> CONRAD: You're forgetting Mr. Bradby that those men have brains. Rotten food, terrible quarters and killing labors do things to their minds.
>
> BRADBY: [Benignly] I'll never understand why the state doesn't send me a doctor who could keep the prisoners fit for work, instead of wasting time trying to see what makes the wheels go round in their heads.
>
> CONRAD: You're running one of the worst prison farms in the country here.
>
> BRADBY: But one of the most profitable. We're making money for the state here at Sunny Grove.
>
> CONRAD: By turning men and women into savages.

The unperturbed Bradby saunters out to address the new arrivals, which include Larry and Jean. The sinister administrator declares:

> I want you men and women to pay close attention to what I have to say. You're here because you violated the law and you owe a debt to the state. You're going to pay that debt with work. Long hard work. Most of you are first timers. You may find it easier if you know what the score is. There's *no* parole here and *no* time off for good behavior. But there's plenty of time added on for bad.

To emphasize the strict rules at the Farm, sullen matrons Brand (Marjorie Main) and Ames (Anna Q. Nilsson) are standing close by at attention. The dour Brand demands strict attention, telling the restless newcomers, "Pipe down you mugs." Viewing the new crop of slave labor and agitated Jean in particular, Bradby decides, "A little hard work will straighten out your difficulties."

Once segregated to the women's dormitory, innocent Jean is befriended by wise-cracking, tough-acting Shifty Sue (Mae Boley), who is making her fifth return visit to Sunny Grove. Mae brags, "I know every rat hole in the place and every rat who lives in it." The unfeeling Matron Brand returns to set down the law to her cowered charges: "I will now explain the work routine at Sunny Grove. A week in the sewing room, a week in the kitchen, a week in the laundry. You follow the schedule as long as you behave yourselves."

When Jean is taken to the indoctrination physical examination, Dr. Conrad tries to befriend her. He offers a sympathetic warning: "If you fit in with the place, they'll take you for granted after a while, but if you don't...."

The strict prison discipline, enforced by no-nonsense matrons such as Ames (Anna Q. Nilsson) and Brand (Marjorie Main), nearly brings the hard-working Jean to a breaking point. Because she falls behind in her work, she is made to work extra hours, and must survive on corn bread and coffee for her dinner. Near exhaustion, she is carted back to the dorm where Sue and the other girls rally to her side. When Jean expresses concern regarding Larry, whom she has not seen since they reached Sunny Grove, the very experienced Sue attempts to comfort her with sage advice gathered from years as a convict:

> It must be mighty comfortin' knowing your boyfriend is up here at the same time as you.... Husbands, wives and sweethearts should be in jail at the same time. Then you don't have to worry about what they're doing. You'll know.

When it is announced that the women must work extra hours in the laundry daily, they revolt. Sue is one of the ringleaders and she is badly injured in the revolt which is soon quelled. She is taken to the infirmary, while the trouble-shooting Brand menacingly confronts Jean, "Making more trouble Forest. Remember, if we can't tame you with overtime, we've got other ways."

Later, Jean and Larry manage a brief reunion. From their conversation, she finally realizes that Harrison's past is very checkered. (This is verified by loyal friend Cora who comes to visit Jean.) Meanwhile, the conniving Larry offers sadistic Haskins $500 to help him escape. When Larry retrieves his hidden loot, the greedy Haskins follows and demands it all. A fight ensues and Haskins shoots Larry. Before he dies, Harrison confesses, clearing Jean's name and listing Haskins's many misdeeds. Haskins is arrested and Jean is quickly freed. She departs the farm with Roi, who has resigned from the institution.

Variety endorsed this high-grade programmer, "Paramount's contribution to the procession of penal institution epics is first-rate entertainment despite lightweight star names.... Dialogue crackles with vitality and pointedness." Thomas M. Pryor *(New York Times)* complimented, "What makes the film interesting, despite its somewhat time-worn theme, is the vigorous manner in which the story is presented under Louis King's sure directional hand and through the solid performances...." In retrospect, Don Miller *(B Movies,* 1973) championed, "It was the usual prison story — in fact, it was all the prison stories ever seen on the screen rolled into one and done in 69 minutes. And done so well, it became a wonderment that similar yarns weren't as satisfactory, including the more expensive production."

The sterling cast of *Prison Farm* makes this formula piece an engaging study. Where else could one find so much talent in one small production? There were: the long-overlooked and quite talented Shirley Ross (the heroine), the always reliable (and here moustachioed) Lloyd Nolan (the gangster), fine character actor Porter Hall (the weasely warden), expert villain J. Carrol Naish (the dastardly prison guard), veteran actresses May Boley (as the tart-mouthed and seasoned inmate "Shifty" Sue who dies) and Mae Busch (another tough convict). Not to be overlooked was Marjorie Main (as a sharp-eyed camp guard) who would gain later fame as the folksy Ma Kettle in the long-running Universal comedy series, *Ma and Pa Kettle.*

The plight of abused inmates on prison farms would be a recurring subject over the decades for Hollywood. As recently as Robert Redford's *Brubaker* (1981), q.v., it would be the focal theme of a major motion picture.

204. *Prison for Children* (CBS–TV, March 14, 1987), color, 100 min.

Executive producer, David Simons; producer, Lee Rafner; associate producer, Eric Sears; director, Larry Peerce; teleplay, Christopher Knopf; art director, Paul Staheli; set decorator, Tommie Fairbanks; makeup, Cynthia Cruz; music, Basil Poledouris; stunt coordinator, Victor Paul; sound, Robert Allan Wald; camera, Arch Bryant; editor, Sears.

John Ritter (David Royce); Betty Thomas (Angela Brannon); Raphael Sbarge (John Parsons); Kenny Ransom (Thomas Holmes); Jonathan Chapin ("Chaser"); Gordie Wright (Tyrone Roosevelt); Josh Brolin (Boise); James Callahan (Judge Collins); Thomas Zak (Joey Elkins); Aaron Makinen (Hermit); Lorraine Davies (Judy); Jamie Horton (Chris Parsons); Robert Himber (Casey Sellers); Dulcie Camp (Bea Saunders); Mimi Wickliff (Mariann Groves); Archie Smith (Pop Saunders); William Bryant (Will Waylon); Terry Rhoades (Ward); Brad Arkin (Mickey Phillips); Ed O'Brien (Arthur Franklin); Don Spencer (Oliver Beame); Tom Patterson (Hank Sims); Bobby Anderson (Robert Hulsey); Tom Becker (Night Watchman); Walt Conley (Shop Supervisor); Bill Gibson (Brad); Marque Gritta (Marcus); Emery Kedocia (Admissions Attendant); Randy Pybus (Randy); Vern Porter (Dr. Willett); Dutch Shindler (Owen Wilbur); Craig Stout (Barrett); Alan Westbrook (Honeycutt).

Prison for Children harkens back to the crusading melodramas of the 1930s (*Hell's House,* 1932, *Crime School,* 1938, qq.v.) which in the name of social protest paraded forth a rash of cruelties inflicted on youngsters imprisoned in a reformatory. Because a federal juvenile protection law was enacted in 1974, this well-intentioned drama was set in pre–1974 in an unnamed state.

When malcontent fifteen-year-old country boy John Parsons (Raphael Sbarge) is left alone, he burns down the shack he shares with his brother (Jamie

Horton). He then steals a horse. For his assorted crimes, he is sent to a reform school known euphemistically as an Industrial School. Superintendent David Royce (John Ritter) means well, but he must cope with an inept bureaucratic system, corrupt guards and the brutalities enforced by both sides of the law. For the bewildered John Parsons, his matriculation at the school is a nightmare. He is confronted by the mean Chaser (Jonathan Chapin), who controls the other young offenders. Other teen inmates include the mute Joey Elkins (Thomas Zak) and the pint-sized Tyrone Roosevelt (Gordie Wright), a frightened youngster. One of the benign teachers at the horror palace is Angela Brannon (Betty Thomas).

With so many manufactured ingredients, and its range of abhorrent on-premise conditions (rape, physical and psychological assault, drugs, etc.), *Prison for Children* was more numbing than illuminating. *Daily Variety* observed, "Often touching, certainly challenging telefilm does nicely until a *deus ex machina* drops into the proceedings; it's not convincing."

205. *Prison Girl* (Producers Releasing Corp., 1942), 70 min.

Producer, Lester Cutler; director, William Beaudine; based on the story "Gallant Lady" by Octavus Roy Cohen; screenplay, Arthur St. Claire; camera, Marcel Le Picard; editor, Fred Bain.

Rose Hobart (Dr. Rosemary Walsh); Sidney Blackmer (Steve); Claire Rochelle (Nellie); Lynn Starr (Linda); Jane Novak (Lucy Walker); Vince Barnett (Baldy); Jack Baxley (Sheriff Verner); Crane Whitley (Pete Saunders); John Ince (Judge Stevens); Frank Brownley (Luke Walker); Richard Clarke (Nick Morelli); Spec O'Donnell (Ben Walker); Inez Cole (Jane); Pat McKee (Jed Hicks); Ruby Dandridge (Sarah); Henry Hastings (Genesis).

A preposterous minor league melodrama from poverty row studio Producers Releasing Corporation (PRC). *Prison Girl* had enough plotline for several movies.

Dr. Rosemary Walsh (Rose Hobart), sentenced to prison on a mercy killing charge, is later forced to join convicts Nellie (Claire Rochelle) and Jane (Inez Cole) in a breakout engineered by Nellie's boyfriend, Nick Morelli (Richard Clarke). Rosemary, with only one more month to serve, intends to return to prison. However, she comes across a shack in which an elderly man is suffering from a broken leg. She mends his limb just as a local physician, Steve (Sidney Blackmer), arrives to help the patient. Steve recognizes her as a wanted person, but, nevertheless, offers to hide Rosemary at his home. Before long, the couple have fallen in love. He convinces her to marry him. However, at the marriage bureau a clerk recognizes her. Steve knocks the man out and the couple flees. Later, she travels to New York, where she asks Nick and Nellie for assistance. Meanwhile, Steve has been arrested for harboring a criminal. Learning of Steve's fate, Rosemary returns by bus, intending to clear him of any charges. Outside the small town where the trial is in progress, the bus is wrecked. Rosemary is unhurt and tends to the injured passengers. The trial is recessed to permit Steve to offer his medical services at the accident scene. Thereafter, the jury acquits Steve and the governor pardons the heroic Rosemary. The couple can now marry.

Variety dismissed the quickie movie. "Miss Hobart stands out in an inconsistent cast.... Film is overlong, photography poor." Actress Rose Hobart (b. 1906) was best known for her work in *Liliom* (1930) and *Dr. Jekyll and Mr. Hyde* (1932).

A.k.a.: *Gallant Lady*.

206. *Prison Girls* (United Producers, 1973), color, 94 min.

Producers, Nicholas J. Grippo, Burton C. Gershfield; director, Thomas DeSimone; screenplay, Lee Walters; art director, Robinson Royce; music supervisor, Christopher Huston; assistant director, Gershfield; sound, William Kaplan; sound re-recording, Erwin Kadden; camera, Gerhard Hentschel; supervising editor, Ron Ashcroft; editor, Paul Young.

With: Robin Whitting, Angie Monet, Tracy Handufss, Maria Arrold, Liz Wolfe, Linde Melissa, Dorothy Dick, Jamie McKenna, Carol Peters, Claire Bow, Donna Sutter, Ushie Digard, Susan Landis, Bolivia Tiernan, Lois Darst, Ilona Lakes, Susan Sterling, Joni Johnston, Lisa Ashbury, Jason Williams, Howard Alexander, Lee Blackmore, John Barnum, Chesley Noone, L. D. Dicksman, Rick Loots, Arnie Renfro, Steve Wilete, Brent Blasdell.

This soft-core pornography entry had the "virtue" of being lensed in the 3-D process which required filmgoers to wear Polaroid glasses.

At the Santa Helena Women's Correction Center, a liberal psychiatrist, Dr. Vivian Reinhardt, arranges to release six model prisoners for a weekend furlough. It is an experiment to help these women (whose paroles are pending) adjust to the outside world. The police ask permission to shadow one of the convicts, Cindy, hoping she will take them to her gangster boyfriend who has recently murdered a bank guard during a holdup.

The women separate for their forty-eight hours of freedom. Kay Rivers, a former hooker, returns to her pimp, only to find that he has found others to take her place. Nonetheless, she comes under his control once again. The seemingly frigid Tracy has a reunion with her husband and together they enjoy their first sexual climax. Joyce, serving a sentence for the manslaughter death of her husband, visits her understanding brother-in-law. A motorcycle gang bursts in to his apartment and forces the young man to rape his sister-in-law. Toni meets with a wealthy male friend, only to have her lesbian cellmate Gertie show up. Soon the trio are engaged in a sexual threesome. Cindy finally locates her boyfriend who wants her to leave the country with him. The police arrive on the scene and in the shootout both Cindy and her lover die. Returning to prison, the surviving five women accuse the psychiatrist of causing Cindy's death by allowing the police to follow her. The doctor is distraught over the situation.

A. H. Weiler *(New York Times)* noted jocularly, "[*Prison Girls*] vividly illustrates this observer's conviction that soft-core pornography can't be much of a help either to serious penology or dedicated thrill-seekers.... With the encumbrances of a one-D script and this 3-D process, ... [the actresses are] likely to generate more headaches than kicks.

When *Prison Girls* debuted in England in mid–1974, it was shorn of seventeen minutes of running time and was shown flat, without the 3-D process. Tony Rayns (British *Monthly Film Bulletin*) was amused by the (bowdlerized) results: "But even if *Prison Girls'* images offer little but a parade of freakishly enlarged breasts ... and its dramatic groin grind boils down to the standard variations on the theme ... there are rich compensations in its characterisations, and the sumptuously ripe dialogue."

Three years later came the more penitentiary-oriented *Prison Babies*. It was produced and directed by Ted Roter and featured Kristi Fletcher, Sally Petersen, Maria Karina, Karne Cooknell, Hilary Scott, Patrick Wright and Peter Balakoff (a.k.a. Ted Roter). It dealt with the sadistic goings-on the Redland State Home of Girls where young porno star Kathy (Kristi Fletcherr) is a new arrival. The female warden is a tyrant. According to Robert H. Rimmer *(The X-Rated Videotape*

Guide, 1986), "Because of the environment of the story there is quite a bit of lesbian sex, but Ted Roter has produced a 'thinking' style adult film which is closer to life than most."

207. *Prison Nurse* (Republic, 1943), 65 min.

Producer, Herman Schlom; director, James Cruze; based on the novel by Dr. Louis Berg; screen story, Adele S. Buffington; screenplay, Earl Felton, Sidney Salkow; art director, John Victor Mackay; costumes, Irene Saltern; music director, Alberto Columbo; assistant director, Phil Ford; camera, Ernest Miller; supervising editor, Murray Seldeen; editor, William Morgan.

Henry Wilcoxon (Dale); Marian Marsh (Judy); Bernadene Hayes (Pepper Clancy); Ben Welden (Gaffney); Ray Mayer (Jackpot); John Arledge (Mousie); Addison Richards (Warden Benson); Frank Reicher (Dr. Hartman); Minerva Urecal (Sutherland); Selmer Jackson (Parker); Fred Kohler, Jr. (Miller); Norman Willis (Deputy).

For some reason, Hollywood scenarists have frequently assumed that setting an action yard in a prison was a good excuse to exercise their bent for incredible plot contrivances. Sylvester Stallone's *Lock Up* (1989), q.v., is one example. The far less overblown *Prison Nurse* is another.

Three nurses—sweet Judy (Marian Marsh), smart-mouthed Pepper Clancy (Bernadene Hayes) and matronly Sutherland (Minerva Urecal)—are among the volunteers arriving to assist Dr. Hartman (Frank Reicher) in curbing an epidemic of typhoid fever at a men's prison supervised by Warden Benson (Addison Richards). Among the convicts, Judy spots Dale (Henry Wilcoxon), whom she recognizes as a renowned surgeon who had been imprisoned for a mercy killing. Initially the embittered Dale refuses to assist the medical team, but when Dr. Hartman is stricken, Dale changes his mind. Meanwhile, he and Judy fall in love and his crushed spirits are revived.

On the day before his release is to be discussed by the parole board, convict/gangster Gaffney (Ben Welden) and two cronies (Ray Mayer, John Arledge) undertake a breakout, forcing Dale at gunpoint to join them. They kill a guard in the process and then escape in a prison ambulance. Dale later gains control of the situation and orders Gaffney to drive back to the prison. Instead, the enraged Gaffney crashes the ambulance and is himself killed. Thereafter, the last surviving other member of the breakout is gunned down by pursuing policemen. Dale is tried for first degree murder and sentenced to die. At the last moment, Judy locates the diary of one of the escapees and the details therein clear Dale of any conspiracy in the escape plan. He is awarded a parole. He and Judy look forward to their new life together.

"Henry Wilcoxon and Marian Marsh are the starrers who, with the expert directorship of Cruze, turn this third-rate story into one of more creditable proportions. . . . There's a vague suggestion of a sociological background to the plot, but that's quickly lost as the story goes on" *(Variety)*.

Prison Nurse was directed by industry veteran James Cruze (1884–1942), famous for such silent epics as *The Covered Wagon* (1923) and *Old Ironsides* (1926). Cruze would leave Hollywood in 1938 after completing a trio of Republic features, including *Prison Nurse.*

Marian Marsh and Henry Wilcoxon in *Prison Nurse* (1938).

208. *Prison Train* (Equity, 1938), 66 min.

Producer, B. F. Zeidman; director, Gordon Wiles; story, Mathew Broden; screenplay, Spencer Towne; art director, Frank Sylos; music director, David Chudnow; special effects, Howard Anderson; camera, Marcel Le Picard; editor, Edward Schroeder.

Fred Keating (Frankie Terris); Linda Winters [Dorothy Comingore] (Louis Terris); Clarence Muse (George); Faith Bacon (Maxine); Alexander Leftwich (Manny Robbins); James Blakely (Joe Robbins); Sam Bernard (Steward); John Pearson (Red); Nestor Paiva (Sullen); Val Stanton (Morose); Peter Potter (Bill Adams); Kit Guard (Guard); Franklyn Farnum (District Attorney); George Lloyd (Bull); Harry Anderson (Hardface).

For many prisoners, the trek to the "big house" is the last taste of freedom they will savor for many years. In *Prison Train,* the cross country ride to Alcatraz Prison proves to be a fatal one-way excursion. This unassuming independent movie was a far cry from another movie which dealt with murder on the high rails, the upper case, star-studded *Murder on the Orient Express* (1974).

Tough mobster Frankie Terris (Fred Keating) heads a numbers racket. His chief competitor, ambitious nightclub owner Manny Robbins (Alexander Leftwich), is engineering a set-up for Terris to take a bum rap. This will allow Manny to supplant Frankie as chief of the gaming mob. Meanwhile, Robbins's son, Joe (James Blakely), dares to romance Frankie's sister, Louise (Linda Winters [Dorothy Comingore]), the latter unaware of her brother's underworld activities. The angered Terris kills Joe and, as a result, he is sentenced to a life term at Alcatraz Prison. En route by train to the island fortress, Robbins, who has sworn revenge, maneuvers to have his gang diverted to a siding. Frankie has learned of Robbins's plan and is ready to retaliate. He yanks a gun from one of manny's henchmen — George (Clarence Muse), who is posing as a train steward — and shoots Robbins. Later, he falls from the train and is killed. Federal agent Bill Adams (Peter Potter), aboard the train to watch over the convict passengers, is on hand to console Louise, who had been aboard to be with her brother.

Variety disapproved of the humble results. "It gets involved and ponderous, with numerous intercuts of speeding train, grinding engine wheels, and swaying cab inserted to detract from what little interest there is." *Harrison's Reports* pointed out, "For the most part, the director has done a competent job; the only fault is that at times he strives for effect by using closeups and in so doing slows up the action. The love interest is mildly pleasant...."

Linda Winters (1913–1971), a.k.a. Kay Winters, would gain greater screen fame as Dorothy Comingore, who played the second Mrs. Kane in *Citizen Kane* (1941). Peter Potter (c. 1904–1983) became well known as a west coast disc jockey and as the host of "Juke Box Jury," an enduring radio and TV entry.

A.k.a.: *People's Enemy.*

209. *Prison Warden* (Columbia, 1949), 62 min.

Producer, Rudolph C. Flothow; director, Seymour Friedman; screenplay, Eric Taylor; art director, Carl Anderson; set decorator, James Crowe; makeup, Bob Meeding; music, Mischa Bakaleinikoff; assistant director, James Nicholson; sound, Philip Faulkner; camera, Henry Freulich; editor, James Sweeney.

Warner Baxter (Victor Burnell); Anna Lee (Elisa Burnell); James Flavin (Captain Pete Butler); Harlan Warde (Al Gardner); Charles Cane (Bill Radford); Reginald Sheffield (English Charlie); Harry Antrim (Dr. Stark); William "Bill" Phillips (Lanning); Frank Richards (Cory); Jack Overman (Henly); Charles Evans

(Governor); Harry Hayden (Greene); John R. Hamilton (Webb); Clancy Cooper (McCall); Edgar Dearing (Lieutenant Davis).

Columbia Pictures, like Warner Bros., retained a strong interest in prison yarns over the decades. In the late 1940s–early 1950s, the studio produced several genre programmers, including: *Prison Warden Convicted* (1950—a remake of *The Criminal Code*, 1931), *Chain Gang* (1950) and *State Penitentiary* (1950), qq.v. *Prison Warden* presents a rarity among Hollywood "big house" movies; a humanitarian administrator dedicated to the welfare of his charges.

Young and attractive Elisa Burnell (Anna Lee) loves her middle-aged spouse, Victor (Warner Baxter), a public health official. However, she was not in love when she married him three months earlier. Her ulterior motive then had been that, when he accepted the appointment of warden, she as his wife would be in a position to assist her boyfriend, Al Garner (Harlan Warde). The latter, whom she believes is innocent, is serving a five-year term for forgery. Meanwhile, now that he is wed, Victor does not want the chief administrator's post at the penitentiary. However, the governor (Charles Evans) persuades him that conditions at the institution have so deteriorated he need's Victor's assistance to undertake immediate reforms. Victor reluctantly accepts the post.

Once installed at the prison, Elisa persuades her husband to appoint Gardner as her chauffer, a decision which annoys the corrupt captain of the guards, Pete Butler (James Flavin). The latter wanted one of his pet criminals to have the job. Moreover, Butler has ambitions of becoming warden himself, which would allow him to continue his unprinciples practices of selling favors to the prisoners. When two of Butler's convict favorites attempt to kill Victor when he examines working conditions at the rock pile, Gardner saves his life. Gardner is made the chauffeur and he confides to Elisa that he intends to escape by driving across the border— with Elisa. She is against this and begs him to wait for a parole.

Convinced that he will not be paroled, Gardner springs into action. One day while driving Elisa to a nearby beauty shop, he decides to execute his plan. Before heading for the border, he stops in his old hometown to retrieve hidden loot. (This action makes Elisa finally realize that Gardner was guilty all the time.) When Gardner attempts to smash through one of the road blocks, Elisa tries to stop him. He pushes her out of the vehicle and drives on. The police shoot at his car which goes out of control and crashes, with Gardner dying. Elisa recovers from her injury and continues her work at the prison with Victor.

Variety was respectful of this mild, assembly-line excursion. "There are enough substantial elements to keep the chase devotees interested. A prison break, a plot to kill a newly appointed warden and several scenes of prison brutality are good embellishments for the action trade." On the other hand, Howard Thompson *(New York Times)* found the going tedious and thought the proceedings "wouldn't even rattle a paper bag." Thompson suggested, "What this film really needed was a mass, hysterical jailbreak, led, if there's any justice, by the warden himself." The *Hollywood Reporter* noted, "The prison background and the details of the yard afford ample opportunity for fisticuffs and gun display, but until the finale chase they are frankly ignored."

Veteran star Warner Baxter (1889–1951), who was nearing the end of his physical/emotional rope (and his performances showed it!) would return to the genre in *State Penitentiary* the final film of his long screen career.

210. The Prisoner of Shark Island (20th Century-Fox, 1936), 95 min.

Producer, Darryl F. Zanuck; associate producer, Nunnally Johnson; director, John Ford; based on the life of Dr. Samuel A. Mudd; screenplay, Johnson; art director, William Darling; set decorator, Thomas Little; costumes, Gwen Wakeling; music director, Louis Silvers; assistant director, Edward O'Fearna; sound, W. D. Flick, Roger Hemen; camera, Bert Glennon; editor, Jack Murray.

Warner Baxter (Dr. Samuel Alexander Mudd); Gloria Stuart (Mrs. Peggy Mudd); Joyce Kay (Martha Mudd); Claude Gillingwater (Colonel Jeremiah Dyer); Douglas Wood (General Ewing); Fred Kohler, Jr. (Sergeant Cooper); Harry Carey (Commandant of Fort Jefferson); Paul Fix (David Herold); John Carradine (Sergeant Rankin); Francis McDonald (John Wilkes Booth); Arthur Byron (Mr. Erickson); O. P. Heggie (Dr. McIntire); John McGuire (Lovett); Paul McVey (Hunter); Francis Ford (Corporal O'Toole); Ernest Whitman (Buck Tifford); Frank Shannon (Judge Advocate Holt); Frank McGlynn, Sr. (Abraham Lincoln); Arthur Loft (Carpetbagger); Maurice Murphy (Orderly); Paul Stanton (Orator); Ronald [Jack] Pennick (Signal Man); Merrill McCormick (Commandant's Aide); James Marcus (Blacksmith); Jan Duggan (Actress); Lloyd Whitlock (Major Rathbone); Leila McIntyre (Mrs. Lincoln); Dick Elliott (Actor); Murdock MacQuarrie (Spangler); Bud Geary, Duke Lee, Robert E. Homans (Sergeants); Robert Dudley (Druggist); Wilfred Lucas (Colonel); Cecil Weston (Mrs. Surratt); Cyril Thornton (Maurice O'Laughlin); Beulah Hall Jones (Blanche); J. M. Kerrigan (Judge Maiben); Etta McDaniel (Rosabelle Tilford); J. P. McGowan (Ship's Captain); Harry Strang (Mate); and: Frank Baker, Whitney Bourne, Robert Parrish.

Despite its somber theme, this is a forceful melodrama; it grips the spectator, and holds his attention throughout. John Ford has directed it with skill, especially the scenes that show mob hysteria. Some of the situations are so touching that one cannot hold back tears.

(Harrison's Reports)

During the Civil War in April 1865, Dr. Samuel Mudd (Warner Baxter) of Maryland accidentally becomes involved with crazed actor John Wilkes Booth (Francis McDonald). The latter had assassinated President Abraham Lincoln (Frank McGlynn, Sr.) at Ford's Theater in Washington, D.C. and had broken his leg making his escape. While fleeing, Booth stops at Mudd's house. The latter mends Booth's leg, not knowing the man's real identity. Booth is later killed while resisting arrest. Yankee soldiers discover telltale clues in Mudd's yard (i.e. Booth's boot) and arrest the physician as one of the alleged conspirators. Although he protests his innocence, as does his wife Martha (Gloria Stuart), mob rule wins out at the military court hearing. Mudd is sentenced to life imprisonment at Fort Jefferson on the island of Dry Tortugas, which is surrounded by shark-infested waters and swamps. Once incarcerated there, the arrogant Yankee officers vent their spleen by beating and mistreating him. Mudd's loyal black servant, Buck Tifford (Ernest Whitman) maneuvers a job at the compound to be near his master. Buck helps Mudd to escape in a boat chartered by his wife. However, Buck and Tifford are caught, brought back to the Fort, and thrown into a pit to die.

Later, an epidemic of yellow fever breaks out and when the prison's doctor (O.P. Heggie) dies, the Fort Commandant (Harry Carey) entreats Dr. Mudd to help with the medical crisis. Even without any promises of reward, the aristocratic Mudd agrees to assist. He works tirelessly to combat the outbreak of disease. As a result, he saves many of the infected men, although he becomes ill himself. Later, the contrite Union officers show their appreciation by petitioning President

Andrew Johnson to grant Mudd's release. He is pardoned and returns to his family and home.

Frank S. Nugent *(New York Times)* granted that *The Prisoner of Shark Island,* filled with a passion for its plea of justice, had the virtues of "directness" and "sincerity." However, Nugent argued, "[F]or all its vaunted biographical accuracy, the new photoplay is scarcely more than a well-fabricated edition of the Dreyfus-Devil's Island series that has become part of the screen's tradition. If it is history, it has repeated itself too often." *Variety* perceived the movie as a "histronic and technical credit to all concerned." However, reported the trade paper, "[I]ts box office potentialities may be only moderate. Minimum of femme appeal accounts for that."

One of the virtues of any John Ford–directed production is the marvelous ensemble work by the supporting cast. *The Prisoner of Shark Island* is no exception, especially the work of John Carradine as the dastardly Sergeant Rankin and Claude Gillingwater as the irrascible Colonel Dyer.

The grisly horrors of the military prison at Fort Jefferson (off the southwest coast of Florida in the Gulf of Mexico) would be replayed in the telefeature *The Ordeal of Dr. Mudd* (1980), q.v., which did not live up to its predecessor. *Hellgate* (1952), q.v., is an unofficial remake of *The Prisoner of Shark Island.*

When *The Prisoner of Shark Island* was initially released, it was promoted with the ad line: "The true story of America's hidden shame!" Much was made of associating this chapter from history with the fates of Dreyfus on Devil's Island and the imprisoned Jean Valjean of Victor Hugo's *Les Misérables.*

211. *Prisoners in Petticoats* (Republic, 1950), 60 min.

Associate producer, Lou Brock; director, Philip Ford; story, Raymond Schrock, George Callahan; screenplay, Bradbury Foote; art director, Frank Arrigo; set decorators, John McCarthy, Jr., George Milo; costume supervisor, Adele Palmer; makeup, Bob Mark; music, Stanley Wilson; sound, Dick Tyler; camera, Ellis W. Carter; editor, Harold Minter.

Valentine Perkins (Beverly Brent [Joan Grey]); Robert Rockwell (Mark Hampton); Danni Sue Nolan (Francis White); Anthony Caruso (Nickey Bowman); Tony Barrett (Steve London); David Wolfe (Sam Clarke); Alex Gerry (Professor Grey); Michael Carr (Danny); Queenie Smith (Old Beatrice); Bert Conway (Shack); Rudy Rama (Connie); Marlo Dwyer (Candy Carson); Russ Conway (Detective Blake); Marta Mitrovich (Sadie).

The best element of this flimsy gangster yarn is its exploitive title.

Beverly Brent (Valentine Perkins) is employed as a pianist at the Bohemia Club, unaware that its owner, Nickey Bowman (Anthony Caruso), and his mob are gangsters. After a racetrack robbery, one of Nickey's underlings, Steve London (Tony Barrett), double-crosses his boss and grabs the loot. When Bowman's muscle men close in, Steve stashes the money with naïve Beverly. She later deposits the suitcase—still not knowing its contents—with her father, Professor Grey (Alex Gerry). Meanwhile, Mark Hampton (Robert Rockwell) of the district attorney's office, who has been following Bowman's gangland activities, traces the money to Beverly. She is brought to police headquarters for questioning but, even when threatened with a prison term, will not reveal the money's whereabouts. (In actuality she is Joan Grey and is fearful that her small town father will be dragged into her scandal.)

In prison, Beverly encounters Francis White (Sue Nolan), Nickey's girlfriend, who broke her parole intentionally so she could be sent to the same prison as Beverly.

Francis helps Beverly to escape and, as both Bowman and Hampton anticipated, she retrieves the money. In a final showdown, Bowman and his mob are overcome. With the case solved, Beverly is freed. She and Mark pursue a romance.

Even by Republic Pictures's standards this was a shoddy entry. The cast ambled through their paces, with the exception of the convict Old Beatrice (Queenie Smith), who breathes life into the proceedings during her few oncamera moments. Beatrice is an old-timer in the prison and is always happy to talk to newcomers, especially about their criminal records.

> BEATRICE: At least you did something.
>
> BEVERLY: I didn't do anything.
>
> BEATRICE: That's it girl! You stick to it! Don't tell 'em nothing.

Then Beatrice, with a wonderful glint to her eyes, recalls her career as a pyromaniac and confides, "How I'd like to see one more good fire before I die." Later, the garrulous Beatrice observes, "What goes on here? Everybody used to like it here. Now they're all talking about leaving."

Rarely in prison pictures—not even in PRC or Monogram entries of the 1940s—has a prison setting been so shoddy. The set looks more like a boarding house, as we see the inmates at work (cleaning, scrubbing) or lounging in their private rooms.

Variety dismissed this time waster with, "Both story and acting are unbelievable, as is the direction. . . . There's little attempt to develop interest in the circumstances that get the girl out of her fix. . . ."

212. *Purgatory* (New Star Entertainment, 1989), color, 93 min.

Executive producers, Dimitri Villard, Robby Wald; producer, Ami Artzi; associate producers, Patricia Shorten, Elizabeth Rowley, Peter Smook; director, Artzi; screenplay, Felix Kroll, Paul Aratow; production designer, Robert van der Coolwijk; set decorator, Eva Strack; music, Julian Laxton; assistant director, Howard Rennie; stunt coordinator, Mark Myron; camera, Tom Fraser; second unit camera, Jerry Lotter; executive editor, Skip Scholinik; editor, Ettie Feldman.

Tanya Roberts (Carly Arnold); Julie Pop (Melanie); Hal Orlandini (Commandant Beldsoe); Rufus Swart (Paul Cricks); Adrienne Pearce (Janine); Marie Human (Kirsten); David Sherwood (Stern); Clare Marshall (Ruth Arnold); Hugh Rouse (Rivers); John Newland (Ambassador Whitney).

Following in the tradition of *Red Heat* (1985), q.v., and scads of other foreign-lensed exploitation features, *Purgatory* was yet another softcore pornography excursion into women in bondage. The advertisements for this poorly-executed feature boasted that *Purgatory* was "The Women's Prison That's One Step from Hell!"

Peace Corps workers Carly Arnold (Tanya Roberts) and pal Melanie (Julie Pop) are based in an African nation. When a military coup turns the country into a dictatorship opposed to foreigners, she and Melanie find themselves arrested on bogus drug charges. Despite the valiant efforts of Carly's mother (Clare Marshall) to bribe the court, Carly and Melanie are given eleven-year sentences and dispatched to a dilapidated prison officially known as Rampot Prison (but better known as Purgatory). There the brutal Commandant Beldsoe (Hal Orlandini), who insists he is a graduate of the Harvard School, exploits the prettier of his inmates for his own sexual pleasures as well as using them as prostitutes to service his clients. Carly survives the ordeal, but Melanie, who has been raped by an assortment of black prison guards, commits suicide. Later, Carly and fellow prisoners rebel and during the breakout settle the score with their sadistic keepers.

Kirk Honeycutt *(Hollywood Reporter)* reported, "For an exploitation film, all this lurid nonsense is suprisingly tame. Most of the violence occurs offscreen, the partial nudity is fleeting and the escape holds little suspense." The *New York Daily News* was equally unimpressed, especially about co-star Tanya Roberts, the one-time member of TV's "Charlie's Angels." "Not only does she go to whining and weeping at the drop of a truncheon but proves exceedingly discreet in the gratuitous-nudity department, shows zero enthusiasm for her 'work detail' chores as a loaned-out hooker at a local hotel, and even performs her token upchuck scene with a decided lack of conviction." *Daily Variety* agreed, "Poorly lit pic limps listlessly to a tired escape-from-stir climax, with time out for typical political content.... Filmmaker Ami Artzi's direction is leaden and he doesn't know how to have fun with an exploitation subject."

Purgatory was filmed in South Africa.

213. *Red Heat [Rote Hitze]* (International Screen, 1985), color, 106 min.

Executive producer, Monica Teuber; producer, Ernst R. van Theumer; associate producer, Paul Hellerman; director, Robert Collector; screenplay, Collector, Gary Drucker; art directors, Livia Kovats, Ernst Wurzer; costumes, Erika Navas, Monika Hinz, Margi Ogris Thiel; makeup, Britta Kraft, Ingrid Thier; music, Tangerine Dream; assistant directors, Barbara Schubert, Hartmut Landsiedel; stunt coordinator, Willy Neuner; technical adviser, Dr. Lorey Perry, Jr.; sound, Hans Kunzi; sound re-recording, Milan Bor; sound editor, Cornnia Dietz; foley, Mel Kutbay; special effects director, Helmut Graef; camera, Wolfgang Dickmann; additional camera, Jiri Stibr; editor, Anthony Redman.

Linda Blair (Chris Carlson); Sylvia Kristel (Sofia); Sue Kiel (Dr. Heda Kliemann); William Ostrander (Lieutenant Michael Grainger); Elisabeth Volkmann (Warden Einbeck); Albert Fortell (Ernst); Herb Andress (Werner); Barbara Spitz (Meg); Kati Marothy (Barbara); Dagmar Michal-Schwarz (Lillian); Sissy Weiner (Uta); Norbert Belcha (Kurt); Sonja Martin (Evelyn); Evelyn Engleder (Eva); John Brett (Roger); Michael Troy (Howard); Helmuth Janatach (Lecturer); Elvira Neustadt (Limmer); Fritz von Friedel (BND Agent).

In the late 1970s and well into the 1980s, the bulk of the softcore pornography women-behind-bars pictures were produced in Europe, spawning such entries as: *Escape from Cell Block Three, 10 Violent Women, Women Unchained, Women in Fury, Amazon Jail, Condemned to Hell.* One of the most widely distributed continental co-productions was *Red Heat,* starring American Linda Blair.

American college student Chris Carlson (Linda Blair) flies to West Berlin to be with her fiancée, U.S. Army Lieutenant Michael Grainger (William Ostrander). When he admits that he plans to re-enlist rather than carry through their marriage plans immediately, they argue and Chris bolts from the hotel. While out walking that night, she comes across East German operatives kidnapping a defector, Dr. Hedda Kliemann (Sue Kiel). Chris is also grabbed and, along with Hedda, is smuggled across the border. After a vicious interrogation, the vulnerable Chris signs a confession which admits she is a CIA agent. She is sentenced to three years at a People's Correctional Prison.

Arriving at the foreboding prison, she is advised by a terse guard who recites the harsh rules in jagged English:

Never complain. Never curse a guard. Never strike a fellow inmate. Never sit on your bed or mattress until lights out.... Each day thirty minutes of exercise. One letter to write a month.

Any infraction and new trial and longer sentence. Always refer to self as 'the prisoner Carlson.' Never refer to yourself personally. You are no longer an individual, but a property of the state.

The bleak jail is supervised by hard-hearted Warden Einbeck (Elisabeth Volkmann), a manipulative tyrant who uses the likes of tough convict Sophia (Sylvia Kristel) and her underlings to make life miserable for political prisoners like Chris. Part of the warden's plan is not only to have Chris *et al.* tormented by their fellow inmates, but to pressure them into rebelling so their sentences can be lengthened. At Chris's induction interview with the sadistic warden, the latter offers a frightening prophecy of the hell in store for young Chris. The threats are all the more ominous for what is left unsaid: "I always care about my girls, especially an American. Three years is a long time. We'll get to know each other pretty well."

Chris is introduced into the crowded dormitory where many have to sleep on thin mattresses strewn on the dirty floor. She is assigned to work in the prison factory at $1.50 per month and must listen to endless lectures on the virtues of Communism. After Hedda realizes that Chris has been a dupe of the East German government, the two imperiled women become friends.

Time passes and Chris becomes hardened to the prison regimen. In fact, she becomes the leader of a prisoner riot, prompted by the suicide of another Sofia-tormented inmate Barbara (Kati Marothy). For their participation in the uprising, the political prisoners have their sentences extended. Meanwhile, Grainger had discovered Chris's whereabouts, although he can get no action through the military bureaucracy. Joined by two Army pals and aided by Hedda's brother (Albert Fortell), Michael sets out to rescue Chris. She, in turn, it currently recuperating in the prison hospital, a minimum security section where Sofia plans to kill her. Grainger and his squad break in and rescue Chris and a few of the other women. in the mêlée, Sofia is shot by Einbeck. Michael smuggles Chris back into West Germany.

For Linda Blair, who first performed in the prison genre in *Born Innocent* (1974), q.v., and later made the well-remembered *Chained Heat* (1983), q.v., the R-rated *Red Heat* was decidedly déjà vu. (To Blair's credit, the twenty-six-year-old, chubby-faced actress did her best to inject her threadbare role with freshness, energy and proper reactions.) Putting aside the fact that the political situation has changed drastically in Germany since the making of this opus, there is much about this re-hash that is overly familiar. But then, audiences who are attracted to this type of fare, would be disappointed if the expected was not presented in all its standard variations.

Despite its shortcomings ("the often clumsy dialog"), *Variety* predicted, "[F]ilm is steeped in an erotic atmosphere which should titillate the libido of male audiences. A spy story, prison brutality, lesbianism and some action sequences are further commercial enhancements." Kim Newman (British *Monthly Film Bulletin*) decided, "The details of life in a East German prison (assembly-line drudgery, organised bullying of politicals, elaborate tattoos to signify memberships of Sofia's clique) are fairly convincing." For Newman, "The film really belongs to Sylvia Kristel [the star of the *Emmanuelle* series].... Swanning around the prison in red underwear to match her lipstick, hair and the scar Linda Blair gives her, Kristel also gets the best lines, as when she reminisces about murdering her stepfather 'because he ate my pet snake!'"

Amidst all the standard ingredients of an innocent coming to maturity in a cesspool environment, there are a few worthwhile observations on the human condition. One time-worn prisoner tells the heroine: "Practicality is all that matters if you want to survive here." Later, Hedda advises Chris: "The world is an ugly place even if you deny it."

Filmed in West Berlin, *Red Heat* was an international co-production shot in both English and German versions. It remains a popular staple on cable TV and in a videocassette version.

214. *Red Hot Tires* (Warner Bros., 1925), 6,600'.

Director, Erle C. Kenton; story, Gregory Rogers [Darryl F. Zanuck]; screenplay, Edward T. Lowe, Jr.; camera, Charles J. Van Enger.

Monte Blue (Al Jones); Patsy Ruth Miller (Elizabeth Lowden); Fred Esmelton (Honorable R. C. Lowden); Lincoln Stedman (George Taylor); Charles Conklin (Coachman); Jimmy Quinn (Al Martin); Tom McGuire, William Lowery, Malcolm Waite (Crooks).

This light-hearted silent comedy used a jail as the means of drawing the hero and heroine closer together.

Impressionable Al Jones (Monte Blue) is so distracted when he first spots comely Elizabeth Lowden (Patsy Ruth Miller) that his car crashes into a steamroller. He takes to driving a horse and buggy. The next time he encounters the fetching young lady—who loves to speed in her roadster—her car causes his horse to bolt, and he is injured. After taking him to the hospital, her father (Fred Esmelton), the local police chief, jails her for reckless driving. Al, wanting to be with his sweetheart, argues his way into an adjoining cell. When he is released, he schemes to be readmitted, unable to bear being away from his beloved. Later when the rambunctious Elizabeth is kidnapped by crooks (Tom McGuire, William Lowery, Malcolm Waite), Al comes to her rescue. The happy couple elope in her speedster.

Mordaunt Hall *(New York Times)* endorsed this unpretentious, light-hearted entry: "Fully three quarters of *Red Hot Tires* ... is enjoyable, and the latter chapters are only weakened by the not unusual inclusion of speeding cars.... There are some good comedy scenes in the jail when Jones discovers that a garter serves as a sort of catapult to send a note to pretty Elizabeth, and she gets one to him by tossing her shoe through the prison bars."

215. *Reform School* (Million Dollar Production, 1939), 58 min.

Producer, Harry M. Popkin; director, Leo C. Popkin; story, Hazel Jamieson, Joe O'Donnell; screenplay, Zelda Young, Jamieson, O'Donnell; camera, William Hyers; editor, Bart M. Rauw.

Louise Beavers (Mother Barton); Reginald Fenderson (Freddie Gordon); Monte Hawley (Jackson); Freddie Jackson (Eddie); Eugene Jackson (Pete); Eddie Lynn (Joe); De Forrest Covan (Bill); Bob Simmons (Johnny); Maceo Sheffield (Mr. Stone); Edward Thompson, Vernon McCalla (Reform School Officials); Alfred Grant (Jones the Guard); Milton Hall (Jackie Rogers); Clifford Holland (Slim); Edward Patrick (Mr. Gordon); Charles Andrews (Gas Station Attendant); Harold Garrison (Guard); Edward Tony (Tony).

Character star Louise Beavers was the drawing card of this all-black economy production which paralleled such Hollywood establishment pictures as *Crime School* (1938) and *Hell's Kitchen* (1939), qq.v.

When Freddie Gordon (Reginald Fenderson) and five of his young Harlem pals create too many problems in their neighborhood, they are dispatched to the state reform school. Conditions there are unfavorable to rehabilitation, until sympathetic Mother Barton (Louise Beavers) brings reforms to the institution.

Variety reported, "Story is of familiar pattern and elemental in both plot and dialog.... Direction and story are deliberate in making plot and situations understandable, and players enunciate lines clearly and sharply—although at times delivery seem over-dramatic."

216. *Reform School Girl* (American International, 1957), 71 min.

Executive producer, James H. Nicholson; producers, Robert J. Gurney, Jr., Samuel Z. Arkoff; director/screenplay, Edward Bernds; art director, Don Ament; music, Ronald Stein; camera, Floyd Crosby; editor, Richard C. Meyer.

Gloria Castillo (Donna Price); Ross Ford (David Lindsay); Edward Byrnes (Vince); Ralph Reed (Jackie); Jan Englund (Ruth); Yvette Vickers (Roxy); Helen Wallace (Mrs. Trimble); Donna Jo Gribble (Cathy); Luana Anders (Josie); Diana Darrin (Mona); Nesdon Booth (Deetz); Wayne Taylor (Gary); Sharon Lee (Blonde); Jack Kruschen (Mr. Horvath); Linda Rivera (Elena); Elaine Sinclair (Midge); Dorothy Crehan (Matron); Claire Carleton (Mrs. Horvath); Lillian Powell (Mrs. Patton); Sally Kellerman (A Girl).

> For the prurient-minded, there's mucho leg display, and for the immature audiences, there's a plaintive, adolescent philosophy about non-squealing.
>
> *Variety*

When seventeen-year-old Donna Price (Gloria Castillo) embarks on a harmless joyride with boyfriend Gary (Wayne Taylor), and another couple—Vince (Edward Byrnes) and Josie (Luana Anders)—she has no idea what lies in store for her. Before long, Gary and Josie have been left behind, and Donna is riding with reckless Vince who soon hits and kills a pedestrian. Vince threatens to murder her if she squeals, so she says nothing at her hearing. She is sent to a correctional facility for girls.

Because the manipulative Vince is worried that Donna might still incriminate him, he arranges for Josie to be sent to the same reformatory, filling her with hate for Donna by lying that she was the one who informed on Josie's car stripping activity. Upon her arrival at the reformatory, Josie corrals many of the hardened young inmates to her side and they proceed to terrorize the innocent Donna. In a later rumble, Donna, in self defense, stabs one of her attackers with a scissors. For this misdeed, Donna is to be sent to the State Prison for Women. However, at the last minute, the staff psychologist (Ross Ford) learns the reason for Donna not having informed on Vince. Meanwhile, Josie sends information to Vince that Donna has told on him. The infuriated Vince attempts to break into the reformatory, but is arrested by the police. When the true facts are learned, Donna is freed.

The impressionable reviewer for *Harrison's Reports* decided, "The ganging up of the girls in the reformatoy against the young heroine, who suffers rather than squeal, is realistic and exciting.... The photography is excellent."

To be noted in a tiny role is Sally Kellerman in her first big screen performance. *Reform School Girl* was issued on a double-bill with *Rock Around the World*, creating an entertainment package aimed to draw teenage audiences into drive-in theaters.

217. *Reform School Girls* (New World Pictures, 1986), color, 94 min.

Executive producers, Gregory Hinton, Leo Angelos; producer, Jack Cummins; director/screenplay, Tom DeSimone; production designer, Becky Block; set decorator, Tom Talbert; music, Martin Schwartz; sound, Steve Nelson; camera, Howard Wexler; editor, Michael Spence.

Linda Carol (Jenny); Wendy O. Williams (Charlie); Pat Ast (Head Matron Edna); Sybil Danning (Warden Sutter); Charlotte McGinnis (Dr. Norton); Sherri Stoner (Lisa); Denise Gordy (Claudine); Laurie Schwartz (Nicky); Tiffany Helm (Fish); Darcy DeMoss (Knox).

Director Tom DeSimone was no stranger to this sub-genre of prison pictures, having directed, among others, *Prison Girls* (1973) and the very popular *The Concrete Jungle* (1982), qq.v. The exploitable sexploitation actress Sybil Danning and paraded through *Chained Heat* (1983), q.v. and the inestimable Pat Ast had camped through the Off Broadway spoof, *Women Behind Bars*. Wendy O. Williams, the busty lead singer of the punk rock group The Plasmatics, was cast in the satirical *Reform School Girls* as an overripe teenage inmate. According to producer Jack Cummins, *Reform School Girls* was not just "another trashy 'B' movie." Rather, he insisted (tongue-in-cheek), "[W]hat we're attempting to do here is to exploit exploitation."

The virginal Jenny (Linda Carol) finds herself behind bars at the Pridemore Reform School. She must cope with the corrupt warden (Sybil Danning) who revels in brandishing a rifle; submit to the butch and sadistic head guard, Edna (Pat Ast), who insists, "The name of the game is power, girls"; and survive dormitory life with the likes of leather-clad, rugged Charlie (Wendy O. Williams), the bully convict of the cellblock who insists, "I'm all the stud you need!" Jenny's only ally in the institution is the vulnerable, traumatized Lisa (Sherri Stoner), a victim of the brutal penal system.

Definitely not made to please reviewers, the R-rated *Reform School Girls* captured no critical endorsements for its deliberately clichéd odyssey filled with deliberate caricatures. Patrick Goldstein *(Los Angeles Times)* complained, "*Girls* is far too feeble to qualify as a raunchy prison parody.... [The] predominantly female cast seems to have been chosen more for their profiles than their personalities.... [It] is so witless that its funniest line comes from the ad campaign, 'So young ... so bad ... so what?' So what, indeed." Jami Bernard *(New York Post)* warned, "The action is divided between the dormitory and the showers, and consists of chewing food with the mouth open, branding buttocks, squashing kittens, beating each other with firehoses, and brushing each other's teeth with razor-embedded toothbrushes. It's as appealing as it sounds.... I've always been highly amused by women's prison movies, from Eleanor Parker on down to Linda Blair. But the sadism here is overdone and frankly, if you've seen one branding, you've seem them all.... Better to put this film into isolation and throw away the key." Leo Seligsohn *(Newsday)* argued, "In the old days, it was simply called trash. These days, it's called a spoof. But anyone who thinks *Reform School Girls* is a spoof must think World War II was a take-off on the earlier conflagration.... Under the guise of mocking yesteryear's junk genre, the film is a mega-garbage scam that mocks

Gloria Castillo and Jan Englund in *Reform School Girl* (1957).

its audience.... Trading on bad acting, shrieking, flesh and sadism ... it's spoof-proof." The amused reviewer for *Variety* branded the film "tame titillation" and noted, "*Reform School Girls* don't have it so bad. For one thing, they don't have to wear uniforms—or much else for that matter. They talk dirty, play dirty and are allowed to take long, long showers. They can even earn special privileges from the head matron for consenting to various requests."

218. *Reformatory* (Columbia, 1938), 59 min.

Producer, Larry Darmour; director, Lewis D. Collins; screenplay, Gordon Rigby; assistant director, Carl Hiecke; sound, Tom Lambert; camera, James S. Brown, Jr.; editor, Dwight Caldwell.

Jack Holt (Robert Dean); Bobby Jordan (Pinkey Leonard); Charlotte Wynters (Dr. Adele Webster); Grant Mitchell (Arnold Frayne); Tommy Bupp (Fibber Regan); Frankie Darro (Louie Miller); Ward Bond (MacGrady); Sheila Bromley (Mrs. Regan); Paul Everton (Governor Spaulding); Lloyd Ingraham (Dr. Blakely); Joe Caits (Jim Leonard).

Wendy O. Williams *(left)*, Sybil Danning *(2nd from right)* and Pat Ast *(right)* in *Reform School Girls* (1986).

Robert Dean (Jack Holt), the effective assistant warden at a tough prison, is requested by Governor Spaulding (Paul Everton) to bring an enlightened regime to the infamous Garfield Reform School where the youngsters endure bad food, squalid living conditions and assorted corporeal punishment. Dean accepts the challenge, and once installed at the institution, cleans house, aided by staff psychiatrist, Dr. Adele Webster (Charlotte Wynters). He establishes an honor system, has the youths dress in quasi-military outfits and forbids corporeal punishments. His sweeping changes include the removal of brutal head guard MacGrady (Ward Bond).

The angered MacGrady arranges to have tough kid Louie Miller (Frankie Darro) sentenced to a term at the youth prison, ordering him to cause chaos. Louie gains influence over Fibber Regan (Tommy Bupp) and convinces him to join in an escape attempt. Truant Pinkey Leonard (Bobby Jordan), once the toughest kid in the "joint" has come to understand Dean's reform program and now considers Dean his mentor. He tries to prevent the breakout. The escape goes through, although Miller drowns and Pinkey is injured. At the last, Fibber admits the truth, which clears Dean's reputation with the authorities. He now pushes forward with his reform program.

Hacked out by Columbia Pictures, *Reformatory* had nothing fresh to offer on the subject. "It is imitative of nearly all reformatory yarns and not as good as most of them.... This is just another yarn, with the politics psychiatry angle and honor system woven into one. Like most such pix, it resolves into a quick finish, too" *(Variety)*. The disgruntled *New York Times* reviewer (B. R. Cristler) admitted, "[I]f it wasn't for the bars on certain windows, you could hardly tell *Reformatory* ... from Hotchkiss or V.M.I.... [By] the time we reached the end it wouldn't have surprised us to hear the seniors burst into a class yell or a chorus of alma mater." Vance King *(Motion Picture Herald)* seemed to be stretching the film's potential with exhibitors when he suggested, "Motion pictures of boys in crime are not new, but treatment of this kind permits a showmanship campaign of a novel character, pointing up the introduction of the honor system."

Bobby Jordan of the Dead End Kids had become a staple of such reformatory reform dramas: *Crime School* (1938) and *Hell's Kitchen* (1939), qq.v. Frankie Darro had appeared in *Mayor of Hell* (1933) and would be in *Boys' Reformatory* (1939), qq.v.

219. *Renegade Girls* (New World, 1974), color, 83 min.

Producer, Evelyn Purcell; director/screenplay, Jonathan Demme; art director, Eric Thiermann; music, John Cale; camera, Tak Fujimoto; editors, Johanna Demetrakis, Carolyn Hicks.

Juanita Brown (Maggie); Erica Gavin (Jackie Wilson); Roberta Collins (Belle); Barbara Steele (Warden McQueen); Ella Reid (Pandora); Rainbeaux Smith (Lavelle); Warren Miller (Randolph); Lynda Gold (Crazy); and: John Aprea, Desiree Cousteau, Mickey Fox, Carmen Argenziano, George Armitage, Cindy Cale, Layla Gallaway, Essie Hayes, Valley Hoffman, Keisha, Gary Littlejohn, Dorothy Love, Hal Marshall, Carol Miller, Leslie Otis, Tobi Carr Rafelson, Amy Randall, Bob Reese, Mike Shack, Cynthia Songey, Ann Stockdale, Irene Stokes, Joe Viola, Patrick Wright.

The ad campaign boasted, *"Women's Prison U.S.A. —Rape, Riot & Revenge! ... White Hot Desires Melting Cold Prison Steel!"* Jonathan Demme (b. 1944) made his official feature film directorial debut with *Renegade Girls*. David Quinlan *(The Illustrated Guide to Film Directors,* 1983) judged that this movie has "a style which transcended its origins. It also had Erica Gavin, just about the most animated actress [softcore pornography director] Russ Meyer ... ever used, and the extraordinary Barbara Steele as the villainess. Demme made the most of the personalities of the actresses...."

Jackie Wilson (Erica Gavin) is imprisoned at Connorville Maximum Security Prison, a brutal women's penitentiary where the demented, wheelchair-bound Warden McQueen (Barbara Steele) is in charge. (The sadistic warden is not above dreaming of herself as a sexy cabaret performer strutting her stuff.) When a prison breakout is attempted, vulnerable Jackie is made the scapegoat and the prison doctor subjects her to excrutiating shock treatments. Later, she and Maggie (Juanita Brown) steal a car while on work assignment and escape. When they discover the doctor intends to conduct a lobotomy on a fellow convict, they return to rescue her, after robbing a gang of bank robbers. They drive a van through the prison gates and rescue the imperiled inmate just in time. They grab the physician and warden as hostages and flee. When the guards shoot at the vehicle, the hostages are killed but the prisoners escape.

In *The Psychotronic Encyclopedia of Film* (1983), Michael Weldon enthused, "Audiences expecting another forgettable women's prison drive-in feature were a bit surprised to find politics and feminism mixed with the usual skin, shocks and lowbrow humor in this cult film." Unlike most such entries in this sub-genre, *Renegade Girls* showed the liberated, enterprising "heroines" of this piece to be resourceful females who refused to be put down by either males or other women.

Co-star Juanita Brown had appeared in *Willie Dynamite* (1973), *Foxy Brown* (1974) and *Black Starlet* (1974), all part of the blaxploitation cycle in Hollywood.

A.k.a.: *Caged Heat!*

220. *The Revenge of Al Capone* (NBC–TV, Feb. 26, 1989), color, 100 min.

Executive producers, Robert Lovenheim, John Levoff; producer, Vicki Niemi-Gordon; co-producer, Tracy Keenan Wynn; director, Michael Pressman; teleplay, Wynn; production designer, Stephen Storer; set decorator, Sharon Viljoen; costumes, Heidi Kacjenski; music, Craig Safan; music editor, Jerelyn Golding; assistant directors, Dennis Maguire, Christine Larson; stunt coordinator, Edward J. Ulrich; sound, Joseph Geisinger; sound editor, Sam Horta; ADR editor, Golding; special effects coordinator, Eddie Surkin; camera, Tim Suhrstedt; second unit camera, Geoff Schaaf; editor, Jeff Freeman.

Ray Sharkey (Al Capone); Keith Carradine (Agent Michael Rourke); Jayne Atkinson (Elizabeth Rourke); Debrah Farentino (Jennie); Charles Haid (Alex Connors); Jordan Charney (J. Edgar Hoover); Scott Paulin (Eliot Ness); Charles Hallahan (Muldowney); James Handy (Hotchkiss); Robert Benedetti (Mayor Cermak); Alan Rosenberg (Frank Nitti); Neil Gray Giuntoli (Dutch Schultz); Peter Noel Duhamel (Newberry); Ton Amendola (Zangara); Christopher Carroll (Judge); Donald Craig (President Franklin D. Roosevelt); John Di Santi (D'Andrea); Bradford English (Warden Johnston); Elaine Joyce (Chanteuse); William Long, Jr. (Captain); Michael Medeiros (Coletti); Raymond O'Keefe (Desk Sergeant); James Brunner (Reporter); Katie Brenner (Amanda); Jeffrey Concklin (Reporter); Nick Corello (Driver); Kimberly Cullum (Becky); Troy Evans (Harry Lang); Marc Figueroa (Bugsy Siegel); Scott Edmund Lane (Reporter); Heath Jobes (Miami Newsman); Dave Matzke (Henchman); Nicholas Mele (Lucky Luciano); Ron Gilbert (Schultz's Lawyer); Joe Gilbride (Henchman); Gary Gordon (Cop); Michael Hungerford (Henry Miller); Burr Middleton (Reporter); Reno Nichols (Tourist); Conn O'Farrell (Sergeant Callahan); Steven Jason Oliver (Newsman); Judith Piguet (Nurse); Eugene Pressman (Reporter); Michael Pressman (Agent); Charles Prior (Snitch); Michael Prokoput (Atlanta Guard); Debbie Lyman Ross (Schultz's Girl); David Stentstrom (Fred Clawson); Bob Swain, Kirk Thornton (Reporters); Merritt Yohnka (Agent).

It used to be assumed that when a criminal—even a big shot crime czar—was imprisoned that it effectively put an end to his wave of lawlessness. *The Revenge of Al Capone* attempts to depict how an infamous Chicago mobster continued to rule his gang from behind bars, whether it be a Chicago jail, the penitentiary at Atlanta or even Alcatraz Prison. Unfortunately, this overblown study of Al Capone (1899–1947) was so distorted by grandiose overacting, feckless scripting and the distortion of historical facts, that its grim message was lost.

The narrative opens in Miami in 1947 with Treasury Department special agent Michael Rourke (Keith Carradine) summoned to the mansion of Al Capone (Ray Sharkey), the one-time public enemy number one who is now nearing death by syphilis. During this bizarre reunion, the decrepit Capone, whose mind is wandering, asks his one-time enemy, "Why did you do it me?... Why did you send me to prison.... I never figured it would end like this."

The scene flashes back to 1932 in Chicago where mobster Capone, a global celebrity of sorts, has been sentenced to a long prison term for income tax invasion. He is amused, rather than upset, by his sentence. ("I got eleven years for not paying my taxes. That's a national pastime, not a crime.") However, the megalomanic criminal has a particular hatred of federal agent Michael Rourke (Keith Carradine), who has made a vendetta of putting Scarface Capone behind bars. Even when incarcerated at the Cook County jail, Al sends out word to his underlings to revenge him on the lawman. Thus on Christmas Eve, two hoods break into Rourke's home and attempt to murder him, his wife Elizabeth (Jayne Atkinson) and their two children. Instead, Michael kills the two punks.

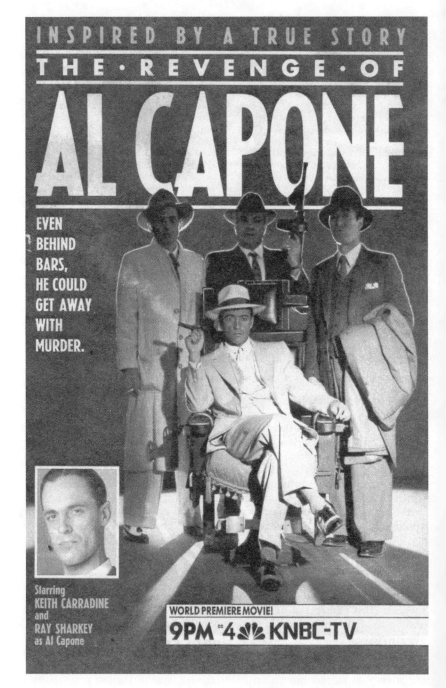

Advertisement for *The Revenge of Al Capone* (1989).

While the FBI works to strengthen its case against Capone, Rourke comes into conflict with special agent Eliot Ness (Scott Paulin), the latter a particular favorite of the dictatorial bureau chief, J. Edgar Hoover (Jordan Charney). Meanwhile, a raid on one of Capone's speakeasies brings Rourke into contact with attractive club worker Jennifer (Debrah Farentino). Before long, Rourke is being unfaithful to his wife as he pursues his romance with Jennie.

It seems no matter where Capone is incarcerated, his criminal empire flourishes. One of the gangster's chief helpers is the notorious Frank Nitti (Alan Rosenberg), ever anxious to become kingpin himself. While doing his best to eliminate his chief competitor, Dutch Schultz (Neil Gray Giuntoli), Nitti is faithful to Capone's murderous commands. (It is the ranting Capone, dressed in a smoking jacket, who orders Nitti to continue a reign of terror: "I need certain people to know that I'm still in charge. I want 'em to know that just because I'm in here doesn't mean that I can't still make things happen!") Meanwhile, Rourke is framed by Jennifer into a compromising position in a hotel room where news photographers arrive to record his adultery. He is temporarily suspended from the bureau and loses his wife. As for Jennie, who loved Michael but cares for money and power more, she is rewarded with her own club in Havana.

Finally, the federal authorities relocate Capone to the newly opened Alcatraz Prison, the maximum of the maximum security penitentiaries "set aside for only the most dangerous prisoners, incorrigibles prone to violence and murder." As Rourke insists, "This is the only place that could handle him." After his release from the island rock, he retires to Florida where he lives a reclusive life.

The scene shifts back to the present with Rourke unaware that the still manipulative Capone has ordered Jennifer to be present in the house during his conversation with the now middle-aged Rourke. She remains hidden during the meeting, but listens intently as Capone asks Rourke if he really loved the betraying Jennifer. Michael, not wanting to admit the truth, denies that he ever did. The amused Capone then lies by advising Rourke that it does not matter, since she is dead.

The two antagonists bid goodbye for the last time. The senile Capone says: "No hard feelings, huh. We only kill each other."

Henry Sheehan *(Hollywood Reporter)* branded this entry "a formless, plotless mess." He explained, "[A] casual viewer might be hard-pressed to describe just exactly what the title of the telefilm refers to, as the 'revenge' never amounts to much more than a minor subplot. But then, this drama is all subplots, minus the storytelling spin required to bind them. . . . And although some bits and pieces do have a modestly spicy tang, the end result is a lot of narrative nibblings while awaiting a main course that never appears." Chris Williams *(Los Angeles Times)* judged, "*Revenge* intends to be taken as ironic romantic tragedy as well as bloody gangland saga, and comes up short all over. *Daily Variety* jibed, "Fact and fiction blend — or blur — in Tracy Keenan Wynn's look at yet another Untouchable and Al Capone and how Capone tried to bump off fictitious agent Michael Rourke and family for putting him behind bars. Looks like Capone's revenge is the continuing films and vidpix in which he's featured."

The soap opera-ish *The Revenge of Al Capone* was promoted with "Even behind bars, he could get away with murder. . . . Inspired by a true story." Tracy Keenan Wynn had authored several prison genre films, including *The Glass House* (1972) and *The Longest Yard* (1974), qq.v. Among those who have played Al

Capone on screen are: Rod Steiger in *Al Capone* (1959), Neville Brand in *Scarface Mob* (1959) and *Spin of a Coin* (1962), Jason Robards in *The St. Valentine's Day Massacre* (1967), Ben Gazzara in *Capone* (1975) and Robert De Niro in *The Untouchables* (1987). (Paul Muni played an Al Capone–like gangster in *Scarface*, 1932.)

221. *Revolt in the Big House* (Allied Artists, 1958), 79 min.

Producer, David Diamond; director, R. G. Springsteen; screenplay, Daniel Hyatt, Eugene Lourie; art director, David Milton; set decorator, Joseph Kish; wardrobe, Roger J. Weinberg; makeup, John Holden; assistant director, Herb Mendelson; sound, Charles Schelling; special effects, Herman Townsley; camera, William Margulies; editor, William Austin.

Gene Evans (Gannon); Robert Blake (Rudy); Timothy Carey (Kyle); John Qualen (Doc); Sam Edwards (Al); John Dennis (Red); Walter Barnes (Starkey); Frank Richards (Jake); Emile Meyer (Warden); Arlene Hunter (Girl); Frank Ferguson (Lawyer); Robert Shayne (Mickey); Sam Edwards (Al); Les Johnson (Detective); Bob Stratton, John Close, Robert Bice, John Mitchum, Fred Kohler, William Haade (Guards); Sam Finn, John Indrissano, John Lomma (Convicts); and: Francis De Sales, Ed Gelb.

No sooner is major racketeer Lou Gannon (Gene Evans) imprisoned on a twenty-year term, than he takes over as king of the convicts, replacing Kyle (Timothy Carey). Lou also begins formulating an escape plan. After convict Al (Sam Edwards) reneges on his role in Lou's planned prison break, he is killed by Gannon and Kyle. Meanwhile, Rudy (Robert Blake), Gannon's young Mexican cellmate, who had been innocently tricked into participating in a holdup (which led to his prison sentence), is eager to win an early parole for good behavior. However, the manipulative Gannon tricks him into fighting with another convict. Gannon plants a knife in Rudy's pocket which leads Starkey (Walter Barnes), the captain of the guards, to believe Rudy killed Al. Starkey places him into solitary confinement. This embitters Rudy who now agrees to join in the breakout bid.

The convicts are unaware that the warden (Emile Meyer) has heard rumors of the potential prison break and has already ordered guards to be stationed on the outside to fire at anyone trying to pass through the gate. The break gets underway when Kale dynamites the main gate. Rudy and Doc (John Qualen) hold the guards hostages and learn from Starkey of the massacre that will occur once the fleeing convicts reach the front gate. While rushing to warn the others, Rudy spots Gannon climbing over the back prison wall. He now realizes that Gannon's plan all along was to sacrifice the others for his own escape. In the ensuing fight, Rudy is badly injured. While Gannon climbs over the walls, the dying Rudy warns the other convicts. Kyle runs through the main gate alone and is machine-gunned. Gannon also dies once he climbs over the wall.

Variety approved of this economy actioner. "A well-concocted prison story, *Revolt in the Big House* is, by any standard, more impressive than its budget.... Director R. G. Springsteen skillfully handled his actors, making the most of a good, well-planned ... screenplay." *Hollywood Reporter* endorsed, "A straight-lined uncluttered story of prison life." *Film Daily* confirmed, "It is the best prison-escape picture in many moons.... Performances on the warden and guard sides are as realistic and credible as those on the criminal side."

For ex–*Our Gang* comedy series actor Robert Blake, *Revolt in the Big House* would be one of his major adult assignments. He would return to the genre in his even more impressive characterization within *In Cold Blood* (1967), q.v. Location work for *Revolt in the Big House* was accomplished at California's Folsom Prison.

Gene Evans and Robert Blake in *Revolt in the Big House* (1958).

222. *The Right Way* (Producers Security Corp., 1921), 7 reels.

Presenter, Thomas Mott Osborne; supervisor, Edward A. MacManus; director, Sidney Olcott; screenplay, Basil Dickey.

Edwards Davis (The Father); Helen Lindroth (The Mother); Joseph Marquis (The Rich Boy); Vivienne Osborne (The Sweetheart); Sidney D'Albrook (The Poor Boy); Annie Ecleston (His Mother); Helen Ferguson (His Sweetheart); Elsie McLeod (His Sister); Tammany Young (The Smiler); Thomas Brooks (The New Warden).

A strong message picture produced by Thomas Mott Osborne, who had been both a warden at Sing Sing Prison and at the U.S. Naval Prison at Portsmouth, New Hampshire. Mott was a leading advocate of prison reform and a champion of the Mutual League, an association of ex-convicts in New York State whose code was based on the honor system. *Variety* reported of this proselytizing essay, "As it stands, besides being an argument for a progressive prison system, it is a thoroughly interesting human story, with the play and interplay of character upon character and a crescendo dramatic effect up to the climax."

The slum-bred Poor Boy (Sidney D'Albrook) is sentenced to a reformatory for a minor offense. There he acquires the skills of a professional criminal. Because of a snitch, the Poor Boy later finds himself sent to prison where he endures the old method of punishment, ranging from silence to hard labor and brutality. Meanwhile, the Rich Boy (Joseph Marquis) is sent to the same prison, now under a new warden (Thomas Brooks). There he encounters the Poor Boy who has been reincarcerated for attacking a stool pigeon. When the two young men learn that The Smiler (Tammany Young) has been erroneously sentenced to die for the killing of the stool pigeon, they escape. They find evidence to clear the condemned man, but they are too late to save their friend who dies in the electric chair. For their efforts they are paroled.

Reissue title: *Within Prison Walls.*

A.k.a.: *Making Good.*

223. *Riot* (Paramount, 1969), color, 97 min.

Producer, William Castle; associate producer, Dona Holloway; director, Buzz Kulik; based on the novel *The Riot* by Frank Elli; screenplay, James Poe; production designer/art director, Paul Sylbert; makeup, Charles Blackman; assistant director, Danny McCauley; music, Christopher Komeda; songs: Komeda and Robert Wells, Johnnie Lee Willis, Deacon Anderson and Blackman; sound, John Wilkinson, Clem Portman; camera, Robert Hauser; editor, Edwin H. Bryant.

Jim Brown (Cully Briston); Gene Hackman (Red Fletcher); Ben Caruthers (Joe Surefoot); Mike Kellin (Bugsy); Gerald S. O'Loughlin (Grossman); Clifford David ("Big Mary" Sheldon); Bill Walker (Jake); Ricky Summers ("Gertie"); Michael Byron (Murray); Jerry Thompson (Deputy Warden Fisk); M. Gerri, John Neiderhauser (Homosexuals); Frank A. Eyman (The Warden); and: Lee Joe Barta, Jack Baxter, Barry Bruce, Earl Donald Christenson, Bobby Favors, Danny Flores, Ralph Gipson, Herman Gorablenkow, Frances D. Gray, Earl Henderson, Charles E. Hart, Thomas B. Ingles, Kenneth Kelly, Baqui Montes, Dwight Palmer, Jess Pina, Levi Robertson, Jack Story, Clair Sullivan, John Targett, Louis Taylor, Thomas Weldon, Trent Wood, Don Ramone-Wooton, Duane Edward Young.

Until *Riot,* the black man in prison had been an incidental character, usually depicted as hymn-singing and subservient, even when a hardened criminal on death row (E.g., *The Last Mile,* 1932, *I Am a Fugitive from a Chain Gang,* 1932, *Mutiny in the Big House,* 1939, qq.v.) However, in *Riot,* ex-football star and rising Hollywood player Jim Brown *starred* as a black prisoner caught up not only in dealing with the rigorous life of a convict, but as a minority group member who must cope with murderous racial discrimination behind bars. *Riot* had a strong effect on the prison genre, which thereafter always included ethnic strife as another hazardous obstacle to survival in the big house. This was also one of the first prison movies to blatantly depict homosexuality behind bars.

Muscular Cully Briston (Jim Brown), an intense black convict of few words, is relegated to the isolation tank, where he becomes drawn into a riot instigated by Red Fletcher (Gene Hackman). Once they take several guards hostage, the rioters control a good part of the 1,200-convict penitentiary. The conniving Fletcher insists the uprising is based on a list of grievances. Actually, he is delaying for time so that he can make his breakout through a tunnel shaft that extends beyond the prison walls. When the media focuses on the prisoners' complaints, Deputy Warden Fisk (Jerry Thompson) is forced to negotiate with Fletcher and his followers. During a party given by the rioters, the stool pigeon convicts who informed on their peers are sentenced to death by a kangaroo court. Some of the rioters get drunk on homemade raisin jack brew and crazed Joe Surefoot (Ben Carruthers) wants to murder the squealers now. Cully stops him from killing the hostages.

The warden (Frank A. Eyman) returns from his vacation and announces radical measures to regain order. Meanwhile, Red and eleven others, including Briston, reach the tunnel. However, when they emerge outside, they are welcomed by machine-gun fire and gas grenade explosions. Briston, Fletcher and Surefoot have gas masks, and they reach the foot of a guard tower. After Surefoot murders a guard, he attempts to knife Briston. Fletcher stops him. Fletcher and Surefoot struggle to the death. Briston alone escapes.

Vincent Canby *(New York Times)* judged, "*Riot* is not a great movie, but it is a respectable one. . . . [Director Buzz] Kulik employs just about every obligatory scene in the old con vs. keeper confrontation, including a few variations. At the height of the riot, there is a gaudily photographed bacchanal on what is known as 'queen's row.' (Members of the old Warner Brothers stock company used to sublimate such desires by making knives out of tea keetles.)" *Variety* had mixed reactions to this new style prison picture: "Concept vacillates between apparent attempt to tell a straightforward escape story, and temptation to linger and exploit violence, perversion, etc., using loaded character setups as specious motivation. No social document, this, but not a potboiler, either."

Riot was filmed on location at Arizona State Penitentiary with prison warden Frank A. Eyman and several hundred inmates/personnel participating in the movie. The picture was adapted from the 1967 book by ex-convict Frank Elli, based on a real life incident at a Minnesota prison. In the novel, Cully Briston had been a white convict.

Jim Brown would appear in another prison drama, *The Slams* (1973), q.v., a more brutal but far lesser distillation of the genre.

224. *Riot in Cell Block 11* (Allied Artists, 1954), 80 min.

Producer, Walter Wanger; director, Don Siegel; screenplay, Richard Collins; art director, David Milton; set decorator, Robert Priestly; music, Herschell Burke Gilbert; assistant director, Austen Jewell; dialogue director, Jim Leicester; sound, Frank Webster, Sr.; camera, Russell Harlan; editor, Bruce Pierce.

Neville Brand (Dunn); Leo Gordon (Crazy Mike Carnie); Emile Meyer (Warden Reynolds); Robert Osterloh (The Colonel); Carleton Young (Captain Barrett); Frank Faylen (Senator Haskell); Joel Fluellen (Al); Ward Wood (Bacon); Roy Glenn (Delmar); Alvy Moore (Gator); William Phipps (Mickey); John Tarangelo (Manuel); Dabbs Greer (Schuyler); James Anderson (Acton); Whit Bissell (Snader); Benny Burt (Doc); Paul Frees (Monroe); Frank Hagney (Roberts); Don Keefer, Harold J. Kennedy, William Schallert (Reporters); Jonathan Hale (Russell); Robert Patton (Frank); Joe Kerr (Mac); Robert Burton (Ambrose).

Among other things, *Riot in Cell Block 11* broke two cardinal Hollywood rules: the good guys lost and there were no women in the picture. Furthermore, the picture clearly had something to say about a serious subject, prison reform, and it spoke seriously, soberly and, above all, realistically. Filmed at Folsom Prison, the picture's cast included many convicts. The producer, Walter Wanger, and one of the leading actors, Leo Gordon, were both former convicts. . . .

(Stuart M. Kiminsky, *Don Siegel: Director,* 1974)

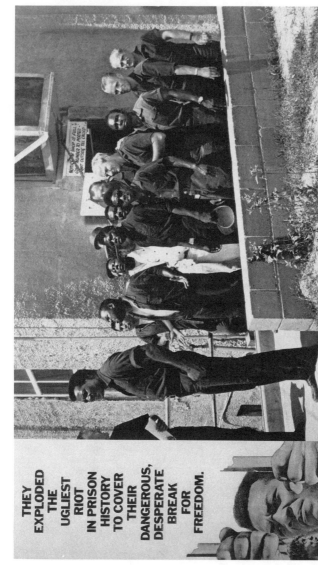

THEY EXPLODED THE UGLIEST RIOT IN PRISON HISTORY TO COVER THEIR DANGEROUS, DESPERATE BREAK FOR FREEDOM.

PARAMOUNT PICTURES presents A WILLIAM CASTLE PRODUCTION

RIOT starring JIM BROWN / GENE HACKMAN

FEATURING MIKE KELLIN / GERALD S. O'LOUGHLIN / BEN CARRUTHERS / CLIFFORD DAVID / AND FEATURING INMATES OF ARIZONA STATE PRISON / SCREENPLAY BY JAMES POE / BASED UPON A NOVEL BY FRANK ELLI / PRODUCED BY WILLIAM CASTLE / DIRECTED BY BUZZ KULIK

TECHNICOLOR® A PARAMOUNT PICTURE

RESTRICTED—Persons under 16 not admitted, unless accompanied by parent or adult guardian.

Next to *Brute Force* (1947), q.v., the realistic and well-staged *Riot in Cell Block 11* is the most graphic prison uprising picture to be produced in Hollywood. "*Riot in Cell Block 11* is a tough, believable account of what happens when convicts are pushed around too much. . . . [The filmmakers] have made a movie of unrelenting violence, but the uproar finds its justification in their purpose: the correction of abuses in penal establishments" (*New Yorker* magazine). *Time* magazine endorsed: "*Riot in Cell Block 11* is the best prison movie produced in years." *Newsweek* magazine proclaimed it "virtually a model of movie realism . . . the film is full of criminological insights." Lowell E. Redellings *(Hollywood Citizen News)* applauded the movie because it is "told in an almost factual manner, endowed with a fine documentary flavor, and devoid of the usual clichés and hackneyed situations of most prison films." Edward Schallert *(Los Angeles Times)* confirmed, "There is a tremendous grip to those sequences which witness the spread of the riot. The film gains most throughout because it has something rather definite to say about the subject it deals with."

In a large state prison, a riot is spreading from cell block to cell block. Among the leaders are the clever and powerful Dunn (Neville Brand) and his homicidal lieutenant, Crazy Mike Carnie (Leo Gordon). The Colonel (Robert Osterloh) opposes violence and writes out the prisoners' demands, while Schuyler (Dabbs Greer), the black Al (Joel Fleullen), Gator (Alvy Moore), and Roberts (Frank Hagney) go along with the protest for better food, improved living conditions, constructive use of time, etc. Among the eight guards held hostages are Monroe (Paul Frees), Acton (James Anderson) and Snader (Whit Bissell).

Appreciating the very dangerous situation, the unflinching but understanding Warden Reynolds (Emile Meyer), Captain Barrett (Carleton Young) and the others negotiate with Dunn, the inmates' spokesman. Senator Haskell (Frank Faylen) and the press arrive to hear the demands. Because of the escalating violence, the state militia is summoned. Dunn's eleven-point ultimatum is heard and the governor finally signs the prisoners' petition. Thereafter, the riot subsides. The convicts return to the cells. The last to enter his steel cage is Dunn, who now faces an extra thirty years to his sentence. Prison life goes on.

Shot in sixteen days at a total cost of $300,000, *Riot in Cell Block 11* proved to be a major hit for the little major studio, Allied Artists. A. H. Weiler *(New York Times)* enthused, "The grim business of melodrama behind prison walls, so often depicted in standard, banal fashion in films, is given both tension and dignity in *Riot in Cell Block 11*. . . . [It] is a realistic and effective combination of brawn, brains and heart. . . . [It] punches and preaches with authority." *Variety* lauded the production because, "The picture doesn't use formula prison plot. There's no inmate reformed by love or fair treatment, nor unbelievable boy-meets-girl, gets-same angle. Nor are there any heroes and heavies of standard pattern. . . ." The trade paper added, "It has been some time since the market has had a real good prison melodrama of this voltage."

Don Siegel would later direct *Escape from Alcatraz* (1980), q.v. Emile Meyer would play another hard-nosed warden in *Revolt in the Big House* (1960), q.v. Leo Gordon would portray a convict again in *The Steel Jungle* (1956), q.v. Neville Brand would have a turn-about role in *Birdman of Alcatraz* (1962), q.v., playing a prison guard.

Opposite: Advertisement for *Riot* (1969).

Leo Gordon in *Riot in Cell Block 11* (1954).

225. *Riot in Juvenile Prison* (United Artists, 1959), 71 min.

Producer, Robert E. Kent; director, Edward L. Cahn; screenplay, Orville H. Hampton; art director, William Glasgow; music, Emil Newman; camera, Maury Gertsman; editor, Eddie Mann.

Jerome Thor (Dr. Paul Furman); Marcia Henderson (Grace Hartwell); Scott Marlowe (Eddie Bassett); John Hoyt (Colonel Walton); Dick Tyler (Stu Killion); Virginia Aldridge (Kitty); Dorothy Provine (Babe); Jack Grinnage (Dink); George Brenlin (Matches); Ann Doran (Bess Monahan); Richard Reeves (Andy Quillan); Al McGranary (Governor); Paul Jasmin (Bobby).

After slugging Colonel Walton (John Hoyt), the martinet warden of a detention home for juveniles, several teenaged boys attempt to escape. In the process, the guards shoot in self-defense and two of the youths die. The publicity and furor over the incident leads the governor (Al McGranary) to appoint Dr. Paul Furman (Jerome Thor) in charge of the institution. The psychiatrist introduces several radical new policies, including making the facility co-ed. Matron Grace Hartwell (Marcia Henderson) is among those who insist that Furman's regime will fail. Although, Eddie Bassett (Scott Marlowe), the punk leader of the boys, refuses to cooperate with Furman's reform regime, the other youths do and the reform program appears to be succeeding. Then news leaks out of more trouble: Stu Killion (Dick Tyler)—who is Eddie's rival for control of the others—sexually attacks Eddie's girlfriend Kitty (Virginia Aldridge). Furman is ousted and Walton is reinstated. The latter brings back his strict, brutal policies. His actions lead Eddie to organize a riot during which hostages are taken. The panicked governor appeals to Furman for assistance and he restores order. With harmony reigning, Furman pursues a romance with Grace.

Riot in Juvenile Prison proved that there was nothing new under the sun in Hollywood. The same story had been told for decades, only with less blatant emphasis on sex and violence. *Variety* reported, "The attempted rape and the fights over girls make possible sensational campaign, but weakness in the screenplay will keep film at the bottom half of double bills.... The use of a large number of youthful extras gives the film some size and the spacious private-school-type setting relieves the picture of prison pallor."

Edward L. Cahn (1907–1963) was no stranger to the prison genre, having directed: *Experiment Alcatraz* (1950), *Betrayed Women* (1955) and *Girls in Prison* (1956), qq.v.

226. *The River Pirate* (Fox, 1928), 67 min.

Presenter, William Fox; director, William K. Howard; based on the book by Charles Francis Coe; screenplay; John Reinhardt, Benjamin Markson; titles, Malcolm Stuart Boylan; assistant director, Gordon Cooper; camera, Lucien Andriot; editor, Jack Dennis.

Victor McLaglen (Sailor Fritz); Lois Moran (Marjorie Cullen); Nick Stuart (Sandy); Earle Foxe (Shark); Donald Crisp (Detective Sergeant Caxton); Robert Perry (Gerber).

Sandy (Nick Stuart) a product of Manhattan's slum-filled waterfront, is erroneously sentenced to a reformatory. Once there he encounters Sailor Fritz (Victor McLaglen), a callous convict assigned to the institution to instruct the boys in the art of sailmaking. After Fritz is paroled he helps his young friend escape from the reformatory and teaches him a new trade—pilfering from warehouses. Meanwhile, Sandy meets Marjorie Cullen (Lois Moran), the ward of a police detective (Donald Crisp). She attempts to get Sandy to go straight. Later, Fritz is captured during a robbery, while Sandy escapes. The young man abandons his life of crime to marry Marjorie. In a spoken epilogue, an elderly reader tells the audience that the preceding story was fiction and that Fritz is released from prison in time to attend Sandy and Marjorie's wedding.

Based on a 1928 novel by Charles Francis Coe, Fox Films's *The River Pirate* was a silent picture with talking sequences, a music score and sound effects. *Variety* reviewed, "The fascinating thing about the picture is the entirely impersonal way this bazarre [sic] history is presented. No preachment against the injustice of shipping petty juvenile delinquents to the reformatory. They don't glorify the dock thief, or point a moral of this trade." The *New York Times* wrote approvingly, "This is a well-knit production capably served by Mr. McLaglen, for, although it again calls for sympathy for the lawless specimens, one usually feels sympathy for any part that Mr. McLaglen plays."

227. *Road Gang* (Warner Bros., 1936), 65 min.

Director, Louis King; story, Abem Finkel, Harold Buckley; screenplay, Dalton Trumbo; art director, Hugh Reticke, Jr.; camera, L. William O'Connell; editor, Jack Killifer.

Donald Woods (James Larrabee); Carlyle Moore, Jr. (Bob Gordon); Kay Linaker (Barbara Metcalfe); Harry Cording (Sam Dawson); Ed Chandler (1st Guard); Marc Lawrence (Pete); Olin Howland (Doctor); Joe King (Winston); Henry O'Neill (Metcalfe); Addison Richards (Warden); Charles Middleton (Mine Warden); Edward Van Sloan (Dudley); Eddie Schubert (Buck Draper); William B. Davidson (Marsden); Herbert Heywood (Convict);

George Lloyd, Donald Woods and Carlyle Moore, Jr. in *Road Gang* (1936).

Joseph Crehan (Shields); George Lloyd (Hymie Sebold); John Irwin (Old Convict); and: Ben Hendricks, Edward Le Saint, Tom Manning, Constantine Romanoff, Tom Wilson.

Idealistic James Larrabee (Donald Wood) is commissioned by a Chicago newspaper to prepare a series of articles exposing corruption in his southern state—in particular, the dishonest regime of political boss, Shields (Joseph Crehan). Metcalfe (Henry O'Neill), Shields's partner and the father of Larrabee's fiancée Barbara (Kay Linaker), attempts to bribe James not to write the newspaper exposés, but he is unsuccessful. As a result, Shields frames Larrabee and his friend Bob Gordon (Carlyle Moore, Jr.) on both a grand larceny charge and, later, on a homicide rap. Shields buys off the defendants' lawyer who persuades his clients to plead guilty, insisting he will insure they receive light sentences. Instead, the two men must serve five years on a road gang.

Once submerged in the arduous life on the road gang, Bob attempts to escape and dies trying. When Larrabee is caught smuggling a story out of the camp detailing the horrendous conditions there, he is reassigned to the mines, where he is treated roughly by the sadistic administrator (Charles Middleton). Meanwhile, Barbara meets with Winston (Joe King), the editor of the Chicago paper and they, in turn, apply to the attorney general for relief. The latter has long had a vendetta against Shields and pushes to get Larrabee freed and to have Shields and his cronies thrown out of office. This is accomplished after the convicts in the mines revolt and break James out to freedom so he can tell his story to the world. Later, James is hired as a staff reporter on the Chicago paper and plans to marry Barbara.

Noting the parallels between *Road Gang* and the same studio's earlier *I Am a Fugitive from a Chain Gang* (1932), q.v., Frank S. Nugent *(New York Times)* thought the new picture "a routine check-up." Nugent reasoned, "Possessing neither the crusading strength of *Fugitive* nor the arresting vigor of Paul Muni's bitter performance, the new photoplay is a minor melodrama in all departments." Nugent also noted, "Credit the Warners with tact; they may level their lances and go crusading, but they never say where or against whom." *Variety* acknowledged that "the picture has a 'serious' implication. It is special pleading for humanity in handling prisoners." However, added the trade paper, "other films have probed deeper and analyzed the causes more keenly. Except for a couple of lines of dialog the financial profits made from convict labor by politicians and business men (and the real cause of the brutalities) is not explored."

One of the more graphic sequences in this minor league actioner occurs when Carlyle Moore, Jr. attempts to flee the barbarous prison camp by climbing the prison's barbed wire. A guard, noting his progress, turns on the electricity and Moore is electrocuted. More sinister in the picture is shifty-eyed Charles Middleton (1878–1948), the character actor who excelled at portraying sinister prison guards: *I Am a Fugitive from a Chain Gang* (1932); *Hell's Highway* (1932), *Jailbreak* (1936), *Blackmail* (1939), qq.v.

228. *Road to the Big House* (Screen Guild, 1947), 74 min.

Producer, Walter Colmes; associate producer, Selwyn Levinson; director, Colmes; screenplay, Aubrey Wiseberg; art director, Frank Sylos; set decorator, George Bahr; assistant director, Ralph Slosser; camera, Walter Strenge; editor, Jason Bernie.

John Shelton (Eddie); Ann Doran (Agnes); Guinn [Big Boy] Williams (Butch); Dick Bailey (Sutter); Joe Allen, Jr. (Bates); Rory Mallinson (Fred); Eddy Fields (Kelvin); Walden Boyle (Prosecutor); Keith Richards (Harvey); Jack Conrad (Collins); Charles Jordan (Benson); C. Montague Shaw (Judge); John Doucette (Danny); Mickey Simpson (Case).

There is not a single new element in the entire film, except its errors.

(Film Daily)

In 1933, bank clerk Eddie (John Shelton) steals $200,000 from his working place to appease his nagging, money-hungry wife Agnes (Ann Doran). He is sent to jail for his crime, but the money which he had hidden is not recovered. Several greedy inmates in the penitentiary are eager to share in Eddie's money hoard and, through outside contacts, help him to escape. However, he is later recaptured. When he is released after fifteen years, he finds that his long-suffering wife has discovered the funds and returned it.

Brimming over with stock footage and corny dialogue, *Road to the Big House* failed to make its O'Henry type story twist pay off. *Variety* dismissed it as a "trite melodrama, unfolded in uninteresting manner.... Walter Colmes' production and direction doesn't build interest."

229. *Saint of Devil's Island* (Lloyd Young, 1960), color, 69 min.

Producer, Lloyd Young; director, Douglas Cox; story, Young; screenplay, H. Kenn Carmichael; art director, William Sherman; music, Perry Botkin; sound, Sidney McCollum; camera, Jules Podilla; editor, George E. Swink.

Eartha Kitt (Annette); Scott Forbes (Jacques Le Dreux); Bing Russell (Gerard); Lance Fuller (Francois); Richard Cutting (Major Charles Pean); Vito Scotti (Louis); and: William Carrlon, Angel Richardson, Vicki Vaughn, Richard Verney.

French sculptor Jacques Le Dreux (Scott Forbes) kills his wife in the heat of passion when he catches her with her lover. As a result, he is sentenced to eight years on Devil's Island. Once at the hellhole prison, he plots his escape with other convicts, including Louis (Vito Scotti) and Francois (Lance Fuller). One of the men's wives, Annette (Eartha Kitt), a singer who performs in the local Paradise club, finds a boat for them. The escape fails and her husband dies in the breakout. Stashed back in solitary, Jacques encounters Gerard (Bing Russell), a trustee convict, who tells him about the work of Major Charles Pean (Richard Cutting) and his Salvation Army–sponsored "House of Hope," geared to help the libertees (the prisoners who have finished their sentences but must remain on Devil's Island for a term equal to their original punishment).

After completing his original sentence, Jacques encounters Annette doing volunteer work at the House of Hope and the two fall in love. Francois reappears on the scene, determined to escape. Jacques tries to tell the desperate convict that Pean has gone to Frances to petition the government to abolish Devil's Island. But Francois is not to be dissuaded and persists with his revolt. Jacques quells the rebellion with his loudspeaker announcement that Pean's objective has succeeded. Devil's Island will be closed and all prisoners will be returned to France.

A little seen programmer whose sole virtue is the appearance of songstress/actress Eartha Kitt in another of her bizarre screen characterizations. The British *Monthly Film Bulletin* rated this "a naïve, turgidly handled and somewhat muddled mixture of penal colony brutalities and scriptual homilies, stuffed to the brim with lines like 'You mustn't punish yourself. Whatever our guilt we can all be forgiven,' and 'You can only hate so much; you must come to the end of hating.'"

230. *San Quentin* (Warner Bros., 1937), 70 min.

Associate producer, Samuel Bischoff; director, Lloyd Bacon; story, Robert Tasker, John Bright; screenplay, Peter Milne, Humphrey Cobb; art director, Esdras Hartley; costumes, Howard Shoup; music, Heinz Roemheld, Charles Maxwell, David Raksin; orchestrators, Joseph Nussbaum, Ray Heindorf; song, Harry Warren and Al Dubin; technical adviser, Doc Stone; sound, Everett A. Brown; special effects, James Gibbons, H. F. Koenekamp; camera, Sid Hickox; editor, William Holmes.

Pat O'Brien (Captain Stephen Jameson); Humphrey Bogart (Joe "Red" Kennedy); Ann Sheridan (Mae DeVilliers [May Kennedy]); Barton MacLane (Lieutenant Druggin); Joseph Sawyer ("Sailor Boy" Hansen); Veda Ann Borg (Helen); James Robbins (Mickey Callahan); Joseph King (Warden Taylor); Gordon Oliver (Captain); Garry Owen (Dopey); Marc Lawrence (Venetti); Emmett Vogan (Lieutenant); William Pawley, Al Hill, George Lloyd, Frank Faylen (Convicts); Max Wagner (Prison Runner); Ernie Adams (Fink); Raymond Hatton (Pawnbroker); Hal Neiman (Convict #38216); Glen Cavender (Convict Hastings); William Williams (Convict Conklin); George Offerman, Jr. (Young Convict); Lane Chandler (Guard); Edward Peil, Sr. (Deputy); Dennis Moore (Convict Simpson); John Ince (Old Convict); Ray Byrd (Policeman on Phone); Ray Flynn (Police Officer); Claire White, Jack Mower (Couple in Car); Douglas Wood (Chairman of Prison Board); Ernest Wood (Attorney); Saul Gorss (Clerk); Jerry Fletcher (Hoffman); Ralph Dunn (Head Guard); Frank Fanning (Cop in Radio Car); Bob Wilkie (Young Convict in Riot).

With prison conditions and convict escape attempts so much in the U.S. news in 1937, it was little wonder that Warner Bros. intensified its output of topical prison movies. It seemed as if the studio was singlehandedly providing filmgoers with a guided tour of America's most heinous penal institutions. There was *Alcatraz Island* (1937), q.v., *Blackwell's Island* (1937), and now *San Quentin*.

Although director Lloyd Bacon took advantage of cost-saving (and adding of realism) location filming at the infamous California penitentiary to capture masses of convicts in the exercise yard, etc., *San Quentin* carried its own special disclaimer:

> The story, all names and characters and incidents portrayed in this production are fictitious. No identification with actual persons living or deceased is intended or should be inferred.
>
> No portrayal or scenes in which recognition of any individual is possible was made of any actual prison inmate or in any penal institution.

Morale among prisoners at San Quentin is at a low ebb. The evil Lieutenant Druggin (Barton MacLane) has been in temporary command of the guards and his mean ways has earned him the enmity of the embittered convicts. One of them, Venetti (Marc Lawrence), is near the breaking point and, in the exercise yard, he discusses this arch enemy with another inmate:

> VENETTI: Some day I'm going to kill that guy. Stick 'em [i.e. the prisoners] in solitary. Put us all in the cooler. Beat our brains out. Take a bath in our blood, it will make you sleep better.

Even the benign Warden Taylor (Joseph King) is well aware of Druggin's shortcomings. (Why he has not fired the maladjusted keeper can only be attributed to plotline necessity.) Taylor advises his out-of-control subordinate that he is *not* going to be made permanent captain of the guards:

> You're not the man for the job, you've proved that. You're as good as any officer I've known on handling the general routine of a prison. But you can't handle these convicts. You don't know men. A while ago it was small riots, now it's open rebellion. The public is demanding they be stopped and they're right.

The laissez-faire Taylor has selected Captain Stephen Jameson (Pat O'Brien) to be Yard Chief of San Quentin. Jameson is on leave from the Army to handle this new assignment. Excited by the challenge, he cavalierly insists to his drinking buddies one night before embarking on his new command, "You can't rib me about the prison routine. What's the difference if it's behind stone walls or any army camp?"

Arriving at the foreboding facility, bright-eyed, enthusiastic Jameson is counseled by the progressive-thinking (albeit inept) warden: "What we need is the self-respect belonging to a properly disciplined group. Now many of these men are here just because they had bad breaks. They're not born criminals and we don't want to turn them into criminals."

Strutting through the prison yard filled with sinister men, the buoyant Jameson addresses his new charges, "I'm not much for making speeches. I don't believe in them. I figure actions count a lot more than words. All I ask for is order and discipline. If anyone feels like getting funny, I guarantee I'll get the last laugh."

Druggin does his best to undermine Jameson's new regime, but Stephen holds firm. If things are not difficult enough for the new disciplinarian chief, soon he must contend with the arrival of a new convict, Joe "Red" Kennedy (Humphrey

Bogart). Joe just happens to be the brother of club singer May Kennedy (Ann Sheridan), the attractive young woman Jameson loves. Joe is a tough cookie who quickly takes the measure of his new environment, figuring he is tougher than anything the prison can offer. In the exercise yard, he discusses prison life with another inmate, "Sailor Boy" Hansen (Joseph Sawyer), the latter a hardened criminal who treats his own return to prison like coming home. However, even Sailor Boy is apprehensive about his latest lock up in the big house.

> HANSEN: Wait till you've been here a stretch. You'll feel like you're in a telephone booth with four other guys and no phone.

> JOE: [Bragging] I'll be out of here like a fish. I got pals on the outside who can pull wires. I'll never sit in a cell and go stir crazy. I got too many pals who want me in circulation.

But Joe quickly discovers that San Quentin is no joke and that Jameson is no scoutmaster. The rebellious Joe spends a month in solitary confinement for his misdeeds. When he is allowed a visit from May, he puts the blame on Jameson for the "arbitrary" punishment. Joe pressures May to sneak him money and when she is caught doing so by the security guards, she is severely reprimanded by Jameson. He insists that he is not being unduly hard on Joe and that, "I've handled men all my life. I think I know something about them. That's my job. That's why I'm here."

Later, Stephen proves his mettle when a convict goes berserk in the yard and shoots a guard with a contraband gun. The courageous Jameson walks into the midst of the tough crowd and takes the weapon away from the crazed inmate. His action gains him tremendous respect with the convicts. However, later when some of the men are denied the privilege of working on the road gang (which breaks up their daily routine) they begin a riot. Newspaper headlines blare forth "Convicts On Strike!" The nervous prison board wants to make Jameson their scapegoat, but he refuses to be cowed. Instead, he offers them a lesson in modern penology:

> There are two types of men in this prison. The first type, no matter what you do for them, they'll never reform. They're habitual criminals. They've spent most of their lives in prison. They're very clever at earning credit to get themselves the softest jobs. They ask to go on the road gang primarily with the hope of escape. Now the second group are definitely trying to reform and they're sincere and they deserve rewards. And if I stay here, I'm going to see they get them.

All of Jameson's continued efforts to reform Joe are destroyed when fellow convicts insist to Joe that May is having sexual relations with Jameson in order to get special favors for her brother. In desperation Joe decides to participate in an escape, along with Sailor Boy. The latter is shot by pursuing guards, but the wounded Joe makes it back to the city where he confronts Jameson at May's apartment. In the scuffle that follows, Joe wounds Stephen. However, he comes to his senses. He realizes that Jameson and May are really in love. Understanding now that Jameson has meant well all along, he accepts that his continuing to remain at large imperils Jameson's reform efforts at San Quentin.

The remorseful Joe hitchhikes back to the penitentiary. Arriving at the main gate, he collapses, but revives enough to alert the gate guards: "Tell Jameson I come back. Tell the cons to play ball with him. He's a swell guy."

John T. McManus *(New York Times)* recognized that *San Quentin* was "another of those Warner Brother screen parables of prison life, this one dealing entertainingly enough and briskly, too, with the rehabilitation of a misanthropic mug.... The picture accents several points that the new criminology recognizes." McManus also noted, "Warners have brought these matters to the attention of the cinema public before, and probably will continue to do so as long as the Hays office taboo against out-and-out gangster picture prevails." *Variety* cut through the film's social message, observing, "*San Quentin* is stark, authentic-looking prison melodrama that misses being big entertainment because of a love story that is none too strong and a plot that is only moderately forceful." The trade paper added, "[Director Lloyd] Bacon has attempted to picture prison routine as it exists. This is more interesting on the whole than the plot situations."

By now Warner Bros. was a master at handling the prison genre. They were the best in Hollywood, proving that practice makes perfect. Between location footage and soundstage recreations, Warner Bros.' penitentiary movies had the look and smell of (theatrical) reality. Their expansive cellblock sets and the inevitable sequences of restless men milling in the exercise yard or marching to the chow hall always had the ring of truth, at least by moviegoer standards. With moist-eyed stars like Pat O'Brien to play altruistic keepers—in contrast to brutal guards like Barton MacLane—the stock company of studio convicts (Joe Sawyer, Marc Lawrence, et al.) could snarl through their rebellious paces very convincingly. One of the pretty distractions of such Warner Bros. prison melodramas was the frequent presence of rising star Ann Sheridan (1915–1967), who also appeared in *Alcatraz Island* (1937) and *Castle on the Hudson* (1940), qq.v. In *San Quentin*, the husky-voiced star performed the catchy song "How Could You" in a nightclub sequence.

231. *San Quentin* (RKO, 1946), 66 min.

Executive producer, Sid Rogell; producer, Martin Mooney; director, Gordon M. Douglas; screenplay,, Lawrence Kimble, Arthur A. Ross, Howard J. Green; art directors, Albert A. D'Agostino, Lucius O. Croxton; set decorators, Darrell Silvera, Tom Oliphant; music, Paul Sawtell; music director, C. Bakaleinikoff; assistant director, John Pommer; sound, Earl A. Wolcott, Roy Granville; camera, Frank Redman; editor, Marvin Coil.

Lawrence Tierney (Jim); Barton MacLane (Nick Taylor); Marian Carr (Betty); Harry Shannon (Warden Kelly); Carol Forman (Ruthie); Richard Powers [Tom Keene] (Schaeffer); Joe Devlin (Broadway); Tony Barrett (Marlowe); Lee Bonnell (Carzoni); Robert Clarke (Tommy); Raymond Burr (Torrance); and Rodney Bell, Larry Nunn.

Neither in quality or in entertainment value does RKO's programmer *San Quentin* bear any relationship to Warner Bros.' earlier (1937) effort, *supra*. The 1946 picture does have actor Barton MacLane from that prior film; this time playing a hardened convict. This mild production was from Martin Mooney, who had created a slew of prison pictures in the early 1940s.

The Inmate's Welfare League, an organization founded and maintained by convicts within California's San Quentin Prison, has come under media criticism. To counter the public outcry that he is pampering the convicts, Warden Kelly (Harry Shannon) of San Quentin brings a paroled ex-convict, Jim (Lawrence Tierney), who founded the League, and the notorious criminal/convict Nick Taylor (Barton MacLane), who had been "reformed" by the group, to a San Francisco press club dinner. En route, Taylor, assisted by an outside pal, Marlowe (Tony Barrett), escapes. In the process, the warden is shot and wounded.

Rodney Bell, Larry Nunn and Harry Shannon in *San Quentin* (1946).

News of this happening brings further pressure on the warden to disband the League. Jim volunteers to track down Taylor. The tight-lipped Jim uncovers that the escapee has headed to Fresno where he has embarked on a crime rampage. Jim follows Taylor to Fresno, not knowing he is being trailed by Schaeffner (Richard Powers [Tom Keene]), a detective who believes Jim is part of Taylor's mob. Schaeffer locates Taylor, but is shot during the confrontation. The police think Jim shot Schaeffer and he must hide from the law while continuing his pursuit. The showdown occurs at a deserted gun club where, in a shootout, Jim kills Marlowe. Taylor is then turned over to the police. The League is vindicated.

A. H. Weiler *(New York Times)* pinpointed the film's essential problem, reporting that it "suffers the curse of a split personality. For the storyline of this offering forks between seriously extolling self rehabilitation among convicts and straight cops-and-robbers adventure. And, rather early in its course, the yarn ... strays from its noble intentions to settle down to a traditional manhunt." In *The RKO Story* (1982), Richard B. Jewell and Vernon Harbin note in retrospect, "The picture had just enough social message to satisfy the critics, and plenty of action to please audiences looking for a red-blooded manhunt saga."

In the film's prologue, Lewis E. Lawes, the former warden of Sing Sing Prison, extols the praises of this film's rehabilitation message. *San Quentin* provided the feature film debut of actor Raymond Burr. For tough guy actor Lawrence Tierney (who made his reputation as *Dillinger,* 1945), *San Quentin* was a contribution of his two-fisted characterizations.

232. *Say It with Songs* (Warner Bros., 1929), 95 min. (Also silent version, 5,699′).

Director, Lloyd Bacon; story, Darryl F. Zanuck, Harvey Gates; adaptors/dialogue, Joseph Jackson; titles, De Leon Anthony; music director, Louis Silvers; songs: Buddy G. DeSylva, Lew Brown, Ray Henderson and Al Jolson; Dave Dreyer, Jolson and Billy Rose; camera, Lee Garmes; editor, Owen Marks.

Al Jolson (Joe Lane); Davey Lee (Little Paul [Joe Lane, Jr.]); Marion Nixon (Katherine Lane); Fred Kohler (Fred, Joe's Cellmate); Holmes Herbert (Dr. Robert Merrill); John Bowers (Surgeon); Kenneth Thompson (Arthur Phillips); Frank Campeau (Officer).

The tremendously popular stage star Al Jolson (1885–1950) had increased his standing with the public by headlining the motion picture *The Jazz Singer* (1927), in which his mammy-style singing could be heard by filmgoers. Having thus helped to launch the talkie revolution in Hollywood, the exuberant Jolson starred in several other equally mawkish yarns for Warner Bros. One of his more sentimental entries was *Say It with Songs,* a grandly improbable yarn, thankfully filled with many song solos by "the singing fool."

Hot-tempered, harum scarum radio entertainer and songwriter Joe Lane (Al Jolson) discovers that the duplistic manager of the studio, Arthur Phillips (Kenneth Thompson), has been making improper advances to Joe's wife, Katherine (Marion Nixon). The incensed Lane, who used to be a prize-fighter, engages Phillips in a fight and the latter is accidentally killed. At the trial, the Lanes's little boy, Junior, (a.k.a. "Little Pal," Davey Lee), innocently provides adverse testimony. Joe is sentenced to prison on a manslaughter charge.

Once in jail, the remorseful Joe is advised by his cellmate Fred (Fred Kohler) of the stigma attached to ex-convicts. Fred, who is divorced, advises Joe that he should do the same with his patient wife.

> What chance has a woman got being married to a convict? When I just come up here, my wife worked and slaved like a dog to take care of herself and the kid. But whenever they found out where her husband was, they'd either fire her or felt sorry for her, which was worse.
> What's the use of [a woman] waiting for a guy who's going to be an ex-convict all the rest of his life? Every time she turned her back, somebody would be saying, 'There goes Mrs. Jones. Her husband was a jailbird.'

Having been so advised, Joe realizes, "You know it's worse for them than for us taking the wrap."

When the loyal Katherine next visits, Joe urges her to divorce him. A thoughtful guard explains to the perplexed Katherine, "Don't mind *that*, lady. They all get that way in here!" However, Joe perseveres and the couple are divorced.

By the time Joe is released from prison, Katherine has married Dr. Robert Merrill (Holmes Herbert), an eminent orthopedic surgeon. Junior is now attending the swank McKinley School for Boys and Joe pays him a clandestine visit there. He is so overjoyed at seeing his offspring that he returns to the school frequently. One day, when Joe leaves the private day school Junior follows his father and wanders onto a city street. He is hit by a car, with the accident leaving his legs paralyzed and him speechless. Joe, who has been hiding his ailing son, is eventually so distraught that he carries his boy to Dr. Merrill's office. He nobly promises that if the doctor will operate and cure his boy, he will turn the child back over to Katherine. The operation restores the boy's ability to walk, but he still cannot talk. Merrill tells Katherine that perhaps a shock may restore the youngster's voice. She plays a recording of Joe singing Junior's favorite song, "Little Pal." This causes the boy to dream that his beloved dad is with him once again. The boy awakens and now can talk. At the finale, a jubilant Joe is again singing on the airwaves. As he concludes his successful broadcast, he tells his listening wife and son that he will be right back home.

While granting that "one is impressed with his [Al Jolson] remarkable personality," Mordaunt Hall *(New York Times)* admitted, "The story . . . at first gives promise of being quite original, but in the later episodes it lapses into sentimentality that makes it somewhat tedious. . . ." He termed the film's dialogue "maladroit" and that precocious child actor Davy Lee "is forced to utter lines and go through acting that is suitable as entertainment only for immature mentalities." As for the behind-bars sequences, Hall decided, "When the inevitable prison garb and bars are brought into the scenes the story becomes wishy-washy, with tears on all sides. . . ." *Variety* was more generous when it judged, "He plays more naturally [in *Say It with Songs*] and looks the human Al Jolson on the screen, even in the betterment of his make up, than previously."

Of all the improbable scenes in *Say It with Songs* perhaps none are so incredible as those lensed behind the prison walls. Even the receptive *Variety* reporter had to admit it was a bit much to swallow "to have a prisoner sing to synchronized music" as in *Say It with Songs*. In the course of *Say It with Songs,* the heroic underdog (Al Jolson), a respectful inmate (with cap in hand and smile planted firmly on his face) sings the maudlin "Why Can't You?" His persuasive rendition of this tearjerking melody turns even the most hardened convicts into marshmallows. The state prison is so progressive (compared to the then harsh reality) that the administration has a Christmas variety show which boasts a national radio hookup. Joe entertains the very well behaved convicts with "One Sweet Kiss" and a reprise of "Little Pal." Compared to most convicts who in the 1920s left prison more hardened, more embittered men, Joe emerges from his several years behind bars, a calmed, less impulsive version of his former irresponsible self.

For the record, Al Jolson performed seven numbers in *Say It with Songs:* "Little Pal," "I'm in Seventh Heaven," "Why Can't You," "Used to You," "Just One Sweet Kiss," "I'm Ka-ra-zy for You" and "Back in Your Own Back Yard."

Seven years later, another screen singer, crooner Bing Crosby would go to prison in the course of *Pennies from Heaven,* q.v., which was equally unconvincing in its depiction of penitentiary life. Hollywood just kept insisting that gullible moviegoers would buy *anything.*

233. *Scared Straight! Another Story* (CBS–TV, Nov. 6, 1980), color, 100 min.

Executive producer, John T. Reynolds; producer, Arnold Shapiro; associate producer, William Watkins; director, Richard Michaels; teleplay, Thomas S. Cook; art director, John Kuri; music, Dana Kaproff; camera, Hector Figueroa; editor, Harry Keramidas.

Cliff DeYoung (Paul Lipton); Stan Shaw (Carl Jones); Terri Nunn (Lucy Loring); Randy Brooks (Sam); Tony Burton (Rafer); Linden Chiles (John Loring); Don Fullivlove (Smash); Eric Laneuville (James); William Sanderson (Harlan); Nathan Cook ("Doctor"); John Hammond (Rak); Michael

Fairman (Warden Livermore); S. John Launer (Judge Wadsworth); Bebe Drake-Massey (Jean Lewis); Al White (Ken Sharp); Kevyn Major Howard (Robert Davis); Scott Edmund Lane (D. A. Harding); Carolyn Coates (Mary Loring); Jean Demter Barton (Mrs. Rakowski); Sonny Gibson (Officer Rawlins); Chuck Lyles (Tyrone); Doug Cronin (1st Inmate); Rodni Hardison (2nd Inmate); Jerico (3rd Inmate); Dan Halleck (4th Inmate).

In 1978 Arnold Shapiro produced *Scared Straight!* a powerful documentary about the Juvenile Awareness (Encounter) Program created by inmates of Rahway State Prison in New Jersey. The forceful offering won an Oscar and two Emmy Awards. A decade later, Shapiro produced this telefeature, inspired by the facts which led up to his acclaimed documentary.

Troubled youngsters, Terri Nunn (Lucy Loring) and John Hammond (Rak), as well as several black ghetto youths—James (Eric Laneuville), Sam (Randy Brooks) and Smash (Don Fullilove)—are heading for a life of crime. Guidance counselor Paul Lipton (Cliff DeYoung) arranged for the impressionable youths to visit Rahway Prison where they endure a shocking encounter session with hardened criminals (Stan Shaw, Tony Burton, William Sanderson, et al.). The inmates attempt to shock the teenagers into appreciating just how hellish prison can be and how much better it would be for them to straighten out their lives now. This leads to a reconciliation between Lucy and her father (Linden Chiles) and the reformation of Rak. However, one of the slum kids, Smash, eventually ends as an inmate himself.

Daily Variety acknowledged that the made-for-television feature "was a unique attempt to fictionalize the content and impact" of the documentary original. However, the trade paper admitted, fictionalization tended to sugarcoat the storyline to a certain degree." *TV Guide* magazine rated this recreation three stars." Most impressive in the teledrama was Stan Shaw as convict Carl Jones, who provides a hauntingly harsh monologue of the horrors of prison life, all geared to scare his young listeners straight."

234. *See You in Jail* (First National, 1927), 60 min.

Producer, Ray Rockett; director, Joseph Henabery; based on the story by William H. Clifford; screenplay, Gerald Duffy; camera, George Folsey.

Jack Mulhall (Jerry Marsden); Alice Day (Ruth Morrisey); Mack Swain (Slossom);

George Fawcett (Marsden, Sr.); Crauford Kent (Roger Morrisey); John Kolb (Jailer); William Orlamond (Inventor); Leo White (Valet); Carl Stockdale (Attorney); Burr McIntosh (Judge Hauser); Charles Clary (Rollins).

When his milk distributor father (George Fawcett) disowns him, reckless playboy Jerry Marsden (Jack Mulhall), needing some quick money, is easily persuaded to substitute for Wall Street millionaire Roger Morrisey (Crauford Kent) in a court hearing. Before he realizes it, Jerry is sentenced to prison for Morrisey's speeding violation. However, it proves to be a scant hardship, for here the elite of convicts have every comfort of home, and Jerry—thought to be the well-known capitalist—is welcomed with open arms. Meanwhile, Jerry falls in love with Morrisey's comely sister Ruth (Alice Day) and organizes his fellow inmates into a company to promote the product of an eccentric inventor (William Orlamond). Eventually Jerry is released from jail. He pushes aside the objections of the annoyed Morrissey, who found that Jerry's impersonation cost him dearly, and plans to marry Ruth. In addition, Marsden, Sr. agrees to purchase the new-fangled invention from Jerry's firm.

The *New York Times*'s Mordaunt Hall admitted that *See You in Jail* "is far from being an airtight narrative" but that it possesses "some good fun." Hall was amused by the storyline convicts who "seem to look upon their short sentences as something deserving of a chevron that marks them as members of an upper social strata." *Variety* rated this "Another light comedy" in which "There's very little action. . . . However, it's all cheerful, handled in good taste and gives an agreeable screen hour."

This theme of the upper crust dallying in prison would be repeated in RKO's *Millionaires in Prison* (1940), q.v., and the concept of resourceful convicts turned entrepreneurs would be resurrected in *Buy & Cell* (1988), q.v.

235. *Short Eyes* (Paramount, 1977), color, 104 min.

Executive producer, Marvin Stuart; producer, Lewis Harris; associate producers, Walker Stuart, Martin Hirsh; director, Robert M. Young; based on the play by Miguel Pinero; screenplay, Pinero; production designer, Joe Babas; set decorator, Pat Prather; costumes, Paul Martino; music, Curtis Mayfield; music arranger, Rick Tufo; songs: Mayfield; H.P. Denenberg and Hirsh; assistant director, Robert Colesberry; technical consultant, Keith Davis; sound, Bill Daly; sound re-recording, Richard Vorisek; sound editor, Maurice Schell; camera, Peter Sova; additional camera, Bob Kaylor, Eddie Marritz; editor, Edward Beyer.

Bruce Davison (Clark Davis); Jose Perez (Juan); Nathan George (Ice); Don Blakely (El Raheem [Johnson]); Shawn Elliott (Paco); Tito Goya (Cupcakes [Julius Micado]); Joe Carberry (Longshore [Charly Murphy]; Kenny Steward (Omar); Bob Maroff (Mr. Nett, the Keeper); Keith Davis (Mr. Brown, the Keeper); Miguel Pinero (Go Go); Willie Hernandez (Cha Cha); Tony De Benedetto (Tony); Bob O'Connell (Captain Allard); Mark Margolis (Mr. Morrison); Richard Matamoros (Gomez); Curtis Mayfield (Pappy); Freddie Fender (Johnny); Harry Baker, Bob Balhatchet, Brodie Barr, Sam Barton, Thommie Blackwell, Richard Robinson Brown, Johnny Barnes, Ted Butler, Yusef Bulos, Carlos Corrasso, George Cox, Richard De Fabees, Nick De Marini, Shelley Desai, Orlando Dole, Charles Douglass, Juan Feliciano, Ernie Fierron, Fred Greene, Luis Guzman, Eddie Earl Hatch, Gerald Jaffe, Donald C. Hawkes, Lee Jines, Sherman Jones, Gordon Keys, Ruben Luciano, Leroy Lessane, Jose Machado, Pedro O'Campo, Ruben Ortiz, Edwin Perez, Rodney Rincon, Ramon Rodriguez, Joseph Rosario, Ronald Salley, Richard Spore, Joe Terra, Roy Thomas, Alberto Vasquez, Andre Waters (Inmates).

The stark and brutal *Short Eyes* is one of the American cinema's most naturalistic prison dramas, delving sharply into the social strata of a society within a society: that of convicts. It is based on the 1974 play by Miguel Pinero, which won the New York Drama Critics Circle Award for Best American Play. It "is so tightly and effectively constructed within its small enclosed landscape that not until it's over does one realize that this prison melodrama reaches well beyond the walls of the Manhattan Men's House of Dentention, where it's set. . . . *Short Eyes* has the natural eloquence and wisdom that one is supposed to find in street people — but seldom does" (Vincent Canby, *New York Times*).

"The Tombs" is the nickname for New York City's dilapidated male prisoner detention center, which has a high undercurrent of racial tension. The cynical, bigoted Officer Nett (Bob Maroff) allows a fist fight to progress between white "Longshore" Murphy (Joe Carberry) and political activist Black Muslim El Raheem (Don Blakely). However, when the latter seems to be winning, the white supremist Nett puts a stop to it.

A new prisoner is introduced into the crowded, filthy cellblock. The know-it-all

Longshore indoctrinates Clark Davis (Bruce Davison) into the practical protocol of his hazardous new environment:

> Niggers and spics don't give us honkies too much trouble. Good floor. Dynamite hack on all shifts. Stay away from the black guards. It's okay to rap with the blacks, but don't get too close to them. We're the minority here, so be cool. Ricans are funny people. Took me a long time to figure them out. And you know what, I realize I still got to learn about them. They get this big brother attitude about white folks in prison, but they'll also back the niggers to the T.

The authoritarian Nett takes an instant dislike to the bewildered Clark, "With you, I smell trouble.... To get a degenerate like you on my floor!... I'm goin' to bust your fuckin' face up so hard."

It develops that Nett's eight-year-old niece had once been raped and he has a burning hatred of all child molesters, the crime for which Clark is awaiting sentencing. Nett wastes no time in broadcasting to the other inmates about the newcomer's police record, knowing that convicts have a traditional antagonism towards a "short eyes" (the nickname with which such offenders are branded). Meanwhile, the paternalistic Pappy (Curtis Mayfield) stops a fight between two Puerto Ricans, but later the hustling "Go Go" (Miguel Pinero) plants a weapon in Pappy's cell and the older man is sent to solitary confinement. As punishment, the black inmates break Go Go's arm.

Further in the day the frightened Clark decides he has a sympathetic listener in the Puerto Rican Juan (Jose Perez). He pours out his troubled background of child abuse. By now, Davis is so confused by the blend of his past misdeeds and his present charges that he is not even sure if he committed the latest offense. His revelations eventually disgust Juan, who, nevertheless, warns Davis to have himself transferred immediately to protective custody *if* he wants to survive. Later, the cellblock takes Clark's possessions and subjects him to physical/verbal abuse. Thereafter, Davis is taken to a police lineup where a witness is scheduled to make a positive identification. In the interim, the powerful Puerto Rican Paco (Shawn Elliott) attempts to rape the young Cupcakes (Tito Goya), the pretty boy of the block.

Davis returns from the lineup and it appears that, through a technicality, he may escape prosecution. At the block council, the men decide Davis's fate. Neither Juan nor Ice (Nathan George), the leader of the blacks, wants to participate in Clark's death. Ice stands aside while Paco holds Juan back. The men seize Clark and the frightened man, in turn, threatens to report this attack. El Raheem cannot carry out his promise to kill Davis, but Longshore blithely cuts Davis's throat. Nett turns the other way during the murder. Eventually Captain Allard (Bob O'Connell) arrives in the block to announce that Davis's death is officially a suicide and to offhandedly mention that Clark was innocent of the charge made against him.

Cupcakes is given his release on bail. The streetwise Juan advises him to forget all about the recent murder.

The critics were duly impressed by the uncompromising realism of this drama, filmed within the actual inner city holding jail. *Variety* ranked the movie "a bold, direct, powerful, often brutal no-holds-barred slice of prison life. It is not a pretty or romantic sight.... There is never a doubt that the mostly black and Puerto

Miguel Pinero in *Short Eyes* (1977).

Rican inmates ... are criminals, prone to reveling in their past behavior." Canby *(New York Times)* perceived, "[T]he theatrical origins contribute to the claustrophobic atmosphere that is essential to the point of *Short Eyes,* which is about a kind of overcrowding that is the physical equivalent to emotional desperation. There's no way out." John Pym (British *Monthly Film Bulletin*) judged that the movie "has a ring of authoritative truth which, for all the film's faults, one cannot ignore.... The film's black moral — that in order to retain their sanity, the inmates have to find a scapegoat, someone whom they can persecute — seems in the end in no way commonplace.... The faults of the film derive mainly from Pinero's need to underline his moral."

Another fault of *Short Eyes* is its overuse of slang which occasionally makes the dialogue difficult to decipher. Then too, the characters sometimes lapse into lyrical poetic imagery which strikes one as too premeditated and out-of-place given the hellish setting. From their demeanor, it is evident that many of the cast's extras are real-life ex-convicts who passionately respond to this re-creation of bad times in their lives. The mixture of rough language, tough confrontations and the graphic slicing of Davis's throat give *Short Eyes* a haunting reality that is difficult to forget. Because of its intense realism (all the prisoners seem to be either homosexual, racist, or generally embittered) and the lack of traditional genre distractions, *Short Eyes* was too harrowing to be commercially successful.

Besides playwright/scenarist Miguel Pinero's appearance as Go Go in *Short Eyes,* musician Curtis Mayfield (who wrote the film's score) plays the bespectacled Pappy, while another musician, Freddy Fender, is seen as Johnny.

A.k.a.: *Slammer.*

236. *Silence* (Paramount, 1931), 60 min.

Directors, Louis Gasnier, Max Marcin; based on the play by Marcin; screenplay, Marcin; camera, Charles Rosher.

Clive Brook (Jim Warren); Marjorie Rambeau (Mollie Burke); Peggy Shannon (Norma, Jim's Sweetheart/Norma, Jim's Daughter); Charles Starrett (Arthur Lawrence); Willard Robertson (Phil Powers); John Wray (Harry Silvers); Frank Sheridan (Joel Clarke); Paul Nicholson (Walter Pritchard); J. M. Sullivan (Father Ryan); Ben Taggart (Alderman Conners); John Craig (Fake Chaplain); Charles Trowbridge (Mallory); Wade Boteler, Robert E. Homans (Detectives).

For time immemorial, men rotting away in jails have claimed they were innocent and had been falsely imprisoned. In Paramount's potboiler, *Silence*, the opposite is the case.

An aged Cockney prisoner, Jim Warren (Clive Brook) is fast approaching the date of his execution for the murder of Harry Silvers (John Wray). A chaplain (John Craig) comes to visit him in his cell, and Warren recalls the strange events that led to his present perilous situation.

Two decades earlier he had been freed from prison, helped by saloon proprietress Mollie Burke (Marjorie Rambeau) who has police friends. The aggressive Mollie wants to marry Jim, but his heart belongs to Norma (Peggy Shannon). The night before they are to be married, the police pursue Jim to Norma's apartment, about to corral him for a robbery. He hides the money at Norma's and then flees. Meanwhile, detectives (Wade Boteler, Robert Homans) arrive on the scene and eventually discover the hidden money. Years pass and Norma has died. Her child by Jim, young Norma (Peggy Shannon) is engaged to marry Arthur Lawrence (Charles Starrett). When Harry Silvers, Warren's one time pal, attempts to blackmail Phil Powers (Willard Robertson), the substitute parent of young Norma, the distraught woman shoots the crook. Warren takes the blame for this crime and ends in prison awaiting execution.

It develops that the clergyman to whom he confesses is really a newspaper reporter, sent to unearth the true facts of the case.

Silence was based on Max Marcin's 1924 melodrama. Mordaunt Hall *(New York Times)* was not persuaded by the contrived theatrics. He found it "rather mechanical" and the surprise ending "hardly plausible." As for leading man Clive Brook, a rather stuffed-shirt British actor, he judged, "Mr. Brook is efficient but he is sorely handicapped by the dialogue and to a certain extent by the direction." *Variety* found it "a literal piece with little if any of the modern subtleties...."

237. *Sing Sing Nights* (Monogram, 1935), 65 min.

Director, Lew Collins; based on the novel by Harry Stephen Keeler; screenplay, Marion North, Charles Logue; camera, Archie Stout; editor, Carl Pierson.

Conway Tearle (Floyd Cooper); Mary Doran (Anne McCaigh); Hardie Albright (Howard Trude); Boots Mallory (Ellen Croft); Ferdinand Gottschalk (Professor Varney); Berton Churchill (Governor Duane); James Thomas (Robert McCaigh); Lotus Long (Li Sung); Henry Kolker (Kurt Nordon); Richard Tucker (Attorney General); George Baxter (Sergei Krenwicz).

Sing Sing Nights is a silly whodunit that made for more effective fiction reading than screen viewing.

Gallivanting global news correspondent Floyd Cooper (Conway Tearle) has amassed a reputation as an amazing American reporter. Unheralded is the fact that this lowlife plays footloose with women's affections and embarks on crooked dealings at a moment's notice. When the wealthy scoundrel is finally murdered, there are three bullets in his body and three suspects—Howard Trude (Hardie Albright), Robert McCaigh (Jameson Thomas), Sergei Krenwicz (George Baxter)—each of whom has confessed to the homicide. Because the prosecution cannot determine who the real killer is, *all three* are sentenced to die in the electric chair. Later, Professor Varney (Ferdinand Gottschalk), the inventor of a newly perfected lie detector, insists that his machine can discern who the real murderer is. All three defendants recount their story to the criminologist who later reveals to the authorities who the real culprit is. The killer is electrocuted and the other two are pardoned by the governor (Berton Churchill).

Frank S. Nugent *(New York Times)* berated this "old-school murder mystery disguised under the flamboyant title of *Sing Sing Nights*. . . . This one is bad, indeed." *Variety* complained of the "Careless acting and direction, plus a hopelessly improbable continuity" and berated Conway Tearle for his scenery chewing.

238. *Six Against the Rock* (NBC–TV, May 18, 1987), color, 100 min.

Executive producers, George Eckstein, Merrill Karpf; producer, Terry Carr; associate producer, Adrienne Luraschi; director, Paul Wendkos; based on the book by Clark Howard; teleplay, John Gay; production designer, Peter M. Wooley; set decorator, Gary Moreno; costumes, Milton Mangum; makeup, Byrd Holland, Jack C. Petty; music, William Goldstein; assistant directors, Leonard Bram, Bruce Alan Solow; stunt coordinator, Fred M. Waugh; sound, Jock Putnam; sound re-recording, David Fluhr; sound editor, Deni King; special effects, John Eggett; camera, Philip Lathrop; editor, Rod Stephens.

David Carradine (Bernard Coy); Howard Hesseman (Joseph "Dutch" Cretzer); David Morse (Marvin Hubbard); Charles Haid ("Crazy" Sam Shockley); Jan-Michael Vincent (Miran "Buddy" Thompson); Paul Sanchez (Dan Durando); Richard Dysart (Warden Johnston); Dennis Farina (Birdman of Alcatraz); John Mahon (Officer Bill Miller); J. P. Bumstead (Officer Cecil Corwin); Tom Reese (Captain Weinhold); Ian Patrick Williams (Lieutenant Bergen); Lee Anthony (Lieutenant Joe Simpson); Scanlon Gail (Officer Baker); Eric Server (Officer Lageson); Greg Norberg (Associate Warden); H. Ray Huff (General Stilwell); Don Matheson (General Merrill); Wayne Grace (Officer Bristow); Newell Alexander (Officer Faulk); Thad Geer (Mail Guard); Ron Hayden (Officer Burdette); Joe Howard (Officer Fish); Fred Lerner (Officer Burch); Johnny Weissmuller, Jr. (Buckner).

> The ingredients are here—a fine cast, compelling premise, a heavy dose, by TV standards, of blood and death, and fingernail-to-the-nub levels of tension. *Six Against the Rock* is the kind of film that can truly be promoted, and that can hook the audience that's been drawn in.
>
> *(Daily Variety)*

On May 2, 1946, routine goes on as usual at the maximum security compound of Alcatraz Prison. However, six convicts are planning the impossible—to break out of the island fortress. They are: Joseph "Dutch" Cretzer (Howard Hesseman), serving life imprisonment for bank robbery and murder, Dan Durando (Paul Sanchez), age nineteen, serving ninety-nine years for a murder he committed at the age of fifteen; Marvin Hubbard (David Morse), age thirty-three, who is serving twenty years for armed robbery; Miran "Buddy" Thompson (Jan-Michael Vincent), who is serving twenty-nine years to life for killing a police officer and who has eight escape attempts to his record; hillbilly Bernard Coy (David Carradine) who works in the prison library; and "Crazy" Sam Shockley (Charles Haid), age thirty-seven, who is serving a life sentence for kidnapping and robbery and is most of the time confined to solitary.

Coy explains to Durando why he is willing to risk breaking out:

> You know how many bars there are on in front of my cell? Twelve. You know how many steps it is from my cage to the yard door? Forty-one. You know how many cells there are on the corridor? Fourteen. I used to tell myself when I run out of things to count that is the day I start dying. Well, I'm running out, Kid. I run out a long time ago and I am dying. So are you. You just don't know it yet. Is that what you want? To die an old man in this stink hole without ever seeing your folks again, without ever seeing nothing?

Coy has been developing the details for his bid for freedom for over seven years. As the plan is put into execution, his very impressed collaborator Hubbard, marvels: "It took him eight months to get them metal pieces out of the machine shop. Eight months hiding 'em in the toilet, and eight months storing 'em in his cell, so he could make it through them bars."

Later, after the six men have put their scheme into operation and four guards are held hostage, one of the terrorized keepers asks the distraught Coy if the dangerous plan is worth it. "If I have to wake up one more morning in a cement cage 9' × 6', not even knowing if it's daylight outside. You better believe it's worth it!"

As events progress, the escapees find the keys to the outside wall, which the captured guards had hidden in a cell toilet. Realizing the situation is out of hand, Warden Johnston (Richard Dysart) summons help from the Marine detachment based on the mainland. Meanwhile, the convicts negotiate for a boat to escape from the prison island. A guard on the gun tower is killed in the volley of gunfire; and the vicious Cretzer goes berserk, killing the guard hostages.

By the next morning, the standoff continues. The military squad arrive and plot their strategy. There is concern that if grenades are used, innocent prisoners will be killed. The determined Warden Johnston insists, "There are no innocent prisoners in Alcatraz." By May 4th, the iron-willed warden has lost all patience. He orders the soldiers, "Hit hard and hit fast. If we have to, we'll blast 'em all to hell."

When the attack is over, Coy, Cretzer and Hubbard are dead and Thompson and Shockley are later executed in the gas chamber at San Quentin. Durando receives a life sentence for his part in the bloody riot. (He would be paroled in 1973.)

A final title card quotes:

> The first hours belong us. The last to God and the straightest shot.
>
> (Bernard Paul Coy)

Despite its efforts to be a realistic, gripping drama, something went amiss with *Six Against the Rock*. Many viewers knew from past genre studies that the escape attempt would fail, which thus robbed the story of any true suspense. One never has a real sense that this is a functioning prison; it all seems so staged, including the men parading about in their jailhouse costumes. *Daily Variety* analyzed, "[T]o truly satisfy that audience, it would have needed a remarkable escape story and/or insight character studies of the men caught in this deadly struggle."

This telefeature, which received a three-star rating from *TV Guide* magazine, was based on the 1977 book by Clark Howard. Howard had dedicated his factual study "To the men, guards and convicts alike, who did time on Alcatraz. And to the men who died there." In his author's note to the book, Clark put into perspective the enormity of this daring, ingenious escape which transpired in the midst of San Francisco Bay, while intrigued observers watched from nearby shorelines.

> The siege of Alcatraz lasted forty-one hours. Ending it required the combined efforts of prison guards not only from Alcatraz but also from San Quentin, Leavenworth, McNeil Island, and Englewood prisons, along with forces of the San Francisco Police Department, the United States Army, Navy, Air Corps, and Coast Guard, and finally, two assault companies of U.S. Marines.

It was one of the faults of this essentially pedestrian TV recreation that the viewer never felt any sense of the overwhelming odds confronting these desperate convicts. Then too, because the character delineations were so one-dimensional, audiences werre drawn to identify with the performers' professional personae. While _Six Against the Rock_ is far better than the parallel segment in _Alcatraz: The Whole Shocking Story_ (1980), q.v., it pales in comparison to the far superior prison breakout yarn, _Escape from Alcatraz_ (1908), q.v.

239. _6,000 Enemies_ (Metro-Goldwyn-Mayer, 1939), 60 min.

Producer, Lucien Hubbard; director, George B. Seitz; story, Wilmon Menard, Leo L. Stanley; art directors, Cedric Gibbons, Daniel B. Cathcart; set decorator, Edwin B. Willis; wardrobe, Dolly Tree; music, Edward Ward; montage, Peter Ballbusch; camera, John Seitz; editor, Conrad A. Nervig.

Walter Pidgeon (Steve Donegan); Rita Johnson (Anne Barry); Paul Kelly (Dr. Malcolm Scott); Nat Pendleton ("Socks" Martin); Harold Huber (Joe Silenus); Grant Mitchell (Warden Parkhurst); John Arledge (Phil Donegan); J. M. Kerrigan (Dan Barrett); Adrian Morris ("Bull" Snyder); Guinn "Big Boy" Williams (Maxie); Arthur Aylesworth (Dawson); Raymond Hatton ("Wibbie" Yern); Lionel Royce ("Dutch" Myers); Tom Neal (Ransom); Willie Fung (Wang); Helena Phillips Evans ("Peachie"); Esther Dale (Matron); Selmer Jackson (Judge); Ernest Whitman (Willie Johnson); Frank Lackteen (Bolo); Robert Emmett Keane (Sam Todd); Horace MacMahon (Boxcar); Jack Mulhall (O'Toole); Ernie Adams, George Magrill, Drew Demarest (Henchmen).

You may not believe the contrived nonsense of _6,000 Enemies_ for a moment of its hour's running time. However, this programmer is so slickly constructed and boasts such a personable cast, that it is still thoroughly enjoyable.

Debonair assistant district attorney Steve Donegan (Walter Pidgeon) has an enviable conviction record, having caused many criminals to be sentenced to prison. Among his latest cases is that of Anne Barry (Rita Johnson), a bookkeeper at Maritime Import Company. She is charged with embezzlement, but insists it is a frame-up. Thanks to Donegan's production-line legal prowess, she is convicted. This case is his 500th court victory and it leads to his election as district attorney. Now he embarks on his real war against the underworld.

Conniving gangster Joe Silenus (Harold Huber), wanting to end Steve's onslaught against his criminal empire, conspires to have Donegan.framed for bribery. Steve finds himself sentenced to a one-to-ten year prison term. He is ordered incarcerated at the state penitentiary, full of vengeful prisoners he caused to be there. Even before he arrives, it is arranged that inmate "Socks" Martin (Nat Pendleton) and his boys will kill the newcomer, if no one else does it before them.

Meanwhile, a new warden had been installed at the penitentiary. However, experienced Dr. Malcolm Scott (Paul Kelly) wonders about Warden Parkhurst's avuncular attitude, a manner garnered from his years supervising a relatively simple youth reformatory:

> SCOTT: You keep calling them boys. They're not boys, they're men. Bad men. Habitual criminals.
>
> PARKHURST: Boys, doctor. That's how I want to think of them. I handled a lot of them in the reformatory.
>
> SCOTT: But this *isn't* the reformatory. This is state prison. These men are two-timers, lifers, killers.... We're sitting on dynamite in this place. We have 2,000 more men than we can handle. The closer you pack them, the harder they blow up.

Steve quickly discovers how imperiled his life is. No sooner does he enter the prison yard (as prisoner #80975), than the inmates try to kill him by dropping a heavy plank on him. Later, they try to scald him to death. It is Anne, housed in the women's quarters of the prison, who saves Steve's life from the next death attempt. He is so preoccupied and her case had made so little impression on him, that he scarcely recognizes her. Once he does, it is love at second sight and he promises to help have her case reopened.

Scott quickly assesses that Steve's survival chances would be much better if he remained in the infirmary, even though it is filled with unpredictable lunatics. However, the jaunty Donegan, who used to be a prizefighter and then a plumber's assistant, insists on pursuing the latter career as his penitentiary occupation. Meanwhile, Donegan's younger brother, Phil (John Arledge), also a lawyer, is investigating Silenus and his empire, in the hopes of prosecuting him and proving Steve's innocence.

Things go poorly for Steve. The first time he enters the general mess hall, the embittered convicts almost riot. Later, in defending himself, Steve gets into trouble with the prison authorities. He is hauled before the self-absorbed warden, a man who exists in his own safe little world. While consuming his gourmet dinner, the administrator advises the undaunted Steve:

> This is a tough old world Donegan, and the way to get along in it is by adjustment.... Harmony. When we fail, we must be helped. Therefore, in sending you to solitary for a period of two weeks, I do so in no spirit of malice. We're all in this thing together.

Later, Scott hits on a plan to provide Steve with new respect from his peers. He arranges for him to fight Martin in a prison-approved boxing match. Donegan is unconvinced that this makes sense, considering Socks's pugilistic reputation.

> SCOTT: These men admire courage.
>
> STEVE: You mean I've got to be killed to be admired by these murderers?
>
> SCOTT: If they see you take a beating, maybe it will satisfy their lust for blood.

At the match, Steve puts up a good fight, but is beaten. Nevertheless, the convicts now respect him. An inmate spokesman tells the exhausted Donegan the good news:

CONVICT: The boys down there ask us to say we ain't got nothin' against yeah.

While Phil rushes to the prison to tell his brother of the evidence he has gathered against Silenus, he is murdered by Silenus's men just as he reaches the prison gate. The penitentiary guards capture the hoodlums. A riot breaks out, with prisoners attempting to escape and general mayhem ensuing. Scott is among the hostages held by the prisoners. Using his ingenuity, Steve quells the riot and Silenus and his mob are jailed. Anne is pardoned and she and Steve marry.

6,000 Enemies is filled with sharp moments that either reflect on the penal system or on the prison genre itself. There is the tour of old biddy socialites visiting the prison and being titillated by encountering real, live prisoners. They excitedly ask their tour guide, "Can we watch them eat in their cages?" There is the dour prison matron (played by Esther Dale, a frequent genre player) who incessantly tells the female convicts in the laundry workshop, "Dummy up! Dummy up!" When Anne Barry first encounters Steve Donegan in the prison, she knows all about his recent problems on the outside, explaining, "We get news, even up here."

B. R. Christler *(New York Times)* had sat through too many prison films to enjoy the current entry. He insisted, "[W]e've been sentenced to so many prison pictures by now, we begin yammering at the sight of a stone wall... The present stretch becomes a pretty tough one before it's over...." *Variety* was less jaded. "[D]irector George B. Seitz maintains interest throughout with a breezy and suspenseful pace, although at times yarn digs deeply into over-theatric situations. Prison sets and episodes are realistic, with a mess hall riot particularly well executed."

Clichés and plot contrivances aside, *6,000 Enemies* is one of the most casually enjoyable of the prison genre entries. It makes its preachment subtly, focuses on action, and uses the stereotypes of the convention to provide humor and insight.

240. *Skidoo* (Paramount, 1968), color, 97 min.

Producer/director, Otto Preminger; story, Erik Kirkland; screenplay, Doran William Cannon, (uncredited): Elliott Baker, Stanley Ralph Ross; art director, Robert E. Smith; set decorator, Fred Price; costumes, Rudi Gernreich; makeup, Web Overlander; music/songs, Harry Nilsson; music arranger, George Tipton; music editor, Fred Prior; assistant directors, Erich von Stroheim, Jr., Wallace Jones, Al Murphy, Steve North; sound, Glenn Anderson, Franklin Milton, Lloyd Hanks; sound effects editor, Donn Higgins; special effects, Charles Spurgeon; camera, Leon Shamroy; editor, George Rohrs.

Jackie Gleason (Tony Banks); Carol Channing (Flo Banks); Frankie Avalon (Angie); Fred Clark (Tower Guard); Michael Constantine (Leech); Frank Gor-

shin (Man); John Phillip Law (Stash); Peter Lawford (Senator); Burgess Meredith (Warden); George Raft (Captain Garbaldo); Cesar Romero (Hechy); Mickey Rooney ("Blue Chips" Packard); Groucho Marx ("God"); Austin Pendleton (Fred, the Professor); Alexandra Hay (Darlene Banks); Luna ("God's" Mistress); Arnold Stang (Harry); Doro Merande (Mayor); Phil Arnold (Mayor's Husband); Slim Pickens, Robert Donner (Switchboard Operators); Richard Kiel (Beany); Tom Law (Geronimo); Jack Rosenstein ("Eggs" Benedict); Stacy King (The Amazon); Renny Roker, Roman Gabriel (Prison Guards); Harry Nilsson (Tower); William Cannon (Convict); Stone Country (Themselves); Orange County Ramblers (Green Bay Packers).

The only possible reason to view this clinker is to watch (and sigh) as an amazing range of talent sinks beneath the weight of this laughless comedy.

Ex-mobster Tony Banks (Jackie Gleason) and his wife, Flo (Carol Channing), own a respectable business (a car wash) and reside in suburban San Francisco. His peaceful life soon takes bizarre turns. His teenage daughter, Arlene (Alexandra Hay), is enamored of hippie Stash (John Phillip Law), which drives Banks frantic. Then gangland figure Hecky (Cesar Romero) and his son Angie (Frankie Avalon) appears to advise Tony that their mobster boss, "God" (Groucho Marx), has a task for Tony. He is to eliminate "Blue Chips" Packard (Mickey Rooney), a jailed underworld figure, who is about to testify before a Senate crime commission in exchange for the promise of a first-class life in solitary confinement. Tony refuses this one last assignment, until his good friend, Harry (Arnold Stang) is killed as a threat to get Tony to accept the hit job.

While Tony is infiltrating the prison where Blue Chips is housed, Flo allows Stash and his hippie pals to camp on her front lawn. Thanks to accidentally swallowing LSD belonging to his cellmate, the Professor (Austin Pendleton), Tony experiences a drug trip. This hallucinatory experience shocks him into realizing killing is wrong. Thereafter, Banks and the Professor feed the prison population LSD-laced soup and make their breakout in garbage cans attached to balloons made from plastic trash bags. The flying twosome land their "crafts" on "God's" (Groucho Marx) yacht where Darlene is being held hostage. Meanwhile Flo and Stash—along with a contingent of flower children—arrive to rescue Darlene. "God" escapes on a raft with the Professor. Tony and Flo are reunited with Darlene, the latter planning to wed Stash.

The scenes of prison life in this labored farce were sad attempts at satire that comedians Jackie Gleason, Mickey Rooney and Austin Pendleton could not enliven, unless the viewer's funnybone is tickled by seeing overstuffed Gleason and pint-sized Rooney rushing around in prison stripes. Having the likes of Burgess Meredith as the warden, Fred Clark as a guard and Frank Gorshin and Michael Constantine as prisoners did not boost his lampoon of life in the big house. *Variety* rated this gigantic misfire as "a dreary, un-funny attempt at contemporary comedy. Over-produced, under-directed and lifelessly-paced...."

Some of the prison sequences were lensed at Lincoln Heights Jail in Los Angeles.

241. *Slammer Girls* (Lightning Pictures, 1987), color, 80 min.

Producer, Chuck Vincent; associate producer, Jeanne O'Grady; director, Vincent; screenplay, Craig Horrall, Vincent, Rick Marx, Larue Watts; additional dialogue, Watts; costumes, Eddie Heath; makeup, Eva Polyka; music, Ian Shaw, Kai Joffe; assistant directors, Bill Slobodian, John Weidner; camera, Larry Revne; editor, Marc Ubell [Chuck Vincent].

Devon Jenkin (Melody Campbell); Jeff Eagle (Raquel [Harry Wiener]); Jane Hamilton (Miss Crabapples); Ron Sullivan [Henri Parchard] (Governor Caldwell); Tally Brittany [Chanel] (Candy Treat); Darcy Nychols (Tank); Stasia Micula (Mosquito);

Sharon Cain (Rita); Beth Broderick (Abigail); Sharon Kelly (Professor); Kim Kafkaloff (Ginny); Philip Campanaro (Gary); Michael Hentzman (Russell); Louis Bonanno (Cabby); Jane Dorskey (Jailer); Sheila Shick (Susan); Peter Rado (Sergeant Santini); Captain Haggerty (Sally); David Reingold (Aide); Bill Slobodian (Priest); Scott Baker (Doctor); John Boyd (Conductor); Frank Manceso (Cop); Marla Machent (Hooker); Donna Davidge (Cauliflower); Joel Nagle (Orderly); Beatrice Lynn (Potato); Carol Ford (Druggie Con); Chris McNami (Obese Con); Isabelle Cullinen (Lonely Con); Jackyln Sydney (Tough Con);

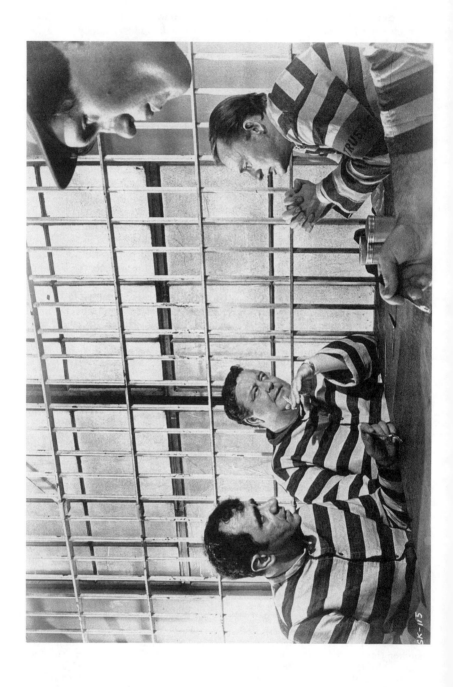

Larry Catanzano (Laundry Supervisor); Dave Mazzeo (Reporter); Lloyd T. Williams, Ron Chalon, Jay Lanno, Andy Kristie (Guards); Adam Fried, Joe Prichard (Laundry Men); Sara Warrington (Little Girl); Sheryl Marshall, Scarlet Smith, Carol Cross (Shower Girls); Steve Lazaroff, Rick Kessler, Michael Knight, Gary Zelman, Joel Von Ornsteiner, Todd Green (Guards).

The R-rated *Slammer Girls* was made in 1985, but not released until 1987. Intended as a broad satire of softcore pornography/women-behind-bars movies, it is pretty lame material which "comes off as silly rather than funny. . . ." (*Variety*). Depending on how tolerant a mood the viewer is in, this weak farce can be occasionally amusing or downright boring. Compared to the chauvinistic films it wants to satirize, there is relatively little nudity, raunch or down-and-dirty tussling.

The picture opens with a political message telecast by Jackson Caldwell (Ron Sullivan), a candidate for state governor. As part of his campaign platform, he insists:

> I represent humanity. I want to protect the common man from the murderers and the thugs and the perverts that roam this state. If I'm elected governor, I'll work for stiffer sentences.
>
> Now this chair [pointing to an electric chair positioned on the stage] cost the state a mere $10,000. Compare that to $30,000 a year per prisoner times twenty. With just one flick of this switch we can save the state $500,000. How can we as tax payers continue not to flip that switch?
>
> This man here [pointing to a hulking, hooded brute] was an executioner. Do you realize that the word "executioner," one of the world's oldest professions, is practically missing from Webster's Dictionary?
>
> Thank you. When you go to the poll this Tuesday, please put the word "death" back in the dictionary.

No sooner does Caldwell wins the election, than he is shot in the groin by a mysterious blonde woman with a tousled Dolly Parton hairdo. After a massive hunt, the chief suspect, the virginal Melody Campbell (Devon Jenkins), is captured by the police on her wedding night. She is sentenced to twenty years in the slammer. The state prison's newly appointed head administrator vows, "Miss Campbell will get no special privileges while I'm warden. She will be brutally abused like all the other prisoners!"

Still protesting her innocence, Melody is discharged at the foreboding prison early one morning. She is greeted by the sinister head Matron Crabapples (Jane Hamilton):

> CRABAPPLES: We've been expecting you, Melody. Your reservation has been confirmed. Your room is ready. . . .
>
> MELODY: You don't understand. I was framed!
>
> CRABAPPLES: [After slapping Melody] Put that back in an old Susan Hayward movie. I want it clear who runs things around here. . . . Me!

The frightened Melody is inducted into the dormitory bullpen, full of toughies, weirdos, and burnouts. "Welcome to death's door," says one hospitable

Opposite: **Michael Constantine, Jackie Gleason, Frank Gorshin and Richard Kiel in *Skidoo* (1968).**

inmate. Melody is just in time to witness a fellow inmate being escorted off to die in the electric chair, with the convict insisting, "I want to live. . . . I want to live." After the condemned prisoner has paid for her crime, taps blow. Later, Crabapples returns to the dormitory to advise the other inmates to watch over Melody, "[Y]our new playmate. Keep your eyes on her, girls. If she acts up, you *all* die." Before long, Melody is dragged by the others to the showers, the favorite recreational activity for the convicts.

Meanwhile, reporter Harry Weiner (Jeff Eagle) of the *Bad News Tribune,* discovers that Governor Caldwell has a vested interest in capital punishment; he owns the firm that manufactures the electric chairs. Going undercover in drag as a convict named Raquel, Harry joins the prison population, intent on learning the truth of why Melody shot the Governor.

In the coming days, Melody receives the brunt of Crabapples's sadistic punishments. The head matron holds an auction to determine how many whip lashes Melody will receive. Later, the abused heroine is dumped into solitary confinement, where another punished soul down the corridor says, "Welcome to Loch Ness." In the distance yet another inmate can be heard singing, "Nobody Knows the Trouble I've Seen." Melody has scarcely been released back into general population before she participates in a would-be breakout. It fails, and as ringleader, she is sent to solitary again. As she is being led away, a sympathizing jailmate reasons, "Look at the bright side. You'll be able to get in touch with your feelings and sort things out."

When Melody is released from the lockup, she admits, "I'm a hard core criminal. I've done my time . . . the pits . . . I'm a con!" Soon, Melody, Raquel/Harry and the girls plot their escape. They make it over the walls and flee via a taxi cab. However, Melody is caught. When brought before the Governor she admits she did shoot him, explaining she is his illegitimate daughter whom he abandoned years ago. With everything now resolved, the Governor serves as best man as Melody and Harry marry at the prison, with the approving inmates looking on. Melody and Harry plan to collaborate on a best-seller about her prison experiences, which they intend to adapt for the movies.

Despite the strained humor, the failed satire, and the very bad acting, there are a few moments of inspired lunacy within *Slammer Girls.* When Melody has her prison mug shot taken, the photographer uses a backdrop of tropical trees. When she is about to be fingerprinted, the matron insists, "Give me five!" Among the lunatic inmates is Abigail (Beth Broderick), an attorney/convict who refuses to get herself sprung from prison because she is doing so well defending fellow convicts at $10,000 per case. There is the pregnant convict, who insists she has gotten in the family way playing with a rubber doll. Finally, whenever things get dull on convict row, one of the girls is certain to suggest, "Let's go to the showers. Let's go to the showers."

Variety's reviewer offered a parting caveat. "Filmmaker Chuck Vincent makes a similar mistake as the unsuccessful New World spoof in the same vein, *Reform School Girls* [1986, q.v.], in thinking that exaggeration and hambone 'acting' is funny or campy. In fact, the original women's prison films, whether from the '50s or '70s, definitively provide the drama and/or laughs without need of highlighting."

A.k.a.: *The Big Slammer.*

242. *The Slams* (Metro-Goldwyn-Mayer, 1973), color, 91 min.

Producer, Gene Corman; director, Jonathan Kaplan; screenplay, Richard L. Adams; art director, Jack Fisk; wardrobe, Jodie Tillen; music, Luther Henderson; assistant directors, Thalmus Rasulala, Nate Long; sound, Bill Kaplan; camera, Andrew Davis; editor, Morton Tubor.

Jim Brown (Curtis Hook); Judy Pace (Iris Daniels); Roland "Bob" Harris (Captain Stambell); Paul E. Harris (Jackson Barney); Frank De Kova (Campiello); Ted Cassidy (Glover); Frenchie Guizon (Macey); John Dennis (Sergeant Flood); Jac Emil (Zack); Quinn Redecker (Warden); Betty Cole (Mother); Robert Phillips (Cobalt); Jan Merlin (Saddler); Dick Miller (Cab Driver); and: Carmen Argenziano, Rudy Challenger, John Lipton.

Like the cycle of black exploitation features, Jim Brown's movie career has risen and begun a downslide since the time of *Riot* (1969), q.v. Nevertheless, the blood-and-guts *The Slams* (which *Variety* labeled a "racial prison meller for people who hate people") was far and away better than Brown's other genre piece of 1973, the weak *I Escaped from Devil's Island,* q.v.

Rugged Curtis Hook (Jim Brown) has stolen $1,500,000 in mob money and thrown away a stash of heroin, both of which he took from the syndicate who was preying on the black ghetto. His double-crossing confederates wound Hook during a chase to the death. When his van crashes, Curtis is hospitalized and then transferred to the California Penal Institution, better known as "the Slams." The underworld has ordered a contract on Hook's life, but the new convict refuses to cooperate with the FBI who pressure him to testify about the Mafia.

Inside the prison walls, tough Hook refuses to associate with white hoodlum Campiello (Frank De Kova) and his underlings or with the competing black group headed by Macey (Frenchie Guizon). Hook is on his own in the big house, with no one to turn to, especially not vicious Captain Stambell (Roland "Bob" Harris), who offers to break Hook out of prison to retrieve the hidden loot for himself. Curtis's only option is to escape. He relies on his girlfriend, Iris Daniels (Judy Pace) and old pal Jackson Barney (Paul E. Harris) to help execute his crafty plan which calls for misleading the prison guards as to his escape route. Stambell discovers Hook about to make his break and the inmate kills his greedy keeper, puts his clothes and ID bracelet on the corpse and drops it into a cement mixer. Hook successfully climbs over the wall and is soon enjoying the good life on the high seas with accommodating Iris.

At least in the much higher caliber *Riot,* the violence and gore was an integral part of the storyline of explosive convicts going wild. However, in *The Slams,* the bloodshed, sadism and tough confrontations are gratuitous efforts to live up to the demands of the blaxploitation idiom. Prison life in *The Slams* goes beyond a macho excursion in survival; it is gore for the sake of gore. (Granted there are a few wry touches such as the prison guard who is concerned that carrying out his job will spoil his fresh manicure, or the guard captain's oozing remains disturbing a group of prison officials.)

When *The Slams* was finally released in England in 1981 in an eighty-seven minute version, Paul Taylor (British *Monthly Film Bulletin*) was appreciative of the tongue-in-cheek nature he perceived in this vicious entry. "Shake off a few of the cobwebbed clichés of the prison race-war, indulgently overlook the gratuitously brattish homages to [director Alfred] Hitchcock . . . and one finds an action-caper that licks along at a fair pace, leaking endearingly ironic (if not downright black) humour in the most unexpected places."

243. *Smashing the Money Ring* (Warner Bros., 1939), 57 min.

Producer, Bryan Foy; director, Terry Morse; based on the story "Murder in Sing Sing" by Jonathan Finn; screenplay, Anthony Coldeway, Raymond Schrock; camera, James Van Trees; editor, Frank Magee.

Ronald Reagan (Lieutenant Brass Bancroft); Margot Stevenson (Peggy); Eddie Foy, Jr. (Gabby Watters); Joe Downing (Dice Mathews); Charles D. Brown (Parker); Elliott Sullivan (Danny); Don Douglas (Gordon); Charles Wilson (Kilrane); Joe King (Saxby); William B. Davidson (Warden); Dick Rich (Guard Davis); Max Hoffman, Jr. (Guard Shelden); John Hamilton (Night Captain); Ralph Sanford (Night Clerk); Sidney Bracey (Pop); Jack Mower (Night Guard); Nat Carr (Prison Doctor); Don Turner (Joe); Frank Mayo (Van Doctor); George Chesebro (Convict); Tom Wilson (Convict #18701); Jack Wise (Runner); Al Herman (Convict #15222); Dutch Hendrian (Fats); Lee Phelps (Gate Guard); John Ridgely (Policeman); Monte Vandegrift, Bob Perry (Guards); Ralph Dunn, Pat O'Malley (Custodians); Milton Frome (Bailiff).

As his third of four Brass Bancroft action programmers that Ronald Reagan made for Warner Bros. between 1938–1940, the actor starred in *Smashing the Money Ring*. If the plot premise seemed somewhat familiar, the viewer would be correct as it had been used before in *Jailbreak* (1936), q.v., and would be reprocessed yet again for *Murder in the Big House* (1942), q.v.

Crafty convict Dice Mathews (Joe Downing) and his gang use the prison's press to print counterfeit money. Through their outside connections they put the phoney bills into circulation. Mathews decides that a gambling ship owned by an ex-convict would be an excellent distribution site. The ship's owner, fearing that this illegal activity will lead to big trouble, has himself jailed. Meanwhile, U.S. Secret Service agents, Lieutenant Brass Bancroft (Ronald Reagan) and his associate, Gabby Waters (Eddie Foy, Jr.), who have been investigating the case, encounter the ship owner's daughter, Peggy (Margot Stevenson). The lawmen believe her when she insists that her father is innocent. Just as the governor is about to pardon the man, Peggy's dad is found dead. Brass is determined to solve the case and arranges to enter the prison, posing as a convict. He is soon taken into the counterfeiters' confidence and uncovers the corrupt elements among the guards. However, Brass's identity is revealed and he is taken for a one-way ride after a prison break. Thanks to Gabby and a backup force, Brass survives the ordeal. He and Peggy become engaged.

Variety admitted, "Picture is weighted down with more than its share of incredulous events and familiar developments." The trade paper added that the gambit of the hero/detective going undercover in a prison was an overworked ploy. Bosley Crowther (*New York Times*) only gave the film a passing nod. "It is cheap action melodrama, compounded of the usual prison-picture theatrics, and might—by a liberal estimate—have some appeal for the Junior G-Man trade."

244. *So Young, So Bad* (United Artists, 1950), 91 min.

Producers, Edward J. Danziger, Harry Lee Danziger; director, Bernard Vorhaus; screenplay, Jean Rouverol, Vorhaus; music, Robert W. Stringer; camera, Don Malkames; editor, Carl Lerner.

Paul Henreid (Dr. Jason); Catherine McLeod (Ruth Levering); Grace Coppin (Mrs. Beuhler); Cecil Clovelly (Mr. Riggs); Anne Jackson (Jackie); Enid Pulver (Jane); Anne Francis (Loretta); Rosita [Rita] Moreno (Dolores).

In the same year that Warner Bros. produced *Caged,* q.v., United Artists released this independent production. However, for *Variety* there was no competition:

"Such a subject lends itself to strong exploitation, but the film misses out principally due to its reliance on stock stir situations and a lack of imaginative scripting. As a result it emerges as routine supporting fare."

Dr. Jason (Paul Henreid) is the new psychiatrist at a girls' reformatory. He focuses his attention on four newcomers: Loretta (Anne Francis), a young mother, and Dolores (Rosita [Rita] Moreno), both arrested for vagrancy; and Jackie (Anne Jackson) and Jane (Enid Pulver), both sentenced for stealing. The compassionate Dr. Jason meets with each of these inmates and from their discussions he determines which duties at the reformatory would best help them to adjust. However, the ironhanded superintendent, Mr. Riggs (Cecil Clovelly), and Mrs. Beuhler (Grace Coppin), the sadistic head matron, countermand his suggestions. Social worker Ruth Levering (Catherine McLeod) observes the clash of wills and advises the doctor that it is useless to try to alter things.

Despite the obstacles, Jason perseveres. Later, he and Ruth gain incriminating evidence against Riggs for his brutalities against the young women. The frightened Riggs agrees to allowing Jason and Ruth to operate the institution as they see fit, if they will forget his past misdeeds. The two idealists make immediate reforms and the reformatory undergoes a miraculous change. The impact on the girls is amazing, as they are now filled with hope, rather than despair. Meanwhile, Riggs has been hoping for an opportunity to regain control. His chance occurs when Dolores commits suicide after Mrs. Beuhler cuts off her hair. In reaction, the frightened Loretta and Jackie escape. Riggs suspends Jason and Ruth and brings them up on charges before an investigating committee. Dr. Jason urges the girls to tell the inquiry board the truth about the brutalities they endured, but they are cowed into submission by Riggs. When Loretta and Jackie learn of Jason's plight, they return to the reformatory and confess the truth. Riggs and Mrs. Beuhler are arrested. Dr. Jason and Ruth, by now in love, take over responsibility for the reformatory.

Harrison's Reports ranked this "ordinary," and the direction as "not outstanding." The trade journal insisted, "As in Warner Brothers' *Caged,* to which this story bears a strong resemblance, the cruelty and inhumanity shown by the sadistic prison authorities towards the inmates are exaggerated to a point where it becomes difficult to believe that such conditions can possibly exist in this day and age." The *New York Times* was extremely harsh to this New York-filmed production, labeling it a "miserably inept little item." In fact, the overly-reactive reviewer contended, "*Caged* was pretty awful — that it is downright embarrassing to watch. It looks as though all of the performers . . . are rank and unencourageable amateurs."

Contrary to the critics' predictions, *So Young, So Bad* proved to be very marketable and profitable. It also helped to spawn the careers of three very talented actresses: Anne Francis, Anne Jackson and Rosita [Rita] Moreno. Like *Caged,* this independently-produced feature helped to carry the cycle of young women-behind-bars into a new decade of depiction and exploitation. Unfortunately, as the 1950s progressed, the quality of the genre pieces diminished, leading to such tawdry items as *Girls in Prison* (1956), *Reform School Girl* (1957) and *Girls Town* (1959), qq.v.

245. *Space Rage* (Vestron, 1985), color, 77 min.

Producer, Morton Reed; associate producers, Damean Lee, Patrick Wells; reshoot producer, Eric Barrett; director, Conrad E. Palmisano; reshoot director, Peter

McCarthy; screenplay, Jim Lenaben; art directors, Cliff Cunningham, William Pomeroy; reshoot art director, Richard Rollison; set decorator, Diana Allen Williams; reshoot makeup, Terry Smilyn; music, Billy Ferrick, Zander Schloss; music supervisor, Katherine Guittner; assistant director, Leon Dudevoir, Denis Stewart; stunt coordinator, Bruce Paul Barbour; sound, Nolan Roberts; re-recording, Wayne Heitman, Mathew Iadarola; reshoot sound, Calvin Allison; sound editor, Linda Fock; special effects, Roger George, Frank DeMarco; camera, Tim Suhrstedt; reshoot camera, Tom Richmond; editor, W. Peter Miller.

Richard Farnsworth (Colonel); Michael Pare (Grange); John Laughlin (Walton); Lee Purcell (Maggie); Lewis Van Bergen (Drago); William Windom (Governor Tovah); Frank Doubleday (Brain Surgeon); Dennis Redfield (Quinn); Harold Sylvester (Max Bryson); Wolfe Perry (Billy Boy); Ricky Superan (Kirk); Nick Palmisano (Carny); Rick Weber (Nose); Eddie Pansullo (Mean Guard); Paul Linke (Duffy); Gene Hartline (Bubba); Alan Graf (Tiny); Paul Keith (Dr. Wohlburg); R. J. Ganzert (Talahasse); Bob Lesser (Salesman); George Fisher (Felon #1); Tom Rosales (Felon #3); Hank Worden (Old Codger); Victory Palmisano (Little Girl); Esther Palmisano (Mother); James Faracci (Driver); Jim Bentley (Bob Smith); Susan Madigan (Mary Smith); William Madigan (Charlie); Dorothy Dells (Judge); Carl Strano (Prosecutor); Rick Seman, Greg Elam, Bruce Paul Barbour, Jerry Willis (Stunts).

If *Terminal Island* (1973), q.v., seemed crude, then by comparison to *Space Rage,* the former is a gem. Both blend science fiction with the prison genre, dealing with futuristic societies and how they cope with the institutionalization of criminals. Despite the presence of some "name" performers (Richard Farnsworth, William Windom, Michael Pare), *Space Rage* was such a botched product that much of it was reshot. Nevertheless, the resultant film was sliced to a thankfully brief seventy-seven-minute version. *TV Guide* magazine rated it only one star, while *TV Movies and Video Guide* (1989) judged it a "bomb."

Some time in the future, Grange (Michael Pare) is caught robbing the Bank of Luna in Los Angeles. He is sentenced to the Penal Mining Colony #5 in New Botany Bay where the convicts dig for bauxite and beryllium. His term is "forever."

Delivered by space craft, he arrives at Boxima Centauri 3, where Governor Tovah (William Windom) addresses the new crop of slave labor:

> You may have noticed that we have no walls here. There is a very good reason for that. There is nowhere to go. The only way off this planet is through the shuttle port, some two hundred kilometers over some formidable desert. We do only two things here: we fulfill our mining quotas and we prevent escape attempts. We have never failed at either one.

Should any of the more feisty convicts attempt the impossible—an escape—the prison camp has a ready reserve of bounty hunters, including macho Walton (John Laughlin) and the older Colonel (Richard Farnsworth). It is the no-nonsense Walton who tells the overstuffed Governor, "My job would be a hell of a lot easier if you'd clean up those barracks. You feed those men cheap booze and bad dope and then you put them at the mercy of the barracks' card sharps and pimps. Hell, no wonder they bust out!"

Needless to say, rebellious, virile Grange is among those who join in a breakout, which leads to an all out riot. In flight he encounters the comely Maggie (Lee Purcell) which makes him question his goal of leaving the penal planet.

It is hard to say which aspect of *Space Rage* is more deadly: the convoluted and puerile script, the leaden acting, the impoverished sets (the overcrowded barracks are tacky at best), or the vain attempts at injecting a commercial science fiction element into the anemic chase-and-pursue theatrics. Stitching the conventions of the prison genre into the proceedings did not spice up the weak broth.

246. *State Penitentiary* (Columbia, 1950), 66 min.

Producer, Sam Katzman; director, Lew Landers; story, Henry E. Helseth; screenplay, Howard J. Green, Robert Libott, Frank Burt; art director, Paul Palmentola; set decorator, Sidney Clifford; makeup, Bob Meading; music director, Mischa Bakaleinikoff; assistant director, Carter DeHaven, Jr.; sound, John Westmoreland; camera, Ira H. Morgan; editor, James Sweeney.

Warner Baxter (Roger Manners); Onslow Stevens (Jim Evans); Karin Booth (Shirley Manners); Robert Shayne (Stanley Brown); Richard Benedict (Tony Gavin); Brett King (Kid Beaumont); John Bleifer (Jailbreak Jimmy); Leo T. Cleary (Warden); Rick Vallin (Guard); Rusty Wescoatt ("Flash" Russell); William Fawcett (Bill Costello); John Hart ("Sandy" O'Hara).

Using a semi-documentary style (with occasional voice-over narration), *State Penitentiary* was a brisk programmer which covered its plot loopholes through speedy action. *Variety* rated it "an obvious little melodrama" and noted that veteran director Lew Landers "spots okay action among the prison inmates and generally keeps the film moving and the players performing acceptably."

Aviation engineer Roger Manners (Warner Baxter) is wrongly accused of embezzling $400,000 from his stockholders and is sent to prison. Even after he is imprisoned, federal agent Jim Evans (Onslow Stevens) continues to hound Roger as well as his attractive young wife, Shirley (Karin Booth). It belatedly occurs to both Roger and Shirley that Manners's partner, Stanley Brown (Robert Shayne), might be the actual culprit. Shirley travels to Florida where Brown is now residing, hoping to trick the truth out of the scoundrel. Meanwhile, Roger becomes the butt of convict hatred when he helps to quell a prison riot. Later, after unsuccessfully begging the warden (Leo T. Cleary) and Evans to free him for a few days to prove Brown's guilt, Roger escapes. Evans pursues and catches up with Roger, but relents and allows Manners to prove his innocence. They head to Florida together. They reach Evans' home just as Jim is attempting to wrest a gun away from Shirley who has uncovered the needed evidence. Evans is caught and imprisoned and Roger is finally set free.

State Penitentiary was shot at the State Penitentiary at Carson City, Nevada. This was the final feature for debonair, dependable Warner Baxter (1889–1951) who had won an Academy Award in 1929 for playing the Cisco Kid in *In Old Arizona*. Baxter had starred in such other genre entries as *The Prisoner of Shark Island* (1936), and *Prison Warden* (1949), qq.v.

247. *The Steel Cage* (United Artists, 1954), 80 min.

Producers, Berman Swarttz, Walter Doniger; director, Doniger; based on the book *The San Quentin Story* by Warden Clinton T. Duffy, Dean Jennings; *The Hostages*: adaptors, Doniger, Swarttz; screenplay, Oliver Crawford; *The Chef*: adaptors, Swarttz, Doniger; *The Face*: adaptor, Scott Littleton; screenplay, Guy Trosper; camera, John Alton, Joseph Biroc; editors, Chester Schaeffer, Everett Dodd.

Paul Kelly (Warden Clinton T. Duffy);

Maureen O'Sullivan (Mrs. Duffy); Walter Slezak (The Chef); John Ireland, Lawrence Tierney (The Ringleaders); Kenneth Tobey (The Artist); Arthur Franz (The Priest); and: Stanley Andrews, Morris Ankrum, Don Beddoe, Robert Bice, George Chandler, George Cooper, Elizabeth Fraser, Ned Glass, Herb Jacobs, Henry Kulky, Alan Mowbray, Charles Nolte, Gene Roth, James Seay, George E. Stone, Lyle Talbot, Charles Tannen, Ben Weldon.

John Hart, Warner Baxter, Brett King, Richard Benedict and Rusty Westcoatt in *State Penitentiary* (1950).

Earlier in 1954 Paul Kelly and Maureen O'Sullivan had co-starred in Warner Bros.' *Duffy of San Quentin,* q.v., based on the prison warden's book, *The San Quentin Story* (1950). That low-budget entry had done sufficiently well to en-courage producers Berman Swartz and Walter Doniger (who also directed) to spin off the movie into a teleseries. Several episodes were filmed and, when they failed to sell as a TV series, they were strung together as *The Steel Cage,* released theatrically by United Artists Pictures. Paul Kelly as Warden Clinton T. Duffy in-troduces the three tales, stating that prisoners, like any individuals, are looking for three things in life: humor, freedom and spiritual solace.

The Chef: a gourmet cook (Walter Slezak) has a rotten temper, which is why he landed in jail in the first place. When he is released after serving his time, his fellow convicts, who miss his excellent cooking in the prison kitchen, arrange with an outside contact (Alan Mowbray) to trap the cook into losing his equilibrium with the result that the man ends in jail again. Thanks to the understanding warden (Paul Kelly) and his wife (Maureen O'Sullivan), the hapless convict earns another chance at freedom.

The Hostages: Two convicts (John Ireland, Lawrence Tierney) are the ringleaders of a planned escape. However, when Tierney causes the death of Ireland's younger brother, also an inmate, the two engage in a deadly fight. Both end up dead.

The Face: A talented artist (Kenneth Tobey), who is also an agnostic, is serving a life sentence. A young priest (Arthur Fanz) asks him to restore a damaged painting in the prison chapel. In the course of the repairs, a deranged convict attempts to murder the clergyman. The artist, whose work in God's house has given him new spiritual insights, saves the priest's life at the cost of his own. The harrowing experience gives the man of cloth a new appreciation for life's caprices.

Variety judged, "The entertainment is spotty and slowly paced . . . and mostly on the grim side."

The Steel Cage played on a double-bill with the cop melodrama, *Shield for Murder*. The advertisements for *The Steel Cage* noted, "*The Strangest City in the World!* . . . *Raw Life.* . . . *Real Life.* . . . *Inside San Quentin Prison!*"

248. *The Steel Jungle* (Warner Bros., 1956), 86 min.

Producer, David Weisbart; director/screenplay, Walter Doniger; art director, Leo K. Kuter; music, David Buttolph; assistant director, Don Page; camera, J. Peverell Marley; editor, Folmar Blangsted.

Perry Lopez (Ed Novak); Beverly Garland (Frances Novak); Walter Abel (Warden Keller); Ted de Corsia (Steve Marlin); Kenneth Tobey (Dr. Lewy); Allison Hayes (Mrs. Archer); Gregory Walcott (Guard Weaver); Leo Gordon (Lupo); Kay Kuter (Stringbean); Bob Steele (Dan Bucci); Ralph Moody (Andy Macklin); Stafford Repp (Beakeley); Billy Vincent (Harry); Charles Cane, Fred Graham (Detectives); Carey Loftin (Truck Driver); Jack Kruschen (Helper); Edward Platt (Judge Wahller); Lyle Latell (Bailiff); Richard Karlan (C.O.D.); Frank Gerstle (Kadinski); Tom McKee (Sergeant Hayes); Eddie Baker (Schiller); Joel Smith (Newspaperman); Lane Bradford (Guard); Malcolm Atterbury (Mailman); Mack Williams (Lieutenant Bryant); Robert Bray (Lieutenant Soberman); Peter Gray (Lieutenant Murray); and: Mickey Simpson.

> [T]he story itself offers little that is original, but it holds one's attention throughout because of the competent direction and acting. The action moves along at a pretty fast pace. . . . No one in the cast means anything at the box-office, but the acting is good.
>
> *(Harrison's Reports)*

Because he refuses to squeal on his confederates, small time bookie Ed Novak (Perry Lopez) is sentenced to a year in the penitentiary. Once inside prison, he encounters tough Steve Marlin (Ted de Corsia), the head of the gambling syndicate, who is now serving time for income tax evasion. When Ed berates Marlin for not protecting him when he was arrested, the menacing hoodlum retaliates by having his convict cronies beat up Novak. Warden Keller (Walter Abel) interrogates Ed about his ordeal, but he refuses to disclose anything. Later, Ed witnesses Marlin and his thugs murdering a guard. Again Keller questions Novak and again he refuses to admit anything. Meanwhile, the warden lets news leak to Marlin that Ed had talked, hoping this might break the deadlock. It only leads to Marlin's men pummeling Ed yet again.

As protection, Ed details all the facts he knows about Marlin in a letter which he entrusts to prison psychiatrist Dr. Lewy (Kenneth Tobey). Marlin learns of this and has his outside gang members kidnap Novak's pregnant wife, Frances (Beverly Garland). The hoodlums warn Novak she will be held hostage until the incriminating letter is turned over to Marlin. Still later, Marlin lies about having just released Frances and Ed turns over the letter. Next, Marlin and his men attempt to kill Ed. The rumpus leads to a confrontation with the prison guards and, in the shootout, Marlin and his underlings die. The wounded Lopez finally agrees to turn state's evidence, hopeful of an early parole so he can be reunited with Frances.

Mickey Simpson *(center)* and Beverly Garland with unidentified actor in *The Steel Jungle* (1956).

There was not much unique about this pedestrian action offering. *Variety* reported, "The melodramatics are regulation, but the freshness of the casting is a help. . . . Some prison fight scenes develop the proper suspense feel. . . . One of the sturdier elements of the undistinguished *The Steel Jungle* was Gregory Walcott as a tough, crooked prison guard."

Walter Doniger had scripted and directed such genre fare as: *Duffy of San Quentin* (1954) and *The Steel Cage* (1954), qq.v.

249. *Stir Crazy* (Columbia, 1980), color, 111 min.

Executive producer, Melville Tucker; producer Hannah Weinstein; associate producer, Francois deMenil; director, Sidney Poitier; screenplay, Bruce Jay Freidman; production designer, Alfred Sweeney; costumes, Patricia Edwards; makeup, Richard Cobos; music, Tom Scott; songs, Michael Masser and Randy Goodrum; Scott and Rob Preston; choreographer, Scott Salmon; assistant directors, Daniel J. McCauley, Joseph Moore, Don Wilkerson; stunt coordinator, Mickey Gilbert; sound, Glenn Anderson; sound effects, Jeff Bushelman, Pat Somerset; camera, Fred Schuler; editor, Harry Keller.

Gene Wilder (Skip Donahue); Richard Pryor (Harry Monroe); Georg Stanford Brown (Rory Schultebrand); JoBeth Williams (Meredith); Miguel Angel Suarez (Jesus Ramirez); Craig T. Nelson (Deputy Ward Wilson); Barry Corbin (Warden Walter Beatty); Charles Weldon (Blade); Nicholas Coster (Warden Henry Sampson); Joel Brooks (Len Garber); Jonathan Banks (Jack Graham); Erland Van Lidth de Jeude (Grossberger); Lee Purcell (Susan); Karmin Murcelo (Theresa Ramirez); Franklyn Ajaye (Young Man in Hospital); Estelle Omens (Mrs. R. H. Broache); Cedrick Hardman (Big Mean); Henry Kingi (Ramopn); Pamela Poitier (Cook's Helper); Alvin Ing (Korean Doctor); Joseph Massengale (Ceasar Geronimo); Herman Poppe (Alex); Luis Avalos (Chico); Esther Sutherland (Sissie); James Oscar Lee (Kicker); Rod McCary (Minister); Claudia Cron (Joy); Bill Bailey (Announcer); Donna Benz (Nancy); Grand Bush (Big Mean's Sidekick); Thomas Moore (Judge); Danna Hansen (Mrs. Sampson); Gwen Van Dam (Mrs. Beatty); Herb Armstrong (County Jail Guard); Herbert Hirschman (Man at Dinner Party); Don Circle (Bank Teller); Kenneth Menard (Repairman); Billy Beck (Flycatching Prisoner); Lewis Van Bergen (Guard).

Gene Wilder and Richard Pryor had previously joined forces onscreen for the action train comedy *Silver Streak* (1977), proving that the mixture of a white and black comedian could lead to a satisfying buddy picture. The success of that lucrative box office hit led the two to reunite for this genre spoof, directed by Sidney Poitier. "As with its predecessor, the fun here is fast and intermittent, now taking a swing at the conventions of the prison-movie, now distilling wacky and special joys from the fanciful interplay of its unjustly jailed birds" (John Coleman, *New Statesman*).

In New York City would-be actor Harry Monroe (Richard Pryor) and ambitious playwright Skip Donahue (Gene Wilder) both lose their jobs. Skip convinces Harry that they move to California and try their show business luck out west. En route, they stop in the hick town of Glenboro for car repairs. To pay the exorbitant garage bill, they accept jobs as singing-dancing chickens, promoting the services of a local bank. Two crooks use their uniform to undertake a bank heist. Skip and Harry, on purely circumstantial evidence, are sentenced to 125 years in prison. The thought of being incarcerated frightens the men, especially Harry ("This ain't funny any more. I hate confinement.")

Inducted into Glenboro State Prison, Skip and Harry are nervous about coping with the tough inmates on their cellblock: the tyrannical Jack Graham (Jonathan Banks), the homosexual Rory Schultebrand (Georg Stanford Brown),

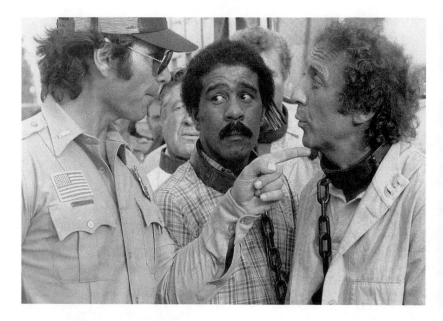

Lewis Van Bergen, Richard Pryor and Gene Wilder in *Stir Crazy* (1980).

the hulking mass murderer Grossberger (Erland Van Lidth de Jeude) and enterprising Mexican Jesus Ramirez (Miguel Angel Suarez). One day domineering Warden
Beatty (Barry Corbin) orders Skip to ride his mechanical bucking bull as punishment. Amazingly Skip proves to be dexterous and the amazed warden realizes that
in Skip he has the key to winning the intra-prison rodeo competition. Thanks to
the advice of conniving Jesus, Skip uses his position of worth to demand that
Harry, Rory and Jesus be part of his rodeo team. This leads to the group executing
an elaborate escape during the rodeo as well as Skip throwing the competition to
his rival. In the midst of their escape, Skip and Harry learn that the actual bank
robbers have been caught. Now Skip, dreaming of his play writing career again,
invites the comely Meredith (JoBeth Williams), legal assistant to his attorney (Joel
Brooks) to the opening night of his forthcoming play—whenever that may be.

The highlight of *Silver Streak* had been a marvelous sequence in which Gene
Wilder, to escape pursuing lawmen, disguises himself as a jiving black man,
coached in his masquerade by con artist Richard Pryor. Determined to match that
wonderful comic moment, *Stir Crazy* has a parallel scene in which Wilder's Skip
Donahue and Pryor's Harry Monroe are first introduced to the jailhouse cellblock.
Having firmly in mind that this is a dangerous place for even rough and tough
convicts—and they know they are wimps—the duo dredge out a masquerade of
bravado, hoping to fool the inmates into believing the newcomers are macho
dudes.

SKIP: What are you doing?

HARRY: Gettin' bad. Better get bad Jack, cause if you ain't bad, you're fucked.
If you're bad, they don't mess with ya.

As the goofy twosome proceed along the cell tier, Skip gets into the swing of things, jivin' along to his own rhythm:

SKIP: We're bad. We don't want no shit . . . no shit.

Later, one of the two poor souls, Harry, tries to convince Skip of how desperate their situation is, pointing out that this is no macho fantasy trip. "You don't get it Skip, do you? You think this is the Count of Monte Cristo or something, man. We're in trouble! This is the *real* deal!"

Eventually, the scatter-brained Skip, having endured the intricate induction process and succumbing to the deadening impact of the hopeless daily stir-life routine, has a bright revelation: "Harry, we're in prison!"

Many of the standard prison conventions are lampooned in hit-or-miss style in *Stir Crazy*. (With Sidney Poitier directing, the comedy is very broad indeed, the undertones are never subtle, and the stars are too frequently left to their own creative devices.) Within the plotline, there are the two underdogs (Wilder, Pryor), who protest their innocence to the end—when they are finally freed. There is the heroes' constant fear of being sodomized by their brutal peers. The convict population runs the stereotyped gamut: the psychotic killer (Jonathan Bank), the very gay inmate (Georg Stanford Brown) who has a yen for Harry, the gargantuan convict (Erland Van Lidth de Jeude) with a heart of gold, and to reflect the ethnic confrontations of post–1960s prison dramas, there is the enterprising Mexican (Miguel Angel Suarez). The heartless warden is shown as corrupt (he bullies his prisoners, refusing the chance of parole to any who do not participate in the annual rodeo games, and he diverts prize money from the competition to his own accounts). The deputy warden (Craig T. Nelson) is a tyrant to his charges and a wimpering toady to his superiors.

David Ansen (*Newsweek* magazine) judged that *Stir Crazy* was "only intermittently funny." He analyzed the problem as belonging to scripter Bruce Jay Friedman. "He's trying for a formula film and can't land on the right formula. Is it a buddy movie, a caper comedy, a parody of prison films, an urban-cowboy neo–Western, a New York vs. Sun Belt comedy? Unfortunately it's more of a shambles than any of the above, albeit a fairly genial one." Archer Winsten *(New York Post)* assessed, "Wilder and Pryor do . . . [their] respective stuff as before, with audience responses extremely mixed. To some it's uproarious. Others sit on their hands, as the saying goes. This is doubtless a factor of the special response to wide-eyed, curly headed Gene Wilder and street-wise, word-flinging Richard Pryor." Carrie Rickey (*Village Voice*) perceived, "Wilder is . . . burdened by an impossible role—a composite of *Cool Hand Luke*, Sullivan of *Sullivan's Travels*, and the quarterback of *The Longest Yard*. Even a gifted comedian like Wilder can't cope with the changes of character the scenario demands. . . . It would be easy to say that when the scene shifts to prison, the movie's tone begins vacillating between slapstick and serious and confuses the audience—but a movie like *Sullivan's Travels* does precisely that, very effectively, leaving viewers laughing at the serious parts and crying at the jokes. No such luck here." Richard Corliss (*Time* magazine) summarized the shenanigans with: "Recipe for a popular movie: take a series of stock situations, two gifted farceurs, and stir. Crazy!"

Stir Crazy earned $58,364,420 in domestic film rentals paid to the distributor. Wilder and Pryor would reteam again for *See No Evil, Hear No Evil* (1989).

250. *The Story of Molly X* (Universal, 1949), 82 min.

Producer, Aaron Rosenberg; director/ screenplay, Crane Wilbur; art. directors, Bernard Herzbrun, Emrich Nicholson; set decorators, Russell A. Gausman, A. Roland Fields; costumes, Rosemary Odell; makeup, Bud Westmore, Frank Westmore; music, Milton Schwarzwald; assistant director, Jesse Hibbs; technical adviser, Dr. Norman Fenton; sound, Leslie I. Carey, Glenn D. Anderson; special camera, David S. Horsley; camera, Irving Glassberg; editor, Edward Curtiss.

Jue Havoc (Molly X); John Russell (Cash Brady); Dorothy Hart (Anne); Connie Gil-christ (Dawn); Cathy Lewis (Molly's Roommate); Elliott Lewis (Rod Markle); Charles McGraw (Captain Breen); Wally Maher (Chris); Sandra Gould (Inmate in Sewing Room); Sara Berner (Laundry Worker); Isabel Jewell (Matron in Laundry); Katherine Warren (Matron); Richard Egan (Detective); Paul Bryar (Detective/Guard); Kathleen Freeman (Inmate, the High School Graduate); Nipper (The Dog); Anne Pearce (Laundry Worker Rescued by Molly); Ida Moore (Elderly Inmate); Stanley Andrews (Judge); Hal March, Bud Wolfe (Accomplices); Lee Phelps (Plainclothesman).

> The novelty in the story is that the central character is a sort of female gangster....
> The melodramatic plot wastes no time in love interest, but its unfoldment is so
> routine and mechanical that it fails to generate more than mild excitement at best,
> for it is neither a fresh nor a vigorous reworking of old situations.
>
> *(Harrison's Reports)*

After the killing of her gangland husband in Kansas City, Molly (June Havoc) moves to San Francisco and embarks on a series of crimes with two pals—Cash Brady (John Russell) and Rod Markle (Elliott Lewis)—of her late spouse. Meanwhile, Anne (Dorothy Hart), Markle's jealous girlfriend insists that Molly is interested in Rod. Markle admits he loves Molly and, with him in this mood, Molly gets him to admit he killed her husband. She guns him down. Brady helps her dispose of the body and the murder weapon. However, Anne tips off San Francisco Police Captain Breen (Charles McGraw) and he arrests the two fugitives. They are found guilty on a lesser charge, since the prosecution is unable to prove they murdered Markle. Brady is sentenced to San Quentin and Molly to Tehachapi.

Molly bridles at the prison's regimen, albeit enlightened. Eventually, she has a change of heart and develops into a model prisoner. Breen is still insistent on charging Molly with Markle's murder and arranges for Anne to be inducted into Tehachapi as an inmate. Anne is unsuccessful at pressuring Molly into a confession.

When Molly is paroled she finds work in Los Angeles and settles into a simple life. Through Anne she learns that Cash has been charged with Markle's murder. Molly rushes to San Francisco, finds the hidden gun and hands it over to Breen. She confesses to Rod's murder. However, a contrite Cash reveals that Molly had actually only wounded Rod and that he had completed the killing. The rehabilitated Molly can now start a new life.

Initially entitled *Tehachapi, The Story of Molly X* was to have originally starred Ginger Rogers. When she dropped out of the project, June Havoc, sister of Gypsy Rose Lee, took over the dramatic assignment. It was perhaps the best role of her screen career. However, the generally dreary movie failed to win over the critics. Bosley Crowther *(New York Times)* was almost snide in dismissing the entry, insisting it "carries a great deal more sentiment than conviction." As for the prison ambiance, he decided, "[T]he females with whom she [Havoc] is surrounded in his penal institute seem not much more wicked or unsocial than the young ladies in a Connecticut finishing school." *Variety* weighed that *The Story of*

June Havoc and Dorothy Hart in *The Story of Molly X* (1949).

Molly X, even with its theme of the plight of female ex-convicts' adjustment to civilian life, was "a standard type of gangster yarn" and that "the performances generally have a stiltedness that is consistent with the whole production." As for Havoc, the trade paper decided, "[H]er performance isn't enough to sustain *Molly* beyond the dualer situations."

The Story of Molly X* was shot on location at Tehachapi, California's (model) Institution for Women located at the base of the Tehachapi Mountains on the Mojave Desert where fresh air and sunshine were part of the rehabilitation process. Dr. Norman Fenton, the state's assistant director of the department of corrections, served as technical adviser. Other location footage included lensing at the Top of the Mark Restaurant in San Francisco. This picture provided the screen debut of the husband-and-wife acting team of Cathy Lewis and Elliott Lewis and offered an early appearance of future leading man, Richard Egan (1921–1987). Veteran director/scriptor Crane Wilbur (1887–1973) would later helm the genre piece, *Inside the Walls of Folsom Prison* (1951), q.v.

251. *Strange Alibi* (Warner Bros., 1941), 63 min.

Associate producer, William Jacobs; director, D. Ross Lederman; story, Leslie T. White; screenplay, Kenneth Gamet; camera, Allen G. Siegler; editor, Frank Magee.

Arthur Kennedy (Joe Geary); Joan Perry (Alice Devlin); Jonathan Hale (Chief Sprague); John Ridgely (Tex); Florence Bates (Katie); Charles Trowbridge (Governor Phelps); Cliff Clark (Captain Reddick); Stanley Andrews (Lieutenant Pagle); Howard Da Silva (Monson); Wade Boteler (Captain Allen); Ben Welden (Durkin); Joe Downing (Benny McKaye); Dick Rich (Big Dox); Paul Phillips (Crips Vossen); Joe King (Warden Morrel); Paul Stanton (Prosecutor).

> Originality was in short supply in *Strange Alibi*. . . . Exposing crime in high places was one of the studio's favourite themes, but as expounded here . . . it was singularly unconvincing.
>
> (Clive Hirshhorn, *The Warner Bros. Story,* 1979)

Honest police detective Joe Geary (Arthur Kennedy) stages a public argument with his boss, Chief Sprague (Jonathan Hale), so that he can establish himself as being on the outs with the law. He resigns from the force and promptly joins a gambling syndicate. He soon uncovers that its leaders are two corrupt policemen: Captain Reddick (Cliff Clark) and detective Lieutenant Pagle (Stanley Andrews). The latter is suspicious of Joe and follows him to a clandestine meeting with Sprague. Pagle kills Sprague, knocks out Geary and places the murder weapon in his hand. Joe is arrested and sentenced to life imprisonment. There his life is hell on earth, because it is known that he is a former cop.

Meanwhile, Joe's girlfriend, Alice Devlin (Joan Perry) works to find evidence to prove his innocence. Through a friend, Katie (Florence Bates), who owns a dockside cafe, Geary learns that the man who could establish his innocence has shown up again. Desperate to vindicate himself, Joe escapes from prison, but discovers that his key witness has been murdered. Later, Joe communicates with Governor Phelps (Charles Trowbridge), and, through a trick forces Reddick and Pagle to confess. Granted a pardon, Joe is reinstated on the police force. He and Alice marry.

Variety gave a back-handed compliment, "Plot is far from new, but hasn't been so frequently and nauseatingly repeated as a number of the others WB uses in its swiftie group. . . . [Director D. Ross] Lederman has had to dive into the stock barrel for a load of trite court and prison stuff which bogs the picture right down in the center." Theodore Strauss *(New York Times)* conceded that Arthur Kennedy provided a "credible performance" and that this unpretentious entry was of the "'I wuz framed' school of cops-and-robbers epics." As far as the penitentiary segment of the story went, Strauss jibed, "What brutality is committed there [behind prison walls] in the name of justice, only the Warners know."

252. *Sullivan's Travels* (Paramount, 1942), 91 min.

Producer, Preston Sturges; associate producer, Paul Jones; director/screenplay, Sturges; art directors, Hans Dreier, Earl Hedrick; costumes, Edith Head; makeup Wally Westmore; music, Leo Shuken, Charles Bradshaw; music director, Sigmund Krumgold; sound, Harry Mills, Walter Oberst; special effects, Farciot Edouart; camer, John Seitz; editor, Stuart Gilmore.

Joel McCrea (John L. Sullivan); Veronica Lake (The Girl); Robert Warwick (Mr. Lebrand); William Demarest (Mr. Jones); Franklin Pangborn (Mr. Casalais); Porter Hall (Mr. Hadrian); Byron Foulger (Mr. Valdelle); Margaret Hayes (Secretary); Robert Greig (Sullivan's Butler); Eric Blore (Sullivan's Valet); Torben Meyer (The Doctor); Victor Potel (Cameraman); Richard Webb (Radio Man); Charles Moore (Chef); Almira Sessions (Ursula); Esther Howard (Miz Zeffie); Frank Moran (Tough Chauffeur); Georges Renavent (Old Tramp); Harry Rosenthal (The Trombenick); Alan Bridge (The Mister); Jimmy Conlin (Trustee); Jan Buckingham (Mrs. Sullivan); Robert Winkler (Bud); Chick Collins

(Capital); Jimmie Dundee (Labor); Pat West (Counterman at Roadside Lunch Wagon); J. Farrell MacDonald (Desk Sergeant); Edward Hearn (Cop at Beverly Hills Station); Arthur Hoyt (Preacher); Paul Newlan (Truck Driver); Roscoe Ates (Counterman at Owl Wagon); Robert Dudley (One-Legged Bum); Monte Blue (Cop in Slums); Harry Tyler (Railroad Information Clerk); Dewey Robinson (Sher- iff); Madame Sul-te-wan (Harmonica Player); Jess Lee Brooks (Black Preacher); Harry Seymour (Entertainer in Air Raid Shelter); Chester Conklin (Old Bum); Frank Mills (Drunk in Theatre); Edgar Dearing (Cop, Mud Gang); Emory Parnell (Man at Railroad Shack); Julius Tannen (Public Defender); Gus Reed (Mission Cook); Perc Launders (Yard Man); Billy Bletcher (Entertainer in Hospital).

One would not expect to find a quasi-realistic chain gang prisoners sequence in the midst of such a wild and wacky comedy as *Sullivan's Travels*. However, eccentric and extremely talented filmmaker Preston Sturges (1898–1959) was noted for accomplishing the unexpected. Thus it becomes almost logical within this brilliant satire, which successfully bursts several balloons of American pomposity, to have the hero's cross-country odyssey interrupted by a sojourn among unfortunate convicts toiling in the swamps of the deep South. These scenes, along with the films *I Am a Fugitive from a Chain Gang* (1932), q.v., and *Hell's Highway* (1932), q.v., represent one of the most memorable depictions of man's brutality to man and an individual's overwhelming need to survive. The film stars the underrated Joel McCrea and that wispy beauty, Veronica Lake, along with the Preston Sturges stock company of adroit pranksters.

Sullivan's Travels opens with a special card:

> To the memory of those who made us laugh: the motley mountebanks, the clowns, the buffoons, in all times and in all nations, whose efforts have lightened our burden a little, this picture is affectionately dedicated.

Acclaimed film director John L. Sullivan (Joel McCrea) is noted for his profitable screen comedies. (As one approving studio executive proudly observes, "They don't stink with messages!") While the studio is hopeful that his next project will be *Ants in Your Pants of 1941,* Sullivan is determined to make a social statement in his next motion picture. He intends to make the "meaningful" *Oh Brother, Where Art Thou?* He has a vision about this project. "I want this picture to be a commentary on modern conditions, stark realism, the problems that confront the average man. I want this picture to be a document. I want to hold a mirror up to life. A true canvas of the suffering of humanity."

Studio executives Mr. Lebrand (Robert Warwick) and Mr. Hadrian (Porter Hall) are aghast at Sullivan's dangerous turnabout. They insist that the well-bred, wealthy filmmaker knows nothing about the "other half." Even Sullivan's pompous butler (Robert Greig) is against his employer's whim. "The poor know all about poverty, and only the morbid rich would find the subject glamorous.... They rather resent the invasion of their privacy."

Undaunted, Sullivan dresses in tramp's clothing and embarks on his excursion into hardship. The worried studio insists on having a staff and luxurious trailer follow him. The aggravated Sullivan makes a deal with his bosses. If they will give him two weeks alone, he agrees to meet them at a designated place and provide them with all the publicity and media photographs they desire. His attempts at hitchhiking end with him finding himself back in Hollywood. Wanting breakfast, he orders food at a diner and finds he cannot pay for it. Another patron, the Girl

Joel McCrea and Veronica Lake in *Sullivan's Travels* (1941).

(Veronica Lake), insists on paying his bill. She is down on her luck, having come to Hollywood to break into pictures. She is discouraged and plans to return home.

Sullivan is attracted to the stranger and finally confesses his real identity. He insists on taking her to his mansion, where he promptly falls in love with this movie extra. He explains his new mission. ("I'm going to feel how it is to be in trouble.") She fears he is too innocent to be on his own, so she, also dressed as a tramp, goes with him on his trek out into the hinterlands. After several adventures they return to Los Angeles. The enthusiastic director is eager to have one more adventure, this time planning to hand out money to tramps. One of the vagrants assaults him, stealing his money and shoes. The thief is later killed under the wheels of a train. Because of the shoes, it is assumed the corpse is that of the filmmaker. Sullivan's friends and associates mourn his passing. (His greedy wife [Jan Buckingham], from whom he was separated, quickly remarries.)

Meanwhile, Sullivan has awakened from his misadventure. The shaken man goes a bit crazy when a railroad guard strikes him and he hits back. He is arrested and sentenced to a prison camp for six years. Arriving at the hellhole compound, an elderly trustee (Jimmy Conlin) takes pity on the bewildered newcomer. He explains the harsh set-up and how to survive the whims of the brutal chain gang boss, the Mister (Alan Bridge):

> It ain't easy at first, but after a while you don't mind. We ain't so bad off. He ain't too bad according to his likes. He has to deal with some bad hombres. He gave us chicken last Thanksgiving and some turkey once and there ain't another mister who takes his gang to the picture show.

The old man's rationalizations in order to find contentment in the midst of his plight touches and amazes Sullivan. Following the old man's advice, he adjusts to the rigors of chain gang life, finally seeing life from another perspective. When he is caught reading a newspaper—a forbidden act—Sullivan is shoved into the sweat box. He survives that and the endless toil on the work detail. One evening he is part of the contingent of convicts taken to a black congregation's church where the audience watch a vintage Mickey Mouse cartoon. As the characters scamper about the screen, the prisoners break into laughter. Even Sullivan begins guffawing. A revelation suddenly hits him. Comedy is perhaps the best tonic in the world, able to distract people from their woes and humdrum existence.

Anxious to return to his world, he concocts a scheme to gain attention. He "admits" to the prison bosses that he killed John L. Sullivan and is put on trial. The engendered publicity gets his story into the national media. The girl and the studio executives see a photograph of Sullivan in the papers and rush to his defense. His identity is proven and he is freed. Now the studio executives expect that Sullivan's highly publicized, sobering experiences can be translated into an appropriately serious film. However, much to the surprise of studio executives, including Mr. Jones (William Demarest), who thinks Sullivan has gone "stir crazy," Sullivan insists he wants to make comedies: "There is a lot to be said for making people laugh. . . . Did you know that's all some people have? It isn't much, but it's better than nothing in this cockeyed caravan. Boy!"

Bosley Crowther *(New York Times)* approved of *Sullivan's Travels*. He described the film as "a beautifully trenchant satire upon 'social significance' in pictures, a stinging slap at those fellows who howl for realism on the screen and a deftly sardonic apologia for Hollywood's make-believe." He cited favorably the sequence where Joel McCrea's hero "learns about cruelty and poverty in a brutal convict camp. There he discovers that laughter is the only anodyne for grief—and subsequently returns to Hollywood a gladder and wiser man." *Variety* championed that *Sullivan's Travels* "is a curious but effective mixture of grim tragedy, slapstick of the Keystone brand and smart, trigger-fast comedy. Being unusual and satisfying entertainment, it is surefire audience material. . . . [Sturges] goes against many of the rules, but gets excellent, refreshing results." The trade papers did note, however, that "with the possible exception of the chain gang sequence which is a little long, he [Sturges] keeps his audience on the go and on edge."

When *Sullivan's Travels* was released on videocassette in the spring of 1989, Richard Schickel (*Video Review* magazine) enthused about the genius of filmmaker Preston Sturges and his "great comedies" made between 1940–1944. "Two things seem certain me: *Sullivan's Travels* is the best movie about moviemakers ever made, and we have had to wait far too long for its video appearance. . . . No moviemaker more richly deserves the renaissance he is now enjoying and which the video release of *Sullivan's Travels* climaxes."

253. The Sun Sets at Dawn (Eagle Lion, 1950), 71 min.

Producers, Helen H. Rathvon, Paul H. Sloane; director/screenplay, Sloane; art director, William Flannery; set decorator, George Sawley; makeup, Marie Clark; music/music director, Leith Stevens; assistant director, William McGarry; sound, William Lynch; camera, Lionel Lindon; editor, Sherman Todd.

Sally Parr (The Girl); Philip Shawn (The Boy); Walter Reed (The Chaplain); Lee Fredericks (Blackie); Houseley Stevenson (Pops); Howard St. John (The Warden); Louise Lorimer (The Warden's Wife); Raymond Bramley (The Deputy Warden); Charles Meredith (*Associate Press* Reporter); Jack Reynolds (E.P. Reporter); King Donovan (National News Service Reporter); Charles Arndt (*Globe Express* Reporter); Sam Edwards (*Herald* Reporter); Percy Helton (Feature Syndicate Reporter); Perry Ivan (Forty-Six).

A young man (Philip Shawn) is sentenced to be electrocuted for the killing of a political boss. He insists he is innocent. However, as the day arrives for his execution, the only people who believe his plea are the warden (Howard St. John), the prison chaplain (Walter Reed) and the young man's girlfriend (Sally Parr). At a nearby diner (which also serves as the local post office), several members of the press discuss the bizarre case in which the defendant will be the first victim of the state's electric chair. The newsmen all agree that the only man who might have committed such a crime, if the convicted man is really innocent, was Blackie (Lee Fredericks), a notorious criminal thought to be dead. The reporters adjourn to the prison to witness the electrocution. However, after the victim is strapped into the chair, a faulty mechanism prevents the execution from occurring.

Meanwhile, a trustee (Perry Ivan) picks up the institution's mail at the diner/post office and recognizes a customer—despite face-altering plastic surgery—as being Blackie. The trustee, who has an old score to settle with Blackie, exposes the latter and, although he himself is killed, the accused is brought before the warden. Blackie confesses to having murdered the politician who was blackmailing him. By now, the condemned man has been strapped into the electric chair *for a second time*. The warden quickly pulls the main switch to the prison's electicity, thus sparing the young convict's life.

Certainly the concept behind the bleak *The Sun Sets at Dawn* was intriguing. However, argued A. H. Weiler *(New York Times)*, the offering is "cliché-ridden and often overly sentimental ... the players rarely rise above the situations in which they are placed. Except for one flurry of action, this somber little item plods along at snail's pace." *Variety* agreed that this was "a slowly-paced programmer.... Production, direction, writing and playing are strictly run-of-the-mill...."

254. Swamp Women (Favorite Films, 1956), 73 min.

Producer, Bernard Woolner; director, Roger Corman; screenplay, David Stern; music, Willis "Bill" Holman; camera, Fred West; editor, Ronald Sinclair.

Marie Windsor (Josie); Beverly Garland (Vera); Carole Mathews (Lee); Jil Jarmyn (Billie); Touch [Mike] Connors (Bob); Susan Cummings (Marie); and Jonathan Haze, Edward [Ed] Nelson, Lou Place.

This mildly exploitive item from director Roger Corman was filmed on location in Louisiana. The ad lines read: *"Branded Women!... Notorious Women!... Scarlet Women!"* Surprisingly, several of the cast already had or would have, prominent film/TV careers.

Dedicated policewoman Lee (Carole Mathews) goes undercover by getting

Beverly Garland and Touch (Mike) Connors in *Swamp Women* (1956).

jailed. She is hoping that three prisoners—Josie (Marie Windsor), Vera (Beverly Garland) and Marie (Susan Cummings)—will reveal the whereabouts of a cache of stolen diamonds. The tough gals stage a jailbreak and Lee goes with them as they flee through the swamps. In the hostile environment, they not only cope with chomping alligators, slithering snakes, and steaming weather, but they soon are battling each other. The law closes in and the appropriate arrests are made.

Variety decided the production values were "mostly sub-standard" and that Roger Corman's direction was "somewhat over-melodramatic," but that this low-budget movie did "fully utilize the bayou area to pictorial advantage."

A.k.a.: *Cruel Swamp*.

TV title: *Swamp Diamonds*.

255. *Sweet Sugar* (Dimension, 1972), color, 85 min.

Producer, Charles S. Swartz; director, Michael Levesque; story, R. Z. Samuels; screenplay, Don Spencer; music, Don Gere.

Phyllis Elizabeth Davis (Sugar); Ella Edwards (Simone); Timothy Brown (Ric); Pamela Collins (Dolores); Cliff Osmond (Burgos); Angus Duncan (Dr. John); James Whitworth (Mario); and: Juan Antillon Baker, Nicholas Baker, Albert Cole, Ramon Coll, Laurencio Cordero, Antonio Casas Figueroa, Frank Garcia, Jackie Giroux, James Houghton, Nicky Jacobstahl, Luis Jimenez, Elvira Oropeza, Ana Maria Rivera, Diane Rojas, Darl Severen.

There were several other similar non–Hollywood pictures made in the Philippines in this period that were far better than *Sweet Sugar;* for example Roger

Corman's New World Pictures's *The Big Bird Cage* (1972) and *The Big Doll House* (1972), qq.v. However, this softcore pornography entry, dealing with ferocity, voodoo and killings on a prison farm, continues to turn up on cable TV for viewer amusement. Like others of this kind, its cinematography is grainy, the canned background music atrocious and its female performers are lithe of body but too frequently dumb of mouth. Its nonsensical plotline rigidly adheres to the prescribed genre formula: foolishly enslaved prisoners on a working plantation in the tropics eventually revolt against their sadistic, chauvinistic guards and escape to freedom, proving by the finale that they are far tougher than their captors. Its fantasy/bondage format would be almost unacceptable if made in today's atmosphere of women's liberation.

When prostitute Sugar (Phyllis Elizabeth Davis) is arrested in Costa Rica on a trumped-up marijuana charge, she has the dubious choice of remaining in jail for a year until her trial (possibly) occurs, or agreeing to be transported, along with the other female prisoners, to a distant plantation to work in the cane fields for two years. She reluctantly chooses the latter, although once she arrives at the forbidding compound, she has second thoughts. The guards, like pudgy Burgos (Cliff Osmond), are brutal and constantly after the women for sex. The handsome owner is a sophisticated brute named Dr. John (Angus Duncan), who, when not seducing his comely charges, is conducting vicious experiments on the cowering inmates. Eventually, feisty Sugar leads the other girls in revolt and they make a break for freedom. En route, they have their revenge on their former captors.

Since all the conventions are followed slavishly, the few joys the picture offers beyond the gratuitous nudity and s & m bondage are the moments of atrociously amusing and or double entendre dialogue.

For example, when Sugar is first jailed, she is eager to prove to the other cellmates that she is not just another hooker.

> INMATE: It happens to all us girls. It's part of our dues [i.e., being jailed].
>
> SUGAR: I don't owe anything.

Or:

> INMATE: You must have some righteous customers.
>
> SUGAR: I am *not* a hooker!
>
> INMATE: Honey, no matter who you put out for, it's still 'business.'
>
> SUGAR: Not if you're *really* a woman.

When Sugar is housed at the plantation, she is ordered up to the main house to meet Dr. John. She finds the young overseer taking a bubble bath.

> SUGAR: You are a nice looking man, doctor. Well formed.
>
> DOCTOR: Ah, you are a perceptive woman, Sugar. You must be aware of why I asked you here.
>
> SUGAR: Oh, I have an inkling.
>
> DOCTOR: No doubt a woman of your capacity will fully enjoy what I have to offer.

SUGAR: Not interested.

DOCTOR: It's only because you don't understand how far the proposal extends.

SUGAR: [Giving the doctor, now standing up nude, the once over twice] Oh, I can see how far it extends.

DOCTOR: There's more to it than meets the eye.

Strangely, the least effective moments of *Sweet Sugar* are those dealing with the regimen at the work farm. When the new batch of female prisoners arrive, the head guard is most perfunctory in his induction speech: "We got one job here, cutting cane. Meet your quota and everything will be fine. . . . Today you can rest, tomorrow we'll work your asses off."

Later, another guard, equally unmenacing and just as apathetic, instructs the new cane field workers on the use of their "tool": "Ladies, this is your machete. From now on your machete is your best friend. Keep it clean, keep it oiled and if you need more than one [swipe], your blade isn't tough enough."

To the film's credit, statuesque Phyllis Elizabeth Davis plays her lead role with tongue-in-cheek sauciness.

A.k.a. *Chain Gang Girls*.

256. *Take the Money and Run* (Cinerama, 1969), color, 85 min.

Executive producer, Sidney Glazier; producer, Charles H. Joffe; associate producer, Jack Grossberg; director, Woody Allen; screenplay, Allen, Mickey Rose; art director, Fred Harpman; set decorator, Marvin March; wardrobe supervisor, Erick M. Hjemvik; makeup, Stanley R. Dufford; music, Marvin Hamlisch; music director, Kermit Levinsky; music supervisor, Felix Giglio; assistant directors, Louis A. Stroller, Walter Hill; sound, Richard Vorisek; music/sound effects editors, John Strauss, Sanford Rackow; sound, Bud Alper; rerecording, Vorisek; special effects, A. D. Flowers; camera, Lester Shorr, (uncredited) Fouad Said; second unit camera, Fred Hoff-

man; supervising film editor, Ralph Rosenblum; editors, James T. Heckert, Ron Kalish, Paul Jordan.

Woody Allen (Virgil Starkwell); Janet Margolin (Louise); Marcel Hillaire (Fritz); Jacquelyn Hyde (Miss Blaire); Lonny Chapman (Jake); Jan Merlin (Al); James Anderson (Chain Gang Warden); Howard Storm (Fred); Mark Gordon (Vince); Micil Murphy (Frank); Minnow Moskowitz (Joe Agneta); Nate Jacobson (Judge); Grace Bauer (Farmhouse Lady); Ethel Sokolow (Mother Starkwell); Henry Leff (Father Starkwell); Don Frazier (Psychiatrist); Mike O'Dowd (Michael Sullivan); Jackson Beck (Narrator).

In his early years as a film director, Woody Allen (b. 1935) was wonderfully fresh, inventive and unpretentious. His first venture as director (in addition to being the scenarist and star) was *Take the Money and Run*. Despite its crude, episodic style and its economy production trappings, it is a marvelous satire on the prison genre, one unduplicated by many far more expensive productions: e.g. *Doin' Time* (1985) and *Buy & Cell* (1988), qq.v.

Tracing the life of failed gangster Virgil Starkwell (Woody Allen) the narrator (Jackson Beck) traces the man's humble beginning. Virgil was a victim of his tenement surroundings, his overdominant mother (Ethel Sokolow) and his milquetoast father (Henry Leff). Always an outsider, he drifts from youthful minor crimes to a life of major criminal offenses. As the result of a botched armored car holdup, he is sentenced to state prison. There he attempts to escape, having carved a pistol from a bar of soap and darkened it with shoe polish. Everything goes well until he makes his break and his soap gun produces bubbles due to a sudden cloudburst of rain. He later volunteers to be a human guinea pig for a new vaccine (which temporarily turns him into an Orthodox rabbi).

Once released, he turns to purse snatching and robbing small shops to support himself. One day in the park, he encounters the innocent Louise (Janet Margolin), a laundress. It is love at first sight. The new emotion baffles the feckless ex-convict:

> Here I'm lying through my teeth. I can't tell Louise that I was in jail, that I rob and steal and never did an honest's day work in my life cause other people hold those things against you. After fifteen minutes I wanted to marry her. And after a half hour, I completely gave up the idea of snatching her purse.

He tells Louise that he is a cellist with the Philharmonic Orchestra. To pay for his first date with Louise, he robs a bubble gum machine of loose change. Determined to be a big-time criminal, he next attempts to rob a bank, but the tellers cannot read his holdup note and insist that it must be notarized. He is captured and given ten years in a maximum security state prison. The hardened criminal vows: "The prison has not been built that can hold me. I'll get out of this one if it takes my entire life here."

He becomes a model prisoner and is assigned to work in the laundry, where he fumbles operating the automatic folding machine. Almost by error, he is part of a breakout, and escapes. He and Louise marry and move to another state where they live on her savings. They have a baby boy and Virgil, the proud family man, accepts a regular daytime job at an insurance company. However, one of the randy employees, Miss Blair (Jacquelyn Hyde), discovers Virgil's background and attempts to blackmail him. His efforts to get rid of this pest are as futile as his past criminal career.

Virgil has an inspiration. "I came up with an idea for robbery that was so fantastic and so brilliant that when it was over, it was considered a real work of art by all the guys in my cellblock."

He develops an ingenious plan to rob the Unity Fidelity Trust Company, casting his gang as members of a bogus film crew at work filming the bank and thus distracting the guards. However, Virgil cannot even get to the scene of the crime on time.

> VIRGIL: I'm going to be late for the robbery.
>
> LOUISE: So you'll be five minutes late. They can start without you.
>
> VIRGIL: Jeez. I'm the leader.

The robbery fails and this time the captured Virgil is sentenced to ten years of hard labor on the Ross County chain gang. The sadistic warden (James Anderson) greets his unfortunate new recruits:

> You men come here cause you commit crimes that render you unfit to live in decent society. That's too bad. I think you're gonna find you made a mistake you're gonna regret.
> Now our job, me and the boys, is to see you get some civilization in ya. So when you leave here, you're gonna think twice about performing anti-social acts. Now my advice to you is to obey the rules and do the job. You got any complaints, you come to me. Now we don't like troublemakers. If things get a little too tough for you, you

take off to Florida. Show 'em what direction Florida is boys. [The guards shoot their rifles into the air.]

Now you got any questions?

Virgil has one: "Do you think a girl should pet on the first date?"

Virgil is sent to work at a rock quarry where he joins the men in singing a spiritual about going to Mississippi to see Liza. His attempts at breaking rock prove ineffectual as the metal head keeps slipping off his sledge hammer. Meal time comes and the narrator notes "The men get one hot meal a day, a bowl of steam." For a minor infraction of the rules, troublemaker Virgil is placed in the dreaded sweat box, locked up with an aggressive insurance salesman.

Finally Virgil and five other convicts, all chained together, break free from the prison camp. As they escape, one of them orders "Okay, spread out!" (and they all fall down). They flee on foot, on bicycles, always one step ahead of the law. During the next months, Virgil becomes a wanted desperado. He is soon elected Gangster of the Year and, as a result, is invited to swanky banquets and to universities as a guest speaker. However, luck is against Virgil. During a holdup, the victim proves to be an old friend from prison who is now a policeman. Virgil is collared and sentenced for fifty-two counts of robbery. He receives eight hundred years in jail.

Once again, in a cell, Virgil philosophizes: "I think crime definitely pays and that, you know, it's a great job. The hours are good. You're your own boss. You travel a lot and you get to meet interesting people and I think it's a good job in general."

An interviewer asks Virgil, who is whittling away at an object, how he spends his time in prison. The criminal replies: "I've been making a lot of stuff in shop. [He holds up a soap gun.] Do you know if it's raining out?"

When initially released, *Take the Money and Run* was not a critical hit. *Variety* observed that the film "scatters its fire in so many directions it has to hit at least several targets. . . . [S]atire on documentary coverage of criminal flop is overextended and eventually tiresome." The British *Monthly Film Bulletin* complained, "[O]n the whole Allen's comedy seems dispirited, disjointed and quite without the visual panache it needs to make it work." Despite the mixed reviews, *Take the Money and Run,* made on a tight budget of $1,600,000, was profitable. Nancy Pogel (*Woody Allen,* 1987) noted, "[I]t is such a commercial success that Allen's managers . . . were able to launch Allen as a director, actor, and writer of his own films." Pogel perceived:

> *Take the Money and Run* . . . finds a humble little-man main character caught between two unsavory possibilities. He is no freer outside than inside prison, and his confinement becomes a representative contemporary predicament. . . . Virgil's confinement also involves a reflexive burlesque context, a comment on films and filmmaking.

In *The Films of the Sixties* (1980) Douglas Brode observes,

> Perhaps no other artist has had his mind so completely conditioned by watching films. . . . When the picture shifts to the jail sequence, it is obvious that what we see is not based on any experiences with real jails but with movie jails: the prisoners speak in movie prison jargon . . . and look like the guys who used to back up George

Raft and John Garfield. . . . This absorption with films came to a head in one of the best scenes in *Take the Money,* when Virgil tries to confuse the police by hiring a rejected European director . . . to pretend he is filming a robbery. . . . On the surface, this was merely another funny scene—but there was a lot going on beneath that surface.

As Woody Allen's reputation as an auteur grew over the decades, *Take the Money and Run* became a semi-cult favorite. Every enthusiast has his favorite sequences in this send-up of prison (and gangster) films. For this author, there are three superior moments. One occurs when Louise comes to see her beloved in prison. In the visitors' room she pushes a hard boiled egg through the mesh wire separating her from Virgil. Another happens during the chain gang segment when the whimsical warden orders mischievous Virgil to be whipped. The guard lashes out at the offender's shadow, leading the angered boss to shout, "Don't beat the shadow, beat him!" Yet another comic gem transpires when Virgil is being frisked by arresting officers. He is ticklish and begins laughing uproariously.

257. *Terminal Island* (Dimension, 1973), color, 88 min.

Executive producer, Lawrence H. Woolner; producer, Charles S. Swartz; director, Stephanie Rothman; screenplay, Rothman, Swartz, Jim Barnett; art director, Jack Fish; makeup, Rafaella Patterson; music, Michael Andres; assistant director, John Broderick; sound, Roger Daniel; camera, Daniel Lacambre; editor, John O'Connor.

Don Marshall (A. J. Thomas); Phyllis Davis (Joy Lang); Ena Hartman (Carmen Sims); Marta Kristen (Lee Phillips); Barbara Leigh (Bunny Campbell); Sean David Kenney (Bobby Farr); Geoffrey Deuel (Chino); Tom Selleck (Dr. Norman Milford); Ford Clay (Cornell); Clyde Ventura (Julian "Mother" Dylan); Frank Christi (Roy Teale); Roger E. Mosley (Monk); Albert Cole (Finney); Sandy Ward (Guard); Jim Whitworth (Vander); Chris Allen (Dana); Richard Taylor (Newsman); Richard Stahl (TV Announcer); and: Randy Boone, Jo Morrow, Ray Saniger

Sometimes a trashy, poorly-acted, badly photographed low-budget feature film becomes a minor cult favorite, almost by accident. Such was the case with the helter-skelter *Terminal Island,* directed by Stephanie Rothman. It not only was one of the few motion pictures to combine the science fiction and prison genres, but it had the fortune of casting then relatively unknown Tom Selleck in a feature role. When he became famous as the star of TV's "Magnum, P.I." (1980–88), the picture became a popular item on (cable) television and in videocassette format. *Terminal Island* also co-starred Roger E. Mosley, who would co-star on the Hawaiian-based detective series with Selleck. It was distributed by Dimension Pictures which had also filmed *Sweet Sugar* (1972), q.v., in the Philippines.

Set some time in the future in which California has abolished capital punishment, the state rids itself of the most incorrigible of prisoners by the cost-saving device of dumping them on a desolate island (laced with electronically controlled mine explosives), some forty miles off the coastline. Here, at the San Bruno Maximum Security Prison, the inmates fend for themselves in the wilds. If they attempt to flee the island, they must contend with rough waters, ravenous sharks, and patrolling guard boats which have orders to shoot the escapees. As one administrator sums it up, "It's where we dump the garbage." According to the revised California Penal Code, prisoners sent to this point of last resort are declared legally dead.

There were seventy-five prisoners on the island when it opened, now there are forty survivors. Among the inmates living at and outside the compound are: Lee Phillips (Marta Kristen), who blew up a bank; Bobby Farr (Sean David Kenney), who killed his partner; Joy Lang (Phyllis Davis), who poisoned her husband; Dr. Norman Milford (Tom Selleck), guilty of a mercy killing; Bunny Campbell (Barbara Leigh), who murdered her parents with an ice pick; Julian "Mother" Dylan (Clyde Ventura), a rebellious biker; Roy Teale (Frank Christi), a homicidal maniac who has killed eleven people; and black misfeasor A. J. Thomas (Don Marshall).

A new prisoner, Carmen Sims (Ena Hartman), is being dropped off at the prison colony. The arrival of this self-sufficient, tough black woman causes the various factions to splinter further apart. Milford is a laissez-faire type who only begrudgingly provides medical attention to his peers. Monk and Bobby are lovers and find Carmen's appearance an intrusion to their relationship. (Bobby is the tribal lord, who also is involved romantically with Bunny.) Well-coiffed Joy, the leader of the blonde prisoners on the isle, informs Carmen "We're the property of every man on the island." In this chauvinistic state, the women pull the plows to grow the crops and they are sex objects used to gratify the men's needs. Tempers quicken and the convicts are soon pitted one against the other. (Among the splinter groups is a faction of rebelling females.) As the combatants die, their bodies are dumped over the cliff after primitive burial rites. The escalating conflict concludes with Bobby's death, he being blown up in his chief's hut. Monk is left blinded and becomes a servant for the others' needs. Later, word arrives that Milford is to be offered a new trial back on the mainland, but he refuses to go. "I don't want to go back ever. This is home now."

As the remaining inmates settle back into a peaceful existence, a new prisoner (Chris Allen) is unloaded by prison guards at the island.

Reviewing this crudely made feature in *The Psychotronic Encyclopedia of Film* (1983), Michael Weldon reported, "It's a variation on the usual sadistic prison movie with sex and a little feminism added."

258. *There Was a Crooked Man* (Warner Bros., 1970), color, 126 min.

Executive producer, C. O. Erickson; producer/director, Joseph L. Mankiewicz; based on the story "Prison Story" by David Newman, Robert Benton; screenplay, Newman, Benton; art director, Edward Carrere; set decorator, Keogh Gleason; costumes, Anna Hill Johnstone; makeup, Perc Westmore; music, Charles Strouse; song, Strouse, Lee Adams; stunt coordinator, Roger Creed; assistant directors, Don Kranze, Bill Green, Chris Seitz; sound, Al Overton, Jr., George Hause; special effects, John Barton; camera, Harry Stradling, Jr.; editor, Gene Milford.

Kirk Douglas (Paris Pitman, Jr.); Henry Fonda (Sheriff Woodward Lopeman); Hume Cronyn (Dudley Whinner); Warren Oates (Floyd Moon); Burgess Meredith (The Missouri Kid); John Randloph (Cyrus McNutt); Arthur O'Connell (Mr. Lomax); Martin Gabel (Warden Francis E. Le Goff); Michael Blodgett (Coy Cavendish); Claudia McNeil (Goldie, the Madam); Alan Hale, Jr. (Tobaccy Watkins); Victor French (Whiskey); Lee Grant (Mrs. Bullard); C. K. Yang (Ah-Ping Woo); Pamela Hensley (Edwina); Bert Freed (Skinner); Barbara Rhoades (Miss Jessie Brundidge); J. Edward McKinley (Governor); Dora Merende (Churchgoer); Gene Evans (Colonel Wolff); Jeanne Cooper (Prostitute); and: Bart Burns, Ann Doran, Byron Foulger, Karl Lukas, Larry D. Mann, Paul Newlan, Paul Prokop.

The credits split the screen, and in so doing, become a metaphor of the film which itself is split; it is part Western, part prison drama with the distinction as thin as the line that divides the murals on the left of the frame from the credits on the right. At the beginning, one does not know it will evolve into a prison drama....

(Bernard F. Dick, *Joseph L. Mankiewicz*, 1983)

The R-rated *There Was a Crooked Man* is an intriguing, if not always fully realized dark satire. It depicts the culpability of men on both sides of the law. As its frame of reference, it employs a crude 1880s territorial prison out west where life was tough, the prisoners rough, and the keepers even more resolute and corrupt. As a reflection on the genre and as a study of man's crassness and greed, it is definitely worth viewing, as is any production by acclaimed filmmaker Joseph L. Mankiewicz (b. 1909), the Academy Award winner who had the misfortune to also supervise *Cleopatra* (1963). *There Was a Crooked Man* was scripted by David Newman and Robert Benton who had written *Bonnie and Clyde* (1969). Benton later turned director and won an Academy Award for *Kramer vs. Kramer* (1979).

Paris Pitman, Jr. (Kirk Douglas) is the only survivor of a bank robbery and hides the $500,000 loot in a snake-infested hole. Later, he is captured by the persevering Sheriff Woodward Lopeman (Henry Fonda) at a brothel and sentenced to ten years at the Arizona Prison. The epicine Warden Francis E. Le Goff (Martin Gabel) welcomes the new inmates which include young Coy Cavendish (Michael Blodgett), sentenced to die for killing a man in a pool hall fight and aging con artists Cyrus McNutt (John Randolph) and Dudley Whinner (Hume Cronyn) who are homosexual lovers. The fastidious Le Goff greets the new charges: "Welcome to the territorial prison, gentlemen. I shall assume we all have one thing in common, a burning desire to be elsewhere."

The dandified administrator, who relies on snuff to perk his sagging interest in his dreary duties, rattles off the house rules. "No singing, no whistling. Any man who can walk is required to work on the rock piles. All prisoners required to attend hangings."

The braggart Pitman shares a crowded, dank cell with McNutt, Whinner, Cavendish, the killer Ah-Ping Woo (C. K. Yang), the irascible Floyd Moon (Warren Oates) and an aging convict, the Missouri Kid (Burgess Meredith). It is the latter who advises the newcomers, "You haven't pulled much time in the pokey. If you want something, you'll pay for it." Pitman quickly alerts his fellow prisoners that only he knows where the loot is hidden; a factor guaranteed to protect him from harm. Meanwhile, the greedy Warden summons Pitman to his office and suggests that if Paris will share the money with him, Le Goff will permit him to escape. Le Goff explains: "Truth is, I find the atmosphere of this place stifling, depressing, boring. I am sure you feel the same, but not for the same reasons."

Before Pitman's escape occurs, the warden is murdered by Ah-Ping. A new warden is appointed, none other than Woodward Lopeman. One of the guards is amazed that Lopeman volunteered for this dangerous, hopeless assignment. "Nobody asks to be warden of this prison. Even Daniel didn't walk into the lion's den."

Lopeman assures the convicts that a new progressive regime is in order. "From now on, if something is bothering you, come tell me."

Soon the arduous corporeal punishment (quarry work) is abandoned for all except Pitman, whom Lopeman intends to whip into conformity. The convicts are put to work building a new structure for themselves in the prison yard and, in the course of events Pitman saves Lopeman's life. Later, the governor (J. Edward McKinley) visits the improved facility and it is then that Paris decides to escape.

A conniving user, he allows three of his fellow convicts to die (including Floyd and Coy), before he flees. Lopeman follows in pursuit, angry that he had trusted Pitman to be a model prisoner. After Paris beds Mrs. Bullard (Lee Grant), a woman who claims to have once slept with Billy the Kid, he retrieves his money cache. He is bitten by a rattlesnake and dies. Lopeman arrives on the scene. He packs the corpse on the back of a horse, escorts it back to the prison, and then rides off toward Mexico, his saddlebag full of the stolen bounty. A final title card reads, "And he lived happily ever after."

Many critics were confused by the mixed message of this black comedy. *Variety* carped that it "has a crooked plot that is neither comedy nor convincing drama. . . . It is the type of action drama in which neither the actors nor director appear to believe the script or characters. . . . The territorial prison is supposedly a place of appalling filth, degradation and hopelessness, but the $300,000 set . . . looks like a set . . . and [nothing] suspends the basic disbelief. No one sweats while working on the rock pile, and there are none of the symbolic touches of neo-realism, such as rats." Pauline Kael (*New Yorker* magazine) was extremely negative. "This example of commercialized black-comedy nihilism seems to have been written by an evil two-year-old, and it has been directed in the Grand Rapids style of filmmaking. . . . There's nobody to root for but Kirk Douglas, a red-haired, jokester-killer." Vincent Canby (*New York Times*) asserted, "One of the movie's bothersome idiosyncracies is that it wants to utilize its myths and to work against them. Thus, the film, which begins as a broad satire, turns into fairly straight melodrama involving prison riots and such things, before ending on a note of gentle cynicism. . . ."

In retrospect, Bernard F. Dick (*Joseph L. Mankiewicz*, 1983) found much worthwhile within *There Was a Crooked Man:*

> [T]he film was also a sendup of the 1960s, when anyone who wore rimless glasses was an activist; and anyone who preached prison reform and looked like Henry Fonda was incorruptible. . . . Once the action moves inside the stockade, the film takes on the conventions of the prison drama; or rather its plot conventions since Mankiewicz makes even less of an attempt to emulate the style of the prison drama than he did of the Western. However, the [filmmakers] . . . had seen enough prison films — *Brute Force* (1947) for one — to supply the necessary motifs. . . . The criminals, who make the great escape at the end, must be a diversified lot. . . . While the Dudley-Cyrus relationship exists in prison films . . . it is more characteristic of the Western. . . . Inevitably, there will be a clash between the warden and the convict.

With its offbeat prison setting, *There Was a Crooked Man* exposes and exploits many of the myths of the prison genre: crooked guards, corrupt warden, homosexuality (between prisoners, as well as between guards and prisoners), convict rebellion at bad food and worse living conditions, the tough convicts who (seemingly) become model prisoners, executions, the big breakout, etc. Several of the players had been in prison dramas before. Hume Cronyn was the well-remembered vicious Captain Muncey of *Brute Force* (1947), q.v. Burgess Meredith who excelled here as the old codger prisoner/philospher had been a convict in *Castle on the Hudson* (1940), q.v. Henry Fonda had performed in such penitentiary dramas as *You Only Live Once* (1937), q.v., and *Let Us Live* (1939), q.v.

259. *Those High Grey Walls* (Columbia, 1939), 81 min.

Producer, B. B. Kahane; director, Charles Vidor; story, William A. Ullman, Jr.; screenplay, Lewis Meltzer; camera, John Stumar; editor, Gene Milford.

Walter Connolly (Dr. MacAuley); On-slow Stevens (Dr. Norton); Paul Fix (Nightingale); Bernard Nedell (Redlands); Iris Meredith (Mary MacAuley); Oscar O'Shea (Warden); Nicholas Soussanin (Lindy); Don Beddoe (Jockey).

> Warmth, simplicity and freshness are qualities so unusual to the prison film that their presence ... has all the surprise of a violet's growing in the gravel of a jailhouse.... [The filmmakers] have spun the story smoothly, spotlighting the prison background in significant bits of action but never letting it overshadow its quiet central....
>
> (Frank S. Nugent, *New York Times*)

Small town Dr. MacAuley (Walter Connolly) is sentenced to prison for having treated a wounded criminal, whom he has known from the latter's childhood, and not reporting it to the police. MacAuley is a model prisoner who comes to the attention of prison physician Dr. Norton (Onslow Stevens) and is eventually given a post at the infirmary. When the pregnant wife of one of the convicts goes into labor during a visit to her husband at the penitentiary, MacAuley tricks Norton—who has been traumatized by a failed delivery years ago—into assisting with the successful birth of the child. Later, when the two doctors, now friends, are performing an operation on a prisoner, high strung convict Redland (Bernard Nedell) breaks into the hospital at gunpoint. He is intent on escaping with the physicians as his hostages. The doctors convince the convict to wait till they complete their surgery; the onlooker passes out at the sight of blood and is captured. Next, when a prisoner dies from an overdose of a sedative, MacAuley is suspected. However, the convicts, eager to repay the doctor for his many services to them, uncover the real culprit among their numbers. Finally Dr. MacAuley is paroled and returns to his daughter (Iris Meredith) and to his civilian life.

Variety endorsed this programmer. "Effective prison melodrama that does not seem to require femme interest or the support of romantic flavor." The trade paper complimented the acting of Connolly, Stevens and Nedell, but suggested, "In view of the 80 minutes running time, some of the pen routine could have been edited out for better results."

Veteran character actor Walter Connolly had starred as a prison warden in Columbia's *Penitentiary* (1938), q.v., a remake of *The Penal Code* (1931), q.v.

260. *Those Three French Girls* (Metro-Goldwyn-Mayer, 1930), 72 min.

Director, Harry Beaumont; story, Dale Van Every, Arthur Freed; adaptors/continuity, Sylvia Thalberg, Frank Butler; dialogue, P. G. Wodehouse; art director, Cedric Gibbons; wardrobe, Rene Hubert; songs, Joseph Meyer and Freed; choreographer, Sammy Lee; sound, Douglas Shearer; camera, Merritt B. Gerstad; edi-tor, George Hively.

Fifi D'Orsay (Charmaine); Reginald Denny (Larry); Cliff Edwards (Owly); Yola D'Avril (Diane); Sandra Ravel (Madelon); George Grossmith (Earl of Ippleton); Edward Brophy (Yank); Peter Gawthorne (Parker).

This nonsensical musical comedy farce worked a jail house sequence into its frothy plotline.

In Paris, an aristocratic Britisher, Larry (Reginald Denny) comes to the rescue of three French girls—Charmaine (Fifi D'Orsay), Diane (Yola D'Avril) and Madelon (Sandra Ravel) when their landlord is evicting them for nonpayment of their rent. Before the mêlée concludes, the quartet end in jail. There Larry encounters Owly (Cliff Edwards) and Yank (Edward Brophy), two earthy doughboys who remained in France after World War I. The trio, plus the girls, escape from their confines and head for Larry's estate. There, Larry's gout-plagued uncle, the Earl of Ippleton (George Grossmith), romances the beguiling Charmaine. However, it develops that the elderly Earl is a bounder and it is Larry whom Charmaine loves.

Variety complimented the three leading ladies—especially vivacious Fifi D'Orsay—for parading around in their scanties, but complained, "It has no story to speak of. Various sequences and performances are the only sales point." The trade paper added, "In between the fashion shows and bathrooms is a load of slapstick which could be found in the 1919 vaults of any short subject producer." Mordaunt Hall *(New York Times)* was more forgiving of this "incongruous mixture," but admitted it was "a production with its broth spoiled by too many cooks."

Joseph Meyer and Arthur Freed wrote two songs ("Six Poor Mortals" and "You're Simply Delish") for this whimsical confection.

261. *Three on a Match* (NBC–TV, Aug. 2, 1987), color, 100 min.

Executive producer, Donald P. Bellisario; producer, Stuart Segall; associate producer, David Bellisario; director/teleplay, Donald P. Bellisario; production designer, Bill Malley; set decorator, Brenda Meyers-Ballard; costumes, Tom Bronson; makeup, John Inzeralla; music, Ian Freebairn Smith; stunt coordinator, Diamond Farnsworth; second unit directors, Don Baer, Russell Solberg; sound, Keith A. Wester; special effects, Phil Cory; camera, Jack A. Whitman; second unit camera, Stan McLain; editor, Arthur W. Forney; additional editor, Leon Ortiz-Gil.

Patrick Cassidy (Scott Crossfield); David Hemmings (Maxwell "Newt" Newton); Bruce A. Young (Ripper); Everett McGill (Boss); Mitch Pileggi (Bull Tully); Lance LeGault (Hornet); Dendrie Allyn Taylor (Mary Lou); Deborah Pratt (Sissy); Diana Bellamy (Bonnie); Raynor Scheine (Skeeter); Jim Haynie (Judge Winthrop); Kendall Conrad (Sarah Winthrop); John Calvin (Mark); Joseph Adams (Chad); David Hart (Ray Bob); Geraldine Pratt (Mama); B. J. Hopper (Judge Tully); Elliott Keaner (Chester); Jason Saugier (Billie Joe); Trellis Septor (Kip); Louis Bourgeois (Guard); Jeffrey Hays (Crowley); Duane Bennet (Georgie); Ken Gerson (Attendant).

Even in the remedial-prone decades following *I Am a Fugitive from a Chain Gang* (1932), q.v., and *Cool Hand Luke* (1967), q.v., life in a southern prison camp is no picnic. The Boss (Everett McGill) is a sadistic keeper who delights in having his guards torment the prisoners. (For example, the men are made to walk a thin wooden plank over crocodile-packed waters.) A trio of disgruntled convicts—Scott Crossfield (Patrick Cassidy), Maxwell "Newt Newton" (David Hemmings) and Ripper (Bruce A. Young)—escape and make it cross country to Los Angeles. They are hardly there before a twist of fate sends the three back to the prison camp. This time the men make good their escape, thanks to the help of a computer-generated breakout scheme.

Daily Variety judged the telefeature a "disjointed, rambling story. . . . If all this sounds like quite a drag, it is." The made-for-television movie was geared as a pilot for a "The Fugitive"-type series that never materialized. It was scripted/directed by Donald Bellisario who had created "Magnum P.I."

262. *Three Sevens* (Vitagraph, 1921), 5 reels.

Presenter, Albert E. Smith; director, Chester Bennett; based on the novel *Three Sevens: A Detective Story* by Perley Poore Sheehan; screenplay, Calder Johnstone; camera, Jack MacKenzie.

Antonio Moreno (Daniel Craig); Jean Calhoun (Joan Gracie); Emmett King (Major Jerome Gracie); Geoffrey Webb (Gary Lee); DeWitt Jennings (Warden Samuel Green); Starke Patterson (Brewster Green); Beatrice Burnham (Amy Green).

On the basis of circumstantial evidence, Daniel Craig (Antonio Moreno) is sentenced to prison. Once incarcerated, Craig, now convict #777, joins with other inmates in rebelling against the cruel warden, Samuel Green (DeWitt Jennings). As a result of the inmate revolt, Green is made to resign. A new administrator, Major Jerome Gracie (Emmett King) convinces Craig to persuade the men to capitulate. They do. Daniel falls in love with Gracie's daughter, Joan (Jean Calhoun). Thereafter, it develops that the ex-warden's son (Starke Patterson) committed the crime for which Craig was being punished. Daniel is freed and pursues his romance with Joan.

Distributed modestly by the once-powerful Vitagraph film studio, *Three Sevens* did not receive much critical notice.

263. *Too Young to Die?* (NBC–TV, Feb. 26, 1990), color, 100 min.

Executive producers, Frank Von Zerneck, Robert M. Setner; producers, Susan Weber-Gold, Julie Anne Weitz; associate producers, Paul Alan Mones, Timothy McFlynn; director, Robert Markowitz; story, David Hill; teleplay, Hill, George Rubino; production designer, Donald Light Harris; set decorator, William Vail; makeup, David A. Simon; music, Charles Bernstein; music editor, Susan Mick; second unit director, Peter L. Bergquist; assistant director, Ray Marsh, James J. Fitzpatrick; sound, Jacob Goldstein; sound effects editor, Rich Harrison; camera, Eric Van Haren Noman; editors, Harvey Rosenstock, Eric Sears.

Michael Tucker (Buddy Thornton); Juliette Lewis (Amanda Sue Bradley); Brad Pitt (Billy Cattan); Michael O'Keefe (Sergeant Michael Midwick); Emily Longstretch (Jean); Alan Fudge (District Attorney); Laurie O'Brien (Amanda's Mother); Tom Everett (Judge Harper); Dean Abston (Harvey); J. Stephen Brady (Brian); Mark Davenport (Mickey); Lew Hopson (Star); Annabelle Weenick (Birdie Jewel); Charles C. Stevenson, Jr. (Pastor); Charles David Richards (Billings); Hank Woessner (Boss); Tim de Zaen (Patron); Jeremy Bailey (Police Officer); C. W. Hemingway (Gas Station Attendant); Taylor Fry (Sally); Bradley Pierce (Wes); Don Pugsley (Booking Officer); James Schendel (Foreman); Redmond M. Gleason (Janitor).

> Based on the sort of tawdry crime story that rates a paragraph in the tabloids—a white-trash teen and her boyfriend kidnap and kill a guy for a little money—*Too Young to Die?* contains TV's best portrayal of lower-middle-class life since the adaptation of *The Executioner's Song.*
>
> (*Entertainment Weekly* magazine)

The legal fate of minors who commit murder is the subject of this harrowing telefeature. (Nothing reminds the viewer so much that this capital offense defendant is a frightened teenager, as when she meets her attorney for the first time and asks him if he has any sugar-coated candies.) Although the bulk of the narrative concerns the seamy facts leading up to the brutal homicide, several sequences feature the overwhelmed fifteen-year-old murderess (Juliette Lewis) in jail. A haunting scene finds the young girl taken, in chains, to the prison's death row. The horror in her young eyes as she looks down the corridor and notices the door leading to the death room is unforgettable.

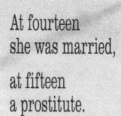

At fourteen
she was married,

at fifteen
a prostitute.

At sixteen
she was
on death row.

**too young
to die?**

Inspired by a true story.

Michael Tucker
"L.A. Law"

Advertisement for *Too Young to Die?* (1990).

Fourteen-year-old Amanda Sue Bradley (Juliette Lewis) of Tulsa, Oklahoma, is ignored by her mother (Laurie O'Brien) and raped by her stepdad (Dean Abston). When her elders impulsively relocate to California, Amanda is abandoned and left to fend for herself. Wandering the streets, she soon meets two people. Jean (Emily Longstretch), a sympathetic young waitress, offers friendship, practical help and guidance. On the other hand, scuzzy Billy Cattan (Brad Pitt), one step above a street person himself, soon introduces Amanda to a life of drugs, booze and prostitution. She hates what she is becoming, but feels helpless to break out of the new mold.

One night all that changes when she meets young Army Sergeant Michael Midwick (Michael O'Keefe). He is recently divorced, the father of two, and very lonely. He allows Amanda to move into his house and before long their platonic relationship turns romantic. The two are happy together until the drifting Billy reenters her life. He alerts Michael's superior officers to the solider's unorthodox domestic situation and Michael is commanded to break off the relationship at once. Rejected once again, Amanda is drawn back into her love-hate relationship with Billy. Later, on a vicious whim, the vengeful Billy and the benumbed Amanda kidnap Michael (and his new girlfriend). On a deserted oilfield, Amanda finds herself stabbing Michael to death. She and Billy are caught. Her trial lawyer is Buddy Thornton (Michael Tucker) a compassionate man who must rise to the occasion in dealing with a murder case and trying to have his teenage defendant judged as a minor, not as an adult. The court verdict is guilty and Amanda is sentenced to be executed in the gas chamber.

A postscript to the telefeature alerts:

> In 1989, the United States Supreme Court decided that states have the right to execute minors who are sixteen years and older for capital offenses.
> There are presently twenty-eight teenagers on death row waiting to die.

Ray Loynd *(Los Angeles Times)* observed, "The production is hard as a cue ball—no distracting subplots, no wasted motion.... The film makers aren't debating capital punishment but they are dramatizing a rigorous question: Should minors guilty of capital crimes be sentenced to death?" *Daily Variety* lauded the performances of Juliette Lewis who "whizzes from childlike innocence via surly avenged to defeated kid with astonishing credibility in a surefire perf." The trade paper noted, "Amanda Sue's case, 'based upon certain actual events and persons,' loses some of its poignancy when the telefilm turns into a statement." Michael Tucker, co-star of the TV series "LA Law" (1986–   ), turned in a solid performance as the attorney who is full of questions and doubt.

264. *The Traveling Executioner* (Metro-Goldwyn-Mayer, 1970), color, 95 min.

Producer/director, Jack Smight; screenplay, Garrie Bateson; art directors, George W. Davis, Edward Carfagno; set decorators, Robert R. Benton, Keogh Gleason; wardrobe, Norma Burza, Edward Marks, Kitty Mager, Marilyn Matthews; makeup, Fred Williams; music, Jerry Goldsmith; assistant directors, Michael Daves, Alan Rudolph; sound, Jerry Jost, Hal Watkins; camera, Phillip Lathrop; editor, Neil Travis.

Stacy Keach (Jonas Candide); Marianne Hill (Gundred Herzallerliebst); Bud Cort (Jimmy); Graham Jarvis (Doc Prittle); James J. Sloyan (Piquant); M. Emmet Walsh (Warden Brodski); John Bottoms

Stacy Keach in *The Traveling Executioner* (1970).

(Lawyer); Ford Rainey (Stanley Mae); James Greene (Gravey Combs); Sammy Reese (Priest); Stefan Fierasch (Willy Herzallerliebst); Logan Ramsey (La Follette); Charles Tyner (Virgil); William Mims (Lynn); Val Avery (Jake); Walter Barnes (Sheriff); Charlie Briggs (Zak); Paul Gauntt (Jeremy); Claire Brenner (Woman Passerby); Scottie MacGregor (Alice Thorn); Tony Fraser (1st Child); Martine Fraser (2nd Child); Lorna Thayer (Madam); Pat Patterson (Roscoe).

The Traveling Executioner is certainly one of the more unique and macabre tales turned out by Hollywood. It focuses on a flim flam man who is an executioner in the 1910s. It is one of the few American features films to deal with this unusual occupation as it focuses on a theatrical con artist / executioner and his delicate relationship with his shy assistant / successor. *Variety* overenthusiastically projected great response to this offbeat black comedy / drama, insisting, "Kooky enough to attract the young, literate enough to hold them, yet sufficiently broad and deep to appeal to older audience. . . ." However, neither the unconventional film nor its charismatic performance by Stacy Keach drew many filmgoers into theatres.

In 1918, Jonas Candide (Stacy Keach) has a unique profession. Boasting his own electric chair, he moves from prison to prison, charging the institutions $100 per execution. At Alabama's Fairweather Prison he is commissioned by Warden Brodski (M. Emmet Walsh) to electrocute Willy Herzallerliebst (Stefan Gierasch) and his sister Gundred (Marianne Hill). After Willy's death, Gundred seduces Candide, playing for time in hopes that her petition for a pardon may still be granted. This leads the infatuated Jonas to convince prison Dr. Prittle (Graham Jarvis) to conspire with him to fake Gundred's death. The greedy physician demands a high fee so Jonas, risking everything, gambles and works as a pimp to acquire the needed funds. Still requiring more money, he seeks a bank loan, but is refused by the banker (Logan Ramsey). Later, the distraught Jonas kills a guard and frees Gundred. While he is retrieving his equipment, Gundred makes her own plans. Her sentence is commuted to a life term. On the other hand, Jonas is ordered executed. His executioner is his bashful, young helper, Jimmy (Bud Cort), a mortician who handles his duties so badly that the electric chair burst into flames.

Variety cautioned of this R-rated entry, "There are some sensibilities that will be affronted, but the important fact is that any offense will be more of a glancing blow than outright gouging."

The Traveling Executioner, which was a box office failure, was shot on location at Kilby Prison near Montgomery, Alabama.

265. *Triple Trouble* (Monogram, 1950), 66 min.

Producer, Jan Grippo; director, Jean Yarbrough; screenplay, Charles R. Marion; additional dialogue, Bert Lawrence; art director, David Milton; set decorator, Raymond Boltz, Jr.; music director, Edward Kay; sound, Tom Lambert; camera, Marcel Le Picard; supervising editor, Otho Lovering; editor, William Austin.

Leo Gorcey (#23322 [Terrence Aloysius] "Slip" Mahoney); Huntz Hall (#233323 [Horance Debussy] "Sach" Jones); Billy Benedict (Whitey); David Grocey (Chuck); Buddy Gorman (Butch); Gabriel Dell (Gabe Moreno); Bernard Gorcey (Louie Dumbrowski); Richard Benedict (Skeets O'Neil); Pat Collins (Bat Armstrong); Effie Lairch (Ma Armstrong); Paul Dubov ("Pretty Boy" Gleason); Joseph Turkel (Benny the Blood); George Chandler (Squirrely Davis); Eddie Gribbon (Hobo Barton); Lyn Thomas (Shirley O'Brien); Jonathan Hale (Judge); Joseph Crehan (Warden Burnside); Eddie Foster, Frank Marlowe (Ma's Henchmen); Edward Gargan (Murphy); Tom Kennedy (Convict); Lyle Talbot (Guard).

One night while Slip (Leo Gorcey), Sach (Huntz Hall) and the boys are returning home from a costume paty, they intercept thieves robbing a warehouse. While they are trying to stop the criminals, the police arrive and accuse them of the crime. Meanwhile, out on bail, one of the group, Whitey (Billy Benedict), notices a similarity between a voice he overhears on his shortwave radio and that of a prisoner whom he had heard on a live broadcast from the state penitentiary. The voice is giving directions for a pending burglary. It occurs to Slip that if he could track down the inmate, he could prove their innocence. Thus he and Sach decide not to contest the charges against them ("I desire to wave away this probation," Slip grandiloquently insists), and they end up with a three-year prison sentence.

Once jailed, Slip and Sach encounter Bat Armstrong (Pat Collins) the prisoner who had been making the broadcasts to lead his gang on the outside to likely robbery sites. To entrap the crafty inmate, Slip and Sach convince Bat that Louie Dumbrowski (Bernard Gorcey) has a stash of money at his sweetshop in his safe. When the heist only nets Armstrong's gang $75.00, the jailed hoodlum quickly deduces he has been duped by Slip and Sach. Bat decides to have the duo escape with him and then to kill them when on the outside. Whitey overhears Bat's radio message to his associates. When they break out of the big house, Whitey, Chuck (David Gorcey) and Butch (Buddy Gorman) are on hand to capture Bat.

Foreshadowing many of the routines they would use in the subsequent *Jail Busters* (1955), q.v., the untiring Bowery Boys play mild havoc with the prison genre, succeeding with a few laughs despite impoverished settings and scant production values. While out on bail and convinced he will soon be imprisoned, Sach devours a book entitled *My Thirty Years Behind Prison Walls*. This leads his curious mentor/cohort Slip to wonder aloud.

SLIP: Why do you read that propaganda?

SACH: Maybe it will help condition me for my prison career.

When they are inducted into the state penitentiary, both Slip and Sach think it is a lark, nothing they can't handle. To make their adjustment easier among the tough inmates, they pretend to be the fearsome Pretty Boy Gleason and Benny the Blood, a masquerade that soon blows up in their faces. When brought before Warden Burnside (Joseph Turkel), dim-witted Sach inquires, "Can I have the Sunday funnies delivered to me?" He also informs the head administrator, "I want an outfit with a belt in the back."

As the newcomers are led down the cellblock to their new home, Sach has a revelation:

SACH: Hey, this place is full of convicts!

SLIP: What did you expect, chorus girls?

Undaunted, Slip is disappointed by his new living accommodations. "I want a room with a view. Oh, this room's crowded."

No sooner does the good-natured Slip encounter another prisoner, than he decides to make friends:

SACH: Hi, what you doin' here?

CONVICT: Twenty years.

To keep their nourishment up, kindly Louie brings the boys behind bars of his famous homemade chicken soup with matzoh balls. Unfortunately, Slip and Sach never get to taste it; the warden consumes it himself.

After days of prison routine drudgery, Sach is still the optimist, finding time to play hopscotch in jail. In a more perceptive moment, he admits, "We got everything we want on the inside, except to be on the outside." On the other hand, enterprising Slip has adjusted to the prison routine. While joyfully absorbed in winning at a game of cards, he observes, "There's nothing like having a full house in the big house." Still later, in true genre fashion, the boys are sent to solitary confinement for being caught wandering the halls without permission. One of the highlights of this picture is Sach's solid imitation of James Cagney from *White Heat* (1949), q.v.

Triple Trouble is certainly no Laurel and Hardy's *Pardon Us* (1931), q.v., or even Wheeler and Woolsey's *Hold 'em Jail* (1932), q.v. However, for any enthusiast of the long-enduring Bowery Boys series, *Triple Trouble* is an extension of sorts for the lead actors who had performed years before in *Crime School* (1938), *Angels with Dirty Faces* (1938), and *Hell's Kitchen* (1939), qq.v.

Variety insisted, "Formula is pat" but admitted, "Gorcey gives his role the characterization it demands, mugging throughout, while Hall does a convincing job as his exasperating buddy."

266. *Turning to Stone* (Canadian Broadcasting Corp., 1985), color, 98 min.

Executive producer, Sid Gerber; producer, John Kastner; associate producer, Harris Verge; director, Eric Till; teleplay, Judith Thompson; art director, Russell Chick; set decorator, Alan Laurie; costumes, Jennifer Alles; makeup, Jean Grossley; music, John Welsman; sound, Eric Hoppe; re-recording, Joe Grimaldi; sound effects, Barry Backus, Terry Burke; sound editor, Tom Berner; special effects, Douglas Waidle; camera, Vic Sarin; editor, Tom Beiner.

Nicky Guadagni (Allison Campbell); Shirley Douglas (Lena Novak); Anne Anglin (Sharon); Jackie Richardson (Dunky [Dunkirk]); Bernard Behrens (Professor Derek Campbell); Kim Renders (Marcie); Ann Holloway (Cora Hemarick); Erin Flannery (Debbie); Lynn Deragon (Mrs. Grover, a Guard); Diane Gordon (Molly); and: Barbara Budd, Colleen Collins, John Friesen, Paul Gross, Kay Hawtrey, Cathy Loan, Lulomir Mykytiuk, Steve Pernie, Maria Vagratsis.

On the surface, this unpretentious entry from the Canadian Broadcasting Corporation appears to be yet another in the long string of pictures depicting the horrors endured by a naïve young girl while coping with prison life. For some, it was just a north-of-the-border distillation of the classic Hollywood entry, *Caged* (1950), q.v. However, the cumulative impact of this low-keyed drama is tremendously affecting. As the luckless victim of *Turning to Stone*, Nicky Guadagni offers a resilient performance that carefully delineates the growing desperation of a well-bred young woman forced to deal with a deadly social structure (i.e. prison). The actress effectively captures how, in the process of surviving, the heroine becomes far tougher than she had ever anticipated. Her frightening realization at what has happened to her is gripping and sticks in the mind. This is a production not to be missed.

Canadian Allison Campbell (Nicky Guadagni) is a respectable, responsible, college graduate. Now a career woman, she is arrested by the police when she is caught at the airport with a stash of cocaine that her boyfriend had entrusted to her. He flees the scene and naïve Allison is left to deal with the consequences. She is sentenced to a term in prison.

No sooner is Allison introduced into the cellblock than Dunkirk (Jackie Richardson), a black prisoner, gives her advice on survival: "If you find your friends you make it through smooth. But if you don't find your friends . . . then there won't be diddly squat left to you."

Each prisoner can furnish her cell with accessories (TVs, record players, aquariums, etc.) as she is able. Each cell has a curtain, so the inmates may have some privacy. However, Allison quickly learns that in this bizarre social structure, the individual is only relevant in relationship to the group. Among the personalities there is the tough Lena Novak (Shirley Douglas), who rules the block and has a relationship with the sensitive Sharon (Anne Anglin). There is also nutty Cora Hemarick (Ann Hollaway), who wants to be treated like a person.

At first when Allison's well-bred father, Professor Derek Campbell (Bernard Behrens), visits his daughter he is angry at her stupid actions that led to her confinement and is embarrassed by the stigma that reflects badly on him as a parent. Allison, on her part, refuses to deal verbally with the trauma she is experiencing as she tries to survive in this unfamiliar, hostile environment. She lies to her emotionally-repressed father: "It's just like being in a boarding school, really. It's not so bad."

But soon she breaks down, sobbing: "Dad, I don't think I'm going to make it. I really can't. . . . They talk about cutting people, doing people like it was nothing. They all hate me. I can't say anything right. I don't think I'm going to make it."

Professor Campbell is extremely uneasy about hearing such confessions. Not only has he no background to help him relate to her turmoil, but he has convinced himself that life in this prison is really not so bad.

Later, Allison talks with the blonde, guitar-strumming Marcie (Kim Renders), who has been in prison four years to date. In contrast to Allison, Marcie's family is too poor to spend money on transportation to visit their daughter in jail. Marcie reasons: "It's almost better in a way [not seeing them personally], cause you can say things in letters you can't say face to face."

Dunkirk, who understands how to deal with her peers, volunteers to be Allison's "girl guide," fully understanding that Allison is straight. She saves her friend from an attack by the vicious Lena.

Having accepted emotionally that she is in prison, Allison decides she just wants to serve her time and avoid any hassles with the keepers and the other inmates. She refuses to help Marcie smuggle a letter out (through Allison's dad) to Marcie's seven-year-old son. Another convict is Debbie (Erin Flannery) who has herself committed to segregation to protect herself from harm by hostile inmates. Although she is physically protected, there is nothing to help the mental punishment. (She will be in segregation for the remaining two years of her stay.) One day by chance she and Allison meet and discuss her plight:

DEBBIE: Twenty-three hours a day in this box. I'm really in a bad head space. All I do all day long is think about different ways of killing myself. And that's not very nice is it?

ALLISON: Isn't this going to drive you crazy?

DEBBIE: Yeah. Up here you may get demons in your head, but at least they're not going to turn around and knife you.

Allison's maladjustment to the prison regimen is monitored by the administration, who insist she is being overly gloomy. Actually, Allison is retreating from her daily anxieties. She is paranoid at being hurt by the vicious Lena and her pals, frightened to tell the keepers about what is going on for fear of reprisals, and bewildered how to get through each day. When Marcie in the next cell tries to kill herself by slashing her wrists, Allison is too scared to call for help.

There is a cellblock social and at first Allison refuses to attend. She later relents and is accosted by other resentful prisoners. Lena comes to her rescue, but soon makes it clear that she wants to control Allison. When Lena attempts to rape her, Allison fends her off by saying if she leaves her alone, her dad will do Lena favors.

When Professor Campbell next comes to the prison, Allison instructs him on the tasks he must accomplish on the outside for Lena. When he at first refuses (i.e. paying inflated sums to purchase Lena's arts and craft work, which he has no use for), she begs him to cooperate, insisting: "It's not your world. We have to play their way."

As time passes, Allison finds herself doing things that months ago would never have entered her mind. She steals drugs from another inmate's purse. Lena and her stooges think Marcie is the culprit and when they march to her cell to beat up the victim, they order Allison to divert the keepers stationed at the cell-bar entrance to the dormitory. A frightened Allison complies. Dunkirk is disgusted by the changes in Allison.

Later on, the hardened Lena, in a rare moment of sharing, confides to Allison her philosophy on life in prison:

> I'll tell you . . . any animal in the jungle who is not capable of ripping out the throats of the other animals gets his own throat ripped.
> I was thrown in this system when I was fourteen for promiscuity. It took me about five years of getting bashed around before I learned. You learn to go cold, that's all. But you always keep something warm. Something somewhere. You know?

More time passes and the ever-demanding Lena now pressures Allison and her Dad to pick up drugs from Lena's boyfriend on the outside. This is going one step too far for Professor Campbell. He refuses, telling Allison she must stop letting her environment pull her down. Fearing Lena's reprisals, the near hysterical Allison asks to be put in segregation, but the quarters are full. The spiteful Lena has Sharon beat up Allison. When the Professor next visits and sees what has happened to his daughter, he relents and cooperates. However, Allison has reached a decision; rather than break she is turning herself around. She tells the guards about Lena's assorted activities. Now that she becomes a "bug," she must be placed in the emotionally stressful segregation.

As she is led away to her new prison within a prison, Professor Campbell expresses: "Allison, you're very very brave. I'm proud of you, Allison."

However, once in this special seclusion, the lonely, monotonous routine begins to affect Allison. She feels like a little child existing in a plastic bubble; a deprived soul who has lost most of her privileges. Depressed, restless and sullen, yet determined to somehow survive, she waits out the endless hours.

> GUARD: It was your choice.
> ALLISON: Was it?

So ends the narrative of another warm human being "turned to stone."

With so much insight to offer, it is a shame that *TV Guide* magazine rated this effective psychological study only one star in its four star rating system.

267. *20,000 Years in Sing Sing* (First National/Warner Bros., 1933), 81 min

Producer, Robert Lord; director, Michael Curtiz; associate director, Stanley Logan; based on the book by Warden Lewis E. Lawes; screenplay, Courtney Terrett, Lord, Wilson Mizner, Brown Holmes; art director, Anton Grot; costumes, Orry-Kelly; music, Bernhard Kaun; music director, Leo F. Forbstein; camera, Barney McGill; editor, George Amy.

Spencer Tracy (Tom Connors); Bette Davis (Fay); Lyle Talbot (Bud); Arthur Byron (Warden Paul Long); Grant Mitchell (Dr. Ames); Warren Hymer (Hype); Louis Calhern (Joe Finn); Sheila Terry (Billie); Edward J. McNamara (Chief of Guards); Spencer Charters (Daniels); Nella Walker (Mrs. Long); Harold Huber (Tony); William LeMaire (Black Jack); Arthur Hoyt (Dr. Meeker); Sam Godfrey (2nd Reporter); George Pat Collins (Mike); and: Lucille Collins, Jimmie Conlon, Rockliffe Fellowes, Clarence Wilson.

In 1932, the high-profile Warden Lewis E. Lawes authored a popular book on his experiences as head administrator of Sing Sing Prison in Ossining, New York. Warner Bros. Pictures, always eager for new material to translate into gritty, brisk drama, purchased the screen rights to Lawes's work. Over the next decade the resourceful studio found several occasions to adapt the material into screenplays.

What makes *20,000 Years in Sing Sing* such a landmark genre film, above and beyond its intriguing cast, is its straightforward manner of presenting prison life. Unlike later movies (including the remake of this film, *Castle on the Hudson* [1940], q.v.), there is no apology for the state of the penal system. At this point in time, the general consensus was that prisons were built to punish society's offenders, and if there were flaws to the American approach to penology, that was too bad. If the offenders incarcerated in prison happened to be rehabilitated by their experiences, so much the better. If not, the convicts had been justly punished for their wrongs. All that said, it was the general belief that once having served his sentence, an ex-convict should not be stigmatized for his past misdeeds. In short, if a man could survive the challenge of life behind the high walls, then he deserved a fresh start.

This mixed attitude of retribution and forgiveness would undergo drastic changes in the later 1930s, yet another reaction to the all-encompassing Depression. By the end of the decade, a new sentiment, which had some enunciation in *The Criminal Code* (1931), q.v., and *The Last Mile* (1932), q.v., had become prevalent. No longer were prisoners merely wrongdoers getting their just desserts. They were now victims (of the topsy-turvy capitalistic system), abused by authority figures (the keepers) and unforgiven by a hypocritical public once they had paid their debts to society. They had become the underdogs.

No such emotional/intellectual complications inhibit one's "enjoyment" in viewing *20,000 Years in Sing Sing*. It is a robust production slickly directed by Michael Curtiz and starring a rugged Spencer Tracy, who had made his screen debut in Fox's *Up the River* (1930), q.v. Because gangster yarns were then so popular with moviegoers, *20,000 Years in Sing Sing* mixes that genre with the prison study, admirably depicting how a cocky hoodlum undergoes a change of heart once behind the intimidating walls of Sing Sing Prison. In the course of this drama, the anti-hero/mug has the opportunity to right wrongs and to die relatively

Lyle Talbot and Spencer Tracy in *20,000 Years in Sing Sing* (1933).

content, knowing he has set matters straight. Thus in a relatively brief running time, this adventure tale reveals how a hot-headed gangster survives the test of manliness (coping with the prison system) and comes to terms with himself. In its peculiar way, it is an upbeat narrative of the human spirit.

Cocky Tom Connors (Spencer Tracy) is on a train bound for Sing Sing Prison. Besides police guards, the notorious gangster has several reporters accompanying him, all anxious for noteworthy quotes to publish in their papers.

> REPORTER: That's your castle on the Hudson.
>
> CONNORS: Sing Sing. What a lousy name! It sounds like a chop suey joint.
>
> REPORTER: Don't let it get you down. . . . [There is] no tailor shop nor speakeasy.
>
> CONNORS: Nothing gets me down. If I don't like the joint, I'll move out. . . . I'll kick my way out with moccasins on.

Connors is confident that his slimy lawyer, Joe Finn (Louis Calhern), will find a means of getting him released from his five-to-thirty year prison term. Finn is on hand to make a deal with Warden Paul Long (Arthur Byron). The mouthpiece blithely hands the administrator $5,000 worth of bonds, insisting, "We'd like to know he [Tom Connors] could buy things in the commissary. So we made up a little purse."
The offended warden takes the bond and burns it:

I'm running this prison and, while I'm running it, I run it without politicians and without bribes. People on the outside are supposed to be treated free and equal, but they aren't. In here, they really are. In here, one inmate is as good as another inmate, but no better.

The no-nonsense warden then focuses on his new charge:

There aren't any big shots in here, except me. And remember this, if two men in this place know anything, I know it. . . .

I'm going to show you it's a privilege to work. A privilege you've got to earn. . . . You talk about callouses. I'm going to let you sit in your cell on your hard iron bench till you get callouses where you can't show it. And you're going to pray to God to let you work, to break rock, shovel coal, pick up garbage. Anything to get out of your cell. And then you're going out into that rock pile gag and swing a sledge until you can't stand up and you're going to thank heaven for the privilege.

This leads to challenges and counter-challenges between the two adversaries.

TOM: Now I'll tell you something. If I find I got a chance to crash my way out of here, and I have to rub somebody out to do it, I'd just as soon rub you out as the next guy.

WARDEN: Yes, I know. If I were in the same place and had a chance, I'd probably do the same thing. But the point is, Connors, you haven't got a chance, not one in a million. . . .

One of these days, you'll learn Connors that no man has a spot in this world except in relation to the people around him. That you've got to be useful to live.

After three months of confinement in his cell, Connors is allowed a visit from his girlfriend Fay (Bette Davis). Already there are changes in the man; he is going a bit stir crazy:

Gee, it's swell to see you! . . . I sit in that cell all day and think about you till I think I'll go crazy. . . . I'd give a million bucks to be with you for a little while. Do you love me? . . . Well, don't come up here dolled up like that anymore. You'll get me foaming at the mouth like a cream puff.

When another convict, Bud (Lyle Talbot), plans a prison break, Tom refuses to join in the plan, not because he is that reformed, but because it is scheduled to occur on a Saturday (a day notorious for being bad luck for Tom). As it turns out the escape fails. Connors assures the warden, "Don't think because I'm playing it smart, that I'm getting soft." Nevertheless, before much further, Connors is undergoing a positive transformation. He is adapting to prison routine and a mutual respect develops between the warden and the convict.

When Warden Long receives a telegram that Fay is seriously injured as the result of an automobile accident, he allows Tom to leave the prison to visit her. A grateful Tom promises to return that night (which is a Saturday). Connors rushes to see Fay in New York City and she tells him that the accident was caused by Finn, who was making advances to her in the speeding car. At that juncture, Finn arrives and attempts to buy Fay off from legally proceeding against him. Tom and Finn fight and Fay, who has a gun hidden under her pillow, shoots the lawyer. Connors goes into hiding.

A scandal erupts at the prison in which the warden is blamed for letting a dangerous convict like Tom out on leave. Concerned at fulfilling his promise to Long, Tom returns to the prison and is later tried for Finn's murder. Refusing to incriminate Fay, Connors is sentenced to die in the electric chair. As he tells a prison guard, "I worked my way through this joint right up to the death house. And when I graduate, it will be to the other door."

Once in the death house, Tom becomes friendly with the other convicts, including the harmonica playing Hype (Warren Hymer). The men joke about their fate and wile away the hours, as, one by one, they are systematically killed by the state. Just before he is scheduled to be electrocuted, Fay visits him for the final time. She begs him again to allow her to tell the truth. He refuses, reasoning: "This is a chance for me to do something decent in my life. You can't take that away from me. I love you."

Accompanied by the warden and the prison chaplain, Tom walks the last mile to his death. It is a Saturday.

Mordaunt Hall *(New York Times)* reported, "In this rapidly paced film there are some extraordinarily interesting glimpses of prison routines.... The various scenes which give a comprehensive idea of the way Warden Long, of the picture, rules the prison are compelling.... This film also shows how the glum, stubborn inmate is affected by hearing the cries and cheers of other prisoners who have done their toil and are enjoying games." *Variety* was more matter-of-fact in its response. "Sing Sing's warden can have no complaint against the Warner picture. He extended WB every cooperation in the filming and permitted cameras within his prison for actual scenes, including of prisoners in the mob scenes.... Picture deals more with conditions at a prison like Sing Sing than it does to story.... Far-fetched, but it sells. Considerable comedy dots the action, making the picture nearest things to such comedies as *Up the River* and *Big House*."

Warner Bros. would remake *20,000 Years in Sing Sing* as *Castle on the Hudson* (1940), q.v., with John Garfield, Ann Sheridan and Pat O'Brien in the key roles. While the storyline would be very similar in structure, the focus was switched to the braggart gangster (Garfield) being a pawn of his environment and a victim of the Depression's grip.

268. *Two Seconds* (First National, 1932), 68 min.

Director, Mervyn LeRoy; based on the play by Elliott Lester; adaptor, Harvey Thew; art director, Anton Grot; music director, Leo F. Forbstein; camera, Sol Polito; editor, Terrill Morse.

Edward G. Robinson (John Allen); Preston Foster (Bud Clark); Vivienne Osborne (Shirley Day); J. Carrol Naish (Tony); Guy Kibbee (Bookie); Adrienne Dore (Annie); Frederick Burton (Judge); Dorothea Wolbert (Lizzie); Edward McWade (The Doctor); Berton Churchill (The Warden); William Janney (A College Boy); Lew Brice, Franklin Parker, Frederick Howard (Reporters); Helena Phillips (Mrs. Smith); June Gittleson (Fat Girl); Jill Bennett, Luana Walters (Tarts); Otto Hoffman (Justice of the Peace); Harry Woods (Executioner); Gladys Lloyd (Woman); John Kelly, Matt McHugh (Mashers).

Edward G. Robinson (1893–1973) provided many dynamic performances during his six decades of filmmaking. While he is best remembered for his riveting role as the grasping gangster in *Little Caesar* (1930), he was equally fascinating in the well-regarded *Two Seconds*. Like the structurally similar *The Blue Angel* (1930), *Two Seconds* traces the mental collapse of a hardworking man because of his vicious, selfish love mate. In *Two Seconds*, the shrew eventually causes the distraught hero to murder her. As a result he is sentenced to the electric chair. The gripping moments leading up to the man's execution remain a landmark in the cinema's depiction of legalized homicide. Once seen, it cannot be forgotten.

John Allen (Edward G. Robinson) is on death row in a state prison. He is about to be electrocuted for the murder of his wife. The warden (Berton Churchill) announces: "All set. Then we will start the parade." The warden has warned the excited press—just arrived to witness the execution—that there are to be no photographs taken of the condemned man. Another witness at the penitentiary is a young college man (William Janney) who is conducting research for his sociology class. He wonders why no one is allowed to talk to the convict. The staid prison physician (Edward McWade) explains:

> Because Allen is living on his nerve now. If he talks at all, it will simply be to keep up his courage. He really doesn't expect an answer. If you gave him one, it would throw him off and we'd have a devil of a time with him. Hysteria and all that fighting to keep out of the chair.

There follows a brief discussion between the matter-of-fact doctor and the earnest college student about Allen's final moments on earth:

> DOCTOR: His body will be paralyzed, but his brain will continue to function for maybe two seconds.
>
> STUDENT: Gee, those will be the longest two seconds he ever lived!
>
> DOCTOR: Long enough for him to relive his whole life.

Allen is strapped into the electric chair. A buzzing sound is heard. The prisoner's mind flashes back over his life.

Allen, who has ambitions of becoming something respectable and important in life, and his pal, Bud Clark (Preston Foster), are both happy-go-lucky riveters. One night, while out on the town, John stops in at a dance hall where he meets one of the flashy hostesses, Shirley Day (Vivienne Osborne). Sensing she has met an easy victim, Shirley convinces the naïve Allen that she has noble ambitions for her life, if only she finds the right opportunities. Despite Bud's warnings about the selfish Shirley, Allen insists there is nothing to worry about, because he has no intentions of marrying Shirley. However, the gold digger has other plans, as she reasons, "I found out a Mrs. can get away with things a Miss can't." One night, the scheming Shirley gets John so drunk that he does not even realize he has wed her. Upset by his rash act, he determines to make the best of the bad situation.

Later, while working on the girders of a new skyscraper, John and Bud have sharp words about Shirley. As Allen leans towards Clark to strike him, the latter moves instinctively, loses his footing, and falls to his death. Stunned by the event, John becomes too nervous to return to work. Soon he is sitting about the apartment in a daze while the money-hungry Shirley returns to her dance hall job. Before long, she is dating other men and tormenting Allen with lurid details of how she is earning their money. Later, he wins a substantial bet on the horse races. After paying back her lover (J. Carrol Naish), he berates Shirley ("You were born rotten!") and then shoots her.

At his trial, the deranged defendant makes no defense. However, he jumps to his feet to provide the judge (Frederick Burton) with an hysterical rationale of the sordid situation: "If you'd burned me when I was living off her, that was the right time to do it. . . . That's when you should have given me the chair! Don't you see you're killing me at the wrong time?. . . Now that I've squared things off you want to kill me."

The scene flashes back to the present. The executioner pulls the switch. A buzzing sound is heard. The witnesses jump. The end.

Mordaunt Hall *(New York Times)* assessed, "Edward G. Robinson contributes a remarkably forceful portrayal. . . . It is a production that is minus any comedy relief, being glum and gruesome, but adroitly done, a film that compels attention and one that is ably cast." *Variety* was more critical, "*Two Seconds* is more of a laboratory cross-section of a humdrum individual's mental stance on life, done in celluloid, than a picture. . . . Combination of the tragic ending, always b.o. [box office] poison for the masses, and the slow progression are too much to be offset by the technical niceties, nor even the star's draw and his excellent support."

While *Two Seconds* was considered just "another" picture from the Warner Bros. factory, it holds up amazingly well today, with Edward G. Robinson's mesmerizing performance a riveting experience for the viewer. Preston Foster had played the role of Bud Clark in *Two Seconds* on Broadway. Edward G. Robinson's then wife, actress Gladys Lloyd had a brief bit in *Two Seconds*.

269. *Unchained* (Warner Bros., 1955), 75 min.

Producer/director, Hall Bartlett; based on the book *Prisoners Are People* by Warden Kenyon J. Scudder; screenplay, Bartlett; music, Alex North; orchestrator, Maurice de Packh; song, North and Hy Zaret; assistant director, Bob Farfan; sound, Hal Bumbaugh; camera, Virgil E. Miller; editor, Cotton Warburton.

Elroy [Crazylegs] Hirsch (Steve Davitt); Barbara Hale (Mary Davitt); Chester Morris (Warden Kenyon J. Scudder); Todd Duncan (Bill Howard); Johnny Johnston (Eddie Garrity); Peggy Knudsen (Elaine); Jerry Paris (Joe Ravens); John Qualen (Leonard Haskins); Bill Kennedy (Sanders); Henry Nakamura (Jerry Hakara); Kathryn Grant (Sally Haskins); Bob Patten (Swanson); Don Kennedy (Gladstone); Mack Williams (Mr. Johnson); Saul Gorss (Police Captain); Tim Considine (Win Davitt).

Unchained is based on the 1952 book by Kenyon J. Scudder, the chief administrator of the California Institution for Men at Chino. Scudder who was approaching retirement as this film was released, spent thirteen years transferring Chino into a pathfinding penal experiment. Under Scudder's guidance, this 2,600 acre, $20,000,000 facility became the world's largest minimum security prison, a model institution without bars, walls or armed guards. "The picture has good exploitation potentialities. . . . [Its] story of an inspiring experiment in prison reform [is] both interesting and thought-provoking" (Jack Moffett, *Hollywood Reporter*).

Among the prisoners transferred from San Quentin Prison to Chino is Steve Davitt (Elroy [Crazylegs] Hirsch), a man convicted of almost killing a man he suspected of stealing from him. The newcomers are greeted by Warden Kenyon J. Scudder (Chester Morris) who explains the liberal rules and regulations of this pilot program prison. Before long, hot-tempered Steve is tussling with bully Sanders (Bill Kennedy) who has roughed up another inmate, Eddie Garrity (Johnny Johnston).

When Davitt's patient wife Mary (Barbara Hale) visits Steve, he admits he intends to escape. Mary meets with Scudder and without revealing what her husband has stated, asks the superintendent to watch out over her spouse. It is Scudder who comes to Steve's rescue when he gets into another fight with Sanders. Later, a fellow prisoner, Bill Howard (Todd Duncan), suggests that Steve compete for the election of dormitory representative on the Men's Council. Steve has ulterior motives for accepting, reasoning that his new position would help his breakout plans. He wins the post and gains new self-respect from the responsibilities of the job. It is the new-found sense of responsibility that causes him to abandon his escape plans. However, when the parole board denies his release, he angrily decides to break out immediately. Howard attempts to stop him and Davitt knocks him out. Part way into his fight, he realizes what he is doing. He returns, apologizes to Bill and determines to serve out his time with a positive spirit.

Some critics were adverse to the obvious preachment of *Unchained*, not to mention the conventional plot ploys. "[O]ne of those films—so very earnest, so very sincere—that makes you wish it might have been better.... Passions, conflict rarely overflow into action; they are answered instead by sane, sound arguments" (*Saturday Review* magazine). Howard Thompson *(New York Times)* accepted the film "as a camera tour of the largest 'wall-less' prison in the world" but argued that "the background remains far more intriguing and unconventional than any of the case histories described." Thompson found two structural faults with the picture: "[F]irst of all the glaring contrast with the recent prison riots. Secondly, Chino itself as seen here, operates primarily as a transient testing-ground for less serious offenders." On the other hand, *Variety* endorsed, "There's a public service flavor to this melodrama that raises it a notch above the usual prison thriller."

One of the unique aspects of *Unchained* was its title song, "Unchained Melody" sung in the picture by Todd Duncan. It was nominated for an Academy Award and became a popular hit, with versions by Les Baxter, Al Hibbler, Roy Hamilton, June Valli, and the Righteous Brothers. The film's star, Elroy Leon "Crazylegs" Hirsch (b. 1923) had been a champion football player as a member of the Los Angeles Rams. He starred in *Crazylegs* (1953), a biography about his life and was later the general manager (1960–1969) of the Rams. For strong-jawed Chester Morris (1901–1970), *Unchained* was a return to the prison genre, since he had starred in the seminal study, *The Big House* (1930), q.v.

270. *Under the Gun* (Universal, 1951), 84 min.

Producer, Ralph Dietrich; director, Ted Tetzlaff; story, Daniel B. Ullman; screenplay, George Zuckerman; art directors, Bernard Herzbrun, Edward L. Ilou; set decorator, John Austin; costumes, Orry-Kelly; makeup, Del Armstrong; music, Joseph Gershenson; assistant director, John Sherwood; sound, Leslie I. Carey, Jack A. Bolger, Jr.; special effects, David Horsley; camera, Henry Freulich; additional camera, John Herman; editor, Virgil Vogel.

Richard Conte (Bert Galvin); Audrey Totter (Ruth Williams); John McIntire (Sheriff Langley); Sam Jaffe (Gower); Shepperd Strudwick (Milo Bragg); Gregg Martell (Nero); Phillip Pine (Gandy); Don Randolph (Sherbourne); Royal Dano (Nugent); Richard Taber (Five Shot); and: Bob Greer.

"The astounding story of a prison law that put a gun in the hands of a convict ... and gave him a pardon if he *used* it" (Advertisement for *Under the Gun*).

Truculent racketeer Bert Galvin (Richard Conte) meets cafe singer Ruth Williams (Audrey Totter) while visiting Miami Beach. He persuades the comely miss to come back to New York with him to sing in his club. While driving northward, they stop in a southern town where years earlier Bert had been a murder

Bob Greer and Richard Conte in *Under the Gun* (1950).

suspect in a still unsolved case. The victim's brother confronts Galvin and, in a shootout, is killed by the gangster. Redneck Sheriff Langley (John McIntire) arrests Galvin. However, Bert's lawyer, Milo Braff (Shepherd Strudwick), is convinced that Ruth's testimony will clear his client. Instead, she proves to be a bad witness on the stand. As a result, Bert is sentenced to twenty years in prison.

At the prison farm, Bert is assigned to a road gang supervised by a trustee Nugent (Royal Dano). According to prison rules, Nugent carries a gun and, if he should shoot an escaping prisoner, he wins a pardon. Galvin convinces the weak-minded Five Shot (Richard Taber) to attempt an escape. As anticipated, he is shot dead by Nugent, who is soon paroled. Bert wins the job of the new "shooter." Next, he makes a deal with philosophical convict Gower (Sam Jaffe), promising to send $25,000 to the man's impoverished family if he will attempt to escape. Gower agrees and, once the money is paid, Bert gives the inmate thirty days to make his break. Despite careful planning, Gower is shot dead and, as a result, Bert is paroled.

Galvin returns to Miami where he forces Ruth at gunpoint to return to New York with him. Meanwhile, Langley discovers a diary Gower kept which outlines his deal with Bert. Longley orders road blocks set up, which Bert crashes through. He next flees by motorboat, but is eventually killed by the police. Ruth is rescued.

Despite its resourceful cast, this entry won few endorsements from the critics. "This gangster-prison melodrama is not cheerful entertainment, and the plot is on the improbable side.... The action for the most part is slow-moving, but it keeps one tense" (*Harrison's Reports*). Bosley Crowther *(New York Times)* wondered, "But we can't for the life of us figure any reason for such an aimless tale, except to indulge in bleak sadism. The marksmanship is infinitely better than the film." *Variety* reported, "Ted Tetzlaff's direction gets a nice element of suspense into the story-telling and crams quite a bit of action into the chase sequences. Conte gives his tough role a strong performance but his co-star, Miss Totter, rates only a few scenes.

Location filming for *Under the Gun* was accomplished in Florida. During a nightclub sequence, there is a rendition of "I Cried for You."

271. *Up the River* (Fox, 1930), 92 min.

Presenter, William Fox; director, John Ford; stager, William Collier, Jr.; story, Maurine Watkins; screenplay, Watkins, (uncredited): Ford, William Collier, Sr.; set designer, Duncan Cramer; wardrobe, Sophie Wachner; assistant directors, Edward O'Fearna, Wingate Smith; song, Joseph McCarthy, James F. Hanley; sound, W. W. Lindsay; camera, Joseph H. August; editor, Frank E. Hull.

Spencer Tracy (St. Louis); Warren Hymer (Dannemora Dan); Humphrey Bogart (Steve Jordan); Claire Luce (Judy Field); Joan Marie Lawes (Jean); Sharon Lynn (Edith La Verne); George MacFarlane (Honest John Jessup); Gaylord [Steve] Pen-dleton (Morris); Morgan Wallace (Frosby); William Collier, Sr. (Pop); Robert Emmett O'Connor (The Warden); Louise MacIntosh (Mrs. Massey); Edythe Chapman (Mrs. Jordan); Johnny Walker (Happy); Noel Francis (Shopie); Mildred Vincent (Annie); Mack Clark (Whitelay); Goodee Montgomery (Kit); Althea Henley (Cynthia); Carol Wines (Daisy Elmore); Adele Windsor (Minnie); Richard Keene (Dick); Elizabeth Keating (May); Helen Keating (June); Robert Burns (Slim); John Swor (Clem); Pat Somerset (Beauchamp); Joe Brown (Deputy Warden); Harvey Clark (Nash); Black and Blue (Slim and Klem); and: Robert Parrish.

With prison breaks in the U.S. such a highly publicized reality, Broadway fastened on the topical subject in two stark plays, *The Criminal Code* (1929) and *The Last Mile* (1930). Both of these grim studies of distraught convicts would be translated onto the screen. However, before they arrived in film versions, Metro-Goldwyn-Mayer jumped the gun with *The Big House* (1930), q.v. Not only was that motion picture a commercial and critical hit, but it started Hollywood on its own cycle of prison stories. While MGM was preparing *The Big House,* Fox Films had its own prison yarn, *Up the River* in pre-production. Fox hired Spencer Tracy, then on Broadway in *The Last Mile,* to spend a few weeks away from his stage work to star in the project. His co-star was another Broadway refugee, Humphrey Bogart. In *John Ford* (1978), the director recalled for author Peter Bogdanovich the genesis of this picture which started out as a screen story by Maurine Watkins and which was almost cancelled when *The Big House* beat Fox to the theaters with Hollywood's first big prison drama talkie:

> [D]ay by day, Bill Collier ... and I rewrote the script. There was so much opportunity for humor in it that eventually it turned out to be a comedy—all about what

Warren Hymer, Humphrey Bogart, William Collier, Sr., and Spencer Tracy in *Up the River*
(1930).

went on inside a prison; we had them playing baseball against Sing-Sing, and these
two fellows broke back *in* so they'd be in time for the big game. We did it in two
weeks; it was Tracy's and Bogart's first picture — they were great — just went right in,
natural.

Two feisty convicts, St. Louis (Spencer Tracy) and the dim-witted Dannemora
Dan (Warren Hymer) break out of jail. As Dan confides to his pal, "I hate all
prisons. The food is bad." After a disagreement, they go their separate ways. Later,
Dan undergoes religious conversion in Kansas City and joins the Brotherhood of
Hope. However, this reformation is short-lived. When he spots high-living St.
Louis parading about town with two attractive young women, he gets into a fight
with his one-time pal. As a result, they both are sentenced to a term at Bensonata
Penitentiary.

According to one disgruntled Bensonata inmate, "It's getting to be a day
nursery. Just one week before the big game and they had to pardon the pitcher!"
But big-spending St. Louis, who carries a walking stick, does not find everything
to his satisfaction. He warns the warden (Robert Emmett O'Connor): "I shoot
straight. When I decide to go, I'll warn you."

He also has a few demands: "If you don't mind, I don't like to sleep too high
up. I'd like an airy cell with southern exposure, sunshine, running water."

Meanwhile, Judy Field (Claire Luce) framed on a bogus charge, finds romance
in prison with convict Steve Jordan (Humphrey Bogart), a well-bred young man
who is serving a term on a manslaughter charge. About to be paroled, Steve promises to wait for Judy's release some five months in the future. He advises her,

"When we get out of here, we're just a couple of ex-convicts. We'll have to start over at the bottom of the ladder."

When freed, Steve returns to his small New England hometown where his family thinks he has been away on a trip to China. He is followed there by a crooked stock salesman, Frosby (Morgan Wallace), who once was Judy's boyfriend. Frosby confronts Steve and threatens to blackmail him unless he agrees to help him swindle the local citizens. Learning of this, St. Louis and Dan escape during the annual prison variety show. They reach New England in time to save Steve's family and his neighbors from being swindled. Having accomplished their mission, they ride a freight train back to prison. The two convicts are pleased to reach their destination:

ST. LOUIS: Home again!

DAN: And I'm glad to be back!

Upon approaching the front gate of Bensonata Prison, Dan asks the guards: "Okay to come in?"

The boys are in time to wish Judy well, now that she is paroled, and to tell her that Steve is waiting for her. They then rush onto the playing field where St. Louis is the star pitcher and wins the big baseball game for their alma mater. (During the game, the players are handcuffed on the bench until it is time for them to play. The Bensonata crew's mascot is a donkey with zebra stripes painted on it. The opposing squad arrives for the match in an armored prison wagon, corralled by armed guards!)

Mordaunt Hall *(New York Times)* assessed, "Whatever may be one's opinion of depicting levity in a penitentiary, this screen offering often proved to be violently funny.... It has a number of clever incidents and lines, but now and again it is more than a trifle too slow.... The serious details of prison life are glossed over quickly. *Variety* judged, "Comedy prison picture that can follow *Big House, Numbered Men* and the others because of its laugh contents. It's even suited to a quick follow-up in the serious prison dramas because of a satirical breeziness.... Life just can't be this joyous in stir, but it is good entertainment. Picture's out is that the majority of the auditors [i.e. the audience] won't authoritatively know the difference. While the laughs square everything."

Up the River is quite an amazing amalgam of genres. It is part serious prison picture, part comedy, part musical (the annual prison variety show in which Black and Blue perform a tap routine and William Collier, Sr. does funny routines), part romance and a little bit underworld drama. Occasionally *Up the River* is an indirect preachment, as when the condescending do-gooder Mrs. Massey (Louise MacIntosh) parades through the prison confines, thinking in her patronizing manner that she is doing such wonders for the unfortunate inmates.

Spencer Tracy and Warren Hymer would reteam in the prison drama *20,000 Years in Sing Sing* (1933), q.v. Humphrey Bogart would appear in such other genre pieces as *San Quentin* (1937), *Crime School* (1938), *The Big Shot* (1942), qq.v., and in one of his final films, the comedic *We're No Angels* (1955) he would be an escapee from Devil's Island.

Twentieth Century–Fox would remake *Up the River* (1938), *infra*, with far lesser results.

For the record, the precious young actress playing the warden's sassy young daughter Jean was actually Joan Marie Lawes, the daughter of Warden Lewis E. Lawes of Sing Sing Prison.

272. *Up the River* (20th Century–Fox, 1938), 75 min.

Producer, Sol M. Wurtzel; director, Alfred Werker; based on the story by Maurine Watkins; screenplay, Lou Breslow, John Patrick; art directors, Bernard Herzbrun, Chester Gore; costumes, Sophie Wachner; music director, Samuel Kaylin; song, Sidney Clara and Harry Akst; choreographer, Nicholas Castle, Geneva Sawyer; camera, Peverell Marley; editor, Nick Demaggio.

Preston Foster (Chipper Morgan); Tony Martin (Tommy Grant [Graham]); Phyllis Brooks (Helen); Slim Summerville (Slim Nelson); Arthur Treacher (Darby Randall); Alan Dinehart (Warden Willis); Eddie Collins (Fisheye Conroy); Jane Darwell (Mrs. Graham); Sidney Toler (Jeffrey Mitchell); Bill "Bojangles" Robinson (Memphis Jones); Edward Gargan (Tiny); Robert Allen (Ray Douglas); Dorothy Dearing (Martha Graham); Charles D. Brown (Warden Harris).

> In comparison with recent crop of prison melodramas, this one plays everything within the prison walls with strokes of broad comedy and humor. Wisely passing up the strict routine and discipline passages....
>
> *(Variety)*

Eight years after Fox Films had produced the popular *Up the River* it remade the property starring Preston Foster and crooner Tony Martin. Much of what seemed new and fresh with the original comedy picture now appeared a bit forced and somewhat trite in this distillation which combined the prison genre with that of celluloid college football tales and musical comedy.

Con artists Chipper Morgan (Preston Foster) and Darby Randall (Arthur Treacher) are caught practicing their cardsharp activities on an ocean liner. They are sentenced to a ten-year term at Rockwell Penitentiary and are welcomed back with open arms by the good-natured warden (Alan Dinehart) and inmates who need their prowess on the gridiron in upcoming football games. Their cellmate is young, earnest Tommy Grant [Graham] (Tony Martin) who is determined to break out of prison when he learns that confidence man Jeffrey Mitchell (Sidney Toler) intends to fleece his mother (Jane Darwell). Not even his convict girlfriend, Helen (Phyllis Brooks) can stop his wild plan. To save the day, Chipper and Darby sneak out of the prison dressed as women visitors. They rush to Tommy's hometown to prevent Mitchell from swindling any of the townfolk. Satisfied with their success, they rush back to the prison to participate in the big football game which they win against State. The warden, who had bet $100 on the competition, breathes a sigh of relief.

To exploit Tony Martin's abilities as a tenor, he is made the star of the prison follies, singing the ballad "It's the Strangest Thing." The variety show also encompasses a tap dance by Bill "Bojangles" Robinson, a chorus line of convicts in drag, and the antics of Eddie Collins as the prisoner/master of ceremonies, Fisheye Conroy.

Rating the remake of *Up the River,* the amused B. R. Cristler (*New York Times*) joshed, "Though the picture is a rowdy and irresponsible comedy, it has its cute side; the very idea of Arthur Treacher as a star halfback, for instance, is cute."

In *John Ford* (1978) author Peter Bogdanovich quotes the director as saying of the 1938 edition, "They tried to remake it some years later—well...."

273. *The Valachi Papers* (Columbia, 1972), color, 123 min.

Executive producer, Nino E. Krisman; producer, Dino De Laurentiis; director, Terence Young; based on the book by Peter Maas; screenplay, Stephen Geller; art director, Mario Carbuglia; set decorators, John Godfrey, Ferdinando Ruffo; costumes, Ann Roth, Giorgio Desideri; makeup, Gianetto De Rossi, Mirella Sforza; music, Riz Ortolani; assistant directors, Christian Raoux, Girgio Gentili; sound, Roy Mangano; special effects, Eros Baciucchi; camera, Aldo Tonti; editor, John Dwyre.

Charles Bronson (Joseph Valachi); Lino Ventura (Vito Genovese); Joseph Wiseman (Salvatore Maranzano); Jill Ireland (Maria Valachi); Walter Chiari (Dominick "The Gap" Petrilli); Gerald S. O'Loughlin (FBI Agent Ryan); Amedeo Nazzari (Gaetano Reina); Guido Leontini (Tony Bender); Allesandro Sperli (Giuseppe Masseria); Maria Baxa (Donna Petrillo); Pupella Maggio (Rosanna Reina); Fausto Tozzi (Albert Anastasia); Mario Pilar (Salerto); Franco Borelli (Buster from Chicago); Angelo Infante (Charles "Lucky" Luciano); Fred Valleca (Johnny Beck); John Alarimo (Steven Ferrigno); Arny Freeman (Penitentiary Warden); Giancomino De Michelis (Little Augie); Sylvester Lamont (Commander of Fort Monmouth); Sabine Sun (Jane); Isabelle Marchal (Mary Lou); Imelde Marani (Donna's Girl Friend); Jason McCallum (Donald Valachi); Saro Urzi (Masseria); Frank Gio (Frank); Steve Belouise (Vinnie); Anthony Dawson [Antonio Margheriti] (Federal Investigator); Don Koll (State Trooper).

Sometimes a convict is so useful to the law that he receives special treatment while a prisoner. Such was the case with Joseph Valachi, whose amazing confessions formed the basis of Peter Maas's best selling book *The Valachi Papers* (1969). Italian filmmaker Dino De Laurentiis turned the chronicle into a splashy, gory, confusing screen recitation of the lives and times of the rich and famous among the Mafia. One of the several disconcerting factors about this international co-production was the use of English language lip-synching for several of the European cast members.

In 1962, despite the death threat from a $20,000 contract offered for his assassination by gangster chief/fellow convict Vito Genovese (Lino Ventura), Joseph Valachi (Charles Bronson) agrees to reveal to FBI agent Ryan (Gerald S. O'Loughlin) the details of his years of service within the Mafia.

In 1929, Brooklyn-born petty criminal Valachi encounters Dominick Petrilli (Walter Chiari) in prison. The latter, when they are both released, introduces Joe to Mafioso Salvatore Maranzano (Joseph Wiseman). Maranzano brings Valachi into his criminal organization and makes him a driver for Gaetano Reina (Amedeo Nazzari). After Reina is murdered by Maranzano's rivals, Valachi becomes Maranzano's driver. Two years later, Maranzano, who has segmented the Cosa Nostra in the U.S. into separate family units, is murdered by his own competitors, including Lucky Luciano (Angelo Infanti). Valachi flees and is hidden by Reina's widow (Pupella Maggio) and thereafter marries the woman's daughter, Maria (Jill Ireland). Valachi and Petrilli later strike an accord with Luciano and Genovese. After Luciano is imprisoned and Genovese relocated to Italy, Albert Anastasia (Fausto Tozzi) is placed in power. Some years later, Genovese returns to America and asserts his power. In 1957, Anastasia is murdered, and Genovese calls a meeting of the full organization. Thereafter, both Genovese and the prosperous Valachi are sent to prison on a phony drug charge. Genovese is convinced Valachi was responsible for the tip-off. In 1963 Valachi testifies in front of a Senate Commission. The enraged Genovese increases the contract price on Valachi's life to $100,000. Nevertheless, Valachi survives in prison (living in luxurious seclusion with protection). He dies in 1971 of a heart attack, some six months after Genovese.

Because *The Valachi Papers* was released in the same year as *The Godfather* and dealt with much of the same subject (the former based on facts; the latter on fiction), the two movies were constantly compared. Everyone agreed that the exploitive *The Valachi Papers* was not in the same league as the award-winning *The Godfather,* the latter of which far outdistanced the former in box office revenue. "Unfortunately, because Valachi never attempts to understand his own role, other than that he is a protector of 'The Family's' interest, he is virtually an undefined character, leaving little for Bronson to do" (Michael Kerbel, *The Village Voice*). "*The Valachi Papers* is a stiff. It may be possible to make a duller gangster melodrama, but I would hate to sit through the attempt" (Gary Arnold, *Washington Post*). More sympathetic was Bruce Williamson (*Playboy* magazine): "Bronson's unsentimentalized yet human portrayal sets the tone for an atmospheric gangland drama in which cowardice, treachery and cruelty are shown to be precisely that — without redeeming virtues."

The Valachi Papers originally began filming in New York, but after a series of "accidents" plague the production, the lensing was moved to Rome where the movie was finished. This was one of a number of features to co-star Bronson and his actress wife, Jill Ireland. *The Valachi Papers* earned $8,381,542 in domestic film rentals paid to the distributor.

A.k.a.: *Joe Valachi: I Segretti Di Cosa Nostra.*

274. *Vendetta* (Concorde Pictures, 1986), color, 88 min.

Producers, Jeff Begun, Ken Solomon, Ken Dalton; associate producers, Richard Harrison, Greg Hinton; director, Bruce Logan; screenplay, Emil Farkas, Sion Maskell, Laura Cavestani, John Adams; art director, Chris Clarens; set decorator, Timothy Ford; costumes, Meg Mayer; assistant director, Elliot Rosenblatt; sound, Dennis Carr; camera, Robert New; second unit camera, Bryan Greenberg; editor, Glenn Morgan.

Karen Chase (Laurie Collins [Cusack]); Lisa Clarson (Bobo); Lisa Hullano (China); Linda Lightfoot (Wanda); Sandy Martin (Kay Butler); Michelle Newkirk (Bonnie Cusack); Marianne Taylor (Star); Marshall Teague (Paul Donahue); Kim Shriner (Steve Nelson); Roberta Collins (Miss Dice); Greg Bradford (Joe-Bob); Mark von Zech (Randy); Pleasant Gehman, Rose Flores, Kerry O'Brian, Marsky Reins, Boom Boom Dixon (Screaming Sirens); Holly Butler (The Movie Star); Bruce Logan (Director); Hoke Howell (Deputy Curly); Will Hare (Judge Waters); Mark Rosenblatt (Bailiff); Charles Joseph Martin (Willie); Marta Kober (Sylvia); Renee Jacque Kino (Amy); Cynthia Harrison (Debra); Kelita Kelly (Sandy); Reggie Bennett (Conchita); Kim Collins (Betty); Ginger Johnston (Dakota); Jack Kosslyn (Warden Haines); Ken Solomon (Coroner); Dave Nicholson (District Attorney); Eugene Robert Glazer (David Greene); Joshua Brooks, J. W. Fails (Parking Attendants); Gamy L. Taylor (Judge); Adzine Melliti (Gino); Joanelle Nadine Romero (Elena); Dixie Lee (Rosie); Durga McBroom (Widow); Topaz (Disc Jockey); Tracette St. Julian (Celebrity Take-Off); Carol Porter, Kathleen Stevens, Lynell Carter, Patti Burdo, Patrice Davis, Shawni Davis (Girls in Shower).

In Los Angeles, attractive college girl Bonnie Cusack (Michelle Newkirk) shoots her date, who attempted to rape her, with his own gun. As a result, she is found guilty of second degree manslaughter and sentenced to two years at Duran Correctional Institute. Hardly has the blonde newcomer matriculated into her strange environment, than she is taunted as "fresh meat" in the showers by some inmates, and challenged during her daily routine by other hostile convicts. A tough guard confronts the rebellious Bonnie:

GUARD: This is a prison, not an ice hockey rink. You can't just start punching anyone who walks by.

BONNIE: I don't understand what's happening to me. I just want everyone to leave me alone.

One of Bonnie's chief adversaries is lesbian drug dealer Kay Butler (Sandy Martin), a rugged inmate who finds it exasperating that Bonnie will not submit to her authority. As punishment, Kay and her friends beat Bonnie up, feed her drugs and then, when the guards are occupied elsewhere, dump her over the side of an upper story cellblock tier.

When Bonnie's stuntwoman sister, Laurie (Karen Chase), learns the news, she is at first stunned, and then demands revenge. Because the prison authorities refuse to investigate this "suicide," she takes matters into her own capable hands. She steals a white Lincoln car from a posh restaurant parking lot, drives recklessly along city streets, and as a finale, breaks into the display window of a chic jewelry shop. This activity earns her a prison sentence at Duran Correctional Institute.

Once at Duran, using her professional surname of Collins, Laurie gains the friendship of several inmates, hoping they will tell her who killed Bonnie. As she uncovers the names of the death gang, she eliminates them one by one in bloody combat, using her stuntwoman skills to gain the upper hand. Her last prey is Kay. In their final confrontation Kay gains the upper hand and is about to smash Laurie over the head with a wrench. Miss Dice (Roberta Collins), head of security, arrives in time to shoot Kay to death. Laurie is freed and drives away with her boyfriend (Marshall Teague).

Certainly the acting in *Vendetta* is not remarkable (although better than usual for such films) and the violence is gratuitously uninspired. The women prisoners are stereotyped and the harsh prison conditions (vicious inmates, brutal male guards who rape the convicts, etc.) are typical of such movies. However, there are some choice lines of dialogue:

INMATE: This is prison. You just can't pick up your marbles and go home.

Or:

INMATE #1: New fish is here!

INMATE #2: Fresh off the ice!

INMATE #3: Holy mackerel!

Or the male guard who inquires of a female prisoner: "Wouldn't you like to play with my nightstick?"

There is also a slight novelty factor in having *Vendetta*'s heroine be an agile stuntwoman out for revenge, rather than the usual undercover cop. In describing this "B" picture, *Variety* noted, "*Vendetta* is too violent and humorless to qualify as the usual woman-behind-bars pic.... Considering the genre, most of the cast turn in very credible performances, even if they don't look much like prisoners...." As for voyeuristic filmgoers, the trade paper cautioned, "There is also a lot less flesh exposed here than in most other women prisoner films, but that which is shown looks seamy, not sexy." Jay Robert Nash and Stanley Ralph Ross noted in *The Motion Picture Guide: 1987 Annual* (1988), "As is usual for these films, any similarity between this prison and the real thing is strictly coincidental; the women here can wear just about any outlandish costume they can devise, and they have almost free run of the place. Of course, all the obligatory scenes are there: long showers, rapist guards, brutal beatings, and more showers; plus, this prison allows conjugal visits, so we can have more sex. . . . [T]hese films are as seedy as they come, but for fans of exploitation, the ultimate extension of what they want."

Roberta Collins had appeared in such genre entries as *The Big Doll House* (1972) and *Sweet Sugar* (1972), qq.v.

A.k.a.: *Angels Behind Bars.*

275. *We Who Are About to Die* (RKO, 1937), 82 min.

Producer, Edward Small; director, Christy Cabanne; based on the novel by David Lamson; screenplay, John Twist; art directors, Van Nest Polglase, Feild Gray; costumes, Edward Stevenson; sound, Denzil A. Cutler; camera, Robert Planck; editor, Arthur Roberts.

Preston Foster (Matthews); Ann Dvorak (Connie); John Beal (John Thompson); Ray Mayer (Bright Boy Schulz); Gordon Jones (Slim Tolliver); Russell Hopton (Mac Andrews); J. Carrol Naish (Nick); Paul Hurst (Tip Fuller); Frank Jenks (Clyde Beasley [Dick Williams]); John Wray (Jerry Daly); Barnett Parker (John Barkley); Willie Fung (Kwong); John Carroll (Joe Donahue); DeWitt Jennings (Mike Brannigan, the Watchman); Landers Stevens (Warden Lawson); John "Skins" Miller (Macy); Howard Hickman (Prison Chaplain); Robert Emmett O'Connor (Mitchell); Frank M. Thomas (Carter); Ralph Byrd (Crime Lab Worker).

One of the worst nightmares an individual can experience is to be convicted of a capital offense crime of which he is innocent and be faced with an impending death sentence. The torment of time slipping away in lockup, with no one believing he is innocent, is a horrendous fate. This theme is well executed in *We Who Are About to Die,* a programmer from RKO starring that capable, underrated performer, John Beal, and boasting a fine supporting cast, including ex–Warner Bros. star Ann Dvorak.

Engineer John Thompson (John Beal) quits his job at the Carter Aircraft Plant in Logan City when his employer (Frank M. Thomas) refuses to test his new plane design. The angered Thompson intends to relocate to California and have his girlfriend Connie (Ann Dvorak), who works at a local travel agency, join him there. However, things go amiss when John innocently becomes the pawn of a gang—Bright Boy Schultz (Ray Mayer), Mac Andrews (Russell Hopton), Clyde Beasley (Frank Jenks) and Nick (J. Carrol Naish)—who rob the payroll office at the aircraft plant. The paymaster is killed and, in the escape, the robbers run over a little boy. Because the gang used Thompson's work smock (which contains his payroll voucher) for the holdup and because John had a revenge motive, he is arrested on circumstantial evidence. The prosecution railroads him into a death sentence. He is sent to the state prison to be hung. Meanwhile, loyal Connie attempts to convince police official Matthews (Preston Foster) to reopen the case and help free John.

On death row, the stunned Thompson, whose protests of innocence fall on deaf ears, must cope with impending doom. Like the others, he vainly hopes for a reprieve, a petition of clemency, a pardon—anything! Beyond this cellblock, one can hear the workmen preparing the gallows for its next victim. Each pounding

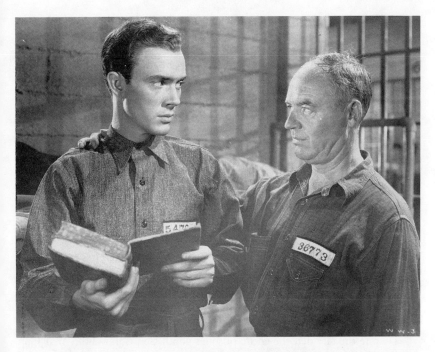

John Beal and John Wray in *We Who Are About to Die* (1937).

of the hammer makes the condemned convicts shudder. Thompson's philosophical cellmate (John "Skins" Miller) advises: "Size don't make a prison. It's not having freedom. If this cell were a hundred feet square and had everything in it you wanted, you'd still want to be outside. It works on you until you gotta get out."

Others on this death row include Kwong (Willie Fung), the snobbish Britisher, John Barkley (Barnett Parker); and the very earthy Tip Fuller (Paul Hurst). The latter has a prideful attitude about being a member of such an exclusive group. When a near catatonic prisoner is brought into their part of the prison Tip complains, "Bringing that guy here is an insult to death row." Another inmate, Slim Tolliver (Gordon Jones), receives word of his reprieve just as his much-anticipated (last) supper of southern fried chicken arrives. One of the traditions on death row, besides endless inmate chatter about the law not knowing that hanging does not hurt, is that a man, about to take the final last walk, should distribute his possessions (especially books) to the other men on the block.

Meanwhile, a few of the gang who robbed Carter's plant have been jailed on other charges. Bright Boy is in another wing of the prison, where, upon learning through the grapevine (messages circulated throughout the prison by inmates tapping on the cell-bars or on wash basins, employing Morse code) that Thompson is soon to be hung, confides to his cellmate, Joe Donahue (John Carroll): "Gee, there must not be nothing tougher than not to know what they got on you. You can't fight back, you can't pay off. You can't even plead guilty."

Another of the imprisoned gang, the cold-blooded Nick, keeps his own counsel, insisting: "Ah, the only way to get along in a place this . . . is to ride your own beat."

Soon it is Kwong's turn to be hung. The prison chaplain (Howard Hickman) promises the condemned man that his last wish will be fulfilled; to have his bones rest with his ancestors in China. Fong, clutching a statue of Buddha, bravely walks the last mile, ready to face the executioner and the crowd of "ghouls" who have gathered to witness his demise.

Eventually, Donahue learns enough from Bright Boy to figure out that there is new evidence in Thompson's case. He passes along the information to John through the grapevine. The near-hysterical Thompson begs the guards to take him to the warden, so he can plead his new defense. However, the keepers refuse. Meanwhile, there is a small riot among the inmates protesting the treatment of Thompson. In the course of quelling it, Thompson's roommate makes a break for freedom, but is shot down by the guards. For his participation in the ruckus, John is placed in solitary confinement. Later, Bright Boy is killed within the prison so he will not say anything further.

On the outside, Connie and the now-convinced Matthews gather clues to prove John's innocence. They find new evidence by using new procedures at the crime lab as well as administering truth serum to Clyde in the prison infirmary. The trail leads them to Mac Alper (who was never caught) and to Nick (who is now out of prison). While the time for John's execution fast approaches, Matthews locates Alper, who, by now, has killed Nick. There is now sufficient evidence to prove Thompson is not guilty. If only they can get word to the prison in time.

Despite the fact that the entire prisoner population is now aware that John is really innocent, the execution is to proceed on schedule. The distraught Thompson screams at the chaplain: "You and all the others, waiting for me to get killed with a rope! They don't kill us that way. No! They kill us slow, taking their time, pounding our brains out."

By now the other death row prisoners are frenzied with anger at the pending injustice. Ringleader Tip shouts out:

> What these bulls got we ain't got? Brass buttons, that's all. For a bunch of mugs that ain't allowed to pack guns, they sure do a lot of leading with their chins, especially when they run around here getting excited thinking we're about to blow the lid.

Tip stages the revolt, but after freeing several of the others, he knocks Thompson out and places him back in his cell so he will be safe. The prison guards counter with volleys of tear gas.

As a result of the uprising, Thompson's execution has been delayed and Matthews is able to reach the warden with the new evidence. John is soon pardoned. He and Connie plan to marry and move to California.

At the time of release, film reviewers were too surfeited with prison movies to appreciate the better qualities of this low-budget entry. Frank S. Nugent *(New York Times)* complained, "The picture . . . uses every standby of the formula prison story." By way of backhanded compliment, Nugent observed, "There is enough of the morbid in us to compel a certain interest in the spectacle of men in steel cages waiting for an impersonal guard of honor to conduct them to death. The callous humor of some of them, the cringing of others, the defiant outcries of the rest ... continue to fascinate us, just as they make me wonder how it is that every film of a murderer's row suggests that the resident homicide specialists are good chaps at heart, but misunderstood." *Variety* had mixed feelings. It decided the movie was "an action melodrama of considerable tension" but that it was "Another Death House story.... [B]asically the plot and the situational formula is old stuff." The trade paper concluded, "Some of the details and some of the broad emphasis might easily be attacked as 'theatrical' rather than realistic, but the thing is held together by Director [Christy] Cabanne, and in general the illusion is sustained."

The film's title refers to a quote in the front of one of prisoner John Barkley's books. It reads "Morituri Te Salutamus," the customary final salutation of gladiators in ancient Rome.... "We Who Are About to Die, Salute You." David Lamson, the author of the book (1935) on which this motion picture was based, had spent thirteen months in San Quentin Prison on death row, before the Supreme Court reversed his murder conviction and freed him. RKO not only changed the storyline of Lamson's book, but also, fearful of upsetting any penal/jurisprudential officials, placed a disclaimer at the start of the film insisting it was all fiction and any similarity to living persons was coincidental, etc.

276. *Weary River* (First National, 1929), 90 min.

Presenter, Richard A. Rowland; director, Frank Lloyd; story, Courtney Ryley Cooper; screenplay, Bradley King; dialogue, Tom J. Gerahty; art director, John H. Hughes; wardrobe, Max Ree; song, Louis Silvers and Grant Clarke; camera, Ernest Haller; editors, Edward Schroeder, Paul Perez.

Richard Barthelmess (Jerry Larabee); Betty Compson (Alice); William Holden (Warden); Louis Natheaux (Spadoni); George [E.] Stone (Blackie); Raymond Turner (Elevator Boy); Gladden James (Vaudeville Manager).

As Hollywood converted to talkies, there was a great emphasis on musical pictures now that moviegoers could both see *and* hear production numbers. Stars who had enough difficulty coping with the new demands of talking oncamera, were suddenly pushed into displaying their "skills" at singing and dancing. One of the victims of this short-lived cycle was Richard Barthelmess (1895–1963), a former D. W. Griffith star who had made a strong impression with such silent photoplays as *Broken Blossoms* (1919), *Way Down East* (1920) and *Tol'able David* (1921). For his sound debut, Barthelmess was cast in *Weary River*, a prison film follow-up to his earlier *The Noose* (1928), q.v., one of the two films (the other was *The Patent Leather Kid*) for which he had been Oscar-nominated in the 1927–28 season.

His home lot (First National) proudly boasted of *Weary River*:

> All these years the wealth of Richard Barthelmess' rich voice has been concealed. Now, *Vitaphone* unearths this hidden treasure for you to enjoy. *Vitaphone* brings you a Barthelmess so much greater it's like discovering a *New Star*. A voice so sensationally fine he could have won stardom on it alone. You and millions of others have gone just to see him act. Now you can *hear* him *talk* and play the piano. You'll enjoy *Two Great Stars* when you see and *hear Richard Barthelmess* talking and playing in *Weary River*.

(The studio's hoopla did not mention that this film, a silent film with some talking sequences and a synchronized musical score, used John Murray to dub Barthelmess's singing of "Weary River" and that Frank Churchill played the piano, not the star.)

Of lesser importance, according to the studio, was the plotline of *Weary River*. The promotional material trumpeted: "An epic of a down-and-outer whose plaintive music reaches through prison's bars to find love and a new life a thousand miles away! Weary River reminds you of the story *The Noose* — it's every bit as big."

Established bootlegger Jerry Larrabee (Richard Barthelmess) is railroaded to prison on a false charge by a rival underworld figure (Louis Natheaux). Once there, and with much time on his hands, Jerry becomes interested in music and forms a prison band. Later, the musical group is heard over a nationwide radio hookup. So great is audience response to Jerry's performing that a movement is soon underfoot to have him paroled. When the governor grants him his freedom, Larrabee attempts a career in vaudeville, but fails. He then tries job after job, but his criminal record haunts him. Discouraged, he returns to his former gang, as well as resuming his relationship with his onetime blonde girlfriend, Alice (Betty Compson). Wanting her man to stay clear of the underworld, she begs the warden (William Holden) of the prison, who once told her to forget Jerry, to intercede. He arrives on the scene in time to save Jerry from new difficulties with the law. With his past behind him, Larrabee proves — by singing the maudlin "Weary River" yet again — that show business is the proper career path for him.

Mordaunt Hall *(New York Times)* was dissatisfied with *Weary River,* explaining, "The chief attribute of this banal jailbird tale is that it has some interesting prison sequences.... It is a pity that Mr. Barthelmess should waste his talent on such a hopeless hodge-podge as this. His acting, even in the would-be lachrymose scenes is not without merit.... William Holden is dignified as the ubiquitous Warden." On the other hand, *Variety* was enthusiastic, "Measured from any angle *Weary River* is a money picture.... Barthelmess emerges as possibly the first of the veteran film stars to register a clean-cut wow in the articulate cinema.... The advantage of *Weary River* ... is that it is artistic without being hard to 'get.' Its problem is definite, simple: its telling intelligently aimed at those old heart strings and that sentimental barometer, the adam's apple." *Photoplay* magazine reported, "The chief interest of *Weary River* lies in the fact that Richard Barthelmess talks and sings the chief role. He really talks.... Barthelmess does splendidly in his first talking appearance."

Weary River was based on the real-life case of Harry Snodgrass, who, while in a Missouri prison, was heard over the radio performing "The Prisoner's Song" and later became a "name" in midwestern vaudeville. Later in 1929, Al Jolson, the talkie's first great star would go to prison in the course of *Say It with Songs* (1929), q.v.

277. *Weeds* (De Laurentiis Entertainment Group, 1988), color, 115 min.

Executive producers, Mel Pearl, Billy Cross; producer, Bill Badalato; associate producers, Fred Baron, Patti Carr, Ken Kitch; director, John Hancock; screenplay, Dorothy Tristan, Hancock; production designer, Joseph T. Garrity; art director, Pat Tagliaferro; set decorator, Francine Mercadante; costumes, Mary Kay Stolz; makeup, Edouard F. Henriques; music, Angelo Badalamenti; songs, Melissa Ethelridge and Orville Stoeber; choreographer, Jerry Evans; assistant director, Paul Deason; stunt coordinator, Joe Dunne; sound, James Thorton; special effects, Mike Menzel, Marvin Gardner, Rick Barefoot; camera, Ian Weincke; editor, Dennis O'Connor.

Nick Nolte (Lee Umstetter); Lane Smith (Claude); William Forsythe (Burt, the Booster); John Toles-Bey (Navarro); Joe

Mantegna (Carmine); Ernie Hudson (Bagdad); Mark Rolston (Dave); J. J. Johnson (Lazarus); Rita Taggart (Lillian Bingington, the Newspaper Critic); Orville Stoeber (Lead Guitar); Essex Smith (Thurman); Cyro Baptista (Percussion); Sam L. Waymon (Keyboard); Anne Ramsey (Mom Umstetter); Ray Reinhardt (Pop Umstetter); Amanda Gronich (Bagdad's Girlfriend); Felton Perry (Associate Warden); Barton Heyman, Walter Charles (*Waiting for Godot* Players); William Lucas, Reggie Montgomery (Rabble Rousers); Amy C. Bass (Graduate Student); Nicholas Wyman (Associate Warden); Richard Olsen (Derrick Mann); Drew Elliott (Fisher Cobb); Charlie Rich (Himself); Arnold Johnson, Gerald Orange, Leonard Johnson, Paul Herman, Frank Gio, Gift Harris, Paul Weeden, Maximo Cerda (Inmates); Richard Portnow, Michael Luciano, Daniel Kent (Guards); Howard Spiegel (House Manager); Louis Criscuolo (Waiter); Denny Burt (Caterer); Raymond Rivera (Busboy); Bill Badalato (Doorman); John Bonitz (Dean); Billy Cross (Pound Attendant); Rhesa Stone (Saleswoman); James Deuter (Motel Manager); Kirsten Baker (Kirsten); John Ring, Robert Miano, Sam Stoneburner (Parole Board).

There is a core of deep feeling that holds *Weeds* together and it's a good thing, too because this prison drama cum musical cum backstage story is one of the strangest hybrids to come along in some time.

Variety

Lee Umstetter (Nick Nolte) is serving a life sentence at San Quentin Prison for armed robbery and aggravated assault which he committed while a teenager. Despairing of ever being freed, this life's loser attempts suicide twice. With so much spare time, the man who never got beyond the sixth grade begins reading voraciously. Within a few years, his intellect is so stimulated that he is discussing philosophical concepts with other educated inmates. When he attends a performance of *Waiting for Godot* performed for the prisoners by a local troupe, he is so inspired that he writes his own play. His subject matter is the dehumanization of prisoners by their environment. In order not to upset the warden, he sets the drama in France. ("We wouldn't want to give anyone ideas that atrocities occur in this penal institute would we?") He begs to have his work, *Weeds,* performed for the inmates. As a friend says: "Maybe this could be an example to some of these inmates. They might be inspired to do their time positive instead of getting worse in here. Maybe they could be inspired like Lee and get their minds off criminal thoughts."

Prison officials agree to the proposal. Lee's motley crew of performers include Burt the Booster (William Forsythe), Navarro (John Toles-Bey), Bagdad (Ernie Hudson), Lazarus (J. J. Johnson) and Dave (Mark Rolston) with other convicts (Cyro Baptista, Orville Stoeber, Essex Smith, Sam L. Waymon) providing the music. The production is enthusiastically received by the prison audience and soon San Francisco drama critic Lillian Bingington (Rita Taggart) comes to review the show. She responds not only to the raw creativity of the work, but to Umstetter himself. She works to get Lee paroled. Meanwhile, members of Lee's cast are paroled and their leaving is a bitter reminder that he is still behind bars.

Eventually, Lee is paroled and he moves to San Francisco to live with Lillian. Arriving at her apartment, he enthuses: "Tell me the truth. Did I die and go to heaven? I mean, I can turn on the TV, when I want. I can stay up late. I can drink or eat what I want. Go buy something if I want, if I had the money."

At her prompting, he gathers together his cast of ex-convicts and they take their play on tour, performing mostly on college campuses. At the end of each night's performance he has a question-and-answer session with the ex-convicts/actors, so the audience can ask questions about prison life. By now, Lee considers himself a professional and his newfound integrity demands that he admit to himself and to the cast that he "borrowed" many of his ideas for his drama from Jean Genet's *Death Watch,* as well as from the writings of Saul Bellow. Encouraged by Lillian and the cast, Lee rewrites his play, resetting it from France to the United States and bringing more of his and his friends' experiences into use. He also added more songs to the production. Meanwhile, after Navarro is killed in a car accident, Lee recasts his part with unknown New York actor Carmine (Joe Mantegna), inventing a criminal background for the player to use in his program biography.

After several false starts, the play bows Off Broadway where influential critic Fisher Cobb (Drew Elliott) gives the play a negative review. Later, the troupe perform their work at a New York state prison where the inmates respond so heatedly to the realism onstage that they begin to riot. In the mêlée, Lee and other cast members, who are still dressed in their prison costumes, attempt to leave, but the guards confuse them with the real prisoners. When Lee is injured by a vicious guard, Burt comes to his assistance but is killed in the process. The riot is quashed finally and the actors, now identified, are permitted to leave. The generated publicity from the chaos leads to Lee's play being given a Broadway showcase.

Variety reported, "Although script . . . musters a good deal of passion about the plight of prisoners, it ignores many of the basic elements of good drama. . . . [R]elationships outside prison are pasted together with homilies and declarations of love without the action and events to back it up. Film tends to address issues too directly in a head-on style that becomes preachy. . . . Nolte, like the film itself, has moments of great conviction, mostly when he isn't trying too hard."

When released for home viewing, Jeffrey Lyons (*Video Review* magazine) judged *Weeds* to be a "gripping tale that never reverts to the formulaic. . . . The men that Nolte assembles for his theater group are depicted with all the flaws and foibles that make them real too—in fact, real enough to underscore why society sometimes seems so skeptical about rehabilitation and why it's difficult for many ex-cons to find the inner strength to finally make something of their lives. . . . *Weeds* is a different kid of underdog story." In *Roger Ebert's Movie Home Companion* (1989), the author observed "There's never a moment when there's much doubt about the outcome, but the movie gets there by a series of small delights and surprises." Ebert also found, "Unfortunately, the whole prison sequence at the end of the film is also less than convincing, and so are the recycled '60s leftist panaceas that pass, in that sequence, as electrifying truth-telling. It's all a little too pat. *Weeds* is a movie that is best when it observes small moments of human truth, and at its worst when it tries to inflate them into large moments."

Weeds was based on the real life story of Rick Cluchey, the author of *The Cage,* and West Coast critic, Barbara Bladen. Director John Hancock, who was artistic director for the San Francisco Actor's Workshop, had been responsible for helping Cluchey bring his drama to the state in 1965. Hancock and his wife, Dorothy Tristan, co-authored the screenplay. Many of the prison scenes for *Weeds* were filmed at the Statesville Correctional Institution in Illinois. *Weeds* was not a commercial success.

278. *When Dreams Come True* (First Division, 1929), 75 min.

Producer, Trem Carr; director, Duke Worne; based on the story "Sunburst Valley" by Victor Roussea; screenplay, Arthur Hoerl; camera, Hap Depew; editor, J. S. Harrington.

Helene Costello (Caroline Swayne); Rex

Lease (Ben Shelby); Claire McDowell (Martha Shelby); Danny Hoy (Jack Boyle); Ernest Hilliard (Jim Leeson); Buddy Brown (Billy Shelby); George Periolat (Robert Swayne); Emmett King (Judge Clayburn); Ranger (Dream Lad, a Horse); Rags (A Dog).

Every good whodunit requires a few stumbling blocks along the way to the solving of the mystery. Locking the hero in jail was one favorite way for scenarists to create an obstacle for the star to overcome before he proceeded to uncover the killer.

In the deep South, impoverished blacksmith Ben Shelby (Rex Lease) is smitten with Caroline Swayne (Helene Costello), the daughter of well-to-do Robert Swayne (George Periolat). The latter opposes his offspring's mixed-classes romance, suggesting there may be some question about the legitimacy of Ben's birth. The angered Ben confronts Swayne and soon thereafter the man is found murdered in his barn. Ben is arrested and imprisoned. He later escapes and discovers that Swayne's horse breeding partner, Jim Leeson (Ernest Hilliard) is the real culprit. Meanwhile, Dream Lad (Ranger, the Horse) wins the big race and Ben and Caroline are reunited.

Variety reported of this independent silent production by Rayart Pictures, "Plenty of action, the high spot an exciting race.... Too many breaks for the hero are crammed into the final reel...."

279. *When the Clock Strikes* (United Artists, 1961), 72 min.

Producer, Robert E. Kent; director, Edward L. Cahn; screenplay, Dallas Gaultois; makeup, Harry Thomas; wardrobe, Einar Bourman, Barbara Maxwell; music, Richard La Salle; music director, Lloyd Young; assistant director, Herbert S. Greene; sound, Dean Thomas; camera, Kenneth Peach, Sr.; editor, Grant Whytock.

James Brown (Sam Morgan); Merry Anders (Ellie); Henry Corden (Cady, Lodge Owner); Roy Barcroft (Sheriff); Peggy Stewart (Mrs. Pierce); Jorge Moreno (Martinez); Francis De Sales (Warden); Max Mellinger (Postman); Eden Hartford (Waitress); Jack Kenny (Café Proprietor).

The execution of a convicted criminal can sometimes lead to strange repercussions as this contrived whodunit attempted to illustrate.

Grocer Sam Morgan's (James Brown) testimony is responsible for helping to convict a man of murder. He has second thoughts whether the man leaving the scene of the crime was really the defendant or not. He is now speeding to the prison where the man is to be executed at midnight. Along the way, he gives a ride to a young woman named Ellie (Merry Anders) whom he leaves at a nearby lodge. Because of a bad storm and felled trees which block the highway, he cannot reach the prison and returns to the lodge. There Ellie admits she is the wife of the man about to be executed. At midnight a stranger, Martinez (Jorge Moreno), arrives at the lodge, having failed in his attempt to reach the prison to confess to the warden. He admits he actually killed the person for whom Frank Pierce has been executed. The following morning Martinez is arrested by the arriving police. In going through Pierce's final effects, Sam and Ellie discover a post office box key which they assume contains the money Pierce stole two years earlier. They telephone to the post office to have the package sent to them at the lodge. Meanwhile, the actual Mrs. Pierce (Peggy Stewart) shows up at the retreat and after announcing her identity, states that Frank had killed her father. Later, Cady (Henry Corden), the greedy hostel owner, wanting the hidden loot for himself, locks Ellie in a vacant room and attempts to shoot Sam. However, it is Mrs. Pierce who is murdered when she tries to intervene. Sam calls the sheriff (Roy Barcroft) to have Cady arrested for murder.

With such a jumbled plotline, it was no wonder that the cast found it difficult to give credibility to the story. As *Variety* noted, "It gets very involved, and the characters are consistently jumping to peculiar conclusions and saying and doing irrational things." *Harrison's Reports* weighed, "The skimpy-budgeted black-and-white production moves at a sick snail's pace, has little or no suspense, action or comic relief. The pitiful dialogue is repetitious, the acting amateurish, the photography justly uninspired." This was one of several budget features to co-star James Brown and Merry Anders.

A.k.a.: *The Clock Strikes Three.*

280. *Where Is My Wandering Boy Tonight?* (Equity Pictures, 1922), seven reels.

Producer, B. F. Zeidman; directors, James P. Hogan, Millard Webb; suggested by the song "Where Is My Wandering Boy Tonight?" by Robert Lowry; story/screenplay, Gerald C. Duffy; art director, Henry Scott Ramsey; camera, David Abel.

Cullen Landis (Garry Beecher); Carl Stockdale (Silas Rudge); Virginia True Boardman (Martha Beecher); Patsy Ruth Miller (Lorna Owens); Kathleen Key (Veronica Tyler); Ben Beeley (Stewart Kilmer); Clarence Badger, Jr. (R. Sylvester Jones).

Based on the popular song, "Where Is My Wandering Boy Tonight?" (1877), this sentimental silent picture concerns young Garry Beecher (Cullen Landis), a country lad who yearns for some real excitement in his life. Ignoring his mother (True Boardman) and his girlfriend, Lorna Owens (Patsy Ruth Miller), he becomes infatuated with an attractive chorus girl, Veronica Tyler (Kathleen Key). He follows her to New York City where he discovers she has a millionaire boyfriend. Intent on gaining money to lavish on her, he robs his former employer and returns with lavish presents for his golddigging friend. When Veronica sets her sights on an expensive diamond necklace and Garry cannot make payments on it, Veronica turns on him. He is arrested for grand larceny and sentenced to ten years at Sing Sing Prison.

While Garry's heartbroken mother pines for her "lost" son, Garry adjusts to the sobering regimen of prison. At one point, Beecher saves the warden from an attack by a vicious prisoner. Later, when there is a major convict breakout, Garry flees from the prison in order to rescue the warden yet again, this time from an oncoming freight train. The prison administrator arranges Garry's pardon and the redeemed young man returns to his loyal, small town sweetheart on Christmas Eve and to the waiting arms of his joyful mother.

Variety judged this independent production to be a "fairly entertaining picture" but noted, "The extra footage of a number of scenes give the picture a tendency to be draggy." The trade paper cited as one of the movie's best sequences, "The prison break, with the convicts escaping on a locomotive and the final smash of that engine with another in a head-on collision, furnishes a real thrill."

281. *The Whipping Boss* (Monogram, 1924), 5,800′.

Director, J. P. McGowan; story, Jack Boyle, P. J. Caldeway; screenplay, P. J. Hurn; camera, Walter Griffin.

Wade Boteler (The Whipping Boss); Eddie Phillips (Jim); J. P. McGowan (Livingston); Lloyd Hughes (Dick Forrest);

Barbara Bedford (Grace Woodward); Billy Elmer (Spike); Andrew Waldron (Timkins); George Cummings (Brady); Lydia Knott (Jim's Mother); Clarence Geldert (Jacknife Woodward).

Occasionally in the "innocent" era of the Roaring Twenties, Hollywood produced features dealing with the exploitation of convict labor, a subject that would become a recurrent theme in the next decade of American filmmaking. One such entry was *The Whipping Boss,* directed by Australian-born J. P. McGowan (1880–1952). He would direct many westerns and action pictures during his long career, in some of which he performed as an actor (as in this picture).

In Oregon the state law permits penal authorities to lease prisoners to private companies as a labor force. Among the prisoners so dispensed is Jim (Eddie Phillips), who is sent to slave in a lumber camp. When he becomes ill and cannot work, he is badly whipped by the company's sadistic enforcer, the Whipping Boss (Wade Boteler). Jim's mother (Lydia Knott) learns of her son's plight. She arrives in town where Dick Forrest (Lloyd Hughes), head of the local branch of the American Legion, agrees to help her. After Dick obtains an order for Jim's release, the frightened owner of the camp, Livingston (J. P. McGowan), orders his whipping boss to remove telltale evidence that could incriminate them. The whipping boss sets fire to the stockade, unmindful that the prisoners are still chained there. Forrest and his Legionnaires arrive in time to save the men. Thereafter, Livingston and the whipping boss are arrested, tried and sentenced to prison. Jim is freed. Meanwhile, Dick becomes engaged to Grace (Barbara Bedford), the daughter of the head (Clarence Geldert) of the logging company. The latter vows to rid the lumber camps of inhumane working conditions.

282. *Whirlpool* (Columbia, 1934), 73 min.

Director, Roy William Neil; story, Howard Emmett Rogers; screenplay, Dorothy Howell, Ethel Hill; camera, Benjamin Kline; editor, Richard Cahoon.

Jack Holt (Buck Rankin); Jean Arthur (Sandra Morrison); Allen Jenkins (Mac); Donald Cook (Bob Andrews); Lila Lee (Helen Morrison); Rita La Roy (Thelma); John Miljan (Barney Gaige); Willard Robertson (Judge Morrison); Ward Bond (Farley); Oscar Apfel (Editor).

For some, being sent to prison not only physically cuts one's ties to society, but emotionally as well. In this "B" picture, a man forces the situation by letting his loved ones believe he has died behind the high walls. To be noted in this quickie tearjerker are rising star Jean Arthur and fading silent screen personality Lila Lee.

Small town carnival owner Buck Rankin (Jack Holt) marries country girl Helen (Lila Lee). Deciding to start a new life, he intends to sell his operation to his hyperactive assistant Mac (Allen Jenkins). While on the midway one day, some customers start a brawl and Buck strikes one of them, who hits his head on a blunt object and dies. Rankin is sentenced to twenty years in the state penitentiary. What upsets rugged Buck the most is learning from loyal Helen, who visits him in prison, that she is expecting a baby. He tries to make her divorce him, but she refuses. Not wanting to ruin her life or that of their child, Buck later contrives to send his wife a letter, ostensibly from the warden, stating he has died in an escape attempt.

Years pass. When Buck is finally released he reencounters Mac and together they embark on lives as racketeers in the nightclub business, soon becoming wealthy. Buck's grown daughter Sandra (Jean Arthur), now a newspaper reporter, is sent by her paper to interview the notorious Rankin about a murder case in which he is scheduled to testify as a key witness. She recognizes Buck from a picture her mother has kept and reveals her identity to her father. She tells him about her life and her fiancée, Bob Andrews (Donald Cook). Not wanting to drag Helen — now married to Judge Morrison (Willard Robertson) — or Sandra into the scandal, he refuses to testify. However, Barney Gaige (John Miljan), the mouthpiece for the defendant in the case, confronts Buck and warns him that unless he testifies, he will make public Buck's past life. Buck kills Gaige, destroys all the incriminating evidence, and then shoots himself. Sandra bravely refuses to tell her mother about the tragic episode.

While granting that the film's start "is brisk enough," Andre Sennwald *(New York Times)* admitted that part way through the contrived tale, "the new film earns a sleepy ho-ho-hum from its audience." He was not particularly impressed by the star's stay behind bars. "In prison he walks with the men in gray, smokes cigarettes through tight lips and wistfully examines the sky." The more easily pleased *Variety* judged this "a piece of film merchandise that's well above fair in entertainment appeal. . . . Nice cutting job sustains a good pace and maintains action without leaving anything of importance missing or upsetting continuity."

Veteran star Jack Holt (1888–1951) would star in several genre films: *Hell's Island* (1930), *Reformatory* (1938) and *Prison Camp* (1940), qq.v.

283. *White Heat* (Warner Bros., 1949), 114 min.

Producer, Louis F. Edelman; director, Raoul Walsh; suggested by the story by Virginia Kellogg; screenplay, Ivan Goff, Ben Roberts; art director, Edward Carrere; set decorator, Fred M. MacLean; costumes, Leah Rhodes; makeup, Perc Westmore; music, Max Steiner; orchestrator, Murray Cutter; assistant director, Russell Saunders; sound, Leslie G. Hewitt; special effects, Roy Davidson, H. F. Koenekamp; camera, Sid Hickox; editor, Owen Marks.

James Cagney (Arthur Cody Jarrett); Virginia Mayo (Verna Jarrett); Edmond O'Brien (Vic Pardo [Hank Fallon]); Margaret Wycherly (Ma Jarrett); Steve Cochran ("Big Ed" Somers); John Archer (Phillip Evans); Wally Cassell (Giovanni Cotton Valetti); Fred Clark (Daniel Winston, the Trader); Ford Rainey (Zuckie Hommell); Fred Coby (Happy Taylor); G. Pat Collins (Herbert, the Reader); Mickey Knox (Het Kohler); Paul Guilfoyle (Roy Parker); Robert Osterloh (Tommy Ryley); Ian MacDonald (Bo Creel); Ray Montgomery (Ernie Trent); Jim Toney (Brakeman); Leo Cleary (Fireman); Murray Leonard (Engineer); Terry O'Sullivan (Radio Announcer); Marshall Bradford (Chief of Police); Milton Parsons (Willie Rolf the Stoolie); John Pickard, Eddie Phillips (Government Agents); Bob Foulk (Plant Guard); Perry Ivins (Dr. Simpson); Nolan Leary (Gas Station Owner); Grandon Rhodes, John McGuire (Psychiatrists); Harry Lauter (Radio Patrolman, Car A); Ray Bennett, Harry Strang, Jack Worth, Bob Fowke, Art Foster, Arthur Miles (Guards); Sid Melton (Russell Hughes); Fern Eggen McGrath (Clocker); George Spaulding (Judge); Buddy Gorman (Popcorn Vendor); Claudia Barrett (Cashier); De Forrest Lawrence (Jim Donovan); George Taylor (Police Surgeon); Stanton Herzog (Accountant); Carl Harbrough (Foreman).

If imitation is the sincerest form of flattery, than James Cagney's Cody Jarrett in *White Heat* stands as Hollywood's most memorable screen convict. Even to this day, when impressionists/comics wish to gain a quick laugh, they mimic Cagney's famous salutation "Top of the world, Ma!" from *White Heat*. Cagney had played many tough gangsters onscreen before. He had been a movie inmate in *Angels with Dirty Faces* (1938), q.v., and *Each Dawn I Die* (1939), q.v. However, it was in *White Heat* that he created his most deeply-etched portrayal. His Cody Jarrett is a complex psychotic hoodlum, a man (over)loyal to his mother and friends, but without regard for human life. This hardened criminal is more at home with fellow inmates in the slammer than he is roaming free outside the walls. As he moves from his cell to the food hall and on to the work plant, he is relatively relaxed and confident, at peace with the simple routine and the structure in which he is a kingpin among the convicts. (And no studio could provide a better prison set or a more convincing set of prisoners than could Warner Bros.)

Thanks to James Cagney's oversized performance in *White Heat,* he paints a cold-blooded felon who can take it as well as he can dish it. Cagney's Cody Jarrett endures as the screen's most intricate characterization of a prisoner.

On the California state line, homicidal gangster Cody Jarrett (James Cagney) leads his gang on a daring mail train robbery during which he viciously kills four trainmen. He disappears in hiding with his gang, along with his beautiful but calculating wife Verna (Virginia Mayo) and his doting mother, Ma Jarrett (Margaret Wycherly). However, when Federal agents close in, the crafty Jarrett turns himself in for a lesser crime committed in Illinois on the same day. He is given a one-year prison sentence.

His scheme does not fool the FBI, who assign veteran agent Hank Fallon (Edmond O'Brien) to go undercover as criminal Vic Pardo. He jokes to his superior (John Archer):

> Look at me. College degree, lovable personality and I spend most of my time in prison, an undercover specialist. Eight sentences in five years! Sing Sing, Leavenworth. . . . I joined the department to put criminals behind bars and here I am stir crazy.

On the other hand, the serious FBI official warns Hank about the complexity of his newest assignment:

> When he was a kid, he used to fake headaches in order to get his mother's attention away from the rest of the family. It worked. As he grew up the fancy headaches became real until now they tear him to pieces. And there goes our case! Any minute he's liable to crack open at the seams. So you'll be working against time.

Vic is transferred to the state prison housing Cody and becomes the man's cellmate, soon earning his friendship. Meanwhile, with Cody out of the way, scheming Verna begins a romance with Big Ed Somers (Steve Cochran), one of Cody's gang. Ed arranges for a prison inmate, Roy Parker (Paul Guilfoyle), to drop a steel beam on Cody, but Vic pulls him to safety. Next, Ma visits her son and reports Verna's disloyalty, promising to take care of the situation. However, when she attempts to stop the affair, she is shot dead (actually by Verna). Cody learns of her death in the prison dining hall and the news drives him berserk. He engineers a daring breakout, taking Vic and several of his gang with him.

As soon as he encounters Somers on the outside, he shoots the man dead. Verna survives — for the time being — convincing the gullible Cody of her alleged loyalty. Cody and his men execute a rash of robberies, with Vic as his chief helper. Later, in partnership with the Trader (Fred Clark), Jarrett plans to rob the payroll office at a large chemical plant. Vic communicates the news to his colleagues. At the robbery site, Vic is recognized by one of the gang's new helpers and Cody tries to kill the traitor. Pardo escapes and informs his superior about the Trader and Verna

James Cagney in *White Heat* (1949).

is brought in for questioning. Later, the gang is caught at the plant's gates with most of them getting killed or being forced to surrender. The wounded, hysterical Cody crawls to the top of a large, gas-filled tank where he shouts gleefully, "Made it, Ma! Top of the World!" He then shoots his gun into the combustible chemicals and is blown to bits in the explosion.

The advertisement for this film blasted, "James Cagney is Red Hot in *White Heat!*" and both the critics and public agreed. "The tight-lipped scowl, the hunched shoulders that rear themselves for the kill, the gargoyle speech, the belching gunfire of a trigger-happy paranoic — one with a mother complex, no less — these are the standard and still popular ingredients that constitute the Cagney of *White Heat.* . . . Production is first rate, and Raoul Walsh's direction has kept the pace sharp and exciting for the nearly two-hour length." Hollywood Reporter endorsed, "There is punch in every line, sock in every action sequence. . . . Cagney's performance of the psychopathic killer is one of the best in his large gallery of distinguished acting portraits." Bosley Crowther *(New York Times)* lauded, "Mr. Cagney has made his return to a gangster role in one of the most explosive pictures that he or anyone has ever played. . . . Mr. Cagney achieves the fascination of a brilliant bull-fighter at work, deftly engaged in the business of doing violence with economy and grace. His movements are supple and electric. . . . [Y]ou should see the sweet and loving things he does to handsome Virginia Mayo. . . . Or you should scan the exquisite indifference with which he 'lets a little air' into the trunk compartment of an auto in which is locked a treacherous 'friend.'

In retrospect, Danny Peary in *Guide for the Film Fanatic* (1986) noted of Cagney's anti-hero lead, "How pathetic he is during his headache bouts, when he staggers across the floor like a wounded animal, mewing and moaning. How terrifying, pathetic and sympathetic he is in the classic prison-cafeteria scene when he learns that Ma is dead. It's interesting that [director Raoul] Walsh treats the story's potential hero — undercover policeman Hank Fallon . . . as the story's villain, no better than a filthy spy. Walsh obviously felt for Cody, who's at least honest where his friends are concerned. So Walsh gives Cody a 'happy' ending. . . ." In *The Films of the Forties* (1975), Tony Thomas weighs, "Even without James Cagney *White Heat* would be a rattling good crime movie, exciting and vivid in its pacing, thanks to the direction of action expert Raoul Walsh. But with Cagney and his extraordinary portrait of the evil, mercurial Jarrett, the film becomes a fascinating experience."

In summing up the unforgettable characterization of Cody Jarrett, David Thomson in *A Biographical Dictionary of Film* (1975) writes:

> [M]ost fascinating of all was the way Cagney 'choreographed' Jarrett when suffering from one of his 'headaches': he staggered endlessly, moaning and shrieking until some half a dozen prison warders were needed to restrain the rapt, seething doll. All the naïvety of Cagney's character was brought out in these cries and *White Heat* is one of his finest films.

White Heat received an Academy Award nomination for Best Motion Picture Story. For the record, the film showing at the drive-in that Cody and his mother attend is Warner Bros.' *Task Force* (1949), which the characters, when they are not busily plotting their future, claim to have enjoyed very much.

284. *Why Must I Die?* (American International, 1960), 86 min.

Executive producer, Richard B. Duckett; producer, Richard Bernstein; associate producer, Gabriel de Caesar; director, Roy Del Ruth; story, George W. Waters; screenplay, Waters, Bernstein; additional dialogue, Herbert G. Luft; set decorator, Ted Driscoll; costumes, Marjorie Corso; makeup, Harry Thomas; music, Dick LaSalle; music coordinator, Al Simms; song, Duane Eddy and Lee Hazelwood; assistant directors, Richard Dixon, Arthur Broidy; sound, S. G. Houghton; camera, Ernest Haller; editor, John Hoffman.

Terry Moore (Lois King); Debra Paget (Dottie Manson); Bert Freed (Adler); Julie Reding (Mitzi); Lionel Ames (Eddie); Richard LePore (Sinclair); Selette Cole (Peggy Taylor); Dorothy Lovett (Mrs. Benson); Phil Harvey (Kenny Randall); Fred Sherman (Red King); Robert Shayne (Charlie Munro); Damian O'Flynn (Dennison); Holly Harris (Mrs. Bradley); Mark Sheeler (Jim); Jean Burton (Trixie); Abigail Shelton (Dawn).

One of the stranger careers in Hollywood is that of actress Terry Moore (b. 1929). She began in pictures with *Maryland* (1940), using her real name Helen Koford. Later, she appeared under the screen name of Judy Ford and, still later, as Jan Ford. She made her first big impression with moviegoers as the ingenue of *Mighty Joe Young* (1949) and was later Oscar-nominated as Best Supporting Actress for *Come Back, Little Sheba* (1952). As late as *Peyton Place* (1957) she was still playing a teenager (!) on screen. In the onslaught of renewed interest over the bizarre death of eccentric billionaire Howard Hughes (1905–1976), she claimed/

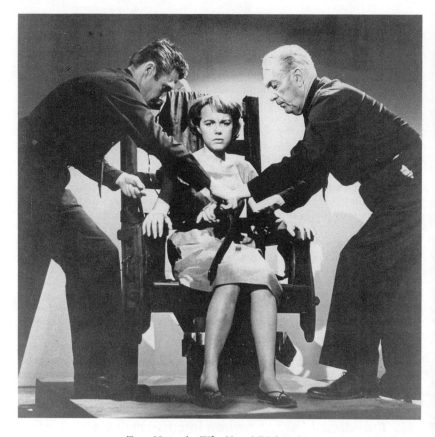

Terry Moore in *Why Must I Die?* (1960).

admitted that she and Hughes had once been married. In the late 1980s she hosted a syndicated TV interview show and produced/starred in occasional motion pictures. Back in 1960 her production company packaged *Why Must I Die?*, an obvious rip-off of Susan Hayward's Oscar-winning *I Want to Live!* (1958), q.v., but which, nevertheless, contains a gripping if strident performance by Ms. Moore.

Aspiring nightclub singer Lois King (Terry Moore) acts as lookout on a robbery heist engineered by her aging safecracker dad, Red King (Fred Sherman), and a punk hoodlum named Eddie (Lionel Ames). The safe proves to be empty and Lois abandons the criminal element to return to show business. Her career advances and soon she is hired as vocalist at the Cocatoo Club by its owner, Kenny Randall (Phil Harvey). At this juncture, Eddie appears with his tough companion Dottie Manson (Debra Paget), an experienced safecracker. They force Lois into helping them engineer a robbery of the Cocatoo's safe. During the robbery, Randall appears on the scene unexpectedly and is killed by Dottie, using Lois's gun. Shortly thereafter, Lois arrives at the club to warn Kenny and discovers his corpse. She instinctively picks up the weapon and is found in this incriminating position by the night watchman, who overhears her sobbing "I killed him" not realizing what she really means. Lois is arrested, tried and sentenced to die in the electric chair.

Despite everything, her attorney, Adler (Bert Freed), still believes in her innocence and urges the police to locate the missing Eddie and Dottie Manson. Meanwhile, Dottie robs a liquor store and, in the process, murders a blind news vendor. She is sentenced to the same prison as Lois. Adler engineers a confrontation between Lois and Dottie, but the latter insists she knows nothing about the robbery/killing for which Lois is charged. Red finally tracks down Eddie and, while pressuring him to confess, Eddie falls from a fire escape and dies. At the prison, Dottie's cellmates discover that she is guilty and threaten her life. A near-crazed Dottie rushes through the prison corridors screaming that she is guilty, not Lois. However, her confession is too late. Lois has already been dragged screaming to the electric chair to die. A disillusioned Adler wonders aloud who is going to be held responsible for the state's crime against Lois King.

Why Must I Die?, made under the working title *The Girl on Death Row*, opened on a double bill with the horror thriller *The House of Usher*. Eugene Archer *(New York Times)* was not impressed. "Miss Moore plays this hopeless role as if every scene were her last, apparently convinced that the road to the death house is paved with Oscars.... Her performance is only slightly more ridiculous than the one given by Debra Paget.... Lurid and salacious in writing and direction, *Why Must I Die?* is *I Want to Live* squared." *Harrison's Reports* rated *Why Must I Die?* as "an ugly, badly scripted and amateurishly acted account.... Pretty Terry Moore is overly melodramatic as the wronged girl.... Debra Paget is unconvincing as the vicious female safecracker-murderess."

Why Must I Die? was promoted with the ad lines, "The True Story of a Girl on Death Row.... Only the motion picture screen would dare tell this shocking story!" Needless to say, it won no Oscar nominations for Ms. Moore or the film.

285. *Within These Walls* (20th Century–Fox, 1945), 71 min.

Producer, Ben Silvey; director, H. Bruce Humberstone; story, Coles Trapnell, James B. Fisher; screenplay, Eugene Ling, Wanda Tuchock; art directors, Lyle Wheeler, Richard Irvine; set decorators, Thomas Little, Ernest Lansing; music, David Buttolph; music director, Emil Newman; special effects, Fred Sersen; camera, Glen Mac-Williams, Clyde DeVinna; editor, Harry Reynolds.

Thomas Mitchell (Michael Howland); Mary Anderson (Anne Howland); Edward Ryan (Tommie Howland); Mark Stevens (Steve Russel); B. S. Pully (Garry Bowser); Roy Roberts (Martin Deutsch); John Russell (Rogers); Norman Lloyd (Peter Moran); Edward Kelly (Tommy Callahan); Harry Shannon (McCaffrey, Assistant Warden); Rex Williams (Hobey Jenkins); Ralph Dunn (Pearson); Dick Rush (Station Agent); William Halligan (Collins); Freddie Graham (Stunt Guard); and: Louis Bacigalupi, Joseph Bernard, Lennie Bremen, Jack Daley, James Flavin, Eddie Hart, Paul Newlan, Steve Olsen, Bob Perry, Otto Reichow, Dick Rich, Frank Scannell, Harry Strang, Charles Wagenheim, Max Wagner.

In its aim to present a new perspective on the standardized prison melodrama, 20th Century–Fox fashioned *Within These Walls*, a decently-crafted diatribe against overstern penal discipline (as being as erroneous as too lax a control over convicts). In this modest picture, it is the martinet warden (excellently played by Thomas Mitchell) who is rehabilitated by his penitentiary ambiance.

Noted as a no-nonsense criminal lawyer/judge, stern Michael Howland

(Thomas Mitchell) is asked to take charge of the state penitentiary and to overcome its wave of convict riots and staff corruption. Joined by his daughter Anne (Mary Anderson) and his seventeen-year-old son, Tommy (Edward Ryan), Howland arrives at the prison where the inmate population greets him with hisses and boos. Howland ruthlessly begins his reform program, ridding the prison of dishonest guards, punishing unruly convicts by placing them in solitary confinement and using the reward of special privileges only when justified.

While these changes are happening, Howland's daughter is being romanced by Steve Russell (Mark Stevens), a model prisoner (he actually is innocent of the embezzlement charge he accepted on behalf of his married brother), who has been made the warden's chauffeur. Meanwhile, Howland's ne'er-do-well son, needing to pay off debts, accepts bribes from the prisoners to accomplish special favors. When the warden learns that his delinquent offspring helped some of the men attempt a break, he lectures him sternly and sends him off to college. Once there Tommy quickly drops out and is drawn into a life of crime. He ends up being arrested for a robbery and is sentenced to ten years in the penitentiary. The heartbroken Howland insists that his son will receive no special treatment while an inmate, and, to prove his point, has the young man put into solitary confinement when he acts rebellious. Later, several convicts, learning of Tommy's relationship to the boss keeper, maneuver him into helping them with an escape. During the attempted breakout, Tommy sacrifices his life to save his father's. The distraught father gains revenge on the responsible prisoners, shooting it out with the convicts in the prison yard.

As a result of this trauma, Howland belatedly sees that stern discipline (i.e., of convicts, of growing children) must be tempered with kindness if it is to be effective. As a new group of prisoners arrive for induction, the warden has a fresh perspective on how to deal best with them.

Variety ranked this an "Actionful film, ably produced and directed.... Mitchell gives an excellent performance, one that is partly sympathetic and partly not." A. H. Weiler *(New York Times)* found Mitchell's pivotal performance "restrained and impressive" but warned that the move is "slowly-paced and uneven entertainment laboring under an occasionally over-imaginative plot." In summation, Weiler found *Within These Walls* "serious but not sizzling melodrama."

286. *Women in Chains* (ABC–TV, Jan. 25, 1972), color, 73 min.

Producer, Edward K. Milkis; associate producer, Wally Samson; director, Bernard L. Kowalski; teleplay, Rita Larkin; art director, Bill Ross; music, Charles Fox; music supervisor, Kenyon Hopkins; camera, Howard R. Schwartz; editor, Argyle Nelson.

Ida Lupino (Tyson); Lois Nettleton (Sandra Parker [Sally Porter]); Jessica Walter (Dee Dee); Belinda J. Montgomery (Melinda); Penny Fuller (Helen Anderson); John Larch (Barney); Neile Adams (Leila); Hazel Medina (Althea); Katherine Cannon (Alice); Lucille Benson (Billie); Joyce Jameson (Simpson); Barbara Luna (Barbara); Judy Strangis (Maggie); Alice Baches (Mrs. Foster); and: Barbara Baldwin, William Bryant, Hollie Hayes, Noah Keen, June Whitley Taylor.

The potential was here for a rip-roaring teledrama exploiting the toughness of life behind bars. Ida Lupino, who had played the snarling chief prison administrator in *Women's Prison* (1955), q.v., reprised a very similar role to far less advantage. (The part had originally been offered to Eleanor Parker of *Caged* [1950], q.v., who rejected the role.) Lois Nettleton appeared as the earnest parole officer who wants to investigate charges of brutality in a woman's prison for herself, spurred on by the mysterious death of an inmate she had known. She has herself locked up on phoney charges, only to discover that the one person who can establish her legitimacy has been killed and that, because she is asking too many questions, she may be the next victim. *TV Movies and Video Guide* (1989) rated it "average," explaining, "Good production tries hard, but script is unbelievable, performances uneven."

In *Ida Lupino* (1977), Jerry Vermilye assessed the actress's work as the quietly malevolent, middle-aged Claire Tyson, head matron at the prison:

> It is one of the actress's best television performances, this unctious sadist who relishes her work so much that she has systematically refused all promotion possibilities to remain where she is. 'My girls are special,' she purrs to a group of new inmates. 'They help me run this block.' . . . Disobedient women are dealt with forcefully here, from Tyson's physical abuse of the inmates to a ruthless, unofficial 'death contract.' . . . [Lupino] makes every scene count with the use of steel-willed, wry-humored understatement. . . . [H]er scenes with the vibrant Nettleton fairly crackle with barely controlled animosity.

287. *Women in Prison* (Columbia, 1939), 59 min.

Director, Lambert Hillyer; story, Mortimer Braus; screenplay, Saul Elkins; costumes, Robert Kalloch; camera, Benjamin Kline; editor, Dick Fantl.

Wyn Cahoon (Ann Wilson); Scott Colton (Bob Wayne); Arthur Loft (Barney Morse); Mayo Methot (Daisy Saunders); Ann Doran (Maggie); Sarah Padden (Martha Wilson); Margaret Armstrong (Mrs. Tatum); John Tyrrell (Jerry Banks); Bess Flowers (Florence); Dick Curtis (Mac); Eddie Fetherston (Manny); John Dilson (Henry Russell); Lee Prather (District Attorney); Beatrice Curtis, Beatrice Blinn, Leona Valde, Mary Russell, Rae Daggett, Gertrude Webber (Prisoners); Helen Keers, Eleanor Woods (Matrons); Thurston Hall (Chairman of Board); Frank Cordell (Texan); Lee Shumway (Detective); Bud Geary (Cop); Al Rhein (Dealer); Gene Stone (Waiter); Grace Goodall (Board Member).

Gangster Barney Morse (Arthur Loft) has an excellent reason for wanting Daisy Saunders (Mayo Methot) paroled from prison. She had been part of his bank robbery gang, but had double-crossed him and hidden the $100,000 loot before being captured by the police. Morse wants that cash. However, Daisy prefers serving out her ten-year term and then enjoying a luxurious life with her stolen money. Because prison superintendent Martha Wilson (Sarah Padden) refuses to cooperate with Barney in releasing Daisy, he arranges for Wilson's daughter, Ann (Wyn Cahoon), to be framed on a charge of manslaughter while drunk driving. She is sentenced to ten years at the prison run by her mother. There the other prisoners make life a living hell for her. Martha is afraid of being accused of showing partiality and must stand quietly during her daughter's torment.

Morse revisits the warden and offers to establish Ann's innocence if she will release Daisy. Wilson refuses the deal. Meanwhile, Daisy has a change of heart, wanting to help the young woman who is suffering because of her. She and Ann escape from prison. Later, Daisy, who has told Ann where the loot is hidden, is killed by Barney's underlings. Ann, with the help of her boyfriend, Bob Wayne (Scott Colton), sets a trap by leading Barney to the money and then leading him into confessing Ann's frame-up. The criminals are caught, and Ann is released.

Frank S. Nugent *(New York Times)* quickly dismissed this potboiler. "Justice triumphs in *Women in Prison*, and it's just too bad it couldn't have been a melodramatic triumph as well. But you can't have everything and, what with a minor script and a very minor cast, Columbia was lucky to get off as well as it did." *Boxoffice* magazine judged, "Entire effort has a synthetic quality."

Columbia's *Women in Prison,* made under the working title *Forgotten Women,* was shot at the same time as the studio's *Penitentiary* (1938), q.v., and utilized several of the same sets. Mayo Methot (1904–1951) as the floozie jailbird stole the acting honors in this lightweight entry. She is best recalled as the third wife (1938–1945) of Humphrey Bogart.

288. *Women of San Quentin* (NBC–TV, Oct. 23, 1983), color, 100 min.

Executive producer, David Gerber; producers, Stephen Cragg, R. W. Goodwin; director, William Graham; story, Mark Rodgers, Larry Cohen; teleplay, Rodgers; production designer, Stan Jolley; set decorator, Charles Rutherford; costumes, Richard W. Hoffman; makeup, Larry Roberts; music, John Cacavas; music editors, Jeff Garson, Wayne Artman; assistant directors, Ed Milkovich, John Perrin Flynn; technical adviser, Anthony Newland; technical consultant, Peggy Kernan; stunt coordinator, Bill Couch; sound, Jacques Nosco; sound re-recording, Tom Dahr, Rick Alexander; sound editor, Ron Horwitz; camera, Robert Steadman; editor, Ronald J. Fagan.

Stella Stevens (Lieutenant Janet Alexander); Debbie Allen (Carol Freeman); Hector Elizondo (Captain Mike Reyes); Amy Steel (Elizabeth Larson); Rosana DeSoto (Adela Reynosa); Gregg Henry (Williams); William Allen Young (Larry Jennings); Yaphet Kotto (Sergeant Therman Patterson); Rockne Tarkington (Bill William Jefferson); William J. Sanderson (Vince Contee); Tracee Lyels (Marion); Jenny Gago (Gloria); Mike Gomez (Mexican Gang Member); Charlie Stavola (Associate Warden); Wesley Thompson, Matt Landers (Young Men); Charles Allen-Anderson (Black Gang Member); Ahmad Hurradin (Anthony De Haven); Francisco Laguervela (Assistant District Attorney); Reverend Johnathan Rhode (Black Minister); James S. Diggs (Band Leader); Orwin C. Harvey (Sheriff's Deputy); Bob Minor (J. W. Power); Charles Watson, Al Stevenson, Earl Billings, Javier Grajeda, J. P. Bumstead, William Steis, Larry Charles White, James N. Dalton, Dennis R. McKibbin, Jackie Hendrickson, George Newman, Ron McCall, Gordon D. Roetker, Martin Witkosy (Officers); Eugene Lawrence, William D. Pipkin, Douglas E. Monticue, Don Sanders, Leroy Ortez, Robert W. Shaw (Inmates).

Who would have thought they would make a soap opera about female guards at San Quentin Prison? But they did! "Stodgy drama gives prison life just the reputation it needs: dull.... Director William A. Graham plays it lax—the tension is nil.... [D]rags from cliché to cliché" *(Daily Variety).*

The narrative opens at the California Correctional Institute Training School where new guards are being educated. They are told:

> Actions by the criminal justice system against lawbreakers are designed to serve three purposes beyond the immediate punitive one: (1) the removal of dangerous people from the community; (2) deter others from criminal behavior; (3) give society the opportunity to attempt to turn lawbreakers into law abiding citizens.

Among the new guards assigned to San Quentin Prison is Elizabeth Larson (Amy Steel) of Portersville, California. Her superior is veteran keeper, Lieutenant Janet Alexander (Stella Stevens) of the East Block. On her first day there, the nervous Liz is taken on a tour of duty by experienced Sergeant Therman Patterson (Yaphet Kotto):

The prisoners will expect you to treat everybody fair. Imagine that? They never treated anyone fair in their whole lives and they have their victims to prove it. And then, they're going to get all uptight if they're not being treated fair and equal.

. . .By the same token when a female officer shows ordinary human sympathy or friendliness, some of the male officers will say that, ah, she's showing favoritism or maybe falling in love with the con.

Patterson also explains: "We have a no-hostage policy. We try and stall them as long as we can to get guns into place, as many as we can make available and then we order them to release the hostage or hostages. Then we go in, one way or the other."

Meanwhile, it develops that Janet, whose late husband was a police officer, is considering leaving the prison to accept a $39,000 position as Special Advisor on Corrections to the Governor, which would mean moving to Sacramento, one hundred miles away. Having endured so much work pressure over the years, she is ready for a change. She feels that she has become just as much a prisoner as the convicts. "We're part of the system too." However, two factors make her hesitant to accept the new post. She is good at her work and she will miss being close to her lover, prison Captain Mike Reyes (Hector Elizondo). Reyes tries to persuade Janet to remain at San Quentin:

> But there are things you and the other women officers can do in prison that men can't do. They look at a man in this uniform and their gut response is it's the enemy. They look at a woman in this uniform and their gut response is it's still a woman.

Liz becomes friendly with Carol Freeman (Debbie Allen), who had attended law school before becoming a guard. Liz tells her co-worker why she chose this unique profession, having previously been a waitress and assorted other meaningless positions: "If I got this job and I could do it, it's a way to get my life together and I'd finally have something I could be proud of."

Carol, a divorcée with children, has been dating lawyer Larry Jennings (William Allen Young), who would prefer she quit this dangerous profession and become a homemaker or perhaps return to her lawyering career. Carol speaks frankly about the dangers of their job: "I've been there two-and-one-half years and there are still mornings when I walk in there wondering if I'll make it out at night."

Carol also confesses how her professional demeanor has changed over the years:

> I came in wanting to be liked by the officers and the inmates and I thought that maybe, somehow, in some small way, I could make it better. It didn't take me long to adjust. When I saw what they had done on the streets in their files and what they did to each other in their cells and they just heap their pent-up hate on me, and nothing was left to the imagination. All I heard was like voices from hell. The other officers enjoyed the show, I'll tell you.
>
> For a while I hated anything that even smelled like a man. Oh yeah, after that I knew what it was all about. Hey, the cons could stay on lock down forever. If I put someone in segregation, I didn't care if he was there for good. If the state wanted to reopen the gas chamber, I would help them fill it up. Nobody could live with that much anger. I couldn't. So I learned to accommodate. First, I just forced myself to smile back, to do favors. Then I realized I was getting to know them, the bad, the

good, the freaks. And when you get to know them, you can understand them. And when that happens, things just to fall into place and just like that, you belong.

A black prisoner, J. W. Power (Bob Minor), who ran the Black Liberation Front from inside San Quentin, and two guards are gunned down in an ambush as they are heading to a San Francisco courtroom where Power was to testify. This action leads to friction among the ethnic factions at the prison, as well as a realignment of the BLF by members both inside and out of San Quentin. Inmate Vince Contee (William J. Sanderson), leading a white faction, stages a hostage situation by grabbing guard Adela Reynosa (Rosana DeSoto), who after being released is badly shaken by the situation. However, she forces herself to resume her dangerous duties. Meanwhile, rumors spread that on Black History Day, the Chicano prisoners, who are divided between two inmate gang leaders, plan to hit the black populaton at the prison. Because of the feared pending riot, Janet has agreed to stay on until everything has cooled down. However, she is disgruntled about her continued responsibilities: "Every decision I make involves somebody's life. It's too heavy. It's not worth it!"

On the appointed day, there is a riot in the yard, with several prisoners killing each other. However, Liz proves resilient in the heated situation, helping to calm down the agitated prisoners. Janet rushes into the breach, knowing the convicts respect her. She informs the ring leaders, "Whichever way it goes, I'm going to be the last person to leave this yard." The riot is quelled. Liz feels confident of herself in her keeper capacity. As for Janet, much to Reyes's satisfaction, she decides to remain working at San Quentin.

Despite the mawkish soap opera qualities of *Women of San Quentin,* the telefeature has it plus sides. Stella Stevens is very convincing as the tough but sympathetic veteran maximum security guard. Amy Steel is refreshingly buoyant as the timorous newcomer who makes good in a dangerous occupation. While the contrasting feelings of the male and female guards and male inmates regarding women guards may be patly expressed, their exposition offers some insight into a little-explored region of the prison drama: i.e. what makes an individual undertake such a dangerous occupation. Additionally, the delineation of hard-lined convicts of many ethnic and moral persuasions is very well handled by the cast.

Much of the location work for this telefeature was accomplished at San Quentin Prison and at the Colorado Territorial Correctional Facility.

289. *Women Without Names* (Paramount, 1940), 62 min.

Producer, Eugene Zukor; director, Robert Florey; based on the play by Ernest Booth; screenplay, William R. Lipman, Horace McCoy; art directors, Hans Dreier, William Flannery; camera, Charles Lang; editor, Anne Bauchens.

Ellen Drew (Joyce King); Robert Paige (Fred MacNeil); Judith Barrett (Peggy Athens); John Miljan (Assistant District Attorney John Marlin); Fay Helm (Millie); John McGuire (Walter Ferris); Louise Beavers (Ivory); James Seay (O'Grane); Esther Dale (Head Matron Inglis); Marjorie Main (Mrs. Lowry); Audrey Maynard (Maggie); Kitty Kelly (Countess); Virginia Dabney (Ruffles); Helen Lynch (Susie); Mae Busch (Rose); Frank M. Thomas (Warden Rynex); Thomas E. Jackson (Detective Sergeant Reardon); Joseph Sawyer (Principal Keeper Grimley); Eddie Saint (Priest); Wilfred Lucas, Dick Elliott, Ruth Warren (Roomers); Harry Worth (Trailer Salesman); Lillian Elliott (Mrs. Anthony); George Anderson, Henry Roquemore, John Harmond, Arthur Aylesworth, Leila McIntyre, Helen MacKellar, Mary Gordon (Jurors); Eddie Fetherston, Allen Fox, Ralph McCullough, Allen

Conner, Jack Egan, Paul Kruger (Re-   Douglas Kennedy (Secretary); James Flavin
porters); Blanche Rose (Jail Matron);   (Guard).

Joyce King (Ellen Drew), who inherited a boarding house that she can barely afford to maintain, works at a drive-in restaurant. One evening on duty, she meets road engineer Fred MacNeil (Robert Paige). It is love at first sight, even after Joyce explains that she has just finished serving three years on probation for having been (innocently) involved in a robbery with her ex-husband, Walter Ferris (John McGuire). The couple decide to marry and to drive to Tennessee where Fred is to start a new construction assignment. Meanwhile, Ferris arrives at Joyce's apartment with his new girlfriend Peggy Athens (Judith Barrett). Police Detective Sergeant Reardon (Thomas E. Jackson) follows Ferris there and, when he attempts to arrest the man, Ferris kills him. Walter leaves the murder weapon, and he and Peggy rush off. Thereafter, Joyce and Fred return to the apartment and, through circumstantial evidence, witnesses and police insist that MacNeil is the killer and Joyce is his accomplice. He is sentenced to be executed at the same prison where Joyce is to spend her life in the women's wing.

The bewildered Joyce is taken to the dormitory by Head Matron Inglis (Esther Dale), who explains: "This is where you'll stay unless your conduct makes it necessary for us to transfer you to a cell. Now if you behave yourself, you'll get well treated here."

However, the frightened newcomer is soon reduced to tears. A veteran prisoner, Ivory (Louise Beavers), attempts to comfort her:

> Oh, that's all right honey. I've been in jail about nine times myself. And every time I arrive, I turns on the rain like you does. I think there's something about a jail that just naturally makes you weep. At first, that is. But you'll soon get over it.

When word spreads about the extent of Joyce's criminal record, she gains immediate respect from the others. Inmate Maggie (Audrey Maynard) enthuses — sarcastically: "You should be very popular here. Most of the fish in this jail are just small fry. We've never had any cop killers before!"

Meanwhile, Fred is locked on death row, desperately hoping that some new evidence will turn up to prove his innocence. A tough keeper, Grimley (Joseph Sawyer), snarls: "Make yourself comfortable. This will be your last hotel room." However, a fellow inmate suggests that Fred keep his mind focused on the good times from the past: "It will all come back to you after a few nights in here. You'll remember things you never even noticed. I killed a night watchman, but I kinda wish it had been first page stuff like your job."

When MacNeil protests that he is innocent, his cellblock confidant responds: "Well, that's the way I talked too. 'I didn't do it.' You try to kid yourself that you didn't, so you can kid everybody else. Funny thing. You can't kid about murder."

Further on, Peggy Atkins is jailed at the same prison for having circulated bad checks. Her boyfriend Ferris has yet to be picked up by the police. Peggy, who has the advantage of knowing all about Joyce, is jealous that she was once Ferris's wife. She immediately turns viciously on the confused Joyce who has no idea of her relationship to Ferris. Before long the two are caught fighting and Joyce, labeled the attacker by crafty Peggy, is placed in solitary confinement for a month. The other inmates turn against Peggy and, thus pressured, she confesses to Inglis that she started the battle royale. When Joyce is released back into general population and holds no grudge against Peggy, the latter becomes friendly with her onetime enemy.

Meanwhile, Assistant District Attorney John Marlin (John Miljan), who had prosecuted Joyce and Fred, is now running for District Attorney. He hopes to gain public endorsement by showing that he is tough on criminals and, if elected, he would see to it that the prison was run strictly. He arranges, through bribes to corrupt matron Mrs. Lowry (Marjorie Main) and Grimley, for Joyce and Fred to have a final reunion on the night before he is to die. He has reporters on hand to document the prison's "easy" policies: i.e. allowing two such dangerous culprits to fraternize. The event backfires, as the warden fires the miscreant keepers and the press is disgusted by Marlin's tactics.

Next, Peggy confesses to Joyce the truth about who killed the police detective. They demand that Marlin hear the new evidence. Marlin arrives at the prison, but refuses to accept Peggy's story, knowing this turnabout would not help him win the election. Peggy and Joyce steal the warden's gun and force Marlin to drive them out of the prison. Peggy and Joyce rush to a local newspaper, which is eager for an exclusive story on the case. The editor helps Peggy trap Ferris into meeting her and confessing the truth in front of witnesses.

With all matters cleared, Joyce and Fred are released and leave for their new life in Tennessee.

Variety reported of this economy production, "Miss Drew is capable in the lead, and shows more ability than the direction provides. Paige carries role of condemned man in good fashion, while Judith Barrett hits a high spot as the jealous meanie...." Bosley Crowther *(New York Times)*, obviously surfeited with such fare, noted jocularly, "This department has been noticing the surprising high order of social refinements which have been creeping into the run of women's prison pictures of late. Conditions in the institutions seem definitely better than last year, even if the pictures themselves are not.... [O]therwise this is just a routine melodrama, lurid but completely implausible...."

For any seasoned viewer of prison dramas, one of the joys of screening a new entry is to judge how salty is the range of eccentric inmates, how dastardly are the matrons, how much tough talk occurs. The unpretentious *Women Without Names,* which falters in its wild, melodramatic plot, scores well on several other levels. Louise Beavers, who had also played an inmate named Ivory in *Ladies of the Big House* (1932), q.v., is very effective as the folksy, piano-playing convict. Then there is the flavorful Countess (Kitty Kelly), a pretentious snob, who has a sharp word for every person and every situation. When Peggy Atkins is introduced into the dormitory, the Countess sizes up the newcomer and acidly observes: "If I may be permitted an observation, this is a respectable ladies jail, not an insane asylum. Are you sure, you're in the right place?"

Later, the Countess, avidly playing a rubber of bridge, explains the process of adapting to prison routine, for those less astute than she: "It's a matter of becoming acclimatized. It's just a matter of adjustment."

In *Women Without Names,* there are a few surprises among the performers playing guards. Not only is the warden (Frank M. Thomas) a sympathetic sort, but Esther Dale, who played several nasty matrons (e.g. *Condemned Women*, 1938, q.v.), is extremely tolerant and empathetic to her charges. In this film, it is Marjorie Main as the pinched-faced Mrs. Lowry who is the sinister keeper, much like she was in *Prison Farm* (1938), q.v. Joseph Sawyer, most frequently cast as a tough pug of a gangster, is seen here as the unconscionable principal keeper, who taunts the imprisoned hero into saying, "You're not a man! You're not human! You won't shut my face till you get me on the end of the rope!"

There is even a decent attempt at revealing convict philosophy. When the condemned hero is nearing his last hours and desperately wants one last meeting with his sweetheart, he confides to an understanding guard: "I hate to go like this. I feel like she's inside, holding on to my heart. . . . Don't think I'm yellow, but do you think it hurts much? . . . I could take it a lot better if I could only see her one more time."

When Fred and Joyce are permitted a final get-together, he fantasizes: "I think if we could get out into the world in a crowd of strange people and tell them who we are, we could convince them we're innocent. They could help us. Ah, it's just a crazy dream."

290. *Women's Prison* (Columbia, 1955), 80 min.

Producer, Bryan Foy; director, Lewis Seiler; screenplay, Crane Wilbur, Jack De-Witt; art director, Gary Odell; set decorator, Louis Diabe; music director, Mischa Bakaleinikoff; assistant director, Carter De-Haven, Jr.; sound, George Cooper; camera, Lester H. White; editor, Henry Batista.

Ida Lupino (Amelia Van Zant); Jan Sterling (Brenda Martin); Cleo Moore (Mae); Audrey Totter (Joan Burton); Phyllis Thaxter (Helen Jensen); Howard Duff (Dr. Clark); Warren Stevens (Glen Burton); Barry Kelley (Warden Blackburn); Gertrude Michael (Sturgess); Vivian Marshall (Dottie) Ross Elliott (Don Jensen); Mae Clarke (Saunders); Adelle August (Grace); Don C. Harvey (Captain Tierney); Edna Holland (Sarah); Lynne Millan (Carl); Mira McKinney (Burke); Mary Newton (Enright); Diane DeLaire (Head Nurse); Jana Mason (Josie); Lorna Thayer (Woman Deputy); Murray Alper (Mug); Ruth Vann, Mary Lou Devore (Girl Patients); Eddie Foy, III (Warden's Secretary), and: Jean Harvey.

Bryan Foy had produced many prison melodramas during his tenure at Warner Bros.; Lewis Seiler had directed several genre studies at the same studio: *Crime School* (1938), *You Can't Get Away with Murder* (1939), *Dust Be My Destiny* (1939), qq.v. They teamed for Columbia's *Women's Prison,* a production that bore striking similarities to Warner Bros.' far superior *Caged* (1950), q.v. The script was by Crane Wilbur, who had written/directed the prison pictures *The Story of Molly X* (1949), q.v., at Universal and *Inside the Walls of Folsom Prison* (1951), q.v., at Warner Bros.

Housewife Helene Jensen (Phyllis Thaxter) is sentenced to a term in prison for the accidental killing of a child during an automobile accident. Once behind bars, the guilt-ridden, frightened woman, bewildered by her harsh surroundings, is the object of torment by the institution's head guard, the tense Amelia Van Zant (Ida Lupino). The latter, frustrated by a loveless existence, is resentful of her charges who have romance in their lives. Several of the inmates—including Brenda Martin (Jan Sterling), Mae (Cleo Moore) and Joan Burton (Audrey Totter)—rally to Helen's defense, as does prison physician, Dr. Clark (Howard Duff). It is Clark who warns the embittered Amelia that Helene is near the breaking point, and the newcomer almost dies from trauma. However, Clark nurses her back to health.

Glen Burton (Warren Stevens), a prisoner in the men's section, finds a way to sneak into the women's quarters one day for a reunion with is wife Joan. (Both of them had been convicted for participating together in a robbery.) When Joan

becomes pregnant as a result of this visit, the prison's warden, Blackburn (Barry Kelly), becomes alarmed, fearing repercussions from the prison board. Blackburn threatens Amelia with the loss of her job if she does not reveal how Glen snuck through security. Amelia, in turn, interrogates Joan and, when the latter refuses to talk, she beats her severely. This leads to Joan having a miscarriage and to her death.

The enraged women prisoners, led by Brenda, revolt. They overcome the matrons and hold Amelia hostage. Glen returns to the women's section, bent on killing Van Zant. However, the guards use tear gas to restore order. By now the traumatized Van Zant has lost her rationality and has become a ranting maniac. Dr. Clark assures the inmates that reforms will be immediately instituted. Helene wins her freedom.

Variety acknowledged, "Psychological aspects of life behind bars, particularly as far as femmes are concerned, get a generous probing in *Women's Prison*. Film is frequently depressing.... At times the melodrama runs a bit heavy.... While femme players ... are far from glamorous in the drab prison garb, they register well in their respective assignments." A. H. Weiler *(New York Times)*, while admitting the filmmakers had done their homework in studying prison conditions and past genre entries, felt, "[I]t's scarcely a riot or a revelation, though." He added, "There's also the recognizable gallery of 'fish'...." He did acknowledge, "Of course, there are vague variations on the normal, tidy gaol tale. In this case the women's prison of the title is a coeducational institution."

In retrospect, Jerry Vermilye in *Ida Lupino* (1977) judged, "*Women's Prison*, with its cardboard characters and predictable plot turns, was merely cheap sensationalism, though briskly directed by Lewis Seiler. In Lupino's capable hands, frigid Amelia Van Zant, who takes out her frustrations on the female inmates, becomes a truly hateful villainess, without any redeeming features." Jim Morton, in his essay "Women in Prison Films" for *Re/Search: Incredibly Strange Films* (1986), judged that Ida Lupino "spectacularly played" her part as the cruel warden in *Women's Prison* and that her "role as the sadistic warden remains the definitive performance for all WIP [women in prison] films to follow." For many, now viewing this taut picture for the first time, Lupino's strident performance (with lesbian undertones) verges on the camp, her climatic mad scene a repeat of a similar sequence in *They Drive by Night* (1940).

Ida Lupino would play a comparable sadistic role in the made-for-television feature, *Women in Chains* (1972), q.v.

291. *You Can't Beat the Law* (Monogram, 1943), 64 min.

Producer, Lindsley Parsons; associate producer, Ralph M. Like; director, Phil Rosen; screenplay, Al Beich; additional dialogue, Charles Marion; art director, David Milton; music director, Edward Kay; sound, Glen Glenn; camera, Mack Stengler; editor, Carl Pierson.

Edward Norris (Johnny Gray); Joan Woodbury (Amy Duncan); Jack La Rue (Cain); Milburn Stone (Frank Sanders); Charles Jordan (Creeper); Kenneth Harlan (Warden Jones); Robert Homans (Duncan); George Kamel (Jumpy); William Castello (Rico); Mauritz Hugo (Harry); Sam Bernard (Red); Paul McVey (Wayne); Bryant Washburn (Governor); Selmer Jackson (Bedford); Inna Gest (Patricia Bedford); Tristram Coffin (Lawyer); Dick Rush

Opposite: Howard Duff, Phyllis Thaxter, Jean Harvey, Gertrude Michael and Ida Lupino in *Women's Prison* (1955).

(Tailor); Ray Miller (Penalty Guard); Cyril Ring (District Attorney); John Elliott (Judge); Jack Gardner (Convict); Charles McMurphy (Guard Murphy).

Irresponsible playboy Johnny Gray (Edward Norris) is framed and sentenced to San Quentin Prison after a stolen car is used in a holdup actually committed by gangster Rico (William Castello). Others sent to jail at the same time are Rico's three henchmen who participated in the actual robbery with their boss: Harry (Mauritz Hugo), Red (Sam Bernard), and Creeper (Charles Jordan). Gray is angered at being falsely imprisoned and losing the respect of his wealthy fiancée (Inna Gest). As such he becomes an unruly prisoner. He is assigned to the same cell as the tough convict Cain (Jack La Rue), who is planning a breakout with his underlings.

Meanwhile, due to his inhumane methods, Warden Jones (Kenneth Harlan) is replaced by the kindly Frank Sanders (Milburn Stone), a former guard. The empathetic Sanders wins Gray over by changing his cell and allowing him to work in the prison yard gardens. There, he meets Amy Duncan (Joan Woodbury), daughter of a veteran keeper (Robert Homans) at the institution. Later, Rico's men in prison are helped by their boss on the outside to make a prison break. Rico is killed and the others are badly wounded. One of the dying confederates confesses that they had framed Johnny. Gray is immediately freed.

Rather than return to his meaningless life of philandering, Johnny remains at the prison as a guard. By now he is in love with Amy, but believes that she loves Sanders. Later, Cain stages a breakout attempt, using Gray as a shield. The new guard is able to convince the men to return to their cells. Thereafter, Sanders admits he and Amy were never in love, and Johnny pursues his romance with her.

The diplomatic *Harrison's Reports* weighed, "A fair program prison melodrama; it holds one's interest. . . . A mild romance has been worked into the plot."

While the paltry sets are tacky, the cast lackluster, and the plot clichéd, *You Can't Beat the Law* has occasional fun moments, most of them provided by veteran actor (screen gangster) Jack La Rue. At one juncture he advises recalcitrant newcomer Edward Norris: "Listen kid. As long as you keep your nose clean, you won't get hurt. Get curious and it won't go so good for you. It's getting so every kid who busts open a cigarette machine, gets in here."

There is also a nice flavor to the interaction between Norris and the experienced, kindly guard, played with competence by Milburn Stone:

> NORRIS: I was framed in here. What do you think about that?
>
> STONE: Well, I don't think it's very original. Every man will tell you that about himself. You're here to do time and on the pain of death, we're here to see that you do. We're here as your friends.
>
> A.k.a. *Prison Mutiny.*

292. *You Can't Get Away with Murder* (Warner Bros., 1939), 78 min.

Producer, Samuel Bischoff; director, Lewis Seiler; based on the play *Chalked Out* by Warden Lewis E. Lawes and Jonathan Finn; screenplay, Robert Buckner, Don Ryan, Kenneth Gamet; art director, Hugo Reticker; costumes, Milo Anderson; music, Heinz Roemheld; orchestrator, Hugo Friedhofer; assistant director, William Kissel; dialogue director, Jo Graham; sound, Francis J. Scheid; camera, Sol Polito; editor, James Gibbon.

Humphrey Bogart (Frank Wilson); Billy Halop (Johnnie Stone); Gale Page (Madge Stone); John Litel (Attorney Carey); Henry Travers (Pop); Harvey Stephens (Fred Burke); Harold Huber (Scappa); Joseph Sawyer (Red); Joseph Downing (Smitty); George E. Stone (Toad); Joseph King (Prin-

cipal Keeper); Joseph Crehan (Warden); John Ridgley (Gas Station Attendant); Herbert Rawlinson (District Attorney); Lane Chandler, Robert E. Homans (Guards); Eddy Chandler (Keeper); Frank Faylen (Spieler); Robert Strange, Robert Emmett O'Connor (Detectives); Tom Dugan, Eddie "Rochester" Anderson (Convicts); Emory Parnell (Cop).

Hard-working Madge Stone (Gale Page) supports her younger brother, Johnnie (Billy Halop), and is concerned because of his acquaintanceship with a crook, Frank Wilson (Humphrey Bogart). On the other hand, Madge's boyfriend, Fred Burke (Harvey Stephens), a private policeman, has the offer of a new post in Boston and wants to marry Madge and take her and Johnnie with him. Meanwhile, Johnnie and Wilson steal a car and later he helps Wilson rob a gas station. Next, Johnnie steals Fred's gun, which Wilson grabs for himself. On a subsequent robbery, Frank uses the gun to kill the pawnshop owner and leaves the weapon there. Johnnie and Frank are arrested for holding up the gas station and sentenced to Sing Sing Prison, while, on circumstantial evidence, Burke is convicted of murder and sentenced to die. Both before and after they are inside the maximum security prison, Wilson threatens Johnnie to keep quiet about what he knows—or else! When Frank plans a prison break, he takes Johnnie with him, planning to kill him once they are on the outside. The break fails and the two are trapped in a boxcar where Wilson shoots Johnnie. Before he dies, Johnnie confesses the whole situation. Now it is Wilson's turn to go to the electric chair, while Burke is freed.

Having witnessed the travails of Dead End Kid member Billy Halop in *Crime School* (1938), *Angels with Dirty Faces* (1938) and *Hell's Kitchen* (1939), qq.v., B. R. Christler (*New York Times*) found it difficult to take *You Can't Get Away with Murder* very seriously. "It is certainly no use pretending ... [this film] isn't one of those deathhouse melodramas where the big punch line in the final sequence is when the warden says: 'Get the Governor on the wire.'... [W]e have seen Billy [Halop] reclaimed so often for society that we are beginning to think he is a sociological pushover.... One thing though ... Billy has finally reached man's estate; he is now being sent to penitentiaries instead of reform schools." *Variety* was just plain bored: "[It] is an obvious and uninteresting melodrama behind the walls of Sing Sing. It's ponderous and slow moving in development, and fails to reach climactic heights in final prison break.... Bogart turns in a standard portrayal of the tough gangster, while Halop stresses his toughness throughout. Best characterization is by Henry Travers, an old lifer who is prison librarian."

293. *You Only Live Once* (United Artists, 1937), 86 min.

Producer, Walter Wanger; director, Fritz Lang; story, Gene Towne; screenplay, Towne, Graham Baker; art director, Alexander Toluboff; costumes, Helen Taylor; music/music director, Alfred Newman; song, Louis Alter and Paul Francis Webster; assistant director, Robert Lee; sound, Frank Maher; camera, Leon Shamroy; editor, Daniel Mandell.

Sylvia Sidney (Joan Graham); Henry Fonda (Eddie Taylor); Barton MacLane (Stephen Whitney); Jean Dixon (Bonnie Graham); William Gargan (Father Dolan); Warren Hymer (Muggsy); Charles "Chic" Sales (Ethan); Margaret Hamilton (Hester); Guinn "Big Boy" Williams (Rogers); Jerome Cowan (Dr. Hill); John Wray (Warden); Jonathan Hale (District Attorney);

Ward Bond (Guard); Ben Hall (Messen-   ronas); Walter De Palma (Bit); Jack Carson
ger); Jean Stoddad (Stenographer); Wade   (Gas Station Attendant).
Boteler (Policeman); Henry Taylor (Kozde-

The very ironic *You Only Live Once* is a classic study of a man haunted by his past, in this case as an ex-convict. It shows society punishing him for his past criminal record and, in the hysteria of mob rule, condemning him to die for a crime he did not commit. Like William Shakespeare's star-crossed lovers, Romeo and Juliet, the hero and heroine of this screen piece are doomed to tragedy, dying in one another's arms. This superbly-crafted motion picture remains a masterpiece of naturalistic understatement. With a minimum of sets and the expert use of shadows, its prison scenes are more starkly memorable than many far higher-budgeted features which boasted huge cellblock settings. This production also used to full effectiveness moviegoers' expectation and acceptance of such stereotyped genre characters as: the understanding warden, the compassion prison chaplain, the falsely imprisoned hero, stir-happy convict, and that most frequent of scenarists' pawn, the prison doctor.

Young Joan Graham (Sylvia Sidney) is the very efficient secretary to public defender Stephen Whitney (Barton MacLane). While he is enamored of her, she loves drifter Eddie Taylor (Henry Fonda), a small-time criminal, who is constantly in trouble with the law. Taylor has been found guilty of such charges as stealing an automobile for a joyride, or being arrested for grand larceny. Most recently, he has been imprisoned for driving the getaway car for bank robbers. Joan persuades Whitney to speed up Eddie's release which he does, against his better judgment.

Eddie has mixed emotions about his future. He tells the warden (John Wray): "Don't worry, I'm checking out of this little hotel for keeps."

However, being no stranger to the scarred life as an ex-convict, he also points out to the sympathetic administrator: "I cheered the first time I got out and they rammed it right down my throat. They're not all like you on the outside. If they were, these places would be haunted houses."

Joan and Eddie optimistically begin their life together, buying a house and he working as a trucker, a position found for him by Whitney. One day Eddie is late to work and is fired. Frantic to support his pregnant wife and to keep the house, he looks vainly for a new job. Meanwhile, he runs into an old prison friend who later holds up an armored truck. The man kills several victims and escapes with $1,000,000. The sole clue is Eddie's hat (with the initials E. T.) which the man had taken when he and Eddie last met. Based on this circumstantial evidence and his prison record, Eddie is arrested, convicted and sentenced to die in the electric chair.

On the evening he is to be electrocuted, Eddie feigns illness and has himself transferred to the infirmary. From there he makes a break, using the prison physician, Dr. Hill (Jerome Cowan), as a shield. Meanwhile, the warden is advised that the armored car, and the real robber has been found submerged in a river. The evidence clears Eddie of the crime. However, he does not believe the warden, who pleads with him to drop his gun. When the prison chaplain, Father Dolan (William Gargan), approaches Eddie, the distraught Eddie shoots him and makes good his escape.

Now on the outside, Eddie has Joan join him and they flee. They are now notorious fugitives with a $5,000 reward offered for their capture. Later, after giving her baby over to the care of her sister, Bonnie (Jean Dixon), Joan returns to Eddie. The couple are cornered by the police near the Canadian border. They are both shot by the police and die in each other's arms.

Frank S. Nugent *(New York Times)* wished that the film had been as powerful as director Fritz Lang's *Fury* (1963), but conceded that "within the somewhat theatrical limits of its script, it is an intense, absorbing and relentlessly pursued tragedy.... Mr. Lang's intuitive sense of camera angle, pace and mood raises it to dramatic stature.... The picture tries vagrantly to blame society for their tragedy, but its arguments are none too persuasive." *Variety* was more appreciative, terming the feature "another wallop." The trade paper explained, "Narrative is full of stark and bitter moments, but these bite no more deeply than deftly wrought scenes of tenderness. Though Lang plies the caustic liberally the film derives its strongest appeal from the romantic sequences." The Britisher Basil Wright (*The Spectator*) perceived, "The social problem involved is a real one. Melodramatics makes it unreal. No compromise is possible—especially when the film ends in a double death, to a full female choir, and the voice of the murdered priest calling from heaven: 'Eddie you are free!'" On the other hand, Wright praised, "[T]he film has all the production values one had learned to expect from Lang. It is well constructed, suspense and action alternate in a quickening pulse of excitement reel by reel, and all the characters are excellently directed.... In the piling up of details, in the choice of camera angles, and in the elaboration of suspense and tension, Lang has no equal."

You Only Live Once was the first of several feature films to base its concept on the legend of Bonnie and Clyde. In retrospect, Ronald Bergen in *The United Artists Story* (1986) assessed this classic study as "an unrelentingly sombre blend of Hollywood romanticism and German expressionism. The German Lang kept a cold eye on the subject of a fugitive couple moving through the shadowy Depression landscape, but the American Lang was gradually forced into religiosity and melodramatics." In *The Films of Fritz Lang* (1979), Frederick W. Ott enunciated, "*You Only Live Once* reworked the Langian themes of fate and revenge.... It is a visual masterpiece. Especially fine is the master shot of the rain-swept street in front of the bank.... Memorable, too, is the shot of the condemned man ... in his cell on Death Row. The later afternoon sun strikes the vertical bars of his cage, casting ominous Caligari-like shadows on the prison floor."

Producer Walter Wanger (1894–1968) would return to the prison genre with such studies as: *Riot in Cell Block 11* (1954) and *I Want to Live!* (1958), qq.v.

Index

*References are to entry numbers except **boldface** references which indicate photographs and their page number.*

475